TONE
HOW
E HO

G

&

INTRODUCING HONG KONG

Local diners enjoying dim sum at Lin Heung Tea House (p183)

Rumours of Hong Kong's demise have been greatly exaggerated. More than 10 years after its handover from Britain to China, this entrepreneurial, irrepressible and singular trading city is booming again.

After plagues real, financial and political, normal service has resumed. This tiny territory is punching well above its size and weight once more, only these days with a self-confidence it never had under its former masters. Hong Kong has never been busier. Nor has it ever felt as comfortable with its status, as a part once again of its original motherland but separate, too, largely governing its own affairs and much better off for it. Almost 7 million people call a territory of 1100 sq km home, squeezing onto only 10% of the available land space. A flood of mainland and international visitors, meanwhile, crowds in to see what all the fuss is about. Multitudes seek standing or sitting room here, bringing with them smog, odour, clutter and clatter.

Hong Kong means different things to different people. For some it is the view from the Peak by day or Hong Kong Island's skyline by night as the skyscrapers flush their neon rainbows, competing like tetchy cuttlefish to out-display each other. It can be about a lingering morning of tea and bite-sized dim sum, or a multidish Chinese banquet. Others – hikers, birders, climbers – say nothing beats the Hong Kong countryside for its beauty, facilities and accessibility.

It is all these things, of course; a city of teeming streets and empty wilderness, dazzling modernity and traditional observances. Brash, buccaneering and Westernised, yet conservatively minded and Chinese to its core, Hong Kong surprises, delights and confounds with its cheerful contradictions and energetic inconsistency.

CITY LIFE

In so many ways Hong Kong has rediscovered its prehandover mojo. The most pressing task for many these days, as in 1997, is to work hard, make money and spend it almost as fast in the malls, teeming markets and at boisterous, happy, restaurant banquets with friends and family. Real estate once again seems like a one-way bet and the other favourite Hong Kong punt, on the horses, is as popular as ever. Don't get your hair cut on a Wednesday (race day) in Hong Kong, they say, for fear the barber will be more intent on the form than your scalp.

But things are changing, too. It's not just the ever-mushrooming skyline or the creeping harbour reclamation (nothing new there). Nor is it the burgeoning population *(plus ça change)*. Hong Kong's people have found their voice, demonstrating in numbers over a hamfisted government's attempts to tell them what to do. Their discontent may have subsided with the booming economy and the arrival of a more popular chief executive, but there's a new-found belief in Hong Kong that the aspirations of the people must be met.

While Hong Kong remains very far from being a democracy and its elections little more than stage shows, for the first time the election for top dog was actually contested and the two candidates engaged in televised debate (a first for both Hong Kong and China).

On his 2007 election Donald Tsang, the incumbent chief executive, promised to move towards democracy and some even talked of universal suffrage by 2012. While that's unlikely, the fact that Tsang could say it suggests his ultimate masters in Beijing accept this debate cannot be stifled.

Perhaps it is Hong Kong's (and China's) greatest achievement in 10 years of 'one country, two systems' that such potentially explosive threats to the Mainland's one-party system can be talked of openly and seriously here.

Despite important caveats and concerns about Mainland meddling (not least in Hong Kong's media and legal affairs), it permits Hong Kong's citizens and businesspeople the extensive freedoms of commerce, expression, worship and association it promised in the handover agreement.

Witness the open and graphic protests against the repression of a Chinese spiritual group, the Falun Gong, that go unmolested here, but which would lead to arrest, beatings and maybe worse just over the border.

For most folk, however, addressing everyday concerns is a more pressing matter. An unskilled underclass fears competition from incoming mainlanders. The education system is not delivering opportunities for all, while Hong Kong's air quality and environmental record are woeful, as is the rapacious destruction of Hong Kong's heritage.

Progress in most instances is slow. The smoking ban is taking effect (but with some significant exemptions) but otherwise there's little more than lip service paid towards making Hong Kong a more sustainable and healthy city. For all this, Hong Kong's citizens feel they have a greater voice in the way their city is run and, more than ever before, they are making it heard.

Bustling Lan Kwai Fong (p204), the centre of much of Hong Kong's nightlife

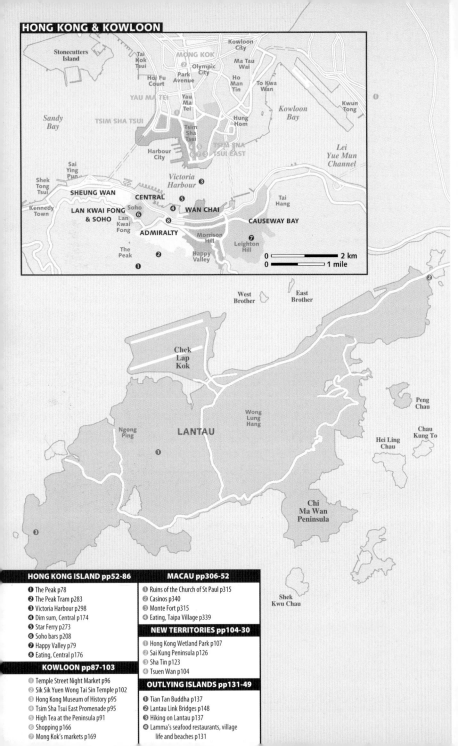

HONG KONG & KOWLOON

Stonecutters Island
Tai Kok Tsui
MONG KOK
Kowloon City
Ma Tau Wai
Olympic City
Park Avenue
Hoi Fu Court
YAU MA TEI
Ho Man Tin
To Kwa Wan
Yau Ma Tei
Kwun Tong
Sandy Bay
TSIM SHA TSUI
Tsim Sha Tsui
Hung Hom
Kowloon Bay
Lei Yue Mun Channel
Harbour City
TSIM SHA TSUI EAST
Sai Ying Pun
Shek Tong Tsui
Victoria Harbour ❸
Tai Hang
Kennedy Town
SHEUNG WAN
CENTRAL ❺
WAN CHAI
LAN KWAI FONG & SOHO ❻
Soho
Lan Kwai Fong
❹
❽
CAUSEWAY BAY
ADMIRALTY
Morrison Hill
Leighton Hill ❼
The Peak ❷
Happy Valley
❶
0 — 2 km
0 — 1 mile

West Brother
East Brother

Chek Lap Kok

Peng Chau

Wong Lung Hang
LANTAU
Chau Kung To
Ngong Ping ❶
Hei Ling Chau
❸
Chi Ma Wan Peninsula
Shek Kwu Chau
❷

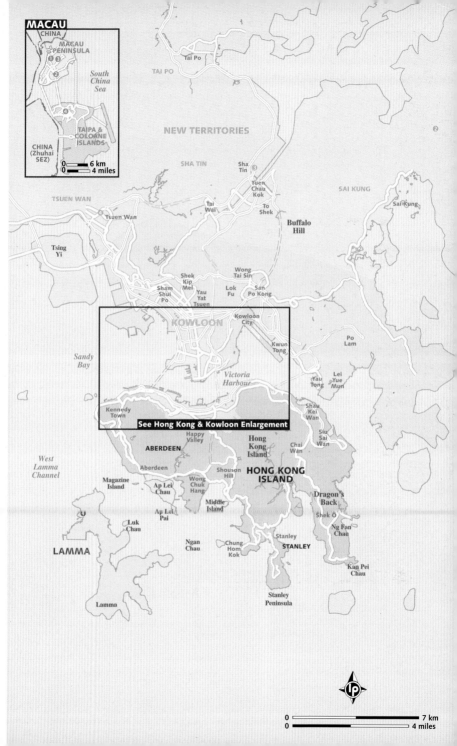

HIGHLIGHTS

HONG KONG ISLAND

The towering skyscrapers climbing from the busy harbour up the steep, jungle-clad hills of Hong Kong Island are an unforgettable sight. The financial and political heart of Hong Kong is also a playground for shoppers, with its many swish malls, and for partygoers, who converge nightly on Soho and Lan Kwai Fong.

❶ The Peak
Home to the rich, you'll find great views and cool breezes up here (p78)

❷ The Peak Tram
This hair-raising funicular ride will whisk you to the Peak (p283)

❸ Victoria Harbour
Float on one of the busiest waterways in the world (p298)

❹ Dim sum, Central
Don't leave Hong Kong before you've done yum cha (tea and dim sum) (p174)

❺ Star Ferry
Floating Hong Kong heritage and a sightseeing bargain (p273)

❻ Soho bars
Hong Kong's coolest bars hide along the alleyways of Soho (p208)

❼ Happy Valley
A night at this atmospheric city horseracing track is a must (p79)

❽ Eating, Central
Head to Central for a bite to eat – for anything from bargain noodles to haute cuisine (p176)

KOWLOON

The bustling hotel and shopping district of Kowloon, facing Hong Kong Island across the harbour, is home to traditional neighbourhoods, old-fashioned shops, lively markets, modern malls and many of Hong Kong's finest museums, galleries and arts venues.

❶ Temple Street Night Market
Browse for quirky souvenirs and grab some
street snacks (p96)

**❷ Sik Sik Yuen Wong Tai Sin
Temple**
See worshippers divine their futures or have
yours foretold (p102)

❸ Hong Kong Museum of History
Hong Kong's life story, from molten lava to
the present day (p95)

❹ Tsim Sha Tsui East Promenade
Could this be the best view in the world? Quite
possibly (p95)

❺ High tea at the Peninsula
Dainty nibbles and fine tea while soothed
by a string quartet (p91)

❻ Shopping
Stroll the Golden Mile (the southern end
of Nathan Rd) for electronics and clothing
bargains (p166)

❼ Mong Kok's markets
Fashion, bargain basement computer goods
and even flower and goldfish markets (p169)

MACAU

This sleepy former Portuguese colonial backwater has become China's Las Vegas almost overnight. It may be all about gaming to most mainland visitors, but the historic delights and wonderful Macanese food are its most powerful drawcards if you're not here to try your luck.

❶ Ruins of the Church of St Paul
The fine carvings on the face of this church are a captivating historical fragment (p315)

❷ Casinos
Take your pick from the busiest casino town in the world (p340)

❸ Monte Fort
The old cannons command fine views from this atmospheric fortress (p315)

❹ Eating, Taipa Village
Hands down the best selection of Portuguese and Macanese food in Macau (p339)

❶ Hong Kong Wetland Park
Wander the futuristic galleries and watch king-fishers dive in silence in this serene haven (p107)

❷ Sai Kung Peninsula
Great seafood, remote beaches, empty trails and amazing views await (p126)

❸ Sha Tin
Fantastic horseracing and Hong Kong's best museum (p123)

❹ Tsuen Wan
Captivating temples and important heritage sites nestle beneath Hong Kong's tallest mountain (p104)

NEW TERRITORIES

The vast areas of wilderness are one of the big attractions of the New Territories, whose mountain trails and nature reserves offer tempting escapes from the city clamour. Crumbling walled villages, massive temple complexes and a few good museums are the other key reasons to explore.

1 Tian Tan Buddha
Great views, vegetarian food and a giant bronze Buddha (p137)

2 Lantau Link Bridges
The spectacular Tsing Ma Bridge (p148) links Lantau with the New Territories

3 Hiking on Lantau
Lose the crowds along Lantau's remote, rugged trails (p137)

4 Lamma's seafood restaurants, village life and beaches
Stroll gently to a seafood lunch on car-free Lamma (p131)

LANTAU & LAMMA

Intimate peeps at traditional village life, convenient but sparsely populated towns and beaches, brooding misty mountains and peaceful Buddhist temples are just some of the delights of the outlying islands.

CONTENTS

THE AUTHORS

Andrew Stone

In 2000 Andrew quit a perfectly good job in London in a bid to travel and make it as a freelance writer. His first destination was Hong Kong, where he spent an unforgettable year and a bit. He made his home on sleepy Lamma Island, his base for exploring Hong Kong, China and the wider region. He has returned every year since to research various guidebooks, magazine and newspaper articles about this very special city.

ANDREW'S TOP HONG KONG DAY

The perfect day begins with laps of the Four Seasons pool (p250); well, I can dream can't I?, earning a leisurely dim sum breakfast at City Hall Maxim's Palace (p180).

Seeking fresh breezes and an easy stroll, I board the Peak Tram (p78) for a circuit of Victoria Peak before taking the jungle path down through Pok Fu Lam Country Park (p225). The mountainous bus trip to Shek O (p86) offers a thrilling white-knuckle ride. Perhaps I'll jump off early and get to Shek O by scaling the Dragon's Back along the Hong Kong Trail (p225). After a quick dip at the beach, I head to the sights and smells of Sheung Wan's dried seafood district (p67), taking in Graham St's captivating little market stalls on the way back to Central.

Then I head to Tsim Sha Tsui for a sunset sharpener with sensational views of the harbour and city skyline at Aqua Spirit (p211). I head to the waterfront just in time for the nightly lightshow (p95) and to catch the Central-bound Star Ferry.

Time to get serious about food now. Yun Fu's cinematic atmosphere (p178) almost wins out over Shui Hu Ju (p181), but then I've always been a sucker for fiery Sichuanese. Afterwards it's time for a bar crawl along Wyndham St, stopping in at the Gecko Lounge (p207) and Yumla (p214) to find a second wind before joining the whooping, hollering madness of Drop (p214).

Chung Wah Chow

Chung Wah was born in Hong Kong. After studying law and working for Greenpeace, she hit the road, pen in hand. She has written for publications in Hong Kong and Taiwan, and loves wandering Hong Kong's countryside and exploring Macau and Guangdong. She wrote the Macau and Excursions chapters.

Reggie Ho

Although born to a food-loving family, Reggie grew up eating only root vegetables and rice. Eventually he embraced the beauty of food while living in New York. Back in Hong Kong he wrote the food column for *HK Magazine* and now edits *South China Morning Post*'s Good Eating guide. He wrote the Eating chapter of this book.

PHOTOGRAPHER
Greg Elms

Greg Elms has been a contributor to Lonely Planet for over 15 years. Armed with a Bachelor of Arts in Photography, Greg was a photographer's assistant for two years before embarking on a travel odyssey. He eventually settled down to a freelance career in Melbourne, and now works regularly for magazines, graphic designers, advertising agencies and, of course, book publishers such as Lonely Planet.

LAST EDITION

Steve Fallon wrote the 11th and 12th editions of this book.

Getting things done in Hong Kong is a breeze. The fantastic transport and city infrastructure, ease of entry and exit, general freedom from crime and disease, widespread use of English and excellent service culture mean you can pretty much rock up here without any forward planning. It's compact, too, which means you won't need to plan complicated journeys, at least around the city itself.

Planning ahead can really help if you're on a budget, however. It's very easy to blow a budget in Hong Kong; your effort will be repaid if you secure a decent, good-value guesthouse ahead of time. Even if you've slightly more to spend, doing your homework on hotels can yield greater comfort and more central locations for no extra cost. Don't forget that hotels can get booked out during the bigger conferences, exhibitions and sporting events.

WHEN TO GO

Hong Kong's subtropical climate can make it a punishingly hot and humid destination during the summer months. June to mid-September is the hottest time when humidity soars. Summer is also typhoon season, when tropical storms sweep rain and high winds off the South China Sea.

Even in late spring and early autumn, wandering Hong Kong's streets can be warm work. The best time to go climate-wise is in early spring (March and April) or late autumn (October and November), when the days are generally warm, fresh and (wind direction and mainland smoke stacks permitting) the air often clearer.

Things can cool down a good deal in winter, when it can often be overcast (as opposed to merely smoggy) and temperatures may even feel chilly enough to don warmer layers.

FESTIVALS

No matter what the time of year, you're almost certain to find some colourful festival or event occurring in Hong Kong. For the most part exact dates vary from year to year, so if you want to time your visit to coincide with a particular event, check the website of the Hong Kong Tourism Board (www.discoverhongkong.com). For tourist high and low seasons in Hong Kong, see p248.

Many Chinese red-letter days, both public holidays and privately observed affairs, go back hundreds, even thousands of years, and the true origins of some are often lost in the mists of time. Most – but not all – are celebrated in both Hong Kong and Macau. For festivals and events specific to Macau, see p351.

For dates of Hong Kong's public holidays, see p293.

January

CHINESE NEW YEAR
Southern China's most important public holiday takes place in late January/early February and is welcomed by a huge international parade at Tamar (now the PLA Central Barracks) site along the waterfront between Central and Wan Chai.

HONG KONG CITY FRINGE FESTIVAL
www.hkfringe.com.hk
The Fringe Club (p218) sponsors three weeks of eclectic performances both local and international between late January and early February.

HONG KONG FASHION WEEK/ WORLD BOUTIQUE HONG KONG
http://hkfashionweekfw.tdctrade.com or www.worldboutiquehk.com
Organised by the Hong Kong Trade Development Council (HKTDC), this fair/event showcases collections from both established and up-and-coming fashion designers, as well as brands from around the world.

February

HONG KONG ARTS FESTIVAL
www.hk.artsfestival.org
Hong Kong's most important cultural event is a month-long extravaganza of music, performing arts and exhibitions by hundreds of local and international artists.

HONG KONG MARATHON
www.hkmarathon.com
This major sporting event dating back to 1997 also includes a half-marathon and 10km race and attracts 30,000 participants.

SPRING LANTERN FESTIVAL
www.discoverhongkong.com/eng/heritage/festivals/index.jhtml
A colourful lantern festival on the 15th day of the first moon (mid- to late February) marking the end of the New Year period and the day for lovers.

March

HONG KONG ARTWALK
www.hongkongartwalk.com
Some 40 galleries in Central, Soho and Sheung Wan throw open their doors on a weekday (usually Wednesday) from 6pm to midnight to expose their art, offer viewers snacks and drinks supplied by the area's restaurants and raise money for charity.

HONG KONG RUGBY WORLD CUP SEVENS
www.hksevens.com.hk
Hong Kong's premier sporting event, this seven-a-side tournament is held over three days at Hong Kong Stadium and attracts teams and spectators from all over the world.

MAN HONG KONG INTERNATIONAL LITERARY FESTIVAL
www.festival.org.hk
This 10-day festival celebrates all things bookish and attracts novelists, short-story writers and poets from around the region and the world.

April

CHING MING
A family celebration held early in the month, this is the time when people visit and clean the graves of ancestors.

KUNG HEI FAT CHOI (AND HAPPY NEW YEAR, TOO)!

The Lunar New Year is the most important holiday of the Chinese year. Expect colourful decorations but not much public merrymaking. For the most part, this is a family festival, though there is a parade on the first day, a fantastic fireworks display over Victoria Harbour on the second evening, and one of the largest horse races is held at Sha Tin on day three.

Chinese New Year, which mainlanders call the Spring Festival, begins on the first new moon after the sun enters Aquarius (ie sometime between 21 January and 19 February) and ends, at least officially, 15 days later. In Hong Kong it is a three-day public holiday.

The build-up to the holiday – the end of the month known as the 'Bitter Moon' since it's the coldest part of the year in Hong Kong – is very busy as family members clean house, get haircuts and cook, all of which are activities prohibited during the holiday. Debts and feuds are settled, and employees get a one-month New Year bonus. You'll see many symbols in Hong Kong at this time of year, all of which have special meaning for people here. Chinese use a lot of indirect language, and 'punning' is very important in the use of symbols. A picture of a boy holding a gàm-yéw (goldfish) and a hàw-fàa (lotus flower) is wishing you 'abundant gold and harmony', since that's what the words can also mean when said in a different tone. Symbols of fùk (bats) are everywhere, since the word also means 'good luck'. The peach and plum blossoms decorating restaurants and public spaces symbolise both the arrival of spring and 'immortality', while the golden fruit of the kumquat tree is associated with good fortune. The red and gold banners you'll see in doorways are wishing all and sundry 'prosperity', 'peace' or just 'spring'.

Punning also carries over into foods eaten during the Lunar New Year holidays. Faat-choy (sea moss) and hò-sí (dried oysters) is a popular dish as the names of the key ingredients can also mean 'prosperity' and 'good business'. Lots of fish, gài (chicken), which also means 'luck', and hàa (prawns, or 'laughter') are served, as are noodles for longevity.

Of course, much of the symbolism and well-wishing has to do with wealth and prosperity. Indeed, 'gùng-háy faatchòy', the most common New Year greeting in southern China, literally means 'respectful wishes, get rich'. The lai-sí packet is very important. It's a small red and gold envelope in which new bills (usually $10 or $20) are enclosed and given as gifts by married people to children and singles.

The first day of Chinese New Year will fall on 7 February in 2008, 26 January in 2009 and February 14 in 2010.

If you're planning to travel around this period, it pays to plan ahead as huge numbers of people move around and trains and planes can get booked solid.

ADVANCE PLANNING

Three weeks before you go, check out some of the key Hong Kong websites and get to know what's going on – both in the headlines and after hours – by reading the local online media (p297). Check to see if your visit coincides with any major holidays or festivals (p15). Make sure your passport and other documents are in order.

One week before you go, book tickets for any major concerts or shows that might interest you at places such as the Hong Kong Cultural Centre (p90) or the Fringe Studio & Theatre (p218). Book a table at Pierre (p177). Remember to cancel the milk.

The day before you go, reconfirm your flight, check the Hong Kong websites for any last-minute changes or cancellations at entertainment venues and buy some Hong Kong dollars. Remember to switch the iron off.

HONG KONG INTERNATIONAL FILM FESTIVAL
www.hkiff.org.hk
This is a two-week extravaganza with screenings of more than 240 films from around the world.

BIRTHDAY OF TIN HAU
www.discoverhongkong.com/eng/heritage /festivals/index.jhtml
A festival in late April/early May in honour of the patroness of fisherfolk and one of the territory's most popular goddesses; in Macau it is known as the A-Ma Festival.

CHEUNG CHAU BUN FESTIVAL
www.cheungchau.org
Taking place around late April/early May, this is an unusual festival that is observed uniquely on Cheung Chau (see p142).

May
BIRTHDAY OF LORD BUDDHA
www.discoverhongkong.com/eng/heritage /festivals/index.jhtml
A public holiday during which Buddha's statue is taken from monasteries and temples and ceremoniously bathed in scented water.

June
DRAGON BOAT FESTIVAL
www.discoverhongkong.com/eng/heritage /festivals/index.jhtml
This festival, also known as Tuen Ng (Double Fifth) as it falls on the fifth day of the fifth moon, commemorates the death of the 3rd-century BC poet-statesman who hurled himself into a river to protest against a corrupt government. Dragon-boat races are held throughout the territory and in Macau, but the most famous are at Stanley.

July
HONG KONG FASHION WEEK FOR SPRING/SUMMER
http://hkfashionweekss.tdctrade.com
This is the spring/summer section of the biannual Hong Kong Fashion week.

August
HUNGRY GHOST FESTIVAL
www.discoverhongkong.com/eng/heritage /festivals/index.jhtml
Celebrated on the first day of the seventh moon (sometime between August and September), when the gates of hell are opened and 'hungry ghosts' (restless spirits) are freed for two weeks to walk the earth. On the 14th day, paper 'hell' money and votives in the shape of cars, houses and clothing are burned for the ghosts and food is offered.

September
MID-AUTUMN FESTIVAL
www.discoverhongkong.com/eng/heritage /festivals/index.jhtml
A colourful festival held on the 15th night of the eighth moon (sometime in September or October) marking an uprising against the Mongols in the 14th century when plans for a revolution were passed around in little round 'moon' cakes, which are still eaten on this day.

October
CHEUNG YEUNG
www.discoverhongkong.com/eng/heritage /festivals/index.jhtml
Celebrated on the ninth day of the ninth month (mid- to late October), and based on a Han dynasty story, where an oracle advised a man to take his family to a high place to escape a plague. Many people still head for the hills on this day and also visit the graves of ancestors.

November

HONG KONG INTERNATIONAL CRICKET SIXES

www.hksixes.com

This two-day tournament pits Hong Kong's top cricketers against select teams from the eight Test-playing nations.

COSTS & MONEY

Hong Kong is a relatively pricey destination. Accommodation is the biggest expense, followed by drinking in Hong Kong's bars. On a very tight budget you could survive on, say, $300 a day, but it would require a good deal of self-discipline. Better to budget something along the lines of $600 if you want to stay in the better class of guesthouse or cheaper midrange hotel and do more than just eat bowls of noodles. If you want to sample the finer hotels and restaurants, you'll be paying the equivalent of most leading world cities. The real bargain compared to the likes of London and even New York is the incredibly cheap taxi fares; in fact, transport generally is excellent value.

INTERNET RESOURCES

The Lonely Planet website, www.lonelyplanet.com, lists many useful Hong Kong links. Other helpful sites:

Asiaxpat (www.asiaxpat.com) A lifestyle site – restaurants, nightlife, trends – but it includes advertorial.

bc magazine (www.bcmagazine.net) Nightlife and entertainment from one of Hong Kong's top nightlife freebies.

Business in Asia (www.business-in-asia.com)

Doing Business in Hong Kong (www.business.gov.hk)

Gay Hong Kong (www.gayhk.com) The nightlife scene in Hong Kong for visitors and locals alike.

HK Clubbing (www.hkclubbing.com)

Hong Kong Leisure and Cultural Services Department (www.lcsd.gov.hk)

Hong Kong Observatory (www.weather.gov.hk)

Hong Kong Tourism Board (www.discoverhongkong.com)

Hong Kong Yellow Pages (www.yp.com.hk)

South China Morning Post (www.scmp.com.hk)

Yellow Pages Maps (www.ypmap.com) Includes maps, phone numbers and addresses.

(UN)SUSTAINABLE HONG KONG

Oh dear. You're in the wrong city in the wrong country. Conspicuous consumption is the main pastime in Hong Kong's malls which, along with everything else, are powered by the dirtiest fuel of all (coal). Let's face it, even though it has great wilderness areas (see p40) Hong Kong isn't exactly a model eco-city and the options to consume sustainable services are very limited.

Hong Kong's efforts to offer recycling facilities are improving, but slowly. Time will also tell if efforts to fine diners who needlessly waste food will make a difference to the city's indulgent dining habits. One of the few things you can do to help make a difference is to order only fish from nonendangered species and preferably sustainable fisheries by consulting the Hong Kong World Wide Find for Nature Fish Identification Guide (www.wwf.org.hk/eng/conservation). The downside is that having long-since exhausted its own inshore fish stocks, much of the fish consumed in Hong Kong is jetted in from other Asian fish markets.

HOW MUCH?

Bowl of wonton noodles: $15 to $30

Copy of *South China Morning Post*: $7

Cup of coffee: from $25

Laundry (5kg): $45 to $60

Litre of bottled water: $10 to $14

Litre of petrol: $14 to $16

MTR fare (Central to Tsim Sha Tsui): $9; $7.90 with Octopus card

Pint of beer: from $40 (happy hour from $25)

Souvenir T-shirt: $40 to $100

Star Ferry fare (Central to Tsim Sha Tsui): 1st/2nd class $2.20/1.70

BACKGROUND

HISTORY

In the very long scale of history, Hong Kong as we know it today has existed for a mere blink of an eye. But there was a lot going on in the region before that wintry morning in 1841 when a contingent of British marines clambered ashore and planted the Union flag on the western part of Hong Kong Island, claiming it for the British Crown.

EARLY INHABITANTS

Hong Kong has supported human life since at least the late Stone Age. Finds uncovered at almost 100 archaeological sites in the territory, including a rich burial ground discovered on the island of Ma Wan in 1997 and three hoards on the west coast of the Tuen Mun peninsula, suggest that the inhabitants of these settlements were warlike. The remnants of Bronze Age habitations (c 1500–220 BC) unearthed on Lamma and Lantau Islands and at around 20 other sites – as well as the eight geometric rock carvings that can still be viewed at various locations along Hong Kong's coastline – also indicate that these early peoples practised some form of ancient religion based on cosmology. Other finds indicate Hong Kong's Stone Age inhabitants also enjoyed a relatively nutritious diet of iron-rich vegetables, small mammals, shellfish and fish harvested far offshore.

THE FIVE GREAT CLANS

Just when the area that is now Hong Kong became an integral part of the Chinese empire is difficult to say. What is certain, however, is that by the time of the Eastern Han dynasty (AD 25–220), Chinese imperial rule had been extended over the region. The discovery of a number of Han coins on Lantau and Kau Sai Chau Islands and at several important digs, including the tomb of a senior Han warrior at Lei Cheng Uk in central Kowloon (see p100) and So Kwun Wat southeast of Tuen Mun, attests to this.

The first of Hong Kong's mighty 'Five Clans', Han Chinese whose descendants hold political and economic clout to this day, began settling the area around the 12th century. The first and most powerful of the arrivals were the Tang, who initially settled around Kam Tin (*tin* means 'field'). The once-moated hamlet of Kat Hing Wai (*wài* means 'protective wall'; see p117), which is probably the most visited of the remaining traditional walled villages in the New Territories, formed part of this cluster.

The Tang were followed by the Hau, who spread around present-day Sheung Shui, and the Pang from central Jiangsu province, who settled in what is now the area around Fanling. These three clans were followed by the Liu in the 15th century and the Man a century later.

The Cantonese-speaking newcomers called themselves *bún-dày* (Punti), meaning 'indigenous' or 'local' – something they clearly were not. They looked down on the original inhabitants, many of whom had been shunted off the land and had moved onto the sea to live on boats. It is thought that today's fisherpeople called, the Tanka, emerged from this persecuted group.

TIMELINE

4000–1500 BC	250 BC–AD 25	12th–16th centuries
Small groups of Neolithic hunter-gatherers and fisherfolk settle coastal areas; a handful of tantalising archaeological finds – tools, pottery and other artefacts – are the only remnants left by these nomads	The aboriginal population, the Yue (a people possibly of Malay stock who migrated from Southeast Asia), begin trading with dynastic China; Chinese imperial rule extends to what is now Hong Kong during the Han dynasty (AD 25–220)	Hong Kong's Five Clans – the Tang, the Hau, the Pang, the Lui and the Man – settle in what is now the New Territories and build walled villages in the fertile plains and valleys

AN IMPERIAL OUTPOST

Clinging to the southern edge of the Chinese province of Canton (now Guangdong), the peninsula and islands that became the territory of Hong Kong counted only as a remote pocket in a neglected corner of the Chinese empire. Among the scattered communities of farmers and fisherfolk were pirates who hid from the authorities among the rocky islands that afforded easy access to the nearby Pearl River.

Hong Kong's first recorded encounter with imperial China in the 13th century was as brief as it was tragic. In 1276 a group of loyal retainers of the Song dynasty (AD 960–1279) smuggled the boy emperor, Duan Zong, south to the remote fringes of the empire after the Song capital, Hangzhou, had fallen to the Mongol hordes sweeping China. Nine-year-old Duan Zong drowned when Mongol ships defeated the tattered remnants of the imperial fleet in a battle on the Pearl River.

The Punti flourished until the struggle that saw the moribund Ming dynasty (1368–1644) overthrown. The victorious Qing (1644–1911), angered by the resistance put up by southerners loyal to the *ancien régime* and determined to solve the endemic problem of piracy, in the 1660s ordered a forced evacuation inland of all the inhabitants of Guangdong's coastal San On district, including Hong Kong.

These turbulent times saw the birth of the Triads (p29). Originally founded as patriotic secret societies dedicated to overthrowing the Qing dynasty and restoring the Ming, they would degenerate over the centuries into Hong Kong's own version of the Mafia. Today's Triads still recite an oath of allegiance to the Ming, but their loyalty is to the dollar rather than the vanquished Son of Heaven.

More than four generations passed before the population was able to recover to its mid-17th-century level, boosted in part by the influx of the Hakka (Cantonese for 'guest people'), who moved here in the 18th century and up to the mid-19th century. A few vestiges of their language, songs and folklore survive, most visibly in the wide-brimmed, black-fringed bamboo hats sported by Hakka women in the New Territories.

ARRIVAL OF THE OUTER BARBARIANS

For centuries, the Pearl River estuary had been an important trading artery centred on the port of Canton (now Guangzhou). Arab traders had entered – and sacked – the settlement as early as the 8th century AD. Guangzhou was 2500km south of Peking, and the Cantonese view that the 'mountains are high and the emperor is far away' was not disputed in the imperial capital. The Ming emperors regarded their subjects to the south as no less than witches and sorcerers, their language unintelligible and their culinary predilections downright disgusting. It was therefore fitting that the Cantonese should trade with the 'outer barbarians', or foreign traders.

Regular trade between China and Europe began in 1557 when Portuguese navigators set up a base in Macau, 65km west of Hong Kong. Dutch traders came in the wake of the Portuguese, followed by the French. British ships appeared as early as 1685 from the East India Company concessions along the coast of India, and by 1714 the company had established offices and warehouses with 'factors' (managers) in Guangzhou to trade for tea, silk and porcelain. By the end of the 18th century, the flags of more than a dozen nations, including Britain, flew over the buildings along 13 Factories St.

1276	1513	1557
Mongol hordes sweep through China and Mongol ships defeat the imperial fleet in the Pearl River; the Song dynasty's boy emperor drowns in Hong Kong	In an attempt to find a sea-trading route to China, Jorge Alvares, a Portuguese explorer, is the first European to visit the region, landing on Lintin island just to the west of Hong Kong Island	The Portuguese settle on Macau, using it as a base to develop and control the trade between China and the West

In 1757 an imperial edict awarded the *cohong* (a local merchants' guild), the monopoly on China's trade with foreigners, restricting the European traders. It was illegal for them to learn the Chinese language or to deal with anyone except merchants of the *cohong*; they could not enter Guangzhou proper but were restricted to Shamian Island in the Pearl River; they were allowed to remain only for the trading season (November to May).

OPIUM & WAR

China didn't reciprocate Europe's voracious demand for its products, especially tea, for the most part shunning foreign manufactured goods. The foreigners' ensuing trade deficit was soon reversed, however, after the British discovered a commodity that the Chinese did want: opium.

The British, with a virtually inexhaustible supply of the drug from the poppy fields of India, developed the trade aggressively. Alarmed to see its silver draining from the country to pay for the opium and the spread of addiction, Emperor Chia Ch'ing (Jiaqing; r 1796–1820) issued an edict in 1799 banning the trade of opium in China, while his son and successor, Tao Kuang (Dao Guang; r 1820–50), banned the drug from Whampoa (now Huangpo) and Macau in 1820.

In Guangzhou the *cohong* and corrupt officials helped ensure the trade continued, and both sides amassed great fortunes. This was all supposed to change in June 1839 with the arrival of Lin Zexu, governor of Hunan and a mandarin of great integrity, who surrounded the British garrison in Guangzhou and cut off their food supplies, forcing them to turn over more than 20,000 chests of the drug.

The British chief superintendent of trade, Captain Charles Elliot, suspended all trade with China while he awaited instructions from London. The foreign secretary, Lord Palmerston, goaded by prominent Scottish merchants William Jardine and James Matheson, ordered the Royal Navy in Guangzhou to force a settlement in Sino-British commercial relations. An expeditionary force of 4000 men under Rear Admiral George Elliot (a cousin of Charles) departed to extract reparations and secure favourable trade arrangements from the Chinese government.

What would become known as the First Opium War (or First Anglo-Chinese War) began in June 1840. British forces besieged Guangzhou before sailing north and occupying or blockading a number of ports and cities along the Yangtze River and the coast as far as Shanghai. To the emperor's great alarm, the force threatened Beijing, and he sent his envoy (and Lin's successor) Qi Shan to negotiate with the Elliots. In exchange for the British withdrawal from northern China, Qi agreed to the Convention of Chuenpi (now Chuanbi), which ceded Hong Kong Island to Britain.

Though neither side, in fact, actually accepted the terms of the convention, a couple of subsequent events decided Hong Kong's fate. In January 1841 a naval landing party hoisted the British flag at Possession Point (now Possession St) on Hong Kong Island. The following month Captain Elliot attacked the Bogue Fort in Humen, took control of the Pearl River and laid siege to Guangzhou, withdrawing only after having extracted concessions from merchants there. Six months later a powerful British force led by Elliot's successor, Sir Henry Pottinger, sailed north and seized Amoy (Xiamen), Ningpo (Ningbo), Shanghai and other ports. With the strategic city of Nanking (Nanjing) under immediate threat, the Chinese were forced to accept Britain's terms.

The Treaty of Nanking abolished the monopoly system of trade, opened five 'treaty ports' to British residents and foreign trade, exempted British nationals from all Chinese laws and ceded the island of Hong Kong to the British 'in perpetuity'.

1757	1773	1840
The *cohong* (local merchants' guild) awarded the monopoly on China's trade with foreigners in Guangdong; European traders' freedom of movement limited between Macau and Shamian Island in Guangzhou	British traders unload 1000 chests from Bengal at Guangzhou, each containing almost 70kg of Indian opium; addiction sweeps China like wildfire, and sales of what the Chinese call 'foreign mud' skyrocket	Start of First Opium War, lasting two years; the war is sparked by an incident the year before when the Chinese forced the British to hand over their opium and publicly burn some 2.3 million catties (almost half a tonne) in the city of Taiping

BRITISH HONG KONG

'Albert is so amused at my having got the island of Hong Kong', wrote Queen Victoria to King Leopold of Belgium in 1841. At the time, Hong Kong was little more than a backwater of about 20 villages and hamlets. It did offer one distinct advantage for the British trading fleet, however: a deep, well-sheltered harbour that went by the Cantonese name *hèung-gáwng* ('fragrant harbour'), so named after the scent from sandalwood incense factories that wafted across the harbour from what is now Aberdeen at the western edge of the island.

As Captain Elliot saw it, from here the British Empire and its merchants could conduct all their trade with China and establish a permanent outpost, under British sovereignty, in the Far East. But the British merchants in Guangzhou and the Royal Navy sided with Lord Palmerston; a small barren island with nary a house on it was not the type of sweeping concession that a British victory was supposed to achieve. Nonetheless, Hong Kong formally became a British possession on 26 June 1843, and its first governor, Sir Henry Pottinger, took charge. A primitive chaotic and lawless settlement soon sprang up.

GROWING PAINS

What would later be called the Second Opium War (or Second Anglo-Chinese War) broke out in October 1856. The first stage of the war was brought to an end two years later by the Treaty of Tientsin (Tianjin), which gave foreigners the right to diplomatic representation in Beijing.

Despite warnings from the Chinese, the British tried to capitalise on this agreement in 1859 by sending a flotilla carrying the first British envoy and minister plenipotentiary up the Pei Ho River to Beijing. The Chinese fired on the armada, which sustained heavy losses. Using this as a pretext, a combined British and French force invaded China and marched on Beijing. The victorious British forced the Chinese to the Convention of Peking in 1860, which ratified the Treaty of Tientsin and ceded the Kowloon peninsula and Stonecutters Island to Britain. Britain was now in complete control of Victoria Harbour and its approaches.

Hong Kong's population had leapt from 33,000 in 1850 to 265,000 in 1900 and the British army felt it needed to command the mountains of the New Territories to protect the growing colony and provide water to it. When the Qing dynasty was at its nadir, the British government petitioned China for a land extension extending Hong Kong into the New Territories. The June 1898 Convention of Peking handed Britain a larger-than-expected slice of territory running north to the Shumchun (Shenzhen) River, and 235 islands, increasing the colony's size by 90%.

A SLEEPY BACKWATER

While the *hong* – Hong Kong's major trading houses, including Jardine, Matheson and Swire – prospered from their trade with China, the colony hardly thrived in its first few decades. Fever, bubonic plague and typhoons threatened life and property, and at first the colony attracted a fair number of criminals and vice merchants. Opium dens, gambling clubs and brothels proliferated; just a year after Britain took possession, an estimated 450 prostitutes worked out of two dozen brothels. Australian 'actresses' were based in Lyndhurst Tce, known as *baak fàa gàai* ('White Flower Street'), in Chinese.

Gradually, however, Hong Kong began to shape itself into a more substantial community. Gas and electrical power companies sprang up, ferries, trams, the Kowloon-Canton Railway

1842	1856	1894
Treaty of Nanking cedes Hong Kong Island to Great Britain; in an angry letter to Captain Elliot, the man responsible for the deal, Lord Palmerston calls it 'a barren island with hardly a house upon it!' '[It] will never be a mart for trade…'	Chinese soldiers board the British merchant schooner *Arrow* to search for pirates, sparking the Second Opium War; French troops support the British in this war, while Russia and the USA lend naval support; the conflict lasts until 1860	Bubonic plague breaks out for the first time in Hong Kong, killing hundreds of mainly local Chinese and leading to a mass exodus from the territory; hundreds die and trade suffers badly as ships avoid the plague-infested port

and the newfangled High Level Tramway (later known as the Peak Tram) provided a decent transport network, and land was reclaimed. Colonials flocked to the races at Happy Valley and visitors were as impressed with the colony's social life as they were with its development. Nonetheless, from the late 19th century right up to WWII, Hong Kong lived in the shadow of the treaty port of Shanghai, which had become Asia's premier trade and financial centre – not to mention its style capital.

The colony's population continued to grow thanks to waves of immigrants fleeing the Chinese Revolution of 1911, which ousted the decaying Qing dynasty and ushered in several decades of strife, rampaging warlords and famine. The civil war in China kept the numbers of refugees entering the colony high, but the stream became a flood after Japan invaded China in 1937.

Hong Kong's status as a British colony would offer the refugees only a temporary haven. The day after Japan attacked the US naval base at Pearl Harbor on 7 December 1941, its military machine swept down from Guangzhou and into Hong Kong.

Conditions under Japanese rule were harsh, with indiscriminate massacres of mostly Chinese civilians; Western civilians were incarcerated at Stanley Prison on Hong Kong Island. Many Hong Kong Chinese fled to Macau, administered by neutral Portugal.

THE ROAD TO BOOMTOWN

After Japan's withdrawal from Hong Kong, and subsequent surrender in August 1945, the colony looked set to resume its hibernation. But events both at home and on the mainland forced the colony in a new direction.

Just before WWII Hong Kong had begun to shift from entrepôt trade servicing China to home-grown manufacturing. The turmoil on the mainland, leading to the defeat of the Nationalists by the victorious Communists in 1949, unleashed a torrent of refugees – both rich and poor – into Hong Kong.

When Beijing sided with North Korea that year and went to war against the forces of the USA and the UN, the UN embargo on all trade with China (1951) threatened to strangle the colony economically. But on a paltry, war-torn foundation, local and foreign businesses built a huge manufacturing (notably textiles and garments) and financial services centre that transformed Hong Kong into one of the world's great economic miracles.

Much of Hong Kong's success depended on the enormous pool of cheap labour from China, often directed by entrepreneurs seeking refuge from the Communist mainland. Working conditions in those early years of economic revolution were often Dickensian: 16-hour days, unsafe working conditions, low wages and child labour were all common. Refugee workers endured, and some even earned their way out of poverty into prosperity. The Hong Kong government, under international pressure, eventually began to establish and enforce labour standards, and the situation gradually improved.

Despite the improvements, trouble flared up in the 1950s and '60s due to social discontent and poor working conditions. Feuding between Communist and Nationalist supporters in Hong Kong led to riots in 1957 and again in 1962 and 1966.

When the Communists came to power in China in 1949, many people were sure that Hong Kong would be overrun. Even without force, the Chinese could simply have ripped down the fence on the border and sent the masses to settle on Hong Kong territory. But though the Chinese government continued to denounce the 'unequal treaties', it recognised Hong Kong's importance to the national economy.

1895	1898	1937
Sun Yat Sen, a newly qualified Chinese doctor from Guangzhou, uses Hong Kong as a base to drive an insurrection in Southern China; it fails and the British ban Sun from the territory and he moves to Japan to continue his bid to foment revolution in China	China hands the New Territories to Hong Kong in the Second Convention of Peking; instead of annexing the 'New Territories', the British agree to sign a 99-year lease, beginning on 1 July 1898 and ending at midnight on 30 June 1997	Pouncing on a country weakened by a bloody civil war, Japan invades China; as many as 750,000 mainland Chinese seek shelter in Hong Kong over the next three years, fleeing their despotic and murderous invaders

In 1967, at the height of the so-called Cultural Revolution, when the ultraleftist Red Guards were in de facto control in China, Hong Kong's stability again looked precarious. Riots rocked the colony, bringing with them a wave of bombings, looting and arson attacks.

Property values in Hong Kong plunged, as did China's foreign-exchange earnings, as trade and tourism ground to a halt. However, the bulk of the population – and, importantly, the Hong Kong police – stood firm with the colonial authorities. By the end of the 1960s, China, largely due to the intervention of Premier Chou Enlai, had come to its senses and order had been restored.

A SOCIETY IN TRANSITION

After 'a testing time for the people of Hong Kong', as the *Hong Kong Yearbook* summed it up at the end of 1967, Hong Kong got on with the business of making money, which included improving the territory's infrastructure. In 1973 the first 'New Town' – Sha Tin – was completed, marking the start of a massive and unprecedented public-housing programme that would, and still does, house millions of Hong Kong people.

Although Hong Kong's stock market collapsed in 1973, its economy resumed its upward trend later in the decade. At the same time many of Hong Kong's neighbours, including Taiwan, South Korea and Singapore, began to mimic the colony's success. Just as their cheap labour was threatening to undermine the competitive edge of Hong Kong manufacturers, China began to emerge from its self-imposed isolation.

The 'Open Door' policy of Deng Xiaoping, who took control of China in the confusion after Mao Zedong's death in 1976, revived Hong Kong's role as the gateway to the mainland and it boomed. Underpinning the boom was the drive to rake in as much profit as possible ahead of 1997, when Hong Kong's once and future master would again take over.

THE 1997 QUESTION

Few people gave much thought to Hong Kong's future until the late 1970s, when the British and Chinese governments met for the first time to decide what would happen in (and after) 1997. Britain was legally bound to hand back only the New Territories – not Hong Kong Island and Kowloon, which had been ceded to it forever. However, the fact that nearly half of Hong Kong's population lived in the New Territories by that time made it an untenable division.

It was Deng Xiaoping who decided that the time was ripe to recover Hong Kong, forcing the British to the negotiating table. The inevitable conclusion laid to rest political jitters and commercial concerns that had seen the Hong Kong dollar collapse – and subsequently be pegged to the US dollar – in 1983, but there was considerable resentment that the fate of 5.5 million people had been decided without their input and that Whitehall had chosen not to provide Hong Kong people with full British passports and the right of abode in the UK.

Despite soothing words from the Chinese, British and Hong Kong governments, over the next 13 years the population of Hong Kong suffered considerable anxiety at the possible political and economic consequences of the handover. In the anxious years leading up to the handover, thousands of Hong Kong citizens emigrated to Canada, the USA, Australia, the UK and New Zealand.

1941	1945	1949
After just over two weeks of fierce but futile resistance, British forces surrender to Japanese forces on Christmas Day, beginning nearly four years of Japanese occupation; internment of Westerners begins; large scale massacres of mostly Chinese civilians	Japan surrenders to the Allies; Hong Kong returns to British rule; the population, numbering about 1.6 million in 1941, has shrunk to about 610,000 by the end of the war, owing in part to enforced wartime deportations by the Japanese	Communist forces are victorious against the Nationalists in China; refugees flood into Hong Kong; by 1947 the population reaches prewar levels and, by the end of 1950, it reaches 2.3 million

ONE COUNTRY, TWO SYSTEMS

Under the agreement signed by China and Britain, which is enshrined in a document known as *The Sino-British Joint Declaration on the Question of Hong Kong*, the 'British-administered territory' of Hong Kong would disappear and be reborn as a Special Administrative Region (SAR) of China. This meant the Hong Kong SAR would be permitted to continue with its current capitalist system, while across the border the Chinese would remain with China's version of socialism. The Chinese catch phrase for this was 'One Country, Two Systems'.

In 1988 the details of this rather unorthodox system of government were spelled out in *The Basic Law for Hong Kong*, the SAR's future constitution. The Basic Law, ratified by the National People's Congress (NPC) in Beijing in 1990, preserved Hong Kong's English common-law judicial system and guaranteed the right of property and ownership. It also included the rights of assembly, free speech, association, travel and movement, correspondence, choice of occupation, academic research, religious belief and the right to strike. The SAR would enjoy a high degree of autonomy with the exception of foreign affairs and matters of defence.

As guarantees of individual freedoms and respect for human rights are written into China's own constitution, few Hong Kong Chinese held much faith in the Basic Law. The guarantees were seen as empty promises and quite a few felt the Basic Law provided Beijing with the means to interfere in Hong Kong's internal affairs to preserve public order, public morals and national security.

Although Hong Kong under the British had never been more than a benignly ruled oligarchy, Whitehall had nevertheless promised to introduce democratic reforms prior to the handover. But it soon became apparent that British and Chinese definitions of democracy differed considerably. Beijing made it abundantly clear that it would not allow Hong Kong to establish its own democratically elected government. The chief executive was to be chosen by a Beijing-appointed panel of delegates; the people of Hong Kong would elect some lower officials. In the face of opposition from Beijing, planned elections for 1988 were postponed.

TIANANMEN & ITS AFTERMATH

The concern of many Hong Kong people over their future turned to out-and-out fear on 4 June 1989, when Chinese troops massacred prodemocracy demonstrators in Beijing's Tiananmen Square. The events horrified Hong Kong people, many of whom had donated funds and goods to the demonstrators. As the Chinese authorities spread out to hunt down activists, an underground smuggling operation, code-named Yellow Bird, was set up in Hong Kong to spirit them to safety overseas.

The massacre was a watershed for Hong Kong. Sino-British relations deteriorated, the stock market fell 22% in one day and a great deal of capital left the territory for destinations overseas.

The Hong Kong government sought to rebuild confidence by announcing plans for a new airport and shipping port; with an estimated price tag of $160 billion, this was the world's most expensive infrastructure project of the day. But China had already signalled its intentions loudly and clearly.

Hong Kong–based Chinese officials who had spoken out against the Tiananmen killings were yanked from their posts or sought asylum in the USA and Europe. Local Hong Kong people with money and skills made a mad dash to emigrate to any country that would take

1962	1967	1971
A bombastic China sends 70,000 people across the frontier between Hong Kong and the New Territories in the space of a couple of weeks, creating the impression that it plans to take Hong Kong back by force	The Cultural Revolution in China reaches its height; riots and bombings rock Hong Kong; a militia of 300 armed Chinese crosses the border, killing five policemen and penetrating 3km into the New Territories before pulling back	A San Francisco–born martial artist called Bruce Lee returns to Hong Kong and takes his first leading role in the kung fu film *Big Boss;* it becomes a smash around the world and marks the beginning of both his international fame and a craze for martial arts movies

them. During the worst period more than 1000 people were leaving each week, especially for Canada and Australia.

Tiananmen had strengthened the resolve of those people who either could not or would not leave, giving rise to the territory's first official political parties. In a bid to restore credibility, the government introduced a Bill of Rights in 1990, and the following year bestowed on Hong Kong citizens the right to choose 18 of the 60 members of the Legislative Council (Legco), which until then had been essentially a rubber-stamp body chosen by the government and special-interest groups.

DEMOCRACY & THE LAST GOVERNOR

Hong Kong was never as politically apathetic as was generally thought in the 1970s and '80s. The word 'party' may have been anathema to the refugees who had fled from the Communists or Nationalists in the 1930s and '40s, but not necessarily to their sons and daughters.

Born and bred in the territory, these first-generation Hong Kong youths were entering universities and colleges by the 1970s and becoming politically active. Like student activists everywhere they were passionate and idealistic, agitating successfully for Chinese to be recognised as an official language alongside English. They opposed colonialism, expressed pride in their Chinese heritage and railed against the benign dictatorship of the Hong Kong colonial government. But their numbers were split between those who supported China – and the Chinese Communist Party – at all costs and those who had reservations or even mistrusted it.

The first to consider themselves 'Hong Kong people' rather than refugees from China, this generation formed the pressure groups emerging in the 1980s to debate Hong Kong's future. By the end of the decade they were coalescing into nascent political parties and preparing for the 1991 Legco (legislative council) elections.

The first party to emerge was the United Democratic Party, led by outspoken democrats Martin Lee and Szeto Wah. The pair, initially courted by China for their anticolonial positions and appointed to the committee that drafted the Basic Law, subsequently infuriated Beijing by publicly burning copies of the proto-constitution in protest over the Tiananmen massacre. Predictably, China denounced them as subversives.

Chris Patten, Hong Kong's 28th – and last – British governor arrived in 1992, pledging to his sceptical citizens to get democracy back on track. China reacted badly, first levelling daily verbal

1982	1984	1988
The prime minister of Great Britain, Margaret Thatcher, visits Beijing and Hong Kong and begins talks on the future of Hong Kong; China starts to expand Shenzhen, the village bordering Hong Kong, and nominates it as a special economic zone	In December 1984, after more than two years of closed-door wrangling, China and Britain announce that the UK has agreed to hand back the entire colony just after midnight on 30 June 1997 (a decision made without consulting the territory's people)	The detail of the 'One Country, Two Systems' policy is revealed in the joint declaration, confirming that Hong Kong people would govern Hong Kong and retain prehandover social, economic and legal systems for 50 years following the handover in 1997

attacks at the governor, then threatening the post-1997 careers of any prodemocracy politicians or officials. When these tactics failed, China targeted Hong Kong's economy. Negotiations on certain business contracts straddling 1997 suddenly came to a halt, and Beijing scared off foreign investors by boycotting all talks on the new airport programme.

Sensing that it had alienated even its supporters in Hong Kong, China backed down and in 1994 gave its blessing to the new airport at Chek Lap Kok. It remained hostile to direct elections, however, and vowed to disband the democratically elected legislature after 1997.

In August 1994 China adopted a resolution to abolish the terms of office of Hong Kong's three tiers of elected bodies: the legislature, the municipal councils and the district boards. A Provisional Legislative Council was elected by Beijing, which included pro-Beijing councillors who had been defeated by democratic ones in the sitting Legco. The rival chamber met over the border in Shenzhen, as it had no authority in Hong Kong until the transfer of power three years later. This provisional body served until May 1998, when a new Legislative Council was elected partially by the people of Hong Kong, partially by business constituencies and partially by power brokers in Beijing.

As for the executive branch of power, no one was fooled by the pseudo election, choreographed by China in 1996, to select Hong Kong's first postcolonial leader. But Tung Chee Hwa (1937–), the Shanghai-born shipping magnate destined to become the SAR's first chief executive, won approval by retaining Patten's right-hand woman, Anson Chan, as his chief secretary and Donald Tsang as financial secretary.

China agreed to a low-key entry into Hong Kong, and People's Liberation Army (PLA) troops were trucked straight to their barracks in Stanley, Kowloon Tong and Bonham Rd in the Mid-Levels. On the night of 30 June 1997 the handover celebrations held in the purpose-built extension of the Hong Kong Convention & Exhibition Centre in Wan Chai were watched by millions of people around the world. Chris Patten shed a tear while Chinese Premier Jiang Zemin beamed and Prince Charles was outwardly stoic (but privately scathing, describing the Chinese leaders in a diary leaked years later to the British tabloids as 'appalling old waxworks').

CHINA'S HONG KONG INVASION PLAN

The peaceful agreement that eventually settled the status of Hong Kong was by no means a foregone conclusion in the decades leading up to it. The key negotiators have since revealed just how touchy China felt about Hong Kong and how close it came to retaking the territory by force.

Margaret Thatcher, the British prime minister who negotiated the deal, said later that Deng Xiaoping, then China's leader, told her he 'could walk in and take the whole lot this afternoon'.

She replied that China would lose everything if it did. 'There is nothing I could do to stop you,' she said, 'but the eyes of the world would now know what China is like.'

Lu Ping, the top Chinese negotiator, recently confirmed that this was no bluff on Deng's part. Deng feared that announcing the date for the 1997 handover would provoke serious unrest in Hong Kong, and China would be compelled to invade as a result.

According to Lu, China had also been hours away from invading during 1967, at the height of the chaotic Cultural Revolution, when a radical faction of the People's Liberation Army (PLA) was poised to invade the British colony during pro-Communist riots. The invasion was called off only by a late-night order from Premier Zhou Enlai to the local army commander, Huang Yongsheng, a radical Maoist who had been itching to invade.

1989	1990	1992
Chinese tanks and troops mow down protesting students in Tiananmen Square in Beijing; the massacre propels dissidents to Hong Kong; up to one million Hong Kong people – one in six of the population – brave a typhoon to march in protest	The Basic Law for Hong Kong is ratified; the Bill of Rights is introduced, establishing that the SAR would enjoy a high degree of autonomy with the exception of foreign affairs and matters of defence, which would be the domain of China	Hong Kong's last governor, Chris Patten, arrives in 1992 and loses no time in putting the British plans for limited democracy back on track and angers China's government as he widens their scope; Sino-British relations hit a new low

So the curtain fell on a century and a half of British rule and the new chief executive Tung summed up Chinese feelings about the handover with the words: 'Now we are masters of our own house.'

THE RECENT PAST

Visitors returning to Hong Kong since July 1997 would see and feel little material difference walking around the city today. China has been largely true to its word in allowing Hong Kong the high level of the autonomy it enjoyed under the previous regime. Apart from the ever-higher buildings and the ever-narrowing gap between Kowloon and Hong Kong Island, business goes on as it did before the handover with ever-greater frenzy and bustle in this booming global financial and commercial centre. Perhaps the most striking thing for returning visitors from the West is the influx of a new breed of visitor: mainland Chinese, who now make up more than half the territory's visitor numbers.

Not everything has been rosy since the handover, however, and the mainland stands accused of interfering in Hong Kong's independence over a number of issues. Perhaps it's not surprising. Chinese premier Deng Xiaoping's policy of 'One Country, Two Systems' would always have its fault lines. His deft verbal fudge over the issue of just how much autonomy Hong Kong should enjoy continues to be tested over a series of issues: perceived attempts by the mainland to erode civil liberties and press freedoms; the debate over whether the rule of law is being maintained in the territory; and vocal calls for real democracy and better representation for all the territory's people.

Clearly the mainland government wields huge influence both benign and malign but in most cases still prefers to tread lightly, honouring the spirit of the handover agreement to a great extent. Perhaps the real surprise should be that a monolithic one-party state (and one which theoretically remains a Communist one) has resisted daily tinkering in the affairs of a nakedly capitalistic city state based on the Western rule of law. A measure of just how successful the handover has been came in a 2007 BBC interview with Baroness Thatcher. Marking the 10th anniversary of the handover of Hong Kong from Britain to China, Thatcher, to her own surprise, deemed China's overall performance a success.

There's much debate about how much influence the mainland is bringing to bear overtly or covertly in Hong Kong. But might history one day identify an equal and opposite reaction going on, too? Hong Kong's dazzling status and success arguably contains within it a kind of 'soft' power to influence thinking in the mainland. It might be hard to measure, but in the enclave that sheltered and inspired the fathers of powerful mainland movements (Sun Yatsen and Zhou Enlai) it should not be dismissed.

The fact remains, however, that true democracy still looks to be a long way off. Chinese people might now rule the roost but, more than a decade on from colonial days, the Legislative Council remains essentially toothless and ultimate power rests with the chief executive (and his ultimate masters), just as it did with the British governor.

HONG KONG POST-1997

Hong Kong might be a buoyant, self-confident place these days, but there were some bumps along the way. Almost as soon as the euphoria of the 1997 handover faded things started going badly in Hong Kong. A brutal economic recession, a plague and an ill-fated launch for the new airport helped to sandbag the new Hong Kong SAR in its early years.

1997	2001	2003
The rain falls, Chris Patten cries and Hong Kong returns to Chinese sovereignty; Tung Chee Hwa takes over as chief executive; avian flu breaks out, killing six people and leading to the slaughter of 1.5 million birds in a bid to contain the outbreak	Tung Chee Hwa follows the lead of his Beijing political masters in labelling the Falun Gong a 'vicious cult' and limits the group's activities in Hong Kong, calling into question the true worth of the Basic Law's guarantee of religious freedom in the SAR	Outbreaks of Severe Acute Respiratory Syndrome (SARS) kill nearly 300 people and bring Hong Kong to a virtual halt; the economy is hit hard as visitor numbers dwindle to almost nothing and the city's residents stay home from work and school

THE TRIADS

Hong Kong's Triads, which continue to run the territory's drug, prostitution, people smuggling, gambling and loan-sharking rackets despite the change of government, weren't always the gangster operations they are today.

They were founded as secret and patriotic societies that opposed the corrupt and brutal Qing (Manchu) dynasty and aided the revolution that brought down that dynasty in 1911. The fact that these organisations had adopted Kwan Tai (or Kwan Yu), the god of war and upholder of righteousness, integrity and loyalty, as their patron, lent them further respectability.

Unfortunately, the Triads descended into crime and illicit activities during the civil war on the mainland, and came in droves to Hong Kong after the Communists came to power in 1949. Today they are the Chinese equivalent of the Mafia. Sporting such names as 14K, Bamboo Union, Water Room and Peace Victory Brotherhood, the Triads have been increasingly successful at recruiting disaffected teenagers from Hong Kong's high-rise housing estates.

The Triad armoury is a hellish array of weapons ranging from meat cleavers and machetes to pistols and petrol bombs. If people default on a loan, Triad members encourage repayment by attacking them with large knives in the middle of the street.

The Communists smashed the Triad-controlled drug racket in Shanghai after the 1949 revolution. The Triads have long memories and, before the handover, many Hong Kong–based hoods moved their operations to ethnic Chinese communities in such countries as Thailand, the Philippines, Australia, Canada and the USA. Since 1997, however, many Triads have moved back into Hong Kong and have even expanded their operations into the mainland, establishing links with corrupt government cadres and high-ranking soldiers in the People's Liberation Army (PLA).

The definitive work on the Triads (available in some Hong Kong bookshops) is *Triad Societies in Hong Kong* by WP Morgan, a former subinspector in the Royal Hong Kong Police.

The financial crisis that had rocked other parts of Asia began to be felt in Hong Kong at the end of 1997. A strain of deadly avian flu, which many people feared would become a worldwide epidemic, saw Hong Kong slaughtering some 1.4 million chickens. Following on from this was the 'Chek Lap Kok-up' of 1998, when the much-trumpeted new airport opened to a litany of disasters. Hong Kong was making world headlines again – but for all the wrong reasons.

The credibility of the SAR administration was severely damaged in 1999 when the government challenged a High Court ruling allowing residency rights for the China-born offspring of parents who became Hong Kong citizens after 1997. The ruling was based on certain clauses of the Basic Law – Hong Kong's miniconstitution – that made 1.6 million people from the mainland eligible for right of abode in the territory. The SAR administration appealed to the standing committee of the National People's Congress (NPC), China's rubber-stamp parliament, to 'reinterpret' these clauses. The NPC complied, and ruled according to what the law drafters 'meant' but had somehow failed to write into law. Once again many people felt that the government was acting in its own – and not their – interest.

Meanwhile, chief executive Tung Chee Hwa's popularity declined rapidly. He was increasingly seen as Beijing's lackey, often dictatorial and aloof but strangely weak and indecisive in times of crisis. One example of the latter was his condemnation of Falun Gong, a spiritual movement that had emerged in China in 1992 and had earned the wrath of the mainland government, which brutally suppressed the movement.

2003	2005	2005
In July an estimated 500,000 people march through Hong Kong to oppose new anti-subversion legislation; one of the major progovernment parties of Legco refuses to vote for the bill, forcing the government to shelve it	Dogged by crises and unpopular with both his citizens and Beijing's leadership, Tung Chee Hwa resigns as chief executive and is replaced by Donald Tsang, who is elected unopposed to the post three months later by the 852-member Election Committee	Prodemocracy Legco members, some of whom had been labelled traitors by Beijing and barred from the mainland after the Tiananmen massacre, are invited to visit the mainland by its government in a significant goodwill gesture to Hong Kong democrats

DOS & DON'TS

There aren't many unusual rules of etiquette to follow in Hong Kong; in general, common sense will take you as far as you'll need to go. But on matters of identity, appearance, gift-giving and the big neighbour to the north, local people might see things a little differently than you do. For pointers on how to conduct yourself at the table, see p174.

- Clothing – beyond the besuited realm of business, smart casual dress is acceptable even at swish restaurants, but save your bikini for the beach and keep your thongs/flip-flops in the hotel.
- Colours – these are often symbolic to the Chinese. Red symbolises good luck, virtue and wealth (though writing in red can convey anger or unfriendliness). White symbolises death, so think twice before giving white flowers.
- Face – think status and respect (both receiving and showing): keep your cool, be polite and order a glass of vintage Champagne at the Pen or Mandarin. That'll show 'em.
- Gifts – if you want to give flowers, chocolates or wine as a gift to someone, they may appear reluctant for fear of seeming greedy, but insist and they'll give in. Don't be surprised if they don't open a gift-wrapped present in front of you, though; to do so would be impolite. Cash is the preferred wedding gift and is given in the form of *lai-si* (p16).
- Name cards – Hong Kong is name-card crazy and in business circles it is a must. People simply won't take you seriously unless you have one (be sure to offer it with both hands). Bilingual cards can usually be printed within 24 hours; try printers along Man Wa Lane in Sheung Wan or ask your hotel to direct you. Expect to pay about $200 for 100 cards.

THE CLAMOUR FOR DEMOCRACY

Despite his poor standing in the polls, Tung was returned for a second five-year term in March 2002 and moved to reform the executive branch, instituting a cabinetlike system within which secretaries would be held accountable for their portfolios.

Controversy continued to dog his time in office, however, most notably in March 2003, with the government's failure to contain the Severe Acute Respiratory Syndrome (SARS) epidemic at an early stage, provoking a torrent of blame. The outbreak killed 299 people, infected 1755 and all but closed Hong Kong down for weeks.

In July 2003 the government came under fire yet again over a deeply unpopular piece of new legislation. Called Article 23, which Beijing had added to Hong Kong's Basic Law in the aftermath of the Tiananmen student movement of 1989, the bill dealt with acts 'endangering public security', such as treason, subversion and sedition. In the face of massive public protests – of 500,000 people or more – the government shelved the bill indefinitely.

At the end of the following year the government was forced to scrap the sale of a public-housing property fund worth US$2.7 billion just hours before it was due to list when a court sided with an elderly tenant's challenge to the sale. It was a major blow to investors – something not lost on the leadership in Beijing.

Soon after, Chinese President Hu Jintao called on Tung to 'reflect on the past' and 'learn from his mistakes', a severe scolding by Chinese political standards. In March 2005 Tung announced his resignation as chief executive, citing overwork as the reason. His interim replacement was the bow-tie-wearing chief secretary Sir Donald Tsang, who straddled both Hong Kong's regimes as financial secretary from 1995 to 2001 and had been knighted under Chris Patten in 1997. Tsang was elected uncontested in June 2005, two weeks after the nomination period closed.

2006	2007	2007
A flood of pregnant mainland Chinese women entering Hong Kong to give birth and claim citizenship strains Hong Kong's maternity resources; a ban on heavily pregnant women entering the territory is introduced early the following year	Donald Tsang stands for election, for the first time facing an opponent; thanks in part to his popularity, but largely due to the limited voting system stuffed with probusiness and pro-Beijing voters, he wins easily and begins his second term as chief executive	A green paper examining the possible introduction of greater representation to create a more democratic system is released; democracy campaigners accuse the government of dragging out any move towards universal suffrage

Compared to the lacklustre Tung, Tsang was a welcome replacement for many. On good terms with the Beijing powerbrokers, he also sustained very high public approval ratings beyond the usual political honeymoon period (helped no doubt by a resurgent economy, and bullish stock and housing markets).

In 2007 Tsang stood again for election, and was elected with ease. He was the first chief executive not to stand unopposed. His contestant, prodemocracy activist Alan Leong, came a distant second, but for many who yearn for a truly democratic Hong Kong it is a sign of hope that Hong Kong people may one day see a government truly elected by them rather than by a cabal dominated by those loyal to local business and to the mainland powers that be.

Yearnings for democracy aside, more than 10 years on from the handover, the mood in Hong Kong is buoyant, thanks in large part to a resurgent economy taking an ever-fatter tithe from China's boom.

In the later years of the decade Hong Kong has a spring in its step and most of its citizens are proud to say they are citizens of the SAR as well, crucially, as subjects of China, however confusing and problematic that dual identity might sometimes seem.

ARTS

The epithet 'cultural desert' can no longer be used to describe Hong Kong. There are both philharmonic and Chinese orchestras, Chinese and modern dance troupes, a ballet company, several theatre groups, and numerous art schools and organisations. Government funds also allow local venues to bring in top international performers, and the number of international arts festivals hosted here seems to grow each year. Local street-opera troupes occasionally pop up around the city. Both local and mainland Chinese opera troupes can also sometimes be seen in more formal settings.

There are two art forms enjoying something of a renaissance in Hong Kong: fine arts (especially painting) and literature. The former is due to the influx of contemporary work – a lot of it derivative but some of it very good indeed – from the mainland and a new-found maturity inherent in much local painting. Home-grown literature in English, which has been quietly simmering away for the past decade or so, has been recently brought to the boil by the annual – and very successful – Man Hong Kong International Literary Festival (p37).

CINEMA

While painting and literature are enjoying a new lease of life in early 21st century Hong Kong, the art of film making has lost its lustre. Once the 'Hollywood of the Far East', churning out 245 films in 1994 alone and coming in third behind Hollywood and Mumbai, Hong Kong now produces only a few dozen films each year. What's more, up to half of all local films go directly to video format, to be pirated and sold as DVDs in the markets of Mong Kok and Shenzhen. Imports now account for between 55% and 60% of the Hong Kong film market.

Modern Hong Kong cinema arrived with the films of Bruce Lee, who first appeared in *The Big Boss* (1971), and the emergence of kung fu as a film genre. The 'chop sockey' trend

---

HONG KONG'S BABY BOOM

Functioning as part of 'one country' (China), with 'two systems' (a marriage of modern Chinese and British colonial legacies) throws up many political, social and legal tensions and anomalies. One of the most striking in recent times has been the flood of mainland women who have been coming to Hong Kong specifically to give birth.

It stems from a 2001 ruling by Hong Kong's highest court, which held that a child born in Hong Kong to parents from mainland China has the right to reside in Hong Kong. An unexpected consequence was a trickle and then a flood of pregnant mainlanders who came to the territory to give birth, attracted by virtually free healthcare, education and housing. It also offered a way to escape punitive fines imposed, under China's one child policy, on mainlanders who have more than one child.

Tens of thousands of mainlanders started taking this opportunity, putting unprecedented strain on Hong Kong's maternity services and causing resentment in Hong Kong. Such was the strain on the region's hospitals that in February 2007, authorities introduced new rules to make it harder for mainland women to come to Hong Kong to give birth.

continued through the 1970s and into the early '80s, when bullet-riddled action films took over. Two directors of this period stand out. King Hu directed several stylish Mandarin kung fu films in the early 1970s, and the films of today still take his work as a reference point for action design. Michael Hui, along with his brother Sam, produced many popular social comedies, including *Private Eyes* (1976) and *The Pilferers' Progress* (1977; directed by John Woo). In terms of actors, the comedic martial artist Jackie Chan was making his mark during this period, with kung fu movies such as *Snake in the Eagle's Shadow* (1978) and *Drunken Master* (1978) – both directed by Yuen Wo Ping – but he later moved on to police-related stories such as *The Protector* in 1985 and the highly popular *Police Story* series.

Overall, however, it was an uphill battle, with market share declining in the face of foreign competition. The upturn came in the mid-1980s, with John Woo's *A Better Tomorrow* series. Also prominent were the historical action films by Tsui Hark, including *Once Upon a Time in China* (1991), featuring great action design and a stirring score.

The new wave of Hong Kong films in the 1990s attracted fans worldwide, particularly John Woo's blood-soaked epics *Hard Boiled* (1992) and *The Killer* (1989). Woo was courted by Hollywood and achieved international success directing films such as *Face/Off* (1997) and *Mission Impossible 2* (2000). Jackie Chan, whose blend of kung fu and self-effacing comedy is beloved the world over, is one of several local stars to make it in Hollywood. He starred in *Crime Story* (1993), Stanley Tong's better-than-average action flick *Rumble in the Bronx* (1996), and teamed up with Owen Wilson in *Shanghai Noon* (2000) and *Shanghai Knights* (2003). Lamma native Chow Yun Fat featured in *The Replacement Killers* (1998), *Anna & the King* (1999) and *Crouching Tiger, Hidden Dragon* (2000). Jet Li, star of *Lethal Weapon 4* (1998) and *Romeo Must Die* (2000), is another Hong Kong boy who has made a splash overseas.

top picks

HONG KONG FILMS

- *Chungking Express* (1994) – a New Wave cop flick that isn't a cop flick. Director Wong Kar Wai creates two separate (but connected) stories about cops dealing with love and relationships – the first with a drug-smuggling femme fatale in a blonde wig and the second, starring Tony Leung with a Jean Seberg–like Faye Wong. Powerful (and, at times, very funny) stuff.

- *Infernal Affairs* (2002) – Andrew Lau and Alan Mak's star-studded, utterly gripping and multi-award winning thriller made such an impact here it was heralded as Hong Kong cinema's saviour on its release. A cop (Tony Leung) and a Triad member (Andy Lau) have penetrated each other's organisations, leading to a heart-stopping and bloody witch-hunt in each tribe. Neither of the other films in the subsequent trilogy, nor Martin Scorsese's Oscar-winning remake *The Departed,* ever quite matched it for tension or style.

- *In the Mood for Love* (2000) – Wong Kar Wai's triumphant (and exceedingly stylish) tale of infidelity and obsession stars Maggie Cheung and Tony Leung as two neighbours in 1960s Hong Kong who discover their spouses are having an affair together.

- *Made in Hong Kong* (1997) – Fruit Chan's low-budget film that went on to win a number of awards is the story of a moody young gang member whose life is turned upside down when he finds the suicide note of a young girl. It's a pretty bleak take on Hong Kong youth post-1997.

- *Once Upon a Time in China* (1991) – the ultimate kung fu film, Tsui Hark's first in a series of five follows hero Wong Fei Hung (Jet Li) as he battles corrupt government officials, violent local gangsters and evil foreign entrepreneurs in order to protect his martial arts school and the people around him in 19th-century China.

Wong, director of the cult favourite *Chungking Express* (1994), received the Palme d'Or at the Cannes Film Festival in 1997 for his film *Happy Together*. Wong Kar Wai's sublime *In the Mood For Love* (2000) raised Hong Kong film to a new level and earned its star, Tony Leung, the Best Actor award at Cannes. Its follow-up, also starring Leung, was the beautifully shot but confusing and indulgent *2046* (2004), the title of which refers to a hotel room number and not some time in the mid-21st century. Other memorable recent films include Yau Ching's *Ho Yuk* (Let's Love Hong Kong; 2002), the story of three alienated women pursuing or being pursued or not being pursued by each other; *Infernal Affairs* (2002); (see above); and *It Had to Be You* (2005) by Andrew Loo Wang-Hin and Maurice Li Ming-Man, a screwball comedy in which restaurant coworkers spar, plot against and then fall in love with one another. Other directors to watch out for include Peter Chan Ho-sun, who made *He's a Woman, She's a Man* (1994), *Comrades, Almost a Love Story* (1996) and *The Love Letter* (1999); Chan Muk Sing (the *Gen-Y Cops* series); and Stanley Kwan who made *Full Moon in New York* (1989).

Hong Kong has been the setting of many Western-made films, including: *Love is a Many-Splendored Thing* (1955), starring William Holden, and Jennifer Jones as his Eurasian doctor paramour, with great shots on and from Victoria Peak; *The World of Suzie Wong* (1960), with Holden again and Nancy Kwan as the pouting bar girl from Wan Chai; *Enter the Dragon* (1973), Bruce Lee's first Western-made kung fu vehicle; *The Man with the Golden Gun* (1974), with Roger Moore as James Bond and filmed partly in a Tsim Sha Tsui topless bar; *Year of the Dragon* (1985), with Mickey Rourke; and *Tai-Pan* (1986), the less-than-successful film version of James Clavell's doorstop novel (don't miss the bogus typhoon footage). Other foreign films shot partly or in full here include *Double Impact* (1991), *Mortal Kombat* (1995), *Rush Hour 2* (2001), with great shots of the harbour, and *Tomb Raider: The Cradle of Life* (2003), in which Lara Croft parachutes from Two International Finance Centre. An excellent source for spotting familiar locations is the two-part freebie *Hong Kong Movie Odyssey Guide* from the Hong Kong Tourist Board (HKTB).

The Hong Kong Film Awards, the territory's own 'Oscars', take place during the two-week Hong Kong International Film Festival, held in April and now in its third decade.

PAINTING

Contemporary Hong Kong art differs enormously from that produced in mainland China, and for good reason. Those artists coming of age in Hong Kong after WWII were largely (though not entirely) the offspring of refugees, distanced from the memories of economic deprivation, war and hunger. They were the products of a cultural fusion and sought new ways to reflect a culture that blended two worlds – the East and the West.

In general, Chinese are interested in traditional forms and painting processes – not necessarily composition and colour. Brush strokes and the utensils used to produce them are of vital importance and interest. In traditional Chinese art, change for the sake of change was never the philosophy or the trend; Chinese artists would compare their work with that of the master and judge it accordingly.

The influential Lingnan School of Painting, founded by the watercolourist Chao Shao-an (1905–98) in the 1930s and moved to Hong Kong in 1948, attempted to redress the situation. It combined traditional Chinese, Japanese and Western artistic traditions to produce a unique and rather decorative style, and basically dominated what art market there was in Hong Kong for the next two decades. An important figure of this time was Luis Chan (1905–95), the first Hong Kong Chinese artist to paint in the Western style.

WWII brought great changes not only to China but to Hong Kong, and the postwar generation of artists was characterised by an intense search for identity – Hong Kong rather than Chinese. It also set the stage for the golden age of modern Hong Kong art to come.

The late 1950s and early '60s saw the formation of several avant-garde groups, including the influential Modern Literature and Art Association, which counted Lui Shou-kwan (1919–75), Irene Chou (1924–) and Wucius Wong (1936–) among its members. Very structural, but at the same time inspired, the association spawned a whole generation of new talent obsessed with romanticism and naturalism. The Circle Art Group, founded in 1963 by Hon Chee Fun, was influenced by Abstract Expressionism and characterised by its spontaneous brushwork. Two other important names of this period were contemporaries Gaylord Chan (1925–) and Ha Bik-Chuen (1925–).

Like young artists in urban centres everywhere, Hong Kong painters today are concerned with finding their orientation in a great metropolis through personal statement. They are overwhelmingly unfussed with orthodox Chinese culture and older generations' attempt to amalgamate East and West. To their mind the latter is now over and done with; judging from their work, they are now looking for something that is uniquely Hong Kong. Among those painters to watch out for are Victor Lai (1961–), a figurative artist much influenced by Francis Bacon and the German Expressionists; David Chan (1950–), who studied under Lui Shou-kwan and experiments with calligraphy and graphics; Wilson Shieh (1970–), who uses traditional

Chinese *gùng-bàt* (fine-brush) painting techniques and forms to examine contemporary themes; Francis Yu (1963–), one of Hong Kong's most important oil painters, who combines Western and Chinese elements (especially characters) in his work; and Cheng Chi-fai (1971–), who uses oils to capture uniquely Hong Kong landscapes and city scenes.

The best place to view the works of modern Hong Kong painters is the Contemporary Hong Kong Art Gallery in the Hong Kong Museum of Art (p90) in Tsim Sha Tsui. Commercial galleries that specialise in local art are Grotto Fine Art and Hanart TZ Gallery (see the boxed text, opposite).

The best sources for up-to-date information on contemporary Hong Kong and other Asian art are the bimonthly *Asian Art News* (www.asianartnews.com) and the Asia Art Archive (Map p70; ☎ 2815 1112; www.aaa.org.hk; 11/F Hollywood Centre, 233 Hollywood Rd, Sheung Wan; ◷ 10am-6pm Mon-Sat).

SCULPTURE

Hong Kong's most celebrated sculptor of recent years was Antonio Mak, who died tragically at the age of 43 in 1994. Working primarily in bronze, Mak focused on the human figure as well as on animals important in Chinese legend and mythology (eg horses and tigers), and was greatly influenced by Rodin. His work employs much visual 'punning'; for example, in his *Mak's Bible from Happy Valley*, a racing horse is portrayed with a winglike book made of lead across its back. The word 'book' in Cantonese has the same sound as 'to lose (at gambling)'. The painter Ha Bik-Chuen (p33) has also worked extensively in mixed media and bronze.

Salisbury Gardens, leading to the entrance of the Hong Kong Museum of Art (p90) in Tsim Sha Tsui, is lined with modern sculptures by contemporary Hong Kong sculptors. Dotted among the greenery of Kowloon Park (p91) is Sculpture Walk, with 30 marble, bronze and other weather-resistant works by both local and overseas artists, including a bronze by Mak called *Torso* and one by Britain's late Sir Eduardo Paolozzi (1924–2005) called *Concept of Newton*.

MUSIC

Classical

Western classical music is very popular among Hong Kong Chinese. The territory boasts the Hong Kong Philharmonic Orchestra and Hong Kong Sinfonietta as well as chamber orchestras, while the Hong Kong Chinese Orchestra often combines Western orchestration with traditional Chinese instruments. Overseas performers of world repute frequently make it to Hong Kong, especially during the Arts Festival (p15) held in late March or February.

Traditional Chinese

You won't hear much traditional Chinese music on the streets of Hong Kong, except perhaps the sound of the doleful *dì-dáa*, a clarinetlike instrument played in a funeral procession; the hollow-sounding *gú* (drums) and crashing *làw* (gongs) and *bàt* (cymbals) at temple ceremonies and lion dances; or the *yí-wú*, a fiddle with 'two strings' favoured by beggars for its plaintive sound. The best place to hear this kind of music in full orchestration is by attending a concert given by the Hong Kong Chinese Orchestra (www.hkco.org) or a Chinese opera (p36).

Canto-pop

Hong Kong's home-grown popular music scene is dominated by 'Canto-pop' – original compositions that often blend Western rock or pop with traditional Chinese melodies and lyrics. Rarely radical, the songs invariably deal with such teenage concerns as unrequited love and loneliness; to many they sound like the American pop songs of the 1950s. The music is slick and eminently singable – thus the explosion of karaoke bars throughout the territory. Attending a Canto-pop concert is to see the city at its sweetest and most over the top, with screaming, silly dancing, Day-Glo wigs and enough floral tributes to set up a flower market.

Canto-pop scaled new heights from the mid-1980s to mid-1990s and turned singers like Anita Mui, Leslie Cheung, Alan Tam, Priscilla Chan and Danny Chan into household names in Hong Kong and among Chinese communities around the world. The peak of this Canto-pop golden

A GALLERY OF GALLERIES

In addition to the half-dozen commercial galleries below, all of which take part in the annual Hong Kong ArtWalk (p16) megaevent held in early March, nonprofit exhibition spaces on the cutting edge are Para/Site Artspace (Map p70; ☎ 2517 4620; www.ssa07.org; 4 Po Yan St, Sheung Wan; ☒ noon-7pm Wed-Sun), one of the most important artists' cooperatives in Hong Kong; Shanghai Street Artspace (Map p97; ☎ 2770 2157; 404 Shanghai St, Yau Ma Tei; ☒ 1-8pm Tue-Sun), a project of the Hong Kong Arts Development Council, with video assemblages, photography, computer art and mixed media; and the Cattle Depot Artists Village (Map pp88–9; ☎ 2104 3322, 2573 1869; 63 Ma Tau Kok Rd, To Kwa Wan; ☒ 2-8pm Tue-Sun), a one-time slaughterhouse in far-flung To Kwa Wan in east Kowloon that is home to a colony of local artists who live, work and exhibit here. You might also try the Hong Kong Visual Arts Centre (p63) in Hong Kong Park.

- Grotto Fine Art (Map p68; ☎ 2121 2270; www.grottofineart.com; 2nd fl, 31C-D Wyndham St, Central; ☒ 11am-7pm Mon-Sat) This small but exquisite gallery represents predominantly Hong Kong artists whose work covers everything from painting and sculpture to mixed media.
- Hanart TZ Gallery (Map p56; ☎ 2526 9019; www.hanart.com; Room 202, 2nd fl, Henley Bldg, 5 Queen's Rd, Central; ☒ 10am-6.30pm Mon-Fri, 10am-6pm Sat) Hanart is *la crème de la crème* of art galleries in Hong Kong and was instrumental in establishing the reputation of many of the artists discussed in the Painting section of this chapter.
- John Batten Gallery (Map p68; ☎ 2854 1018; www.johnbattengallery.com; Ground fl, 64 Peel St, Soho; ☒ 1-7pm Tue-Sat, 2-5pm Sun) This gallery is charged with the enthusiasm and vision of its director, who is the Hong Kong ArtWalk organiser. He shows Asian painting (especially from the Philippines) and photography that is of consistently good quality.
- Plum Blossoms (Map p68; ☎ 2521 2189; www.plumblossoms.com; Shop 6, Ground fl, Chinachem Hollywood Centre, 1-13 Hollywood Rd, Central; ☒ 10am-6.30pm Mon-Sat) The shop where Rudolf Nureyev used to buy his baubles (and other celebrities continue to do so) is one of the most exquisite and well established in Hong Kong. It promotes Asian (especially Chinese) contemporary artists.
- Schoeni Art Gallery (www.schoeni.com.hk; ☒ 10.30am-6.30pm Mon-Sat); Soho (Map p68; ☎ 2869 8802; 21-31 Old Bailey St); Central (Map p68; ☎ 2542 3143; 27 Hollywood Rd) This Swiss-owned gallery, which has been a feature on Hollywood Rd for almost a quarter-century, specialises in Neorealist and postmodern mainland Chinese art.
- Sin Sin Fine Art (Map p77; ☎ 2858 5072; www.sinsincom.hk; Ground fl, 1 Prince's Tce, Soho; ☒ 10.30am-7.30pm Tue-Sat, 2-7pm Sun) This eclectic gallery owned and run by a local fashion designer shows predominantly Hong Kong, mainland Chinese and Southeast Asian art.

None of these galleries charge an admission fee.

age came with the advent of the so-called Four Kings: thespian/singer Andy Lau, Mr Nice Guy Jacky Cheung, dancer-turned-crooner Aaron Kwok and teen heart-throb Leon Lai.

It never quite reached that altitude again. Subsequent arrivals such as Beijing waif Faye Wong, Sammi Cheung, Kelly Chen and protohunk Nicholas Tse took their turns on the throne for a time. But today most stars are a packaged phenomenon. Stars from the mainland and Taiwan – singer/songwriter Jay Chou is one example – are competing with local stars and gaining new fans here, and the strongest influences on local music are now coming from Japan and Korea.

THEATRE

Nearly all theatre in Hong Kong is Western in form, if not content. Most productions are staged in Cantonese, and a large number are new plays by Hong Kong writers. The plays often provide an insightful and sometimes humorous look at contemporary Hong Kong life and society. The independent Hong Kong Repertory Theatre (www.hkrep.com), formed in 1977, tends to stage larger-scale productions of both original works on Chinese themes or translated Western plays. More experimental troupes are the Hong Kong Players (www.hongkongplayers.com) and the multimedia Zuni Icosahedron (www.zuni.org.hk).

English-language theatre in Hong Kong is for the most part the domain of expatriate amateurs, and plays are more often than not scripted by local writers. Among the more popular venues are the Fringe Club theatres (p218) in Central. The Hong Kong Cultural Centre (p218), the Hong

Kong Academy for the Performing Arts (p217), Hong Kong City Hall (p217) and the Shouson Theatre at the nearby Hong Kong Arts Centre (p217) all host foreign productions, ranging from overblown Western musicals to minimalist Japanese theatre.

Chinese Opera

Chinese opera *(kēk)*, a mixture of singing, dialogue, mime, acrobatics and dancing, is a world away from its Western counterpart, but the themes are pretty much the same: mortal heroes battle overwhelmingly powerful supernatural foes; legendary spirits defend the world against evil; lovers seek escape from domineering and disapproving parents.

Most foreigners will find that Chinese opera performances take some getting used to. Both male and female performers sing in an almost reedy falsetto designed to pierce through crowd noise, and the instrumental accompaniment often takes the form of drumming, gonging and other nonmelodic punctuation. The whole affair can last five to six hours, and the audience makes an evening of it – eating and chatting among themselves.

HONG KONG IN PRINT

- *Chinese Walls* by Sussy Chako (1994) – a harrowing (and courageous) account of incest, infidelity and despair in a dysfunctional Chinese family living in Kowloon by the Chinese-Indonesian author now known as Xu Xi.
- *Dynasty* by Robert Elegant (1977) – a favourite and a rollicking good read, this novel describes the life and times of a young Englishwoman who marries into a family not unlike the Ho Tungs, a powerful Eurasian family dating back to the early colonial period.
- *Gweilo: Memories of a Hong Kong Childhood* by Martin Booth (2004) – this much acclaimed memoir by the late British novelist and biographer captures the spirit and ethos of the Hong Kong of the 1950s, but even newcomers to Hong Kong will wonder how a prepubescent boy – even an especially precocious one – managed to have many of the adventures he claimed to have had or witness so many pivotal events first-hand.
- *The Honourable Schoolboy Spy* by John Le Carré (1977) – the most celebrated novel from the master of the thriller, this is a story of espionage and intrigue as seen through the eyes of one George Smiley, acting head of the British Secret Service in the Hong Kong of the early 1970s.
- *An Insular Possession* by Timothy Mo (1987) – this hefty book follows the careers of two young Americans who are determined to expose the corruption of British opium traders in China by leaving their trading company and starting a newspaper. The First Opium War lands them in precolonial Hong Kong.
- *Love is a Many-Splendored Thing* by Han Suyin (1952) – this novel, set in Hong Kong shortly after the end of the Chinese revolution and proclamation of the People's Republic of China (PRC), is based on a love affair the author had with a British foreign correspondent.
- *Myself a Mandarin* by Austin Coates (1968) – this positively charming work was based on Coates' work as a special magistrate dealing in traditional Chinese law in the New Territories during the 1950s. It's full of revelations about rural Hong Kong Chinese and their culture.
- *Overleaf Hong Kong* by Xu Xi (2005) – this fine collection of a dozen short stories and essays focuses largely on identity and *wàa-kiù* (*huaqiao* in Mandarin), or 'overseas Chinese'.
- *The Road* by Austin Coates (1959) – Coates' first book is a riveting tale of the colonial government's attempt to build a highway across Great Island (which sounds suspiciously like Lantau), and the effect it has on the government, the builders and the islanders.
- *Tai-Pan* by James Clavell (1966) – almost as thick as the *Yellow Pages, Tai-Pan* is a rather unrealistic tale of Western traders in Hong Kong's early days, but it's an easy read. The sequel to *Tai-Pan*, also set in Hong Kong, is another epic called *Noble House* (1981) about a fictitious *hong* (trading house).
- *The Monkey King* by Timothy Mo (1988) – Mo's first novel, set in 1950s Hong Kong, is the often hilarious account of one Wallace Nolasco, a Macanese who marries into a wickedly dysfunctional Cantonese merchant's family.
- *The Train to Lo Wu* by Jess Row (2005) – this perceptive and very subtly written collection of short stories by a former teacher at Chinese University explores the theme of alienation and feelings of being outside a place or community.
- *Triad* by Derek Lambert (1991) – a British police superintendent, who has lost his son to drugs, takes on the Chinese underworld of Hong Kong and a very attractive missionary trying to convert the godfather. Gripping (though violent) police yarn.
- *The World of Suzie Wong* by Richard Mason (1957) – arguably the most famous – if not the best – novel set in Hong Kong, this is the story of a Wan Chai–based prostitute with a heart of gold and the British artist who loves her.

There are three types of Chinese opera performed in Hong Kong. Peking opera *(gìng-kkk)* is a highly refined style that uses almost no scenery but a variety of traditional props. This is where you'll find the most acrobatics and swordplay. Cantonese opera *(yuet-kkk)* is more a 'music hall' style, usually with a 'boy meets girl' theme, and often incorporating modern and foreign references. The most traditional is Chiu Chow opera *(chiu-kkk)*. It is still staged almost as it was during the Ming dynasty, with stories from the legends and folklore of the Chiu Chow (Chaozhou in Mandarin), an ethnic group from the easternmost region of Guangdong province.

Costumes, props and body language reveal much of the meaning in Chinese opera. Check out the enlightening display on the subject at the Hong Kong Heritage Museum (p125), where the HKTB (p289) offers a Chinese opera appreciation course every Saturday from 2.30pm to 3.45pm.

The best time to see Cantonese opera is during the Hong Kong Arts Festival in February/ March; outdoor performances are also staged in Victoria Park on Hong Kong Island during the Mid-Autumn Festival. At other times, you might stumble upon a performance at the Temple Street Night Market (p156) in Yau Ma Tei, but the most reliable venue for opera performances year-round is the Sunbeam Theatre (p218) in North Point.

LITERATURE

Until recently about the only English-language writer Hong Kong could claim as its very own was the late Austin Coates (1922–97), who set two of his books – the autobiographical *Myself a Mandarin* and a novel called *The Road* – in the territory and also wrote a fictionalised account of the life of the celebrated 18th-century Macanese 'taipan' Martha Merop (p350). But there's life in the locally grown English-language literature scene yet, demonstrated by the creation of the Man Hong Kong International Literary Festival for English literature with an Asian focus (held every March).

Anyone who wants a 'taster' of Hong Kong literature since WWII should pick up a copy of the seminal *City Voices: Hong Kong Writing in English 1945 to the Present* (editors Xu Xi and Mike Ingham; 2003), which is a collection of novel excerpts, short stories, poems, essays and memoirs with ties to Hong Kong. *Hong Kong: Somewhere Between Heaven and Earth* (editor Barbara-Sue White; 1996) is a not-dissimilar anthology on Hong Kong but is more historical than literary, with excerpts from such figures as Queen Victoria and the French novelist Jules Verne, and reaching back as far as the Song dynasty (AD 960–1279). *Hong Kong Collage* (editor Martha PY Cheung; 1998) is a collection of stories and other writings by contemporary Chinese writers, most of whom were born and/or raised in Hong Kong.

Given its dramatic setting, its unique mixture of Chinese and Western cultures and its sensitive position at China's back door, Hong Kong has been the setting of legions of fictional books – from thrillers to romances (see the boxed text, opposite).

ARCHITECTURE

Welcome to the most dazzling skyline in the world. We defy you not to be awed as you stand for the first time at the harbour's edge in Tsim Sha Tsui and see Hong Kong Island's majestic panorama of skyscrapers marching up those steep jungle-clad hills.

The spectacle you see is thanks to the fact that in Hong Kong they knock down buildings and replace them with taller, shinier versions almost while your back is turned. The scarcity of land, the pressures of a growing population and the rapacity of developers drive this relentless cycle of destruction and reconstruction.

Over the years Hong Kong has played host to everything from Tao temples and Qing dynasty forts to Victorian churches and Edwardian hotels, not that you'd know it walking down the average street. Commercial imperatives and the almost inexhaustible demand for social housing have resulted in these high-rise forests.

Impressive though it might be on first acquaintance, there are downsides. The bulk of building here is of uninspired office and apartment blocks sprouting cheek by jowl in towns throughout the territory.

The government's risible record in preserving architecturally important buildings went almost entirely unregretted by the public at large until very recently. The destruction of the iconic Star Ferry terminal in Central marked a surprising reversal in public apathy. Heartfelt protests greeted the wrecking balls in late 2006, not that they did any good.

Things aren't getting any better either. Other important historic buildings, such as the Bauhaus market at Wan Chai or the police headquarters in Soho, may not exist by the time you read this. The jury is out on how sensitive the new reclamation of the Central shoreline will be and whether there will be a particularly generous allocation of public space.

About the only bright spot is the preservation and redevelopment of the Marine Police Headquarters in Tsim Sha Tsui. Even this venture is compromised somewhat by the redevelopment of the site into a hotel, shops and new office block.

All this destruction and the grand scale of buildings demanded here does, of course, present architects with a few opportunities to make grand and striking statements. Yet it takes a generous sponsor, usually a bank, to fund buildings that aspire to more than just concrete and glass mediocrity, making truly inspired and inspiring bits of the built environment very much the exception rather than the rule.

TRADITIONAL CHINESE & COLONIAL ARCHITECTURE

About the only examples of precolonial Chinese architecture left in urban Hong Kong are Tin Hau temples dating from the early to mid-19th century, including those at Tin Hau near Causeway Bay, Stanley, Aberdeen and Yau Ma Tei. Museums in Chai Wan and Tsuen Wan have preserved a few Hakka village structures that predate the arrival of the British. For anything more substantial, however, you have to go to the New Territories or the Outlying Islands, where walled villages, fortresses and even a 15th-century pagoda can be seen.

Colonial architecture is also in short supply. Most of what is left is on Hong Kong Island, especially in Central, such as the Legislative Council building (formerly the Supreme Court; p60), built in 1912, and Government House (p59), residence of all British governors from 1855 to 1997. In Sheung Wan there is Western Market (p70), built in 1906, and in the Mid-Levels the Edwardian-style Old Pathological Institute, now the Hong Kong Museum of Medical Sciences (p77) dating from 1905. The Old Stanley Police Station (1859; p84) and nearby Murray House (1848; p84) are important colonial structures in the southern part of Hong Kong Island.

The interesting Hong Kong Antiquities & Monuments Office (Map p94; ☎ 2721 2326; www.amo.gov.hk; 136 Nathan Rd, Tsim Sha Tsui; ◷ 9am-5pm Mon-Sat), housed in a British schoolhouse that dates from 1902, has information and exhibits on current preservation efforts. For further information, an excellent source book is *Colonial Hong Kong: A Guide* by Stephen Vines.

CONTEMPORARY ARCHITECTURE

Hong Kong's verticality was born out of necessity – the scarcity of land and the sloping terrain have always put property at a premium in this densely populated place. Some buildings, such as Central Plaza (p64) and Two International Finance Centre (p61), have seized height at all costs; others are smaller but revel in elaborate detail, such as the Hongkong & Shanghai Bank building (p53). A privileged few, such as the Hong Kong Convention & Exhibition Centre (p64), have even been able to make the audacious move to go horizontal.

It's not unfair to say that truly inspired modern architecture only reached Hong Kong when Sir Norman Foster's award-winning Hongkong & Shanghai Bank building opened in Central in 1985 (on its completion in 1985 it was also the most expensive ever built, costing about $5 billion, or US$668 million). For

top picks

CONTROVERSIAL BUILDINGS

- Bank of China Tower (p58) Architect IM Pei's soaring symphony of triangular geometry is stunning. Pity about the feng shui, which geomancers say throws off aggressive and harmful energies.
- Hongkong & Shanghai Bank building (p53) Sir Norman Foster's award-winning but very expensive 'inside out' 'robot' (apparently that's what it looks like to some) is by contrast a wonderfully inclusive space.
- Hong Kong Cultural Centre (p90) Is it a petrol station or a public toilet? And why are there no windows in the greatest location of all? The debate continues...
- Jardine House (p60) A smart exterior with a nod to the portholes of the ships that pass through the harbour. At least that's the polite interpretation of this house of many orifices.
- Two International Finance Centre (p61) Hong Kong's tallest building (by far) proves that size does matter.

the first time the territory was seeing what modern architecture can and should be: innovative, functional and startlingly beautiful.

For more on Hong Kong's contemporary architecture, pick up a copy of the illustrated pocket guide *Skylines Hong Kong* by Peter Moss or the more specialist *Hong Kong: A Guide to Recent Architecture* by Andrew Yeoh and Juanita Cheung.

ECONOMY

Hong Kong finally began booming once again after a wretched, posthandover slump that saw property prices and the stock market tank and everyone from rich to poor become uncharacteristically bearish. The talk was that Shanghai was the new Asian world city and Hong Kong was doomed to remain a mere backwater.

It took several unexpected body blows to create this gloomy mood – a 1997 run on Asian currencies, September 11 2001 and the deadly SARS epidemic that virtually shut the place down.

You can't keep the irrepressible and hard-working citizens of Hong Kong down forever, though. As China's epoch-making rise continues, entrepreneurial Hong Kong rides its surging wave. It is once again Asia's preeminent city state, taking a fat tithe from its mainland trade in goods and finance. Its container port is busier than ever and its booming stock market continues to underwrite a historic series of mainland public flotations, its unique status and clear rule of law attracting significant deals and, increasingly, investment from the mainland away from Shanghai's exchange.

Hong Kong's Stock Exchange is the seventh largest in the world, with a market capitalisation of about US$1.71 trillion. In 2006, the value of initial public offerings handled here was second highest in the world after London. The easing of travel restrictions from China to Hong Kong hasn't hurt either. Visitor numbers from the mainland have surged by half.

The fact remains, however, that while Hong Kong proudly trumpets its laissez faire economic policies, considerable sections of the economy, including transport and power generation, are dominated by a handful of cartels and monopolistic franchises. Nonetheless, Hong Kong's economy is by far the freest in Asia, enjoying low taxes, a modern and efficient port and airport, excellent worldwide communications and strict anticorruption laws.

Critics would say that while Hong Kong's annual per capita GDP of US$38,000 – the highest in Asia, ranking fifth worldwide (compared to $7600 in China) according to IMF figures – is less impressive than it looks. The distribution of such wealth is far from even. Hong Kong has more billionaires than most other countries, but many more people who struggle to meet much more than fairly basic levels of subsistence.

Hong Kong has moved from labour- to capital-intensive industries in recent decades – service industries employ about 85% of Hong Kong's workforce and make up more than 88% of its GDP. Telecommunications, banking, insurance, tourism and retail sales have pushed manufacturing into the background, and almost all manual labour is now performed across the border in southern China. The shift from manufacturing to services has not been without problems. The change may have seen a dramatic increase in wages, but there has not been a corresponding expansion of the welfare state. On the other hand generous personal tax allowances mean only a little more than 40% of the working population of 3.54 million pays any salaries tax at all and a mere 0.3% pays the full 16%.

Hong Kong has traditionally suffered from a labour shortage. Most of the manual work (domestic, construction etc) is performed by imported labour, chiefly from Southeast Asia. The labour shortage is most acute in the high-tech and financial fields, prompting the government to consider further relaxing restrictions on importing talent from the mainland, a move deeply unpopular with Hong Kong's working class.

ENVIRONMENT & PLANNING

THE LAND

Hong Kong measures 1103 sq km and is divided into four major areas: Hong Kong Island, Kowloon, the New Territories and the Outlying Islands.

Hong Kong Island covers 81 sq km, or just over 7% of the total land area. It lies on the southern side of Victoria Harbour, and contains the main business district, Central. Kowloon is a peninsula on the northern side of the harbour. The southern tip, an area called Tsim Sha Tsui (pronounced jìm-sàa-jéui), is a major tourist area. Kowloon only includes the land south of Boundary St, but land reclamation and encroachment into the New Territories gives it an area of about 47 sq km, or just over 4% of the total. The New Territories occupies 747 sq km, or more than 68% of Hong Kong's land area, and spreads out like a fan between Kowloon and the border with mainland China. What was once the territory's rural hinterland has become in large part a network of 'New Towns'. The Outlying Islands refers to the territory's 234 islands, but does not include Hong Kong Island or Stonecutters Island, which is off the western shore of the Kowloon peninsula and has been absorbed by land reclamation. Officially, they are part of the New Territories and their 228 sq km make up just over 20% of Hong Kong's total land area.

Almost half the population lives in the New Territories, followed by Kowloon (30.1%), Hong Kong Island (19.7%) and the Outlying Islands (2%). A tiny percentage (0.1%, or under 7000 people) live at sea. The overall population density is 6300 people per sq km and may already have reached seven million.

GREEN HONG KONG

When you finally reach it, Hong Kong's countryside is very lush and, although only 12% of the land area is forested, some 415 sq km (or 38% of the territory's total landmass) has been designated as protected country parks. These 23 parks – for the most part in the New Territories and Outlying Islands, but encompassing the slopes of Hong Kong Island, too – comprise uplands, woodlands, coastlines, marshes and all of Hong Kong's 17 freshwater reservoirs. In addition, there are 15 'special areas' (eg Tai Po Kau Nature Reserve), as well as four protected marine parks and one marine reserve.

Hong Kong counts an estimated 3100 species of indigenous and introduced plants, trees and flowers, including Hong Kong's own flower, the bauhinia *(Bauhinia blakeana)*. Hong Kong's beaches and coastal areas are also home to a wide variety of plant life, including creeping beach vitex *(Vitex trifolia)*, rattlebox *(Croatalaria retusa)*, beach naupaka *(Scaevola sericea)* and screw pine *(Pandanus tectorius)*.

One of the largest natural habitats for wildlife in Hong Kong is the Mai Po Marsh (p108). There are also sanctuaries in the wetland areas of Tin Shui Wai (Hong Kong Wetland Park) and Kam Tin.

Wooded areas throughout the territory are habitats for warblers, flycatchers, robins, bulbuls and tits. Occasionally you'll see sulphur-crested cockatoos, even on Hong Kong Island, and flocks of domestic budgerigars (parakeets) – domestic pets that have managed to fly the coop.

The areas around some of Hong Kong's reservoirs shelter a large number of aggressive long-tailed macaques and rhesus monkeys, both of which are nonnative species. Common smaller mammals include woodland and house shrews and bats. Occasionally spotted are leopard cats, Chinese porcupines, masked palm civets, ferret badgers, wild boar and barking deer. An interesting (but rare) creature is the Chinese pangolin, a scaly mammal resembling an armadillo that rolls itself up into an impenetrable ball when threatened.

Frogs, lizards and snakes – including the red-necked keelback, which has not one but *two* sets of fangs – can be seen in the New Territories and the Outlying Islands. Hong Kong is also home to an incredible variety of insects. There are some 200 species of butterflies and moths alone, including the giant silkworm moth with a wingspan of over 20cm.

Hong Kong waters are rich in sea life, including sharks (three-quarters of Hong Kong's 40-odd gazetted beaches are equipped with shark nets) and dolphins, including Chinese white dolphins (see the boxed text, p148) and finless porpoises. Endangered green turtles call on Sham Wan beach on Lamma to lay eggs (see the boxed text, p133), and there are some 80 species of stony coral. One of Hong Kong's few remaining colonies of horseshoe crab lives in Tung Chung Bay, where the first part of the proposed Pearl River delta bridge (p310) will be built.

POLLUTION

Pollution has been and remains a problem in Hong Kong, but it wasn't until the formation of the Environmental Protection Department (EPD) in 1989 that government authorities acted decisively to clean up the mess. The EPD has had to deal with decades of serious environmental abuse and – almost as serious – a population that until recently didn't know (or care) about the implications of littering and pollution.

Three large landfills in the New Territories now absorb all of Hong Kong's daily 9440 tonnes of municipal waste (though they will soon be full). This, as well as the increased use of private garbage collectors and more recycling, appears to be having some effect.

Perhaps Hong Kong's most pressing environmental problem is air pollution, responsible for up to 15,600 premature deaths a year. It seems to get only worse. Ceaseless construction, a high proportion of diesel vehicles, coal-fired power stations and industrial pollution from the industrialised Pearl River delta have made for dangerous levels of particulate matter and nitrogen dioxide, especially in Central, Causeway Bay, Mong Kok and Tung Chung.

Complaints related to air pollution in Hong Kong led to seven million visits to the doctor in 2006 – that's one for every citizen. Unsurprisingly it has become a highly charged political and economic issue. Opinion polls show Hong Kong citizens put it right at the front of the issues they worry about and a new lobby group, the Clean Air Foundation, has challenged the government in court over its lack of action in tackling the problem. An hourly update of Hong Kong's air pollution index can be found on the EPD's website (www.info.g ov.hk/epd).

The Hong Kong and Guangdong provincial governments have signed a joint intent to reduce regional emissions of breathable suspended particulates, nitrogen oxides, sulphur dioxide and volatile organic compounds by more than half by 2010. The switch from diesel fuel to LPG by Hong Kong's taxis and newly registered minibuses has reduced breathable suspended particulates and nitrogen oxides by 13% and 23% respectively in four years, but Hong Kong's ever-growing fleet of buses continues to run overwhelmingly on diesel. It is still a fairly frequent experience not to be able to see across Victoria Harbour during daylight hours.

Water pollution has been one of Hong Kong's most serious ecological problems over the years. Victoria Harbour remains in a pitiful state, suffering from the effects of years of industrial and sewage pollution, though a disposal system called the Harbour Area Treatment Scheme has been collecting up to 70% of the sewage entering the harbour and the *E.coli* count (the bacteria that can indicate the presence of sewage) has stabilised. The percentage of rivers in the 'good' and 'excellent' categories is also increasing.

The quality of the water at Hong Kong's 41 gazetted beaches must be rated 'good' or 'fair' to allow public use, but many beaches here fall below the World Health Organization's levels for safe swimming due to pollution. Since 1998 water has been tested at each beach every two weeks during the swimming season (April to October) and judgements made based upon the level of *E. coli* present in the sample. The list of beaches deemed safe enough for swimming (an average 34 in 2004) is printed in the newspapers and on the EPD's website.

An especially annoying form of pollution in Hong Kong is the noise created by traffic, industry and commerce. Laws governing the use of construction machinery appear strict on paper, but there's often a way around things. General construction is allowed to continue between the hours of 7pm and 7am as long as builders secure a permit.

CHINESE MEDICINE

Chinese herbal medicine remains very popular in Hong Kong and seems to work best for the relief of common colds, flu and for chronic conditions that resist Western medicine, such as migraine headaches, asthma and chronic backache. The pills on sale in herbal medicine shops are generally broad-spectrum, while a prescription remedy will usually require that you take home bags full of specific herbs and cook them into a thick, vile-smelling broth.

It is a widely held belief in China that overwork and sex wear down the body and that such 'exercise' will result in a short life. To counter the wear and tear, some Chinese practise *jeun-bó* (the consumption of tonic food and herbs). This can include, for example, drinking raw snake's blood or bear's bile, or eating deer antlers, all of which are claimed to improve vision, strength and sexual potency. Similarly, the long life of the tortoise can be absorbed through a soup made from its flesh.

Like herbal medicine, Chinese acupuncture is used to treat long-term complaints rather than acute conditions and emergencies. The exact mechanism by which acupuncture works is not fully understood. The Chinese talk of energy channels or meridians, which connect the needle insertion point to the particular organ, gland or joint being treated. The acupuncture point is sometimes quite far from the area of the body being treated, and knowing just where to insert the needle is crucial. Acupuncturists have identified more than 2000 insertion points, but only about 150 are commonly used.

URBAN PLANNING & DEVELOPMENT

In recent years reclamation has continued apace in Victoria Harbour, prompting fears among many that Hong Kong's most scenic (and valuable) spot will soon disappear under concrete. (The harbour is already about half the size it was in the mid-19th century.)

Hong Kong's Court of Final Appeal forced the government to rethink plans for a 26-hectare landfill in January 2004. But despite a mass outcry and protests organised by the Society for Protection of the Harbour (www.friendsoftheharbour.org), two reclamation projects near Central are going ahead and at full tilt. Watch this (and that) space.

For an idea of how Hong Kong will look in the near and distant future, visit the Hong Kong Planning & Infrastructure Exhibition Gallery (p60) near City Hall in Central.

GOVERNMENT & POLITICS

The government of the Hong Kong Special Administrative Region (SAR) is a complicated hybrid of a quasi-presidential system glued awkwardly onto a quasi-parliamentary model. It is not what could be called a democratic system, although it has democratic elements. Sort of.

The executive branch of government is led by the chief executive, Donald Tsang, who was selected to replace Shanghai business tycoon Tung Chee Hwa, following his resignation in March 2005. Uncontested, Tsang was elected by an 800-member election committee dominated by pro-Beijing forces in June and then voted in two years later in a contested election when he comfortably beat prodemocracy activist Alan Leong.

The chief executive selects members (currently numbering 21) of the Executive Council, which serves effectively as the cabinet and advises on policy matters. The top three policy secretaries are the chief secretary for the administration of government, the financial secretary and the secretary for justice. Council members are usually civil servants or from the private sector.

The 60-seat Legislative Council is responsible for passing legislation proposed by the Executive Council. It also approves public expenditure and, in theory, monitors the administration. Council members are elected for four-year terms.

In the September 2004 election, the prodemocracy bloc, including the Association for Democracy and People's Livelihood, the Democratic Party and the Frontier Party, won almost two-thirds of the popular vote, but due to the rules of appointment they took only 25 seats (ie 40% of the total). This is because only half of the 60 council seats are returned through direct election, with the other 30 chosen by narrowly defined, occupationally based 'functional constituencies'. With a few exceptions, 'corporate voting' is the rule, enfranchising only a few powerful and conservative members of each functional constituency.

The judiciary is headed by the chief justice and is, according to the Basic Law, independent of the executive and the legislative branches. The highest court in the land is the Court of Final Appeal, which has the power of final adjudication.

The 18 District Boards, created in 1982 and restructured in 1997, are meant to give Hong Kong residents a degree of control in their local areas. These boards consist of government officials and elected representatives, but they have little power.

Although the stated aim of the Basic Law is 'full democracy', it supplies no definition for this. In April 2004, China's legislators ruled out universal suffrage in Hong Kong's 2007 election of its chief executive as well as for its 2008 Legislative Council election, citing concern that such reforms could undermine political stability and economic development.

Changes to the system can only be made with the agreement of the chief executive and a two-thirds majority of the legislature. With the democratic camp in the minority in the Legislative Council, many are pessimistic about the prospects of installing genuine democracy in Hong Kong. The clamour among the people to be heard may be louder and better organised these days but the government's response, characterised by platitudes and general expressions of a vague desire for democracy, doesn't look much less mealy-mouthed than that of Britain while it was in charge. Hong Kong's (admittedly popular) chief executive Donald Tsang has made noises about a more democratic future some time after 2012, but it's a vague commitment and one that is in any case largely the gift of the mainland.

VERY SUPERSTITIOUS

While Hong Kong may appear as Western as a Big Mac on the surface, many old Chinese traditions persist. Whether people still believe in all of them or just go through the motions to please parents, neighbours or coworkers is hard to say. But Hong Kong Chinese are too astute to leave something as important as joss, or ('luck'), to chance.

For all its worldly ways, Hong Kong is also a surprisingly religious place. The dominant religions in Hong Kong are Buddhism and Taoism, entwined with elements of Confucianism, ancient animist beliefs and ancestor worship. The number of active Buddhists in Hong Kong is estimated at around 700,000.

Feng Shui

Literally 'wind water', feng shui ('geomancy' in English) aims to balance the elements of nature to create a harmonious environment. In practice since the 12th century, it still influences designs of buildings, highways, parks, tunnels and grave sites. To guard against evil spirits, who can move only in straight lines, doors are often positioned at an angle. For similar reasons, beds cannot face doorways. Ideally, homes and businesses should have a view of calm water (even a goldfish tank helps). Corporate heads shouldn't have offices that face westward, otherwise profits will go in the same direction as the setting sun.

Fortune-Telling

There are any number of props and implements that Chinese use to predict the future but the most common method of divination in Hong Kong are the chim ('fortune sticks') found at Buddhist and Taoist temples that must be shaken out of a box onto the ground and then read by a fortune-teller. Palm readers usually examine both the lines and features of the hand (left for men, right for women) but may also examine your facial features. Apparently there are eight basic shapes, but 48 recognised eye patterns that reveal character and fortune.

Numerology

In Cantonese the word for 'three' sounds similar to 'life', 'nine' like 'eternity', and the ever-popular number 'eight' like 'prosperity'. Lowest on the list is 'four', which shares the same pronunciation with the word for 'death'. As a result the right number can make or break a business and each year the government draws in millions of dollars for charity by auctioning off automobile licence plates that feature lucky numbers. The Bank of China Tower was officially opened on 8 August 1988 (8/8/88), a rare union of the prosperous numbers. August is always a busy month for weddings.

Zodiac

As in the Western system of astrology, the Chinese zodiac has 12 signs, but their representations are all animals. Your sign is based on the year of your birth (according to the lunar calendar). Being born or married in a particular year is believed to determine one's fortune, so parents often plan for their children's sign. The year of the dragon sees the biggest jump in the birth rate, closely followed by the year of the tiger. A girl born in the year of the pig could have trouble later in life.

MEDIA

A total of 52 daily (or almost daily) newspapers and upwards of 800 periodicals are published in the well-read territory of Hong Kong. The vast majority of the publications are in Chinese. *Ta Kung Pao, Wen Wei Pao* and *Hong Kong Commercial Daily* all toe the government line and are pro-Beijing. According to independent surveys, the most trusted newspapers are *Ming Pao*, Hong Kong's newspaper of record, and the business-orientated *Hong Kong Economic Journal*.

This is all relative, however; the press is not entirely free and journalists are more inclined to self-censor. Media watchdog Reporters Without Borders placed Hong Kong 58th in its press freedom ranking for 2006, a slump from 18th place in 2002. Mainland Chinese influence, both overt and covert, is corrosive of press freedom but the business interests of many Hong Kong media owners eager to curry favour with the mainland is another factor in the decreasing ability of the Hong Kong media to tell the truth to power and to its own people.

Two English-language dailies, the *South China Morning Post* and the *Hong Kong Standard,* compete for the expatriate and Westernised Chinese markets, though there is also an English-language version of *China Daily* on sale here as well as other international dailies, including the *International Herald Tribune* and the *Financial Times*. For details see p297. For information on Hong Kong radio, see p300, and see p301 for information on television.

FASHION

Not so long ago, the strength of the Hong Kong fashion industry lay in its ability to duplicate designs. Indeed, for many travellers a shopping trip to Hong Kong meant amassing *faux* but authentic-looking Chanel purses, Louis Vuitton bags and Cartier wrist watches.

With the crackdown by the Hong Kong government on such activities and a maturing of the market, the industry has taken on a much more creative role, finding a new voice in everything from haute couture and casual wear to hip street fashion.

The fashion industry here includes: established designers who, for the most part, are couturiers and create one-off made-to-measure outfits; younger 'name' designers, who have popular collections and sell both in Hong Kong and for export; and local brands, covering the spectrum from evening and party wear to casual and streetwear.

Of the established designers a few names stand out, including the New York–based Vivienne Tam, who trained in Hong Kong, and Walter Ma, often cited as the voice of Hong Kong fashion, whose women's wear is both sophisticated and adventurous. Barney Cheng's designs are very luxurious, often embellished with beads and sequins, and he sews for the stars. Other names to watch out for include Lu Lu Cheung, especially her Terra Rosalis line, with subtle, Japanese-influenced pieces; Cecilia Yau and her gowns; Johanna Ho, whose low-key outfits are characterised by elegant straight lines and stylish but classic design; and Dorian Ho, the current darling of the designer fashion pack whose D'Orient line is classic but modern. Blanc de Chine does mostly tailored outfits, which are quietly elegant, very exclusive and distinctively Oriental.

Among the younger designers, Benjamin Lau produces innovative but very wearable pieces noted for their fine cutting. His Madame Benjie line of contemporary ready-to-wear for young women is one of the few in Hong Kong not influenced by trends. The signature pieces of one of the most amusing designers in the game, Pacino Wan, are T-shirts with kooky stencilling and denim jackets and skirts. Ruby Li is another young designer producing pieces for the young and trendy that are fun to wear. Virginia Lai concentrates on evening wear in her Virginia L line. Lu Lu Cheung's assistant designer, Otto Tang, with his cotton uppers, leather pants and torn fishnet stockings, is a name to watch. Grace Choi makes great use of embroidery and beads in her styles.

Today some of the more popular brands are the i.t group (www.izzue.com), with a hip casual-wear line and its 5cm line of easy coordinates and trendy streetwear, and Fait a Main, women's contemporary lines designed by John Cheng and distributed by Lane Crawford. Henry Lau's Spy, with three branches, is funky and provocative. Shanghai Tang has modern off-the-rack designs with traditional Chinese motifs, often dyed in vibrant colours.

See p154 in the Shopping chapter for the rundown on clothes shopping in Hong Kong.

THE WARDROBE OF SUZIE WONG

Neon-coloured Indian saris are beautiful when fastidiously wrapped and tucked, and Japanese kimonos can be like bright cocoons from which a chrysalis coyly peaks. And what's wrong with a sarong with a palm tree and blue lagoon as backdrop?

But there's nothing quite like a cheongsam, the close-fitting sheath that is as Chinese as a bowl of wonton noodle soup. It lifts where it should and never pulls where it shouldn't. And those thigh-high side slits – well, they're enough to give any man apoplexy. It's sensuous but never lewd; it reveals without showing too much.

Reach into any Hong Kong Chinese woman's closet and you're bound to find at least one cheongsam (*qípáo* in Mandarin), the closest thing Hong Kong has to national dress. It's there for formal occasions like Chinese New Year gatherings, work (restaurant receptionists and nightclub hostesses wear them), school (cotton cheongsams are still the uniform at several colleges and secondary schools) or for the 'big day'. Modern Hong Kong brides may take their vows in white, but when they're slipping off for the honeymoon, they put on a red cheongsam.

It's difficult to imagine that this bedazzling dress started life as a man's garment. During the Qing dynasty, the Manchus ordered Han Chinese to emulate their way of dress – elite men wore a loose 'long robe' (*chèung-pò*) with a 'riding jacket' (*máa-kwáa*) while women wore trousers under a long garment. By the 1920s, modern women in Shanghai had taken to wearing the androgynous *changpao*, which released them from layers of confining clothing. From this outfit evolved the cheongsam.

The 'bourgeois' cheongsam dropped out of favour in China when the Communists came to power in 1949 and was banned outright during the Cultural Revolution, but the 1950s and '60s were the outfit's heyday. This was the era of Suzie Wong (the cheongsam is sometimes called a 'Suzie Wong dress') and, although hemlines rose and dropped, collars stiffened and more darts were added to give it a tighter fit, the cheongsam has remained essentially the same: elegant, sexy and very Chinese.

BLUELIST[1] (blu₁list) *v.*
to recommend a travel experience.
What's your recommendation? www.lonelyplanet.com/bluelist

NEIGHBOURHOODS & ISLANDS

top picks

- **Tsim Sha Tsui East Promenade** (p95) Marvel at Hong Kong Island's nightly skyscraper light show.
- **The Peak Tram** (p78; see also p283) Hold on tight for a steep ascent.
- **The Peak** (p78) Admire the views on a walk around Victoria Peak's cooler climes.
- **The Star Ferry** (p91; see also p273) Still the single best and still the best-value Hong Kong experience.
- **Hong Kong Wetland Park** (p107) Skyscrapers at your back, serenity and nature in front.
- **Hiking on Lantau** (p134; see also p226) You may not see a soul on Lantau's wild ridges and coastal paths.
- **A seafood ramble on Lamma** (p131) Build an appetite on a leafy, traffic-free perambulation on low-rise Lamma Island.
- **Tian Tan Buddha** (p137) For a cost-free superlative.

ink of Hong Kong as being divided into four main areas: Hong Kong Island, Kowloon, the New Territories and the Outlying Islands.

The beating commercial and social heart of Hong Kong lies in the first two of these areas – the skyscraper-clad northern edge of Hong Kong Island and the busy commercial and residential district of Kowloon – which face each other across Victoria Harbour. Most of the museums, galleries and other places occupy either the northern side of Hong Kong Island or the southern tip of the Kowloon Peninsula. Beyond these heavily built-up areas, things thin out.

'Think of Hong Kong as being divided into four main areas: Hong Kong Island, Kowloon, the New Territories and the Outlying Islands'.

The land beyond this urban hub, most of it in the New Territories and the Outlying Islands, is generally far more sparsely populated and offers space, greenery and wilderness in abundance, something that surprises and delights many first-time visitors.

This chapter begins in Central on the northern side of Hong Kong Island. As its name implies, this district is where much of what happens (or is decided) in Hong Kong takes place; come here for business, sightseeing, umpteen transport options, and entertainment in the Lan Kwai Fong and Soho nightlife districts.

To the west and contiguous to Central is more traditional Sheung Wan, which manages to retain the feel of pre-war Hong Kong in parts. Rising above Central are the Mid-Levels residential area and the Peak, home to the rich, the famous and the indefatigable Peak Tram. To the east of Central are Admiralty, not much more than a cluster of office towers, hotels and shopping centres these days but still an important transport hub; Wan Chai, a seedy red-light district during the Vietnam War but now a popular entertainment area; and Causeway Bay, the most popular shopping district on Hong Kong Island.

On the southern edge of the island are small popular seaside towns, including Stanley – with its fashionable restaurants, cafés and famous market – and Aberdeen, Hong Kong's original settlement, where you can ride in a sampan (motorised launch) around the harbour or visit nearby Ocean Park, Hong Kong's home-grown amusement and theme park.

North of Hong Kong Island and across Victoria Harbour is Kowloon – its epicentre is the shopping and entertainment district Tsim Sha Tsui. To the east are Tsim Sha Tsui East and Hung Hom, awash with hotels and museums. North of Tsim Sha Tsui are the working-class areas of Yau Ma Tei – where you'll find pawnshops, outdoor markets, Chinese pharmacies, mahjong parlours and other retailers plying their time-honoured trades – and Mong Kok, a somewhat seedy district of street markets and brothels. Beyond are the districts of so-called New Kowloon, containing everything from cheap computers to Hong Kong's largest temple complex, Sik Sik Yuen Wong Tai Sin.

The New Territories, once Hong Kong's country playground, is today a mixed bag of housing estates and some surprisingly unspoiled rural areas and country parks. The area's New Towns are worth visiting for their temples, monasteries and/or museums hidden somewhere below all the skyscrapers. Don't miss the more tranquil areas either: old walled villages, mountains, important wetlands, forested nature reserves; and the idyllic Sai Kung Peninsula.

The Hong Kong archipelago counts hundreds of islands, most uninhabited. Among the so-called Outlying Islands accessible on a day trip from Hong Kong Island are: Cheung Chau, with its traditional village and fishing fleet; Lamma, celebrated for its restaurants and easy country walks; Lantau, the largest island of all, with excellent beaches and country trails; little Peng Chau, laid-back and something of a shopping mecca; Ma Wan and Tsing Yi, the 'anchors' for the two colossal bridges linking Lantau with the New Territories; Tung Lung Chau, with the remains of a 300-year-old fort; and Po Toi, a haven for seafood lovers.

The Transport boxes in this chapter provide quick reference for Mass Transit Rail (MTR), Kowloon-Canton Railway (KCR), Light Rail and bus stations, ferry piers and tram stops in each district. See further details in the Transport chapter, and for suggestions on the best maps and plans, see p295.

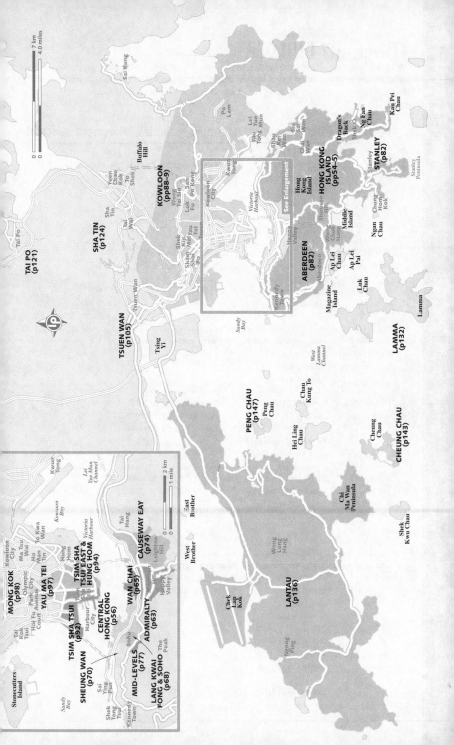

0   7 km
0   4.0 miles

Stonecutters Island

Sandy Bay

TAI PO (p121)

SHA TIN (p124)

KOWLOON (pp88-9)

TSUEN WAN (p105)

Tsing Yi

Buffalo Hill

Po Lam

See Enlargement

HONG KONG ISLAND (pp54-5)

STANLEY (p82)

Kau Pei Chau

Ng Fan Chau

Dragon's Back

Stanley Peninsula

Chung Hom Kok

ABERDEEN (p82)

Ap Lei Chau

Ap Lei Pai

Luk Chau

Middle Island

Ngan Chau

Magazine Island

LAMMA (p132)

Lamma

Happy Valley

Victoria Harbour

Kennedy Town

West Lamma Channel

PENG CHAU (p147)

Peng Chau

Chau Kung To

Hei Ling Chau

Cheung Chau

CHEUNG CHAU (p143)

Chi Ma Wan Peninsula

Shek Kwu Chau

LANTAU (p136)

Chek Lap Kok

Ngong Ping

Wong Lung Hang

Sandy Bay

Kowloon Bay

Lei Yue Mun Channel

East Brother

West Brother

Tai Hang

Leighton Hill

Happy Valley

CAUSEWAY BAY (p74)

0   2 km
0   1 mile

MONG KOK (p98)

Olympic

Ma Tau Wai

Ho Man Tin

To Kwa Wan

Kowloon City

Hung Hom

Kwun Tong

YAU MA TEI (p97)

Tai Kok Tsui

Hoi Fu Park City

Court Avenue

TSIM SHA TSUI (p92)

TSIM SHA TSUI EAST & HUNG HOM (p94)

Victoria Harbour

SHEUNG WAN (p70)

Sai Ying Pun

Shek Tong Tsui

Kennedy Town

CENTRAL HONG KONG (p56)

WAN CHAI (p65)

ADMIRALTY (p63)

MID-LEVELS (p77)

LANG KWAI FONG & SOHO (p68)

Soho

The Peak

ITINERARY BUILDER

Most of the sights, activities and eating and drinking attractions in Hong Kong are concentrated into a fairly tight area comprising of the northern edge of Hong Kong Island and the tip of Kowloon. Beyond these, things spread out into the larger and generally less built-up expanses of Hong Kong Island, the New Territories and the Outlying Islands.

AREA	ACTIVITIES Sightseeing	Museums, Galleries, Monuments & Temples
Central	Hongkong & Shanghai Bank Building (p53) Bank of China Buildings (p58) Legislative Council Building (p60)	Hong Kong Monetary Authority Information Centre (p61) Hanart TZ Gallery (p35)
Sheung Wan & the Mid-Levels	Man Mo Temple (p67) Tai Ping Shan Temples (p71) Queen's Road West Incense Shops (p70)	Dr Sun Yat Sen Museum (p77) Hong Kong Museum of Medical Sciences (p77)
Wan Chai & Causeway Bay	Hong Kong Convention & Exhibition Centre (p64) Noonday Gun (p73) Golden Bauhinia (p64)	Hung Shing Temple (p67)
Tsim Sha Tsui	Former KCR Clock Tower (p90) Nathan Road (p91) Peninsula Hong Kong (p91)	Hong Kong Museum of Art (p90) Hong Kong Museum of History (p95) Hong Kong Science Museum (p96)
Mong Kok, Yau Ma Tei & New Kowloon	Sik Sik Yuen Wong Tai Sin Temple (p102) Chi Lin Nunnery (p102) Jade Market (p98)	Lei Cheng Uk Han Tomb Museum (p100) Tin Hau Temple (p98)
New Territories	Sha Tin Racecourse (p125) Yuen Yuen Institute (p105) Lung Yeuk Tau Heritage Trail (p119)	Hong Kong Heritage Museum (p125) Chinese University of Hong Kong Art Museum (p123) Sam Tung Uk Museum (p106)
The Outlying Islands	Ngong Ping (p135) Cheung Chau Village (p142) Lamma Family Trail (p131)	Pak Tai Temple (p144)

HOW TO USE THIS TABLE

The table below allows you to plan a day's worth of activities in any area of the city. Simply select which area you wish to explore, and then mix and match from the corresponding listings to build your day. The first item in each cell represents a well-known highlight of the area, while the other items are more off-the-beaten-track gems.

Outdoors	Shopping	Eating	Drinking & Nightlife

Graham St Market (p58)
 Hong Kong Zoological & Botanical Gardens (p58)
 Lan Kwai Fong & Soho (p67)
	The Landmark (p162)
	 Lok Cha Tea Shop (p163)
	 IFC Mall (p162)
		Yun Fu (p178)
		 Sichuan Cuisine
		   Da Ping Huo (p184)
		 Lung King Heen
		   (p177)
			Drop (p214)

Western Market (p70)
 Man Wa Lane (p71)
 Possession St (p71)
	Hollywood Rd (p156)
	 Cat St (p70)
		Korea House
		   Restaurant (p182)
		 Gaia Ristorante (p182)
		 Leung Hing Chiu
		   Chow Seafood
		   Restaurant (p183)
			Barco (p208)
			 Club 71 (p208)
			 Rice Bar (p208)

Victoria Park (p75) Happy Valley Racecourse (p79)	Times Square (p166) Walter Ma (p165) Island Beverley (p164)	Forum (p187) Kin's Kitchen (p189)	Champagne Bar (p209) Chinatown (p209) Dusk Till Dawn (p216)

Tsim Sha Tsui East
   Promenade (p95)
 Kowloon Park (p91)
	Harbour City (p168)
	 Curio Alley (p168)
	 Alan Chan
	   Creations (p168)
		Nobu (p191)
		 Hutong (p192)
		 Tsui Wah (p182)
			Aqua Spirit (p211)
			 Balalaika (p211)
			 Cloudnine (p216)

Kowloon Walled
   City Park (p101)
 Lei Yue Mun (p102)
 Yuen Po St Bird Garden
   & Flower Market (p99)
	Temple Street
	   Night Market (p96)
	 Festival Walk Shopping
	   Centre (p170)
	 Golden Computer
	   Arcade (p170)
		Ming Court (p194)	

Hong Kong Wetland
   Park (p107)
 Sai Kung Peninsula
   (p126)
 Tai Mo Shan (p106)
		Sun Keung Kee Roasted
		   Goose & Seafood
		   Restaurant (p197)
		 Honeymoon Dessert
		   (p197)
		 Panda Café (p195)
			The Duke (p212)
			 Poets (p212)

Lantau Peak (p137)
 Cheung Chau Walking
   Tour (p145)
 Lo So Shing Beach (p133)
		Stoep Restaurant (p201)
		 Hometown
		   Teahouse (p199)
		 Rainbow Seafood
		   Restaurant (p199)
			China Beach Club (p213)
			 Morocco's Bar & Restaurant
			   (p212)
			 Island Society Bar (p212)

HONG KONG SPECIAL ADMINISTRATIVE REGION (SAR)

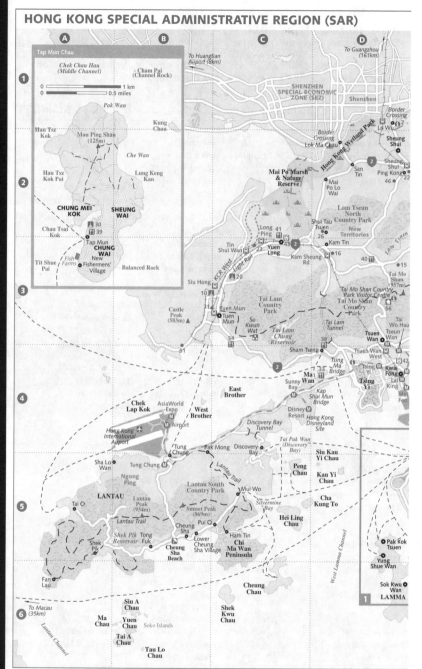

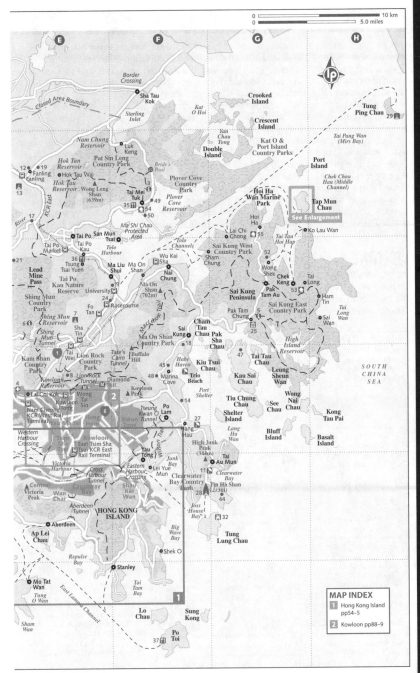

MAP INDEX

1 Hong Kong Island pp54–5
2 Kowloon pp88–9

HONG KONG ISLAND

Hong Kong Island remains every bit as important to the territory as when Britain claimed it for the Empire in 1841. Its importance as the historical, political and economic centre of Hong Kong far outweighs its size (making up just over 7% of the territory's total land area and about a fifth of its population). Though a few old monuments have been preserved here, Hong Kong Island is overwhelmingly a metropolis of dazzling modernity.

Hong Kong's most important district is Central, the commercial heart of Hong Kong pumping away on the northern side of the island. Hong Kong counts its money and spends much of it conspicuously here. Most of the region's major businesses, government offices, many top-end hotels and restaurants, nightlife areas and exclusive residential neighbourhoods are found between Central to the west and Causeway Bay to the east. It is where you'll find the ex-governor's mansion, the stock exchange, the Legislative Council and High Court, the territory's premier shopping districts, the original horse-racing track and a host of other places that define Hong Kong's character.

One of the best ways to see the northern side of the island is to jump on one of the green double-decker trams that trundle between Kennedy Town in the west and Shau Kei Wan in the east. The southern side of Hong Kong Island has a totally different character to that of the north. The coast is dotted with fine beaches – including those at Big Wave Bay, Deep Water Bay, Shek O, Stanley and Repulse Bay – where the water is clean enough to swim.

CENTRAL

Drinking & Nightlife p205; Eating p176; Shopping p156; Sleeping p250

All visitors to Hong Kong inevitably pass through Central (Map p56) – sightseeing, shopping, taking care of errands, en route to the bars and restaurants of Lan Kwai Fong and Soho, or boarding or getting off the Airport Express.

As Hong Kong's business centre, Central has some impressive architecture (p37). It's sky-

HONG KONG SPECIAL ADMINISTRATIVE REGION (SAR)

scrapers can be quite magnificent, especially at night when they put on a lightshow. There's also an assortment of historical civic buildings, churches parks and gardens.

The district was originally named Victoria, after the British sovereign who had ascended to the throne just two years before a naval landing party hoisted the British flag at Possession Point west of here in 1841. But as the 'capital' of the territory, it has been called Central at least since WWII.

Above Central the residential Mid-Levels cling to steep, jungle-clad hill sides; above these soars Victoria Peak, home to the super-rich and a great place from which to look back down on Central.

Though very much open to debate, Central's limits are Garden Rd to the east, somewhere between the disused Central Market and Wing On Centre to the west, Caine Rd and the Hong Kong Zoological & Botanical Gardens to the south, and the harbour to the north.

Central's main thoroughfares going west to east are Connaught Rd Central, Des Voeux Rd Central and Queen's Rd Central. Important streets running (roughly) south (ie uphill) from the harbour are Garden Rd, Ice House St, Pedder St and Pottinger St.

The best way to view Central is from a Star Ferry as it crosses the harbour from Kowloon.

HONGKONG & SHANGHAI BANK (HSBC) BUILDING Map p56
1 Queen's Rd Central; MTR Central (exit K)
Fittingly, the statue of Sir Thomas Jackson in Statue Square is gazing at the stunning headquarters of what is now HSBC (formerly the Hongkong & Shanghai Bank) headquarters, designed by British architect Sir Norman Foster in 1985. The two bronze lions guarding the bank's main entrance were designed by British sculptor WW Wagstaff to mark the opening of the bank's previous headquarters in 1935; the lions are known as Stephen – to the left as you face them – and Stitt, after two bank employees of the time. The Japanese used the lions as target practice during the occupation; you can still see bullet holes on Stitt.

The Hongkong & Shanghai Bank Building is a masterpiece of precision, sophistication and innovation. And why not? It was the world's most expensive building (it cost upward of US$1 billion) when it opened in 1985. The building reflects architect Sir Norman's wish to create areas

top picks

HONG KONG IN A DAY

Introduction
High-rises and mountain peaks overlooking a harbour thick with ferries and junks, Hong Kong is a wealth of cultural delights coupled with the familiarity of the Western world.

Tsim Sha Tsui – start here
On the southern tip of Kowloon, facing the sparkling high-rises of Hong Kong island, this is the perfect start and end place for your day. Jump on the timeless Star Ferry and head over to the island while enjoying the harbour views.

Island by Bus – a cheap thrill ride
Take a bus from Central heading towards Stanley. This hair-raising ride gives you a cheap tour of much of the island.

Stanley Market – bargain souvenirs
Although touristy, Stanley Market is a great place for souvenirs. Wander along the waterfront when you tire of the crowds, then jump back on a bus to Central.

Victoria Peak – spectacular view
Walk from Central to the Peak Tram and enjoy the most spectacular view over Hong Kong city and Kowloon. For a different angle take the bus back down, then take a stroll in the Central area and enjoy the city ambience.

Kowloon – the cultural heart
As the day moves on, Kowloon becomes a vibrant mix of coloured neon and mesmerising markets. Take the MTR to Mong Kok and head south. Nathan Rd is the main strip, but the backstreets contain the hidden delights.

Not Exhausted Yet?
Ride a sampan in Aberdeen; go bargain electronics shopping in Mong Kok; enjoy a change of pace on Lamma Island; lose a fortune in Macau; or find your spiritual side at the Po Lin Monastery on Lantau Island.

doyley

BLUELIST[1] (blu list) v.
to recommend a travel experience.
What's your recommendation? www.lonelyplanet.com/bluelist

of public and private space and to break the mould of previous bank architecture. The ground floor is public space, which people can traverse without entering the

lonelyplanet.com

HONG KONG ISLAND

A **B** Stonecutters **C** **D**
Island

MAP INDEX
1 Aberdeen p82
2 Admiralty p63
3 Causeway Bay p74
4 Central Hong Kong p56
5 Lan Kwai Fong & Soho p68
6 Mid-Levels p77
7 Sheung Wan p70
8 Stanley p82
9 Wan Chai p65

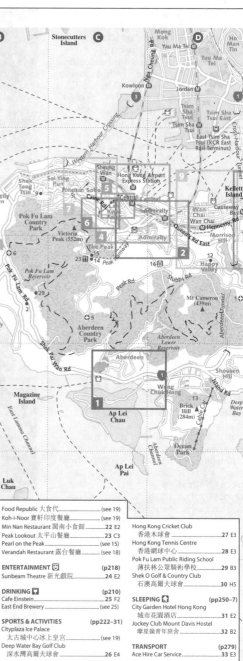

NEIGHBOURHOODS & ISLANDS   HONG KONG ISLAND

INFORMATION
Adventist Hospital 1 D3
Chinese Cuisine Training Institute
中華廚藝學院 2 B3
Home Management Centre
香港家政中心 3 E2
Map Publication Centre 地圖銷售處 4 F2
Matilda International Hospital
明德國際醫院 5 C3
Queen Mary Hospital 瑪麗醫院 6 B3

SIGHTS (pp52–149)
Hong Kong Film Archive
香港電影資料館 7 F2
Hong Kong Museum of Coastal Defence
香港海防博物館 8 G2
Hong Kong University 香港大學 9 B2
Kwun Yam Shrine 觀音廟 10 E4
Law Uk Folk Museum 羅屋博物館 11 G3
Longevity Bridge 長壽橋 .... (see 10)
Lover's Rock 姻緣石 12 D3
Madame Tussauds .... (see 15)
Ocean Park 13 D4
Peak Galleria 14 C3
Peak Tower 15 C3
Police Museum 警察博物館 16 D3
Sam Ka Tsuen Typhoon Shelter
三家村避風塘 17 G2
The Repulse Bay 淺水灣 18 E4
University Museum & Art Gallery
香港大學美術博物館 .... (see 9)

SHOPPING (p165)
Cityplaza 太古城 19 F2

EATING (pp176–201)
Beira Rio Wine Bar & Grill 20 F2
Cafe Deco .... (see 14)
Cococabana 21 E4

Food Republic 大食代 .... (see 19)
Koh-i-Noor 寶軒印度餐廳 .... (see 19)
Min Nan Restaurant 閩南小食館 22 E2
Peak Lookout 太平山餐廳 23 C3
Pearl on the Peak .... (see 15)
Verandah Restaurant 露台餐廳 .... (see 18)

ENTERTAINMENT (p218)
Sunbeam Theatre 新光戲院 24 E2

DRINKING (p210)
Cafe Einstein 25 F2
East End Brewery .... (see 25)

SPORTS & ACTIVITIES (pp222–31)
Cityplaza Ice Palace
太古城中心冰上皇宮 .... (see 19)
Deep Water Bay Golf Club
深水灣高爾夫球會 26 E4

Hong Kong Cricket Club
香港木球會 27 E3
Hong Kong Tennis Centre
香港網球中心 28 E3
Pok Fu Lam Public Riding School
薄扶林公眾騎術學校 29 B3
Shek O Golf & Country Club
石澳高爾夫球會 30 H5

SLEEPING (pp250–7)
City Garden Hotel Hong Kong
城市花園酒店 31 E2
Jockey Club Mount Davis Hostel
摩星嶺青年旅舍 32 B2

TRANSPORT (p279)
Ace Hire Car Service 33 E3

54

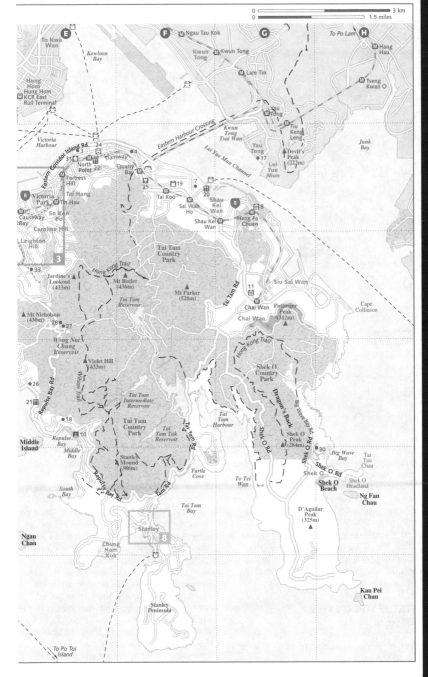

E   To Kwa Wan
Kowloon Bay

F   Ngau Tau Kok
Kwun Tong
Kwun Tong
Lam Tin

G

H   To Po Lam
Hang Hau
Tseng Kwan O

Hung Hom
Hung Hom
KCR East
Rail Terminal

Eastern Harbour Crossing
Kwun Tong Tsai Wan
Yau Tong
Tiu Keng Leng
Yau Tong   17
Devil's Peak (222m)
Lei Yue Mun
Junk Bay

Victoria Harbour

Eastern Corridor Island Rd
3
24
North Point
31
22
Tramway
Quarry Bay
Lei Yue Mun Channel

Victoria Park
8
Tin Hau
Tai Hang
25
19
Tai Koo
7
20
Sai Wan Ho
Shau Kei Wan
8
Heng Fa Chuen
8

Causeway Bay
So Kon Po
Caroline Hill
Shau Kei Wan
M

Leighton Hill

33
Jardine's Lookout (433m)
Mt Butler (436m)
Mt Parker (528m)
11
Siu Sai Wan
Cape Collinson

Hong Kong Trail

Tai Tam Country Park

Tai Tam Reservoir

Mt Nicholson (430m)
28
27
Chai Wan
Pottinger Peak (312m)
Chai Wan

Wong Nai Chung Reservoir

Wilson Trail

Violet Hill (433m)

Hong Kong Trail

Shek O Country Park

26
21
18

Repulse Bay Rd

Tai Tam Intermediate Reservoir

Tai Tam Country Park

Tai Tam Tuk Reservoir

Tai Tam Harbour

Dragon's Back

Shek O Rd

Big Wave Bay Rd

Shek O Peak (284m)
30
Big Wave Bay
Tai Tau Chau

Shek O Rd

Middle Island
Repulse Bay
10
Middle Bay

Shek O
Shek O Beach
Shek O Headland
Ng Fan Chau

South Bay

Repulse Bay Rd

Stanley Mound (386m)

Turtle Cove

To Tei Wan

D'Aguilar Peak (325m)

Tam Rd

Tai Tam Bay

Stanley
8

Ngan Chau
Chung Hom Kok

Kau Pei Chau

Stanley Peninsula

To Po Toi Island

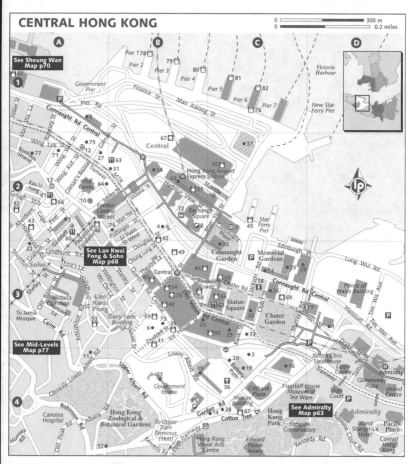

CENTRAL HONG KONG

building; from there, escalators rise to the main banking hall. The building is inviting to enter – not guarded or off limits. Hong Kong Chinese, irreverent as always, call the 52-storey glass and aluminium structure the 'Robot Building'.

It's worth taking the escalator (☉ 9am-4.30pm Mon-Fri, 9am-12.30pm Sat) to the 3rd floor to gaze at the cathedral-like atrium and the natural light filtering through its windows.

STATUE SQUARE Map p56
MTR Central (exit K)

Statue Square, due south of Star Ferry pier, is divided roughly in half by Charter Rd. In the northern part, reached via a pedestrian underpass from the pier, is the Cenotaph (Greek for 'empty tomb'; 1923), a

memorial to Hong Kong residents killed during the two world wars. Due west is the venerable Mandarin Oriental (p251), which opened in 1963 and is consistently voted the best hotel in the world, and to the east the Hong Kong Club Building (1 Jackson Rd), which houses a prestigious club of that name that was still not accepting Chinese members until well after WWII. The original club building, a magnificent four-storey colonial structure, was torn down in 1981 despite public outcry and was replaced with the modern bow-fronted monstrosity there now.

On the south side of Chater Rd, Statue Square has a collection of fountains and covered outside seating areas; it is best known in Hong Kong as the meeting place of choice for tens of thousands of Filipino

CENTRAL HONG KONG

migrant workers on the weekend, especially Sunday, when it becomes a cacophony of Tagalog, Visayan and Ilocano (see boxed text, p60).

The square derives its name from the various effigies of British royalty on display here that were spirited away by the Japanese during the occupation. Only one statue actually remains, a bronze likeness of Sir Thomas Jackson, a particularly successful Victorian chief manager of the Hongkong & Shanghai Bank.

MARKETS Map p56
MTR Central (exit B)
On the lower reaches west of the 800m-long Central Escalator, which transports pedestrians through Central and Soho and as far as Conduit Rd in the Mid-Levels, you'll find narrow streets containing market stalls and open-air canteens centred on the Graham St Market.

It's a compelling place to go if you want to have a close look at the exotic produce that Hong Kong prides itself in selling and consuming. Preserved 'thousand-year' eggs and fresh tofu curd scooped still steaming from wooden tubs are just some of the produce items on display. The squeamish should stay away; fish are cut lengthwise, but above the heart so that it continues to beat and pump blood around the body, keeping it fresher than fresh.

HONG KONG ZOOLOGICAL & BOTANICAL GARDENS Map p56
☎ 2530 0154; www.lcsd.gov.hk/en/ls_park.php; Albany Rd; admission free; ⏲ terrace gardens 6am-10pm, zoo & aviaries 6am-7pm, greenhouses 9am-4.30pm; 🚌 3B, 12 or 40M from Central
Established in 1871 as the Botanic Garden, these 5.6-hectare gardens are a pleasant collection of fountains, sculptures, greenhouses, a playground, a zoo and several fabulous aviaries. Along with exotic trees, plants and shrubs, some 160 species of bird are in residence here – including non-native sulphur-crested cockatoos, which are attractive but damage the local vegetation. The zoo is surprisingly comprehensive, with

more than 70 mammals and 40 reptiles, and is also one of the world's leading centres for the captive breeding of endangered species (there are 16 different species of endangered animal being bred here).

The gardens are divided by Albany Rd, with the plants and aviaries in the area to the east, close to Garden Rd, and most of the animals to the west. The animal displays are mostly primates (lemurs, gibbons, macaques, orangutans etc); other residents include a jaguar and radiated tortoises.

The Hong Kong Zoological & Botanical Gardens are at the top (ie southern) end of Garden Rd. It's an easy walk from Central, but you can also take bus 3B or 12 from the stop in front of Jardine House on Connaught Rd Central or bus 40M from the Central bus terminus below Exchange Square. The bus takes you along Upper Albert Rd and Caine Rd on the northern boundary of the gardens. Get off in front of Caritas House (Map p77; 2 Caine Rd) and follow the path across the street and up the hill to the gardens.

BANK OF CHINA BUILDINGS Map p56
MTR Central
To the east of the HSBC building is the old Bank of China (BOC) building (2A Des Voeux Rd Central), built in 1950, which now houses the bank's Central branch and, on the top three (13th to 15th) floors, the exclusive China Club, which evokes the atmosphere of old Shanghai. The BOC is now headquartered in the awesome Bank of China Tower (1 Garden Rd) to the southeast, designed by Chinese-born American architect IM Pei and completed in 1990.

The 70-storey Bank of China Tower is Hong Kong's third-tallest structure after Two International Finance Centre in Central

TRANSPORT – CENTRAL

MTR Central station on the Island and Tsuen Wan lines is at the heart of the neighbourhood.

Airport Express Hong Kong station below IFC Mall connects by underground walkway with Central MTR on one side and on the other to the central piers ferry terminal.

Bus Buses from all over the island start and end their journeys at Central bus terminus below Exchange Square.

Tram The line runs east and west along Des Voeux Rd Central.

Star Ferry Ferries from Tsim Sha Tsui and Hung Hom in Kowloon arrive at the new Central ferries pier.

Central Escalator Lower terminus at Central Market to the Mid-Levels.

Peak Tram Lower terminus at 33 Garden Rd to the Peak.

Outlying Islands Ferry Ferries to Discovery Bay (pier 3), Lamma (pier 4), Cheung Chau (pier 5), Lantau and Peng Chau (pier 6).

A CHINESE CURE ALL

So you're feeling a bit peaky. Below par. Liverish even. Why not see if a Chinese herbalist can pep you up? Might we suggest the Good Spring Co on Cochrane St, directly beneath the Escalator?

First for the consultation: you will be asked a few questions, your pulse taken, and your tongue examined to reveal how balanced your humours are and whether you have too much heat or cold in your constitution.

According to the prognosis the tonic will very likely be a medicinal tea. This may be a simple herbal infusion, or something containing more exotic ingredients. Some are helpfully described in the window, such as powdered deer's horn, monkey's visceral organs (useful if you need to 'remove excessive sputum') and deer's tail (a marvel if you need to 'strengthen sinews' or 'treat the seminal emission').

Other ingredients might include desiccated deer's penis, dinosaur teeth or horse bezoars (gallstone-like balls formed in horses' stomachs, and the herbalist's poison antidote of choice). The resulting brew is invariably dark brown, sinister in smell and bitter to taste.

What's that you say? You're not feeling quite so bad after all?

and Central Plaza in Wan Chai. The asymmetry of the building is puzzling at first glance but is really a simple geometric exercise. Rising from the ground like a cube, it is successively reduced, quarter by quarter, until the south-facing side is left to rise upward on its own.

Many local Hong Kong Chinese see the building as a huge violation of the principles of feng shui. For example, the bank's four triangular prisms are negative symbols in the geomancer's rule book; being the opposite to circles, these triangles contradict what circles suggest – money, prosperity, perfection. The public viewing gallery (☼ 8am-6pm Mon-Fri) on the 43rd floor offers panoramic views of Hong Kong.

CENTRAL DISTRICT POLICE STATION
Map p68

10 Hollywood Rd; 🚌 **26**
Part of this compound of four-storey buildings dates back to 1864, though other blocks were added in 1910 and 1925. The police moved out in late 2004 and, at the time of writing, the government was considering putting the buildings and the valuable chunk of land on which they sit up for commercial tender, despite a public outcry against the move.

EXCHANGE SQUARE Map p56

8 Connaught Pl; MTR Central (exit A)
West of Jardine House, this complex of three elevated office towers is home to the Hong Kong Stock Exchange and a number of businesses and offices. Access is via a network of overhead pedestrian walkways stretching west to Sheung Wan and linked to many of the buildings on the other side of Connaught Rd. The ground level of the

52-storey Towers I and II is given over to the Central bus and minibus terminus; Tower III is 32 levels high. The stock exchange is located at the main entrance to Towers I and II.

FORMER FRENCH MISSION BUILDING Map p56

1 Battery Path; MTR Central (exit K)
The Court of Final Appeal, the highest judicial body in Hong Kong, is now housed in the neoclassical former French Mission building, a charming structure built by an American trading firm in 1868. It served as the Russian consulate in Hong Kong until 1915 when the French Overseas Mission bought it and added a chapel and a dome. The building was the headquarters of the provisional colonial government after WWII. Tree-lined Battery Path links Ice House St with Garden Rd. Just before the mission building is pretty Cheung Kong Garden, which developers were required to lay out when they built the 70-storey Cheung Kong Centre to the south.

GOVERNMENT HOUSE Map p56

☎ **2530 2003; Upper Albert Rd; MTR Central (exit G)**
Parts of this erstwhile official residence of the governor of Hong Kong, opposite the northern end of the Zoological & Botanical Gardens, date back to 1855 when Governor Sir John Bowring was in residence. Other features, including the dominant central tower linking the two original buildings, were added in 1942 by the Japanese, who used it as military headquarters during the occupation of Hong Kong in WWII. Hong Kong's first chief executive, Tung Chee Hwa, refused to occupy Government House after taking up his position in 1997, claiming the

feng shui wasn't satisfactory, and his successor, Donald Tsang, has followed suit.

Government House is open to the public three or four times a year, notably one Sunday in March, when the azaleas in the mansion gardens are in full bloom.

HONG KONG CITY HALL Map p56
☎ 2921 2840; 1 Edinburgh Pl; MTR Central (exit J3)
Southwest of Star Ferry pier, the recently facelifted City Hall was built in 1962 and is still a major cultural venue in Hong Kong, with concert and recital halls, a theatre and exhibition galleries. Within the so-called Lower Block but entered to the east of City Hall's main entrance, the Hong Kong Planning & Infrastructure Exhibition Gallery (☎ 3102 1242; www .info.gov.hk/infrastructuregallery; 3 Edinburgh Pl; admission free; 🕙 10am-6pm Wed-Mon) may not sound like a crowd-pleaser but it will awaken the Meccano builder in more than a few visitors. The exhibition follows an 18.5-m 'walk' past recent, ongoing and future civil engineering, urban renewal and environment improvement projects, including the massive land reclamation project underway outside along the harbour side, which is leaving City Hall marooned ever further inland.

JARDINE HOUSE Map p56
1 Connaught Pl; MTR Hong Kong (exit B2)
A short distance southeast of Star Ferry pier, this 52-storey silver monolith punctured with 1750 porthole-like windows was

Hong Kong's first true 'skyscraper' when it opened as the Connaught Centre in 1973. Hong Kong Chinese like giving nicknames to things (and people, be they friend or foe) and the centre has been dubbed the 'House of 1000 Arseholes'.

LEGISLATIVE COUNCIL BUILDING
Map p56
8 Jackson Rd; MTR Central (exit G)
The colonnaded and domed neoclassical building on the east side of Statue Square was once the old Supreme Court. Built in 1912 of granite quarried on Stonecutters Island, it has served as the seat of the Legislative Council (Legco) since 1985. Standing atop the pediment is a blindfolded statue of Themis, the Greek goddess of justice and natural law. During WWII it was a headquarters of the Gendarmerie, the Japanese version of the Gestapo, and many people were executed here. Across Jackson Rd to the east is Chater Garden, which was a cricket pitch until 1975.

LI YUEN STREET EAST & WEST
Map p56, Map p68
🕙 10am-7pm; MTR Central (exit C)
These two narrow and crowded alleyways linking Des Voeux Rd Central with Queen's Rd Central are called 'the lanes' by Hong Kong residents, and were traditionally the place to go for fabric and piece goods. Most vendors have now moved to Western

MAID IN HONG KONG

A large number of households in Hong Kong have an *amah*, a maid who cooks, cleans, minds the children and/or feeds the dog, who either lives in or comes in once or twice a week. In the old days *amahs* were usually Chinese spinsters who wore starched white tunics and black trousers, put their hair in a long plait and had a mouthful of gold fillings. Their employers became their families. Today, however, that kind of *amah* is virtually extinct, and the work is now done by foreigners – young women (and increasingly men) from the Philippines, Indonesia, Nepal, Thailand and Sri Lanka on two-year renewable 'foreign domestic helper' (FDH) work visas.

Filipinos are by far the largest group, accounting for some 65% of the territory's 240,000 foreign domestic workers. While the Indonesians descend on Victoria Park and the Nepalese prefer Tsim Sha Tsui on their one day off (usually Sunday), Filipino *amahs* take over the pavements and public squares of Central. They come in their thousands to share food, gossip, play cards, read the Bible, and do one another's hair and nails. You can't miss them around Statue Square, Exchange Square and the plaza below the HSBC building.

Though it doesn't seem very attractive, for young Filipinos a contract to work in Hong Kong is a dream come true, an answer to the poverty of the Philippines, even if the minimum monthly salary is only $3320 (still more than twice what they would earn in Singapore or Malaysia). The work is a chance to attain, eventually, a better standard of life back home. But such opportunity doesn't come without a heavy price. According to Hong Kong-based Asian Migrant Centre (www.asian-migrants.org), as many as 25% of foreign domestic helpers in Hong Kong suffer physical and/or sexual abuse from their employers. If you'd like to learn more, read *Maid to Order in Hong Kong* by Nicole Constable, which is based on interviews the author conducted with *amahs* throughout Hong Kong.

Market (p70) in Sheung Wan, and today you'll find the usual mishmash of cheap clothing, handbags, backpacks and costume jewellery.

ST JOHN'S CATHEDRAL Map p56

☎ 2523 4157; www.stjohnscathedral.org.hk; 4-8 Garden Rd; admission free; ⏱ 7am-6pm; MTR Central (exit J2)

Consecrated in 1849, this Anglican cathedral is one of the very few colonial structures still standing in Central. Criticised for blighting the colony's landscape when it was first erected, St John's is now lost in the forest of skyscrapers that make up Central. The tower was added in 1850 and the chancel extended in 1873.

Services have been held here continuously since the cathedral opened, except in 1944, when the Japanese Imperial Army used it as a social club. The cathedral suffered heavy damage during WWII and after the war the front doors were remade using timber salvaged from HMS *Tamar,* a British warship that used to guard the entrance to Victoria Harbour, and the beautiful stained-glass East Window was replaced. You walk on sacred ground in more ways than one at St John's: it is the only piece of freehold land in Hong Kong. There's usually a free organ concert at 1.15pm on Wednesdays. Enter from Battery Path.

LOWER ALBERT ROAD & ICE HOUSE STREET Map p56, Map p68

MTR Central (exit G)

Lower Albert Rd, where the massive SAR Government Headquarters (Map p56; 18 Lower Albert Rd) is located, has many interesting buildings. The attractive off-white stucco and red-brick structure at the top of the road is the Dairy Farm Building (Map p68), built for the Dairy Farm Ice & Cold Storage Company in 1898 and renovated in 1913.

Today it houses the Fringe Club (p218), the excellent M at the Fringe restaurant (p177) and the illustrious Foreign Correspondents' Club of Hong Kong (☎ 2521 1511; www.fcchk.org). Towering above the Dairy Farm Building on the opposite side of the road is the Bishop's House (Map p68), built in 1851 and the official residence of the Anglican Bishop of Victoria.

From the Dairy Farm Building, Ice House St doglegs into Queen's Rd Central. Just before it turns north, a wide flight of stone steps leads down to Duddell St (Map p56). The

four wrought-iron China Gas lamps at the top and bottom of the steps were placed here in the 1870s and are listed monuments.

ONE & TWO INTERNATIONAL FINANCE CENTRE Map p56

1 Harbour View St; MTR Hong Kong (exit F)

These two tapering, pearl-coloured colossi sit atop the International Finance Centre (IFC) Mall and Hong Kong station, terminus of the Airport Express and the Tung Chung lines. Both were partly designed by Cesar Pelli, the man responsible for Canary Wharf in London. One IFC, which opened in 1999, is a 'mere' 38 levels tall. At 88 storeys, Two IFC, topped out in mid-2003, is Hong Kong's tallest (though not prettiest) building. Given the local penchant for bestowing nicknames on everything, Two IFC has been christened 'Sir YK Pao's Erection', a reference to the owner of the development company that built the tower.

You can't get to the top of Two IFC but you can get pretty high up by visiting the Hong Kong Monetary Authority Information Centre (☎ 2878 1111; www.hkma.gov.hk; 55th fl, Two IFC, 8 Finance St; admission free; ⏱ 10am-6pm Mon-Fri, 10am-1pm Sat), which contains a research library and exhibition areas related to the Hong Kong currency, fiscal policy and banking history. There are guided tours at 2.30 and 3pm Monday to Friday, and 10.30am Saturday.

EXPLORING HONG KONG'S HEART
Walking Tour

1 Legislative Council Building Begin the walk at Statue Square and take in the handsome outline of the neo-classical Legislative Council Building (opposite), one of the few colonial-era survivors in the area and the seat of Hong Kong's modern legislature.

2 Bank of China Tower Begin walking southwest through Chater Garden park and cross over Garden Rd to the angular, modern lines of the Bank of China Tower (p58), with amazing views from the 43rd floor.

3 Flagstaff House Museum of Tea Ware Duck into Hong Kong Park for this free museum (p62) displaying valuable pots, cups and other elegant tea ware. Sample some of China's finest teas down in the serene café.

4 St John's Cathedral From here take elevated walkways west over Cotton Tree Dr, through Citybank Plaza, over Garden Rd and through Cheung Kong Garden to the cathedral (p61), dating from 1849. It is a modest building to earn the title of cathedral, especially so set among the towering corporate cathedrals now surrounding it, but it is an important historic Hong Kong monument all the same.

5 Hongkong & Shanghai Bank Building Follow Battery Path past the Former French Mission Building to Ice House St. Cross over and walk right (east) along Queen's Rd Central to the Hongkong & Shanghai Bank building (p53) and up the escalator, if it's open, to the large airy atrium. Walk through the ground-floor plaza to pat Stephen and Stitt, the two lions guarding the exit to Des Voeux Rd Central. The closest Central MTR station entrance is then a short distance to the north along the pedestrian walkway between Statue Square and Prince's Building.

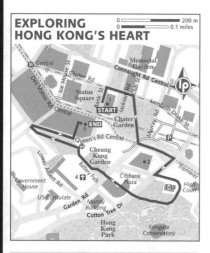

EXPLORING HONG KONG'S HEART

WALK FACTS

Start Statue Square, Central
End Central MTR station (entrance/exit K)
Distance 1.5km
Time 45 minutes
Fuel stop Museum of Tea Ware Café

ADMIRALTY & WAN CHAI

Drinking & Nightlife p209; Eating p183; Shopping p163; Sleeping p252

To the east of Central is Admiralty (Map p63), a district you might not even notice were it not for the dominating Pacific Place shopping centre and several modern buildings of note, including the blindingly gold Far East Finance Centre (Map p63; 16 Harcourt Rd), known locally as the 'Amah's Tooth' in reference to the traditional Chinese maids' preference for gold fillings and caps.

Admiralty is a small district, bordered by Cotton Tree Dr in the west and Arsenal St in the north. Hong Kong Park effectively cuts it off from the Mid-Levels and the Peak to the south, while Harcourt Rd is its barrier to the harbour in the north.

East of Admiralty is Hong Kong Island's most famous district: Wan Chai (Map p65), or 'Little Bay'. Its three main roads are Jaffe, Lockhart and Hennessy Rds. The harbour is the limit to the north, and to the south it's Queen's Rd East. If you choose to believe some of the tourist brochures, Wan Chai is still inseparably linked with the name of Suzie Wong – not bad considering that the book dates back to 1957 and the movie to 1960. Although Wan Chai had a reputation during the Vietnam War as an anything-goes red-light district, today it is mainly a centre for shopping, business and more upscale entertainment. If you want to see how far Wan Chai has come since then, check out the majestic Hong Kong Convention & Exhibition Centre (p64). It's a different world south and southeast of this 'new' Wan Chai. Sandwiched between Johnston Rd and Queen's Rd East are row after row of narrow streets harbouring all sorts of traditional shops, markets and workshops.

HONG KONG PARK Map p63

☎ 2521 5041; www.lcsd.gov.hk/en/ls_park.php; 19 Cotton Tree Dr, Admiralty; admission free; ☼ park 6am-11pm, conservatory & aviary 9am-5pm; MTR Admiralty (exit C1), 🚌 12A runs btwn Chater Rd in Central & Kennedy Rd, alight at the first stop on Cotton Tree Dr

Deliberately designed to look anything but natural, Hong Kong Park is one of the most unusual parks in the world, emphasising artificial creations such as its fountain plaza, conservatory, artificial waterfall, indoor games hall, playground, t'ai chi garden, viewing tower, museum and arts centre. For all its artifice, the 8-hectare park is beautiful in its own weird way and, with a wall of skyscrapers on one side and mountains on the other, makes for some dramatic photographs.

By far the best feature of the park is the delightful Edward Youde Aviary, named after a former Hong Kong governor (1982–86) and China scholar who died suddenly while in office. Home to more than 600 birds representing some 90 different species, the aviary is huge and manages to actually feel like a corner of rainforest in places. Visitors walk along a wooden bridge suspended some 10m above the ground and at eye level with the tree branches, where most of the birds are to be found. The Forsgate Conservatory on the slope overlooking the park is the largest in Southeast Asia.

At the park's northernmost tip is the Flagstaff House Museum of Tea Ware (☎ 2869 0690; www.lcsd.gov.hk/en/cs_mus_lcsd.php; 10 Cotton Tree Dr; admission free; ☼ 10am-5pm Wed-Mon). Built in 1846 as the home of the commander of the British forces, it is the oldest colonial building in Hong Kong still standing in its original spot. The museum, a branch of the Hong Kong Museum of Art, houses a collection of antique Chinese tea ware: bowls, teaspoons, brewing trays, sniffing

cups (used particularly for enjoying the fragrance of the finest oolong from Taiwan) and, of course, teapots made of porcelain or purple clay from Yixing. The ground-floor café makes a great spot to recharge over a pot of fine tea.

The KS Lo Gallery (☎ 2869 0690; 10 Cotton Tree Dr; admission free; ☼ 10am-5pm Wed-Mon), in a small building just southeast of the museum, contains rare Chinese ceramics and stone seals collected by the gallery's eponymous benefactor.

The Hong Kong Visual Arts Centre (☎ 2521 3008; 7A Kennedy Rd; admission free; ☼ 10am-9pm

TRANSPORT – ADMIRALTY

MTR Admiralty station is on the Central and Tsuen Wan lines.

Bus Buses to and from destinations throughout Hong Kong Island operate from Admiralty bus terminus below Queensway Plaza and Admiralty MTR station.

Tram East along Queensway, Johnston Rd and Hennessy Rd (Map p65) to Causeway Bay; west to Central and Sheung Wan.

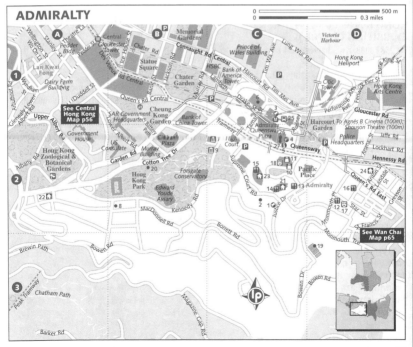

ADMIRALTY

Wed-Mon), housed in the Cassels Block of the former Victoria Barracks, within Hong Kong Park at its eastern edge, since 1992, supports local sculptors, printmakers and potters, and stages temporary exhibitions.

Hong Kong Park is an easy walk from either Central or the Admiralty MTR station.

HONG KONG CONVENTION & EXHIBITION CENTRE Map p65

☎ 2582 8888; www.hkcec.com; 1 Expo Dr, Wan Chai; 🚌 18

Due north of the Wan Chai MTR station, the Hong Kong Convention & Exhibition Centre, which was built in 1988 and extended onto a man-made island in the harbour for the handover in 1997, has been variously compared with a bird's wing, a banana leaf and a lotus petal. For more information, see p38.

CENTRAL PLAZA Map p65

18 Harbour Rd, Wan Chai; 🚌 18

At just under 374m, Central Plaza, which was completed in 1992, is just 3m shorter than the newer Two IFC. The glass skin of the tower has three different colours – gold, silver and terracotta – and the overall impression is rather garish.

Central Plaza functions as one of the world's biggest clocks. There's method to the madness of those four lines of light

shining through the glass pyramid at the top of the building between 6pm and midnight. The bottom level indicates the hour: red is 6pm; white 7pm; purple 8pm; yellow 9pm; pink 10pm; green 11pm. When all four lights are the same colour, it's right on the hour. When the top light is different from the bottom ones, it's 15 minutes past the hour. If the top two and bottom two are different, it's half-past the hour. If the top three match, it's 45 minutes past the hour. So what time is it now?

GOLDEN BAUHINIA Map p65

Golden Bauhinia Sq, 1 Expo Dr, Wan Chai; bus 18, MTR Wan Chai (exit A5)

A 6m-tall statue (including pedestal) of Hong Kong's symbol, called the *Forever Blooming Bauhinia,* stands on the waterfront promenade just in front of the Hong

TRANSPORT – WAN CHAI

MTR Wan Chai station is on the Island line and is the best way to reach this district.

Tram East along Queensway, Johnston Rd and Hennessy Rd to Causeway Bay; west to Central and Sheung Wan.

Star Ferry Wan Chai ferry pier to Hung Hom and Tsim Sha Tsui in Kowloon.

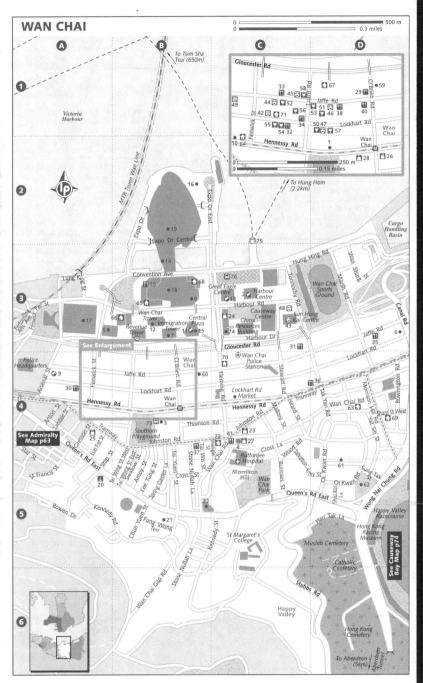

WAN CHAI

0   500 m
0   0.3 miles

lonelyplanet.com

NEIGHBOURHOODS & ISLANDS **HONG KONG ISLAND**

To Tsim Sha Tsui (650m)

Gloucester Rd

Jaffe Rd

Hennessy Rd

Lockhart Rd

Wan Chai

0   250 m
0   0.15 miles

Victoria
Harbour

MTR Tsuen Wan Line

To Hung Hom
(2.2km)

Cargo
Handling
Basin

Expo Dr East

Expo Dr Central

Convention Ave

Lung K

Wan Chai
Tower

Revenue
Tower

Immigration
Tower

Central
Plaza

Great Eagle
Centre

Harbour
Centre

Harbour Rd

Causeway
Centre

Sun Hung
Kai Centre

China
Resources
Building

Harbour Dr

Gloucester Rd

Wan Chai
Sports
Ground

Hung Hing Rd

Tonnochy Rd

Wan Shing

Marsh Rd

Canal Rd

Jaffe Rd

Lockhart Rd

Wan Chai
Police
Station

See Enlargement

Fenwick St

O'Brien Rd

Fleming Rd

Wan Chai

Jaffe Rd

Lockhart Rd

Hennessy Rd

Wan Chai

Police
Headquarters

Gloucester St

Arsenal St

Lockhart Rd
Market

Stewart Rd

Heard St

Mallory St

Tak Yan St

Wan Chai Rd

Morrison Hill Rd

Sam Pei St West

Bowrington Rd

Hennessy Rd

Tramway

Johnston Rd

Thomson Rd

Southorn
Playground

Johnston Rd

Cross La

Ruttonjee
Hospital

Morrison
Hill

Wan Chai
Park

Wood St

Burrows St

Amoy St

Salvation Army St

Cross La

O Kwan

Sung Tak St

Wong Nai Chung Rd

Queen's Rd East

See Admiralty
Map p63

Queen's Rd East

Anton St

Landale St

Swatow St

Tai Wong St West

Tai Wong St East

Ship St

Lun Fat St

Star St

St Francis St

Bowen Dr

Kennedy St

Tai Yuen St

Lee Tung St

Stone Nullah Ln

Spring Garden Ln

Chun Yuen St

Fung Wong
Terr

Kennedy Rd

Wan Chai Gap Rd

Stone Nullah Ln

St Margaret's
College

Muslim Cemetery

Catholic
Cemetery

Happy
Valley

Hong Kong
Racing
Museum

Happy Valley
Racecourse

See Causeway
Bay Map p74

Hong Kong
Cemetery

Stubbs Rd

Hong Kong
Cemetery

To Aberdeen
(5km)

Aberdeen Tunnel

Pedestrian
Arts Ave

Fenwick Pier St

65

WAN CHAI

Kong Convention & Exhibition Centre to mark the return of Hong Kong to Chinese sovereignty in 1997 and the establishment of the Hong Kong SAR. The flag-raising ceremony, held daily at 7.50am and conducted by the Hong Kong Police, has become a 'must see' for visiting tourist groups from the mainland. There's a pipe band on the 1st, 11th and 21st of each month at 7.45am.

HONG KONG ARTS CENTRE Map p63
☎ 2582 0200; www.hkac.org.hk; 2 Harbour Rd, Wan Chai; MTR Admiralty (exit E2)
Due east of the Academy for the Performing Arts is the Hong Kong Arts Centre. Along with theatres, including the important Agnès B Cinema (p217), you'll also find here the Pao Sui Loong & Pao Yue Kong Galleries (☎ 2824 5330; admission free; ☺ 10am-6pm during

exhibitions). Extending over floors Nanshan four and five, there's room to host retrospectives and group shows in all visual media.

HONG KONG DESIGN CENTRE Map p63
☎ 2522 8688; www.hkdesigncentre.org; 28 Kennedy Rd, the Mid-Levels; admission free; ☺ 9am-6pm (variable); 🚌 12A
The design centre, just opposite the Hong Kong Visual Arts Centre, is housed in one of the most graceful colonial buildings in the territory. Built in 1896, it served as a bank, the offices of the Japanese Residents Association of Hong Kong before WWII and a school until it was renovated and given to the Hong Kong Federation of Designers. Even if it does not have any exhibitions open to the public, the exterior and public areas are worth a look.

ACADEMY FOR THE PERFORMING ARTS Map p65

☎ 2584 8500; www.hkapa.edu; 1 Gloucester Rd, Wan Chai; MTR Admiralty (exit E2)

With its striking triangular atrium and an exterior Meccano-like frame that is a work of art in itself, the academy building (1985) is a Wan Chai landmark and an important venue for music, dance and scholarship.

HUNG SHING TEMPLE Map p65

☎ 2527 0804; 129-131 Queen's Rd East, Wan Chai; ⏱ 8am-6pm; 🚌 6 or 6A

Nestled in a leafy nook on the southern side of Queen's Rd East, this narrow and dark temple (which is also called Tai Wong Temple) is built atop huge boulders in honour of a Tang-dynasty official who was well known for his virtue (important) and ability to make predictions of great value to traders (ultra-important).

OLD WAN CHAI POST OFFICE Map p65

Cnr Queen's Rd East & Wan Chai Gap Rd, Wan Chai; 🚌 6 or 6A

A short distance to the east of Wan Chai Market is this important colonial-style building erected in 1913 and now serving as a resource centre operated by the Environmental Protection Department (☎ 2893 2856; ⏱ 10am-5pm Mon-Tue & Thu-Sat, 10am-1pm Wed, 1-5pm Sun).

LAN KWAI FONG & SOHO

Drinking & Nightlife p208; Eating p180

South of Queen's Rd Central and up hilly D'Aguilar or Wyndham Sts is Lan Kwai Fong (Map p68), a narrow, L-shaped pedestrian way that is Hong Kong Island's chief entertainment district. It's popular with expats and Hong Kong Chinese alike. In recent years it has become one of the first ports of call for mainland tour groups: most often they're here

TRANSPORT – LAN KWAI FONG & SOHO

MTR Central station (Map p56) on the Island and Tsuen Wan lines is at the heart of the neighbourhood.

Bus Buses 5 and 5A from Central call at 10 Des Voeux Rd (Map p70); bus 26 runs along Hollywood Rd.

to gawp – not to party. The bars are generally nothing to get excited about – standing out for little more than their similarity – but it's a fun place to do a little pub-crawling, especially at happy hour. Lan Kwai Fong has more pubs and bars than restaurants, while Wyndham St, the latest corner of the area to spring into life, has a slightly more upmarket selection of bars and restaurants. These lead west to Soho (from 'South Of HOllywood Rd'), which is *above* Hollywood Rd, another good hunting ground for good food and nightlife.

SHEUNG WAN

Drinking & Nightlife p208; Eating p182; Shopping p162; Sleeping p250

West of Central, in pockets Sheung Wan (Map p70) still has something of a feel of old Shanghai about it, although that is fast disappearing under the jackhammer, and many of the old 'ladder streets' (steep inclined streets with steps) once lined with stalls and street vendors have been cleared away to make room for more buildings or the MTR. Nevertheless, traditional shops and businesses cling on and the area is worth exploring.

Hollywood Road (Map p68), which got its name from all the holly bushes that once thrived here, is an interesting street to explore. The eastern end is lined with upmarket antique and carpet shops and trendy eateries. However, once you head west of Aberdeen St the scene changes: you'll soon be passing traditional wreath and coffin makers, as well as several funeral shops.

The limits of Sheung Wan are difficult to define, but basically the district stretches from the Sheung Wan MTR station in the east to King George V Memorial Park and Eastern St in the west. The harbour – or, rather, Connaught Rd West – is the northern border, while Hollywood Rd is the southern limit.

MAN MO TEMPLE Map p70

☎ 2540 0350; 124-126 Hollywood Rd; admission free; ⏱ 8am-6pm; 🚌 26

This busy 18th-century temple is one of the oldest and most famous in Hong Kong. Man Mo (literally 'civil' and 'martial') is dedicated to two deities. The civil deity is a Chinese statesman of the 3rd century BC called Man Cheung, who is worshipped as the god of literature and is represented holding a writing brush. The military deity is Kwan Yu (or Kwan Tai), a Han-dynasty soldier born in the 2nd century AD and

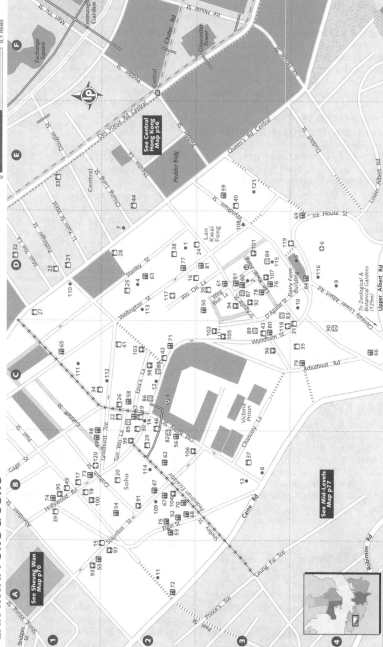

LAN KWAI FONG & SOHO

See Sheung Wan Map p70

See Hong Kong Central Map p56

See Mid-Levels Map p77

Lan Kwai Fong

Soho

Victoria Prison

To Zoological & Botanical Gardens (725m)

200 m
0.1 miles

LAN KWAI FONG & SOHO

now venerated as the red-cheeked god of war; he is holding a sword. Kwan Yu's popularity in Hong Kong probably has more to do with his additional status as the patron god of restaurants, pawnshops, the police force and secret societies such as the Triads (see p29).

Outside the main entrance are four gilt plaques on poles that are carried at proces-

sion time. Two plaques describe the gods being worshipped inside, while others request silence and respect within the temple grounds and warn menstruating women to keep out of the main hall. Inside the temple are two 19th-century sedan chairs shaped like houses, which are used to carry the two gods at festival time. The coils suspended from the roof are incense

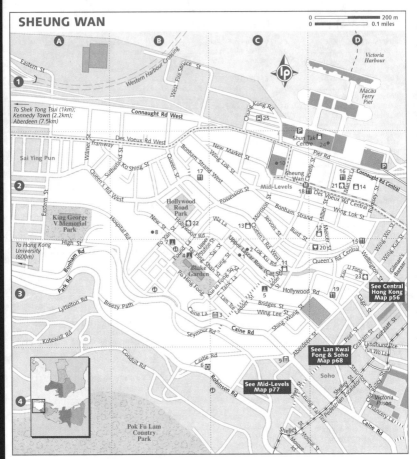

SHEUNG WAN

cones burned as offerings by worshippers. Off to the side are fortune-tellers ready and willing to tell you of your (undoubtedly excellent) fate.

QUEEN'S ROAD WEST INCENSE SHOPS Map p70

🚌 26

Head along Queen's Rd West, about 200m past the end of Hollywood Rd, and you'll find two or three shops selling incense and paper offerings. These are burned to propitiate the spirits of the dead and make a consumer heaven of their hell. There's quite a choice of spirit-world comestibles, including complete mini-sets of kitchenware, cars, gold and silver ingots, the popular hell banknotes, and even computers and personal stereos.

CAT ST Map p70

🕐 9am-6pm; 🚌 26

Southwest of Sheung Wan MTR station and just north of (and parallel to) Hollywood Rd is Upper Lascar Row, the official name of 'Cat St', a pedestrians-only lane lined with antique and curio shops and stalls selling found objects, cheap jewellery, ornaments, carvings and newly minted ancient coins. It's a fun place to trawl through for a trinket or two, but expect more rough than diamonds. There are proper shops on three floors of the Cat Street Galleries (Casey Bldg, 38 Lok Ku Rd; 🕐 10am-6pm Mon-Sat), a small shopping centre entered from Upper Lascar Row.

WESTERN MARKET Map p70

☎ 2815 3586; 323 Des Voeux Rd Central & New Market St; 🕐 9am-7pm; MTR Sheung Wan (exit B)

SHEUNG WAN

When the textile vendors were driven out of the lanes linking Queen's and Des Voeux Rds Central in the early 1990s, they were moved to this renovated old market (1906) with its distinctive four-corner towers. You'll find knick-knacks, jewellery and toys on the ground floor, piece goods on the 1st floor and bolts of cloth on the floors above it.

MAN WA LANE Map p70
MTR Sheung Wan (exit A1)
Just a block east of the Sheung Wan MTR station, this narrow alley is a good introduction to traditional Sheung Wan. Stalls here specialise in name chops: a stone (or wood or jade) seal that has a name carved in Chinese on the base. When dipped in pasty red Chinese ink, the name chop can be used as a stamp or even a 'signature'. The merchant will create a harmonious and auspicious Chinese name for you.

POSSESSION ST Map p70
🚌 26
A short distance west of Cat St, next to Hollywood Road Park and before Hollywood Rd meets Queen's Rd West, is Possession St. This is thought to be where Commodore

Gordon Bremmer and a contingent of British marines planted the Union flag on 26 January 1841 and claimed Hong Kong Island for the Crown (though no plaque marks the spot). Queen's Rd runs in such a serpentine fashion as it heads eastward because it once formed the shoreline of Hong Kong Island's northern coast, and this part of it was called Possession Point.

TAI PING SHAN TEMPLES Map p70
🚌 26
Tai Ping Shan, a tiny neighbourhood in Sheung Wan and one of the first areas to be settled by Chinese after the founding of the colony, has several small temples clustered around where Tai Ping Shan St meets Pound Lane. Kwun Yam Temple (34 Tai Ping Shan St) honours the ever-popular goddess of mercy, Kun Iam – the Taoist equivalent of the Virgin Mary. Further to the northwest, the recently renovated Pak Sing Ancestral Hall (42 Tai Ping Shan St) was originally a storeroom for bodies awaiting burial in China. It contains the ancestral tablets of around 3000 departed souls.

HONG KONG'S WHOLESALE DISTRICT
Walking Tour
1 Dried Seafood Shops Begin the tour at the Sutherland St stop of the Kennedy Town tram. Have a look at (and a sniff of) Des Voeux Rd West's many shops piled with all manner of desiccated sea life.

2 Herbalist Shops Walk south on Sutherland St to Ko Shing St, to browse the positively medieval-sounding goods on offer from the herbal-medicine traders.

TRANSPORT – SHEUNG WAN

MTR Sheung Wan station on the Island line.

Bus Buses 5 and 5A from Central call at 10 Des Voeux Rd; bus 26 runs along Hollywood Rd (Map p68) between Sheung Wan and Central, Admiralty and Wan Chai.

Tram Runs along Des Voeux Rd Central and Des Voeux Rd West.

Macau Ferry Terminal at Shun Tak Centre.

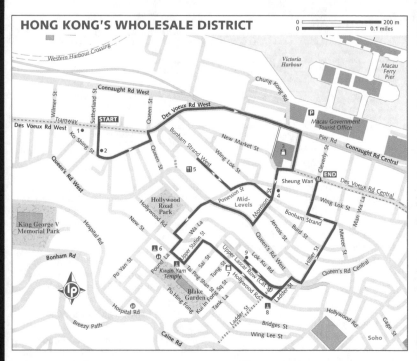

HONG KONG'S WHOLESALE DISTRICT

3 Western Market At the end of Ko Shing St, re-enter Des Voeux Rd West and walk northeast. Continue along Connaught Rd West, where you'll find several floors of market stalls occupying the attractive colonial building housing the Western Market (p70).

4 Birds' Nests, Ginseng & Funeral Offerings Shops At the corner of Morrison St, walk south past Wing Lok St and Bonham Strand, which are both lined with shops selling ginseng root and edible birds' nests. Turn right onto Queen's Rd Central to the shops selling paper funeral offerings for the dead.

5 Leung Hing Chiu Chow Seafood Restaurant Hungry? Turn left into Possession Street and take a detour to Bonham Strand West for a quick Chiu Chow fix (see p183).

6 Pak Sing Ancestral Hall & Kwun Yam Temple Take a left into Hollywood Rd and then right to ascend Pound Lane to where it meets Tai Ping Shan St, where you'll spot two temples (p71). Look to the right for Pak Sing Ancestral Hall and to the left for Kwun Yam Temple.

7 Hollywood Rd Turn left into Tai Ping Shan St, then left to descend Upper Station St to the start of Hollywood Rd's antique shops (see p156). There's a vast choice of curios and rare, mostly Chinese, treasures.

8 Man Mo Temple Continuing east on Hollywood Rd brings you to the Man Mo Temple (p67), one of the oldest in the territory and dedicated to the civil and martial gods Man Cheung and Kwan Yu.

9 Cat St Market Take a short hop to the left down Ladder St to Upper Lascar Row, home of the Cat St Market (p70), well stocked with Chinese memorabilia and inexpensive curios and gift items. Ladder St brings you back to Queen's Rd Central. Cross the road and follow

WALK FACTS

Start Kennedy Town tram (Sutherland St stop)
End Sheung Wan MTR station (entrance/exit B)
Distance 1.9km
Time One hour
Fuel stop Leung Hing Chiu Chow Seafood Restaurant

top picks

HONG KONG'S BEST FREEBIES

- The spectacle from the public viewing gallery viewing deck at the Bank of China (p58).
- Chi Lin Nunnery (p102), where peace and serenity doesn't cost a cent.
- Wednesday is 'admission free' day at six Hong Kong museums: Hong Kong Heritage Museum (p125), Hong Kong Museum of Art (p90), Hong Kong Museum of Coastal Defence (p80), Hong Kong Museum of History (p95), Hong Kong Science Museum (p96) and Hong Kong Space Museum (p91), excluding Space Theatre.
- Hong Kong Zoological & Botanical Gardens (p58) for free walks and gratis squawks.
- Kadoorie Farm & Botanic Garden (p107), where the butterflies (and cows and dragonflies) are free.
- Tian Tan Buddha (p137) for a cost-free superlative.

Hillier St to Bonham Strand. Due north is the Sheung Wan MTR station.

CAUSEWAY BAY

Drinking & Nightlife p210; Eating p187; Shopping p165; Sleeping p255

Causeway Bay (Map p74), which is Tung Lo Wan (Copper Gong Bay) in Cantonese, was the site of a British settlement in the 1840s and was once an area of godowns (a Hong Kong 'business' or 'pidgin English' word for warehouses) and a well-protected harbour for fisherfolk and boatpeople.

The new Causeway Bay, one of Hong Kong's top shopping and nightlife areas, was built up from swampland and reclaimed land from the harbour. Jardine Matheson, one of Hong Kong's largest *háwng* (major trading houses or companies), set up shop here, which explains why many of the streets in the district bear its name: Jardine's Bazaar, Jardine's Crescent and Yee Wo St (the name for Jardine Matheson in Cantonese).

Causeway Bay is primarily for shopping, especially trendy clothing and, to a lesser degree, dining out. The biggest and best shopping centre is in Times Square (p166), an enormous block with offices, four floors of restaurants and 10 retail levels.

Causeway Bay is a relatively small but densely packed district. Canal Rd is its border to the west and Victoria Park is the eastern limit. From north to south it runs from the

harbour and the ty⬛⬛⬛⬛⬛ Rd. Tin Hau, the s⬛⬛⬛⬛⬛ most famous temp⬛⬛⬛⬛⬛ queen of heaven, i⬛⬛⬛⬛⬛ of Victoria Park.

NOONDAY GU⬛

221 Gloucester Rd; M⬛⬛⬛⬛⬛

Noel Coward mad⬛⬛⬛⬛⬛ Gun famous with ⬛⬛⬛⬛⬛ *Dogs and Englishmen* (1924), about colonials who braved the fierce heat of the midday sun while the local people sensibly remained indoors: 'In Hong Kong/they strike a gong/And fire off a noonday gun/ To reprimand each inmate/Who's in late'. Apparently when Coward was invited to pull the lanyard, he was late and it didn't go off until 12.03pm.

Built in 1901 by Hotchkiss of Portsmouth this recoil-mounted 3lb cannon is one of the few vestiges of the colonial past in Causeway Bay and is its best-known landmark. The original six-pounder was lost during WWII; its replacement was deemed too noisy and was exchanged for the current gun in 1961. The gun stands in a small garden opposite the Excelsior Hotel on Gloucester Rd – the first plot of land to be sold by public auction in Hong Kong (1841) – and is fired at noon every day. Eight bells are then sounded, signalling the end of the forenoon watch. The gun also welcomes in the New Year at midnight on 31 December.

Exactly how this tradition got started remains a mystery. Some people say that Jardine Matheson fired the gun without permission to bid farewell to a departing managing director or to welcome one of its incoming ships. The authorities were so enraged by the company's insolence that, as

---

TRANSPORT – CAUSEWAY BAY

MTR Causeway Bay and Tin Hau stations on Central line.

Bus From Admiralty and Central, buses 5, 5B and 26 stop along Yee Wo St.

Green Minibus Bus 40 from Stanley calls along Tang Lung St and Yee Woo St.

Tram Along Hennessy Rd and Yee Wo St to Central and Shau Kei Wan; along Percival St to Happy Valley; along Wong Nai Chung Rd to Causeway Bay, Central, Kennedy Town, and Shau Kei Wan.

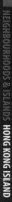

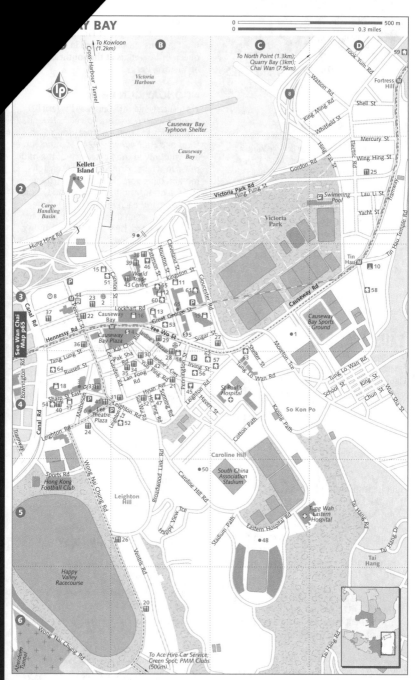

0 ——————————— 500 m
0 ——————————— 0.3 miles

B

C

D

To Kowloon
(1.2km)

Cross-Harbour Tunnel

To North Point (1.3km);
Quarry Bay (3km);
Chai Wan (7.5km)

Fook Yum Rd

59

Victoria
Harbour

Watson Rd

Fortress
Hill

8

King Ming Rd

Whitfield St

Shell St

Causeway Bay
Typhoon Shelter

Hing Fat Rd

Mercury St

Electric Rd

Wing Hing St

25

Causeway
Bay

Gordon Rd

Lau Li St

Kellett
Island

49

2

Cargo
Handling
Basin

Victoria Park Rd

Tsing Fung St

Swimming
Pool

Yacht St

Tin Hau Temple Rd

Tramway

Victoria
Park

Tin Hau

10

Hung Hing Rd

9

Cleveland St

Houston St

Causeway Rd

58

38
39
15
51

Paterson St

World
Trade
43 Centre

46

Kingston St

Gloucester Rd

Causeway
Bay Sports
Ground

Canton Rd

55
11
12

8
44
23
2

37
22

Percival St

Lockhart Rd
29

16

Causeway
Bay

60

13

65

Great George St

P

53

19

1

3

Canal Rd

Hennessy Rd

Yee Wo St

Sugar St

35

5

27

Shelter St

Tung Lo Wan Rd

Moreton Tce

Causeway
Bay Plaza

4

Jardine's Bazaar

Matheson St

28
14

62
57
56

63

School St

King St

Tung Lo Wan Rd

Chun St Wun Sha St

36
64

Tang Lung St

Russell St

Pak Sha Rd

30
35
34

Jardine's Cres

Lan Fong
Rd

Irving St

Bowrington Rd

18

33

Sharp St East

41
40
17

31

Leighton Rd

Hysan Ave

Sunning Rd

45
21

Leighton
Haven St

St Paul's
Hospital

So Kon Po

Kwong Path

Matheson St

Lee
Theatre
Plaza

24

52

Percival St

Cotton Path

Leighton Rd

Caroline Hill

50

South China
Association
Stadium

Sports Rd

Hong Kong
Football Club

Canal Rd

Tramway

Leighton Rd

Wong Nai Chung Rd

Leighton
Hill

Caroline Hill Rd

Happy View Tce

Stadium Path

Eastern Hospital Rd

Tung Wah
Eastern
Hospital

Tai Hang Rd

Tai Hang Dr

5

26

Venfris Rd

48

Tai
Hang

Happy
Valley
Racecourse

20

Wong Nai Chung Rd

Aberdeen Tunnel

6

To Ace Hire Car Service;
Green Spot; PMM Clubs
(500m)

NEIGHBOURHOODS & ISLANDS HONG KONG ISLAND

See Wan Chai Map p65

CAUSEWAY BAY

punishment, Jardine's was ordered to fire the gun every day. A more prosaic explanation is that, as at many ports around the world (including London), a gun was fired at noon daily so that ships' clocks – crucial for establishing longitude and east–west distances at sea – could be set accurately.

The Noonday Gun is accessible via a tunnel through the basement car park in the World Trade Centre, just west of the Excelsior Hotel. From the taxi rank in front of the hotel, look west for the door marked 'Car Park Shroff, Marina Club & Noon Gun'. It's open from 7am to midnight daily.

VICTORIA PARK Map p74
☎ 2890 5824; www.lcsd.gov.hk/en/ls_park.php; Causeway Rd; MTR Causeway Bay & Tin Hau
At 17 hectares, the biggest patch of public greenery on Hong Kong Island, Victoria Park is a popular place to escape to. The best time to stroll around is in the morning during the week, when it becomes a forest

of people practising the slow-motion choreography of t'ai chi. At the weekend they are joined by Indonesian *amahs*, who prefer it to Central (see boxed text, p60).

Between April and November you can take a dip in the swimming pool (☎ 2570 4682; adult/child 3-13 & senior over 60 $19/9; ⏰ 6.30am-10pm with 1hr closure at noon & 5pm Apr-Oct). The park becomes a flower market a few days before the Chinese New Year and is the site of the Hong Kong Flower Show in March. It's also worth a visit during the Mid-Autumn Festival (p17), when people turn out en masse carrying lanterns.

CAUSEWAY BAY TYPHOON SHELTER
Map p74
off Hung Hing Rd, Causeway Bay
Not so long ago the waterfront in Causeway Bay used to be a mass of junks and sampans huddling in the typhoon shelter for protection, but these days it's nearly all yachts. The land jutting out to the west

is Kellett Island, which has been a misnomer ever since a causeway connected it to the mainland in 1956, and further land reclamation turned it into a peninsula. It is home to the Royal Hong Kong Yacht Club (☎ 2832 2817), which retains its 'Royal' moniker in English only.

TIN HAU TEMPLE Map p74
☎ 2721 2326; 10 Tin Hau Temple Rd; ☽ 7am-6pm; MTR Tin Hau (exit B)
Southeast of Victoria Park, Hong Kong Island's most famous Tin Hau temple is relatively small and dwarfed by surrounding high-rises. Before reclamation, this temple dedicated to the patroness of seafarers stood on the waterfront. It has been a place of worship for three centuries, though the current structure is only about 200 years old. The temple bell dates from 1747, and the central shrine contains an effigy of Tin Hau with a blackened face.

CENTRAL LIBRARY Map p74
☎ 3150 1234; www.hkpl.gov.hk; 66 Causeway Rd; ☽ 10am-9pm Thu-Tue, 1-9pm Wed, 10am-7pm some public holidays; ☒ Shau Kei Wan
This architectural monstrosity, a 12-storey neoclassical-postmodern building with Ionic columns, a Roman pediment and sandy-yellow tiles, is both a research and lending library and contains some 1.2 million volumes (p294). It also has some 24 public-access computer terminals where you can check emails and surf the web.

WESTERN DISTRICTS
Beyond Sheung Wan are the districts of Sai Ying Pun and Shek Tong Tsui (Map pp54–5), which are often lumped together as 'Western' by English speakers, and Kennedy Town, a working-class Chinese district at the end of the tramline.

Kennedy Town's maritime connections can still be felt the closer you get to the Praya (officially Kennedy Town New Praya) – from the Portuguese *praia* meaning 'beach' or 'coast',

---

TRANSPORT – WESTERN DISTRICTS

Bus Bus 3B from Jardine House in Central, bus 23, 40 or 40M from Admiralty, and bus 103 from Gloucester Rd in Causeway Bay all stop along Bonham Rd (Map p70).

---

which was commonly used in Hong Kong in the days when Portuguese merchants were a force to be reckoned with on the high seas.

The area wedged between the Mid-Levels and Sheung Wan doesn't have an official name as such but is usually called Pok Fu Lam after the main thoroughfare running through it. It's a district of middle-class housing blocks, colleges and Hong Kong's most prestigious university.

HONG KONG UNIVERSITY Map pp54–5
☎ 2859 2111; www.hku.hk; Pok Fu Lam Rd; ☒ 23 & 40M from D'Aguilar St in Central
Established in 1911, HKU is the oldest and most prestigious of Hong Kong's eight universities. The Main Building, completed in the Edwardian style in 1912, is a declared monument. Several other early-20th-century buildings on the campus, including the Hung Hing Ying (1919) and Tang Chi Ngong Buildings (1929), are also protected.

The University Museum & Art Gallery (☎ 2241 5513; www.hku.hk/hkumag; Fung Ping Shan Bldg, 94 Bonham Rd; admission free; ☽ 9.30am-6pm Mon-Sat, 1.30-5.30pm Sun), to the left of the university's Main Building and opposite the start of Hing Hon Rd, houses collections of ceramics and bronzes, plus a lesser number of paintings and carvings. The bronzes are in three groups: Shang and Zhou–dynasty ritual vessels; decorative mirrors from the Warring States period to the Tang, Song, Ming and Qing dynasties; and almost 1000 small Nestorian crosses from the Yuan dynasty, the largest such collection in the world. (The Nestorians formed a Christian sect that arose in Syria, were branded heretics, and moved into China during the 13th and 14th centuries.)

THE MID-LEVELS
Eating p182; Sleeping p250
The Mid-Levels (Map p77) have relatively little to offer tourists in the way of sights, though there are a few gems, particularly houses of worship, hidden within the forest of marble-clad apartment blocks. Check out the Roman Catholic Cathedral of the Immaculate Conception (Map p77; ☎ 2523 0384; 16 Caine Rd), built in 1888 and financed largely by the Portuguese faithful from Macau; the Jamia Mosque (Map p77; ☎ 2526 0786; 30 Shelley St), erected in 1849 and also called the Lascar Mosque; and the Ohel Leah Synagogue (opposite).

Another district with rather elastic boundaries, the Mid-Levels stretches roughly from Hong Kong University and Pok Fu Lam in the west to Kennedy Rd in the east. Caine Rd is the northern boundary and the Peak the southern one. But the Mid-Levels are as much a state of mind as a physical area, and some people regard the middle-class residential areas further east to be the Mid-Levels as well.

DR SUN YAT SEN MUSEUM Map p70
☎ 2367 6373; www.lcsd.gov.hk/CE/Museum/sysm; 7 Castle Lane, Mid-Levels; adult/concession $10/5, free after 2pm Tue; ☼ 10am-6pm Mon-Wed & Fri-Sat, 10am-7pm Sun; ☒ 3B, alight at the Hong Kong Baptist Church on Caine Rd

Sun Yat Sen was an early 20th-century revolutionary, dedicated to overthrowing the Qing dynasty, and a key figure in modern Chinese history. He had many links with Hong Kong, not least of them being his education here and his formative experience of the colony's order and efficiency (standing in stark contrast to China at the time). The displays here are rather stodgy and worthy but Dr Sun's story is one of the more interesting chapters in China's history, so it's certainly worth a visit. Audio guides cost $10.

HONG KONG MUSEUM OF MEDICAL SCIENCES Map p70
☎ 2549 5123; www.hkmms.org.hk; 2 Caine Lane; adult/concession $10/5, free after 2pm Tue; ☼ 10am-5pm Tue-Sat, 1-5pm Sun; ☒ 3B alight at Ladder St bus stop on Caine Rd

This small museum houses medical implements and accoutrements (including an old dentistry chair, an autopsy table, herbal-medicine vials and chests) and offers a rundown on how Hong Kong cop[...] the 1984 bubonic plague, but is less[...] ing for its exhibits than for its architect[...] is housed in what was once the Patholog[...] Institute, a breezy Edwardian-style brick-and-tile structure built in 1905 and fronted by palms and bauhinia trees. The exhibits comparing Chinese and Western approaches to medicine are unusual and instructive.

OHEL LEAH SYNAGOGUE Map p70
☎ 2589 2621, 2857 6095; 70 Robinson Rd; admission free; ☼ 10.30am-7pm Mon-Thu (by appointment only); ☒ 3B or 23

This renovated Moorish Romantic temple, completed in 1902 when that style of architecture was all the rage in Europe, is named after Leah Gubbay Sassoon, matriarch of a wealthy (and philanthropic) Sephardic Jewish family that traced its roots back to the beginning of the colony. Be sure to bring some sort of ID if you plan to visit the sumptuous interior.

TRANSPORT – THE MID-LEVELS

Bus Bus 26 from Central calls along Hollywood Rd (Map p68); bus 3B from Jardine House in Central and bus 23 from Admiralty stop at Robinson Rd (Map p56).

Green Minibus Bus 8 or 22 from Central call at Caine Rd and Ladder St (Map p70).

Central Escalator (Map p56) For Caine Rd (museum) and Robinson Rd (synagogue).

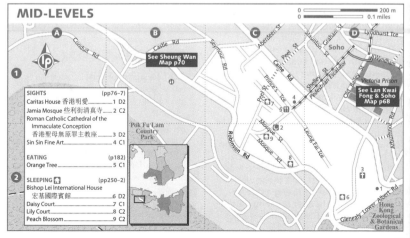

MID-LEVELS

0 ————— 200 m
0 ————— 0.1 miles

See Sheung Wan Map p70

See Lan Kwai Fong & Soho Map p68

Victoria Prison

SIGHTS	(pp76–7)
Caritas House 香港明愛	1 D2
Jamia Mosque 些利街清真寺	2 C2
Roman Catholic Cathedral of the Immaculate Conception 香港聖母無原罪主教座	3 D2
Sin Sin Fine Art	4 C1

| EATING | (p182) |
| Orange Tree | 5 C1 |

SLEEPING	(pp250–2)
Bishop Lei International House 宏基國際賓館	6 D2
Daisy Court	7 C1
Lily Court	8 C2
Peach Blossom	9 C2

Pok Fu Lam Country Park

Hong Kong Zoological & Botanical Gardens

... day in Hong Kong, make ...r climes of the Peak (Map ...point on the island. Not ... of the most spectacular ...ld, it's also a good way to ...Hong Kong and its layout into perspective. Repeat the trip up on a clear night; the views of illuminated Central below and Tsim Sha Tsui across the harbour in Kowloon are superb.

The Peak has been *the* place to live in Hong Kong ever since the British arrived. Taipans (company bosses) built summer houses here to escape the heat and humidity.

When people refer to the Peak, they generally mean the plateau (elevation 370m) with the seven-level Peak Tower, the huge titanium anvil rising above the Peak Tram terminus and containing themed venues, shops and restaurants; they don't mean the summit itself.

Half the fun of going up to the Peak is riding the Peak Tram (see boxed text, right; see also p283). In 1885 everyone thought Phineas Kyrie and William Kerfoot Hughes were mad when they announced their intention to build a tramway to the top, but it opened three years later, silencing the scoffers and wiping out the sedan-chair trade in one fell swoop.

VICTORIA PEAK Map pp54–5

Some 500m to the northwest of the Peak Tram terminus up steep Mt Austin Rd, Victoria Peak (552m) is the highest point on Hong Kong Island. The old governor's mountain lodge near the summit was burned to the ground by the Japanese during WWII, but the gardens remain and are open to the public.

You can walk around Victoria Peak without exhausting yourself. Harlech Rd on the south side and Lugard Rd on the northern slope together form a 3.5km loop that takes about an hour to walk. If you feel like a longer walk, you can continue for a further 2km along Peak Rd to Pok Fu Lam Reservoir Rd, which leaves Peak Rd near the car-park exit. This goes past the reservoir to the main Pok Fu Lam Rd, where you can get bus 7 to Aberdeen or back to Central.

Another good walk leads down to Hong Kong University (p76). First walk to the west side of Victoria Peak by taking either Lugard or Harlech Rds. After reaching Hatton Rd, follow it down. The descent is steep, but the path is clear.

For information on the 50km-long Hong Kong Trail, which starts on the Peak, see p225.

PEAK GALLERIA Map pp54–5

118 Peak Rd; 🚋 Peak Tram

Both the Peak Tower and the neighbouring Peak Galleria are designed to withstand winds of up to 270km/h, theoretically more than the maximum velocity of a No 10 typhoon. You can reach the Peak Galleria's viewing deck, which is larger than the one in the Peak Tower, by taking the escalator to level 3. Inside the centre you'll find a number of expensive restaurants and retail shops, from art galleries to duty-free stores.

PEAK TOWER Map pp54–5

128 Peak Rd; 🚋 Peak Tram

The Peak Tower, with its attractions, shops and restaurants, is a good place to bring the kids. On level 4 there's an outpost of Madame Tussauds (☎ 2849 6966; adult/child $120/70; ⏰ 10am-10pm), with eerie (and scary) wax likenesses of international stars as well as local celebrities, such as Jackie Chan, Andy Lau, Michelle Yeoh and Kelly Chen. There is an open-air viewing terrace with coin-operated binoculars on level 5.

LOVER'S ROCK Map p56

Off Bowen Rd; 🚐 green minibus 24A

A kilometre or so northeast of the Police Museum is what the Chinese call Yan Yuen Sek, a phallus-shaped boulder on a bluff at the end of a track above Bowen Rd. This is a favourite pilgrimage site for childless women and those who think their lovers, husbands or sons could use the help of prayer and a joss stick or two. It's especially

TRANSPORT – THE PEAK

Peak Tram Join the tram at the lower terminus on Cotton Tree Drive (Map p56). The service disgorges passengers in Peak Tower (entrance level 4, exit level 3).

Bus Bus 15 from Central bus terminus below Exchange Square (Map p56), bus 15B from Wan Chai and Causeway Bay (Map p65) via Police Museum, Caine Rd and Ladder St all terminate at the bus station below the Peak Galleria.

Green Minibus Bus 1 from Edinburgh Pl (southeast of City Hall) in Central and bus 24A from Admiralty terminate at the Peak.

NEIGHBOURHOODS & ISLANDS HONG KONG ISLAND

busy during the Maidens' Festival held on the seventh day of the seventh moon (mid-August). The easiest way to reach here is to take green minibus 24A from the Admiralty bus station. Get off at the terminus (Shiu Fai Tce) and walk up the path behind the housing complex.

POLICE MUSEUM Map pp54–5

☎ 2849 7019; www.police.gov.hk/hkp-home /english/museum; 27 Coombe Rd; admission free; ☺ 2-5pm Tue, 9am-5pm Wed-Sun; 🚌 15 or 15B, alight at the stop btwn Stubbs Rd & Peak Rd

Housed in a former police station, this seldom-visited museum in neighbouring Wan Chai Gap, an attractive residential area en route to the Peak, deals with the history of the Hong Kong Police Force, which was formed in 1844. It's small and rather static, although the intriguing Triad Societies Gallery and the very well-supplied Narcotics Gallery are worthwhile.

HAPPY VALLEY

Eating p188

Happy Valley (Map p74) – called *Páau-máa-dáy* (Horse Running Place) in Cantonese – has been a popular residential area for expats since the early days of British settlement, though, having built their houses on what turned out to be swampland, early residents had to contend with severe bouts of malaria. There are some interesting cemeteries to the west and southwest of Wong Nai Chung Rd. They are divided into Protestant, Roman Catholic, Muslim, Parsee and Hindu sections, and date back to the founding of Hong Kong as a colony. The district's most important drawcard, however, is the Happy Valley Racecourse. Happy Valley is essentially the racetrack in the centre of circular Wong Nai Chung Rd and the residential areas to the east and south, where the main streets are Shan Kwong, Sing Woo and Blue Pool Rds.

HAPPY VALLEY RACECOURSE Map p74

☎ 2895 1523, 2966 8111; www.happyvalleyrace course.com; 2 Sports Rd; Races usually held Sep-Jun on Wed & weekends (1st race 7.30pm); 🚊 Happy Valley

Horse racing, worth more than US$1 billion annually, remains the most popular form of gambling in Hong Kong and it is one of the quintessential things to do while you're in town. The punters pack into the stands and trackside, and the atmosphere is electric.

The first horse races were held in 1846 at Happy Valley and became an annual event. Now meetings are held both here and at the newer and larger (but less atmospheric) Sha Tin Racecourse (p125) in the New Territories. For details on placing bets, see p230.

If you know nothing about horse racing but would like to attend, consider joining the Come Horseracing Tour available through Gray Line or Splendid Tours & Travel (p298) during the racing season. The tour includes admission to the Visitors' Box of the Hong Kong Jockey Club Members' Enclosures and buffet lunch. Tours scheduled at night last about 5½ hours, while daytime tours are about seven hours long.

Racing buffs can wallow in the history of the place at the Hong Kong Racing Museum (☎ 2966 8065; www.hkjc.com/english/museum/mu02 _index.htm; 2nd fl, Happy Valley Stand, Wong Nai Chung Rd; admission free; ☺ 10am-5pm Tue-Sun, 10am-12.30pm on racing days), with eight galleries and a cinema showcasing celebrated trainers, jockeys and horseflesh, and key races over the past 150 years. The most important event in the history of the Happy Valley Racecourse – individual winnings notwithstanding – was the huge fire in 1918 that killed hundreds of people. Many of the victims were buried in the cemeteries surrounding the track.

ISLAND EAST

Drinking & Nightlife p210; Eating p189; Sleeping p257

Eastern (Map pp54–5) is a large district that is primarily residential, with some of Hong Kong Island's largest housing estates (eg Tai Koo Shing in Quarry Bay). As elsewhere on the island, however, office towers stand cheek by jowl with residential areas. There are not as many restaurants and nightspots in this area as there are in Central, Wan Chai and Causeway Bay to lure you onto the MTR's Central line, but the shopping is good and there are a handful of top-class museums.

The Eastern District runs from Causeway Bay to Siu Sai Wan, at the eastern end of Hong Kong Island's north coast. Major settlements are North Point, Quarry Bay, Sai Wan Ho, Shau Kei Wan and Chai Wan.

North Point & Quarry Bay

North Point, settled largely by Shanghainese after WWII, is a somewhat down-at-heel district with a couple of interesting markets, and

TRANSPORT – ISLAND EAST

MTR Central line from Causeway Bay.

Tram A more atmospheric alternative to the MTR, clatters sedately from Western Market (p70) in Sheung Wan to Shau Kei Wan.

North Point & Quarry Bay

MTR By far the easiest way to reach this area is to use the Island line with stations at North Point, Quarry Bay, Tai Koo, Sai Wan Ho, Shau Kei Wan, Heng Fa Chuen and Chai Wan. North Point and Quarry Bay are also on Tseung Kwan O line.

Bus North Point: To get to the North Point Ferry bus terminus from Tsim Sha Shui take bus 110 that runs down Canton Rd. From the south of the island, bus 38 comes from Aberdeen bus terminus (by the promenade) or bus 77 from Aberdeen Main Rd, which runs along King's Rd in North Point. Bus 63 (or 65 on Sundays) comes from Stanley (the bus terminus is just up from the market). The only direct bus from Shek O is the 309 on Sundays that runs along King's Rd in North Point.

Shau Kei Wan: To get to Shau Kai Wan bus terminus from Tsim Sha Shui take bus 110, which runs down Canton Rd. From the south of the island, take bus 77 from Aberdeen Main Rd. From Stanley bus 14 passes along Stanley Village Rd and takes you to Shau Kei Wan Rd close to the MTR station. From Shek O bus terminus take bus 9, which terminates at Shau Kei Wan MTR.

Tram If you're coming from Central or Admiralty, North Point has a tram terminus, as does Shau Kei Wan, which is at the end of the line.

Ferry North Point: You can reach North Point by ferry from Kwun Tong, Hung Hom and Kowloon City.

Sai Wan Ho: Ferries from Kwun Tong and Sam Ka Tsuen (by Lei Yue Mun) on the mainland arrive here. There are also Kaito services operating to Tung Lung Chau via Joss House Bay (although in significant quantities only on the weekend).

the Sunbeam Theatre (p218), one of the best places to see and hear Chinese opera. Tong Chong St opposite the Quarry Bay MTR station has had a face-lift in recent years and is something of a restaurant and nightlife strip. The main attraction at Quarry Bay is Cityplaza (p165).

Sai Wan Ho

HONG KONG FILM ARCHIVE Map pp54–5
☎ 2739 2139, bookings 2734 9009, 2119 7383; www.lcsd.gov.hk/en/cs_mus_lcsd.php; 50 Lei King Rd; admission free; ☾ main foyer 10am-8pm Mon-Wed & Fri-Sun, box office noon-8pm Mon-Wed & Fri-Sun, resource centre 10am-7pm Mon-Wed & Fri, 10am-5pm Sat, 1-5pm Sun; MTR Sai Wan Ho
The archive, which opened in 2001, is well worth a visit, even if you know nothing about Hong Kong films and film-making. It preserves, catalogues and studies – there are more than 6300 in the vaults – and related material such as magazines, posters, records and scripts; there's a small exhibition hall with themed exhibits (opening hours vary), including videos with subtitles, and a 127-seat cinema (☎ 2734 9009) that shows Hong Kong and other films here throughout the year for $30 to $50.

To reach the film archive from the Sai Wan Ho MTR station, follow exit A, walk north on Tai On St and west on Lei King Rd.

Shau Kei Wan

HONG KONG MUSEUM OF COASTAL DEFENCE Map pp54–5
☎ 2569 1500; www.lcsd.gov.hk/en/cs_mus_lcsd.php; 175 Tung Hei Rd; adult/concession $10/5, admission free Wed; ☾ 10am-5pm Fri-Wed; MTR Shau Kei Wan
This museum doesn't exactly sound like a crowd pleaser but the displays it contains are as much about peace as war. Part of the fun is just to enjoy the museum's location. It has been built into the Lei Yue Mun Fort (1887), which took quite a beating during WWII, and has sweeping views down to the Lei Yue Mun Channel and southeastern Kowloon.

Exhibitions in the old redoubt, which you reach by elevator from street level, cover Hong Kong's coastal defence over six centuries – from the Ming and Qing dynasties, through the colonial years and Japanese invasion, to the resumption of Chinese sovereignty. There's a historical trail through the casemates, tunnels and observation posts almost down to the coast.

To reach the museum take the MTR to Shau Kei Wan station (exit B2). Then follow the museum signs on busy Tung Hei Rd for about 15 minutes. Bus 85, which is accessible via exit A3 and runs along Shau Kei Wan Rd between North Point and Siu Sai Wan, stops on Tung Hei Rd outside the museum.

Chai Wan

LAW UK FOLK MUSEUM Map pp54–5
☎ 2896 7006; www.lcsd.gov.hk/en/cs_mus_lcsd .php; 14 Kut Shing St; admission free; ☻ 10am-6pm Mon-Wed & Fri-Sat, 1-6pm Sun; MTR Chai Wan
This small museum, a branch of the Hong Kong Museum of History dating from 1990, is housed in two restored Hakka village houses that have been standing in Chai Wan (Firewood Bay) – a district of nondescript office buildings, warehouses and workers' flats – for more than two centuries. The quiet courtyard and surrounding bamboo groves are peaceful and evocative, and the displays – furniture, household items and farming implements – simple but charming.

To reach the museum from the Chai Wan MTR station, follow exit B and walk for five minutes to the west.

ISLAND SOUTH

Drinking & Nightlife p210; Eating p189
Though largely residential, the Southern District (Map pp54–5), which encompasses everything from Big Wave Bay and Shek O in the east to Aberdeen and Ap Lei Chau in the west, is full of attractions. At times it can feel like Hong Kong Island's backyard playground – from the beaches of Repulse Bay and Deep Water Bay and the outdoor activities available at Shek O, to Stanley Market, the shoppers' paradise, and Ocean Park, the large amusement and theme park near Aberdeen.

Shek O lies halfway down a long peninsula in the southeast of Hong Kong Island; Stanley village is at the start of the next peninsula over, but you'll have to travel a bit further south to reach the best beach on Stanley peninsula. Further west along the southern coast is Repulse Bay, with its ever-heaving beach, Kwun Yam shrine, lucky bridge and posh shopping complex, and then Deep Water Bay, a much more serene beach and one of the best places in Hong Kong for wakeboarding (see p229).

Aberdeen is at the western edge of the southern coast. From here, buses return to the northern side of the island either through the Aberdeen Tunnel or Pok Fu Lam Rd along the west coast.

Buses, and to a lesser extent green minibuses, are the best form of transport for getting to and around the southern part of Hong Kong Island. Though some go via the Aberdeen Tunnel, many buses (eg bus 6 to Stanley and Repulse Bay) climb over the hills separating the north and south sides of the island. It's a scenic, winding ride; for the outbound trip,

TRANSPORT – ISLAND SOUTH

Bus Shek O: The easiest way to reach Shek O is to take bus 9 from Shau Kei Wan MTR station (exit A3). Bus 309 (Sunday and holidays only) runs here from Central, below Exchange Square. If you're coming from Stanley, take bus 14 and change to bus 9 on Tai Tam Rd, at the junction with Shek O Rd.

Stanley: From Shau Kei Wan take bus 14 from Shau Kei Wan Rd, a short walk from the MTR station (exit A3). Bus 6, 6A, 6X, 66 or 260 all leave for here from Central, below Exchange Square.

Aberdeen: From Aberdeen buses 73 and 973 run to Stanley. Both from Aberdeen Main Rd and the latter from the bus terminus, too, by the promenade. Buses 73 and 973 also run here from Repulse Bay beach. From Tsim Sha Tsui take bus 973 that leaves from Concordia Plaza by the science museum. Green minibus 40 (24 hours) runs from Times Square to Stanley via Tang Lung St and Yee Woo St in Causeway Bay (Map p74).

Repulse Bay: From Central, below Exchange Square, take bus 6, 6A, 6X, 66 or 260. From Stanley (the terminus is just up from the market) take 6, 6A, 6X, 66 or 260, which go on to Central, or 73 or 973. To get here from Aberdeen take bus 73 or 973 – both stop on Aberdeen Main Rd and the latter at the bus terminus, too. From Tsim Sha Tsui take bus 973 that leaves from Concordia Plaza by the science museum.

Deep Water Bay: From Central, below Exchange Square, take bus 6A, 6X or 260. From Stanley (the terminus is just up from the market) take bus 6A, 6X or 260, which go on to Central, or 73 or 973. To get here from Aberdeen take bus 73 or 973 – both stop on Aberdeen Main Rd and the latter at the bus terminus too. From Tsim Sha Tsui take bus 973 that leaves from Concordia Plaza by the science museum.

make sure you sit on the upper deck on the right-hand side.

Aberdeen

For many years Aberdeen (Map p82) – or Heung Gong Tsai (Little Fragrant Harbour) in Cantonese – was one of Hong Kong's top tourist attractions because of the large number of people (up to 6000, in fact) who lived and worked on the junks and other traditional sailing craft moored in the harbour and in the Aberdeen Typhoon Shelter off Aberdeen Praya Rd to the west. Over the years the number of boats has dwindled as more and more of these boatpeople have moved into high-rises or abandoned fishing as a profession. These days the busy little harbour is still an attractive place to explore. It is also the home to popular floating restaurants (p190) and to Ocean Park (below), Hong Kong's first, and still, thriving, amusement park.

OCEAN PARK Map pp54–5

☎ 2552 0291; www.oceanpark.com.hk; Ocean Park Rd; adult/child 3-11 yr $185/93; ☉ 9.30am-8pm; 🚌 6A, 6X, 70 & 75 from Central, 629 from Admiralty, 72, 72A & 92 from Causeway Bay or 973 from Tsim Sha Tsui

Hong Kong's original amusement park has scrubbed up well against it's shiny, new Disneyland competitor on Lantau (see p141). The resurgent park has invested billions of dollars in revamping its rides and attractions, to good effect. Visitor numbers have been soaring (thanks in part to the influx of mainland visitors) and the arrival of two more young pandas in 2007, a gift from the mainland to mark Hong Kong's 10th year of independence, crowned its renaissance.

This excellent, fully fledged amusement and educational theme park has plenty of white-knuckle rides, such as the celebrated roller coaster called the Dragon, the Abyss 'turbo drop', and a marine park with sea lions and seals, daily dolphin and killer-whale shows, and aquariums. The Atoll Reef is particularly impressive, with over 2000 fish representing 200 species in residence. The walk-through Shark Aquarium has hundreds of different sharks on view and scores of rays. Bird-watchers are also catered for, with aviaries, a flamingo pond and the Amazing Birds Theatre, with regular aerial shows.

The park is divided into two sections. The main entrance is on the lowland side,

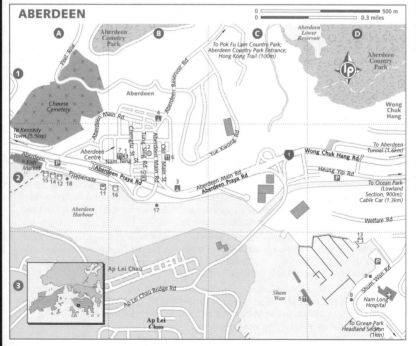

82

ABERDEEN

INFORMATION
HSBC 匯豐銀行 1 B2
Post Office 郵局 2 B2

SIGHTS (pp82–4)
Hung Shing Shrine 洪聖古廟...........3 B2
Tin Hau Temple 天后廟 4 B1

EATING 🍴 (pp190–1)
Jumbo Kingdom Floating Restaurant
    珍寶海鮮舫 5 C3
Shan Loon Tse Kee Fish Ball
    山窿謝記魚蛋 6 B2

Top Deck ....(see 5)
Wang Jia Sha 王家沙 7 B2

SPORTS & ACTIVITIES (pp222–31)
Aberdeen Boat Club
    香港仔遊艇會 8 D3
Aberdeen Marina Club
    深灣遊艇俱樂部 9 D3

TRANSPORT (pp269–86)
Aberdeen Bus Terminus
    香港仔巴士總站.........................10 B2
Aberdeen Sampan Company
    香港仔三舨公司 11 A2

Boats to Ap Lei Chau
    往鴨脷洲街渡 12 A2
Boats to Floating Restaurants
    往海鮮舫街渡 13 D3
Boats to Floating Restaurants
    往海鮮舫街渡 14 A2
Boats to Sok Kwu Wan & Mo Tat Wan
    (Lamma) & Po Toi
    往索罟灣、模達灣、蒲台島船15 A2
Boats to Yung Shue Wan (Lamma)
    往榕樹灣船隻..............................16 B2
Private Sampans..................................17 B2
Private Sampans..................................18 A2

where there are gardens and the Hong Kong Jockey Club Giant Panda Habitat, home to the two new arrivals, Ying Ying and Le Le, and their older cousins An An and Jia Jia. It is linked to the main section on the headland, where most of the attractions are found, by a scenic (and hair-raising) cable car. The headland section affords beautiful views of the South China Sea and at the rear entrance, where a giant escalator will bring you down to Tai Shue Wan and Shum Wan Rd, is the Middle Kingdom, a sort of Chinese cultural village with temples, pagodas and traditional street scenes.

SAMPAN TOURS Map p82
Aberdeen Promenade
Sampan tours can easily be arranged along Aberdeen Promenade, which runs south and parallel to Aberdeen Praya Rd. You can have your choice of private operators, which generally mill around the eastern end of the promenade, or licensed operators registered with the HKTB, such as the Aberdeen Sampan Company (Map p82; ☎ 2873 0310; Aberdeen Praya Rd). The private sampans usually charge $50 per person for a 30-minute ride (about $100 to Sok Kwu Wan and $120 to Yung Shue Wan on Lamma), though you should easily be able to bargain this down if there are several of you. Ferries to several spots on Lamma also operate from the promenade, as well as infrequent services to Stanley and Po Toi island (see the transport section for details, p275).

The promenade is easily accessed from Aberdeen bus terminus. To get to it just take the pedestrian subway under Aberdeen Praya Rd.

DON'T KNOW MUCH ABOUT HISTORY

Hong Kong has a dreadful track record, which persists to this day, when it comes to preserving old buildings. Basically if a structure sits on a 'valuable' piece of land (ie virtually every square centimetre of the built-up areas) or gets in the way of progress (ie money), the wrecker's ball brings it down, and it lives on only in old photographs and the memories of a dwindling population.

It was business as usual, then, when the colonial government announced in 1982 that Murray House, Hong Kong's oldest colonial building, was going to have to make room for the new Bank of China Tower. But because Murray House had a Grade 1 classification, even the government couldn't just smash it to pieces as they had the old Hong Kong Club and the Central Post Office. Instead, the building would be dismantled and its more than 4000 pieces numbered and stored for 'safekeeping' and erection elsewhere. Time passed and when heritage societies demanded to know its whereabouts, the government admitted it had misplaced some of the pieces.

Scene and time change... It's the mid-1990s and the government has found the missing pieces stored in crates in Tai Tam. But there's a big problem. The limestone blocks and pillars had been wrapped in plastic sheeting and the numbers written or etched into their sides had spontaneously erased due to moisture building up on the soft stone. To its credit, the government rolled up its sleeves and spent 3½ years putting the colossal puzzle back together again. And when they'd finished in early 2001, six columns were left over that they didn't know what to do with.

As you approach Murray House, which now contains the Hong Kong Maritime Museum on the ground floor and restaurants on the 1st and 2nd floors, you'll see these idle Ionic columns standing rather forlornly off to the left along the waterfront promenade. Note, too, some of the numbers still visible on the building blocks to the right of the entrance.

AP LEI CHAU Map p82
👤 Ap Lei Chau

On the southern side of the harbour is Ap Lei Chau (Duck's Tongue Island), one of the most densely populated places in the world. It used to be a centre for building junks, but now it's covered with housing estates, including a huge one called South Horizons. There's not much to see there, but a walk across the bridge to the island affords good views. From Aberdeen Promenade you can get a boat across to Ap Lei Chau (adult/child under 12 $1.80/1).

TEMPLES Map p82
Aberdeen Main Rd

If you've got time to spare, a short walk through Aberdeen will bring you to a renovated Tin Hau temple (182 Aberdeen Main Rd; ⏰ 8am-5pm). Built in 1851, it's a sleepy spot, but it remains an active house of worship. Close to the harbour is a Hung Shing shrine (cnr Aberdeen Main Rd & Old Main St), a chaotic collection of altars and smoking, ovenlike incense pots. Both temples are a short walk from Aberdeen bus terminus.

Stanley

About 15km from Central as the crow flies, Stanley's (Map p85) attractive market, beaches, and good pubs and restaurants make it an appealing place to escape the concrete jungle. It had an indigenous population of about 2000 when the British took control of the territory in 1841, making it one of the largest settlements on the island at the time. A prison was built near the village in 1937 – just in time for the Japanese to intern the builders. Stanley Prison is a maximum security facility today. Hong Kong's contingent of British troops was housed in Stanley Fort at the southern end of the peninsula until 1995. It is now used by China's People's Liberation Army (PLA). There's a beach to the northeast of town that never gets as crowded as the one at Repulse Bay. The most important dragon-boat races are held at Stanley during the Dragon Boat Festival (Tuen Ng; p17) in early June.

STANLEY MARKET Map p85
Stanley Village Rd; ⏰ 9am-6pm; 🚌 6, 6A, 6X or 260

No big bargains or big stings, just reasonably priced casual clothes (plenty of large sizes), bric-a-brac, toys and formulaic art, all in a nicely confusing maze of alleys running down to Stanley Bay. It's best to go during the week; on the weekend the market is bursting at the seams with both tourists and locals alike.

MURRAY HOUSE Map p85
Stanley Bay; 🚌 6, 6A, 6X or 260

At the start of the Chung Hom Kok peninsula across the bay from Stanley Main St, the waterfront promenade lined with bars and restaurants, stands this three-storey colonnaded affair. Built in 1848 as officers' quarters, it took pride of place in Central, on the spot where the Bank of China Tower now stands, for almost 150 years until 1982. It was re-erected here and opened in 2001 after, well, a slight glitch (see boxed text, p83).

HONG KONG MARITIME MUSEUM
Map p85

☎ 2813 2322; www.hkmaritimemuseum.org; GF, Murray House; adult/concession $20/10; ⏰ 10am-6pm Tue-Sun; 🚌 6, 6A, 6X or 260

This small but interesting museum occupying the ground floor of Murray House consists of an ancient and a modern gallery charting the shipping history of Hong Kong and is well worth a visit if you've already come to see Murray House. The modern gallery includes some fun interactive displays where you can test your skills at morse code or even pilot a tanker through Hong Kong waters.

HONG KONG CORRECTIONAL SERVICES MUSEUM Map p85
☎ 2147 3199; www.csd.gov.hk/english/hkcsm /hkcsm.html; 45 Tung Tau Wan Rd; admission free; ⏰ 10am-5pm Tue-Sun; 🚌 6, 6A, 6X or 260

With Stanley Prison so close by, it's only natural that there should be a museum devoted to the subject here. The museum, about 500m southeast of Stanley Village Rd, has nine galleries that trace the history of jails, prisons and other forms of incarceration in Hong Kong. The mock cells, gallows and flogging stands will convince most of the error of their ways.

OLD STANLEY POLICE STATION Map p85
88 Stanley Village Rd; 🚌 6, 6A, 6X or 260

The most interesting building in the village itself is this two-storey structure built in 1859. It now contains a Wellcome supermarket.

ST STEPHEN'S BEACH & MILITARY CEMETERY Off Map p85

🚌 **6A or 14**

St Stephen's Beach, which has a café, showers and changing rooms, is south of the village. In summer you can hire windsurfing boards and kayaks from the water-sports centre (see p229). To reach the beach, walk south along Wong Ma Kok Rd. Turn west (ie right) when you get to a small road (Wong Ma Kok Path) leading down to a jetty.

At the end of the road, turn south and walk past the boathouse to the beach. Bus 14 or 6A will take you close to the intersection with the small road.

Well worth a look is Stanley Military Cemetery for armed forces personnel and their families. The oldest graves date back to 1843 and are an intriguing document of the colonial era. The earlier graves show just how much of a toll disease took on European settlers, while the number of graves from the early 1940s serves as a reminder of the many who died in the fight for Hong Kong and during subsequent internment at the hands of occupying Japanese forces. The cemetery is just opposite the bus stop.

TEMPLES & SHRINES Map p85

🚌 **6, 6A, 6X or 260**

At the western end of Stanley Main St, past a tiny Tai Wong shrine and through the modern shopping complex called Stanley Plaza, is a Tin Hau temple (119 Stanley Main St; ⏰ 7am-6pm), built in 1767 and said to be the oldest building in Hong Kong. It has undergone a complete renovation since then, however, and is now a concrete pile (though the interior is traditional). A sign explains that the tiger skin hanging on the wall came from an animal that 'weighed 240 pounds, was 73 inches long, and three feet high [and] shot by an Indian policeman, Mr Rur Singh, in front of Stanley Police Station in the year 1942'.

Behind the Tin Hau temple is huge Ma Hang Estate. If you go across the front of the temple and follow the road, through the barriers and up the hill, you'll reach Kwun Yam Temple (⏰ 7am-6pm). The temple is on the left when you get to the roundabout at the top.

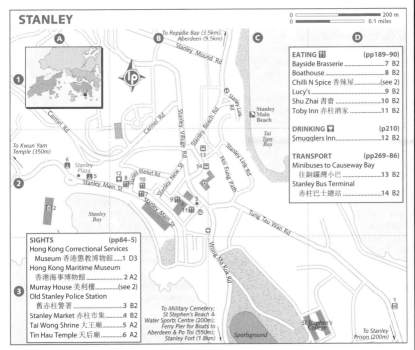

STANLEY

0 ——— 200 m
0 ——— 0.1 miles

To Repulse Bay (3.5km); Aberdeen (9.5km)

Stanley Mound Rd
Stanley Link Rd
Carmel Rd
Carmel Rd
Stanley Village Rd
Stanley Beach Rd
Stanley Main Beach
Tai Tam Bay
To Kwun Yam Temple (350m)
Stanley Plaza
Stanley Market Rd
Stanley New St
Stanley Main St
Hoi Fung Path
Stanley Link Rd
Stanley Bay
Tung Tau Wan Rd
Wong Ma Kok Rd
To Military Cemetery; St Stephen's Beach & Water Sports Centre (200m); Ferry Pier for Boats to Aberdeen & Po Toi (550m); Stanley Fort (1.8km)
Sportsground
St Stephen's College
To Stanley Prison (200m)

EATING 🍴 (pp189–90)
Bayside Brasserie 7 B2
Boathouse 8 B2
Chilli N Spice 香辣屋 ....(see 2)
Lucy's 9 B2
Shu Zhai 書齋 10 B2
Toby Inn 赤柱酒家 11 B2

DRINKING 🍷 (p210)
Smugglers Inn 12 B2

TRANSPORT (pp269–86)
Minibuses to Causeway Bay
往銅鑼灣小巴 13 B2
Stanley Bus Terminal
赤柱巴士總站 14 B2

SIGHTS (pp84–5)
Hong Kong Correctional Services
Museum 香港懲教博物館 1 D3
Hong Kong Maritime Museum
香港海事博物館 2 A2
Murray House 美利樓 ....(see 2)
Old Stanley Police Station
舊赤柱警署 3 B2
Stanley Market 赤柱市集 4 B2
Tai Wong Shrine 大王廟 5 A2
Tin Hau Temple 天后廟 6 A2

Shek O

Sometimes referred to as the 'last real village on Hong Kong Island', Shek O (Map pp54–5), has one of the best beaches on the island. Not as accessible as the beaches to the west (although it is only a 20-minute bus ride from Shau Kei Wan), the beaches here are usually less crowded.

Shek O has all sorts of activities to keep you amused and out of trouble. Shek O Beach has a large expanse of sand, shady trees to the rear, showers, changing facilities and lockers for rent. It's a good spot for swimming with several platforms offshore within a netted swimming area. In the village itself there's miniature golf ($13; 9am-6pm Apr-Sep, 9am-5.30pm Oct-Mar) and from Dragon's Back, the 280m-high ridge to the west of the village, there's both paragliding and abseiling. Walking is possible around Shek O Beach, though the terrain is steep and the underbrush quite thick in spots. You can also take advantage of several bicycle-rental shops (bicycles from $15 a day), including Tung Lok Barbecue Store (2809 4692; Apr-Sep) in the centre of the village.

BIG WAVE BAY Map pp54–5
9 or 309 (Sun only)
This fine and often deserted beach is located 2km to the north of Shek O. To get to Big Wave Bay follow the road north out of town, travel past the 18-hole Shek O Golf & Country Club (2809 4458; Shek O Rd), then turn east at the roundabout and keep going until the road ends.

One of eight prehistoric rock carvings discovered in Hong Kong (see p19) is located on the headland above Big Wave Bay.

Repulse Bay

Repulse Bay (Map pp54–5) is home to some of Hong Kong's richest residents, and the hills around the beach are strewn with luxury apartment blocks. This includes the pink, blue and yellow wavy number with a giant square hole in the middle called the Repulse Bay. This design feature was apparently added on the advice of a feng shui expert.

The long beach with tawny sand at Repulse Bay – Chin Shui Wan (Shallow Water Bay) in Cantonese – is the most popular one on Hong Kong Island. Packed on the weekend and even during the week in summer, it's a good place if you like people-watching. The beach has showers and changing rooms and shade trees at the road side, but the water is pretty murky. Lifeguards keep extended hours here: from 9am to 6pm daily from March to November (8am to 7pm on Saturday and Sunday from June to August).

Middle Bay and South Bay, about 10 and 30 minutes to the south respectively, have beaches that are usually much less crowded.

KWUN YAM SHRINE Map ppp54–5
Repulse Bay Beach; 6, 6A, 6X or 260
Towards the southeast end of Repulse Bay Beach is an unusual shrine to Kwun Yam. The surrounding area has an amazing assembly of deities and figures – goldfish, rams, the money god and other southern Chinese icons, as well as statues of the goddess of mercy and Tin Hau. Most of the statues were funded by local personalities and businesspeople during the 1970s. In front of the shrine to the left as you face the sea is Longevity Bridge; crossing it is supposed to add three days to your life.

THE REPULSE BAY Map pp54–5
109 Repulse Bay Rd; 6, 6A, 6X or 260
The Repulse Bay, a copy of the wonderful old colonial Repulse Bay Hotel, built in 1922 and bulldozed 60 years later, contains a small shopping mall and several food outlets, including the Verandah Restaurant (p190).

Deep Water Bay

A quiet little inlet with a beach flanked by shade trees, Deep Water Bay (Map pp54–5) is located a few kilometres northwest of Repulse Bay; lifeguards keep the same schedule as those at Repulse Bay Beach and in winter – ie December to February – they are on duty daily from 8am to 5pm. There are a few decent places to eat and have a drink, and barbecue pits at the southern end of the beach. If you want a dip in the water, this spot is usually less crowded than Repulse Bay. Opposite the beach is the nine-hole Deep Water Bay Golf Club (see p224). Deep Water Bay Beach is a centre for wakeboarding (see p229).

KOWLOON

It says something about Kowloon (Map pp88–9) that one of the most stirring experiences you can have there is to turn your back on it, stand at the waters edge and look back towards Hong Kong Island's startling skyline. There's a sense that Central's busy but scruffier neighbour is forever gazing enviously across the water at it.

This is not to say you shouldn't spend time here. It is a compelling destination containing some of Hong Kong's best museums, sights, hotels and shopping. It is also where you start to leave behind sleek commercialism for a more absorbing and human-scale neighbourhood life of markets, temples, traditional shopping streets, crumbling tenement blocks.

The name 'Kowloon' is thought to have originated when the last emperor of the Song dynasty passed through the area during his flight from the Mongols in the late 13th century (p20). He is said to have counted eight peaks on the peninsula and concluded that there must therefore be eight dragons there. But the young emperor was reminded that with he himself present, there were actually nine dragons. Kowloon is thus derived from the Cantonese words *gáu*, meaning 'nine', and *lùng*, meaning 'dragon'.

Kowloon proper, the area ceded 'in perpetuity' to Britain by the Convention of Peking in 1860, extends north from the waterfront as far as Boundary St in Mong Kok. It covers about 12 sq km, but land reclamation and encroachment into the New Territories – the so-called New Kowloon – over the past 150-odd years has more than quadrupled its size to almost 47 sq km.

Kowloon's most important area, Tsim Sha Tsui, has none of the slickness or sophistication of Hong Kong Island's Central, except within the confines of its top-end hotels. Tsimsy (as local expats call it) is a riot of commerce and tourism set against a backdrop of crumbling tenement blocks.

In general, Kowloon is unexciting architecturally. Height restrictions for buildings, due to the proximity of the old Kai Tak International Airport in southeastern Kowloon, gave it a much lower skyline than that of northern Hong Kong Island, though that's all changing – and fast. The waterfront Hong Kong Cultural Centre in Tsim Sha Tsui was a bold (and early) stab at turning Hong Kong into something more than a territory obsessed with wealth. The Peninsula Hotel is housed in one of Hong Kong's greatest colonial buildings and, at night, the promenade running east and northeast along Victoria Harbour from Star Ferry pier offers a technicolour backdrop of Central and Wan Chai. There are some green spaces as well, such as Kowloon Park.

TSIM SHA TSUI

Drinking & Nightlife p211; Eating p191; Shopping p166; Sleeping p257

Tsim Sha Tsui (Map p92; roughly pronounced 'jìm-sàa-jéui' and meaning 'Sharp Sandy Point') is Hong Kong's tourist ghetto. It is packed with hotels and inexpensive guesthouses, and the dining and drinking options are plentiful if not as glittering as the ones across the water.

It's also a shopping destination. Clothing and shoe shops, restaurants, camera and electronics stores, and hotels are somehow crammed into an area not much bigger than 1 sq km. Around Ashley, Hankow and Lock Rds is a warren of shops, restaurants and bars. It's a fun area to wander around, particularly in the evening. Nightlife areas include Knutsford Tce and, most recently, Minden Ave.

The hotel and shopping district of Tsim Sha Tsui ('Tsimsy' to locals) lies at the very tip of the Kowloon Peninsula to the south

of Austin Rd. (The area between Austin and Jordan Rds is usually called Jordan by Hong Kong residents, but it can still be considered Tsim Sha Tsui here.) Chatham Rd South separates it from the hotels and shops of Tsim Sha Tsui East and the transport hub of Hung Hom. Tsim Sha Tsui's western and southern boundaries – Victoria Harbour – are lined with top-end hotels, shopping centres and cultural venues.

top picks

KOWLOON

- Star Ferry (p273)
- Avenue of the Stars evening lightshow (p95)
- Afternoon Tea at the Peninsula (p91)
- Tsim Sha Tsui East Promenade (p95)
- Hong Kong Museum of Art (p90)

KOWLOON

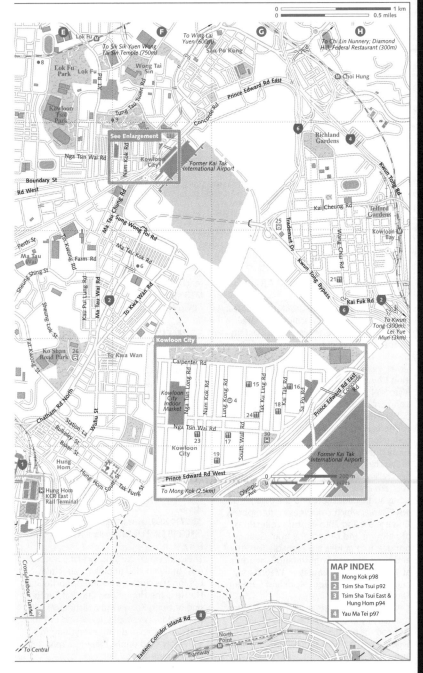

0   1 km
0   0.5 miles

E Lok Fu
To Sik Sik Yuen Wong
Tai Sin Temple (750m)
F To Wing Lai
Yuen (600m)
Sau Po Kong
G
H To Chi Lin Nunnery; Diamond
Hill; Federal Restaurant (300m)

• 8
Lok Fu
Park Lok Fu Rd
Wong Tai
Sin

Kowloon
Tsai
Park

Tung Tau Tsuen Rd

Prince Edward Rd East
M Choi Hung

See Enlargement

Nam Kok Rd
Kowloon
City
Former Kai Tak
International Airport

Concorde Rd

Richland
Gardens 4

Kwun Tong Rd

Nga Tsin Wai Rd

Boundary St
Rd West

Ma Tau Chung Rd
Tung Wong Toi Rd

Kai Cheung Rd
Telford
Gardens

Kowloon
Bay M

Wang Chiu Rd

Perth St
Ma Tau
Kai Pui Lung Rd
Farm Rd
Ma Tau Kok Rd
• 6

25

Trademart Dr

Kwun Tong Bypass

21

Sheung Shing St
To Kwa Wan Rd

Kai Fuk Rd 2
6

To Kwun
Tong (300m);
Lei Yue
Mun (3km)

Sheung Lok St
Kai Pui Lung Rd
Ma Tau Wai Rd

2

Fat Kwong St

Ko Shan
Road Park 26
To Kwa Wan

Kowloon City

Carpenter Rd 15

Kowloon
City
Indoor
Market

Nga Tsin Long Rd
Nam Kok Rd
Lung Kong Rd 4
Tak Ku Ling Rd 16
18
24

Prince Edward Rd East
Concorde
Rd

Chatham Rd North
Station La
Wuhu St
Bulkeley St
Baker St

Hung
Hom

Nga Tsin Wai Rd
23
17
South Wall Rd
30

Kowloon
City
19

1

Hung Hom South
Tak Fung St

Hung Hom
KCR East
Rail Terminal

Prince Edward Rd West
To Mong Kok (2.5km)

Former Kai Tak
International Airport

0   200 m
0   0.1 miles

Olympic
Ave

3

Cross-Harbour Tunnel

MAP INDEX
1 Mong Kok p98
2 Tsim Sha Tsui p92
3 Tsim Sha Tsui East &
   Hung Hom p94
4 Yau Ma Tei p97

8
North
Point M

To Central
Eastern Corridor Island Rd
Tramway

KOWLOON

HONG KONG MUSEUM OF ART
Map p92

☎ 7221 0116; www.lcsd.gov.hk/hkma; 10 Salisbury Rd; adult/concession $10/5, admission free Wed; ☽ 10am-6pm Fri-Wed, to 8pm Sat; ⬛ Star Ferry
To the southeast of the Hong Kong Cultural Centre, the Hong Kong Museum of Art has seven galleries spread over six floors, exhibiting Chinese antiquities, Chinese fine art, historical pictures and contemporary Hong Kong art, and hosting temporary international exhibitions.

The seventh gallery houses the Xubaizhi collection of painting and calligraphy. Highlights include some exquisite ceramics in the Chinese Antiques Gallery, the Historical Pictures Gallery, with its 18th- and 19th-century Western-style paintings of Macau, Hong Kong and Guangzhou, and the Gallery of Chinese Fine Art, which combines contemporary Chinese art and 20th-century collections of painting and calligraphy from Guangdong. Audio guides are available for $10, and there are free English-language tours at 11am and 4pm Sunday to Wednesday and Friday, and at 3pm, 4pm and 5pm on Saturday.

When your feet get tired, take a seat in the hallway and enjoy the harbour views. Or head for the Museum Café. The Museum Bookshop sells a wide range of books, prints and cards. Salisbury Gardens, which leads to the museum entrance, is lined with sculptures by contemporary Hong Kong sculptors. To reach the museum from the Tsim Sha Tsui MTR station, take exit E and walk south down Nathan Rd.

FORMER KCR CLOCK TOWER Map p92
Tsim Sha Tsui Public Pier; ⬛ Star Ferry
Immediately east of Star Ferry pier, this 44m-high clock tower (1915) was once part of the southern terminus of the Kowloon–Canton Railway (KCR). Operations moved to the modern train station at Hung Hom to the northeast in late 1975. The station was demolished in 1978, though you can see a scale model of what it looked like if you visit the Hong Kong Railway Museum (p120) in Tai Po in the New Territories.

HONG KONG CULTURAL CENTRE
Map p92

☎ 2734 2009; www.lcsd.gov.hk/CE/CulturalService/HKCC; 10 Salisbury Rd; ☽ 9am-11pm; ⬛ Star Ferry
The odd, wave-like (and virtually windowless) building clad in pink ceramic tiles behind the clock tower and opposite Star House is the Hong Kong Cultural Centre, one of Hong Kong's most distinctive – if not loved – landmarks. It opened in 1989 and was compared with everything from a cheaply tiled public toilet to a road-side petrol station.

Its controversial design notwithstanding, the centre is a world-class venue, with a

2085-seat concert hall, a Grand Theatre that seats 1750, a studio theatre for up to 535, rehearsal studios and an impressive foyer. The concert hall even has a Rieger Orgelbau pipe organ (with 8000 pipes and 93 stops), one of the largest in the world. On the building's south side is the beginning of a viewing platform from where you can admire Victoria Harbour and the skyline of Central and gain access to the Tsim Sha Tsui East Promenade and Avenue of the Stars (p95).

NATHAN ROAD Map p92
MTR Tsim Sha Tsui

Kowloon's main thoroughfare was named after Sir Matthew Nathan, governor of Hong Kong from 1904 to 1907. As Kowloon was very sparsely populated at the time and such a wide boulevard thought unnecessarily extravagant, it was dubbed 'Nathan's Folly'. Banyans line the road at the northern end near Austin Rd, but the trees that once lined the rest of the street and can be seen in not-so-old photographs were removed in 1976 when the MTR's first line was being built.

Though lacking any tourist sights as such, the lower end of this boulevard is a sight in itself. This 'Golden Mile' is an iconic Hong Kong scene, but not for the opulence suggested by the name. In fact it is a chaotic scrum of tenement blocks stacked with seedy guesthouses awkwardly rubbing shoulders with top-end hotels; touts selling 'copy' watches; tailors plying their trade on street corners; and pavements chock-a-block with consumers scurrying from one shop to another. Anyone who chooses to stay (see p257)at Chungking Mansions, Mirador Mansion or Golden Crown Guest House will have this frenetic scene at their very doorstep.

TRANSPORT – TSIM SHA TSUI

MTR Tsim Sha Tsui station (Map p92) on the Tsuen Wan line empties onto both sides of Nathan Rd. There's also a long tunnel linking it with Tsim Sha Tsui East KCR station (although a couple of travelators make it less of a schlepp).

KCR East Tsim Sha Tsui station (Map p94) is the terminus of the KCR East Rail.

Star Ferry Pier (Map p92) at western end of Salisbury Rd.

Macau Ferries China ferry terminal (Map p92) on Canton Rd.

PENINSULA HONG KONG Map p92
☎ 2920 2888; www.peninsula.com; cnr Salisbury & Nathan Rds; MTR Tsim Sha Tsui

More than a Hong Kong landmark, the Peninsula, in the throne-like building opposite the Hong Kong Space Museum, is one of the world's great hotels (p257). Though it was being called 'the finest hotel east of Suez' just a few years after opening in 1928, the Peninsula was in fact one of several prestigious hostelries across Asia where everybody who was anybody stayed, lining up with (but not behind) the likes of the Raffles in Singapore, the Peace (then the Cathay) in Shanghai and the Strand in Rangoon (now Yangon).

Taking afternoon tea ($240; ⏱ 2-7pm) at the Peninsula is one of the best experiences in town – dress neatly and be prepared to queue for a table.

KOWLOON PARK Map p92
☎ 2724 3344; www.lcsd.gov.hk/en/ls_park.php; 22 Austin Rd; ⏱ 5am-midnight; MTR Tsim Sha Tsui & Jordan

Built on the site of a barracks for Indian soldiers in the colonial army, Kowloon Park is an oasis of greenery and a refreshing escape from the hustle and bustle of Tsim Sha Tsui. Pathways and walls crisscross the grass, birds hop around in cages, and towers and ancient banyan trees dot the landscape.

There's an aviary (⏱ 6.30am-6.45pm Mar-Oct, 6.30am-5.45pm Nov-Feb) and a Chinese Garden and Sculpture Walk, featuring works by local artists. Kung Fu Corner, a display of traditional Chinese martial arts, takes place here from 2.30pm to 4.30pm on Sunday. The renovated Kowloon Park Swimming Complex (☎ 2724 3577, adult/concession $19/9; ⏱ outdoor 6.30am-10pm with 1hr close at noon & 5pm Apr-Oct, indoor 6.30am-9.30pm with 1hr close at noon & 5pm Nov-Mar) is complete with four pools and waterfalls. Visit on a weekday; on weekends there are so many bathers it's difficult to find the water.

HONG KONG SPACE MUSEUM & THEATRE Map p92
☎ 2721 0226; www.lcsd.gov.hk/CE/Museum /Space/index.htm; 10 Salisbury Rd; adult/concession $10/5; admission free Wed; ⏱ 1-9pm Mon & Wed-Fri, 10am-9pm Sat, Sun & public holidays; 🚢 Star Ferry

Just east of the Hong Kong Cultural Centre, this golf-ball-shaped building consists of the Hall of Space Science, the Hall of Astronomy

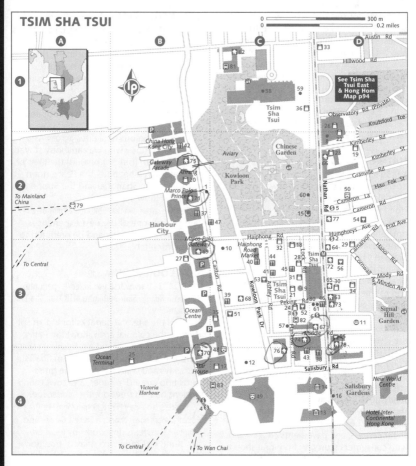

TSIM SHA TSUI

and the large Space Theatre, one of the largest planetariums in the world. Exhibits include a lump of moon rock, rocket-ship models and NASA's 1962 *Mercury* space capsule.

It's not a compelling museum (the Science Museum has a lot more to offer) but if it's raining, a standby option is the Space Theatre, which screens 'sky shows' and Omnimax films on a massive screen; lasting about 40 minutes, they are mostly in Cantonese, but translations by headphones are available. The first show is at 1.30pm weekdays (12.20pm Saturday, 11.10am Sunday), the last at 8.30pm. Tickets are $32/16 for adults/concession ($24/12 in the front stalls); children under three are not allowed entry. Advance bookings can be made by phone up to one hour before show time.

KOWLOON MOSQUE & ISLAMIC CENTRE Map p92

☎ 2724 0095; 105 Nathan Rd; ⏱ 5am-10pm; MTR Tsim Sha Tsui

North of the intersection of Nathan and Haiphong Rds, the Kowloon Mosque & Islamic Centre is the largest Islamic house of worship in Hong Kong. The present building, with its dome and carved marble, was completed in 1984 to serve the territory's 70,000-odd Muslims, more than half of whom are Chinese, and can accommodate 2000 worshippers. It occupies the site of a mosque built in 1896 for Muslim Indian troops.

Muslims are welcome to attend services but non-Muslims should ask permission to enter. Do remember to remove your footwear.

TSIM SHA TSUI

OCEAN TERMINAL Map p92

☎ 2118 8668; www.harbourcity.com.hk; Salisbury Rd; ⏰ 11.30am-9pm; ⏏ Star Ferry
To the north of the clock tower is Star House (3 Salisbury Rd), a frayed-looking retail and

office complex. At its western end is the entrance to Ocean Terminal, the long building jutting into the harbour. It is part of the massive Harbour City shopping complex that stretches for half a kilometre north along Canton Rd and offers priceless views of Tsim Sha Tsui's western waterfront.

The stunning blue-and-white colonial structure on the hill above where Canton and Salisbury Rds meet is the former Marine Police Headquarters, built in 1884. Following a lengthy redevelopment of the site, new shops, cafés and restaurants, together with a luxury hotel, should be open on the site by the time you read this.

TSIM SHA TSUI EAST & HUNG HOM

Drinking & Nightlife p211; Eating p193; Sleeping p260

The large triangular chunk of land east and northeast of Tsim Sha Tsui proper (Map p94), built entirely on reclaimed land, is a cluster of shopping centres, hotels and theatres. There

are none of the old, crumbling buildings of 'real' Tsim Sha Tsui here – and like most reclaimed areas, it has that soulless, artificial feel that will take decades to remove. But two of Hong Kong's most important museums are here, and it offers an excellent vantage point from which to admire the harbour and the Hong Kong Island skyline.

Among the features of Hung Hom, the contiguous district to the northeast, are the massive KCR East Rail station, on Wan Rd; the 12,500-seat Hong Kong Coliseum (☎ 2355 7234; 9 Cheong Wan Rd), which hosts concerts and sporting events; the Hong Kong Polytechnic University (☎ 2766 5100; Hong Chong Rd), opposite the station; and one of the strangest shopping venues in the territory, the Wonderful World of Whampoa (Map pp88–9; ☎ 2128 7710; www.whampoaworld.com; 18 Tak Fung St; ☼ 10am-10pm), a full-scale concrete model of a luxury cruise liner. While presumably not

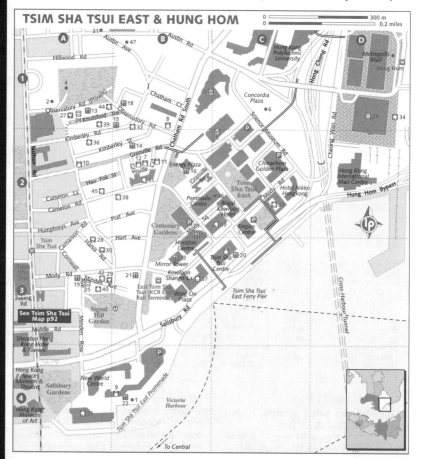

TSIM SHA TSUI EAST & HUNG HOM

very seaworthy, the 'ship' – 100m long and four decks tall – is impressive and works very well for what it was intended to be: a shopping centre with retail outlets, restaurants, a cinema, and a playground on the top deck.

Tsim Sha Tsui East is defined by Chatham Rd South to the west and Salisbury Rd to the south. The limit to the east is Hong Chong Rd, backed by the Hong Kong Coliseum and Hung Hom train station. To the north it ends at Cheong Wan Rd.

Hung Hom is further to the north and northeast and divided by the Hung Hom Bypass into two parts: the station and coliseum on the west side and residential Hung Hom to the east.

TSIM SHA TSUI EAST PROMENADE
Map p94

🚢 **Star Ferry**
One of the finest city skylines in the world has to be that of Hong Kong Island, and the promenade here is one of the best ways to get an uninterrupted view. It's a lovely place to stroll during the day but comes into its own at night, during the nightly Symphony of the Stars, a spectacular sound-and-light show involving 20 buildings on the Hong Kong Island skyline from 8pm to 8.20pm.

Along the first part of the promenade is the Avenue of the Stars, which pays homage to the Hong Kong film industry and its stars, with handprints, sculptures and information

TRANSPORT – TSIM SHA TSUI EAST & HUNG HOM

MTR Take the Tsuen Wan line to Tsim Sha Tsui station (Map p92).

KCR East Tsim Sha Tsui and Hung Hong stations (Map p94) are on the KCR East Rail.

Ferry Star Ferries run from Central and Wan Chai to the Hung Hom ferry pier (Map p94).

boards, a brave but ultimately lacklustre effort to celebrate Hong Kong's film and TV industry.

The promenade officially starts at the New World Centre shopping centre and runs parallel to Salisbury Rd almost to the Hong Kong Coliseum and Hung Hom train station, but you can walk along the water all the way from Star Ferry pier in order to gain access to it. It gets especially crowded during the Chinese New Year fireworks displays in late January/early February and in June during the Dragon Boat Festival (p17).

HONG KONG MUSEUM OF HISTORY
Map p94

☎ 2724 9042; www.hk.history.museum; 100 Chatham Rd South; adult/concession $10/5, admission free Wed; ⏰ 10am-6pm Mon & Wed-Sat, 10am-7pm Sun & public holidays; MTR Tsim Sha Tsui (exit B2)

TSIM SHA TSUI EAST & HUNG HOM

For a whistlestop overview of the territory's archaeology, natural history, ethnography and local history, this museum is well worth a visit, not only to learn more about the subject but to understand how Hong Kong presents its history to itself and the world.

'The Hong Kong Story' takes visitors on a fascinating walk through the territory's past via eight galleries, starting with the natural environment and prehistoric Hong Kong – about 6000 years ago, give or take a lunar year – and ending with the territory's return to China in 1997. Along the way you'll encounter replicas of village dwellings; traditional Chinese costumes and beds; a re-creation of an entire arcaded street in Central from 1881, including an old Chinese medicine shop; a tram from 1913; and film footage of WWII, including recent interviews with Chinese and foreigners taken prisoner by the Japanese.

Free guided tours of the museum are available in English at 10.30am and 2.30pm on Saturday and Sunday.

HONG KONG SCIENCE MUSEUM
Map p94

☎ 2732 3232; www.lcsd.gov.hk/CE/Museum /Science; 2 Science Museum Rd; adult/concession $25/12.50, admission free Wed; ☉ 1-9pm Mon-Wed & Fri, 10am-9pm Sat, Sun & public holidays; MTR Tsim Sha Tsui (exit B2)

Illustrating the fundamental workings of technology, such as computers and telecommunications, and practical demonstrations of the laws of energy, physics and chemistry, the Hong Kong Science Museum is a great hands-on experience capable of entertaining adults as well as children. There are more than 500 displays, although some of them are showing their age.

HONG KONG OBSERVATORY Map p94

☎ 2926 8200; www.hko.gov.hk; 134A Nathan Rd; MTR Tsim Sha Tsui & Jordan

This historic monument, built in 1883, is sadly *not* open to the public. It continues to monitor Hong Kong's weather and sends up those frightening signals when a typhoon is heading for the territory (see boxed text, p288).

YAU MA TEI

Eating p194; Shopping p169; Sleeping p262

Immediately to the north of Tsim Sha Tsui is Yau Ma Tei (Map p97), pronounced 'yàu-màa-dáy' and meaning 'Place of Sesame Plants'.

TRANSPORT – YAU MA TEI

MTR Yau Ma Tei MTR station is on the Tsuen Wan and Kwun Tong lines, and Kowloon MTR on the Tung Chung and Airport Express lines.

Bus Buses 2, 6, 6A and 9 run up Nathan Rd (Map p92).

Today the only plants you'll find in this heavily urbanised neighbourhood are in the window boxes of *tàwng-láu*, the crumbling six-storey tenements that don't have lifts and more often than not have illegal huts on the roof. The narrow streets full of shops and tenement buildings in Yau Ma Tei are much the same as those further south and north in Tsim Sha Tsui and Mong Kok, making this district practically indistinguishable from its neighbours. Yau Ma Tei starts at Jordan Rd and reaches north to somewhere between Waterloo Rd and Argyle St. King's Park and Gascoigne Rd are its borders to the east. To the west it reaches Yau Ma Tei Typhoon Shelter in Victoria Harbour, the West Kowloon reclamation site, and the Kowloon station of the Tung Chung MTR and Airport Express lines.

Yau Ma Tei's narrow byways are good places to check out Hong Kong's more traditional urban society. There are many interesting walks to take along the streets running east to west between Kansu St and Jordan Rd (Map p97), including Nanking St (mahjong shops and parlours), Ning Po St (paper kites and votives, such as houses, mobile phones and hell money, to burn for the dead) and Saigon St (herbalist shops, old-style tailors, pawnshops). On Shanghai St you'll find Chinese bridal and trousseau shops. See p99 for a self-guided walk of this area.

TEMPLE STREET NIGHT MARKET
Map p97

☉ 4-11pm; MTR Yau Ma Tei (exit C)

The liveliest night market in Hong Kong, Temple St extends from Man Ming Lane in the north to Nanking St in the south and is cut in two by the Tin Hau temple complex. While you may find better bargains further north in New Kowloon, and certainly over the border in Shenzhen, it is still a good place to go for the bustling atmosphere and the smells and tastes on offer from the *daai-pàai-dawng* (open-air street stall) food.

People shop here for cheap clothes, watches, pirated CDs, fake labels, footwear,

YAU MA TEI

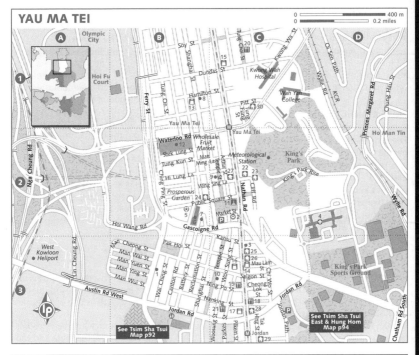

YAU MA TEI

INFORMATION
International Women's League
國際婦女會 1 B3
Kowloon Central Post Office
九龍中央郵局 2 C2
Map Publication Centre
地圖銷售處 3 C3
Queen Elizabeth Hospital
伊利沙伯醫院 4 D2
Yau Ma Tei Police Station
油麻地警署 5 B2

SIGHTS (pp96–8)
Jade Market 玉器市場 6 B2
Jade Market 玉器市場 7 B2
Shanghai Street Artspace
上海街視藝空間 8 B1

Temple Street Night Market
廟街夜市 9 C2
Temple Street Night Market
廟街夜市 10 C3
Tin Hau Temple 天后廟 11 C2
Wholesale Fruit Market 果欄 12 B2

SHOPPING (p169)
Chamonix Alpine Equipment
沙木尼登山用品 13 B1
Chinese Arts & Crafts 中藝 14 C3
Trendy Zone 潮流特區 15 C1
Wing On 永安 16 C3
Yue Hwa Chinese Products
Emporium 裕華國貨 17 C3

EATING (p194)
Bali Restaurant 峇里餐廳 18 C3
Miu Gute Cheong Vegetarian
Restaurant 妙吉祥素食館 19 C3

Tai Pak 西門町台灣麵食 20 C1
Tsui Wah 翠華餐廳 21 C3

SLEEPING (pp262–3)
Booth Lodge 卜維廉賓館 22 C2
Caritas Bianchi Lodge
明愛白英奇賓館 23 C2
Dorsett Seaview Hotel
帝豪海景酒店 24 B2
Eaton Hotel 逸東酒店 25 C3
Hakka's Guest House
嘉應賓館 ....(see 28)
Nathan Hotel 彌敦酒店 26 C3
New Kings Hotel 新高雅酒店 27 C2
New Lucky House 華豐大廈 28 C3
Ocean Guest House 宏洋賓館 ...(see 28)
Rent-a-Room Hong Kong
訂房通 29 C3
YMCA International House
青年會國際賓館 30 C1

cookware and everyday items. Any marked prices should be considered mere suggestions – this is definitely a place to bargain.

You'll also find a surfeit of fortune-tellers, herbalists and, occasionally, some free, open-air Cantonese opera performances.

For street food, head for Woo Sung St, running parallel to the east, or to the section of Temple St north of the temple. You can get anything from a simple bowl of noodles to a full meal. There are also a few seafood and hotpot restaurants in the area.

The market officially opens in the afternoon, but most hawkers set up at about 6pm and start shutting up around 11pm. The market is at its best from about 7pm to 10pm, when it's clogged with stalls and people. If you want to carry on, visit the colourful wholesale fruit market (cnr Shek Lung & Reclamation Sts; ☽ midnight-dawn), which is always a hive of activity.

To reach Temple St market, take exit C2 from the Jordan MTR station and walk along Bowring St or exit C from the Yau Ma Tei MTR station and follow Man Ming Lane.

JADE MARKET Map p97
Battery St; ☽ 10am-4pm; MTR Yau Ma Tei (exit C)
The Jade Market, near the Gascoigne Rd overpass just west of Nathan Rd and split into two parts by the loop formed by Battery St, has some 400 stalls selling all varieties and grades of jade from inside two covered markets. Unless you really know your nephrite from your jadeite, it's probably not wise to buy any expensive pieces here, but there are plenty of cheap and cheerful trinkets on offer as well.

You can reach the market easily on foot from either the Jordan (exit A) or Yau Ma Tei (exit C) MTR stations. Bus 9 from the Star Ferry bus station will drop you off at the Kowloon Central Post Office at 405 Nathan Rd, which is just around the corner from the market.

TIN HAU TEMPLE Map p97
☎ 2332 9240; cnr Public Square St & Nathan Rd; ☽ 8am-6pm; MTR Yau Ma Tei (exit C)
A couple of blocks northeast of the Jade Market, this temple is dedicated to Tin Hau, the goddess of seafarers. The temple complex also houses an altar dedicated to Shing Wong, the god of the city, and to To Tei, the earth god. You'll find a row of fortune-tellers through the last doorway on the right from the main entrance facing Public Square St; signs indicate which ones speak English. An incense spiral that lasts 10 days will set you back a mere $130.

The Yau Ma Tei Police Station (Map p97; 627 Canton Rd), a short distance to the east along Public Square St, was built in 1922 and is a listed building.

MONG KOK
Eating p194; Sleeping p263
Mong Kok (Map p98; Prosperous Point) is one of Hong Kong's most congested working-class residential areas, as well as one of its busiest shopping districts.

Mong Kok starts somewhere between Waterloo Rd and Argyle St to the south and ends

MONG KOK

0 ———————— 300 m
0 ———————— 0.2 miles

INFORMATION	
Hong Kong Trade & Industry Department	
工業貿易署	1 C2

SIGHTS	(pp98-9)
Flower Market 花墟	2 D1
Yuen Po St Bird Garden	
園圃街雀鳥花園	3 D1

SHOPPING 🛍	(p169)
KHS Bicycles 飛球單車行	4 C2
Langham Place Mall 朗豪坊	5 C3
Mong Kok Computer Centre	
旺角電腦中心	6 C3
Tung Choi St (Ladies) Market 女人街	7 C3
Wing Shing Photo Supplies	
永成攝影器材公司	8 C3
Wise Mount Sports 惠峰運動公司	9 D3

EATING 🍴	(p194)
Ming Court 明閣	(see 11)

SPORTS & ACTIVITIES	(p230)
Mong Kok Stadium 旺角大球場	10 D1

SLEEPING 🛏	(pp263-4)
Langham Place Hotel 朗豪酒店	11 C3
Newton Hotel Kowloon 九龍麗東酒店	12 C1
Royal Plaza Hotel 帝京酒店	13 D1

TRANSPORT	(pp269-86)
Buses to China 往中國大陸的士巴士	14 D3
China Travel Service 中國旅行社	15 D3
Trans-Island Chinalink	
環島旅運有限公司	16 C2

To Kowloon Tong (1km)
Boundary Street Recreation Ground
Ki Lung St
Portland St
Choi Hung St
Sai Yee St
Playing Field Rd
Flower Market Rd
Embankment Rd
Cedar St
Tai Nan St
Prince Edward Prince Edward Rd West
Queen Elizabeth School
Hotel Concourse Hong Kong
Nathan Rd
Sai Yeung Choi St
Mong Kok
Lai Chi Kok Rd
Arran St
Bute St
Lien Wan St
Canton Rd
Mong Kok
Mong Kok Rd
Shantung St
Fife St
To Kowloon City (1.5km)
Reclamation St
Fa Yuen St
Argyle St
Hak Po St
Mong Kok
Cherry St
Ferry St
Portland St
Nelson St
Nelson St
Macpherson Playground
Shantung St

See Yau Ma Tei Map p97

TRANSPORT – MONG KOK

MTR Mong Kok and Prince Edward MTR stations are on the Tsuen Wan and Kwun Tong lines.

KCR Mong Kok station is on the KCR East Rail.

at Boundary St in the north – strictly speaking, anything beyond that is the New Territories. The limit to the east is Waterloo Rd as it heads northward to Kowloon Tong and to the west the district of Tai Kok Tsui.

This is where locals come to buy everyday items, such as jeans, tennis shoes, computer accessories and kitchen supplies. Take a look at Fife St, which has an amazing collection of stalls selling old vinyl, books, ceramics, machinery and music scores. Mong Kok is also a good place to buy backpacks, hiking boots and sporting goods (p169). Two blocks southeast of the Mong Kok MTR station (exit D3) is the Tung Choi Street market (see boxed text, p156), which runs from Argyle St in the north to Dundas St in the south.

The streets west of Nathan Rd reveal Hong Kong's seamier side; this is where you'll find some of the city's seediest brothels. Mostly run by Triads, these places are often veritable prisons for young women. The Hong Kong police routinely raid these places, but a look at the rows of pastel-coloured neon strip lights on so many blocks is an indication that it's 'business as usual' despite the change in landlords.

YUEN PO ST BIRD GARDEN & FLOWER MARKET Map p98
Flower Market Rd; 7am-8pm; MTR Prince Edward (exit B1)

This market is a wonderful place to visit, if only to marvel at how the Hong Kong Chinese (especially men) fuss and fawn over their feathered friends. The Chinese have long favoured songbirds as pets; you often see local men walking around airing their birds and feeding them squirming caterpillars with chopsticks. Some birds are also considered harbingers of good fortune, which is why you'll see some people carrying them to the racetrack.

There are scores of birds for sale from the stalls here, along with elaborate cages carved from teak and bamboo. Adjacent to the bird garden is the flower market on Flower Market Rd, which keeps theoretically the same hours but only gets busy after 10am, especially on Sunday.

To get to the bird garden and flower market, from the Prince Edward MTR station, come out of exit B1 and walk east along Prince Edward Rd West for about 10 minutes.

KOWLOON'S TEEMING MARKET STREETS
Walking Tour
1 Yuen Po Street Bird Garden & Flower Market A 10-minute walk away from Prince Edward MTR (exit A), Yuen Po Street Bird Garden is the gathering place for mostly old men who air their caged birds here and feed them grasshoppers with chop sticks. A little further along, Flower Market Rd (left) is lined with fragrant and exotic blooms and plants.

2 Goldfish Market At the end of the street, turn left onto Sai Yee St, then right onto Prince Edward Rd West and left onto Tung Choi St: the first couple of blocks are dominated by bicycle shops but give way to up to a dozen shops trading in these extravagantly hued, and weirdly shaped fish. There's an amazing variety with the real rarities commanding high prices.

3 Tung Choi Street Market Sharpen your elbows. This market (see boxed text, p156), also known as the Ladies' Market, is crammed with stalls and shoppers selling mostly inexpensive clothing. Refuel on Taiwanese at Tai Pak (p194) before continuing south.

4 Temple Street Night Market Beneath the bleaching glare of naked light bulbs, hundreds of stalls (p96) sell a vast array of booty from bric-a-brac to clothes, shoes, luggage and accessories. Turn right at Shanghai St, cut down Hi Lung Lane to Temple St and turn right. The market runs right down to Jordan Rd.

5 Tin Hau Temple Fragrant smoke curls from incense spirals at this atmospheric temple

WALK FACTS
Start Prince Edward MTR station (entrance/exit A)
End Jordan MTR station (entrance/exit A)
Distance 4.5km
Time Two hours
Fuel stop Tai Pak

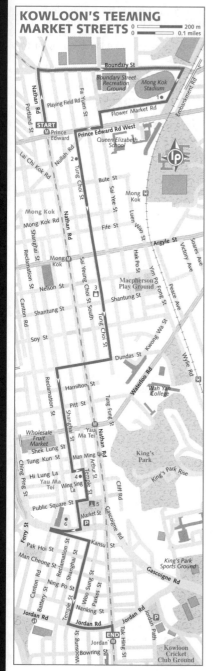

KOWLOON'S TEEMING MARKET STREETS

(p98) to the goddess of the sea. Fortune-tellers nearby use everything from tarot cards, palmistry and even tame sparrows to deliver their predictions. Chinese opera singers sometimes also practise in the area.

6 Jade Market A great place to pick up an inexpensive trinket, this large covered market (p98) contains dozens of stalls selling jade, the much-valued Chinese precious stone. At Jordan Rd turn east, then south into Nathan Rd to find Jordan MTR station.

NEW KOWLOON

Eating p194; Shopping p170

New Kowloon (Map pp88–9) encompasses as many as 20 different neighbourhoods, but only half a dozen are of much interest to travellers. From west to east they are Sham Shui Po, Kowloon Tong, Kowloon City, Wong Tai Sin and Diamond Hill. The majority (and the places of interest described in this section) are within easy reach of an MTR station.

Sham Shui Po

A residential area of high-rises, Sham Shui Po (Map pp88–9) is famous for its market and computer emporiums (p170). North of (and easily accessible from) the district is Lei Cheng Uk Han Tomb, an important archaeological find.

APLIU STREET MARKET Map pp88–9

Apliu St, btwn Nam Cheong & Kweilin Sts; ☉ noon-midnight; MTR Sham Shui Po

From the Sham Shui Po MTR station follow exit A1 and you'll soon fall right into this flea market, which makes a cheaper and more interesting hunting ground than the Temple Street Night Market. Everything from clothing to antique clocks and coins is on sale here, although the real speciality is second-hand electronic goods – radios, mobile phones, stereo systems, amplifiers and spare parts. The market spills over into Pei Ho St.

LEI CHENG UK HAN TOMB MUSEUM

Map pp88–9

☎ 2386 2863; www.lcsd.gov.hk/CE/Museum/History /en/lcuht.php; 41 Tonkin St; admission free; ☉ 10am-6pm Mon-Wed & Fri-Sat, 1-6pm Sun & public holidays; MTR Cheung Sha Wan (exit A3), ☒ 2 from the Star Ferry or 2A from Nathan Rd in Mong Kok, alight in front of the museum

This burial vault dating from the Eastern Han dynasty (AD 25–220) was discovered in 1955 when workers were levelling the hillside for a housing estate. It is one of Hong Kong's earliest surviving historical monuments and, believe it or not, was once on the coast.

The tomb consists of four barrel-vaulted brick chambers that take the form of a cross; they are set around a domed central chamber and many of the bricks contained moulded patterns of fish, dragons and the like. It's encased in a concrete shell for protection and visitors can only peek through a plastic window; it's a bit of a journey for an anticlimactic peek through perspex. The museum also contains a few pottery and bronze pieces taken from the tomb.

From Cheung Sha Wan MTR take exit A3 and walk northeast for 10 minutes along Tonkin St.

Kowloon Tong

As well as containing two of Hong Kong's most prestigious seats of learning – the Hong Kong Baptist University (☎ 3411 7400), Hong Kong's most generously endowed seat of higher learning, and City University of Hong Kong (☎ 2788 7654) – Kowloon Tong (Map pp88–9) also has bridal shops with names like Cité du Louvre, where brides-to-be can buy their finery, have their photos done and even attend the ceremony itself. It is also a neighbourhood of knock-up shops – 'no-tells', as one wag called them, with revolving beds, velvet-flock wallpaper and heart-shaped jacuzzis. They're very popular for 'matinées' and rented by the hour.

FESTIVAL WALK SHOPPING CENTRE
Map pp88–9

☎ 2844 2222; 80-88 Tat Chee Ave; ⏱ 10.30am-10pm; MTR Kowloon Tong

Kowloon Tong can claim Festival Walk, the territory's most luxurious shopping complex, and, in typical Hong Kong fashion, the centre boasts a fair few superlatives itself. Festival Walk has the largest cinema, bookshop and ice-skating rink (p229) in the territory. From the Kowloon Tong MTR station, take exit C2.

Kowloon City

Just west of what was once Kai Tak International Airport, the rather low-rent neighbourhood of Kowloon City (Map pp88–9) has two draw cards: a wonderful park that was once the infamous Kowloon Walled City, and a string of authentic and excellent-value Thai restaurants. The airport sits on a prime chunk of land, slowly being redeveloped.

KOWLOON WALLED CITY PARK
Map pp88–9

☎ 2716 9962, 2762 2084; www.lcsd.gov.hk/en /ls_park.php; Tung Tau Tsuen, Tung Tsing, Carpenter & Junction Rds; ⏱ 6.30am-11pm; 🚌 1 from Star Ferry pier, alight opposite the park at Tung Tau Tsuen Rd

The walls that enclose this beautiful park were once the perimeter of a notorious village that technically remained part of China throughout British rule, as it was never included in the 1898 lease of the New Territories. The enclave was known for its vice, prostitution, gambling and illegal dentists. In 1984 the Hong Kong government acquired the area, rehoused the residents elsewhere and built pavilions and ponds filled with turtles and goldfish and planted exquisite trees and shrubs, including a long hedge coaxed into the form of a dragon. The park opened in 1996. Close to the Carpenter Rd entrance of the park is the renovated Yamen building, once an almshouse. It contains displays on the history of the walled city, with a scale model of the village in the mid-19th century. At the park's north side are the remnants of the original South and East Gates.

TRANSPORT – NEW KOWLOON

MTR The two MTR lines running up the spine of Kowloon are useful for getting around New Kowloon. Key stops on the Tsuen Wan line include Sham Shui Po and Cheung Sha Wan MTR stations; key stops on the Kwun Tong line include Kowloon Tong, Lok Fu, Wong Tai Sin and Diamond Hill MTR stations.

KCR The most important stop on the KCR East Rail line is Kowloon Tong station, which has an interchange with Kowloon Tong MTR station.

Bus Buses 5 and 26 leave from Tsim Sha Tsui to Ma Tau Chung Rd for Kowloon.

Wong Tai Sin

The district of Wong Tai Sin to the north of Kowloon City is known for two things: its enormous and faceless housing estate and one of the most active and interesting temples in the territory.

SIK SIK YUEN WONG TAI SIN TEMPLE
Off Map pp88–9
☎ 2854 4333; Lung Cheung Rd; $2 donation requested; ⏱ 7am-6pm; MTR Wong Tai Sin

An explosion of colourful pillars, roofs, lattice work, flowers and incense, this busy temple is a destination for all walks of Hong Kong society, from pensioners to business-people, parents and young professionals.

Some come simply to pray, others to divine the future with *chim,* bamboo 'for-tune sticks' that are shaken out of a box on to the ground and then read by a fortune-teller (they're available for free to the left of the main temple).

The complex, adjacent to the Wong Tai Sin housing estate, was built in 1973 and is dedicated to the god of that name, who began his life as a humble shepherd in Zhejiang province. When he was 15 an immortal taught Wong Tai Sin how to make a herbal potion that could cure all illnesses. He is thus worshipped both by the sick and those trying to avoid illness. He is also a favourite god of businesspeople. The image of the god in the main temple was brought to Hong Kong from Guangdong province in 1915 and was initially installed in a temple in Wan Chai, where it remained until being moved to the present site in 1921.

Behind the main temple and to the right are the Good Wish Gardens ($2 donation requested; ⏱ 9am-4pm), replete with colourful pavilions (the hexagonal Unicorn Hall, with carved doors and windows, is the most beautiful), zigzag bridges, waterfalls and carp ponds.

Below the main temple and to the left as you enter the complex is an arcade filled with dozens of booths operated by for-tune-tellers, some of whom speak English. Expect a consultation to cost upwards of $100.

The busiest times at the temple are around Chinese New Year, Wong Tai Sin's birthday (23rd day of the eighth month – usually in September) and on weekends. Getting to the temple is easy. From the Wong Tai Sin MTR station, take exit B2 and then follow the signs or the crowds (or both).

Diamond Hill

Spread out below the peak of the same name, the residential district of Diamond Hill is due east of Wong Tai Sin and is worth visiting solely for the nearby nunnery.

CHI LIN NUNNERY Off Map pp88–9
☎ 2354 1604; 5 Chi Lin Dr; admission free; ⏱ nunnery 9am-5pm, garden 6.30am-7pm; MTR Diamond Hill

One of the most beautiful and arrestingly built environments in Hong Kong, this large Buddhist complex, originally dating from the 1930s, was rebuilt completely of wood in the style of the Tang dynasty in 1998. It is a serene place, with lotus ponds, immaculate bonsai tea plants and bougain-villea, and silent nuns delivering offerings of fruit and rice to Buddha and arhats (Buddhist disciple freed from the cycle of birth and death), or chanting behind intri-cately carved screens. The design (involving intricately interlocking sections of wood joined without a single nail) is intended to demonstrate the harmony of humans with nature and is pretty convincing – until you look up at the looming neighbourhood high-rises behind the complex.

You enter the complex through the Sam Mun, a series of 'three gates' representing the Buddhist precepts of compassion, wis-dom and 'skilful means'. The first courtyard, which contains the delightful Lotus Pond Garden, gives way to the Hall of Celestial Kings, with a large statue of the seated Buddha surrounded by the deities of the four cardinal points. Behind that is the main hall, containing a statue of the Sakyamuni Buddha flanked by two standing disciples and two seated Bodhisattvas (Buddhist holy people). Below the complex is a café selling vegetarian snacks and dim sum for $12 to $25.

To reach the nunnery, take exit C2 of Diamond Hill MTR station, walk through the Hollywood Plaza shopping centre and turn east (left) on to Fung Tak Rd. The nunnery is a five-minute walk away.

Lei Yue Mun

Southeast of the old Kai Tak airport is the res-idential neighbourhood of Kwun Tong (Map pp50–1), and a bit further southeast is the rapidly modernising fishing village of Lei Yue Mun (Map pp50–1). *Láy-yèw* means 'carp' and *mùn* is 'gate';

the 'carp gate' refers to the channel separating southeast Kowloon from Hong Kong Island, which is the narrowest entrance to Victoria Harbour. Across the water on the island and looming on the hillside is 19th-century Lei Yue Mun Fort (Map pp54–5), which now contains the Hong Kong Museum of Coastal Defence (p80).

SAM KA TSUEN SEAFOOD PRECINCT
MTR Yau Tong (Exit A2)
The 'village' of Lei Yue Mun is one of Hong Kong's prime seafood venues; around two-dozen fish restaurants line narrow, winding Lei Yue Mun Praya Rd overlooking the typhoon shelter. The area is a colourful and lively place to dine by the water at night and is always busy. To get here from the Yau Tong MTR station, use exit A2 and follow Cha Kwo Ling Rd and Shung Shun St south for 15 minutes or catch green minibus 24M from outside the station. Bus 14C links the Yau Tong Centre halfway down the hill with the Kwun Tong MTR station.

NEW TERRITORIES

Many Hong Kong residents make the New Territories (Map pp50–1) their getaway for the weekend, and the eastern section, notably Sai Kung Peninsula in the northeast and the area around Clearwater Bay further south, has some of Hong Kong's most beautiful scenery and hiking trails. Life in these more rural parts of Hong Kong is more redolent of times past – simpler, slower, often more friendly.

The New Territories was so named because the area was leased to Britain in 1898, almost half a century after Hong Kong Island and four decades after Kowloon were ceded to the crown. For many years the area was Hong Kong's rural hinterland; however, since WWII, when some 80% of the land was under cultivation, many parts of the 'NT' – as the area is known locally – have become urbanised. In the past two decades the speed at which this development has taken place has been nothing short of heart stopping.

The New Territories is large, comprising 747 sq km, or almost 68% of Hong Kong's land area. Strictly speaking, everything north of Boundary St in Kowloon, up to the border with mainland China, is the New Territories. The northernmost part of the New Territories, within 1km of the Chinese frontier, is a 'closed border area' that is fenced and well marked with signs. It marks the boundary of the Hong Kong SAR with the Shenzhen Special Economic Zone (SEZ).

Almost four million people, up from less than half a million in 1970, call the New Territories home – about half the total population of Hong Kong. Most of them live in 'New Towns'. Since its inception in the 1950s, the New Towns programme has consumed more than half of the Hong Kong government's budget, with much of the funding spent on land reclamation, sewage, roads and other infrastructure projects.

Getting to and around the New Territories has never been easier, particularly to the New Towns and areas of interest listed here. The KCR West Rail, which opened in late 2003, is now transporting passengers from Kowloon to the western New Territories as far as Tuen Mun. The MTR goes to Tsuen Wan (on the Tsuen Wan line) in the west and Po Lam in the east, from where you can catch buses and minibuses to explore other parts of the New Territories. Travel to the northern New Territories is simple, fast and cheap with the KCR East Rail, which connects Tsim Sha Tsui, Hung Hom and Kowloon Tong with Sha Tin, Tai Po, Sheung Shui and the Chinese border at Lo Wu. There are also a number of buses linking Hong Kong Island and Kowloon with the New Territories.

Once in the New Territories, buses – run for the most part by the Kowloon Motor Bus Co (KMB; ☎ 2745 4466; www.kmb.com.hk) – and green minibuses – which run on just under 200 routes – are the main ways to get around. For detailed bus route information check the KMB's website.

Catching a taxi is easy – at least to and from the New Towns; there are more than 2840 taxis cruising the streets and country roads of the New Territories. Ferries and *kaidos* (small, open-sea ferries) serve the more remote areas and a few large communities on the coast.

In the far west of the New Territories, the way to go is the KCR's Light Rail, a modern, street-level tram system that connects Tuen Mun with Yuen Long and stops at several interesting places along the way.

TSUEN WAN

Eating p195

Among the easiest destinations in the New Territories to reach, Tsuen Wan (Map p105), or 'Shallow Bay', is an industrial and residential New Town northwest of Kowloon, with some 290,000 inhabitants. It's nothing special, but it does have a fine (though small) museum and some of the most colourful and active temple and monastic complexes in Hong Kong, including the serene Western Monastery (p106) and the vivid Yuen Yuen Institute (opposite), stuffed with all manner of deities.

top picks

NEW TERRITORIES

- Sai Kung's beaches (p126)
- Hong Kong Wetland Park (p107)
- MacLehose Trail (p226)
- Tsuen Wan's monasteries and museums (left)
- Hong Kong Heritage Museum (p125)
- 10,000 Buddhas Monastery (p124)

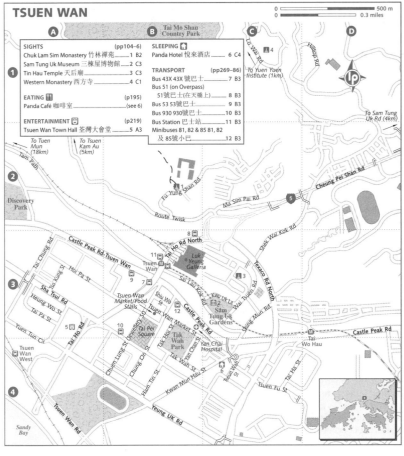

TSUEN WAN

SIGHTS	(pp104–6)
Chuk Lam Sim Monastery 竹林禪苑	1 B2
Sam Tung Uk Museum 三棟屋博物館	2 C3
Tin Hau Temple 天后廟	3 C3
Western Monastery 西方寺	4 C1

EATING	(p195)
Panda Café 咖啡室	(see 6)

ENTERTAINMENT	(p219)
Tsuen Wan Town Hall 荃灣大會堂	5 A3

SLEEPING	
Panda Hotel 悅來酒店	6 C4

TRANSPORT	(pp269–86)
Bus 43X 43X 號巴士	7 B3
Bus 51 (on Overpass)	
51 號巴士(在天橋上)	8 B3
Bus 53 53 號巴士	9 B3
Bus 930 930 號巴士	10 B3
Bus Station 巴士站	11 B3
Minibuses 81, 82 & 85 81, 82	
及 85 號小巴	12 B3

Chung On St, south of the Tsuen Wan MTR station, is famed for its jewellery and goldsmith shops. Tak Wah Park (6.30am-11pm) in the centre of town has ancient trees, footbridges over ponds and ornamental stone mountains. It's a peaceful place and an ideal spot to take a break from the hustle and bustle of the town around it.

The MTR station is on Sau Lau Kok Rd, with the Luk Yeung Galleria shopping centre above it. The main bus station is opposite the MTR on Castle Peak Rd (exit A2), but buses and green minibuses pick up and disgorge passengers throughout the New Town. Tsuen Wan is the last station on the Tsuen Wan MTR line. If you're really in a hurry to get there or back, change to the Tung Chung MTR line at Lai King, which has fewer stops.

YUEN YUEN INSTITUTE Off Map p105
☎ 2492 2220; Lo Wai Rd; 8.30am-5pm;
🚐 green minibus 81

Stuffed with vivid statuary of Confucian and Buddhist deities, the Yuen Yuen Institute, in the hills northeast of Tsuen Wan, is very much on the tourist trail but well worth a

TRANSPORT – TSUEN WAN

MTR Tsuen Wan MTR station on Tsuen Wan line.

KCR Tsuen Wan West station.

Bus Many buses (but not all) from around the new territories arrive at Tsuen Wan's central bus station, including bus 60M from Tuen Mun and 68M from Yuen Long. Bus 51 from Tai Mo Shan and Kam Tin stops along Tai Ho Rd.

visit nonetheless. The main building is a (vague) replica of the Temple of Heaven in Beijing. On the upper ground floor are three Taoist immortals seated in a quiet hall; walk down to the lower level to watch as crowds of the faithful pray and burn offerings to the 60 incarnations of Taoist saints lining the walls. This place is packed out at Chinese New Year. There are also deities representing particular years and birth signs, to which worshippers pray and make offerings.

To reach both the Institute and the Western Monastery, take minibus 81 from Shiu Wo St, two blocks due south of Tsuen Wan MTR station (exit B1). Bus 43X from along Tai Ho Rd, further south of the MTR station (exit D), will drop you off on Sam Tung Uk Rd. The monastery is several hundred metres away and the institute is just up the hill. A taxi from the MTR station will cost $30 to $35.

WESTERN MONASTERY Map p105
☎ 2411 5111; Lo Wai Rd; 8.30am-5.30pm; green minibus 81

A short distance down from the Yuen Yuen Institute, the Buddhist Western Monastery offers a sharp contrast to what's going on up the hill. This is a tranquil complex in which to pass the time, observing points of interest both architectural and spiritual. After being greeted by a Bodhisattva statue in the entrance, the main building lies behind, styled as a classical Chinese palace. This comprises of the Hall of Maitreya and the Great Buddha's Hall above it. Further behind is a another two-storey building where, depending on what time of day you visit, you may witness scores of monks chanting mantras. This building is topped by a spectacular nine-storey pagoda.

CHUK LAM SIM MONASTERY Map p105
☎ 2490 3392; Fu Yung Shan Rd; 9am-4.30pm; green minibus 85

Chuk Lam Sim Yuen (Bamboo Forest Monastery) is one of the most impressive temple complexes in Hong Kong. The temple was completed in 1932 when an aged monk was told by Tou Tei, the earth god, to build it. Ascend the flight of steps to the first temple, walk to the back and enter the second. This second temple contains three of the largest golden Buddhas in the territory (though mere shadows of the big one on Lantau Island, p135). Flanking the trio on

either side is an equally impressive line-up of 12 Bodhisattvas, or Buddhists seeking enlightenment. The third temple contains another large image of Lord Gautama.

Chuk Lam Sim Monastery is northeast of Tsuen Wan MTR station. To reach it, take green minibus 85 from Shiu Wo St, which is two blocks due south of the MTR station (exit B1).

SAM TUNG UK MUSEUM Map p105
☎ 2411 2001; 2 Kwu Uk Lane; admission free; 9am-5pm Wed-Mon; MTR Tsuen Wan

This imaginative and well-tended museum is housed in a restored late-18th-century Hakka walled village, whose former residents, the Chan clan, were only resettled in 1980. Within the complex are a dozen three-beamed houses containing traditional Hakka furnishings, kitchenware, wedding items and agricultural implements, most of which came from two 17th-century Hakka villages in Bao'an county in Guangdong province. There are also special exhibits on such topics as rice farming in the New Territories. Behind the restored assembly and ancestral halls is the old village school, with interactive displays and videos on such topics as Hakka women, traditional crafts and traditional food.

At the Tsuen Wan MTR station, take exit E and walk five minutes southeast along Sai Lau Kok Rd to Kwu Uk Lane and the museum.

TAI MO SHAN
Sleeping p264

Hong Kong's tallest mountain is not Victoria Peak but Tai Mo Shan (Map pp50–1), the 'big misty mountain' that, at 957m, is nearly twice as high as that relative molehill (552m) on Hong Kong Island. Several hiking trails thread up and around it, but you'll need to bring your own food and water. The Countryside Series *North-East & Central New Territories* map is the one you want for this area (p295). If you don't want to go it alone, contact any of the

---

TRANSPORT – TAI MO SHAN

Bus Bus 64K links Tai Mo Shan with Yuen Long and Tai Po Market.

Green Minibus Bus 25K also runs between Tai Po Market and Tai Mo Shan.

---

outfits listed on p225. The Tai Mo Shan Country Park Visitor Centre (☎ 2498 9326; ⏰ 9.30am-4.30pm Sat, Sun & holidays) is at the junction of Route Twisk (the name is derived from 'Tsuen Wan into Shek Kong') and Tai Mo Shan Rd, which is crossed by the MacLehose Trail.

To reach Tai Mo Shan from the Tsuen Wan MTR station, catch bus 51 on Tai Ho Rd North, alighting at the junction of Route Twisk and Tai Mo Shan Rd in Tsuen Kam Au. Follow Tai Mo Rd, which forms part of stage No 9 of the MacLehose Trail, east to the summit. On the right-hand side, about 45 minutes from the bus stop, a fork in the road leads south along a concrete path to the Sze Lok Yuen Hostel (p264).

For information on accessing stages of the MacLehose Trail and the Wilson Trail near Tai Mo Shan, see p226.

NG TUNG CHAI WATERFALL & KADOORIE FARM & BOTANIC GARDEN Map pp50–1

☎ 2483 7200; www.kfbg.org.hk; Lam Kam Rd; admission free; ⏰ 9.30am-5pm; 🚌 64K
The area around the Ng Tung Chai Waterfall is scenic and worth a detour. It is near the village of Ng Tung Chai, which is several kilometres north of Tai Mo Shan and just south of Lam Kam Rd. There is actually a series of falls and streams here reached by taking the path leading to Ng Tung Chai and the Lam Kam Rd from the radio station on the summit of Tai Mo Shan.

Southwest of Ng Tung Chai is the Kadoorie Farm & Botanic Garden, a conservation and teaching centre where farmers receive practical training in crop and livestock management. The gardens are especially lovely, with many indigenous birds, animals, insects and plants in residence.

You can reach Kadoorie Farm most easily on bus 64K, which runs between Yuen Long KCR West Rail station and Tai Po Market KCR East station; get off on Lam Kam Rd near the sign for Ng Tung Chai village. If you walk from Tai Mo Shan to the village of Ng Tung Chai, you can catch green minibus 25K to Tai Po Market KCR East Rail station as well.

TUEN MUN

Eating p195
The largest and most important New Town in the western New Territories, Tuen Mun (Map pp50–1; population 550,000) is linked

TRANSPORT – TUEN MUN

KCR Tuen Mun West Rail station.

Light Rail Tuen Mun is towards the southern end of the useful light rail network. Other major points include Tin Shui Wai, Yuen Long and Siu Hong. The station is linked to the KCR station.

Bus An alternative route along the coast to Tuen Mun is to take bus 60M from Tsuen Wan MTR station (exit A3).

Ferry Services to Tuen Mun ferry pier arrive from Tung Chung, Sha Lo Wan and Tai O (all on Lantau).

with other centres in Kowloon and the New Territories by the KCR West Rail. If you're travelling to Tuen Mun from Tsuen Wan or points in Kowloon or Hong Kong Island by bus, sit on the upper deck on the left side for spectacular views of the Tsing Ma Bridge, which links Kowloon with Lantau Island. In recent years a number of important archaeological discoveries have been made here, notably to the north and west of Tuen Mun town (see p19).

As always in New Towns, the centre of Tuen Mun is dominated by commercial developments and shopping centres. Most buses stop at the station just west of the town hall, where you'll also find the Town Centre station of the Light Rail. The KCR's West Rail interchanges at the Tuen Mun Light Rail station. Ferries to the airport, Tung Chung and Tai O on Lantau depart from the pier to the southwest of the town centre, which is also served by the Light Rail (p282).

HONG KONG WETLAND PARK

Map pp50–1
☎ 3152 2666; www.wetlandpark.com; Wetland Park Rd, Tin Shui Wai; adult/child $30/15; ⏰ 10am-5pm Wed-Tue; 🚃 line 705 or 706
The space and serenity of this 60-hectare ecological park make it a wonderful place to while away half a day. Its nature trails, bird hides and viewing platforms are windows on the wetland ecosystems and biodiversity of the northwest New Territories. The futuristic grass-covered headquarters houses interesting galleries, including one on tropical swamps, a film theatre, a large café and a viewing gallery. It's oddly pleasing to watch in silence as a kingfisher dives and then turns 180 degrees to be faced with a bank of high-rise apartment blocks. If you

have binoculars then bring them, otherwise be prepared to wait to use the fixed points in the viewing galleries and hides.

To reach the Hong Kong Wetland Park, take the KCR West Rail to Tin Shui Wai and board Light Rail line 705 or 706, alighting at the Wetland Park stop. It can also be reached directly from Hong Kong Island, from the Admiralty MTR bus station on bus 967.

MIU FAT MONASTERY Map pp50–1

☎ 2461 8567; 18 Castle Peak Rd; ⊗ 9am-5pm; 🚃 line 751

Miu Fat Monastery in Lam Tei, due north of Tuen Mun town centre, is one of the most well-kept and attractive Buddhist complexes in the territory. Guarding the entrance to the main temple are two stone lions and two stone elephants, and there are attractive gardens outside. This is an active monastery that preserves more of a traditional character than many smaller temples; you'll see Buddhist nuns in droves wearing brown robes.

On the ground floor there's a golden like-ness of Buddha in a glass case; on the 2nd floor are three larger statues of Lord Gau-tama. The 1st floor is a vegetarian restaurant serving set meals and open to all (p196).

At the time of writing a new main com-plex is nearing completion. The soaring structure is 42m high with the top storey resembling a huge crystal lotus blossom that will light up at night.

Miu Fat Monastery is reached by Light Rail line 751 from the Tuen Mun or Town Centre stops to Lam Tei station. The complex is on the opposite side of Castle Peak Rd; cross over the walkway and walk north 150m. Bus 63X, from the Mong Kok MTR station and the Star Ferry terminal in Tsim Sha Tsui, also stops in front of the monastery.

CHING CHUNG TEMPLE Map pp50–1

☎ 2462 1507; Tsing Chung Koon Rd; ⊗ 7am-6pm; 🚃 line 505

Ching Chung Koon (Green Pine Temple) is a peaceful Taoist temple complex northwest of Tuen Mun town centre. The main temple, which is on the left at the far end of the complex past rows of bonsai trees, bamboo and ponds, is dedicated to Lu Sun Young, one of the eight immortals of Taoism who lived in the 8th century. Flanking a statue of him are two of his disciples. Outside the entrance to the main temple are pavilions

containing a bell and a drum to call the faithful to pray or to rest. An annual Bonsai Festival is held here April.

Ching Chung Temple is directly opposite the Light Rail station of that name. To reach it from the Tuen Mun or Town Centre sta-tions, catch line 505.

YUEN LONG

Eating p196

There's nothing special at Yuen Long (Map pp50–1; Yuen Long KCR West Rail), which currently counts some almost 500,000 inhab-itants, but it's an important transport hub and a gateway to the Mai Po Marsh (see the following section). To the west of Yuen Long is the Ping Shan Heritage Trail, one of the best spots to spend a tranquil hour or two in the western New Territories.

MAI PO MARSH

This fragile ecosystem (Map pp50–1) abutting Deep Bay, south of the border with the main-land, simply teems with life. It is a protected network of mud flats, *gày-wài* (shallow shrimp ponds), reed beds and dwarf mangroves, of-fering a rich habitat of up to 340 species of migratory and resident birds, more than a third of them rarely seen elsewhere in the ter-ritory. The area attracts birds in every season but especially winter, when an average 54,000 migratory waterfowl, including such endan-gered species as the Dalmatian pelican, black-faced spoonbill, spotted and imperial eagle and black vulture, pass through the marshes. In the centre is the Mai Po Nature Reserve, jointly managed by the World Wide Fund for Nature Hong Kong and the government's Agriculture, Fisheries & Conservation Department.

Despite its protected status, the marsh's future is precarious. The water quality in Deep Bay is among the worst in the Hong Kong coastal area. The Environmental Protection Department (EPD) has found that levels of dissolved oxygen (DO) in the water have been declining since 1988. As a result, the numbers of crabs and mudskippers, on which the birds feed in winter, have declined. If the lower links of the food chain are seriously imperilled, the birds that depend on Mai Po as a stopping ground during migration could disappear, taking with them endangered mammals such as the leopard cat and otter.

(Continued on page 117)

MEET THE LOCALS

Talk to seasoned travellers from Mumbai or Delhi and they may tell you what dull back-waters London or New York are compared with their home cities. You get the same feeling about Hong Kong citizens, who were weaned on the city's buzz and bustle. They're proud of its go-ahead spirit, philosophical about the shocking air quality and quite restless in the absence of ceaseless activity.

Perhaps the strongest feeling you get talking to Hong Kong people is their love of the energy and contrast offered by the city's kaleidoscopic neighbourhoods. Where else can you barter amid the intimate colour and gore of traditional wet markets while cricking your neck beneath looming corporate monoliths?

Not every contrast is a happy one, though. The vast gulf that divides Hong Kong's mega-rich and those merely getting by is written in the skyline. A very few private houses and executive residential blocks look down on countless ranks of nondescript public housing sprouting from the narrow streets below.

High-rise living (and long working hours) may be the lot of the majority but it's not the whole story. To set sail on the harbour for one of the outlying islands or board a double-decker across to Hong Kong Island's southern shores is to realise just how much space and peace everyone can enjoy in this tiny territory of seven million souls.

Just don't expect solitude in any neighbourhood on weekends, when absolutely every-one heads outdoors. And just think: if plans to merge Hong Kong and its neighbour Shen-zhen into a single megacity bear fruit, you 'aint seen nothing yet.

Tea ceremony at Ngong Ping Village (p137), Lantau

Top-quality produce at the Graham St Market (p180), Central

	Name	Calvin Yeung
	Age	40-something
	Occupation	Designer & Executive Chef of the Aqua Restaurant Group
	Residence	Hong Kong Island

The Landmark shopping mall (p162) in Central is home to fine dining and high fashion (top); Drying fish in the traditional village of Tai O (p138), Lantau (middle); Food stalls in Tsim Sha Tsui (p166), Kowloon (bottom)

What's special about the food in Hong Kong? I like the combination of how seafood is treated and the way traditional Chinese food is celebrated. The approach to seafood is about 'less is more', which keeps it fresh and real tasting… whether that's prawns dried without seasoning in the sun, or fresh fish simply prepared.

What do you do when you're off duty? I enjoy simple home cooking with fresh ingredients. There's lots of good material to work with in Hong Kong's wet markets.

What do you tell visitors to do and see when they come to Hong Kong? Head up the Mid-Levels escalator, explore Lan Kwai Fong, Soho and Sheung Wan. You experience so many different layers of Hong Kong culture old and new: tourist spots, trendy places, tucked-away art galleries, traditional retail stores, such as Chinese medicine tea houses, and ancient architecture.

What's your favourite Hong Kong day out? Eating well on our junk *Aqua Luna*, on the harbour during the best time of year, autumn.

Any grumbles about your home town? Land reclamation! Victoria harbour is a stunning place to be, but I really worry how it will be affected by all this commercial activity.

For you, Hong Kong in a word? Speedy.

Name	Dr Allan Zemun
Age	57
Occupation	Entrepreneur & Property Developer
Residence	Southern Hong Kong Island

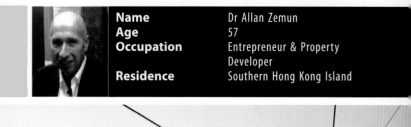

The scenic cable car in Ocean Park (p82), Aberdeen (top); The beach at Repulse Bay (p86) attracts lots of visitors (middle); Causeway Bay (p73) is one of Hong Kong's top shopping and nightlife areas (bottom)

What makes Hong Kong so special? It's the fact that you can have an idea in the morning and make it happen the same day. It is a fantastic city to do business in, probably the best in the world. The possibilities are amazing.

Ten years on from the handover has Hong Kong changed? Hong Kong is better than ever, thanks to China. Everyone was questioning what was going to happen after the handover, but it has clearly benefited Hong Kong. We're now much better integrated with the Mainland economy – the world's 4th biggest.

What's your favourite Hong Kong day out? Taking my boat out to the beaches in Sai Kung (p126), then dinner in Lan Kwai Fong, and spending time with friends in the buzzing bars and clubs.

What are your favourite Hong Kong things? The cable-car ride at Ocean Park (p82), the stunning skyline, and the huge diversity of shopping and eating.

Hong Kong in a word? Vibrant.

The high-rise Central Plaza and the Hong Kong Convention & Exhibition Centre (p64), Wan Chai

Staunton's Wine Bar & Cafe (p208), Soho

Name	Colette Koo
Age	47, going on 27
Occupation	Bar & Club Owner
Residence	Jardine's Lookout

Lan Kwai Fong (p204) is a popular place to go for a drink (top); Peak Cafe Bar (p208), Soho (middle); FINDS Bar & Restaurant (p206), Central (bottom)

What can you expect from a night out in Hong Kong these days? The variety is amazing and the atmosphere is friendly with no hassle.

What's hot? Small and more private bars and clubs are popping up everywhere. Hong Kong's club and bar scene is all about intimate places and spaces.

How should you approach a night out in Hong Kong to get the best from it? Look at it as a moving feast, go with the flow. Expect to go to different places along the way, expect to meet lots of new people and expect to drink!

If you had to choose: nightclub or karaoke? Nightclub… have you heard me sing!?

Ten years on from the handover have you noticed any changes? The party scene has become much more vibrant.

What's your favourite Hong Kong day out? Wake-boarding in the morning, a seafood lunch, chill in the afternoon, have dinner with a few friends and drinks on the terrace at FINDS (p177). If the mood takes us, then Drop (p214) till 5am!

What are your favourite Hong Kong things? The sea, the closeness of everything (including neighbouring countries), the few remaining open markets, the efficiency and convenience. It's safe and the people are kind.

Name	The Hon Leung Kwok Hung (aka Long Hair)
Age	51
Occupation	Legislative Council Member & Political Activist
Residence	Kowloon Bay

Stalls at the Graham St Market (p180), Central (top); Shop with the locals on Nathan Rd, Mong Kok (middle; p169); Find a bargain at the Temple Street Night Market (p96), Yau Ma Tei (bottom)

You spent years demonstrating outside the Legislative Council (and sometimes getting chucked out of it). What are you trying to achieve now that you are an elected member of it? I want to show what a sham the current political system is. Collusion between business and government is as bad as ever and the election of the chief executive by 800 people in a territory of nearly seven million is a joke.

Ten years on from the handover have you noticed any changes? Politically it has got more repressive. I hope that eventually we will see full democracy in Hong Kong but in the short term I'm not optimistic.

If you had to choose: nightclub or karaoke? Definitely karaoke. There are good places all over Hong Kong, although it's becoming an expensive night out for local kids.

What are your favourite Hong Kong things? I'm so busy I don't get much free time to enjoy them. A night of karaoke maybe or a drink in Club 71 (p208), although it hasn't been the same since it moved location and changed its name from Club 64.

(Continued from page 108)

The culprit is the neighbouring city of Shenzhen in mainland China, which is pumping out a rapidly increasing amount of sewage, about half of which is untreated. The only long-term solution to this environmental threat is for Shenzhen to build more sewage-treatment facilities but, as the population of the city expands faster than its infrastructure, this will take time. Meanwhile, the only hope in the short term is that Hong Kong's increasingly wet summers will flush out and dilute many of the pollutants, helping to raise the number of crabs and mudskippers.

Mai Po Marsh comprises some 1500 hectares of wetlands. The part open to visitors, the Mai Po Nature Reserve, is in the centre. For more detailed information about this and other areas, contact the Hong Kong Bird Watching Society (p223).

MAI PO NATURE RESERVE Map pp50–1
☎ 2526 4473; San Tin, Yuen Long; admission $100 (plus $200 deposit); ⊕ 9am-6pm; 🚌 76K from Fanling & Sheung Shui KCR East Rail stations or Yuen Long (On Tat Square station)

The 270-hectare nature reserve includes the Mai Po Visitor Centre (☎ 2471 8272) at the northeastern end, where you must register; the Mai Po Education Centre (☎ 2471 6306) to the south, with displays on the history and ecology of the wetland and Deep Bay; floating boardwalks and trails through the mangroves and mud flats; and a dozen hides (towers or huts from where you can watch birds up close without being observed). Disconcertingly, the cityscape of Shenzhen looms to the north.

Visitors are advised to bring binoculars (they may be available for rent at the visitor centre for $20) and cameras, and to wear comfortable walking shoes or boots but not bright clothing. It is best to visit at high tide (minimum 2m), when birds in their tens of thousands – mostly ducks, gulls, cormorants and kingfishers, but many rare species as well – flock to the area. Ring the weather hotline (☎ 187 8200) or the Hong Kong Observatory (☎ 2926 8200; www.hko.gov.hk/tide/etide _main.htm) for tidal times.

Foreign visitors (but not Hong Kong residents) can visit the nature reserve unaccompanied but numbers are limited, so call well in advance to book a time.

Pay the $100 entrance fee and $200 deposit at the visitor centre; the latter will be returned when you leave the reserve. For Hong Kong residents regular tours are run on weekends and public holidays as well as seasonal ones. Again, these should be booked well in advance. If calling on a weekend or holiday, call the Visitor Centre number above.

The World Wide Fund for Nature Hong Kong (WWFHK; Map p56; ☎ 2526 4473; www.wwf.org.hk; 1 Tramway Path), adjacent to the entrance of the Peak Tram in Central, can arrange guided visits to the marsh; ring between 9am and 5pm on weekdays to book. Three-hour tours ($70) leave the visitor centre at 9am, 9.30am, 10am, 2pm, 2.30pm and 3pm on Saturday, Sunday and public holidays, but are only conducted in English when there are a minimum of 10 visitors.

Bus 76K, which runs between Yuen Long and the Fanling and Sheung Shui KCR East Rail stations, will drop you off at Mai Po Lo Wai, a village along the main road just east of the marsh. The WWFHK car park is about a 20-minute walk from there. Red minibus 17 from San Fat St in Sheung Shui also goes to Mai Po Lo Wai. Alternatively, a taxi from Sheung Shui will cost $60.

KAM TIN
The area around Kam Tin (Fertile Field; Map pp50–1) is where the Tangs, the first of Hong Kong's mighty Five Clans, settled in the 12th century AD and where they eventually built their walled villages (p19).

Walled villages, which usually had moats, are a reminder that Hong Kong's early settlers were constantly menaced by marauding pirates, bandits and imperial soldiers. They remain one of the most popular destinations for visitors to the New Territories.

Kam Tin contains two fortified villages: Kat Hing Wai and Shui Tau Tsuen. Most tourists go to Kat Hing Wai, as it is just off Kam Tin Rd, the main thoroughfare, and easily accessible. Shui Tau Tsuen is larger and less touristy, but don't expect to find remnants of ancient China. For details on Ping Kong, a seldom-visited walled village to the northeast, see p119.

KAT HING WAI Map pp50–1
🚌 64K

This tiny village is 500 years old and was walled in some time during the early Ming

TRANSPORT – KAM TIN

Bus Bus 64K stops along Kam Tin Rd on its way between Yuen Long and Tai Po Market KCR East Rail stations; bus 77K also goes to Yuen Long, Sheung Shui and Fanling.

dynasty (1368–1644). It contains just one main street, off which a host of dark and narrow alleyways lead. There are quite a few new buildings and retiled older ones in the village. A small temple stands at the end of the street.

Visitors are asked to make a donation when they enter the village; put the money in the coin slot by the entrance. You can take photographs of the old Hakka women in their traditional black trousers, tunics and distinctive bamboo hats with black cloth fringes, but they'll expect you to pay (around $10).

Kat Hing is just south of Kam Tin Rd. If travelling from Yuen Long, get off at the first bus stop on Kam Tin Rd, cross the road and walk east for 10 minutes. Alternatively take a taxi from Kam Sheung Rd KCR West station for less than $15.

SHUI TAU TSUEN Map pp50–1
🚌 64K

This 17th-century village, 15 minutes' walk north of Kam Tin Rd and signposted, is famous for its prow-shaped roofs decorated with dragons and fish along the ridges. Tiny traditional houses huddle inside Shui Tau Tsuen's walls.

The Tang Kwong U Ancestral Hall (🕙 9am-1pm & 2-5pm Wed, Sat & Sun) and, just north of it, the Tang Ching Lok Ancestral Hall (🕙 9am-1pm & 2-5pm Wed, Sat & Sun) in the middle of the village, were built in the early 19th century for ancestor worship. The ancestors' names are listed on the altar in the inner hall and on the long boards down the side. The sculpted fish, on the roof of the entrance hall, symbolise luck; in Cantonese, the word for 'fish' (yéw) sounds similar to the word for 'plenty' or 'surplus'. Between these two buildings is the small Hung Shing Temple. South of them is Shui Tau Tsuen's most impressive sight, the renovated Yi Tai Study Hall (🕙 9am-1pm & 2-5pm Wed, Sat & Sun), built in the first half of the 19th century and named after the gods of literature and martial arts. The Tin Hau temple on the outskirts of the

village to the north was built in 1722 and contains an iron bell weighing 106kg.

There's been a lot of building in and around Shui Tau Tsuen in recent years – massive Tsing Long Hwy and the KCR West Rail extension straddle it to the west – and the old sits rather uncomfortably with the new. But the further north you walk beyond the village, the calmer and more tranquil it gets.

To reach Shui Tau Tsuen, which is signposted from Kam Tin Rd, walk north, go under the subway below the Kam Tin Bypass, pass Kam Tai Rd and cross over the river to Chi Ho Rd. Go over the small bridge spanning a stream, turn right and then left to enter the village from the east. The first thing you'll pass is the Yi Tai Study Hall.

FANLING & SHEUNG SHUI

What were two lazy country villages (Map pp50–1) just a few years ago, Fanling and Sheung Shui now form one of the largest New Town conurbations in the New Territories, with some 300,000 inhabitants. Get a feel for what they were once like by walking around the Luen Wo Hu district at the northern end of Fanling. Major sights are thin on the ground here, but there's an important Taoist temple within easy walking distance and, a short bus ride away, a seldom-visited walled village and the Lung Yeuk Tau Heritage Trail (opposite; Map pp50–1). The posh 18-hole Hong Kong Golf Course (see p224) at Fanling will be a draw for some.

Fanling and Sheung Shui are in the north-central New Territories, much closer to the mainland (5km) than they are to Tsim Sha Tsui (20km). They are linked by San Wan Rd, along which the bulk of buses and green minibuses serving the two New Towns travel.

TRANSPORT – FANLING & SHEUNG SHUI

KCR Take the KCR to Fanling and Sheung Shui East Rail stations.

Bus Most onward travel connections depart from, or close to, KCR East Rail stations. Bus 76K to Yuen Long and Mai Po Marsh departs from Pak Wo Rd in Fanling and Choi Yun Rd in Sheung Shui. Bus 73K to Ping Kong stops at Yuen Long Jockey Club Rd in Fanling and Po Shek Wu Rd in Sheung Shui.

Green Minibus Bus 58K heads to Ping Kong from San Wan Rd in Sheung Shui.

FUNG YING SIN TEMPLE Map pp50–1

☎ 2669 9186; 66 Pak Wo Rd, Fanling; ☯ 9am-5pm; 🚉 Fanling

The main attraction in the area is this huge Taoist temple complex opposite the Fanling KCR East Rail station, and connected to it by an overhead walkway and subway. It has wonderful exterior murals of Taoist immortals and the Chinese zodiac, an orchard terrace, herbal clinic and a vegetarian restaurant (ground & 1st fl, Bldg A7; ☯ 10am-5pm). Most important are the dozen ancestral halls behind the main temple, where the ashes of the departed are deposited in what might be described as miniature tombs, complete with photographs.

MARKETS Map pp50–1

Wo Mun & Luen On Sts, Fanling; Chi Cheong Rds, Sheung Shui; ☯ 6am-8pm; 🚌 77K

These two lively markets frequented by Hakka people are worth a look, particularly early (ie before 10am). Sheung Shui market is 250m north of the Sheung Shui KCR East Rail station. To reach Fanling market in the old district of Luen Wo Hui, walk north along Sha Tau Kok Rd for about 1.5km or catch bus 77K from the Fanling KCR East Rail station. This bus carries on to the market in Sheung Shui.

PING KONG Map pp50–1

🚌 77K

This sleepy walled village in the hills south of Sheung Shui is seldom visited by outsiders. Like other walled villages still inhabited in Hong Kong, it is a mix of old and new, and has a lovely little Tin Hau temple in the centre. You can also go exploring around the farming area behind the village compound.

To get to Ping Kong from Sheung Shui, catch green minibus 58K from the huge minibus station south of the Sheung Shui Landmark North shopping centre on San Wan Rd. The centre is a short walk northwest of Sheung Shui KCR East Rail station. Alternatively, bus 77K between Yuen Long and the Sheung Shui and Fanling KCR East Rail stations travels along Fan Kam Rd. Alight at the North District Hospital stop and walk southeast along Ping Kong Rd to the village.

A taxi from the Sheung Shui KCR East Rail station to Ping Kong will cost $20.

LUNG YEUK TAU HERITAGE TRAIL
Walking Tour

1 Lo Wai Begin this walk about a kilometre northeast of the KCR station on Luk Tung St. The first real port of call on this trail are the impressive brick enclosing walls facing this tiny walled village and just to the east a lovely Tin Hau Temple with two 18th-century bells.

2 Tang Chung Ling Ancestral Hall (☯ 9am-1pm & 2-5pm Wed-Mon) was built in 1525 in honour of the founder of the Tang clan, and one of the largest such structures in the New Territories.

WALK FACTS

Start Lok Tung St in Fanling (green minibus 54K from Fanling KCR station)
End Siu Hang Tsuen (green minibus 56K to Fanling KCR station)
Distance 4.5km
Time 2½ to three hours
Fuel stop Fanling market

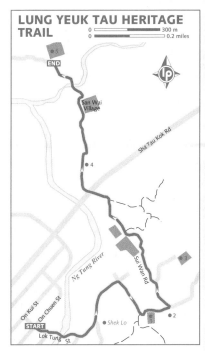

LUNG YEUK TAU HERITAGE TRAIL

The entire hall is richly decorated with fine wood carvings, colourful plaster mouldings and murals.

3 Walled Villages Turning left, away from the hall, heading northwest over the next 800m you'll pass more little villages, including Wing Ning Wai and Wing Ning Tsuen, whose houses are at different heights for feng shui reasons.

4 Sin Shut Study Hall After crossing Sha Tau Kok Rd, keep ahead rather than following the road on the left. Built in 1840 and boasting some fine tiles.

5 San Wai & Siu Hang Tsuen The last walled village on the trail, San Wai and Siu Hang Tsuen now contains mostly modern buildings. From here you can pick up the minibus back to the centre of Fanling. A taxi to the KCR station will cost just over $15. With any number of *daai-pàai-dawng* (street stalls) and noodle shops, Fanling market (p119) is just over 1km northwest of the start of the trail.

TAI PO
Eating p196

Another large residential and industrial New Town, Tai Po (Map p121) is the springboard for excursions into Plover Cove Country Park and Pat Sin Leng Country Park. Four Lanes Square, where four pedestrian streets converge in the centre of town, is a popular shopping area. The Old Tai Po District Office (Wan Tau Kok Lane) was built in 1907 and is one of the oldest examples of Western architecture in the New Territories.

Tai Po lies north and south of the Lam Tsuen River, at the westernmost point of Tolo Harbour, making it an excellent springboard for excursions into Plover Cove Country Park and Pat Sin Leng Country Park. It's an attractive market town and home to the Hong Kong Railway Museum (right).

Bicycles can be rented in season from several stalls around Tai Po Market KCR East Rail station, but try to arrive early – they often run out during the busiest times. There are a number of bicycle shops lining Kwong Fuk Rd northwest of the KCR station.

One cycling route not to miss is the ride to Plover Cove Reservoir (p122) on the northeast side of Tolo Harbour. Another is to the Chinese University of Hong Kong (p123) in Ma Liu Shui, on the southwest side of the harbour.

Allow at least half a day for either trip. There is an inland route to the university, but the coastal route linking the university with Tai Mei Tuk has the best views. Another option is to follow Ting Kok Rd east to the fishing village San Mun Tsai (Map pp50–1).

HONG KONG RAILWAY MUSEUM
Map p121

☎ 2653 3455; 13 Shung Tak St; admission free; ⏱ 9am-5pm Wed-Mon; 🚇 Tai Wo

The museum is housed in the former Tai Po Market train station, built in 1913 in traditional Chinese style, and spills into the outside garden. Exhibits, including a narrow-gauge steam locomotive dating back to 1911, detail the history of the development of rail transport in the territory. There is also much attention paid to the opening of the Kowloon–Canton Railway in 1910 and its original terminus in Tsim Sha Tsui, which moved to Hung Hong in 1975.

You can get to the museum most easily by alighting at Tai Wo KCR East Rail station, walking south through the Tai Wo Shopping Centre and housing estate, and crossing the Lam Tsuen River via Tai Wo Bridge (the small one with the Chinese roof) leading from Po Nga Rd. The museum is just southeast.

LAM TSUEN WISHING TREE Map pp50–1
Lam Kam Rd, Fong Ma Po; 🚌 64K

Until a short time ago Tai Po was the springboard for this large banyan tree, laden with coloured streamers of paper tied to oranges, in the village of Fong Ma Po to the southwest. The idea was to write your wish on a piece of paper, tie it to the citrus fruit and then throw it as high as you could up into the tree. If your fruit lodged in the branches, you were in luck – and the higher it went, the more chance there was of your

TRANSPORT – TAI PO

KCR Take the KCR to Tai Po Market or Tai Wo East Rail stations.

Bus Bus 71K runs between Tai Wo and Tai Po Market KCR East Rail stations.

Green Minibus For onward travel start at Tai Po Market KCR station or Heung Sze Wui St for bus 20K to San Mun Tsai; catch the bus at Tsing Yuen St for bus 25K to Ng Tung Chai (Tai Mo Shan).

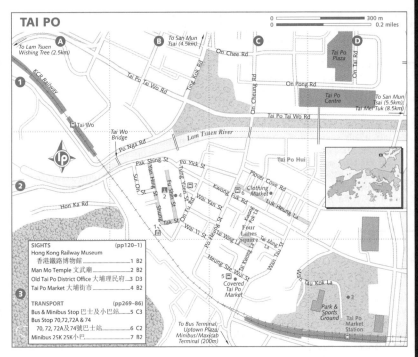

TAI PO

0 _____ 300 m
0 _____ 0.2 miles

To Lam Tsuen
Wishing Tree (2.5km)

To San Mun
Tsai (4.5km)

KCR Railway

On Chee Rd

Tai Po
Plaza

 On Tai Rd

Tai Po Tai Wo Rd

Ling Kok Rd

On Cheung Rd

On Pong Rd

Tai Po
Centre

To San Mun
Tsai (5.5km);
Tai Mei Tuk (8.5km)

Tai Po Tai Wo Rd

Tai Wo

Tai Wo
Bridge

Po Nga Rd

Lam Tsuen River

Pak Shing St

Po Yick St

Tai Po Hui

Sui On St

Tak On St

Kwong Fuk Rd

Kwong
Fuk La

Plover Cove Rd
Clothing
Market

Luk Heung La

Wan Tau Kok La

Hon Ka Rd

Kwong
Fuk Rd

Wai Yan St

Four
Lanes
Square

Tai Ming St

Heung Sze Wui St

Wing La

Kwong La

Wan La

Park &
Sports
Ground

Tai Po
Market
Station

5 Covered
Tai Po
Market

To Bus Terminal;
Uptown Plaza;
Minibus/Maxicab
Terminal (200m)

SIGHTS	(pp120–1)
Hong Kong Railway Museum	
香港鐵路博物館 1 B2	
Man Mo Temple 文武廟 2 B2	
Old Tai Po District Office 大埔理民府 ...3 D3	
Tai Po Market 大埔街市 4 B2	
TRANSPORT	(pp269–86)
Bus & Minibus Stop 巴士及小巴站.........5 C3	
Bus Stop 70,72,72A & 74	
70, 72, 72A及74號巴士站.........................6 C2	
Minibus 25K 25K小巴...................................7 B2	

wish coming true. But things got, er, out of hand just once too often, and in 2005, a week after the end of Chinese New Year, a large branch of the tree came crashing to the ground, dashing most punters' wishes once and for all.

Focus switched to another tree nearby, which became the new arboreal oracle while the original was left to recover. However, this practice soon was stopped, too. In the name of conservation, wish makers can now only tie their wishing papers to Chinese-style wooden racks. You can still buy the wishing papers from vendors but you're unlikely to find any oranges for sale. At least there's a small Tin Hau temple nearby, replete with fortune-tellers, to compensate for your curtailed wish making.

To reach the tree catch bus 64K from the Tai Po Market KCR East Rail station and alight at Fong Ma Po.

TAI PO MARKET Map p121
Fu Shin St; 🕑 6am-8pm; 🚉 **Tai Wo**
Not to be confused with the KCR East Rail station of the same name, this street-long outdoor wet market is a stone's throw from the Hong Kong Railway Museum and is one of the busiest and most interesting markets in the New Territories. Towards the northern end of the same street, the double-hall Man Mo Temple (🕑 8am-6pm) is a major centre of worship for the Tai Po area. It was founded in the late 19th century and, like the Man Mo Temple found in Sheung Wan (p67), it is dedicated to the gods of literature and of war.

PLOVER COVE

The area around Plover Cove Reservoir (Map pp50–1) is good hiking and cycling country and well worth at least a full day's exploring. The village of Tai Mei Tuk, the springboard for most of the activities in the Plover Cove area, is about 6km northeast of Tai Po Market KCR East Rail station.

It may be worthwhile getting a copy of Universal Publications' *Tseung Kwan O, Sai Kung, Clearwater Bay* or else the Countryside Series map *North-East & Central New Territories* (see p295).

Bicycles can be rented at Tai Mei Tuk at several locations, including Lung Kee Bikes (☎ 2662 5266; Ting Kok Rd, Lung Mei village; bicycle rental per day $25; 🕑 9.30am-6pm). A bicycle track along the coast runs from Tai Mei Tuk to Chinese University (opposite) at Ma Liu Shui. Ting Kok Rd in Lung Mei village is also where you'll find a row of popular restaurants (p196). Rowboats are available for hire from Sang Lee Boat Rental (☎ 2660 5402; small/big boat per hr $20/50, 6hr $120/250; ⏰ 9.30am-6pm) on the picture-postcard bay south of the main parking lot on Tai Mei Tuk Rd, where buses and minibuses terminate. Adjacent to the car park is the Tai Mei Tuk Fish Farm (p224), where you can try your luck angling for some freshwater fish.

The Plover Cove Country Park Visitor Centre (Map pp50–1; ☎ 2498 9326; ⏰ 9.30am-4pm Sat, Sun & public holidays), a short distance further east from the car park on Ting Kok Rd, is where the Pat Sin Leng Nature Trail (see below) to Bride's Pool starts.

PAT SIN LENG NATURE TRAIL
Map pp50–1
🚌 75K
This excellent (and easy) 4.4km-long trail, which should take from two to 2½ hours, leads from the Plover Cove Country Park Visitor Centre at Tai Mei Tuk and heads northeast for 4km to Bride's Pool; there are signboards numbered 1 to 22 so there is little danger of getting lost. The elevation gain is only 300m, the scenery is excellent and the two waterfalls at Bride's Pool are delightful, but the place gets packed on the weekend. You can either return to Tai Mei Tuk via Bride's Pool Rd on foot or catch green minibus 20C, which stops at Tai Mei Tuk before carrying on to Tai Po Market KCR station. On Sunday and public holidays only, bus 275R links Bride's Pool with Tai Po. If you carry on north from Bride's Pool to Luk Keng on Starling Inlet, you can catch green minibus 56K, which will take you to Fanling KCR station. Those looking for a more strenuous hike can join stage No 9 of the Wilson Trail (p227) at Tai Mei Tuk on the Plover Cove Reservoir and head west into the steep Pat Sin Leng range of hills

(named after the 'Eight Immortals' of Taoism) to Wong Leng Shan (639m). The trail then carries on westward to Hok Tau Reservoir and Hok Tau Wai (12km, four hours).

PLOVER COVE RESERVOIR Map pp50–1
🚌 75K
Plover Cove Reservoir was completed in 1968 and holds 230 million cubic metres of water; before then Hong Kong suffered from critical water shortages and rationing was not uncommon. Even after the reservoir opened, water sometimes had to be rationed; taps were turned on for only eight hours a day through the dry winter of 1980-81. The reservoir was built in a very unusual way. Rather than build a dam across a river, of which Hong Kong has very few, a barrier was erected across the mouth of a great bay. The sea water was siphoned out and fresh water – mostly piped in from the mainland – was pumped in.

TAI PO KAU
South of Tai Po is the small settlement of Tai Po Kau, which most visitors wouldn't give a second thought were it not for the wonderful nature reserve here. Tai Po Kau Nature Reserve lies south of Tai Po, less than 1km inland from Tolo Harbour. The main entrance and the information centre are at the village of Tsung Tsai Yuen in the northernmost part of the reserve along Tai Po Rd.

TAI PO KAU NATURE RESERVE
Map pp50–1
Tai Po Rd; 🚌 70 or 72
The Tai Po Kau Nature Reserve is a thickly forested 460-hectare 'special area' and is Hong Kong's most extensive woodlands. It is home to many species of butterflies, amphibians, birds, dragonflies and trees, and is a superb place in which to enjoy a quiet walk. The reserve is crisscrossed with four main tracks ranging in length from 3km (red trail) to 10km (yellow trail), and a short nature trail of less than 1km. If possible, avoid the reserve on Sunday and public holidays, when the crowds descend upon the place en masse.

The reserve is supposed to emphasise conservation and education rather than recreation, and about 1km northwest of the reserve entrance and down steep Hung Lam Drive is the Kerry Lake Egret Nature Park

---

TRANSPORT – PLOVER COVE

Bus Take bus 75K (and additionally 74K or 275R on Sundays and holidays) from Tai Po Market KCR East Rail station (Map p121) in Tai Po.

Green Minibus Bus 20C passes through Tai Po Market KCR station and Heung Sze Wui St (Map p121) in Tai Po on its way to Plover Cove.

TRANSPORT – TAI PO KAU

Bus Tai Po Kau Nature Reserve is well served by buses. Bus 70 passes through Jordan and Mong Kok on its way here. Bus 72 can be used to get here from nearby the Sha Tin and Tai Po Market KCR East Rail stations.

KCR A taxi from Tai Po Market KCR East Rail station will cost around $20, and from the University KCR East Rail station about $38.

and the much-touted, over-priced Museum of Ethnology (☎ 2657 6657; www.taipokau.org; 2 Hung Lam Dr; adult/concession $25/15; ☿ 1-6pm Sun & public holidays). In the same complex is the delightful Little Egret Restaurant (p196).

UNIVERSITY

The Chinese University of Hong Kong (Map pp50–1; ☎ 2609 6000; www.cuhk.edu.hk/v6/en/), established in 1963, is in Ma Liu Shui and served by University KCR East Rail station. It is situated on a beautiful campus and its art museum is well worth a visit.

Ma Liu Shui and the Chinese University of Hong Kong are southeast of Tai Po and Tai Po Kau, overlooking Tolo Harbour. The University KCR East Rail station is southeast of the four campuses (Chung Chi Campus, New Asia Campus, Shaw Campus and United Campus). Ferries from Ma Liu Shui ferry pier, opposite the university on the eastern side of Tolo Hwy and about 500m northeast of University station, serve the Sai Kung Peninsula (p126) and Tap Mun Chau (p128) twice daily (p274). A taxi from the station to the pier will cost $12.50.

CHINESE UNIVERSITY OF HONG KONG ART MUSEUM Map pp50–1

☎ 2609 7416; www.cuhk.edu.hk/ics/amm; Sir Run Run Shaw Hall, Central Ave; admission free; ☿ 10am-5pm (closed public holidays); ⊠ University

The Chinese University of Hong Kong Art Museum is divided into two sections. The four-floor East Wing Galleries house a permanent collection of Chinese paintings, calligraphy, ceramics and other decorative arts, including 2000-year-old bronze seals and a large collection of jade flower carvings. The West Wing Galleries stage five to six special exhibitions each year.

A shuttle bus from University station travels through the campus to the administration building at the top of the hill; for the museum, get off at the second stop. The bus runs every 20 to 30 minutes daily and is free except on Sunday ($5) from September to May. From June to August, it costs $1 Monday to Saturday and $5 on Sundays.

SHA TIN

Sleeping p265

Sha Tin (Sandy Field; Map p124) is an enormous New Town (population 637,000) built mostly on land that was once a mud flat and produced some of the best rice in imperial China. Sha Tin retains some traditional Chinese houses, giving parts of it a historical feel absent in most of the other New Towns. Hong Kong Chinese flock to Sha Tin on the weekends to place their bets at the nearby racecourse or to shop at Sha Tin's New Town Plaza (Map p124), one of the biggest shopping centres in the New Territories. For visitors, the drawcards are the temples and one of the best museums in Hong Kong.

Sha Tin lies in a narrow valley on both banks of a channel of the Shing Mun River. Fo Tan, where the racecourse is located, is to the north and northeast, and Tai Wai, where you'll find the Hong Kong Heritage Museum, is to the south. Though once separate villages, they are now extensions of the Sha Tin conurbation. Sha Tin KCR East Rail station is west of (and connected to) New Town Plaza in central Sha Tin. Buses arrive at and depart from the KCR East Rail station, the bus station below New Town Plaza and the one at City One Plaza on Ngan Shing St on the opposite side of the channel. You can rent bicycles from several kiosks in Sha Tin Park, south of New Town Plaza shopping centre, including Power Three Company (Map p124; ☎ 2603 0498; Kiosk No 3; per hr Mon-Fri $20, per hr Sat & Sun $25; ☿ 9am-7pm).

TRANSPORT – SHA TIN

KCR Sha Tin, Tai Wai (Map pp50–1), Fo Tan (Map pp50–1) and Racecourse (Map pp50–1) East Rail stations.

Train Che Kung Temple (Map pp50–1) station.

Bus Buses into and out of Sha Tin leave from/terminate at City One Plaza Sha Tin bus station. Bus 182 links Sha Tin with Wan Chai, Admiralty and Central. Bus 170 connects Sha Tin KCR East Rail bus station with Causeway Bay and Aberdeen. Bus 299 shuttles between Sha Tin and Sai Kung.

10,000 BUDDHAS MONASTERY
Map pp50–1

☎ 2691 1067; www.10kbuddhas.org; admission free; ☼ 9am-6pm; ☒ Sha Tin

Perched on Po Fook Hill about 500m northwest of Sha Tin KCR East Rail station, this quirky temple is well worth a visit. Built in the 1950s, the complex actually contains more than 10,000 Buddhas – some 12,800 miniature statues line the walls of the main temple. Dozens of life-sized golden statues of Buddha's followers flank the steep steps leading to the monastery complex. There are several temples and pavilions split over two levels, as well as a nine-storey pagoda that can be climbed. For sustenance the complex also has a vegetarian restaurant (☼ 10.15am-4pm or 5pm). Be aware the temple may close if it's raining heavily.

To reach the monastery, take exit B at Sha Tin KCR station and walk down the ramp, passing a series of traditional houses at Pai Tau village on the left. Take the left onto Pai Tau St, and turn right onto Sheung Wo Che St. At the end of this road, a series of signs in English will direct you to the left along a concrete path and through bamboo groves to the first of some 400 steps leading up to the monastery. An alternative route down is to take the path from the lower level. This will take you back down to the houses at Pai Tau Village by the rail station.

AMAH ROCK Map pp50–1

This boulder southwest of Sha Tin may look like just a rock, but it's an oddly shaped one and, like many local landmarks in Hong Kong, it carries a legend. It seems that for many years a fisherman's wife would stand on this spot in the hills above Lion Rock Country Park, watching for her husband to return from the sea while carrying her baby on her back. One day he didn't come back – she waited and waited. The gods apparently took pity on her and transported her to heaven on a lightning bolt, leaving her form in stone. The name of the rock in Cantonese is Mong Fu Shek, or 'Gazing out for Husband Stone'. It's a popular place of pilgrimage for girls and young lovers during the Maiden's Festival on the seventh day of the seventh moon (mid-August).

As you take the KCR south from Sha Tin to Kowloon, Amah Rock is visible to the east (ie on the left-hand side) up on the

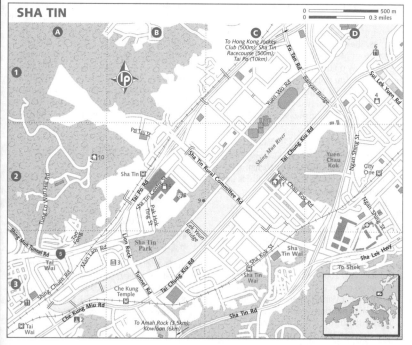

hill-side after Tai Wai KCR East Rail station, but before the train enters the tunnel.

CHE KUNG TEMPLE Map p124

☎ 2691 1733; Che Kung Miu Rd; admission free; ☺ 7am-6pm; ⊠ Che Kung Temple

This large Taoist temple complex, built in 1993, is on the opposite bank of the Shing Mun River channel in Tai Wai. It's dedicated to Che Kung, a Song-dynasty general credited with ridding Sha Tin of the plague; you'll see an enormous and quite powerful statue of the good general in the main temple to the left as you enter the complex. The main courtyard, flanked by eight statues of Taoist immortals, is always a hive of activity.

To reach the temple, take the KCR East Rail to Tai Wai station and change to the Ma On Shan Rail extension, alighting at Che Kung Temple station. The temple is just west of here.

HONG KONG HERITAGE MUSEUM
Map p124

☎ 2180 8188; www.heritagemuseum.gov.hk; 1 Man Lam Rd; adult/concession $10/5, admission free Wed; ☺ 10am-6pm Mon & Wed-Sat, 10am-7pm Sun; ⊠ Sha Tin

Located southwest of Sha Tin town centre, this exceptional museum is housed in a three-storey, purpose-built structure that is reminiscent of an ancestral hall. It has both rich permanent collections and innovative temporary exhibits in a dozen galleries.

The ground floor contains a book and gift shop, the wonderful Children's Discovery Gallery, with eight learning and play zones (including 'Life in a Village', 'Undersea Garden', 'Mai Po Marsh') for kids aged four to 10, a Hong Kong Toy Story hands-on area for tots and an Orientation Theatre, with a 12-minute introductory video in English on the hour. There's also a lovely teahouse (☺ 10am-6pm).

Along with five thematic (ie temporary) galleries, the 1st floor contains the best of the museum's permanent collections: the New Territories Heritage Hall, with mock-ups of traditional shops, a Hakka fishing village and history of the New Towns; the Cantonese Opera Heritage Hall, where you can watch old operas on video with English subtitles, 'virtually' make yourself up as a Cantonese opera character on computer or just enjoy the costumes and sets; and the Chao Shao-an Gallery, devoted to the work of the eponymous water-colourist (1905–98) and founder of the Lingnan School of painting (p33).

The 2nd floor contains another thematic gallery and the TT Tsui Gallery of Chinese Art, an Aladdin's cave of fine ceramics, pottery, bronze, jade and lacquerware, stone carvings, and furniture. You may be interested in some of the gifts various Chinese provinces presented to China for the reunification, which are on display in the hallways.

To reach the Hong Kong Heritage Museum, take the KCR East Rail to Sha Tin station and walk south along Tai Po Rd. If coming from the Che Kung Temple, walk east along Che Kung Miu Rd, go under the subway and cross the footbridge over the channel. The museum is 200m to the east.

SHA TIN RACECOURSE Map pp50–1

☎ 1817 hotline; www.sha-tin.com; Penfold Park; admission on race days public stands $10, members enclosures $100-150; ⊠ Racecourse or Fo Tan

Northeast of Sha Tin town centre is Hong Kong's second racecourse, which opened in 1978 and can accommodate up to 80,000 punters. In general, races are held on Saturday afternoon – and sometimes on Sunday and public holidays – from September to

---

SHA TIN

June; a list of race meetings is available from the HKTB or the racecourse website.

Bets are easily placed at one of the numerous computerised betting terminals run by the Hong Kong Jockey Club (p230). There is a worthwhile horseracing tour available for the interested but uninitiated, through Gray Line or Splendid Tours & Travel (see p298).

The KCR Racecourse station, just west of the track, opens on race days only. Otherwise, get off at Fo Tan station and walk north along Lok King St, and its extension Lok Shun Path, for about 1.5km.

SAI KUNG PENINSULA

Drinking & Nightlife p212; Eating p197; Sleeping p265

The Sai Kung Peninsula (Map pp50–1), in the northeastern New Territories, is the garden spot of the New Territories. It is also one of the last areas left in Hong Kong – the Outlying Islands notwithstanding – reserved for outdoor activities, and 60% of the peninsula is one huge 7500-hectare country park, divided into Sai Kung East and Sai Kung West. Though strictly speaking not on the peninsula, the 28,880-hectare Ma On Shan Country Park is contiguous with it and access is from Sai Kung Town. The hiking is excellent in Sai Kung – the MacLehose Trail (p226) runs right across it – there's sailing galore and some of the best beaches in the territory are here.

The region is washed by Tolo Harbour to the north, Mirs Bay to the east and Port Shelter to the south. On the southern end of the peninsula is High Island Reservoir, once a sea channel and now Hong Kong's second-largest source of fresh water.

A good website devoted exclusively to the area is the district council's www.travelinsaikung.org.hk.

ISLAND HOPPING IN SAI KUNG

You can make any number of easy boat trips from Sai Kung Town, exploring the mosaic of islands that dot the harbour. It's a delightful way to spend a few hours or even an entire day. Most kaidos (small, open-sea ferries) leave from the pier on the waterfront, just in front of Hoi Pong Square.

The easiest (and cheapest) way to go is to jump aboard a 'scheduled' kaido (ie one that goes according to demand and when full) bound for the small island of Yim Tin Tsai ($15, 15 minutes).

On the way, the boat weaves through a number of small islands. The first island to the east of Sai Kung Town is Yeung Chau (Sheep Island). You'll be able to spot a horseshoe-shaped burial plot up on the slope; for reasons dictated by feng shui, the Chinese like to position graves with decent views of the sea. Southeast of Yeung Chau, Pak Sha Chau (White Sand Island) has a popular beach on its northern shore.

Just beyond Pak Sha Chau is the northern tip of the much larger Kiu Tsui Chau (Sharp Island), arguably the most popular island destination. Kiu Tsui Chau has several fine, sandy beaches: Kiu Tsui and, connected to it by a sand spit, Kiu Tau on the western shore, and Hap Mun on the island's southern tip. Both can be reached by kaido ($10) directly from Sai Kung Town.

Yim Tin Tsai (Little Salt Field) is so-called because the original fisherfolk who lived here augmented their income by salt-panning. A few minutes' walk from the jetty up a small flight of steps to the left is St Joseph's Chapel, the focal point of the island. This is Yim Tin Tsai's only house of worship, which is most unusual in an area of Hong Kong where temples devoted to Tin Hau proliferate. Apparently the villagers, who all belong to the same clan, converted to Catholicism 150 years ago after St Peter appeared on the island to chase away pirates who had been harassing them.

Yim Tin Tsai is connected to the much larger island of Kau Sai Chau by a narrow spit of land that becomes submerged at high tide. Kau Sai Chau is the site of the 36-hole Jockey Club Kau Sai Chau Public Golf Course (Map p127; see also p224), a public link that can be reached by the course's direct ferry from Sai Kung (adult/concession $50/30 return), which departs every 20 minutes daily from 6.40am to 9pm; the last boat back is at 10pm. Boats dock in Sai Kung Town at the long pier opposite the new Sai Kung Waterfront Park. The 19th-century Hung Shing Temple at the southern tip of Kau Sai Chau won a Unesco restoration award in 2000.

Beyond Kau Sai Chau is Leung Shuen Wan (High Island), a long trip from Sai Kung Town, and the High Island Reservoir, which was built in 1978 by damming what was once a large bay with dolooses (huge cement barriers shaped like jacks); sea water was then siphoned out and fresh water pumped in. You can see one example of a doloose, weighing 25 tonnes, on display on the pier in Sai Kung Town (Map p127).

If you want to be out on the water for a longer period or to have greater flexibility as to where you go, you can hire your own boat and kaido owners can usually be found trawling for fares. Explain to the kaido owner where you want to go, how long you want to spend there and which way you wish to return. They don't speak much English, but if you point to the islands on Map pp50–1 in this book, they may get the picture. The usual price for this kind of trip is about $120 on weekdays, more on the weekend.

Sai Kung Town

Originally a fishing village, Sai Kung Town (Map p127) is now more of a leafy suburb for people working in Kowloon and on Hong Kong Island, but it still has some of the feeling of a port. Fishing boats put in an occasional appearance, and down on the waterfront there's a string of seafood restaurants that draw customers from all around the territory.

Sai Kung Town is an excellent base for hikes into the surrounding countryside. A *kaido* trip to one or more of the little offshore islands and their secluded beaches is also recommended (see boxed text, opposite). Windsurfing equipment can be hired from the Windsurfing Centre (☎ 2792 5605; ◷ from 9.30am-6pm Sat & Sun, call ahead weekdays) at Sha Ha (off Map p127), just north of Sai Kung Town. Bus 94, heading for the pier at Wong Shek and the springboard for Tap Mun Chau, will drop you off. Or you can walk there from town in about 15 minutes.

Hebe Haven

The very small bay of Hebe Haven (Map pp50–1), which Cantonese speakers call Pak Sha Wan (White Sand Bay), is home to the Hebe Haven Yacht Club (☎ 2719 9682, 2719 3673; www.hhyc.org.hk), which has a large fleet of yachts and other pleasure craft all but choking Marina Cove.

To swim at Trio Beach, opposite the marina, catch a sampan from Hebe Haven to the long, narrow peninsula called Ma Lam Wat; along the way you'll pass a small Tin Hau temple on a spit of land jutting out to the south. The beach is excellent and the sampan trip should only cost a few dollars. You can also walk to the peninsula from Sai Kung Town; it's about 4km.

LIONS NATURE EDUCATION CENTRE
Map pp50–1

☎ 2792 2234; Pak Kong; www.hknature.net/lnec /eng/; admission free; ◷ 9.30am-4.30pm Wed-Mon; ◻ 92

This 34-hectare attraction, 2km northwest of Hebe Haven and just off Hiram's Hwy, is Hong Kong's first nature education centre and comprises everything from an arboretum, a medicinal plants garden and an insectarium, to a mineral and rocks corner and a shell house. We love the Dragonfly Pond, which attracts up to a quarter of the more than 100 dragonfly species found in

SAI KUNG TOWN

0 — 200 m
0 — 0.1 miles

To Sai Kung Park Entrance (50m); Sha Ha (650m); Windsurfing Centre (650m)

Swimming Pool

Tang Shiu Kin Sports Ground

Sai Kung Town Hall

Sai Kung Sports Centre

Fuk Man Rd

Wai Man Rd

Chan Man Rd

Po Tung Rd

Hoi Pong Square

Children's Playground

Fruit Stands

Tin Hau Temple

Sai Kung Market

Wan King Path

Sha Tsui Path

Yi Chun St

Nin Chuen St

Man Nin St

Old Town

See: Cheung St

Hoi Pong St

Pier

Sai Kung Hoi (Inner Port Shelter)

TRANSPORT – SAI KUNG PENINSULA

Sai Kung Town
Bus From Sai Kung Town bus 299 heads to Sha Tin KCR East Rail, bus 92 runs to Diamond Hill and Choi Hung, bus 96R (Sunday and public holidays) heads to Wong Shek, Hebe Haven, and Choi Hung and Diamond Hill MTR stations, while bus 792M calls at Tseung Kwan O and Tiu Keng Leng MTR stations. Bus 94 goes to Wong Shek.
Green Minibus From Sai Kung Town, buses 1A, 1M and 1S (12.30am to 6.10am) go to Hebe Haven and Choi Hung MTR station.

Pak Tam Chung
Bus No 94 from Sai Kung Town.

Hoi Ha
Green minibus Minibus 7 makes the run from Sai Kung Town daily, with the first departure at 8.45am and the last at 6.45pm. A taxi from there will cost around $100.

Hong Kong. You can reach the centre on bus 92 from Diamond Hill MTR and Choi Hung, bus 96R on Sunday and holidays from Diamond Hill to Wong Shek Pier, and green minibus 1A from Choi Hung.

Pak Tam Chung

Pak Tam Chung (Map pp50–1) is the start of the MacLehose Trail (p226).

SAI KUNG COUNTRY PARK VISITOR CENTRE Map pp50–1
☎ 2792 7365; Tai Mong Tsai Rd; ☽ 9.30am-4.30pm Wed-Mon; 🚌 94
While you're in Pak Tam Chung, visit the Sai Kung Country Park Visitor Centre, which is to the south of the village, just by the road from Sai Kung. It has excellent maps, photographs and displays of the area's geology, fauna and flora, as well as its traditional villages and Hoi Ha Wan Marine Park.

SHEUNG YIU FOLK MUSEUM
Map pp50–1
☎ 2792 6365; Pak Tam Chung Nature Trail; admission free; ☽ 9am-4pm Wed-Mon; 🚌 94
This museum is a leisurely 20-minute walk from Pak Tam Chung south along the 1km-long Pak Tam Chung Nature Trail. The museum

is part of a restored Hakka village typical of those found here in the 19th century. The village was founded about 150 years ago by the Wong clan, which built a kiln to make bricks. In the whitewashed dwellings, pigpens and cattle sheds, all surrounded by a high wall and watchtower to guard against raids by pirates, are farm implements, objects of daily use, furnishings and Hakka clothing.

Hoi Ha, Wong Shek, Chek Keng & Tai Long

There are several rewarding hikes at the northern end of the Sai Kung Peninsula starting in the little coves such as Hoi Ha, Wong Shek and Chek Keng, but the logistics can be a bit tricky. Be sure to take along a copy of the *Sai Kung & Clearwater Bay* Countryside Series map or Universal Publications' *Tseung Kwan O, Sai Kung, Clearwater Bay* (p295).

HOI HA WAN MARINE PARK Map pp50–1
☎ 1823 hotline; Hoi Ha; 🚌 green minibus 7
A rewarding 6km walk in the area starts from the village of Hoi Ha (literally 'Under the Sea'), on the coast of Hoi Ha Bay, now part of the Hoi Ha Wan Marine Park, a 260-hectare protected area blocked off by concrete booms from the Tolo Channel and closed to fishing vessels. It's one of the few places in Hong Kong waters where coral still grows in abundance and is a favourite with divers. You can visit anytime, but 1½-hour tours of the marine park are available in English at 10.30am and 2.15pm on Saturday, Sunday and public holidays. Be aware that you must register with the Agriculture, Fisheries & Conservation Department (AFCD; ☎ 1823) in advance, though.

TAP MUN CHAU

Eating p197

Tap Mun Chau (Map pp50–1), which translates as 'Grass Island', is very isolated and retains an old-world fishing village atmosphere. If you have the time (count on a full day), it's definitely worth the trip, and you will be re-

TRANSPORT – TAP MUN CHAU

Ferry Depart from Ma Liu Shui near University KCR East Rail station.

warded with a feeling that's hard to come by in Hong Kong: isolation. The sailing is particularly scenic from Wong Shek, as the boat cruises through the narrow Tai Tan Hoi Hap – more reminiscent of a fjord in Norway than a harbour in Hong Kong.

Delightfully sleepy Tap Mun Chau doesn't have accommodation, but you may get away with pitching a tent. There's only one restaurant on the island (p198), but there are shops selling snacks and drinks. For ferry routes, schedules and fares for Tap Mun Chau, see p274. The island is found off the northeast coast of the New Territories, where the Tolo Channel empties into Mirs Bay, which is Tai Pang Wan in Cantonese. Only Tung Ping Chau to the northeast in Mirs Bay is more remote.

As you approach the pier at Tap Mun village, you'll see fishing boats bobbing about in the small bay and, to the south, people working on fish-breeding rafts. Tap Mun village is noted for its Tin Hau temple, which was built during the reign of Emperor Kang Xi of the Qing dynasty in the late 17th or early 18th century and is northeast from where the boat docks. The Tin Hau birthday festival in late April/early May (p17) is big here, although most of the participants come from elsewhere in Hong Kong. Part of the temple is devoted to the god of war Kwan Tai (or Kwan Yu).

Other attractions here include an easy (and signposted) walk northward to Mau Ping Shan (125m), the island's highest point, a windy pebble beach on the southeastern shore and an odd stone formation called Balanced Rock, a couple of hundred metres south of the beach.

TUNG PING CHAU

Tung Ping Chau (Map pp50–1), sitting in splendid isolation in Mirs Bay in the far northeast of the New Territories, is as remote as it gets in Hong Kong. The distance from Ma Liu Shui to the southwest, from where the ferry serving the island departs, is 25km.

A remote, crescent-shaped island, it is part of Plover Cove Country Park (☎ 2498 9326; ⏲ 9.30am-4pm Sat, Sun & public holidays). The island and the waters around it, which teem with sea life (especially corals), form Hong Kong's fourth marine park.

At one time the island, which is called Tung Ping Chau (East Peace Island) to distinguish it from Peng Chau (same pronunciation in Cantonese) near Lantau, supported a population of 3000, but now it is virtually deserted.

There are a couple of tiny settlements on the northeastern side, including Sha Tau, where you'll find a food stall.

Tung Ping Chau is just 12km from the mainland's Daya Bay nuclear power station and has Hong Kong's only radiation shelter, at Tai Tong just north of the pier.

For ferry routes, schedules and fares for Tung Ping Chau, see p274.

Tung Ping Chau's highest point is only about 40m, but it has unusual rock layers in its cliffs, which glitter after the rain. The island has some sandy beaches on its east coast that are good for swimming. The longest one, to the northeast, is Cheung Sha Wan. There is a small Tin Hau temple on the southwestern coast of the island, and some small caves dotting the cliffs. A good 6km walking trail encircles the whole island.

CLEARWATER BAY PENINSULA

Clearwater Bay Peninsula (Map pp50–1) is a wonderfully untamed and rough-contoured backdrop to urban Hong Kong – at least on its eastern shore. It is wedged in by Junk Bay (Tseung Kwan O) to the west and Clearwater Bay (Tsing Sui Wan) sitting to the east; Joss House Bay (Tai Miu Wan) lies to the south. Junk Bay is now the site of Tseung Kwan O, a New Town built on reclaimed land with a growing population of 325,000 and a sixth MTR line, but the eastern coastline remains fairly unscarred and offers some exceptional walks, fine beaches and one of the most important temples dedicated to Tin Hau on the South China coast.

Clearwater Bay Peninsula is on the southeastern edge of the New Territories. The country park is divided into two parts: a long and narrow finger-shaped section stretching from Joss House Bay in the south almost to Port Shelter, and a half-moon-shaped section to the east between Lung Ha Wan and Clearwater Bay.

BEACHES Map pp50–1
Bus 91 passes Silverstrand Beach (Ngan Sin Wan) north of Hang Hau before reaching Tai Au Mun; if you wish you can get off at

TRANSPORT – CLEARWATER BAY PENINSULA

Bus Bus 91 runs between Diamond Hill and Choi Hung MTR stations to Tai Au Mun.

Green Minibus Bus 103M runs between Tseung Kwan O MTR station and Clearwater Bay. Bus 103 runs to Kwun Tong ferry pier, and bus 16 to Po Lam MTR station.

Silverstrand and go for a dip. If you're heading for Lung Ha Wan, get off the bus at Tai Au Mun village and start walking. From Sai Kung, take bus 92 to where Hiram's Hwy and Clearwater Bay Rd meet and change there to bus 91.

From Tai Au Mun, Tai Au Mun Rd leads south to two fine, sandy beaches: Clearwater Bay First Beach and, a bit further southwest, Clearwater Bay Second Beach. In summer, try to go during the week, as both beaches can get very crowded on the weekend.

CLEARWATER BAY COUNTRY PARK
Map pp50–1
The heart of the country park is Tai Au Mun, from where trails head off in various direc-

tions, though the Clearwater Bay Country Park Visitor Centre (☎ 2719 0032; ⏰ 9.30am-4.30pm Wed-Mon) is to the southeast in Tai Hang Tun. You can take the small road (Lung Ha Wan Rd) north from Tai Au Mun to the beach at Lung Ha Wan (Lobster Bay) and return via the 2.3km Lung Ha Wan Country Trail.

TAI MIU TEMPLE Map pp50–1
☎ 2519 9155; ⏰ 8am-5pm
Further south along Tai Au Mun Rd is this ancient temple dedicated to Tin Hau. It is said to have been first built in the 13th century by two brothers from Fujian in gratitude to the goddess for having spared their lives during a storm at sea. It is particularly busy during the Tin Hau birthday festival in late April/early May (p17).

Just behind the temple is a Song-dynasty rock carving dating from 1274 and recording both the visit of a superintendent of the Salt Administration and the history of two temples in Joss House Bay. It is the oldest inscription extant in Hong Kong.

From Tai Miu, hikers can follow the 6.6km-long High Junk Peak Country Trail up to Tin Ha Shan (273m) and then continue on to High Junk Peak (Tiu Yu Yung; 344m) before heading eastward back to Tai Au Mun.

The territory of Hong Kong (Map pp50–1) consists of 234 islands, in addition to Hong Kong Island. Together these sparsely populated 'Outlying Islands' are the territory's bolt holes and its playgrounds.

Among the magnets that attract local day-trippers and foreign visitors alike are country parks, with hundreds of kilometres of hiking trails, fresh(er) air and examples of some of the last remnants of traditional village life in Hong Kong. Explore them on a weekday and you're likely to have great expanses of these islands all to yourself.

Hong Kong's islands vary greatly in size, appearance and character. Many are little more than uninhabited rocks poking out of the South China Sea, while Lantau is almost twice the size of Hong Kong Island.

From the tranquil lanes of Cheung Chau and Peng Chau to the monasteries of Lantau and the waterfront seafood restaurants of Lamma, Hong Kong's islands offer a world of peace and quiet along with a host of sights and activities. The islands are a colourful encyclopaedia of animal and plant life – a boon for nature lovers. What's more, some of Hong Kong's best beaches punctuate their rocky coasts.

Poisonous snakes are a rare but significant hazard to be aware of on Lamma and Lantau. See p292 for more details.

The islands listed here are all easily accessible from Hong Kong Island daily, and Cheung Chau and Lantau can be reached from Kowloon on the weekend as well. For details on routes, schedule and fares, see p274.

Because the tiny islands of Tap Mun Chau and Tung Ping Chau are best reached from the New Territories, they are covered on p128 and p129.

LAMMA

Drinking & Nightlife p212; Eating p198; Sleeping p265

With no roads or cars, leafy, low-rise Lamma (Map p132) makes a perfect place to find some space, peace and quiet. At 13.6 sq km, the territory's third-largest island after Lantau and Hong Kong Island, Lamma is home to an estimated 5000 fisherfolk, farmers and foreigners, and the hills above the main village, Yung Shue Wan, are strewn with small homes and apartment blocks. Known mainly for the seafood restaurants at Sok Kwu Wan, the island's 'second' village, Lamma also has some good beaches, excellent hiking and lively pubs.

Perhaps the most interesting way for visitors to see a good portion of the island is to follow the 4km-long Family Trail that runs between Yung Shue Wan and Sok Kwu Wan. This takes a little over an hour, and you can return to Central by ferry from Soke Kwu Wan. Those with extra time should carry on to Tung O Wan, an idyllic bay some 30 minutes further south at the bottom of a steep hill, and perhaps return to Sok Kwu Wan via Mo Tat Wan.

Lamma is the closest inhabited island to Hong Kong Island; its northernmost tip is only 3km across the East Lamma Channel from Ap Lei Chau in Aberdeen. There are two main settlements on the island: Yung Shue

top picks

OUTLYING ISLANDS

- Tian Tan Buddha via cable car (p137)
- Cheung Chau's temples and street scenes (p142)
- Tai O's old-world atmosphere (p138)
- Lamma cross-island walk (left)
- Pink dolphin–spotting (p148)

Wan to the northwest and Sok Kwu Wan on the east coast of the island.

There's a HSBC branch (☎ 2982 0787; 19 Main St) and a post office (3 Main St) in Yung Shue Wan. Bicycles are available for rent from Hoi Nam Gift & Bicycle Shop (☎ 2982 0128, 9364 4941; Ground fl, 37 Sha Po Old Village; per hr/day $20/60; ☼ 11am-7pm) in Yung Shue Wan on the main path to Sok Kwu Wan.

YUNG SHUE WAN Map p132

🚢 Yung Shue Wan ferry

Though it's the larger of the island's two main villages, Yung Shue Wan (Banyan Tree Bay) remains a small place, with little more than a main street following the curve of the bay. Plastic was the big industry here at one time, but now restaurants, bars and other tourism-related businesses are the main employers. There is a small Tin Hau temple dating from the late 19th century at the southern end of Yung Shue Wan.

SOK KWU WAN Map p132
🚢 Sok Kwu Wan ferry

If you continue on the Family Trail you'll encounter another pavilion on a ridge, this

TRANSPORT – LAMMA

Ferry Yung Shue Wan pier to pier 4 of Outlying Islands ferry terminal in Central, Pak Kok Tsuen (Lamma) and Aberdeen; Sok Kwu Wan pier to pier 4 of Outlying Islands ferry terminal in Central, Man Tat Wan (Lamma) and Aberdeen.

time looking down onto Sok Kwu Wan (Picnic Bay), with its many fine restaurants, and fishing boats and rafts bobbing in the bay. Although still a small settlement, Sok Kwu Wan supports at least a dozen water-front seafood restaurants that are popular with boaters. The small harbour at Sok Kwu Wan is filled with rafts from which cages are suspended and fish farmed. If entering Sok Kwu Wan from the south (ie from the Family Trail linking it with Yung Shue Wan), you'll pass three so-called 'kamikaze caves', grottoes measuring 10m wide and 30m deep and built by the occupying Japanese forces to house motorboats wired with explosives to disrupt Allied shipping during WWII. They were never used. Further on and near the entrance to Sok Kwu Wan is a totally reno-vated Tin Hau temple dating back to 1826.

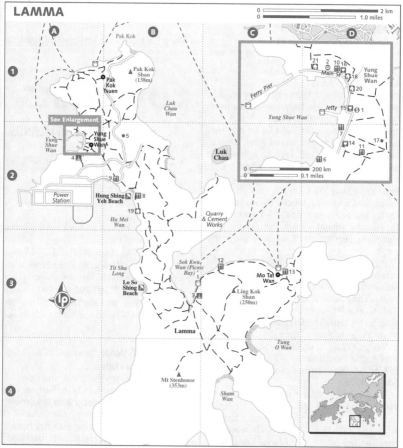

LAMMA'S ENDANGERED TURTLES

Sham Wan has traditionally been the one beach in the whole of Hong Kong where endangered green turtles *(Chelonia mydas)*, one of three species of sea turtle found in Hong Kong waters, still struggle onto the sand to lay their eggs from early June to the end of August.

Female green turtles, which can grow to a metre in length and weigh 140kg, take between 20 and 30 years to reach sexual maturity and always head back to the same beach where they were born to lay their eggs, which takes place every two to six years. Fearing that Sham Wan would catch the eye of housing-estate developers and that the turtles would swim away forever, the area was declared a Site of Special Scientific Interest and closed. It is patrolled by the Agriculture, Fisheries & Conservation Department (AFCD) from June to October. Some eight turtles are known to have nested here since 1997 and some are now being tracked by satellite.

As well as developers, a major hurdle faced by the long-suffering turtles is the appetite of Lamma locals for their eggs. In 1994 three turtles laid about 200 eggs, which were promptly harvested and consumed by villagers. Several years later villagers sold eggs to Japanese tourists for $100 each. There is now a $50,000 fine levied on anyone caught on the beach during the nesting season. Anyone taking, possessing or attempting to sell one of the eggs faces a fine of $100,000 and one year in prison.

Gwài-dáan, or 'turtle egg', by the way, is one of the rudest things you can call a Cantonese-speaking person.

WIND TURBINE Map p132

Standing in elegant contrast to that CO_2 belching, coal-fired power station, Lamma's giant Wind Turbine, close to the top of the ridge just south east of Tai Peng village, makes a stirring sight. There's nothing to actually do here but admire its feathered blades scything the breeze and to take in the dramatic backdrop of freighters setting sail far below, with Hong Kong Island looming in the background. To reach it follow the paths from Yung Shue Wan up to Tai Peng old village and turn right once you hit the concrete roadway linking the power station with Pak Kok.

HUNG SHING YEH BEACH Map p132

🚢 Yung Shue Wan ferry

About a 25-minute walk southeast from the Yung Shue Wan ferry pier, Hung Shing Yeh Beach is the most popular beach on Lamma. But arrive early in the morning or on a weekday and you'll probably find it deserted. The beach is protected by a shark net and has toilets, showers and changing rooms, but the view of the power station across the bay takes some getting used to. There are a few restaurants and drinks stands nearby – the latter open on the weekend only, except in summer – as well as the Concerto Inn (p200), a hotel that also serves so-so Western food.

LO SO SHING BEACH Map p132

🚢 Yung Shue Wan ferry

If you continue south from Hung Shing Yeh Beach, the path climbs steeply until it reaches a Chinese-style pavilion near the top of the hill. From this vantage point, it becomes obvious that the island is mostly hilly grassland and large boulders, though more and more trees are being planted. You will pass a second pavilion offering splendid views out to sea; from here a path leads from the Family Trail down to Lo So Shing Beach, the most beautiful on Lamma. The beach is not very big, but it has a nice cover of shade trees at the back for a break from the sun.

SNAKES ALIVE

Take care when bushwalking, particularly on Lamma and Lantau Islands. Poisonous snakes, the most common being the Bamboo Pit Viper, are a hazard, although they will not attack unless surprised or provoked. Go straight to a public hospital if bitten; private doctors do not stock antivenom. Other fauna to be aware of in the New Territories are wild boars, which can be hugely dangerous if they choose to attack. Steer well clear if you spot one and back off slowly if you've already gotten too close.

MO TAT WAN Map p132

The clean and relatively uncrowded beach at Mo Tat Wan is a mere 20-minute walk east of Sok Kwu Wan along a coastal path. Mo Tat Wan is OK for swimming, but has no lifeguards. You can also reach here by *kaido* from Aberdeen, which continues on to Sok Kwu Wan.

SHAM WAN Map p132

Sham Wan (Deep Bay) is another beautiful bay to the southwest that can be reached from Tung O Wan by clambering over the hills. A trail on the left about 200m up the hill from Tung O leads south to a small and sandy beach. Don't come here from June to October, when Hong Kong's endangered green turtles nest (see boxed text, p133).

TUNG O WAN Map p132

A detour to this small and secluded bay, with a long stretch of sandy beach, while walking to Sok Kwu Wan from Yung Shue Wan or from Sok Kwu Wan itself, is highly recommended. Just before the Tin Hau temple at the entrance to Sok Kwu Wan, follow the signposted path to the right southward, up and over the hill to the tiny village of Tung O. The walk takes about 30 minutes over a rugged landscape, and the first half is a fairly strenuous climb up steps and along a path. Don't do this walk at night unless it's a full moon, as there are only a few street lights at the start in Sok Kwu Wan.

If coming from Mo Tat Wan, take the trail immediately to the west of the pavilion above the beach and follow the signposted path up the hill and through bamboo groves and fields. It takes about 25 minutes to reach the sleepy village of Yung Shue Ha on the fringes of the bay. All of the Chinese who live there are from the same clan and have the surname of Chow. A member of this clan, Chow Yun Fat, the bullet-proof star of many John Woo films, was born and raised in Tung O.

The beach at Tung O Wan is a secluded and unspoiled stretch of sand, punctuated by chunks of driftwood and other flotsam.

LANTAU

Drinking & Nightlife p213; Eating p200; Sleeping p266

Hong Kong's largest island Lantau (Cantonese for 'broken head'; Map p136) is also known by the Chinese as Tai Yue Shan or 'Big Island Mountain' – a name that refers both to its size and elevation. It is home to some of the region's best and most remote beaches, wilderness trails, monasteries and monuments, including the giant Tian Tan Buddha. Part of its appeal is its generous dimensions, ruggedly beautiful terrain and small population.

It is home to about 100,000 people, yet at 144 sq km, it is almost twice the size of Hong Kong Island. Its highest point, Lantau Peak (Fung Wong Shan; 934m), is almost double the height of Victoria Peak. More than half of the surface area – 78.5 sq km, in fact – is designated country park and there are several superb mountain trails, including the 70km Lantau Trail (p226), which passes over both Lantau Peak and Sunset Peak (869m).

Lantau is the last inhabited island west of Hong Kong Island; next stop is Macau and the Zhuhai SEZ. Lantau has many villages, but the main settlements dot the southern coast. From east to west they are: Mui Wo, the 'capital' and the place where most of the ferries dock; Pui O and Tong Fuk along South Lantau Rd; and Tai O on the west coast. The New Town of Tung Chung is on the north coast and accessible from Mui Wo by buses that climb steep Tung Chung Rd. Discovery Bay, a self-contained 'bedroom community' to the northeast, can be reached from Mui Wo by ferry. Not everyone on Lantau resides here of their own accord; the island is home to three prisons.

Rock carvings discovered at Shek Pik on the southwestern coast of Lantau suggest that the island was inhabited as early as the Bronze Age, 3000 years ago, well before the arrival of the Han Chinese; a stone circle uncovered at Fan Lau may date from Neolithic times. The last Song-dynasty emperor passed through here in the 13th century while fleeing the Mongol invaders. He is believed to have held court in the Tung Chung Valley to the north, which takes its name from a local hero who gave up his life for the emperor. Tung Chung is still worshipped by the Hakka people of Lantau, who believe he can predict the future.

Like Cheung Chau, Lantau was once a base for pirates and smugglers, and a trading post for the British long before they showed any interest in Hong Kong Island.

There are some interesting traditional villages, such as Tai O on the west coast; several important religious sites, including the Po Lin Monastery and the adjacent Tian Tan Buddha, the largest outdoor Buddha statue in the world; and some excellent beaches, including Cheung Sha, the longest in Hong Kong.

Until the Lantau Link, the combined road and rail transport connection between Kowloon and Lantau, opened in 1997, the island was accessible only by ferry. That's still the most popular and enjoyable way to go, but today you can reach the island from the rest of the territory by MTR, the Airport Express, a fleet of buses and even by taxi.

HSBC (Map p139; ☎ 2984 8271; Mui Wo Ferry Pier Rd) has a branch in Mui Wo and there's an HSBC ATM (Tai O Market St) in Tai O, which you'll see as you cross the footbridge from the mainland to the island. The main post office (Map p139; Ngan Kwong Wan Rd) is a short distance west of the footbridge crossing the Silver River in Mui Wo.

Bicycles are available for hire ($10 per hour and $25 per day including overnight) at two central locations a short distance from the ferry pier in Mui Wo: Friendly Bicycle Shop (Map p139; ☎ 2984 2278; Ground fl, Shop 12, Mui Wo Centre, 1 Ngan Wan Rd; ☺ 10am-8pm Wed-Mon), just opposite Wellcome supermarket, and Bike Shop (Map p139; ☎ 2984 2002; Ground fl, Shop B, Silver Centre, 10 Mui Wo Ferry Pier Rd; ☺ 10.30am-9pm). They can also be hired from two bike kiosks (Map p139; ☎ 2984 7500, 2984 8232) near the Silvermine Beach Hotel in Mui Wo and from several in Pui O village.

NGONG PING Map p136
🚌 2 from Mui Wo, 21 from Tai O, 23 from Tung Chung, or cable car

Perched 500m up in the western hills of Lantau is the Ngong Ping Plateau, a major drawcard for Hong Kong day-trippers and foreign visitors alike, especially since 1993, when one of the world's largest statues of Buddha was unveiled here.

TRANSPORT – LANTAU

Ferry Mui Wo: Major services from Central leave from pier 6 of the Outlying Islands ferry terminal. Ferries also depart from Chi Ma Wan (also on Lantau), Cheung Chau and Peng Chau.

Chi Ma Wan: Served by the inter-island ferry from Mui Wo, Cheung Chau and Peng Chau.

Tai O: Reached by the service that operates from Tuen Mun in the New Territories via Sha Lo Wan and Tung Chung (both Lantau).

Tung Chung: Reached by a regular service from Tuen Mun. It's also served by the less-frequent service that comes from Tai O and Sha Lo Wan (both Lantau) before going on to Tuen Mun (or vice versa).

Bus Mui Wo: Served by bus 1 from Tai O (from the bus terminus at the end of Tai O Rd), bus 2 from Ngong Ping, bus 3M from Tung Chung (main bus terminus by the MTR station).

Ngong Ping: Other than the cable car the best way to get here is on bus 2 from Mui Wo (opposite the ferry pier) or bus 23 from Tung Chung (main bus terminus by the MTR station).

Tai O: Reached on bus 1 from Mui Wo (opposite the ferry pier), bus 11 from Tung Chung (main bus terminus by the MTR station) or bus 21 from Ngong Ping.

Tung Chung: Served by bus 3M from Mui Wo (opposite the ferry pier), bus 11 from Tai O (from the bus terminus at the end of Tai O Rd) and bus 23 from Ngong Ping.

All buses listed above run along some, or all of, South Lantau Rd, the junction with Tung Chung Rd being the point at which the bus will join or leave the route.

Taxi Telephone the call service on ☎ 2984 1328 or 2984 1368. Sample fares to Ngong Ping and the Tian Tan Buddha from Mui Wo and Tung Chung/Tai O/Hong Kong International Airport are $125/45/145.

MTR Tung Chung station is at the end of the line of the same name.

Airport Express Airport station at Chek Lap Kok.

NEIGHBOURHOODS & ISLANDS OUTLYING ISLANDS

lonelyplanet.com

LANTAU

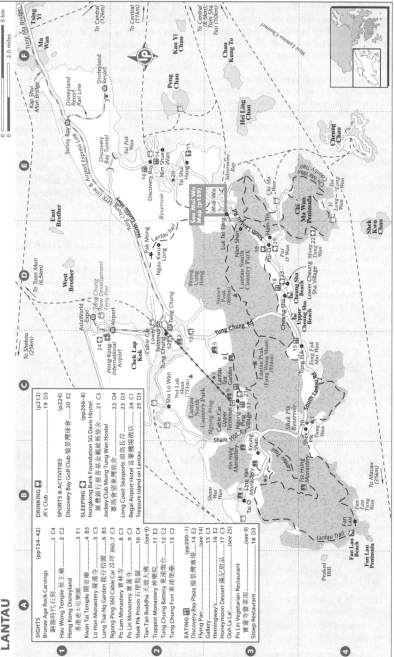

SIGHTS   (pp134–42)
Bronze Age Rock Carvings
銅器時代石刻 1 C4
Hau Wong Temple 侯王廟 2 C2
Hong Kong Disneyland
香港迪士尼樂園 3 F1
Kwan Tai Temple 關帝廟 4 B3
Lo Hon Monastery 羅漢寺 5 C3
Lung Tsai Ng Garden 龍仔悟園 6 B3
Ngong Ping 360 Cable Car 昂坪 360..7 C3
Po Lam Monastery 寶林寺 8 C3
Po Lin Monastery 寶蓮寺 9 C3
Shek Pik Prison 石壁監獄 10 C4
Tian Tan Buddha 天壇大佛 ....(see 9)
Trappist Monastery 神樂院 11 E2
Tung Chung Battery 東涌炮台 12 C2
Tung Chung Fort 東涌砲壘 13 C2

EATING   (pp200–1)
Discovery Bay Plaza 愉景灣商場 14 E2
Flying Pan ....(see 14)
Gallery 15 D3
Hemingway's 16 E2
Honeymoon Dessert 滿記甜品 17 C3
Ooh La La! ....(see 25)
Po Lin Vegetarian Restaurant
寶蓮寺齋菜部 18 D3

DRINKING   (p213)
JK's Club 19 D3

SPORTS & ACTIVITIES   (p224)
Discovery Bay Golf Club 愉景灣球會 ..20 E2

SLEEPING   (pp266–8)
Hongkong Bank Foundation SG Davis Hostel
匯豐銀行慈善基金戴維斯旅舍 21 C3
Jockey Club Mong Tung Wan Hostel
賽馬會望東灣旅舍 22 D4
Long Coast Seasports 浪茄長岸 23 D3
Regal Airport Hotel 富豪機場酒店 ...24 C1
Treasure Island on Lantau 25 D3

136

Po Lin (Precious Lotus; www.plm.org.hk/blcs/en; 9am-6pm) is a huge Buddhist monastery and temple complex that was originally built in 1924. Today it is a fairground as much as a religious retreat, attracting many visitors. Most of the buildings you'll see on arrival are new, with the older, simpler ones tucked away behind them. The 5.7km Ngong Ping 360 (www.np360.com.hk; adult/concession one way $58/28/45, return $88/45/68; 10am-6pm Mon-Fri, 10am-6.30pm Sat & Sun, 9am-6.30pm certain holidays) is a cable car linking Ngong Ping with the centre of Tung Chung (downhill and to the north). The attraction was shut after a 2007 accident, but should have reopened by the time you read this following safety reviews and upgrades.

The ride is well worth taking, offering spectacular views over the airport as it transports you from the high-rise apartments of Tung Chung to the more rural landscapes of Lantau. The lower station is just opposite the Tung Chung MTR station; the upper station is at the new 1.5-hectare Ngong Ping Village just west of the monastery complex. It includes several themed attractions: Walking with Buddha and the Monkey's Tale Theatre, both of which cost $35/18/28 for adults/concession, and the Ngong Ping Tea House. A variety of packages combine the cable-car rides with entrance tickets to the attractions. The journey takes 20 to 25 minutes, each glassed-in gondola carries 17 passengers and the system can move up to 3500 people per hour.

On a hill above the monastery sits the Tian Tan Buddha (10am-6pm), a seated representation of Lord Gautama some 23m high (or 26.4m with the lotus), or just under 34m if you include the podium. There are bigger Buddha statues elsewhere – notably the 71m-high Grand Buddha at Leshan in China's Sichuan province – but apparently these are not seated, outdoors or made of bronze. It weighs 202 tonnes, by the way. The large bell within the Buddha is controlled by computer and rings 108 times during the day to symbolise escape from what Buddhism terms the '108 troubles of mankind'.

The podium is composed of separate chambers on three different levels. On the first level are six statues of Bodhisattvas, each of which weighs around two tonnes. On the second level is a small museum (2985 5248; 10am-6pm) containing oil paintings and ceramic plaques of the Buddha's life and teachings. At busy times priority entry is given to those with meal tickets from the monastery's vegetarian restaurant, Po Lin Vegetarian Restaurant (p201).

It's well worth climbing the 260 steps for a closer look at the statue and surrounding views. The Buddha's Birthday (p17), a public holiday celebrated in late April or early May, is a lively time to visit, when thousands make the pilgrimage. Visitors are requested to observe some decorum in dress and behaviour. It is forbidden to bring meat or alcohol into the grounds.

A 2.5km concrete footpath to the left of the Buddha statue leads to the Lantau Tea Garden, the only one in Hong Kong. The tea bushes are pretty sparse and not worth a detour, but the garden is on the way to the Hongkong Bank Foundation SG Davis Hostel (p249) and Lantau Peak, and there are tea leaves for sale.

LANTAU PEAK Map p136
Known as Fung Wong Shan (Phoenix Mountain) in Cantonese, this 934m-high peak is the second-highest in Hong Kong after Tai Mo Shan (957m) in the New Territories. The view from the summit is absolutely stunning, and on a clear day it is possible to see Macau and Zhuhai, some 65km to the west.

If you're hiking the length or the first several stages of the Lantau Trail (p226) to Ngong Ping, you'll cross the peak. If you want to just climb up from Ngong Ping, the easiest and most comfortable way to make the climb is to spend the night at the SG Davis Hostel (p249), get up at the crack of dawn and pick up the signposted trail at the hostel that runs southeast to the peak. Many climbers get up earlier to reach the summit for sunrise; take a torch and wear an extra layer of clothes, as it can get pretty chilly at the top in the early hours, even in summer.

Another signposted trail leading east from the hostel will take you along the northern slopes of Lantau Peak to Po Lam Monastery at Tei Tong Tsai and then south through a valley leading to Tung Chung, from where you can catch the MTR back to Kowloon or Hong Kong or bus 3M to Mui Wo. This charming walk – if you ignore the airport to the north – also takes you past Lo Hon Monastery as well as Tung Chung Fort and Battery (p141).

top picks

HONG KONG FOR CHILDREN, FROM A TO Z

As well as Hong Kong's two theme parks, Ocean Park (p82) and Disneyland (p141), Hong Kong offers plenty of amazement for kids as well as adults:

- Avenue of the Stars evening lightshow (p95)
- Beaches (p223)
- Cityplaza's Ice Palace skating rink (p229)
- Hong Kong Heritage Museum (p125)
- Junk and sampan trips in Aberdeen Harbour (p83)
- Kowloon Park (p91)
- Noonday Gun (p73)
- Peak Tram (p283)
- Space Museum & Theatre (p91)
- Star Ferry (p273)
- Tsim Sha Tsui East Promenade (p95)
- Zoological & Botanical Gardens (p58)

LUNG TSAI NG GARDEN Map p136

🚌 1 from Mui Wo, 11 from Tung Chung, 21 from Ngong Ping

This magical garden southwest of Ngong Ping, with a lotus pond crossed by a rickety zigzag bridge, was built by a wealthy merchant in the 1930s in a small valley near where the village of Lung Tsai once stood. The site is rather derelict, but atmospheric nonetheless, and the gardens are in excellent condition. You can reach here via a water catchment path and trail from the Tai O Rd, a continuation of South Lantau Rd just west of Keung Shan. Alight from the bus after the Kwun Yam temple on Tai O Rd, which is about 2km past the turn-off for the Tian Tan Buddha. You'll see a country park sign and the start of the water catchment.

TAI O Map p136

🚌 1 from Mui Wo, 11 from Tung Chung, 21 from Ngong Ping

A century ago this mostly Tanka village on the west coast of Lantau was an important trading and fishing port, exporting salt and fish to China. As recently as the 1980s it traded in IIs (illegal immigrants) brought from China under cover of darkness by 'snakeheads' (smugglers in human cargo) in long narrow boats, sending back contraband such as refrigerators, radios and TVs to the mainland.

Today Tai O is in decline, except perhaps as a tourist destination. A few of the salt-pans still exist, but most have been filled in to build high-rise housing. Older people still make their living from duck farming, fishing, making the village's celebrated shrimp paste and processing salt fish, which you'll see (and smell) everywhere. It remains a popular place for locals to buy seafood – both fresh and dried.

Tai O is built partly on Lantau and partly on a tiny island about 15m from the shore. Until the mid-1990s the only way to cross was via a rope-tow ferry pulled by elderly Hakka women. That and the large number of sampans in the small harbour earned Tai O the nickname 'the Venice of Hong Kong'. Though the narrow iron Tai Chung footbridge now spans the canal, the rope-tow ferry is resurrected on some weekends and holidays: drop $1 in the box as you disembark. There are also brief river boat tours (☎ 9629 4581, 9645 6652; per 15/25min $10/20) departing from the footbridge.

Some of the traditional-style village houses still stand in the centre. A fire in 2000 destroyed many of Tai O's famed stilt houses on the waterfront, but when the government tried to raze the rest and relocate residents elsewhere, the move was strongly opposed. The few houses that escaped the fire remain. There are also a number of shanties, their corrugated-iron walls held in place by rope, and houseboats that haven't set sail for years – they'd capsize immediately if they tried.

The stilt houses and the local Kwan Tai temple dedicated to the god of war are on Kat Hing St. To reach them, cross the bridge from the mainland to the island, walk up Tai O Market St and go right at the Fook Moon Lam restaurant. There are a couple of other temples here, including an 18th-century one erected in honour of Hung Shing, patron of fisherfolk; it's on Shek Tsai Po St, about 600m west of the Fook Lam Moon restaurant.

SOUTH LANTAU RD Map p136

🚌 1 from Mui Wo & Tai O, 2 from Ngong Ping, 3 from Tung Chung

Just under 5km southwest of Mui Wo, Pui O is the first of several coastal villages along South Lantau Rd. Pui O has a decent beach, but as it's the closest one to Mui Wo it can get very crowded. The village has several restaurants, holiday flats galore and, in season, stalls renting bicycles. There's also a decent restaurant right on Pui O Beach called Ooh La La! (p201).

Cheung Sha (Long Sand), at over 3km Hong Kong's longest beach, is divided into 'upper' and 'lower' sections; a trail over a hillock links the two. Upper Cheung Sha, with occasional good surf, is the prettier and longer stretch and boasts a modern complex with changing rooms, toilets, showers and a snack bar. Lower Cheung Sha village has a beachfront restaurant, Stoep Restaurant (p201). Long Coast Seasports (☎ 2980 3222; www.longcoast .hk; 29 Lower Cheung Sha Village; ☒ 10am-7pm) is a water-sports centre offering windsurfing, sea kayaking and wakeboarding. Prices vary widely but basic windsurfing costs from $90/240/360 for an hour/half-day/day, while a single kayak rents for $60/180 for an hour/half-day. Beach umbrellas are also available from $50 a day. Some claim because of the Ventura effect on the wind from Tung Chung this is the best windsurfing in Hong Kong, especially from November to March. Long Coast also offers basic accommodation (p267).

The beach at Tong Fuk, the next village over from Cheung Sha, is not as nice, but the village has holiday flats, several shops

and a popular roadside barbecue restaurant called Gallery (p201). To the northwest is the not-so-scenic sprawl of Ma Po Ping Prison.

West of Tong Fuk, South Lantau Rd begins to climb the hills inland before crossing an enormous dam holding back the Shek Pik Reservoir, completed in 1963, which provides Lantau, Cheung Chau and parts of Hong Kong Island with drinking water. Just below the dam is the granddaddy of Lantau's trio of jails, Shek Pik Prison. Below the dam to the south but before the prison is another Bronze-Age rock carving unusual in that it is so far from the coastline.

The trail along the water-catchment area east of Shek Pik Reservoir, with picnic tables and barbecue pits, offers some of the easiest and most peaceful walking on Lantau. From here you can also pick up the switchback trail to Dog's Tooth Peak (539m), from where another trail heads north to Lantau Peak.

CHI MA WAN Map p136
🚢 Inter-island service from Mui Wo and Cheung Chau

Chi Ma Wan, the large peninsula south of Mui Wo that can be reached via the inter-island ferry, is a relatively remote part of

MUI WO (LANTAU)

0 _____ 300 m
0 _____ 0.2 miles

EATING 🍴	(p200)
Bahçe	6 C3
La Pizzeria	7 C3
Silvermine Beach Hotel 銀礦灣酒店	(see 16)

DRINKING 🍷	(p213)
China Beach Club	8 C1
China Bear	9 D3

SPORTS & ACTIVITIES	(p135)
Bike Shop 單車店	10 C3
Friendly Bicycle Shop 老友記	11 C3
Rental Bicycles 租單車站	12 B2
Rental Bicycles 租單車站	13 B2

SLEEPING 🛌	(pp266-8)
Mui Wo Accommodation Kiosks	14 C3
Mui Wo Inn 梅窩酒店	15 C1
Silvermine Beach Hotel 銀礦灣酒店	16 B2

TRANSPORT	(pp269-86)
Bus Terminal & Taxi Rank 巴士總站及的士站	17 C3
Ferries to Discovery Bay 往愉景灣渡輪	18 D3

To Silvermine Cave, Waterfall & Garden (3km)

Wang Tong

To Trappist Monastery (2.3km)

Silvermine Bay Beach

Wang Tong River

▲ Butterfly Hill (67m)

Barbecue Pits & Picnic Tables

Silvermine Bay

Mui Wo Rural Committee Rd

Silver River

Mui Wo Clinic

Ngan Kwong Wan Rd

Ngan Wan Estate

To Peng Chau (5km)

To Tsim Sha Tsui (15km); Central (15.5km)

To Chi Ma Wan (5km); Cheung Chau (8km)

South Lantau Rd

Mui Wo Ferry Pier

Ngan Wan Rd

Pier Rd

SIGHTS	(pp140-1)
Butterfly Hill Watchtower 蝴蝶山更樓	3 A1
Luk Tei Tong Watchtower 鹿地塘更樓	4 A3
Man Mo Temple 文武廟	5 A1

INFORMATION	
HSBC	1 C3
Post Office 郵局	2 B3

Lantau and an excellent area for hiking; just be sure to get a map (p295) as the trails are not always clearly defined or well marked.

The Chi Ma Wan ferry pier is on the northeast coast; the large complex just south of the pier is not a hostel but the Chi Ma Wan Correctional Institution. There's a decent beach to the south at Tai Long Wan. There's budget accommodation at the Jockey Club Mong Tung Wan Hostel (p267) on the peninsula's southwestern coast.

FAN LAU Map p136

Fan Lau (Divided Flow), a small peninsula on the southwestern tip of Lantau, has a couple of good beaches and the remains of Fan Lau Fort, built in 1729 to protect the channel between Lantau and the Pearl River estuary from pirates. It remained in operation until the end of the 19th century and was restored in 1985. The sea views from here are sterling.

To the southeast of the fort is an ancient stone circle. The origins and age of the circle are uncertain, but it probably dates from the Neolithic or early Bronze Age and may have been used in rituals.

The only way to reach Fan Lau is on foot. To get here from Tai O, walk south from the bus station for 250m and pick up stage No 7 of the coastal Lantau Trail (p226), a distance of about 8km. The trail then carries on to the northeast and Shek Pik for another 12km, where you can catch bus 1 back to Mui Wo.

TRAPPIST MONASTERY Map p136

☎ 2987 6292; Tai Shui Hang; 🚢 kaido from Peng Chau

Northeast of Mui Wo and south of Discovery Bay at Tai Shui Hang is the Roman Catholic Lady of Joy Abbey – better known as the Trappist Monastery. The monastery is known throughout Hong Kong for its cream-rich milk, sold in half-pint bottles everywhere, but, alas, the cows have been moved to the New Territories and Trappist Dairy Milk now comes from over the border in China.

The Trappists, a branch of the Cistercian order, were founded by a converted courtier at La Trappe in France in 1662 and gained a reputation as being one of the most austere religious communities in the Roman Catholic Church. The Lantau congregation was established at Beijing in the 19th century. All of the monks here now are local Chinese.

Trappist monks take a vow of absolute silence, and there are signs reminding visitors to keep radios and music players turned off and to speak in low tones. Give the guys a break; they're up at 3.15am and in bed by 8pm.

You can reach the monastery on foot by following a well-marked coastal trail from the northern end of Tung Wan Tau Rd in Mui Wo, but it's much easier to get here by kaido from Peng Chau, Lantau's little island neighbour to the west. For details, see p274.

MUI WO Map p139

🚢 Lantau

Mui Wo (Plum Nest), Lantau's main settlement 'capital', is on Silvermine Bay, so named for the silver mines that were once worked to the northwest along the Silver River. In fact, many foreign residents refer to Mui Wo as Silvermine Bay.

About a third of Lantau's population lives in the township of Mui Wo and its surrounding hamlets. There are several decent places to stay here and, though the options for eating and drinking are few, they are fine.

Silvermine Bay Beach, to the northwest of Mui Wo, has been cleaned up and rebuilt in recent years and is now an attractive place, with scenic views and opportunities for walking in the hills above. There's a complex with toilets, showers and changing rooms open from April to October.

If you have the time, consider hiking out to Silvermine Waterfall, the main feature of a picturesque garden near the old Silvermine Cave northwest of the town. The waterfall is quite a spectacle during the rainy season, when it swells and gushes; the cave was mined for silver in the latter half of the 19th century but has now been sealed off.

En route to the waterfall you'll pass the local Man Mo temple, originally built during the reign of Emperor Shen Zong (1573–1620) of the Ming dynasty and renovated a couple of times in the last century.

You can reach the temple, cave and waterfall by walking west along Mui Wo Rural Committee Rd and then following the marked path north. The 3km walk should take about an hour.

There are several old granite watchtowers in the area, including Luk Tei Tong Watchtower on the Silver River and Butterfly Hill

Watchtower further north. They were built in the late 19th century as safe houses and as coastal defences against pirates.

HONG KONG DISNEYLAND Map p136

☎ 1-830 830; www.hongkongdisneyland .com; adult/senior over 65/child 3-11 Mon-Fri $295/170/210, Sat, Sun & holidays $350/250/200; ⏰ 10am-9pm Apr-Oct, 10am-7pm Nov-Mar; MTR Disney Bay Resort

One of America's most famous cultural exports finally landed in Hong Kong in late 2005 and has been struggling ever since to attract the hoped-for number of visitors. The reason is simple: compared to its US and European sister parks this tiny 100-odd hectare park, divided into four main areas – Main Street USA, Fantasy land, Adventureland and Tomorrowland – offers a decidedly flat experience. Welcome to Anti-climaxland. Or perhaps that should be Lack-lustreland or maybe Merchandisingland.

There's a single real adrenaline-inducing roller coaster ride (Space Mountain) and the rest of the park is made up of lacklustre amusements rammed with Disney shops (selling toys way beyond the budgets of most mainland visitors, the park's target market) and fast-food outlets at every turn.

The full complement of Disney characters patrolling the park and the odd show re-creating great Disney moments from films such as *Pirates of the Caribbean* will doubtless please very young visitors, but take teenagers along and you may face a mutiny of your own making. The resurgent Ocean Park (p82) offers vastly more variety, thrills and amusement for all ages.

Disneyland is linked by rail with the MTR at the new futuristic Sunny Bay station on the Tung Chung line; passengers just cross the platform to board the dedicated train for Disneyland Resort station and the theme park. Journey times from Central/Kowloon/Tsing Yi stations are 10/21/24 minutes.

DISCOVERY BAY Map p136

🚤 Discovery Bay

Lying on the northeastern coast of Lantau, what locals have dubbed 'DB' is very much a world of its own, a dormitory community for professionals who commute to Central. Discovery Bay (Yue Ging Wan in Cantonese) has a fine stretch of sandy beach ringed by high-rises and more luxurious condominiums clinging to the headland to the north – but there is no pressing need to visit except to ogle at residents in their converted golf carts that cost $200,000 a pop. There is a handful of decent restaurants in Discovery Bay Plaza, just up from the ferry pier and the central plaza, and the 27-hole Discovery Bay Golf Club (see p224) perched in the hills to the southwest.

Until recently Discovery Bay existed in splendid isolation, linked only to the outside by ferries from Central, Lantau and Peng Chau and all but inaccessible from the rest of Lantau even on foot. Now buses make the run to and from Tung Chung and the airport at Chek Lap Kok via the Discovery Bay Tunnel and the North Lantau Hwy. A trail leading from the golf course will take you down to Silvermine Bay and the rest of Lantau in a couple of hours.

TUNG CHUNG Map p136

Tung Chung; 🚌 3M from Mui Wo, 11 from Tai O, 23 from Ngong Ping

In recent years change has come to Tung Chung, on Lantau's northern coast, at a pace that can only happen in Hong Kong. This previously all-but-inaccessible farming region, with the small village of Tung Chung at its centre, has seen Chek Lap Kok, the mountain across Tung Chung Bay, flattened to build Hong Kong's international airport and a New Town served by the MTR rise up.

As part of the territory's plans to solve the housing crisis, Tung Chung New Town has now become a 760-hectare residential estate. The targeted population of Tung Chung and the neighbouring New Town of Tai Ho is an astonishing 330,000 by 2012.

These developments and transport improvements have put an end to Tung Chung as a peaceful and secluded spot. But efforts have been made to protect Tung Chung Old Village. Buildings may rise no higher than three storeys and each floor can be no larger than 70 sq metres.

Annals record a settlement at Tung Chung as early as the Ming dynasty. There are several Buddhist establishments in the upper reaches of the valley, but the main attraction here is Tung Chung Fort (Tung Chung Rd; admission free; ⏰ 10am-5pm Wed-Mon), which dates back to 1832, when Chinese troops were garrisoned on Lantau. The Japanese briefly occupied the fort during WWII. Measuring 70m by 80m and enclosed by granite-block walls, it retains six of its muzzle-loading cannons pointing out to sea.

About 1km to the north are the ruins of Tung Chung Battery, which is a much smaller fort built in 1817. All that remains is an L-shaped wall facing the sea, with a gun emplacement in the corner. The ruins were only discovered in 1980, having been hidden for about a century by scrub.

Facing Tung Chung Bay to the southwest in the village of Sha Tsui Tau is double-roofed Hau Wong Temple, founded at the end of the Song dynasty. The temple contains a bell dating from 1765 and inscribed by the Qing-dynasty emperor Qian Long.

CHEUNG CHAU

Drinking & Nightlife p212; Eating p199; Sleeping p266

Once a refuge for pirates, Cheung Chau (Long Island; Map p143) supports a population of some 30,000 people on less than 2½ sq km of territory. Its modest dimensions and winding pathways past temples, beaches, fishing boats and mini chandleries make a delightful destination for a day trip.

Fishing and aquaculture are important industries for a large number of the island's inhabitants, some of whom still live on junks and sampans anchored in the harbour. Bring your camera for some of the best shots of traditional maritime life on the South China coast.

TRANSPORT – CHEUNG CHAU

Ferry Services from Central leave from pier 5 of the Outlying Islands ferry terminal. Ferries can also be taken from Mui Wo and Chi Ma Wan on Lantau and from Peng Chau. Additionally, regular *kaidos* operate between Cheung Chau village (Sampan pier) and Sai Wan in the south of the island.

Archaeological evidence, including a 3000-year-old rock carving uncovered just below the Warwick Hotel, suggests that Cheung Chau, like Lamma and Lantau, was inhabited at least as early as the Neolithic period. The island had a thriving fishing community at the time, and the early inhabitants – Hakka and Cantonese settlers – supplemented their income with smuggling and piracy.

Cheung Chau boasts several interesting temples, the most important being Pak Tai Temple, which hosts the annual Bun Festival, *the* red-letter day on Cheung Chau (see boxed text, below). The island has a few worthwhile beaches, and there are some relatively easy walks, including the one described on p145. When Canton (present-day Guangzhou) and Macau opened up to the West in the 16th century, Cheung Chau was a perfect spot from which to prey on passing ships. The infamous and powerful 18th-century pirate Cheung Po Tsai is said to have had his base here, and you can still visit the cave where he supposedly stashed his booty at the southwestern tip of the island.

CHEUNG CHAU'S BUN FESTIVAL

The annual Bun Festival (*Tàai-pìng chìng jìu* in Cantonese; www.cheungchau.org), which honours the god Pak Tai and is unique to the island, takes place over eight days in late April or early May, traditionally starting on the sixth day of the fourth moon. It is a Taoist festival, and there are four days of religious observances.

The festival is renowned for its bun towers, bamboo scaffolding up to 20m high that are covered with sacred rolls. If you visit Cheung Chau a week or so before the festival, you'll see the towers being built in front of Pak Tai Temple.

In the past, hundreds of people would scramble up the towers at midnight on the designated day to grab one of the buns for good luck. The higher the bun, the greater the luck, so everyone tried to reach the top. In 1978 a tower collapsed under the weight of the climbers, injuring two-dozen people. Now everyone must remain on terra firma and the buns are handed out.

Sunday, the third day of the festival, features a procession of floats, stilt walkers, and people dressed as characters from Chinese legends and opera. Most interesting are the colourfully dressed 'floating children', who are carried through the streets on long poles, cleverly wired to metal supports hidden under their clothing. The supports include footrests and a padded seat.

Offerings are made to the spirits of all the fish and livestock killed and consumed over the previous year. A priest reads out a decree calling on the villagers to abstain from killing any animals during the four-day festival, and no meat is consumed.

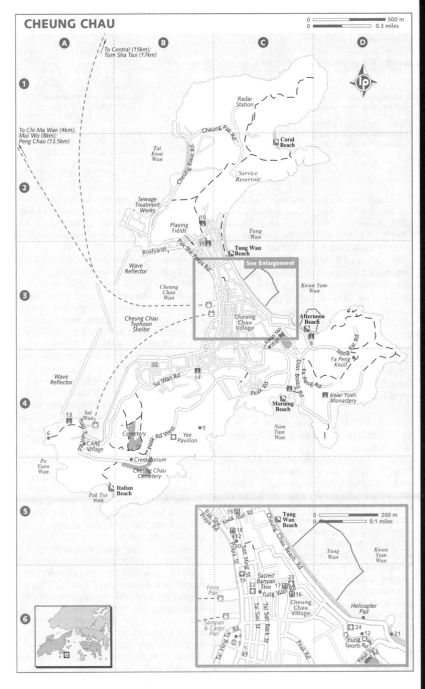

CHEUNG CHAU

0 ————— 500 m
0 ————— 0.3 miles

A **B** **C** **D**

1

To Central (15km);
Tsim Sha Tsui (17km)

Radar
Station

Coral
Beach

To Chi Ma Wan (4km);
Mui Wo (8km);
Peng Chau (13.5km)

*Tai
Kwai
Wan*

Cheung Pak Rd

Service
Reservoir

2

Sewage
Treatment
Works

*Tung
Wan*

Playing
Fields

10

Boatyards

**Tung Wan
Beach**

Wave
Reflector

Pak She Praya Rd

See Enlargement

*Cheung
Chau
Wan*

*Kwun Yam
Wan*

3

Cheung Chau
Typhoon
Shelter

Cheung
Chau
Village

**Afternoon
Beach**

*Ming
Fa Peng
Knoll*

Wave
Reflector

Sai Wan Rd

14

Kwun Yam Wan Rd

Don Bosco Rd

Fa Peng Rd

Kwai Yuen
Monastery

4

13

*Sai
Wan*

Peak Rd West

Peak Rd

**Morning
Beach**

*Nam
Tam
Wan*

6

CARE
Village

Cemetery

5

Yee
Pavilion

*Po
Yuen
Wan*

Crematorium

Cheung Chau
Cemetery

*Pak Tso
Wan*

**Italian
Beach**

5

0 ————— 200 m
0 ————— 0.1 miles

15

Kwok Man Rd

**Tung
Wan
Beach**

Pak She Praya Rd

18

San Hing St

2

Cheung Chau Beach Rd

*Tung
Wan*

*Kwun
Yam
Wan*

20

19

Sacred
Banyan
Tree

23

Ferry
Pier

22

17

16

Tung Wan Rd

Tai San St

Tai San Back St

Cheung
Chau
Village

Helicopter
Pad

6

Sampan
& Cargo
Pier

Tai Hing Tai Rd

3

Praya Rd

24

12

21

Cheung Chau
Sports Rd

Kwun Yam Rd

143

CHEUNG CHAU

Cheung Chau is a bone-shaped island 10km southwest of Hong Kong Island and just off the Chi Ma Wan peninsula on southeastern Lantau. Cheung Chau village, where the ferry docks, is the only real settlement on the island.

There is an HSBC (☎ 2981 1127; Lot 1116, Praya South) branch southeast of the cargo pier, and an ATM (19A Pak She Praya Rd) north of the ferry pier. The post office (2A Tai Hing Tai St) is in the market complex. The market (☼ 8.30am-5pm) is a hive of activity, with meat and fish being sold on the ground floor and a variety of other goods upstairs. There is no transport on Cheung Chau, but you can rent bicycles from a kiosk (☎ 2981 0227) at the northern end of Praya St for $10/30 per hour/day and new two-seat pedal bikes for $30/90.

PAK TAI TEMPLE Map p143
☎ 2981 0663; Pak She Fourth Lane; ☼ 7am-5pm;
🚶 Cheung Chau

This colourful and recently renovated temple from 1783 is the oldest on the island and is the focus of the annual Cheung Chau Bun Festival (p142) in late April or early May. It is dedicated to the Taoist deity Pak Tai, the 'Supreme Emperor of the Dark Heaven', military protector of the state, guardian of peace and order, and protector of fisherfolk. Legend tells that early settlers from Guangdong province brought an image of Pak Tai with them to Cheung Chau and, when the statue was carried through the village, Cheung Chau was spared the plague that had decimated the populations of nearby islands. A temple dedicated to the saviour was built six years later.

BEACHES Map p143
🚶 Cheung Chau

Tung Wan Beach, Cheung Chau's longest and most popular (though not its prettiest)

beach lies at the end of Tung Wan Rd, due east of the ferry pier. The best part of Tung Wan is the far southern end, which is a great area for windsurfing. Just south of Tung Wan Beach, Kwun Yam Wan Beach is known to English speakers as Afternoon Beach and is a great spot for windsurfing.

Windsurfing has always been an extremely popular pastime on Cheung Chau, and Hong Kong's only Olympic gold-medal winner to date, Lee Lai-shan, who took the top prize in windsurfing at the 1996 Olympics in Atlanta, grew up here. At the northern end of Afternoon Beach, the Cheung Chau Windsurfing Water Sports Centre (☎ 2981 8316; www .ccwindc.com.hk; 1 Hak Pai Rd; ☼ 10am-7pm) rents sailboards for between $90 and $150 per hour, as well as single/double kayaks for $60/100. There are also windsurfing courses available for $700 per day. The best time for windsurfing here is between October and December.

At the southeastern end of Afternoon Beach a footpath leads uphill past a Kwun Yam temple, which is dedicated to the goddess of mercy. Continue up the footpath and look for the sign to the Fa Peng Knoll. The concrete footpath takes you past quiet, tree-shrouded villas.

From the knoll you can walk down to signposted Don Bosco Rd; it leads due south to rocky Nam Tam Wan (also known as Morning Beach), where swimming is possible. If you ignore Don Bosco Rd and continue walking west, you'll come to the intersection of Peak and Kwun Yam Wan Rds. Kwun Yam Wan Rd and its extension, School Rd, will take you back to Cheung Chau village.

Peak Rd is the main route to the island's cemetery in the southwestern part of the island; you'll pass several pavilions along the way built for coffin bearers making the hilly climb. Once at the cemetery it's worth dropping down to Pak Tso Wan (Italian Beach), a sandy, isolated spot that is good for swimming. At this point Peak Rd West becomes Tsan Tuen Rd, which continues north to Sai Wan.

CHEUNG CHAU TYPHOON SHELTER
Map p143

🔊 Cheung Chau

A great way to see the harbour and soak up the fishing village atmosphere is to charter a sampan for half an hour (expect to pay $50 to $80 depending on the day, the season and the demand). Most sampans congregate around the cargo pier, but virtually any small boat you see in the harbour can be hired as a water taxi. Just wave and two or three will come forward. Be sure to agree on the fare first.

CHEUNG CHAU VILLAGE Map p143

🔊 Cheung Chau

The island's main settlement lies along the narrow strip of land connecting the headlands to the north and the south. The waterfront is a bustling place and the maze of streets and alleyways that make up the village are filled with old Chinese-style houses and tumble-down shops selling everything from plastic buckets to hell money. The streets close to the waterfront are pungent with the smell of incense and fish hung out to dry in the sun.

CHEUNG PO TSAI CAVE Map p143

🔊 Cheung Chau

This cave, on the southwestern peninsula of the island, is said to have been the favourite hideout of the notorious pirate Cheung Po Tsai, who once commanded a flotilla of 600 junks and had a private army of 4000 men. He surrendered to the Qing government in 1810 and became an official himself, but his treasure is said to remain hidden here.

It's a 2km walk from Cheung Chau village along Sai Wan Rd, or take a kaido (adult/child $3/2 – but dependent on passenger numbers) from the cargo ferry pier to the pier at Sai Wan. From here the walk is less than 200m (uphill).

TIN HAU TEMPLES Map p143

🔊 Cheung Chau

Cheung Chau has four temples dedicated to Tin Hau, the empress of heaven and

patroness of seafarers. Pak She Tin Hau Temple lies 100m northwest of the Pak Tai Temple. Nam Tan Wan Tin Hau temple is just north of Morning Beach; Tai Shek Hau Tin Hau temple is to the west on Sai Wan Rd. Sai Wan Tin Hau temple is west of Sai Wan (Western Bay), on the southwestern tip of the island. You can walk there or catch a kaido from the cargo pier.

ISLAND LIFE
Walking Tour

1 Cheung Chau Ferry Pier Head north along Praya St, where a row of mostly seafood restaurants face the harbour. Praya St becomes Pak She Praya Rd after the turn-off for Kwok Man Rd, and from here you can look out at the many junks and sampans moored in the harbour and typhoon shelter.

2 Pak Tai Temple At Pak She Fourth Lane, turn right and shortly you'll see the colourful temple, built in 1783. The Pak She Tin Hau Temple is behind, about 100m to the northwest. The temple is within the grounds of the Chung Shak-Hei home for the aged.

3 Pak San St & San Hing St You'll pass traditional Chinese houses and several shops selling traditional Chinese medicine, incense and paper hell money to be burned in memory of the dead. Further south, and on the left at the intersection of Pak She St and Kwok Man Rd, is a small Tou Tei shrine, dedicated to the overworked earth god.

4 Rock Carving Turn right and walk along Cheung Chau Beach Rd to a 3000-year-old rock carving of two identical geometric designs, just below the Warwick Hotel. Behind the hotel is Cheung Chau Sports Rd; walk up and when you see a pavilion, turn right onto Kwun Yam Wan Rd and from there onto Peak Rd, which takes you around to the other side of the pavilion.

WALK FACTS

Start Cheung Chau ferry pier (ferry from pier 5 in Central)
End Sai Wan (kaido to Cheung Chau ferry pier)
Distance 4.5km
Time 2½ hours
Fuel stop Hometown Teahouse

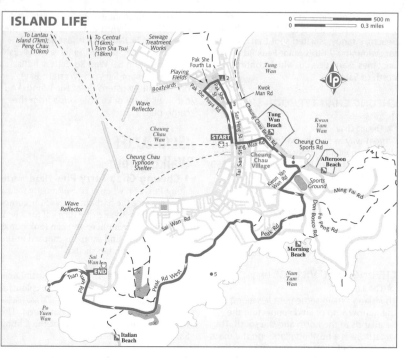

ISLAND LIFE

To Lantau
Island (7km);
Peng Chau
(10km)

To Central
(16km);
Tsim Sha Tsui
(18km)

Sewage
Treatment
Works

Pak She
Fourth La

Playing
Fields

Boatyards

Tung
Wan

Kwok
Man Rd

Wave
Reflector

Tung
Wan
Beach

Kwun
Yam
Wan

Cheung
Chau

Cheung Chau
Sports Rd

Afternoon
Beach

Cheung Chau
Typhoon
Shelter

START

Cheung
Chau
Village

Sports
Ground

Ming Fai Rd

Wave
Reflector

Sai Wan Rd

Peak Rd

Morning
Beach

Sai
Wan

END

Peak Rd West

Nam
Tam
Wan

Po
Yuen
Wan

Italian
Beach

0 ———— 500 m
0 ———— 0.3 miles

(Map p147)

5 Cheung Chau Meteorological Station
Follow Peak Rd West about 500m past Kam
Kong Primary School to the Meteorological Station, offering splendid views of the island and
sea. A bit further south and through the trees
to the left is Cheung Chau Cemetery, affording a
quiet and solemn view out to sea. Stay left
where the path splits in the cemetery.

6 Cheung Po Tsai Cave Follow the signs
for Sai Wan and signs to the Cheung Po Tsai Cave
(p145), a place where pirates of old were supposed to have buried their booty. Return via
the well-signposted *kaido* (adult/child $3/2)
back to Cheung Chau village. Alternatively,
follow Sai Wan Rd around the bay and north
back to the village (20 to 30 minutes).

PENG CHAU

Tiny Peng Chau (Map p147) is fairly flat and
not especially beautiful, but it does have its
charms. It is perhaps the most traditionally
Chinese of the Outlying Islands, with narrow
alleyways, crowded housing, a covered wet
market near the ferry pier, a couple of small
but important temples, and interesting shops

selling everything from Thai goods to New
Age products. There are also a few closet-
sized restaurants whose sea views have unfortunately been ruined by a massive concrete
'wave reflector' and promenade running along
the shore south of the ferry pier.

The appeal of visiting Peng Chau lies in
slacking your pace to match the island's, and
soaking up the traditional sights and sounds,
such as the clatter of mah jong tiles with the
plaintive accompaniment of Cantonese opera
leaking from old transistors.

Until recently the island's economy was
supported by fishing and some cottage industries, notably the manufacture of porcelain,
furniture and metal tubing. These manufacturing industries are now all but dead, hav-

TRANSPORT – PENG CHAU

Ferry Services from Central leave from pier 6 of the
Outlying Islands ferry terminal. Ferries also depart
from Mui Wo and Chi Ma Wan on Lantau and from
Cheung Chau. Additionally, regular *kaidos* operate
to Peng Chau from the Trappist Monastery and
Discovery Bay on Lantau.

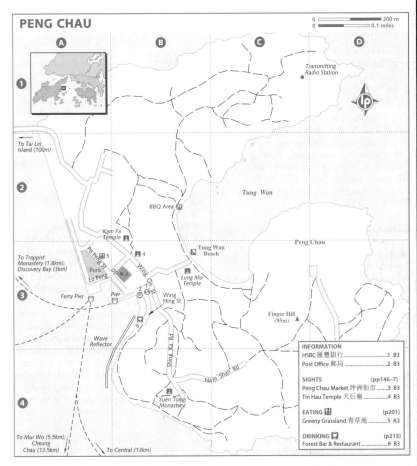

PENG CHAU

To Tai Lei Island (100m)

Transmitting Radio Station

Tung Wan

BBQ Area

Kam Fa Temple

Tung Wan Beach

Peng Chau

To Trappist Monastery (1.8km); Discovery Bay (3km)

Park to Peng

Lung Mo Temple

Ferry Pier

Pier

Wing Hing St

Finger Hill (95m)

Wave Reflector

Shing Ka Rd

Nam Shan Rd

Yuen Tong Monastery

To Mui Wo (5.5km); Cheung Chau (13.5km)

To Central (13km)

INFORMATION		
HSBC 匯豐銀行	1	B3
Post Office 郵局	2	B3
SIGHTS	(pp146–7)	
Peng Chau Market 坪洲街市	3	B3
Tin Hau Temple 天后廟	4	B3
EATING	(p201)	
Greeny Grassland 青草地	5	A3
DRINKING	(p213)	
Forest Bar & Restaurant	6	B3

ing moved to mainland China, though you will find a couple of porcelain and gift shops on Wing Hing and Wing On Sts. There's a branch of HSBC (☎ 2983 0383; 1 Wing Hing St; ☼ Mon, Wed & Fri) nearby. The post office is due west near the start of the promenade.

Looking not unlike a plumped-out horse-shoe jettisoned from Lantau's northeast coast, Peng Chau is just under 1 sq km in area. It is inhabited by around 7000 people, making it far more densely populated than its larger neighbour.

There are no cars on Peng Chau, and you can walk around it easily in an hour. Climbing the steps up to Finger Hill (95m), the island's highest point, and topped with the winged Chinese-style Fung Ping Pavilion, offers some light exercise and excellent views. To get to it from the ferry pier, walk up Lo Peng St, turn right

at the Tin Hau temple, containing a century-old 2.5m-long whale bone blackened by incense smoke, and walk south along Wing On St. This gives way to Shing Ka Rd, and Nam Shan Rd leads from here east up to Finger Hill. The water at otherwise-pleasant Tung Wan Beach, a five-minute walk from the ferry pier, is too dirty for swimming and is not served by lifeguards.

MA WAN

Ma Wan (Map pp50–1, Map p136) was once famous as the gateway to Kowloon, where foreign ships would drop anchor before entering Chinese waters. If you want to get away from it all, Ma Wan is hardly the place to go. It's got a couple of temples devoted to Tin Hau, a long beach on the east coast at Tung Wan and

TRANSPORT – MA WAN

Ferry Services from Central leave from pier 2 of the Outlying Islands ferry terminal. Ferries also depart from Tsuen Wan. The ferry pier is south of Tsuen Wan West KCR station (Map pp50–1).

a massive, high-end residential community called Park Island. Basically you're here to view some startling engineering feats.

Ma Wan is a flat, rapidly developing island off the northeastern tip of Lantau. It is effectively the 'anchor' for the Lantau Link between Hong Kong's largest island and the New Territories.

LANTAU LINK BRIDGES
Map pp50–1, Map p136

🏯 **Ma Wan**

The real reason to come to Ma Wan is to take in the enormity of Tsing Ma Bridge to the east (and, to a lesser extent, Kap Shui Mun Bridge on the west), which forms the rail and road link connecting Lantau with the New Territories via Tsing Yi Island. While catapulting Ma Wan headlong into the next century, the bridge has guaranteed an end to the island's solitude; it now serves as a huge platform for the civil engineering works overhead. Neighbouring Tsing Yi has a special viewing platform for those

particularly interested in seeing the bridge up close (below).

TSING YI

Tsing Yi (Map pp50–1), disfigured by oil depots and extended by land reclamation, serves as a stepping stone for the gigantic Tsing Ma Bridge, at 1377m the world's longest suspension bridge. Don't even think about visiting the beaches.

Tsing Yi is the large island to the east of Ma Wan on the MTR's Tung Chung and the Airport Express lines.

LANTAU LINK VISITORS CENTRE
Map pp50–1

☎ 2495 5825, 2495 7583; admission free; ⏰ 10am-5pm Mon, Tue, Thu & Fri, 10am-6.30pm Sat & Sun; MTR Tsing Yi, 🚐 green minibus 308M
The Lantau Link Visitors Centre and its viewing platform (admission free; ⏰ 7am-10.30pm Sun-Fri, 7am-1.30am Sat) is where you can take in the enormity of Tsing Yi Bridge and the Lantau Link, the combined road and rail transport connection between the New Territories and Lantau. The centre contains models, photographs and videos of the construction process – very much a crowd-pleaser for train spotters and the hard-hat brigade.

The visitors centre is in the northwest corner of Tsing Yi Island just to the south

THE PINK DOLPHINS OF THE PEARL RIVER

Between 100 and 200 misnamed Chinese white dolphins *(Sousa chinensis)* – they are actually bubble-gum pink – inhabit the coastal waters around Hong Kong, finding the brackish waters of the Pearl River estuary to be the perfect habitat. Unfortunately these glorious mammals, which are also called Indo-Pacific humpback dolphins, are being threatened by environmental pollution, and their numbers are dwindling.

The threat comes in many forms, but the most prevalent – and direct – dangers are sewage, chemicals, over-fishing and boat traffic. Some 200,000 cu metres of untreated sewage are dumped into the western harbour every day, and high concentrations of chemicals such as DDT have been found in tissue samples taken from some of the dolphins. Several dolphins have been entangled in fishing nets and, despite the dolphins' skill at sensing and avoiding surface vessels, some have collided with boats.

The dolphins' habitat has also been diminished by the erosion of the natural coastline of Lantau Island during the construction of Hong Kong International Airport, which required land reclamation of 9.5 sq km of seabed and the destruction of many kilometres of natural coastline. The North Lantau Hwy also consumed about 10km of the natural coastline. The Hong Kong Disneyland theme park also required large amounts of reclamation in Penny's Bay.

Hong Kong Dolphinwatch (Map p92; ☎ 2984 1414; www.hkdolphinwatch.com; 15th fl, Middle Block, 1528A Star House, 3 Salisbury Rd, Tsim Sha Tsui) was founded in 1995 to raise awareness of these wonderful creatures and promote responsible ecotourism. It offers 2½-hour cruises (adult/student & senior/child under 12 $360/255/180) to see the pink dolphins in their natural habitat every Wednesday, Friday and Sunday year-round. Guides assemble in the lobbies of the Mandarin Oriental in Central at 8.30am and the Kowloon Hotel in Tsim Sha Tsui at 9am for the bus to Tung Chung via the Tsing Ma Bridge, from where the boat departs; the tours return at 1pm or 1.30pm. About 97% of the cruises result in the sighting of at least one dolphin; if none are spotted, passengers are offered a free trip.

TRANSPORT – TSING YI

MTR Tsing Yi station on Tung Chung line.

Airport Express Tsing Yi station for services from Hong Kong and Kowloon or the airport.

Green minibus For the Lantau Viewing Platform and Visitor Centre take minibus 308M from Tsing Yi MTR station (exit A1).

of Ting Kau Bridge. To reach it, take the MTR to Tsing Yi station, use exit No A1 and board minibus 308M in Maritime Sq, which will drop you off at the centre's car park.

TUNG LUNG CHAU

Standing guard at the eastern entrance to Victoria Harbour is the island of Tung Lung Chau (Map pp50–1), or 'East Dragon Island', whose position was once considered strategic enough for protection. According to the experts the island is Hong Kong's premier spot for rock climbing (p223).

Tung Lung Chau lies to the south of the Clearwater Bay Peninsula across the narrow Fat Tong Mun channel. To the west is Shek O and Big Wave Bay on Hong Kong Island's east coast. In addition, the northwest tip of the island boasts an important rock carving of what is generally thought to be a dragon. It is quite possibly the oldest such carving

TRANSPORT – TUNG LUNG CHAU

Ferry *Kaidos* run from Sai Wan Ho on Hong Kong Island via Joss House Bay on the Clearwater Bay Peninsula in the New Territories. There are single sailings on Tuesday and Thursday, with more regular services only on weekends and public holidays. A weekend and holiday service also operates from Sam Ka Tsuen near Yau Tong MTR.

in the territory and it is certainly the largest, measuring 2.4m by 1.8m. The ferry pier is close by.

TUNG LUNG FORT Map pp50–1
🏛 Tung Lung Chau

Tung Lung Fort, on the northeastern corner of the island, was built in the late 17th or early 18th century and was attacked a number of times by pirate bands before being abandoned in 1810. The fort once consisted of 15 guardhouses and was armed with eight cannons, but little of it remains today except for the outline of the exterior walls. There's an information centre (🕙 9am-4pm Wed-Mon) here.

PO TOI

Eating p201

Po Toi (Map pp50–1) is a solid favourite of weekend holiday-makers with their own seagoing transport. They frequent the seafood restaurants beyond the jetty at Tai Wan, the main settlement, in the island's southwest.

Po Toi is the largest of a group of four or five islands – one is little more than a huge rock – off the southeastern coast of Hong Kong Island. Hong Kong's territorial border lies just 2km to the south.

There's some decent walking on Po Toi, a tiny Tin Hau temple across the bay from the pier, and, on the southern coast, rock formations that (supposedly) look like a palm tree, a tortoise and a monk, and some mysterious rock carvings resembling stylised animals and fish. You can see everything here in an hour.

TRANSPORT – PO TOI

Ferry *Kaidos* run to the ferry pier from Aberdeen and Stanley on Tuesdays, Thursdays, weekends and public holidays.

BLUELIST[1] (blu,list) *v.*
to recommend a travel experience.
What's your recommendation? www.lonelyplanet.com/bluelist

SHOPPING

top picks

- **Alan Chan Creations** (p168)
  Stylish souvenirs from the man who has designed almost everything in Hong Kong.
- **Beatniks** (p166)
  Cool vintage streetwear.
- **Chine Gallery** (p157)
  Top-of-the-crop antique furniture and rugs.
- **Chinese Arts & Crafts** (p164)
  The best place in town for quality Chinese bric-a-brac.
- **Curio Alley** (p168)
  The strip for low-cost trinkets and mementos.
- **Joyce** (p159)
  A tight selection of the best local and international high fashion in one store.
- **Lulu Cheung** (p160)
  Locally designed, sophisticated, understated style.
- **Shanghai Tang** (p160)
  Retro Chinese style for him and her. The accessories and other knick-knacks make perfect presents.
- **Wattis Fine Art** (p158)
  The best place in Hong Kong for antique maps, prints and photographs.

SHOPPING

Hong Kong has long since lost its reputation as a bargain hunter's paradise. While you can still find some bargains, these days you can get pretty much anything that's on sale here a notch cheaper just over the border in China.

Hong Kong trades on its reputation as a place of neon-lit retail pilgrimage, the home of giant temples to consumption where shopping is practically a religion. The city is positively stuffed with glitzy shopping malls towering above the streets.

Any international brand worthy of its logo has at least one outlet here, and there are also a few local brands worth spending your money on. Clothing (off the peg or tailored), shoes, jewellery, luggage and, to a lesser degree nowadays, cameras and electronic goods are the city's strong suites. Excellent art and antiques shops also abound.

Shopping is made very easy here. Opening hours are long and the government has so far resisted introducing a sales tax, so the marked price is the price you'll pay. Credit cards are widely accepted, except in markets, but it's rare for traders to accept travellers cheques or foreign currency as payment. Sales assistants in department or chain stores rarely have any leeway to give discounts, but you can try bargaining in owner-operated stores and certainly in markets.

Hong Kong may be made for shopping but it has to be said that after the first impressions of endless shopping possibilities fade, all this retail floor space starts blending into a rather homogenous whole. The same names do tend to crop up in the countless sleek but identikit malls dotted around the city.

You'll find disappointingly few made-in-Hong Kong, cutting-edge fashion lines or boutiques. Most of the designers with local connections either trained or made their names (and tend to concentrate their activities) overseas. In short, there's not much of a home-grown fashion scene, thanks to the size of the market and an innate conservatism among local shoppers.

The Hong Kong Tourism Board (HKTB) produces a handy 300-page book called *A Guide to Quality Shops and Restaurants*, which lists shops that are HKTB members. It is available for free at its information outlets (p301).

SHOPPING AREAS

The main shopping areas are Central and Causeway Bay on Hong Kong Island and Tsim Sha Tsui in Kowloon. Nathan Rd in Tsim Sha Tsui is the main tourist strip, and one of very few places where you'll find merchants poised to rip you off (see boxed text, p167), especially when buying electronic goods or photographic equipment. Central is good for clothing (usually midrange to top end), as well as books, cameras and antiques. Causeway Bay has a lot of department stores and low-end clothing outlets. For market shopping, see p156.

Warehouse sales and factory extras can be found along Granville Rd in Tsim Sha Tsui, in Causeway Bay and on Ap Lei Chau, the island opposite Aberdeen. Most of these deal in ready-to-wear garments, but there are a few that also sell carpets, shoes, leather goods, jewellery and imitation antiques. Often prices aren't that much less than in retail shops, and it's important to check purchases carefully, as refunds are rarely given and many articles are factory seconds and imperfect.

OPENING HOURS

In the Central and Western districts, daily shop hours are generally from 10am to 7.30pm, and in Causeway Bay and Wan Chai many will stay open until 9.30pm or 10pm. In Tsim Sha Tsui, Mong Kok and Yau Ma Tei, they close around 9pm, and in Tsim Sha Tsui East at 7.30pm. Some smaller shops close for major holidays – sometimes for up to a week – especially during Chinese New Year. Many also close on Sunday. We've included opening hours in reviews only where the hours differ dramatically from these standard times.

Winter sales are during the first three weeks in January; summer sales are in late June and early July.

BARGAINING

Bargaining is a way of life at retail outlets throughout Hong Kong, with the exception of department stores and clothing chain shops, where the prices marked are the prices paid. Some visitors operate on the theory that you can get the goods for half the price originally quoted. Many Hong Kong residents believe that if you can bargain something down that low, then you shouldn't be buying from that shop anyway. If the business is that crooked – and many are, particularly in the Tsim Sha Tsui tourist ghetto – it will probably find other ways to cheat you (such as selling you electronic goods with missing components or no international warranty).

Price tags are supposed be displayed on all goods. If you can't find a price tag, you've undoubtedly entered one of those business establishments with 'flexible' – ie rip-off – prices.

DUTY FREE

The only imported goods on which there is duty in Hong Kong are alcohol, tobacco, perfumes, cosmetics, cars and certain petroleum products. In general, almost anything – from cameras and electronics to clothing and jewellery – will be cheaper when you buy it outside duty-free shops.

WARRANTIES & GUARANTEES

Every guarantee should carry a complete description of the item (including the model and serial numbers), as well as the date of purchase, the name and address of the shop it was purchased from, and the shop's official name chop (stamp).

Many imported items come with a warranty registration with the words 'Guarantee only valid in Hong Kong'. If it's a well-known brand, you can often return this card to the importer in Hong Kong to get a warranty card for your home country.

A common practice is to sell grey-market equipment (ie imported by somebody other than the official local agent). Such equipment may have no guarantee at all or the guarantee may only be valid in the country of manufacture (which will probably be either China or Japan).

REFUNDS & EXCHANGES

Most shops are loath to give refunds, but they can usually be persuaded to exchange purchases that haven't been soiled or tampered with. Make sure you get a detailed receipt that enumerates the goods, as well as the amount and payment method.

There is really no reason to put a deposit on anything unless it is an article of clothing being made for you or you've ordered a new pair of glasses. Some shops might ask for a deposit if you're ordering an unusual item that's not normally stocked, but this isn't a common practice.

SHIPPING GOODS

Goods can be sent home by post, and some shops will package and post the goods for you, especially if it's a large item. It's a good idea to find out whether you will have to clear the goods at the country of destination. If the goods are fragile, it is sensible to buy 'all risks' insurance. Make sure you keep all the receipts.

Smaller items can be shipped from the post office. United Parcel Service (UPS; ☎ 2735 3535) also offers services from Hong Kong to some 40 countries worldwide. It ships by air and accepts parcels weighing up to 70kg. DHL (☎ 2400 3388) is another option.

WHAT TO BUY
Antiques

Hong Kong has a rich and colourful array of Asian, especially Chinese, antiques on offer, but serious buyers will restrict themselves to the reputable antique shops and auction houses only; Hong Kong imports many forgeries and expert reproductions from China and Southeast Asia. Just remember that most of the really good pieces are sold through the auction houses such as Christie's (p158), especially at its auctions in spring and autumn.

Most of Hong Kong Island's antique shops are bunched along Wyndham St and Hollywood Rd in Central and Sheung Wan. The shops at the western end of Hollywood Rd tend to be cheaper in price and carry more dubious 'antiques'. Some of them stock a range of old books and magazines, Chinese propaganda posters, badges from the Cultural Revolution and so on. It's easy to get lost in some of these dusty holes in the wall, but be cautious – tread carefully through this minefield of reproductions. When it comes to buying antiques and curios, there are relatively few places of interest in Kowloon.

For Chinese handicrafts and other goods (hand-carved wooden pieces, ceramics, paintings, cloisonné, silk garments), the main places to go are the large China-run emporiums scattered throughout the territory, such as Chinese Arts & Crafts (p164) and Yue Hwa Chinese Products Emporium (p169).

Carpets

While carpets are not a huge bargain in Hong Kong, it has a good selection of both new and antique silk and wool carpets. Imported carpets from Afghanistan, China, India, Iran, Pakistan, Tibet and Turkey are widely available; some of the new Iranian ones with contemporary designs are stunning. The best carpets have a larger number of knots per square inch (over 550) and are richer in detail and colour than cheaper carpets. Older carpets are dyed with natural vegetable dye. Silk carpets are often hung on the wall rather than used on the floor. The bulk of Hong Kong's carpet and rug shops are clustered around Wyndham St in Central, although there are some large retailers located in Wan Chai as well.

Clothing

The best places to find designer fashions and top-end boutiques are in the big shopping centres and malls, especially Landmark (p162) in Central, Pacific Place (p164) in Admiralty and Festival Walk (p170) in Kowloon Tong. The best hunting grounds for warehouse sales and factory extras are generally in Tsim Sha Tsui at the eastern end of Granville Rd; check out Austin Ave and Chatham Rd South as well. On Hong Kong Island, Jardine's Bazaar in Causeway Bay has low-cost garments and there are several sample shops and places to pick up cheap jeans in Lee Garden Rd. The street markets (see boxed text, p156) in Temple St in Yau Ma Tei and Tung Choi St in Mong Kok have the cheapest clothes. You may also try Li Yuen St East and Li Yuen St West, two narrow alleyways linking Des Voeux Rd Central with Queen's Rd Central. They are a jumble of inexpensive clothing, handbags, backpacks and costume jewellery.

For midpriced items, Causeway Bay and Tsim Sha Tsui, particularly east of Nathan Rd, are good hunting grounds.

Although many people still frequent Hong Kong's tailors, getting a suit or dress made is no longer a great bargain. Remember that you usually get what you pay for; the material is often good but the work may be shoddy. Most tailors will require a 50% nonrefundable deposit and the more fittings you have, the better the result.

Computers

Hong Kong is a popular place to buy personal computers and laptops. While prices are competitive, it is also important to pay careful attention to what you buy and where you buy it.

You may have your own ideas about what kind of computer you want to buy, but if you're just visiting Hong Kong you would be wise to choose a brand-name portable computer with an international warranty, such as Hewlett-Packard, Compaq or Acer.

Be careful: you may be hit with a steep import tax when you return to your home country. Save your receipt; the older the machine, the less you're likely to pay in import duty. The rules in many countries say that the machine is tax exempt if over a year old.

POST-RETAIL THERAPY

If your arms ache from carting around that ancient stone tomb guard you picked up on Hollywood Rd, or those impulse-purchase winkle pickers are starting to pinch, soothe your aches and pains with a massage or spa treatment.

Foot (Map p56; ☎ 2997 7138; www.foothk.com; 8th fl, Regent Centre, 88 Queen's Rd Central; MTR Central, exit D1) Foot reflexology and acupressure plus lymphatic detox and pedicures from $220 for 50 minutes.

Elemis Day Spa (Map p68; ☎ 2521 6660; www.elemisdayspa.com.hk; 9th fl, Century Sq, 1 D'Aguilar St, Central; MTR Central, exit D2) Manages to feel luxurious and utterly soothing without absolutely breaking the bank. Treatments range from basic facials to deep-tissue massage. There are separate sections (and treatment menus) for men and women. Its very Central location is another plus.

Plateau Residential Spa (Map p65; ☎ 2584 7688; www.plateau.com.hk; 11th fl, Grand Hyatt Hong Kong, Wan Chai; MTR Wan Chai) When an afternoon of pampering just isn't enough, stay the night at the Plateau, the Hyatt's rather Zen spa. You can be treated in your room on your futon-style bed and then enjoy wonderful harbour views from your balcony.

The Spa at the Four Seasons (Map p56; ☎ 3196 8888; www.fourseasons.com; Four Seasons Hotel, 8 Finance St, Central; MTR Hong Kong) This vast, ultra high-end spa pretty much offers it all. As well as a full range of beauty, massage and health treatments, there's an ice fountain, hot cups, moxibustion and something called a herbal cocoon room.

Most people buy their computers in Kowloon, where there are loads of centres selling computers and related equipment. There's a much greater choice and prices are lower, but 'caveat emptor' is the phrase to bear in mind as you browse. Hong Kong Island does have a couple of reasonable computer arcades – Windsor House (Map p74; 311 Gloucester Rd, Causeway Bay) and the Wan Chai Computer Centre (p163).

Electronics

Sham Shui Po in northwestern Kowloon is a good neighbourhood to search for electronic items. You can even buy and sell second-hand goods. If you take exit A2 from the MTR at Sham Shui Po station, you'll find yourself on Apliu St, one of the best places in Hong Kong to search for the numerous plug adaptors you'll need if you plan to use your purchase in Hong Kong, Macau and/or the mainland.

Mong Kok is another great neighbourhood in which to look for electronic gadgetry. Starting at Argyle St and heading south, explore all the side streets running parallel to Nathan Rd, such as Canton Rd, Tung Choi St, Sai Yeung Choi St, Portland St, Shanghai St and Reclamation St.

There are also quite a few electronics shops in Causeway Bay, their windows stuffed full of digital cameras, DVD and CD players, and iPods. Locals generally avoid these places – apparently many of these shops are under the same ownership, ensuring that the prices remain high throughout the area.

It's best to avoid the electronics shops in Tsim Sha Tsui, especially those along Nathan Rd or just off it, as many are skilled at fleecing foreign shoppers.

Gems & Jewellery

The Chinese attribute various magical qualities to jade, including the power to prevent ageing and accidents. The circular disc with a central hole worn around many Hong Kong necks represents heaven in Chinese mythology. If you're interested in looking at and possibly purchasing jade, head for the Jade Market (p98) in Yau Ma Tei. Unless you're fairly knowledgeable about jade though, it's probably wise to limit yourself to modest purchases.

Hong Kong carries a great range of pearls, and opals are said to be good value. Diamonds aren't generally a good deal, because the world trade is controlled by a cartel and Hong Kong does not have a diamond-cutting industry.

CLOTHING SIZES

Women's clothing

Aus/UK	8	10	12	14	16	18
Europe	36	38	40	42	44	46
Japan	5	7	9	11	13	15
USA	6	8	10	12	14	16

Women's shoes

Aus/USA	5	6	7	8	9	10
Europe	35	36	37	38	39	40
France only	35	36	38	39	40	42
Japan	22	23	24	25	26	27
UK	3½	4½	5½	6½	7½	8½

Men's clothing

Aus	92	96	100	104	108	112
Europe	46	48	50	52	54	56
Japan	S		M	M		L
UK/USA	35	36	37	38	39	40

Men's shirts (collar sizes)

Aus/Japan	38	39	40	41	42	43
Europe	38	39	40	41	42	43
UK/USA	15	15½	16	16½	17	17½

Men's shoes

Aus/UK	7	8	9	10	11	12
Europe	41	42	43	44½	46	47
Japan	26	27	27½	28	29	30
USA	7½	8½	9½	10½	11½	12½

Measurements approximate only, try before you buy

Diamonds aside, jewellery exporting is big business in Hong Kong, where other gemstones are imported, cut, polished, set and re-exported using cheap labour. In theory, this should make Hong Kong a cheap place to purchase jewellery. In reality, retail prices are only marginally lower than elsewhere.

A couple of reputable jewellery-shop chains, including King Fook (p161) and Tse Sui Luen (p162), will issue a certificate that states exactly what you are buying and guarantees that the shop will buy it back at a fair market price. If you've bought something and want to know its value, you can have it appraised. There is a charge for this service, and some stones (such as diamonds) may have to be removed from their setting for testing. You can contact Hong Kong Jewellers' & Goldsmiths' Association (☎ 2543 9633) for a list of the approved appraisers. One company that does appraisals is Valuation Services (☎ 2869 4350).

The only carved ivory products being sold here *legally* are those that were manufactured

TO MARKET, TO MARKET...

For budget shopping, there's no better place to start than at one of Hong Kong's busy covered markets and street markets.

The biggest one in the territory is the Temple Street night market (p96) in Yau Ma Tei, which basically runs parallel to (and west of) Nathan Rd from Jordan Rd in the south to Man Ming Lane in the north, and is divided by Tin Hau Temple. It is the place to go for cheap clothes, watches, pirated CDs and DVDs, fake labels, footwear, cookware and everyday items, as well as *dàai-pàai-dawng* (open-air street stall food). The best time to visit is between 7pm and 10pm.

The Tung Choi Street market (Map p98; ⏰ noon-11.30pm), two blocks east of Nathan Rd and the Mong Kok MTR station, mainly sells cheap clothing. It is sometimes called the Ladies' Market to distinguish it from the Men's Market (the Temple St night market) because the stalls in the latter once sold only menswear. Though there are still a lot of items on sale for women on Tung Choi St, vendors don't discriminate and anyone's money will do nowadays. Vendors start setting up their stalls as early as noon, but it's best to get here between 1pm and 6pm when there's much more on offer.

There are other bustling markets on Apliu St (Map pp88–9; ⏰ noon-9pm) in Sham Shui Po, one block west of Sham Shui Po MTR station, and in the streets running off Tai Po's Four Lane Sq (Map p121) in the New Territories.

If you're looking strictly for clothing, try Jardine's Bazaar (Map p74) in Causeway Bay. A bit more upmarket and a tourist attraction in its own right is Stanley Market (p84), in the village of that name on southern Hong Kong Island. Another market worth visiting is Western Market (p70) near the Macau ferry terminal in Sheung Wan.

before a 1989 ban came into effect or those made of marine ivory. Ivory retailers must have all sorts of documentation to prove where and when the goods were made.

Leather Goods & Luggage

Most of what gets sent to the Hong Kong market from China is export quality, but check carefully because there is still a lot of rubbish on sale. All the big brand names such as Louis Vuitton and Gucci are on display in Hong Kong department stores, and you'll find some local vendors in the luggage business. If you're just looking for a casual bag or daypack, try Li Yuen St East and Li Yuen St West in Central or Stanley Market (p84).

Photographic Equipment

When shopping for a camera, keep in mind that you should never buy one that doesn't have a price tag. This will basically preclude most of the shops in Tsim Sha Tsui. One of the best spots in Hong Kong for buying photographic equipment is Stanley St in Central, where competition is keen. Everything carries price tags, though some low-level bargaining may be possible. Tsim Sha Tsui has a couple of shops on Kimberley Rd dealing in used cameras and there are plenty of photo shops on Sai Yeung Choi St in Mong Kok.

Watches

Shops selling watches are ubiquitous in Hong Kong and you can find everything from a Rolex to Russian army timepieces and diving watches. As always, you should avoid the

shops that do not have price tags on the merchandise. The big department stores and City Chain (p162) are fine, but compare prices.

HONG KONG ISLAND

Central and Causeway Bay are the main shopping districts on Hong Kong Island, with Wan Chai lagging pretty far behind.

CENTRAL

Central has a mix of midrange to top-end shopping centres and street-front retail; it's popular with locals and tourists alike. This is a good place to look for cameras, books, antiques and designer threads. The Landmark shopping mall in Central has designer boutiques, shops selling crystal and so on. The IFC Mall is for high fashion.

AMOURS ANTIQUES
Map p68   Antiques; Clothing & Accessories
☎ 2803 7877; 45 Staunton St; ⏰ 12.30-9.30pm Sun-Thu, 12.30-10.30pm Fri & Sat; 🚌 26
This wonderful shop stocks antique (well, old) rhinestone jewellery, frocks, and a darling clutch of beaded and tapestry bags dating from early last century. There are also vases, candle holders and Buddha figurines. Good gift-shopping territory.

ARCH ANGEL ANTIQUES Map p68 Antiques
☎ 2851 6848; 53-55 Hollywood Rd; 🚌 26
Though the specialities are antique and ancient porcelain and tombware, Arch Angel packs a lot more into its three floors:

there's everything from mahjong sets and terracotta horses to palatial furniture. It also operates an art gallery, Arch Angel Fine Art (Map p68; ☎ 2854 4255; 38 Peel St), across the road that deals in paintings by Vietnamese artists.

CHINE GALLERY Map p68   Antiques, Carpets
☎ 2543 0023; www.chinegallery.com; 42A Hollywood Rd; 🚌 26
The carefully restored furniture – the lacquered cabinets are fab – at this shop come from all over China, and hand-knotted rugs are sourced from remote regions such as Xinjiang, Ningxia, Gansu, Inner Mongolia and Tibet. It sells statues and collectibles, too.

HOBBS & BISHOPS FINE ART
Map p68   Antiques
☎ 2537 9838; 28 Hollywood Rd; 🕑 10am-5.30pm Mon-Sat; 🚌 26
This shop smelling of beeswax specialises in lacquered Chinese wooden furniture from the 19th and early 20th centuries. Its taste leans towards the sleek and handsome rather than gilded and showy pieces.

HONEYCHURCH ANTIQUES
Map p68   Antiques
☎ 2543 2433; 29 Hollywood Rd; 🕑 closed Sun; 🚌 26
This fine shop, run by an American couple for more than four decades, specialises in antique Chinese furniture, jewellery and Chinese export, and antique English silver. There's a wide range of stock, from the early Chinese dynasties right up to the 20th century.

KARIN WEBER GALLERY
Map p68   Antiques, Fine Art
☎ 2544 5004; www.karinwebergallery.com; 20 Aberdeen St; 🚌 26
Karin Weber has an enjoyable mix of Chinese country antiques and contemporary Asian artworks. She also gives short lectures on antiques and the scene in Hong Kong, and is able to arrange antique-buying trips into Guangdong for serious buyers.

TAI SING FINE ANTIQUES
Map p68   Antiques
☎ 2525 9365; 12 Wyndham St; MTR Central
Tai Sing has been selling quality Chinese antiques for more than half a century, with a special focus on porcelain. Two of the shop's six floors are now devoted to European furniture, including a dandy assembly of Art Deco pieces.

TERESA COLEMAN FINE ARTS
Map p68   Antiques
☎ 2526 2450; Ground fl, 79 Wyndham St; 🚌 26
This is the finest shop in Hong Kong for purchasing antique Chinese textiles, including rare *chi fu*, the formal court robes of valuable silk worn by the Chinese emperor, princes and imperial ministers. The shop also deals in Chinese export paintings from the 18th and 19th centuries and antique fans.

TIBETAN GALLERY Map p68   Antiques
☎ 2530 4863; Shop A, Yu Yuet Lai Bldg, 43-55 Wyndham St; 🕑 closed Sun; 🚌 26
This shop has an impressive selection of Tibetan religious art and artefacts, including mini-altars. You'll also find Tibetan furniture, silverware and rugs. There's a large showroom on the 1st floor.

top picks

SHOPPING IN HONG KONG

The Ladies' Market has plenty for all
This Mong Kok market place is awesome for bargain shopping. From Bruce Lee figurines to Mao lighters, all souvenirs and clothes are cheap. Beware, though, pushy sales people and dense crowds can make it too much for even the most dedicated shopper.

Festival Walk is a cause for celebration
Away from the street markets this huge shopping centre has 216 shops whose goods are limited only by your imagination. Relax by watching a movie in the multiplex or by skating on the indoor ice rink. Check out the futuristic, mirrored escalators.

Shop at Temple Street Night Market and see your future
Temple Street is host to Hong Kong's most famous open-air market. At dusk, this place really comes alive and you can spend hours here. Have your future told by a streetside fortune-teller or catch an impromptu Chinese opera street show or a bite to eat.

kikko01

BLUELIST[1] (blu list) *v.*
to recommend a travel experience.
What's your recommendation? www.lonelyplanet.com/bluelist

WATTIS FINE ART Map p68   Antiques

☎ 2524 5302; www.wattis.com.hk; 2nd fl, 20 Hollywood Rd; ⏱ closed Mon; 🚌 26

No place in Hong Kong has a better collection of antique maps for sale than Wattis Fine Art. The selection of old photographs of Hong Kong and Macau is also very impressive. You enter the shop from Old Bailey St.

CHRISTIE'S Map p56   Auction House

☎ 2521 5396; Room 2203-2208, 22nd fl, Alexandra House, 16-20 Chater Rd; MTR Central (exit J2)

Christie's has regular sales in ceramics, jade, jewellery, stamps, snuff bottles, art, traditional and contemporary Chinese paintings and calligraphy. It holds its spring (May) and autumn (November) pre-auction previews in the Hong Kong Convention & Exhibition Centre in Wan Chai (p64).

BLOOMSBURY BOOKS Map p56   Books

☎ 2526 5387; Shop 102, 1/F Hutchison House, 10 Harcourt Rd; ⏱ closed Sun; MTR Central (exit J3)

The delightful bookshop carries a tremendous selection of business, legal and other professional titles but, in deference to its name, leans on the literary side as well. There's a brilliant children's section.

FLOW ORGANIC BOOKSHOP

Map p68   Books

☎ 2964 9483, 8104 0822; www.flowagain.com; 1st & 2nd fls, 40 Lyndhurst Tce; ⏱ noon-7pm; 🚌 26

Quite what makes this secondhand and exchange bookshop 'organic' is anyone's guess, but it does have a focus on spiritual and New Age literature. On the 2nd floor are Chinese-language books and relaxation tapes and CDs. Enter from Cochrane St.

GOVERNMENT PUBLICATIONS

OFFICE Map p56   Books; Maps

☎ 2537 1910; Room 402, 4th fl, Murray Bldg, 22 Garden Rd; ⏱ closed Sun; 🚌 3B, 12 or 40M

All Hong Kong government publications, including hiking maps, are available from here.

INDOSIAM Map p56   Books; Antiques

☎ 2854 2853; 1st fl, 89 Hollywood Rd; ⏱ 2-7pm; 🚌 26

Hong Kong's first (and only) truly antiquarian bookshop deals in rare titles relating to Asian countries. It's particularly strong

on Thailand, China and the former French colonies (ie Vietnam, Cambodia, Laos).

JOINT PUBLISHING Map p56   Books

☎ 2868 6844; 9 Queen Victoria St; MTR Central (exit A)

This primarily Chinese-language bookshop has a good range of English-language books about China, and CDs and DVDs for studying the language. It's also strong on local and China maps. Most English-language titles are on the mezzanine floor. There are 15 other JP outlets, many in MTR stations, including a branch in Wan Chai (Map p65; ☎ 2838 2081; 158 Hennessy Rd).

TAI YIP ART BOOK CENTRE Map p68 Books

☎ 2524 5963; Room 101-102, 1st fl, Capitol Plaza, 2-10 Lyndhurst Tce; MTR Central (exit C)

Tai Yip has a terrific selection of books about anything that is Chinese and artsy: calligraphy, jade, bronze, costumes, architecture, symbolism. This is a good place to look deeper if you're planning on buying art in Hong Kong. There are outlets in several of Hong Kong's museums, including the Hong Kong Museum of Art (p90).

CARAVAN Map p56   Carpets

☎ 2547 3821; 65 Hollywood Rd; 🚌 26

A shop called Caravan with an owner named Driver? Trustworthy rugsellers travel all over Asia to stock this nicely cluttered shop. The range of Afghan and Tibetan carpets is especially notable among a varied rug range.

MIR ORIENTAL CARPETS Map p68   Carpets

☎ 2521 5641; Ground fl, New India House, 52 Wyndham St; 🚌 26

This two-floor shop is the largest stockist of fine rugs in Hong Kong, with thousands of carpets from around the world flying in and out of the store. It is the top specialist in town for Persian carpets.

CIGAR EXPRESS CENTRAL Map p68   Cigars

☎ 2110 9201; Shop 4A, Ground fl, Cheung Fai Bldg, 45-47 Cochrane St; ⏱ 11am-11pm Mon-Sat, noon-6pm Sun; MTR Central (exit E)

This branch of a Hong Kong chain sells everything from a $30 Honduran Quintero stogy to a hand-rolled Cuban Cohiba Double Corona for $350 a pop.

BOOKSHOP CHAINS

Bookazine (Map p56; ☎ 2522 1785; Shop 309-313A, 3rd fl, Prince's Bldg, 10 Chater Rd; MTR Central, exit G) Largest of these chain stores dotted around the territory. Dependable range of books, magazines and stationery. Also a branch in Admiralty (Map p63; ☎ 2866 7522; Shop C, Upper ground fl, Far East Finance Centre, 16 Harcourt Rd).

Dymocks (Map p56; ☎ 2117 0360; Shop 2007-2011, 2nd fl, IFC Mall, 8 Finance St; MTR Central, exit A) Australian bookshop chain offering a solid mainstream selection of books and magazines in several branches.

Hong Kong Book Centre (Map p56; ☎ 2522 7064; www.swindonbooks.com; Basement, On Lok Yuen Bldg, 25 Des Voeux Rd Central; MTR Central, exit B) Basement shop with a vast selection of books and magazines, particularly business titles.

CIGARRO Map p56   Cigars
☎ 2810 1883; Shop 5, Ground fl, St George's Bldg, 2 Ice House St; MTR Central
There's nothing like a fat cigar to say you're making it big in the city. This smoke shop in Central comes to the rescue with Cuban, Dominican, Nicaraguan and other fine stogies.

BAPE STORE Map p56   Clothing & Accessories
☎ 2868 9448; 10 Queen's Rd Central; MTR Central (exit D1)
How Japanese label Bathing Ape's formerly hard-to-find T-shirts, trainers and other urban wear will sustain their cool, cult reputation with socking great flagship stores like this one is anyone's guess, but it's worth a look if you were born no earlier than the 1980s. Check out the underfloor footwear 'train' as you enter.

BLANC DE CHINE
Map p56   Clothing & Accessories
☎ 2524 7875; Room 201 & 203A, 2nd fl, Pedder Bldg, 12 Pedder St; MTR Central (exit D1)
This sumptuous store specialises in traditional men's Chinese jackets, off the rack or made to measure. There's also a lovely selection of silk dresses for women. The satin bed linens are exquisite (as are the old ship's cabinets in which they are displayed).

BOSSINI Map p56   Clothing & Accessories
☎ 2523 0520; On Lok Yuen Bldg, 27a Des Voeux Rd Central; ⏰ 11am-10pm; MTR Central (exit B)
You'll find plenty of inexpensive, wearable, everyday threads here, in the same kind of cuts and styles as Gap or i.t. A good store for stocking up on T-shirts and other basics.

CARPET CENTRE
Map p68   Clothing & Accessories
☎ 2850 4993; Shop A, Lower ground fl, 29 Hollywood Rd; 🚌 26

No, you're not being asked to don a dhurry… This place has pashmina shawls, ranging in price from $350 to $900, and exotic slippers fit for a sultana. Enter the store from Cochrane St.

H&M Map p68   Clothing & Accessories
☎ 2110 9546; 68 Queen's Rd; MTR Central (exit D2)
This Swedish chain has finally brought its inexpensive, of-the-moment clothing to Hong Kong. The appeal is discount prices with lines that track high-end fashion trends closely, partly with the help of fashion collaborations with the likes of Madonna, Stella McCartney and Kylie Minogue.

JILIAN, LINGERIE ON WYNDHAM
Map p56   Clothing & Accessories
☎ 2826 9295; Ground fl, 31 Wyndham St; MTR Central (exit D2)
Swimwear and a vast range of French and Italian lingerie from gossamer delicates small enough to swallow with a glass of water to rather *outré* corsetry with strings and stays and such. There's even a small range of men's designer smalls if you just can't put up with your man's industrial-sized underpants any longer. Labels stocked include Eres, Argentovivo, I.D. Sarrieri, Cadolle, Aubade, Bacirubati, Pin-up Stars, Jonquil, Revanche de la Femme, Rosa Cha and Grigioperla.

JOYCE Map p56   Clothing & Accessories
☎ 2810 1120; Ground fl, New World Tower, 16 Queen's Rd Central; MTR Central (exit D1)
This multidesigner store is a good choice if you're short of time rather than money: Issey Miyake, Alexander McQueen, Marc Jacobs, Comme des Garçons, Chloë, Pucci, Yohji Yamamoto and several Hong Kong fashion names are just some of the designers whose wearable wares are on

display. There's another branch of Joyce in Admiralty (Map p63; ☎ 2523 5944; Shop 334, 3rd fl, Pacific Place, 88 Queensway). For the same duds at half the price, visit Joyce Warehouse (☎ 2814 8313; 21st fl, Horizon Plaza Arcade, 2 Lee Wing St, Ap Lei Chau; ☺ closed Mon), opposite the Aberdeen waterfront.

LINVA TAILOR Map p68   Clothing & Accessories
☎ 2544 2456; Ground fl, 38 Cochrane St; 🚌 26
This is the place to come to have your very own cheongsam (tight-fitting Chinese dress) tailored. Bring your own silk or choose from Miss Tong's selection. The proprietors are also happy to mail completed items, if you're pushed for time.

LITTLE MISSES & MINI MASTERS
Map p56   Clothing & Accessories
☎ 2156 1118; Shop 307, 3rd fl, Prince's Bldg, 10 Chater Rd; MTR Central (exit G)
Horrible name but this children's shop, owned and managed by expats, has some of the most stylish clothing imaginable for kids. You'll also find a select range of upmarket toys here.

LULU CHEUNG Map p56   Clothing & Accessories
☎ 2537 7515; Shop B63, Basement, Landmark Bldg, 1 Pedder St; MTR Central (exit G)
Local Designer Lulu makes sophisticated, understated women's casual wear and elegant evening gowns using natural fabrics, such as wool, cotton, silk, linen, in muted tones. Cheung also often works with layers and textures using mesh or floral embroidery.

MIU MIU Map p56   Clothing & Accessories
☎ 2523 7833; Shop B24, Basement, Landmark Bldg, 1 Pedder St; MTR Central
Clean lines, the best fabrics and a lush colour palette define the high-end fashion from this Prada spin-off. Great (and pricey) shoes and handbags, too. A range of smaller accessories makes it a good place to hunt for presents.

SHANGHAI TANG
Map p56   Clothing & Accessories
☎ 2525 7333; Basement & ground fl, Pedder Bldg, 12 Pedder St; MTR Central (exit D1)
This stylish shop has sparked something of a fashion wave in Hong Kong with its updated versions of traditional yet neon-coloured Chinese garments. It also stocks accessories and delightful gift items. Custom tailoring is available.

HARVEY NICHOLS Map p56   Department Store
☎ 3695 3389; www.harveynichols.com; Landmark Bldg, 1 Pedder St; MTR Central (exit G)
Britain's Harvey Nichols has brought its diverse, profuse and on-the-pulse range of couture and smart street fashions to Hong Kong, occupying four floors at the Landmark.

LANE CRAWFORD Map p56   Department Store
☎ 2118 3388; Level 3, IFC Mall, 8 Finance St; MTR Central (exit A)
This branch of Hong Kong's original Western-style department store, the territory's answer to Harrods in London, is the flagship now that the store on Queen's Rd Central has closed. There are branches in Admiralty (Map p63; ☎ 2118 3668; 1st & 2nd fls, Pacific Place, 88 Queensway), Causeway Bay (Map p74; ☎ 2118 3638; Ground & 1st fls, Times Square, 1 Matheson St) and Tsim Sha Tsui (Map p92; ☎ 2118 3428; Ground & 1st fls, Ocean Terminal, Harbour City, Salisbury Rd).

THE SWANK Map p56   Department Store
☎ 2868 3804 (ladies), 2810 0769; Shop 202, 2nd fl, Alexandra House, 16-20 Chater Rd; MTR Central (exit H)
A long-standing fashion powerhouse, the Swank stocks a good range of established, mainly European labels, including Kenzo, Sonia Rykel, Christian Lacroix and Givenchy, plus a smattering of up-and-coming talent from Hong Kong and the world's fashion centres.

OCEAN OPTICAL Map p56   Eyeware
☎ 2868 5670; Shop 5, Ground fl, The Cascade, Standard Chartered Bank Bldg, 4-4A Des Voeux Rd Central; MTR Central (exit G)
Both frames and lenses can be cheaper (in some case, much cheaper) in Hong Kong than what you would pay at home, and we do not know of a better optician in Hong Kong than Ocean Optical. There's a branch in Tsim Sha Tsui (Map p92; ☎ 2735 0611; Shop 326, 3rd fl, Ocean Centre, Harbour City, 3-9 Canton Rd).

ANGLO-CHINESE FLORIST
Map p68   Flowers
☎ 2921 2986; Ground fl, Winway Bldg, 50 Wellington St; MTR Central

If you've been invited to someone's home and you wish to bring flowers – as is *de rigueur* here – stop by Anglo-Chinese. Nobody does them better. You'll also find some exquisite bonsai here.

FOOK MING TONG TEA SHOP
Map p56   Food & Drink
☎ 2295 0368; Shop 3006, IFC Mall, 8 Finance St; MTR Central (exit A)
Tea-making accoutrements and carefully chosen teas of various ages and grades, from gunpowder to Nanyan Ti Guan Yin Crown Grade – costing anything from $10 to $9000 per 100g. There's also a branch in Tsim Sha Tsui (Map p92; ☎ 2735 1077; Shop 3225, Level 3, Gateway Arcade, Harbour City, 25-27 Canton Rd).

OLYMPIA GRAECO-EGYPTIAN COFFEE
Map p68   Food & Drink
☎ 2522 4653; Ground fl, 24 Old Bailey St; ☺ closed Sun; ☒ 26
This place has been around since, well, anyone can remember, and it still grinds the best beans in town.

SOHO WINES & SPIRITS
Map p68   Food & Drink
☎ 2530 1182; 37 Staunton St; ☒ 26
Its name notwithstanding, this place's forte is in its large selection of beer and spirits. If it's not here, it probably isn't made or drunk any longer. Its prices tend to be keen, thanks to the shop's hospitality-trade wholesaling business.

THREE SIXTY Map p56   Food & Drink
☎ 2111 4480; 3rd & 4th fl, Landmark Bldg, 1 Pedder St; MTR Central (exit G)
A fabulous addition to Hong Kong's food scene, Three Sixty sells a great range of organic and natural foods, as well as top notch imports of hard-to-find ingredients from all over the world. The prices, of course, are high. There's also a terrific food court with cuisine from all over the world on the upper floor.

WATSON'S WINE CELLAR
Map p68   Food & Drink
☎ 2869 2210; 2 Staunton St; ☒ 26
The choice at this wine emporium is enormous and the staff is always willing to assist. There's a branch in Causeway Bay (Map p74; ☎ 2895 6975; Basement, Windsor House, 311 Gloucester Rd).

LIULIGONGFANG Map p56   Gifts & Souvenirs
☎ 2973 0820; Shop 20-22, Ground fl, Central Bldg, 1-3 Pedder St; MTR Central
Exquisite coloured-glass objects, both practical (vases, candle holders, jewellery) and ornamental (figurines, crystal Buddhas, breathtaking sculptures) from renowned Taiwanese glass sculptor Loretta Yang Hui-Shan are on display and for sale here. There's another branch in Admiralty (Map p63; ☎ 2918 9001; Shop 320, 3rd fl, Pacific Place, 88 Queensway).

MANDARIN ORIENTAL FLOWER & GIFT SHOP Map p56   Gifts & Souvenirs
☎ 2825 4019; Ground fl, Mandarin Oriental, 5 Connaught Rd Central; MTR Central (exit F)
Crockery, cushion covers, chopsticks, tasteful souvenirs and a small selection of jewellery, all of the highest quality, are available, plus the flowers, of course.

MOUNTAIN FOLKCRAFT
Map p68   Gifts & Souvenirs
☎ 2523 2817; 12 Wo On Lane; ☺ closed Sun; MTR Central
This is one of the nicest shops in Central for folk craft. It's piled with bolts of batik and sarongs, clothing, wood carvings, lacquerware and papercuts made by ethnic minorities in China and other Asian countries. The shop attendants are friendly, and prices, while not cheap, are not outrageous either.

WAH TUNG CHINA ARTS
Map p68   Gifts & Souvenirs
☎ 2543 2823; 59 Hollywood Rd; ☺ closed Sun; ☒ 26
Wah Tung, the world's largest supplier of hand-decorated ceramics, has some 18,000 items on display at this showroom, just east of Pacific Place. You'll find everything from brightly painted vases and ginger jars to repro Tang-dynasty figurines.

KING FOOK Map p68   Jewellery
☎ 2822 8573; Ground fl, King Fook Bldg, 30-32 Des Voeux Rd Central; MTR Central (exit C)
King Fook, with a grandiose gilded entrance, stocks a large range of watches, top-end fountain pens and baubles. There's another branch in Tsim Sha Tsui (Map p92; ☎ 2313 2788; Shop G1, Miramar Shopping Centre, 118-130 Nathan Rd).

ROCK CANDY Map p68 Jewellery
☎ 2549 1018; 1 Elgin St, Soho; 🚌 26
Made from black glass and with pin-prick lights illuminating display cases, this goth-glam jewellery shop (and its ubertrendy gewgaws) has to be seen to be believed.

TSE SUI LUEN Map p68 Jewellery
☎ 2921 8800; Ground fl, Commercial House, 35 Queen's Rd Central; MTR Central (exit D2)
This is the most sparkling of Tse Sui Luen's dozen or so outlets and is worth visiting for its sheer opulence or garishness – however you see it. There's another branch in Tsim Sha Tsui (Map p92; ☎ 2926 3210; Shop A & B, Ground fl, 190 Nathan Rd).

HMV Map p56 Music
☎ 2739 0268; 1st fl, Central Bldg, 1-3 Pedder St; MTR Central
This Aladdin's cave of music not only has Hong Kong's largest choice of CDs, DVDs and cassettes, but also a great range of music-related literature. There are branches in Causeway Bay (Map p74; ☎ 2504 3669; 1st fl, Style House, The Park Lane) and Tsim Sha Tsui (Map p92; ☎ 2302 0122; 2nd fl, HK Pacific Centre, 28 Hankow Rd).

EVERBEST PHOTO SUPPLIES
Map p68 Photographic Equipment
☎ 2522 1985; 28B Stanley St; MTR Central
This extremely reliable shop is where many of Hong Kong's professional photographers buy their equipment. Same day or next day China visas are an odd but useful sideline here.

PHOTO SCIENTIFIC
Map p68 Photographic Equipment
☎ 2525 0550; 6 Stanley St; ⏰ 9am-7pm Mon-Sat; MTR Central (exit D2)
This is the favourite of Hong Kong's resident pros. You'll almost certainly find equipment elsewhere for less, but Photo Scientific has a rock-solid reputation with labelled prices, no bargaining, no arguing and no cheating.

IFC MALL Map p56 Shopping Mall
☎ 2295 3308; www.ifc.com.hk; 8 Finance St; MTR Hong Kong
As if Central didn't have nearly enough luxury retail space already, they built this swanky shopping centre with 200 high-fashion boutiques linking the One and Two IFC towers and the Four Seasons Hotel. Outlets include Patrick Cox, Geiger, Longchamp, Kenzo, Vivienne Tam, Zegna…we could go on. The Hong Kong Airport Express Station is downstairs.

LANDMARK Map p56 Shopping Mall
☎ 2525 4142; www.centralhk.com; 1 Pedder St; MTR Central
The most central of all shopping centres, the Landmark has high fashion and good eating in a pleasant, open space. It has become a home almost exclusively to the very high-end fashion brands and boutiques (Gucci, Louis Vuitton, TODs etc) and a handful of worthwhile refreshment stops.

PRINCE'S BUILDING Map p56 Shopping Mall
☎ 2504 0704; www.centralhk.com; 10 Chater Rd; MTR Central
You may find the layout of Prince's Building disorientating, but it's worth a look for its speciality fashion, toy and kitchenware shops. The selection is rather eclectic – from high-end boutiques such as Chanel and Cartier on the ground floor to booksellers, Mothercare, jewellers, stationers and luggage shops on the levels above. It's an especially good place to bring the kids as almost the entire 3rd floor is given over to children's shops.

TOY MUSEUM Map p56 Toys
☎ 2869 9138; Shop 320, 3rd fl, Prince's Bldg, 10 Chater Rd; MTR Central (exit K)
Top-of-the-line teddy bears, action men, Beanie Babies and Pokemon paraphernalia are crammed into a tight space here. There's a great collection of old GI Joes for dads to amuse themselves with and a toy hospital, too.

CITY CHAIN Map p68 Watches
☎ 2259 9020; Ground fl, Man Yee Bldg, 67 Queen's Rd Central; MTR Central (exit D2)
City Chain stocks every type of wristwatch imaginable – from the stylish and dressy to the funky and glitzy. It has some two-dozen outlets in Hong Kong, including one in Admiralty (Map p63; ☎ 2845 9403; Shop 112, 1st fl, Pacific Place, 88 Queensway).

SHEUNG WAN
For antiques and curios, head for Hollywood Rd, which starts in Central and ends up in

Sheung Wan, where there is a long string of shops selling Asian items. Some of the really good spots have genuine finds, but beware of what you buy. Western Market (p70) is a good spot for buying fabrics and curios. There are also a couple of big department stores in the area.

WING ON Map p70   Department Store
☎ 2852 1888; 211 Des Voeux Rd Central; MTR Sheung Wan

'Forever Peaceful' is notable for being locally owned. It carries a range of goods but is especially well known for inexpensive electronics and household appliances. There is another branch located in Tsim Sha Tsui (Map p97; ☎ 2710 6288; 345 Nathan Rd).

LOK CHA TEA SHOP Map p56   Food & Drink
☎ 2805 1360; Ground fl, 290B Queen's Rd Central; 🚌 26

This favourite shop sells Chinese teas of infinite variety, as well as tea sets, wooden tea boxes and well-presented gift packs of various cuppas. A great bonus is that you can try before you buy. Enter the shop from Ladder St.

PO KEE FISHING TACKLE
Map p56   Sporting Goods
☎ 2543 7541; 6 Hillier St; ⏱ closed Sun; MTR Sheung Wan (exit A2)

The guys at Po Kee have had the market cornered – hook, line and sinker – on fishing supplies since 1933, when it served Hong Kong's commercial fishing fleet. Now it exclusively serves sports-fishing enthusiasts.

ADMIRALTY & WAN CHAI

Admiralty, bordering Wan Chai, has one of Hong Kong Island's glitziest shopping malls, Pacific Place, just opposite Admiralty station, to which it is connected by elevated and underground walkways.

Wan Chai is a good spot for medium and low-priced clothing, sporting goods and footwear, but the area caters mainly for locals. The district has little glamour, but it is well worth hunting for bargains.

COSMOS BOOKS Map p65   Books
☎ 2866 1677; Basement & 1st fl, 30 Johnston Rd, Wan Chai; 🚌 6, 6A or 6X

This chain-store branch has a good selection of China-related books in the base-

ment. Upstairs are English-language books (nonfiction is strong) plus one of Hong Kong's best stationery departments. Enter the Wan Chai store from Lun Fat St and the Tsimsy branch from Granville Rd.

KELLY & WALSH Map p63   Books
☎ 2522 5743; Shop 236, 2nd fl, Pacific Place, 88 Queensway, Admiralty; MTR Admiralty

This smart shop has a good selection of art, design and culinary books, and the staff know the stock well. Books for children are shelved in a handy kids' reading lounge. There's also a Central branch (Map p56; ☎ 2810 5128; Shop 305, 3rd fl, Exchange Square Tower I).

KENT & CURWEN
Map p63   Clothing & Accessories
☎ 2840 0023; Shop 372, 3rd fl, Pacific Place, 88 Queensway, Admiralty; MTR Admiralty

Distinguished suits, dress shirts, ties, cufflinks and casual tops for the gentleman who'd rather look to the manor born than arriviste broker.

PACIFIC CUSTOM TAILORS
Map p63   Clothing & Accessories
☎ 2845 5377; Shop 110, 1st fl, Pacific Place, 88 Queensway, Admiralty; MTR Admiralty (exit C1)

This is one of our favourite bespoke tailors in Hong Kong. It'll make or copy anything; turnaround on most items is two or three days, including two fittings. Count on about $4000 for a suit.

VIVIENNE TAM Map p63   Clothing & Accessories
☎ 2918 0238; www.viviennetam.com; Shop 209, 2nd fl, Pacific Place, 88 Queensway, Admiralty; MTR Admiralty (exit F)

This enduring brand from New York–based designer Tam, who was trained in Hong Kong, sells eminently wearable, feminine but also streetwise women's foundation pieces, light gossamer dresses and slinky tops, plus a range of accessories.

WAN CHAI COMPUTER CENTRE
Map p65   Computers
1st fl, Southorn Centre, 130-138 Hennessy Rd, Wan Chai; ⏱ closed Sun; MTR Wan Chai (exit B2)

This place, on the northern edge of Southorn Playground, is a cut above Hong Kong's computer emporiums. The prices on pretty much everything digital are generally keener than the local chain stores.

CHINESE ARTS & CRAFTS
Map p63   Department Store
☎ 2523 3933; Shop 220, Pacific Place, 88 Queensway, Admiralty; MTR Admiralty (exit F)
Mainland-owned CAC is probably the best place in Hong Kong to buy quality bric-a-brac and other Chinese trinkets; it's positively an Aladdin's cave of souvenirs. On Hong Kong Island there's also a branch in Central (Map p68; ☎ 2901 0338; Ground fl, Asia Standard Tower, 59 Queen's Rd Central), Tsim Sha Tsui (Map p92; ☎ 2735 4061; 1st fl, Star House, 3 Salisbury Rd) and a huge branch in Wan Chai (Map p65; ☎ 2827 6667; Lower Block, China Resources Bldg, 26 Harbour Rd).

DESIGN GALLERY Map p65   Gifts & Souvenirs
☎ 2584 4146; Level 1, Hong Kong Convention & Exhibition Centre, 1 Harbour Rd, Wan Chai; 🚌 18
Supported by the Hong Kong Trade Development Council, this shop showcases local design in the form of jewellery, toys, ornaments and gadgets. It's a chaotic but often rewarding gaggle of goodies. A great place to find present-buying inspiration. There's also a branch in the check-in hall at the airport (☎ 2261 2524; TE07, level 7).

HONG KONG RECORDS Map p63   Music
☎ 2845 7088; Shop 252, 2nd fl, Pacific Place, 88 Queensway, Admiralty; MTR Admiralty
This local outfit has a good selection of Cantonese and international sounds, including traditional Chinese, jazz, classical and contemporary music. There's also a good range of DVDs and VCDs of both Chinese films and Western movies with Chinese subtitles. There's also a Kowloon Tong branch (Map pp88–9; ☎ 2265 8299; Shop L1-02, Level 1, Festival Walk, 80-88 Tat Chee Ave).

SUNMARK CAMPING EQUIPMENT
Map p65   Outdoor Gear
☎ 2893 8553; 1st fl, 121 Wan Chai Rd, Wan Chai; ⏱ noon-8pm Mon-Sat, 1.30-7.30pm Sun; 🚌 6, 6A or 6X
Head here for hiking and camping gear and waterproof clothing of all sorts. There's also a small selection of second-hand gear. Enter from Bullock Lane.

PACIFIC PLACE Map p63   Shopping Mall
☎ 2844 8988; www.pacificplace.com.hk; 88 Queensway, Admiralty; MTR Admiralty (exit F)
One of the city's best shopping malls, Pacific Place has, if anything, gone further upmarket recently. There are a couple of hundred outlets, dominated by higher-end men's and women's fashion (from the likes of Burberry, Chanel, Chloé, Loewe, Marc Jacobs and Versace) and accessories (Bottega Veneta, Coach, Fendi, Gucci etc). There's also a Lane Crawford department store.

BUNN'S DIVERS Map p65   Sporting Goods
☎ 3422 3322; Mezzanine, Chuen Fung House, 188-192 Johnston Rd, Wan Chai; MTR Wan Chai (exit A3)
Masks, snorkels, fins, regulators, tanks – Hong Kong's longest-established dive shop also runs dive tours and training courses.

KUNG FU SUPPLIES Map p65   Sporting Goods
☎ 2891 1912; Room 6A, 6th fl, Chuen Fung House, 188-192 Johnston Rd, Wan Chai; 🚌 6, 6A or 6X
If you need to stock up on martial arts accessories or just want to thumb through a decent collection of books, this is the place to go. The staff here is very helpful.

WISE KIDS Map p63   Toys
☎ 2868 0133; Shop 134, 1st fl, Pacific Place, 88 Queensway, Admiralty; MTR Admiralty (exit F)

MIGHTY MICROMALLS
Crammed into old buildings, above MTR stations, up escalators and in back lanes are Hong Kong's malls of microshops, selling designer threads, a kaleidoscope of kooky accessories and a colourful closet of funky footwear. This is where Hong Kong's youngest mall-trawlers go for clothes, trinkets and to capture the moment on sticker machines. The best shopping is done from 3pm to 10pm, when *all* the shops are open.
- Beverley Commercial Centre (Map p94; 87-105 Chatham Rd South, Tsim Sha Tsui; Tsim Sha Tsui MTR) Enter via the passage north of Observatory Rd
- Island Beverley (Map p65; 1 Great George St, Causeway Bay; Causeway Bay MTR)
- Rise Commercial Centre (Map p94; 5-11 Granville Circuit, Tsim Sha Tsui; Tsim Sha Tsui MTR)
- Trendy Zone (Map p97; Chow Tai Fook Centre, 580A Nathan Rd, Mong Kok; Mong Kok MTR)
- Up Date Mall (Map p92; 36-44 Nathan Rd, Tsim Sha Tsui; Tsim Sha Tsui MTR)

Nothing to plug in, nothing with batteries: Wise Kids concentrates on kids generating energy with what's upstairs. Along with stuffed toys, card games and things to build, there are practical items for parents such as toilet-lid locks and carry-alls. There's also a branch in Central (Map p56; ☎ 2377 9888; Shop 301, 3rd fl, Prince's Bldg, 10 Chater Rd).

CAUSEWAY BAY

Causeway Bay has perhaps the largest weekend crowds and the broadest spectrum in terms of price. It is a crush of department stores and smaller outlets selling designer and street fashion, electronics, sporting goods and household items. A good up-and-coming neighbourhood for hip fashions is springing up along Paterson and Kingston Sts close to Victoria Park. Causeway Bay also has a few lively street markets. Jardine's Bazaar (actually a street) and the area behind it are home to stalls and shops peddling cheap clothing, luggage and footwear. The area is also home to the huge Times Square shopping mall.

D-MOP Map p74   Clothing & Accessories
☎ 2203 4130; Shop B, Ground fl, 8 Kingston St; MTR Causeway Bay (exit E)
This is the main outlet for one of Hong Kong's edgier designer lines. It specialises in slinky tops, some out-there *avant garde* one-offs, cool shoes and a handful of hip hipsters from international labels such as Tsubi jeans.

DADA CABARET VOLTAIRE
Map p74   Clothing & Accessories
☎ 2890 1708; Shop F-13A, 1st fl, Fashion Island, 47 Paterson St; ⏰ 12.30-10pm; MTR Causeway Bay (exit E)
Selling bold urban clothing in primary colours also sported by the staff, this is just one of many fine shops in the Fashion Island micromall, where you'll also find branches of shoe god Patrick Cox, Armani Exchange and Gay Giano.

SISTER Map p74   Clothing & Accessories
☎ 2504 1016; Shop 331, 3rd fl, Island Beverley, 1 Great George St; ⏰ 2-11pm; MTR Causeway Bay (exit E)
This 'trendy fashion store' sells young Hong Kong designer wear verging on the wacky, which is saying something given the competition in this mall.

SPY Map p74   Clothing & Accessories
☎ 2893 7799; Shop C, Ground fl, 11 Sharp St East; ⏰ noon-11pm; MTR Causeway Bay (exit A)
Tame yet trendy everyday wear, such as slacks and short-sleeved shirts. Spy also has two other outlets, including one in Tsim Sha Tsui East (Map p94; ☎ 2366 5866; Shop 406-407, 4th fl, Rise Commercial Centre, 5-11 Granville Circuit; ⏰ 2-11pm).

WALTER MA Map p74   Clothing & Accessories
☎ 2838 7655; Ground fl, 33 Sharp St East; ⏰ noon-10pm Mon-Fri, noon-10.30pm Sat & Sun; MTR Causeway Bay (exit A)
Sophisticated but comfortable women's fashions from the daddy of Hong Kong's home-grown fashion industry. It ranges from smart-casual office wear to more glamorous evening wear.

IN SQUARE Map p74   Computers
10th-11th fl, Windsor House, 311 Gloucester Rd; MTR Causeway Bay (exit D1)
This landmark building in Causeway Bay houses dozens of reliable computer shops, selling both hardware and software. There's also space to browse at leisure here, unlike the usual electronics warren.

SOGO Map p74   Department Store
☎ 2833 8338; www.sogo.com.hk; 555 Hennessy Rd; MTR Causeway Bay (exit B)
This Japanese-owned store, in the hub of Causeway Bay, has 12 well-organised floors and more than 37,000 sq metres of retail space. The range is mind-boggling: over 20 brands of ties just for starters. Eclectic departments include the Barbie Counter and the Character's Shop.

MOUNTAINEERING SERVICES
Map p74   Outdoor Gear
☎ 2541 8876; Ground fl, 271 Gloucester Rd; MTR Causeway Bay (exit D1)
This excellent and centrally located shop sells climbing and hiking gear and pretty much everything you need for tackling Hong Kong's hills and country parks.

CITYPLAZA Map pp54–5   Shopping Mall
☎ 2568 8665; www.cityplaza.com.hk; 18 Tai Koo Shing Rd, Tai Koo Shing, Quarry Bay; MTR Tai Koo (exit D2)
The largest shopping centre in eastern Hong Kong Island, with 180 shops (mainly fashion and electronics), Cityplaza is directly

linked up to the MTR. Being further from the main business district, it charges retailers lower rents, which can translate into lower prices for shoppers. There's a Wing On department-store branch here, as well as an ice-skating rink.

KITTY HOUSE GIFTS SHOP
Map p74   Shopping Mall

☎ 2890 6968; Shop 229, Island Beverley, 1 Gt George St, Causeway Bay; MTR Causeway Bay (exit E)

This is just one of the dozens of micro-stores cramming into Island Beverley selling Japanese cartoon ephemera such as Hello Kitty, the cat with no mouth, and an abiding attraction to young locals. A good place for kitschy gifts and toys.

RAINBOW CITY Map p74   Shopping Mall
☎ 2881 1423; 1st fl, Fashion Island; MTR Causeway Bay (exit E)

Japanese cartoons and all manner of cutesy kitsch is splashed across the clothes and bags in vivid technicolour in this store aimed at local teens, tweens and twenty-somethings.

TIMES SQUARE Map p74   Shopping Mall
☎ 2118 8900; www.timessquare.com.hk; 1 Matheson St; MTR Causeway Bay (exit A)

The 10 floors of retail organised by type are slightly less high end than in Central. Fashion brands and outlets include Lane Crawford, Anne Sui, Aquascutum, Birkenstock, Jessica, Marks & Spencer, Vivienne Westwood and Vivienne Tam. There are plenty of electronics and homewares. There are restaurants on the 10th to 13th floors, and snack bars, cafés and a supermarket in the basement.

KOWLOON

Shopping in Kowloon is a bizarre mix of the down at heel and the glamorous, and an afternoon's stroll through its shopping quarters should yield quite a few surprises.

TSIM SHA TSUI

Nathan Rd is the main tourist strip, a huge avenue with side streets full of camera, watch and electronic shops, and leather and silk emporiums. Although this is the part of town where you're most likely to become a victim of sharp practice, Tsim Sha Tsui is also home to

a large number of above-board designer and signature shops. Some of these are found in Nathan Rd, but the bulk are in Harbour City, a labyrinthine shopping complex with a mall that stretches nearly 1km from the Star Ferry terminal north along Canton Rd. Many hotels in Tsim Sha Tsui have very upmarket boutique shopping arcades, most notably the Peninsula and the Hotel Inter-Continental.

SWINDON BOOKS Map p92   Books
☎ 2366 8001; 13-15 Lock Rd; 🚇 Tsim Sha Tsui (exit C1)

This is one of the best 'real' (as opposed to supermarket) bookshops in Hong Kong, with an excellent range and knowledgeable staff. Strong on local books and history in particular.

TRAVELLERS' HOME Map p92   Books
☎ 2380 8380; travelbookshop@yahoo.com.hk; 2nd fl, 55 Hankow Rd; MTR Tsim Sha Tsui (exit A1)

This one-stop shop has become something of a meeting place for travellers in Tsim Sha Tsui. It sells both new and used travel books (roughly 30% and 70%, respectively), schedules travel talks and hosts photo exhibitions. It has a small café corner and a message board.

CHINESE CARPET CENTRE Map p94   Carpets
☎ 2736 1773; Shop L021, Ground fl, New World Centre, 18-24 Salisbury Rd; 🚌 5C or 8

This place has an excellent selection of new Chinese carpets and rugs, many of them handmade, in silk, wool and cotton as well as acrylic. There's another branch in Tsim Sha Tsui East (Map p94; ☎ 2730 7230; Shop 5, Ground fl, Houston Centre, 63 Mody Rd).

BEATNIKS Map p94   Clothing & Accessories
☎ 2739 8494; Shop 1, Rise Commercial Bldg, Granville Circuit; MTR Tsim Sha Tsui (exit B1)

A selective stock ensures a visit to this vintage-clothing outlet isn't like the jumble-sale rummage you get with many second-hand outlets. The focus here is on street styles and left-field cool, rather than on high fashion or couture.

GRANVILLE RD Map p94   Clothing & Accessories
Granville Rd; MTR Tsim Sha Tsui

If you want to hunt for bargains and have the time and inclination to riffle through racks and piles of factory seconds, the dozen or so factory outlet stores along Granville Rd should reward you with prices at a fraction of store prices. It's pot luck as to what labels you will find, although they tend to be familiar, slightly premium mainstream casual and leisure brands (both international and local). Hotspots include UNO OUN (29 Granville Rd), Sample Moon (30 Granville Rd) and the Baleno Outlet Store (24B Granville Rd).

I.T Map p92   Clothing & Accessories
☎ 2736 9152; Shop 1030, 1st fl, Miramar Shopping Centre, 1-23 Kimberley Rd; ☷ noon-10pm; MTR Tsim Sha Tsui (exit B1)
This shop and the women's-only b+ab shop next door both sell stylish mainstream fashion fairly typical of the type that abounds in Hong Kong, although it's a notch up in quality and price from the likes of Bossini. There are i.t shops in all the major shopping areas, including in Causeway Bay (Map p74; ☎ 2506 0186; Shop 517, 5th fl, Times Square, 1 Matheson St).

LIDS Map p92   Clothing & Accessories
☎ 3523 0626; Shop 2, Park Hotel, 61-65 Chatham Rd South; MTR Tsim Sha Tsui (exit G)
This is the place to come for headgear – from baseball caps begging to be turned back to front, to helmets for cyclists, rollerbladers and skateboarders.

SAM'S TAILOR Map p92   Clothing & Accessories
☎ 2367 9423; Shop K, Burlington Arcade, 92-94 Nathan Rd; ☷ 10am-7.30pm Mon-Sat, 10am-noon Sun; MTR Tsim Sha Tsui (exit B1)
It's not certain that Sam's is the best tailor in Hong Kong, but it's the most aggressively marketed and best known. Sam's has stitched up everyone – from royalty and rock stars to us.

WWW.IZZUE.COM
Map p92   Clothing & Accessories
☎ 2992 0612; Shop 2225, 2nd fl, Gateway Arcade, Harbour City, 25-27 Canton Rd; MTR Tsim Sha Tsui (exit E)

DEFENSIVE SHOPPING, BLOW BY BLOW

Hong Kong is *not* a nest of thieves just waiting to rip you off, but pitfalls can strike the uninitiated.

Whatever you are in the market for, always check prices in a few shops before buying. When comparing camera prices, for example, make sure you're comparing not only the same camera body but also comparable lenses and any other accessories included. Always get a manufacturer's guarantee or warranty that is valid worldwide.

The most common way for shopkeepers in Hong Kong to cheat tourists is to simply overcharge. In the tourist shopping district of Tsim Sha Tsui, you'll rarely find price tags on anything. Checking prices in several shops therefore becomes essential. But Hong Kong merchants weren't born yesterday; they know tourists comparison-shop. So staff will often quote a reasonable or even low price on a big-ticket item, only to get the money back by overcharging on accessories.

Spotting overcharging is the easy part, though. Sneakier (but rarer) tricks involve merchants removing vital components that should have been included for free (like the connecting cords for the speakers on a stereo system) and demanding more money when you return to the shop to get them. You should be especially wary if staff want to take the goods into the back room to 'box it up'. Another tactic is to replace some of the good components with cheap or imitation ones.

Watch out for counterfeit-brand goods. Fake labels on clothes are the most obvious example, but there are fake Rolex watches, fake Gucci leather bags, even fake electronic goods. Pirated CDs and DVDs are a positive steal (in more ways than one) but are of poor quality and rapidly deteriorate.

Hong Kong's customs agents have cracked down on the fake cameras and electronic goods, and the problem has been pretty much solved. However, counterfeit brand-name watches remain very common and are constantly being flogged by the irritating touts patrolling Nathan Rd. If you discover that you've been sold a fake brand-name watch by a shopkeeper when you thought you were buying the genuine article, call the police (☎ 2527 7177).

If you have any trouble with a dodgy merchant, call the HKTB's Quality Tourism Services (QTS; ☎ 2806 2823; www.qtshk.com) if the shop is a tourist-board member; the HKTB logo will be displayed on the front door or in some other prominent place. Otherwise, contact the Hong Kong Consumer Council (☎ 2929 2222; www.consumer.org .hk) Monday to Friday between 9am and 5.45pm.

If you are determined to take legal action against a shopkeeper, the Small Claims Tribunal (Map p65; ☎ 2582 4084, 2582 4085; 4th fl, Wan Chai Tower, 12 Harbour Rd, Wan Chai; ☷ 9am-1pm & 2-5pm Mon-Fri, 9am-noon Sat; Wan Chai MTR) handles civil cases involving up to a maximum of $50,000. The Community Advice Bureau (Map p56; ☎ 2815 5444; www.cab.org.hk; Room 16C, Right Emperor Commercial Bldg, 122-126 Wellington St, Central; ☷ 9.30am-4.30pm Mon-Fri) will help you find a lawyer.

Simple, energetic and comfortable styles in this chain of bright, modern boutiques. There are 15 outlets throughout the territory, including a branch in Central (Map p56; ☎ 2868 4066; Upper ground fl, 10 Queen's Rd Central).

STAR COMPUTER CITY Map p92 Computers
2nd fl, Star House, 3 Salisbury Rd; 🚇 Star Ferry
This is the largest complex of retail computer outlets in Tsim Sha Tsui, with some two-dozen shops selling PDAs, laptops, computer games, and all manner of cables and accessories. You could certainly do slightly better on price further north in Mong Kok, but as well as being handier, these outlets are probably a bit more reliable.

ALAN CHAN CREATIONS
Map p92   Gifts & Souvenirs
☎ 2723 2722; www.alanchancreations.com; Shop 5A, Basement, Peninsula Hong Kong, Salisbury Rd; MTR Tsim Sha Tsui
Alan Chan has designed everything – from airport logos to soy-sauce bottles – and now lends his name to stylish souvenirs, such as clothing and ceramic pieces. Some items he has a direct hand in, others he simply approves of. Cool, contemporary Chinese design that should inspire plenty of gift ideas.

CURIO ALLEY Map p92 Gifts & Souvenirs
🕙 10am-8pm; MTR Tsim Sha Tsui
This is a fun place to shop for name chops, soapstone carvings, fans and other Chinese bric-a-brac. It's found in an alleyway between Lock and Hankow Rds, just south of Haiphong Rd.

KING SING JEWELLERY Map p92 Jewellery
☎ 2735 7021; Shop 14, Ground fl, Star House, 3 Salisbury Rd; 🚇 Star Ferry
A long-standing jeweller with a wide selection of diamonds, pearls and gold items, many of them made by its own goldsmiths. The sales staff is pleasant and not pushy.

OM INTERNATIONAL Map p92 Jewellery
☎ 2366 3421; 1st fl, Friend's House, 6 Carnarvon Rd; 🕙 closed Sun; MTR Tsim Sha Tsui (exit B2)
This place has an excellent selection of saltwater and freshwater pearls, and there's a whole lot more on offer than what's on display. The staff is scrupulously honest, helpful and friendly.

PREMIER JEWELLERY Map p92 Jewellery
☎ 2368 0003; Shop G14-15, Ground fl, Holiday Inn Golden Mile Shopping Mall, 50 Nathan Rd; MTR Tsim Sha Tsui
This third-generation family firm is directed by a qualified gemmologist and one of our favourite places to shop. The range isn't huge, but if you're looking for something particular, give it a day's notice to have a selection ready in time for your arrival. Staff can also help you design your own piece.

TOM LEE MUSIC COMPANY
Map p92   Music
☎ 2723 9932; 1-9 Cameron Lane; MTR Tsim Sha Tsui
Tom Lee, who has almost 20 branches across the territory, is Mr Music in Hong Kong and the man to see if you're looking for Western musical instruments, including guitars, flutes, recorders and the odd mouth organ.

GIGA SPORTS Map p92 Outdoor Gear
☎ 2115 9930; Shop 244-247, 2nd fl, Ocean Terminal, Harbour City, Salisbury Rd; 🕙 10am-8pm; 🚇 Star Ferry
This vast sports superstore is Hong Kong's largest, with a wide range of sports equipment, backpacks, clothing and footwear.

TRAVELMAX Map p92 Outdoor Gear
☎ 3188 4271; Shop 270-273, 2nd fl, Ocean Terminal, Harbour City, Salisbury Rd; 🚇 Star Ferry
Travelmax sells both lightweight and cold-weather outdoor gear; kids' sizes are available. There's a good range of Eagle Creek travel products here, too.

DAVID CHAN PHOTO SHOP
Map p92   Photographic Equipment
☎ 2723 3886; Shop 15, Ground fl, Champagne Court, 16 Kimberley Rd; MTR Tsim Sha Tsui (exit B1)
If you've decided to give the digital age a miss altogether or at least still use film cameras, this dealer is one of the most reliable in Hong Kong and sells both new and antique cameras.

HARBOUR CITY Map p92 Shopping Mall
☎ 2118 8666; www.harbourcity.com.hk; 3-9 Canton Rd; MTR Tsim Sha Tsui
This is an enormous place, with 700 shops, 50 food and beverage outlets, and five cin-

emas in four separate zones: for kids, sport, fashion and cosmetics and beauty. There's also a large Lane Crawford department store. Every major brand is represented.

KS AHLUWALIA & SONS
Map p92   Sporting Goods
☎ 2368 8334; 8C Hankow Rd; MTR Tsim Sha Tsui (exit E)
Long established, this store is well stocked with golf gear, tennis racquets, cricket bats, shirts and balls. It's cash only and no prices are marked, so haggle away.

OCEAN SKY DIVERS Map p92   Sporting Goods
☎ 2366 3738; 1st fl, 17-19 Lock Rd; www.ocean skydiver.com; MTR Tsim Sha Tsui (exit C1)
Along with a full range of diving and snorkelling gear, this place is also worth consulting about dive courses and ideal dive sites all around the territories coastline and islands.

YAU MA TEI & MONG KOK
To the north of Tsim Sha Tsui, Yau Ma Tei and Mong Kok cater mostly to local shoppers and offer good prices on clothing, sporting goods, camping gear, footwear, computers and other daily necessities. There's nothing very exotic available here, but for your everyday items they're popular spots, and it is fun to see how the local people shop, and to check out what they are buying.

TRENDY ZONE Map p97   Clothing & Accessories
Chow Tai Fook Centre, 580A Nathan Rd; ⏲ 1-10pm; MTR Mong Kok (exit E2)
A couple of dozen quirky little fashion outlets crowd into this micromall selling new and vintage gear for guys and gals. It's very urban and aimed largely at a teen and twenty-something clientele.

MONG KOK COMPUTER CENTRE
Map p98   Computers
8-8A Nelson St, Mong Kok; ⏲ 1-10pm; MTR Mong Kok (exit E2)
This centre has three floors of computer shops. In general, it's geared more towards the resident Cantonese-speaking market than foreigners, but you can normally get better deals here than in Tsim Sha Tsui. Check out Winframe System (☎ 2300 1238; Shop 106-107) on the 1st floor.

YUE HWA CHINESE PRODUCTS EMPORIUM Map p97   Department Store
☎ 2384 0084; 301-309 Nathan Rd; MTR Yau Ma Tei (exit D)
This enormous place, with seven floors of ceramics, furniture, souvenirs and clothing, has absolutely everything the souvenir-hunting tourist could possibly want, as well as bolts of silk, herbs, clothes, porcelain, luggage, umbrellas and kitchenware. There's also a branch in Tsim Sha Tsui on Kowloon Park Dr (Map p92; ☎ 2317 5333; 1 Kowloon Park Dr) that's entered from Peking Rd.

CHAMONIX ALPINE EQUIPMENT
Map p97   Outdoor Gear
☎ 2770 6746; 1st fl, On Yip Bldg, 395 Shanghai St; MTR Yau Ma Tei (exit B2)
Far-flung but worth the trip, this Mong Kok shop, run by an avid mountaineer, has a wide range of camping, hiking and climbing equipment.

WISE MOUNT SPORTS
Map p98   Outdoor Gear
☎ 2787 3011; Ground fl, 75 Sai Yee St; ⏲ 11.30am-10.30pm; MTR Mong Kok (exit E2)
This is a long-standing family-run shop with camping gear, swimming goggles, pocket knives, compasses, hard-wearing bags and even sports trophies for sale.

WING SHING PHOTO SUPPLIES
Map p98   Photographic Equipment
☎ 2396 6886; 57 Sai Yeung Choi St South; MTR Mong Kok (exit D3)
We've received letters from readers praising the quality of the service and the competitive prices at Wing Shing. We like the hours; the boys in the north always try harder.

LANGHAM PLACE MALL
Map p98   Shopping Mall
☎ 3520 2800; 8 Argyle St; MTR Mong Kok (exit C3)
This 15-storey supermall has some 300 shops that stay open till as late as 11pm. The focal point of the mall is the high-tech Digital Sky where special events take place.

KHS BICYCLES Map p98   Sporting Goods
☎ 2733 7777; 201 Tung Choi St; MTR Mong Kok (exit A2)
A well-stocked shop offering a range of bikes from urban runabouts to rugged mountainbikes and a good range of accessories.

NEW KOWLOON

Shopping venues in New Kowloon run the gamut from glittering shopping malls, such as Festival Walk in Kowloon Tong, to the cut-price computer centres of Sham Shui Po.

PAGE ONE Map pp88–9 Books
☎ 2778 2808; Shop LG1 30, Lower ground fl, Festival Walk, 80-88 Tat Chee Ave, Kowloon Tong; MTR Kowloon Tong (exit C2)

A chain, yes, but one with attitude. Page One has Hong Kong's best selection of art and design magazines and books; it's also strong on photography, literature, film and children's books. There's also a smaller branch in Tsim Sha Tsui (Map p92; ☎ 2730 6080; Shop 3202, 3rd fl, Gateway Arcade, Harbour City, 25-27 Canton Rd).

GOLDEN COMPUTER ARCADE
Map pp88–9 Computers
Basement & 1st fl, 146-152 Fuk Wa St, Sham Shui Po; Sham MTR Shui Po (exit B1)

This centre sells computers and components, as well as software, VCDs and DVDs, all at the lowest prices this side of Shenzhen.

NEW CAPITAL COMPUTER PLAZA
Map pp88–9 Computers
1st & 2nd fls, 85-89 Un Chau St, Sham Shui Po; MTR Sham Shui Po (exit B1)

This emporium of computer shops has a good range of stock and helpful staff who can produce enough English to close a sale.

FESTIVAL WALK Map pp88–9 Shopping Mall
☎ 2844 2222; www.festivalwalk.com.hk; 80-88 Tat Chee Ave, Kowloon Tong; ⏰ 10am-midnight; MTR Kowloon Tong (exit C2)

Festival Walk is a huge and glittering shopping mall with Hong Kong's largest cinema and ice-skating rink. There's a good midrange selection of some 200 shops and around two-dozen restaurants here as well.

BLUELIST[1] (blu list) *v.*
to recommend a travel experience.
What's your recommendation? www.lonelyplanet.com/bluelist

EATING

top picks

EATING

It is hard to have a conversation in Hong Kong without mentioning food, especially when many still greet each other by asking, *'Láy sik-jó faan may?'* (Have you eaten yet?). Dim sum brunch on Sunday is still the way of life for many families and the thickness of the dumpling skin, the consistency of the glutinous rice and the colour of the green vegetable are all part of the discussion. Socialites, or *tai tai,* meet for high tea in the afternoon and, between catching up on the latest gossip, comment on the presentations of their finger sandwiches and scones. Office workers fervently discuss whether to have sushi or pasta for lunch, while the fashionable set inevitably exchanges news on which celebrity chef is due to make an appearance in town. In the last half century, Hong Kong has emerged from a backwater British outpost in the Far East to an epicentre of international trade. The general lifestyle of its population has become cosmopolitan, and so have the things people eat.

Despite its 150 years as a British colony, which ended in 1997, Hong Kong has never lost its Chinese roots. Cantonese food is by far the most popular cuisine in Hong Kong. It originated in Guangdong province, from where most Hong Kong Chinese people can trace their roots. The flavours are more subtle than in other Chinese cooking styles and the sauces are rarely strong.

Spoilt by their locale's generally mild climate, with clearly divided seasons, the Cantonese are almost religious about the importance of fresh ingredients. 'What's in season now?' is often the first question customers pop to the waiter when dining Cantonese. It is common to see tanks in seafood restaurants full of finned and shelled creatures enjoying their final moments on *terra infirma.* Housewives still prefer a live chicken or pigeon plucked from (and plucked in, come to think of it) a market for the evening meal, though the cost of fresh poultry means the supermarket variety still has its market.

Guangzhou, the capital of Guangdong, once known as Canton (from which the adjective 'Cantonese' was derived), was the first Chinese port to open to foreign trades, so Cantonese cuisine has always had the cosmopolitan edge. It has the largest collection of specialised dishes in all of China and is characterised by elaborate preparation and the use of an infinite variety of ingredients. Subtle flavours are combined with a light touch of soy sauce and ginger, enhancing the freshness of the ingredients. Delicate and well-balanced flavours are obtained through cooking methods such as quick stir-frying and steaming.

Wok tossing is a distinctly Cantonese cooking technique that is crucial to the quality of a quick stir-fry. The radiating heat and aroma of the finished dish, known as *wok-hay,* determines the success of a dish. Seasoned Cantonese diners can often guess the size and the age of the wok by tasting the food cooked from it.

Accelerated international airfreights and the increase in foreign travel by local people means there's a lot more experimentation with food these days. Macadamia nuts find their way into scallop dishes, and you're just as likely to find on a menu sautéed cod slices with pinenuts and fresh fruit as you are traditional steamed grouper.

Expensive local dishes – some of which are truly tasty, others that carry with them more of a 'face' value – include abalone, shark's fin and bird's nest. Pigeon is a tasty Cantonese speciality that is served in various ways, but most commonly roasted, chopped finely and eaten with lettuce and hoisin sauce (a sweet, slightly piquant brown paste).

Hong Kong's colonial history has developed few unique food items. *Bo lo bao* (meaning 'pineapple bun' because of its surface pattern) is a cheap-and-cheery, sweet breakfast or afternoon pastry believed to have been inspired by scones. Little-trolley noodles *(chē jái mihn)* owed their origin to mainland immigrant hawkers but are most certainly a Hong Kong invention. But other than these few examples, there aren't many dishes or sauces unique to Hong Kong per se.

Hong Kong chefs, however, pride themselves on innovation: experimenting, improvising and creating. They will instantly seize upon a new ingredient and find ways to use it. For example, asparagus is a vegetable little known in the rest of China, but Hong Kong chefs serve it every day, combining it with baby abalone and olive oil or with caviar and preserved eggs.

In Western dining, hotels play an important role. Short of an established culinary institute Hong Kong has always relied on resource-rich hotel groups to bring in trained non-Chinese chefs. Although such dependency has decreased in the past 30 years or so with the developments of many stand-alone restaurants, the legacy continues. Michelin staples Nobu (p191) and Pierre (p177) both have their footholds in five-star hotels.

For a territory where almost everything has to be imported, embracing outside influences is a way of life. Starbucks is considered hip, Pret A Manger is lunch culture and McDonald's is everyone's childhood memory. Seafarers, colonists, refugees, migrant workers and expatriates have all come here from different parts of the world and enriched – or at least influenced – the culture and the food. To Hong Kong globalisation is nothing new, and neither is mixing flavours on the plate.

HISTORY & CULTURE

The modern history of Hong Kong begins with the First Opium War (p21), but the roots of Hong Kong cuisine were laid long before. Prior to its colonial history, Hong Kong was already home to three major clans: the Punti (Cantonese Chinese) and Hakka (non-Cantonese Chinese) peoples lived in what is the New Territories today, while a humble fisherfolk called the Dan lived on the coast, especially in the south of Hong Kong Island.

Not wanting to have much to do with the local fare, the British brought their own provisions, and in this far corner of the world continued to eat their gammon and sausage, pies and kippers, and wash it all down with milky tea and warm beer.

The local inhabitants, living in walled villages, ate what they could herd and grow or catch from the sea. Produce was abundant. Certain ancient food traditions from these peoples have remained, and the most notable among them is the 'basin dish' *(poon choy)*. The story has it that the last emperor of the Southern Song dynasty (AD 1127–1279), Zhào Bǐng, fleeing from the Mongolians, headed south and ended up in Hong Kong with his entourage. The villagers were gobsmacked by the sudden arrival of their supreme ruler. And although he was only eight, they treated him to the best food they could scrape together, according to the imperial tradition of wastefulness. Not a people overly endowed with beautiful crockery, the villagers resorted to serving the mountain of fine foods to the emperor in a basin. *Poon choy* has become a dish for festival occasions ever since.

The Crown Colony maintained its stability and prosperity for most of its 150 years, even as the mainland skipped from one upheaval to another. Many of the best mainland cooks, especially those from Guangzhou, eventually found refuge in Hong Kong. Given the colony's resources to play around with, they strived for the best and the most exotic, making Hong Kong the 'real' Guangzhou.

With the declaration of the People's Republic of China in 1949, floods of immigrants from Shanghai, Sichuan, Hunan and Peking (Beijing) came looking for safety, jobs and a new life. Their arrival turned Hong Kong into a melting pot of Chinese regional cuisines, and the rest, literally, is history.

HOW HONG KONG PEOPLE EAT

Local brand Doll Instant Noodle once suggested Hong Kong people eat its product five times a day. While not what a dietician would call a sound piece of advice, it was an accurate reflection on how Hong Kong people eat: always in a hurry and up to five meals a day – breakfast, lunch, afternoon tea, dinner and a late-night snack.

In Hong Kong, workers often drop by a small restaurant specialising in breakfast foods such as *jùk*, a rice porridge also known as congee, which is either eaten plain or with a multitude of savoury garnishes and condiments. Office workers often grab a bowl of soup noodles to bring back to work, happily slurping away at their desks. On weekends and holidays everyone goes out for dim sum (aka yum cha) for breakfast, brunch or even lunch.

Lunch in the built-up areas during the week will often be a set lunch consisting of one or two dishes at a fixed price. Or it could be a bowl of soup noodles with shrimp wontons or a plate of rice with roast pork, duck or goose. Or something more elaborate.

Afternoon tea in Hong Kong is especially popular on weekends. It may be an elaborate affair – such as traditional English high tea or dim sum – at a good hotel. Or it may be at the office and comprise little more than tea and biscuits or a steamed bun. Labourers will stop for just a few minutes to pour a cup of tea and eat a custard tart before going back to work.

Dinner is a big event every day, especially dinner in a restaurant. The majority of Hong Kong people live in very small flats with handkerchief-sized kitchens; dining out with friends and family solves the problem of space. This is one reason Hong Kong's restaurants are always so noisy; this is where people come to catch up on all the gossip, make plans, tell jokes and just enjoy life. But still, few dinners are longer than two hours, as Hong Kong people always have somewhere else to go.

Dishes at a Chinese meal are always served together. Tables, which are always round in Chinese restaurants, are often equipped with a lazy Susan. It's not unusual for dishes to be served with tiny saucers filled with various sauces, with *si-yàu* (soy sauce), *gaai-laat* (hot mustard) and *laat-jiù jeung* (chilli sauce) the most common ones. Feel free to stand up, lean over the table and dip if the sauce is on the other side.

Often you'll see several small bottles on the table, usually containing soy sauce and vinegar. The vinegar is usually a dark colour and is easily confused with soy sauce, so taste some first before pouring. Sauces aren't dumped on food – instead the food is dipped into a separate dish. Staff will usually let you know which sauce goes with which dish.

ETIQUETTE

The Chinese are, by and large, casual about etiquette at the table, and they don't expect foreigners to understand all of their dining customs. But there are a few unique ways of doing things here that are useful to know.

The Chinese think nothing of sticking their chopsticks into a communal dish, which can raise sanitation issues. Better restaurants provide separate serving chopsticks or even spoons with each dish; if so, use them.

Leaving chopsticks sticking vertically into the bowl – as unlikely as that sounds – is a bad omen as they resemble incense sticks in a bowl of ashes, a sign of death.

If you absolutely can't manage chopsticks, don't be afraid to ask for a fork; nearly all Chinese restaurants have them. It's less embarrassing than having your food dropping all over the table, or worse yet flying across the room, as it often happens with unskilled chopstick users.

At a Chinese meal, everyone gets an individual bowl of rice or a small soup bowl. It's quite acceptable to hold the bowl close to your

SMOKING

Effective 1 January, 2007, all indoor spaces of restaurants were theoretically smoke free. But in its usually irresolute style, the government has allowed certain places exemption until 1 July, 2009. Nicotine addicts are seeking out these havens, as well as restaurants with unsheltered outdoor spaces where the smoking ban does not reach. In districts such as Soho (p180) and Sai Wan Ho (p189), where restaurants tend to have open fronts, customers often step outside to get their fix.

lips and shovel the contents into your mouth with chopsticks. An alternative is to hold a spoon in one hand and use the chopsticks to push the food onto the spoon. Then use the spoon as you normally would.

If the food contains bones, just put them directly on the tablecloth beside your plate or bowl. And you needn't use a napkin to hide what you're doing; except at very upmarket restaurants most Hong Kong people just spit them on the table.

Chinese make great use of toothpicks – foreign residents of Hong Kong sometimes call them 'Chinese dessert'. The polite way to use them is to cover your mouth with one hand while using the toothpick with the other.

Beer, soft drinks, wine or brandy may or may not be served with the meal, but tea most definitely will. When your waiter or host pours your tea, thank them by tapping your middle and index fingers lightly on the table. When the teapot is empty and you want a refill of hot water, signal the waiter by taking the lid off the pot and resting it on the handle.

DIM SUM

Dim sum (*dím sàm*) is a uniquely Cantonese 'meal', eaten as breakfast, brunch or lunch. The term literally means 'to touch the heart', but 'snack' is more accurate. The act of eating dim sum is usually referred to as yum cha (*yám chàa*), meaning 'to drink tea' as the beverage is always consumed in copious amounts with dim sum.

Each dish, often containing two to four morsels steamed in a bamboo basket, is small and meant to be shared, so the bigger the group the greater the variety you get to try. At some restaurants there can be close to a hundred varieties to choose from.

In old-style dim sum places you don't need a menu; just stop the waiter and choose something from the cart. Modern venues give you an order slip, but it's almost always in Chinese only. However, as dim sum dishes are often readymade, the waiters should be able to show you samplings to choose from. When a dish arrives, the server will mark it down on a bill they leave on the table. Dim sum restaurants are normally brightly lit and very large and noisy.

VEGETARIANS & VEGANS

Chinese vegetarian food has undergone a renaissance in recent years and it is consumed by devout Buddhists and the health-conscious alike. Out of Buddhist piety many Hong Kong people will become vegetarians on the first and 15th day of the lunar month.

Chinese chefs are masters at adding variety to vegetarian cooking and creating 'mock meat' dishes. Dishes formed to resemble (and taste like) spare ribs or chicken are made from layered pieces of dried beancurd and gluten or fashioned from mashed taro root.

Large monasteries, notably Po Lin (p201) on Lantau, often have vegetarian restaurants, though you will also find many restaurants in Kowloon and on Hong Kong Island. For the most part they are Cantonese or Shanghainese and strictly vegetarian, as they are owned and operated by Buddhists.

Western vegetarian food is reasonably hard to come by here if you want anything more complex than a salad or penne in tomato sauce, though there are options in Central and the island of Lamma. Some Indian restaurants are exclusively vegetarian, but most in Hong Kong offer a combined menu.

Otherwise, this city is not particularly vegetarian-friendly. Seemingly meatless dishes often have hidden meat elements in them (see boxed text, p194).

COOKING COURSES

Hong Kong is a good place to hone your skills in the art of Chinese cookery.

Chinese Cuisine Training Institute (Map pp54–5; ☎ 2538 2200; www.ccti.vtc.edu.hk; 7th fl, Pokfulam Training Centre Complex, 145 Pok Fu Lam Rd, Pok Fu Lam; $620) Four-hour afternoon course that surveys the full spectrum of Chinese cooking.

Home Management Centre (Map pp54–5; ☎ 2510 2828; www.hec.com.hk; 10th fl, Electric Centre, 28 City Garden Rd, North Point) Wednesday English-language class teaches three simple Chinese recipes in two hours for $85.

On the website go to the Electric Living/Home Management Centre section.

The Peninsula Academy (Map p92; ☎ 2920 2888; The Peninsula, Salisbury Rd, Tsim Sha Tsui) Every two months one of the chefs from the historical five-star hotel teaches a different cuisine, ranging from Japanese to French to Cantonese. The $1000 per head fee (including high lunch) makes it popular among *tai tai*.

Towngas Cooking Centre (Map p74; ☎ 2576 1535; www.towngascooking.com; Basement, Leighton Centre, 77 Leighton Rd, Causeway Bay; $300 to $350) Classes in a vast range of Chinese cooking styles and other culinary subjects. There's also a Tsim Sha Tsui branch (Map p94; ☎ 2367 2707; Shop L030, New World Centre, 18-24 Salisbury Rd).

PUBLICATIONS

The best sources for travellers looking for more restaurant recommendations than we are able to make here are the biannual *Good Eating* guide by the South China Morning Post (special@scmp.com), published in March and October, and the annual *HK Magazine Restaurant Guide* by in the HK Magazine (asiacity@asia-city .com.hk), published n February or March. Both offer reviews and listings of hundreds of eateries throughout the territory. *The Guide: Hong Kong's Restaurant Guide* from bc magazine (www .bcmagazine.net) has reviews of 300-plus Hong Kong restaurants in all price categories. The Hong Kong Tourism Board (HKTB; p301) distributes an annual booklet called *Best of the Best Culinary Guide*, featuring award-winning local dishes and where to find them. Lonely Planet's *World Food Hong Kong*, while not a restaurant guide per se, will take you on an indepth culinary tour of the territory.

SNACKING ON STREET-SAVVY SAVOURIES

Dim sum is not the exclusive province of the tea restaurants; some street stalls serve dim sum until the wee hours, to help partygoers soak up the booze. What they serve are usually the more common items, such as steamed shrimp dumplings (*hàa gáau*), steamed pork and shrimp dumplings (*siù máai*) and steamed rice-flour rolls with shrimp, beef or pork (*chéung fán*). The dim sum is served alongside other street-food items, such as curried fish balls, grilled squids, poached pig's colon and – it's no euphemism – stinky tofu (*chau dau fū*), tofu fermented with shrimp shell and deepfried.

PRACTICALITIES

Opening Hours

With the exceptions of local tea restaurants (*chàa chàan tèng*), most Hong Kong restaurants open from around 11.30am to 3pm for lunch and 6pm to 11.30pm for dinner. The restaurants reviewed below follow these standard opening hours unless otherwise stated.

How Much?

You can make a meal out of wonton noodles and some greens and it would cost you no more than $30, and fast-food chains such as Café de Carol (www.cafedecoralfastfood.com), Fairwood (www.fairwood.com.hk) and MX (www.maxims.com.hk/html/fastfood) would serve you a Western set (soup, main and coffee) for less than $40. Otherwise, a proper sit-down lunch costs at least $80 and for dinner about $120 per head. Upscale restaurants will set you back at least $700 per person for dinner.

Booking Tables

Most restaurants midrange or above will take reservations. Booking is a must for private kitchens (see p184) and very popular places that serve two or even three seatings a night.

Tipping

Tipping is not a must in Hong Kong restaurants as waiters supposedly get full salaries and every bill includes a 10% service charge. But the service charge almost always goes into the owner's coffers so if you like the service, tip as you see fit. Most people leave behind the small change.

Self-Catering

The two major supermarket chains, Park'N'Shop and Wellcome, have megastores around that offer grocery as well as takeaway cooked food. Their gourmet counterparts

include: Great Food Hall (Map p63; ☎ 2918 9986; Basement, Two Pacific Place, Admiralty; ☯ 10am-10pm); Citysuper, with a handful of branches, including Causeway Bay (Map p74; ☎ 2506 2888; Basement One, Times Square, Causeway Bay; ☯ 10.30am-10pm); Oliver Delicatessen in Central (Map p56; ☯ 8.30am-8pm), as well as Sheung Wan and Admiralty; and Taste (Map pp88–9; Festival Walk, Kowloon Tong; ☯ 7am-midnight). The relatively new Three Sixty (Map p56; ☎ 2111 4480; 3rd & 4th fl, Landmark Bldg, 1 Pedder St; ☯ 7am-9pm; MTR Central, exit C) offers organic produce, mostly imported and generally expensive.

HONG KONG ISLAND

Catering facilities on Hong Kong Island run the gamut from Michelin-level restaurants in five-star hotels to Asian fusion enjoyed at pavement cafés, to an embarrassment of ethnic cuisines – from Indian and Mexican to Chiu Chow and Vietnamese – served in tiny little holes in the wall upstairs, downstairs or in some obscure chamber.

CENTRAL

From one end to the other, Central can offer a diverse range of dining experiences covering everything from *daai-pàai-dawng* (open-air street-stall food) and affordable ethnic food to funky Western restaurants with celebrity chefs. Lan Kwai Fong and Soho are still going strong, and the part of Wyndham St linking the two areas is growing in full force.

AMBER Map p56   Modern European $$$$
☎ 2132 0066; 7/F, The Landmark Mandarin Oriental; 15 Queen's Rd Central; weekend brunch $348; ☯ also open for breakfast 6.30-10.30am; MTR Central (ex it G)
Amber is the name as well as the colour tone of the restaurant's interior. In the light of day it serves as a power restaurant for three-Martini lunches; at night the brightest light sources are the tubular ceiling light installation and the flat-screen computer wine menu customers use to pick their bottles according to regions, varietals and, less importantly, price ranges. The menu is rather cryptic and every name is at least 12 words long, but once that oven-roasted Sisteron baby-spring-lamb shoulder or soy-and-maple-glazed bluefin tuna melts in your mouth, every syllable is fine.

PIERRE Map p56   Modern French $$$$
☎ 2825 4001; Mandarin Oriental, 5 Connaught Rd; 🕙 dinner only Sat, closed Sun; MTR Central (exit F)

The godfather of fusion, Pierre Gagnaire, has finally brought his revolutionary cuisine to the city that embodies the concept. Consider this: Le Rouge – red-pepper jelly, duck foie gras and 'red' red tuna, red belotta 'Croque-Monsieur', Niora paste, chorizo, light butternut squash chutney, red beetroot and raspberry ice cream. Every bite hits your taste buds like a pianist working the keys. Dessert might be a caramelised rocket salad – and it works. The décor, with portholes and chandelier, reminds one of a fine restaurant on a cruise liner, especially when adding the harbour view.

CAFÉ DES ARTISTES Map p68   French $$$
☎ 2526 3880; 1st fl, California Tower, 30-32 D'Aguilar St; 🕙 dinner only Sun; MTR Central (exit D2)

This bright and airy eatery has evolved from a rather stuffy provincial French restaurant to a casual modern French haunt. Perched on the 1st floor and surrounded by breezy, bright windows overlooking Lan Kwai Fong, the restaurant boasts a large bar and secluded terrace area perfect for enjoying the immaculate foie gras dishes and diving into fresh seafood from the ice-bar.

FINDS Map p68   Scandinavian $$$
☎ 2522 9318; 2nd fl, Lan Kwai Fong Tower, 33 Wyndham St; set lunch from $98; 🕙 dinner only Sun; MTR Central (exit D2), 🚌 26

This wonderful place, whose name stands for – would you believe? – 'Finland', 'Iceland', 'Norway', 'Denmark' and 'Sweden', serves seasonal Scandinavian food. We love the *scapas* (Scandinavian tapas, for lack of a better term; $50 to $90), especially the tartare of Baltic herring and terrine of pork confit with leek. The surrounds – faux igloo walls, icicles-cum-chandelier, lots of blue tones – will have you thinking that global warming has worked in reverse in old Hong Kong.

LUNG KING HEEN Map p56   Chinese $$$
☎ 3196 8888; Four Seasons Hotel, 8 Finance St, Central; set lunch $400, dinner $880; MTR Central (exit A)

It's not just the view that you should come for, it's the plump and fresh crustaceans and the divine roast duck ($560 each, good for six people), whose aroma lingers on long after you've devoured every bit of the bird.

M AT THE FRINGE Map p68   International $$$
☎ 2877 4000; 1st fl, South Block, Fringe Club, Dairy Farm Bldg, 2 Lower Albert Rd; 🕙 dinner only Sat & Sun; MTR Central (exit D2)

No one seems to have a bad thing to say about Michelle's. The menu changes constantly and everything is excellent, be it lobster soufflé ($168) or slow-baked salted lamb ($248). It's worth saving room for dessert, if you have that kind of self-restraint. Reservations are a must. At lunch starters/mains/desserts are a uniform $68/112/58.

MOZART STUB'N Map p68   Austrian $$$
☎ 2522 1763; 8 Glenealy; 🕙 closed Sun; MTR Central (exit D2)

This classy, almost fastidious Austrian (do *not* say German) establishment has excellent food and wines and a delightful atmosphere. The dishes may sound Teutonic, but they are served in sensible portions.

OLÉ SPANISH RESTAURANT & WINE BAR Map p68   Spanish $$$
☎ 2523 8624; 1/F, Shun Ho Tower, 24-30 Ice House Street; tapas $50-130; MTR Central (exit D2)

Any Spaniard living in the city would point to this restaurant as the best Spanish restaurant in town. Every tile and vase oozes Iberian air, and if you sit by the window looking at the colonial-style Bishop's House across the street, you might forget that you're in Asia. The paella ($360) is great for two to share.

TOKIO JOE Map p68   Japanese $$$
☎ 2525 1889; Ground fl, 16 Lan Kwai Fong; 🕙 dinner only Sun; MTR Central (exit D2)

This place serves sushi and sashimi that's among the freshest in Hong Kong, though there is a full range of hot dishes (including *yakitori*) available as well. There are set lunches for $125 to $190. Joe's flashier kid brother, Kyoto Joe (Map p68; ☎ 2804 6800; Ground fl, 21 D'Aguilar St), just down the hill, is somewhat more expensive and modern, and a venue for drinking as much as dining. There's a *robotayaki* (barbecue) bar out back.

VA BENE Map p68   Italian $$$
☎ 2845 5577; 17-22 Lan Kwai Fong; set lunch $198; 🕙 dinner only Sat & Sun; MTR Central (exit D2)

This smart restaurant bears a striking resemblance to a neighbourhood trattoria in

Venice. It's a good choice for a special date or an extravagant celebration. Book ahead; dress smart.

YUN FU Map p68 — Northern Chinese $$$

☎ 2116 8855; Basement, Yu Yuet Lai Bldg, 43-45 Wyndham St; 🚌 26

No other place does Chinese food in such a fun way. Entering the restaurant through the stone staircase feels like travelling in a time tunnel, to the period of *Crouching Tiger, Hidden Dragon*. After an exotic cocktail garnished with dry seahorses or lizards ($88), your appetite should be whetted for goose liver soaked in dark soy sauce ($98) and sliced duck fillet wrapped in tofu paper ($88). If you're a veggie, why not a whole roasted bamboo shoot served in the bark?

ZUMA Map p56 — Japanese $$$

☎ 3657 6388; Level 5 & 6, The Landmark, 15 Queen's Rd Central; 🕐 closed Sun; MTR Central (exit G)

This uberchic dining import from London markets itself as authentic but not traditional Japanese cuisine, and has miles of space in which to serve it. There is a robata counter, sushi bar and a terrace. Up the game with *sashimi omakase* of rock lobster, Dungeness crab, sea urchin, monkfish liver, abalone, oscietra caviar and tuna belly, each of which'll set you back $880.

ASSAF Map p68 — Lebanese $$

☎ 2851 6550; Shop B, Ground fl, Lyndhurst Bldg, 37 Lyndhurst Tce; 🕐 noon-midnight; 🚌 40M

This welcoming and cosy place specialises in meze and other tasty titbits; the set dinners are a mixture of six to eight different items. There are good-value set lunches ($78) and dinners (vegetarian/meat $155/178) as well. The Assaf brothers also own the Beyrouth Cafe Central (Map p68; ☎ 2854 1872; 39 Lyndhurst Tce), a simple place that does takeaway sandwiches, kebabs and so on for $45.

CHINA TEE CLUB Map p56 — International $$

☎ 2521 0233; Room 101, 1st fl, Pedder Bldg, 12 Pedder St; 🕐 11.30am-8pm Mon-Sat; MTR Central (exit D1)

This civilised tea house-cum-restaurant serving both Asian and Western favourites is perfect for a meal or a cuppa after finishing your shopping at Shanghai Tang (p160) or Blanc de Chine (p159) below. The food is

only passable but you can't beat sipping tea or diving into laksa or Hainan chicken rice in an ambience that makes you feel like you had travelled back to 19th-century Hong Kong. Pasta and vegetarian dishes are $90 to $105.

HABIBI Map p56 — Egyptian $$

☎ 2544 6198; Shop B & D, Ground fl, 112-114 Wellington St; 🕐 dinner only Sat, closed Sun; 🚌 40M

Whether or not Habibi serves strictly authentic Egyptian food is a moot point – the halal food is very good and the setting is the Cairo of the 1930s – all mirrors, tassels, velvet cushions, ceiling fans and hookahs. Habibi's casual and takeaway section, Habibi Café (Map p56; ☎ 2544 3886; 🕐 11am-midnight), in Shop A next door is a lot cheaper, with meze from $25 to $58, meze platters $85 to $110, mains $45 to $160 and a weekday set lunch $60.

HUNAN GARDEN Map p56 — Hunanese $$

☎ 2868 2880; 3rd fl, The Forum, Exchange Sq, Connaught Rd, Central; MTR Central (exit A)

This elegant place specialises in spicy Hunanese cuisine, which is often hotter than the Sichuan variety. The Hunanese fried chicken with chilli is excellent, as are the seafood dishes. Views, overlooking the harbour or into the heart of Central, are a bonus. Set meals start from $398 for two.

IVAN THE KOZAK

Map p68 — Ukrainian, Russian $$

☎ 2851 1193; Lower ground fl, 46-48 Cochrane St; 🚌 40M

Blinis and borscht are probably not what spring to mind when you're considering an ethnic dining experience in Hong Kong, but the food here – down-home dishes such as Ukrainian-style borscht, beef Stroganoff, stuffed cabbage rolls and *vareniki* (Ukrainian dumpling) – is surprisingly authentic and the décor cosy. There's live folk music nightly. Caviar goes for $65 to $850 for 30g.

JIMMY'S KITCHEN Map p68 — International $$

☎ 2526 5293; Basement, South China Bldg, 1-3 Wyndham St; MTR Central (exit D1)

High on nostalgia and one of the oldest names in the game, Jimmy's, a Hong Kong feature for seven decades, rests on its laurels. The baked onion soup ($58), chargrilled king prawns ($235), seven-pepper steak ($290) and a whole medley of desserts (including its famous baked Alaska, $58 per person) all compete for the diners' attention. There's a branch in Tsim Sha Tsui (Map p92; ☎ 2376 0327; 1/F, Kowloon Centre, 29-39 Ashley Rd).

KOH-I-NOOR Map p68   Indian $$
☎ 2877 9706; 1st fl, California Entertainment Bldg, 34-36 D'Aguilar St; ☽ dinner only Sun; MTR Central (exit D2)
Fine Indian cuisine in sophisticated presentation and service is what you get here, as well as sophisticated prices. The most expensive dish is the leg of lamb ($300), which is great for sharing. But the weekday vegetarian/meat lunch-time buffet is a steal at $55, while biryani dishes are $62. There are branches around town, including Tsim Sha Tsui (Map p94; 1/F, 3-4 Peninsula Mansion, 16C Mody Rd) and Tai Koo Shing (Map pp54–5; Shop 001, G/F, Cityplaza, 1111 King's Rd), and prices may be a little lower at those locations.

LA KASBAH Map p68   Middle Eastern $$
☎ 2525 9493; 4-8 Arbuthnot Rd; ☽ 6.30-11.30pm Mon-Sat; ☷ 40M
La Kasbah is a Frenchified Maghreb caravanserai serving dishes from Algeria, Tunisia and Morocco, which effectively means meze and tajine or couscous. It's good stuff, but expensive for what it is. The bar, Medina, opens till 2am.

LUK YU TEA HOUSE Map p68   Dim Sum $$
☎ 2523 5464; 24-26 Stanley St; ☽ 7am-11pm; MTR Central
This old-style teahouse is a museum piece in more ways than one. Most of the staff have been here since the early Ming dynasty and are as grumpy and ill-tempered as an emperor deposed. The booths are uncomfortable, it's not cheap, prices aren't marked on the English menu, but the dim sum, served from 7am to 6pm, is really quite delicious.

POST 97 Map p68   International $$
☎ 2186 1817; 1st fl, Cosmos Bldg, 9-11 Lan Kwai Fong; ☽ 9.30am-1am Mon-Thu, 9.30am-2.30am Fri & Sat, 9.30am-1am Sun; MTR Central (exit D2)
Since its renovation, this all-day brasserie and café above the Fong has lost a little of that bohemian charm and become a bit nondescript, but it still offers a view of the bustling Lan Kwai Fong. The all-day

breakfast items such as egg benedict ($85) are still there, and new items such as detox salad ($98) are welcome additions. Weekend brunch ($150) with bottomless coffee and pick-me-ups such as Bloody Mary is a draw.

QING Map p70   Vietnamese, Western $$
☎ 2815 6739; 3 Mee Lun St; ☽ noon-midnight Mon-Fri, noon-2am Sat, closed Sun; ☷ 26
Time seems to just stand still at this place, which resembles a street-side bistro in Hanoi. Blocked out from traffic, the outdoor tables here offer an ambience that is increasingly hard to find in hyperactive Hong Kong. Go light with the Vietnamese-style rice-paper rolls or indulge in a steak smothered with Roquefort – it's all up to you, and the wine is always fab.

RUGHETTA Map p68   Italian $$
☎ 2537 7922; Basement, Carfield Commercial Bldg, 75-77 Wyndham St; pasta $110-168; ☽ dinner only on Sun; ☷ 26
This basement restaurant with a branch in New York City serves faultless 'Roman' (read earthy Italian) cuisine – though it may suffer after being discovered by the cheap lunch crowd.

SHALOM GRILL Map p56   Kosher $$
☎ 2851 6300; 2nd fl, Fortune House, 61 Connaught Rd Central; ☽ no dinner Fri; ☷ 5B
If it's Ashkenazic and Sephardic glatt kosher food you're after, the Shalom Grill can oblige. Don't expect cordon bleu, but if you're in the mood for felafel or gefilte fish (or you answer to a Higher Authority on matters culinary), this is the place to visit. Shabbat dinner and Saturday lunch can be prearranged and paid for in advance. For something lighter, sandwiches are $45 to $55.

SONG Map p68   Vietnamese $$
☎ 2559 0997; Lower ground fl, 75 Hollywood Rd; ☽ dinner only Sat, closed Sun; ☷ 26
This very stylish though somewhat cramped Vietnamese eatery, down an unnamed alleyway between Peel and Aberdeen Sts, serves refined (some might say overly so) Vietnamese food to the denizens of Soho.

THAI LEMONGRASS Map p68   Thai $$
☎ 2905 1688; 3rd fl, California Tower, 30-32 D'Aguilar St; weekday set lunch $118-138; ☽ dinner only Sun; MTR Central (exit D2)

This quiet, discreet and very smart place serves up such treats as pomelo salad, spicy green papaya salad and mussels in red curry. It is Thai food with a lot of style and a price to match, but it is worth the bucks.

YUNG KEE RESTAURANT

Map p68 Cantonese $$

☎ 2522 1624; 32-40 Wellington St; roast goose from $100; ⊙ 11am-11.30pm; MTR Central (exit D2)

This long-standing institution is probably the most famous Cantonese restaurant in Central. Its signature roast goose has been the talk of the town since 1942 (the restaurant farms its own geese for quality control), and its dim sum (2pm to 5.30pm Monday to Saturday, 11am to 5.30pm Sunday) is excellent. Set meals cost $300 to $550 per person.

BON APPETIT Map p68 Vietnamese, Thai $

☎ 2525 3553; 14B Wing Wah Lane; ⊙ 10am-midnight Mon-Sat; MTR Central (exit D2)

Cheap but tasty dishes for those on a rock-bottom budget – and a scrum of office workers trying to squeeze a decent meal into a short break at lunch time – are available at this Vietnamese and Thai nook in Wing Wah Lane, the northern extension of Lan Kwai Fong. Dishes such as filled baguettes and rice and noodles are generally less than $50, but you may also spend a little more on seafood such as crab curry ($150).

GRAHAM ST MARKET

Map p56 Produce Market $

Graham St; ⊙ 6am-8pm; ⊜ 5B

The stalls and shops lining Graham St south of (and up the hill from) Queen's Rd Central to Hollywood Rd are positively groaning with high-quality vegetables and fruit, as well as meat, seafood and other comestibles. But being in Central, the prices are generally higher than wet markets further west in Sheung Wan and Kennedy Town.

CITY HALL MAXIM'S PALACE

Map p56 Dim Sum $

☎ 2521 1303; 3rd fl, Low Block, Hong Kong City Hall, 1 Edinburgh Pl; dim sum $23-42, compulsory tea fee per person $11; ⊜ 13

For many years HK Magazine readers voted this place as the best dim sum restaurant in town, and while probably not everyone

would agree, this establishment does offer food of solid quality. The ambience is civilised but not snobbish, and at busy lunch time there is always a nice buzz to the place. Dim sum ladies walk around with trays of food ready to be served, saving you from having to read the menu. At night the restaurant serves more formal Cantonese cuisine and is a popular venue for Chinese banquets.

MAK'S NOODLE Map p68 Noodle Bar $

☎ 2854 3810; 77 Wellington St; ⊙ 11am-8pm; ⊜ 40M

This noodle shop sells excellent wonton soup, and the beef brisket noodles, more of a Western taste than a Chinese one, are highly recommended. Go for lunch or eat early; it's shut tight by 8pm. Branches: Causeway Bay (Map p74; ☎ 2895 5310; 44 Jardines Bazaar; ⊙ 11am-midnight; MTR Causeway Bay, exit F), Tai Kok Tsui (Map pp88–9; ☎ 2740 4129; Shop K09, G/F, Olympian City Phase 2; ⊙ 10am-10pm; MTR Olympic, exit D3), Tsim Sha Tsui (Map p92; ☎ 2730 0710; Shop C03, 2/F, Gourmet Express, China Hong Kong City, 33 Canton Rd; ⊙ 7am-10pm; MTR Tsim Sha Tsui, exit A1).

SOHO

Soho is awash in restaurants; in fact, there is nothing but eateries lining Elgin St. Most of them are in the middle and top-end range. The area is accessible by the Central Escalators, or bus 26 can be caught from Caroline Centre (Map p74) in Causeway Bay or Pacific Place (Map p63), Admiralty.

CECCONI'S CANTINA Map p68 Italian $$$

☎ 2147 5500; 43 Elgin St

If the décor of this restaurant is a little too cold and showroom-like, the food more than makes up for it. Few would be able to resist such sophisticated dishes as roasted figs with goats curd, flat pancetta and honey mustard dressing, and peppered duck and confit leg with sweet potato and lime jus.

STONEGRILL Map p68 International $$$

☎ 2504 3333; Ground fl, 28 Elgin St; set lunch $100, set dinner $400-500

Don't complain when your food arrives half-cooked – it's supposed to be that way. Steak or fish comes sunny-side up and sizzling on a slab of stone; you turn it over to suit your taste. Whether you consider this a half-baked idea or fall for it, you'll love the excellent New York–style bar. There is also a pasta selection.

VEDA Map p68 — Indian $$$
☎ 2868 5885; 8 Arbuthnot Rd; 🕙 dinner only Sun; 🚌 40M from Wan Chai for Pacific Place, Admiralty
We've heard talk that this uberstylish and pricey eatery is not measuring up to the same standards as when it first opened its doors and introduced Hong Kong to 'innovative Indian' (eg chicken in coriander and cashew-nut paste, fish steamed with mint). Sunday brunch ($198) still seems to pack in the punters, though. The weekday lunch buffet is $98.

CARAMBA! Map p68 — Mexican $$
☎ 2530 9963; 26-30 Elgin St; 🕙 noon-midnight
Mexican is a cuisine as diametrically opposed to Chinese as you can imagine, but with a blinding selection of tequilas, this cantina provides a cosy and intimate venue for a fix of chilli ($95), fajitas, enchiladas and quesadillas ($55 to $68). There's brunch from noon to 6pm on the weekend.

CHILLI FAGARA Map p68 — Sichuanese $$
☎ 2893 3330; Shop E, Ground fl, 45-53 Graham St; 🕙 dinner only Sat & Sun
This new hole-in-the-wall in Soho serves reasonably authentic Sichuan fare and is a welcome addition to the short list of quality local eateries open in this part of Central. Make sure you try all three Sichuan tastes: màa (spicy), laat (hot) and táam (mild).

CRU WINE & GRILL Map p68 — Australian $$
☎ 2803 2083; 44 Staunton St; 🕙 8am-11pm
Since the first day this two-storey, open-front restaurant opened, there hasn't been a day when it is not packed out. It's all in the food (and not the service, for sure). You can't beat a big hot plate of tasty fettuccini marinara or spaghetti with clams, tomato and chorizo for under $100. Even a ribeye steak is only $250, which is a bargain for this town, and especially this neighbourhood. Vegetarian options aplenty.

NEPAL Map p68 — Nepalese $$
☎ 2869 6212; Ground fl, 14 Staunton St
This was one of the first ethnic restaurants to find its way to Soho, and Nepalese flavours and treats remain in abundance

here. There are some 14 vegetarian choices on the menu.

OLIVE Map p68 — Greek, Middle Eastern $$
☎ 2521 1608; Ground fl, 32 Elgin St
We've received very mixed reports about the food at this Greek(ish) Soho restaurant, but with ace Australian chef Greg Malouf behind the wheel (if from afar), we know it's been a success. Give it a go and stick to the mixed meze ($108).

PEAK CAFE BAR Map p68 — International $$
☎ 2140 6877; 9-13 Shelley St; 🕙 11am-2am Mon-Fri, 9am-2am Sat, 9am-midnight Sun
The fixtures and fittings of the much-missed Peak Cafe, established in 1947, have moved down the hill to this comfy restaurant and bar with excellent nosh and super cocktails. The only thing that's missing now is the view. There are also sandwiches ($68 to $98) and pizza ($88 to $98).

SHUI HU JU Map p68 — Sichuanese $$
☎ 2869 6927; Ground fl, 68 Peel St; 🕙 6pm-midnight
This restaurant, which could almost be in Off Soho, serves earthy dishes from Sichuan that have only been gently toned down. The décor is a delight – traditional Chinese with tables separated by latticed screens. It's like dining in one of the neighbouring antiques shops.

ARCHIE B'S NEW YORK DELI
Map p68 — American Deli $
☎ 2522 1239; Lower ground fl, 7 & 9 Staunton St; 🕙 11am-11pm
This little place just off the Central Escalator serves as authentic East Coast American delicatessen food as you'll find west of the US of A. It's pretty much an eat-and-run kind of place, but the few tables in the small alleyway just off Staunton St may have you lingering over your kosher dill pickle or Dr Brown's Cream Soda.

LIFE Map p68 — Vegetarian $
☎ 2810 9777; 10 Shelley St; 🕙 delicatessen & shop 8am-10.30pm Mon-Fri, 9am-10.30pm Sat & Sun, café & rooftop noon-midnight Mon-Fri, 10am-midnight Sat & Sun
This place is a vegetarian's dream, serving vegan food and dishes free of gluten,

ALL-DAY DINING

For a city that is so bustling and vibrant, the amount of late-night dining options in Hong Kong is surprisingly short. Most of the eateries that open late are local tea restaurants (chàa chàan tèng), one of the most famous being fast-food chain Tsui Wah, which has branches in Central (Map p68; ☎ 2525 6338; 15-19 Wellington St; 🕑 6.30am-4am; MTR Central, exit D2), Causeway Bay (Map p74; ☎ 2834 2438; 491-493 Jaffe Rd; 🕑 24hr; MTR Causeway Bay, exit B) and Yau Ma Tei (Map p97; ☎ 2384 8388; 77-83 Parkes St; 🕑 24hr; MTR Jordan, exit A), as well as elsewhere. The menu is more limited at night, but the signature fish-ball vermicelli in shark-bone broth ($25) is always available.

In recent years, other styles of off-hour eateries have sprung up. Flying Pan in Central (Map p68; ☎ 2140 6333; 9 Old Bailey St), Wan Chai (Map p65; ☎ 2528 9997; 81-85 Lockhart Rd) and Lantau (Map p139; ☎ 2987 7749; Discovery Bay Plaza, Discovery Bay; 🚢 from Central Pier) serves 24-hour Western breakfasts. Meanwhile Hotdog (Map p68; ☎ 2543 3555; Shop D, L/G Hollywood Hse, 27-29 Hollywood Rd, Central) offers a broad range of franks served on soft buns ($25 to $35, condiments $2 to $6) 'round the clock.

A few hotel coffee shops have experimented with 24-hour dining but given up on the idea in the end, apparently having failed to capture the business they had hoped for. One that still persists is Cafe One (Map p74; ☎ 2839 3311; The Park Lane Hong Kong, 310 Gloucester Rd; MTR Causeway Bay, exit E), which features an à la carte menu comprising everything from wonton noodles ($68 per bowl) to linguine al vongole ($88). There are also the omnipresent 7-Eleven and Circle K convenient stores, which, depending on the locations, serve sushi, sandwiches and microwaveable foods. Some branches of McDonald's and Wellcome supermarkets are open 24 hours.

---

wheat, onion and garlic. There's a delicatessen and shop on the ground floor, a café on the 1st and additional seating in the rooftop garden. Delicious takeaway salads from the deli counter costs $50 to $75 and the large size one can feed a small family.

SHEUNG WAN & THE MID-LEVELS

West of Central, Sheung Wan stands out for two quite disparate cuisines: Chinese (in particular, Chiu Chow) and Korean. For some reason the district has always been a 'Little Korea' and is the best place on Hong Kong Island to look for bulgogi (Korean barbecue) and kimchi (spicy fermented cabbage). Restaurants in the Mid-Levels cater mostly to local residents who don't feel like making the trek down to Soho or Central.

GAIA RISTORANTE Map p70   Italian $$$

☎ 2167 8200; Ground fl, Grand Millennium Plaza, 181 Queen's Rd Central, Sheung Wan; 🕑 till 1am Fri & Sat; MTR Sheung Wan (exit E2)

At least one bon vivant friend considers this the best restaurant in Hong Kong. We love the wood and tile floors, the thin-crust pizzas and the outside tables in the lush plaza.

ORANGE TREE Map p77   Dutch $$

☎ 2838 9352; 17 Shelley St; 🕑 6-10.30pm; 🚌 40M from Wan Chai For Pacific Place, Admiralty

Modern Dutch food served in a breezy russet setting in the higher reaches of the Central Escalator. Don't get stuck on the sausages – there are lighter dishes like smoked eel. For dessert there are always delicious poffertjes (Dutch pancakes) on the menu.

GRAND STAGE Map p70   Cantonese $$

☎ 2815 2311; 2nd fl, Western Market, 323 Des Voeux Rd Central, Sheung Wan; dishes $68-128, dim sum $14.8-29.8; 🕑 11.30am-6.15pm & 7pm-midnight; MTR Sheung Wan (exit C)

This wonderful place, with balcony and booth seating overlooking a huge dance floor in Western Market, features ballroom music and dancing at high tea (2.30pm to 6.15pm) and dinner. The food is fine, but come here primarily to kick your heels up.

KOREA HOUSE RESTAURANT

Map p70   Korean $$

☎ 2544 0007; Ground fl, Honwell Commercial Centre, 119-121 Connaught Rd Central, Sheung Wan; 🕑 noon-11pm; MTR Sheung Wan (exit C)

Korea House, in situ since 1965, is acknowledged as having some of the most authentic Korean barbecue, kimchi and appetisers (side dishes to a barbecue sizzled at your table) in Hong Kong, and is always filled with Korean expats – the ultimate stamp of approval. Enter from Man Wa Lane.

LEUNG HING CHIU CHOW SEAFOOD
RESTAURANT Map p56   Chiu Chow, Seafood $$
☎ 2850 6666; 32 Bonham Strand West, Sheung Wan; ⏰ 11am-midnight; MTR Sheung Wan (exit A2)
The staple ingredients of Chiu Chow cuisine – goose and duck but especially fish and shellfish – are extensively employed and delectably prepared at this very local place.

LIN HEUNG TEA HOUSE
Map p56   Cantonese $
☎ 2544 4556; Ground fl, 160-164 Wellington St, Sheung Wan; ⏰ 6am-10pm; MTR Sheung Wan (exit E2)
This old-style Cantonese restaurant on the corner of Aberdeen St, packed with older men reading newspapers, extended families and office groups, has decent dim sum (from $12 to $16) served from trolleys. It's a very local place, but staff can rummage out an English menu. The signature braised stuffed duck ($150) is a must try if you come for dinner, but advance booking is needed.

THE PEAK
You'd hardly venture all the way up Victoria Peak for a meal; food here takes its place in the queue behind the views and all the attractions of the Peak Tower. But there are a few options from which to choose.

PEARL ON THE PEAK
Map pp54–5   Australian $$$
☎ 2849 5123; Shop 2, Level 1, The Peak Tower, 128 Peak Rd; 🚋 Peak Tram
This place has all the trappings of a tourist restaurant, so you're bound to end up here one way or the other. It is somewhat of a branch of Pearl Restaurant in Melbourne, and the signature air-freight pearl meat flash fried with shiitake, chive buds, ginger and soy served on a mother of pearl shell ($198) would be quite enjoyable eaten with the view. Otherwise there is everything from pasta to curry, with twists of Oz.

CAFE DECO Map pp54–5   International $$
☎ 2849 5111; Levels 1 & 2, Peak Galleria, 118 Peak Rd; set lunch $88; ⏰ 11.30am-midnight Mon-Thu, 11.30am-1am Fri & Sat, 9.30am-midnight Sun; 🚋 Peak Tram
With its spectacular harbour views, Art Deco furnishings and live jazz from 7pm

to 11pm Monday to Saturday nights, this place need not have made too much effort with the menu. But the food, while an East-meets-West eclectic thing, is above average, with the bistro dishes, sushi and sashimi plates ($152 to $298) and oyster bar scoring extra points. Breakfast and brunch are served from 9.30am to 2.30pm Saturday and Sunday.

L16 Map pp54–5   Thai $$
☎ 2520 1616; Shop 1, G/F, The Peak Galleria, 118 Peak Rd; ⏰ 11am-11pm Mon-Sat, 9am-11pm Sun; 🚋 Peak Tram
The Thai food here is not the most authentic – a jaded palate might even find the tom yum and pomelo salad lacking in heat – but it's the location and the sophistication that will get you through the door. Besides, there is another restaurant inside this restaurant. A branch of Zen, an upscale Cantonese restaurant whose Admiralty flagship (Map p56; ☎ 2845 4555; Shop 001, LG/F, Pacific Place, 88 Queensway; MTR Admiralty, exit F) draws quite a crowd, takes up the inner space. The soya marinated chicken is highly recommended.

PEAK LOOKOUT
Map pp54–5   International, Asian $$
☎ 2849 1000; 121 Peak Rd; ⏰ 10.30am-midnight Mon-Thu, 10.30am-1am Fri, 8.30am-1am Sat, 8.30am-midnight Sun; 🚋 Peak Tram
East meets West at this swish colonial-style restaurant, with seating indoors in a glassed-in veranda and on the outside terrace – there's everything from Indian and French to Thai and Japanese on offer. We'll stick to the oysters ($140 to $225 a half-dozen), the barbecue and the views which are to the south of the island, not the harbour. Breakfast is available on the weekend from 8.30am.

ADMIRALTY & WAN CHAI
Wan Chai, and to a lesser extent Admiralty, is a happy hunting ground for ethnic restaurants. Name your cuisine and MTR, bus or tram it down to the Wanch. You're certain to find it here.

NICHOLINI'S Map p63   Italian $$$$
☎ 2521 3838; 8th fl, Conrad Hong Kong, 88 Queensway, Admiralty; set lunch/dinner $288/688; MTR Admiralty (exit F)

This refined restaurant's approach to northern Italian cuisine has won it praise from Italian expats – a certain stamp of approval. Simple yet superb antipasti and shellfish dishes are firm favourites here. It also has an excellent bar.

PETRUS Map p63 French $$$$

☎ 2820 8590; 56th fl, Island Shangri-La Hotel, Pacific Place, Supreme Court Rd, Admiralty; set lunch from $310, set dinner from $800; MTR Admiralty (exit F)

With its head (and prices) in the clouds, Petrus is one of the finest Western restaurants in Hong Kong. Expect traditional (not nouvelle) French cuisine, some over-the-top décor and stunning harbour views. Coat and tie required for men.

CINE CITTÀ Map p63 Italian $$$

☎ 2529 0199; Ground fl, Starcrest Bldg, 9 Star St, Wan Chai; ☾ dinner only Sat & Sun; MTR Admiralty (exit F)

This very flash restaurant with an Italian-film theme is in an area of southwest Wan Chai that is slowly becoming something of a restaurant and nightlife district. The crowd here is more unhip hotel bar than Lan Kwai Fong, though.

FISH BAR Map p63 Seafood $$$

☎ 2841 3858; 7/F, JW Marriott Hotel Hong Kong, 88 Queensway, Admiralty; MTR Admiralty (exit F)

Seafood by the pool is what you get here, and the harbour view is a bonus. The signature jumbo shrimp cocktail with avocado and cocktail sauce ($148) gets you ready for the seasonal selection of imported fish, cooked in your preferred recipes. The oysters are so fresh they shrivel when poked by a fork. Carnivores may still find solace in the freshly grilled rib-eye steak.

H ONE Map p63 Mediterranean, International $$$

☎ 2805 0638; Shop 4008-4010, Podium Level 4, IFC Mall, 8 Finance St; ☾ closed Sun; MTR Central (exit A)

The nameplate outside proclaims the restaurant 'the ultimate dining experience', and besides wood-fired pizzas, handcrafted pasta, handcrafted breads and specialities, such as Wagyu beef cheek and roasted northern Thai–style chicken massaged with tamarind and spices, there are also 'kick-ass curries' and 'dum dum biryani' and tandoori. Over-confidence aside, this glass-encased restaurant does offer the ultimate view.

PRIVATE KITCHENS

Private kitchens, or speakeasy restaurants, have become a characteristic of Hong Kong dining, though the hype has died down in recent years. Originally, private kitchens were unlicensed, clandestine eateries hidden in high-rise flats and serving meals for relatively low prices, but the raves gained regulators' notice and now many private kitchens are licensed eateries. But they still tend to be at hidden locations.

Sichuan Cuisine Da Ping Huo (Map p68; ☎ 2559 1317; L/G Hilltop Plaza, 49 Hollywood Rd, Central; ☾ 2 seatings 6.30-9pm, 9-11pm) This pioneer of the private kitchen scene, owned by Sichuanese couple Wang Hai and Wong Siu-king, now operates out of a commercial space and even has a specialised wine fridge. Happily, all the great dishes such as màa pàw dau fû (stewed beancurd with minced pork and chilli), gòng baau gài ding (sautéed diced chicken and peanuts in sweet chilli), daam daam mìn (noodles in savoury sauce) continue to be served for $250 per head (set menu), and Wong, a trained Chinese opera singer, still sings for customers after she finishes in the kitchen.

Xi Yan (Map p65; ☎ 2575 6966; 3/F, 83 Wanchai Rd, Wan Chai; lunch per head $48, dinner from $360; ☾ by booking only; MTR Wan Chai, exit A3) This former advertising executive converted his office into a private kitchen and achieved so much success he is currently also running casual walk-in restaurants Xi Yan Sweets (Map p63; ☎ 2833 6299; Shop 1, G/F, 8 Wing Fung St, Wan Chai; MTR Admiralty, exit F) and Xi Yan – Tastes (Map p74; ☎ 2881 6693; GOD, 2/F Leighton Centre, 77 Leighton Rd; MTR Causeway Bay, exit A). Both open noon to 11pm and dishes are $18 to $148.

Club Qing (Map p68; ☎ 2536 9773; 10/F Cosmos Bldg, 8-11 Lan Kwai Fong; MTR Central, exit D2) A restaurant that could easily be mistaken for a museum of dynastic Chinese artefacts, Club Qing serves menus that are degustation style, with eight to 10 courses, starting from $400 per person. It can go all the way up to $1500 if you're into whole braised Yoshihama abalone and shark's fin soup. Less politically incorrect treats include baked prawns with lemon grass and baked rib 'fingers' in Club Qing style.

THE GRILL Map p65 — Grills $$$

☎ 2584 7623; 11/F, Grand Hyatt, 1 Wan Chai Rd, Wan Chai; ⏰ 11.30am-10pm; MTR Wan Chai (exit A5)

You come here in the day to chill out with a salad and a cocktail and you come in the evening to heat things up with the all-you-can-eat barbecue ($460 to $490). Stationed chefs are doing the cooking for you so that you have time to dive into the seafood mountain.

YÈ SHANGHAI Map p63 — Shanghainese $$$

☎ 2918 9833; Shop 332, Level 3, Pacific Place, 88 Queensway, Admiralty; MTR Admiralty (exit F)

This groovy place takes street-level Shanghainese cuisine and gives it a tweak here and there. The cold drunken pigeon ($100) is a wine-soaked winner and the steamed dumplings are perfectly plump, but sometimes this restaurant goes for clattery style over substance. There's live music from 9.30pm to 11.30pm Thursday to Saturday.

CAFÉ TOO Map p63 — International $$

☎ 2829 8571; 7th fl, Island Shangri-La Hotel, Pacific Place, Supreme Court Rd, Admiralty; ⏰ 6.30am-10.30pm; MTR Admiralty (exit F)

This immensely popular food hall has a half-dozen kitchens preparing dishes from around the world, seating for 250 grazers and one of the best lunch/dinner buffets ($250/350 Monday to Saturday, $290/380 Sunday) in town. There's lighter fare as well, including sandwiches ($120 to $180) and rice and pasta dishes ($120 to $170).

CHE'S CANTONESE RESTAURANT
Map p65 — Cantonese $$

☎ 2528 1123; 4th fl, The Broadway, 54-62 Lockhart Rd, Wan Chai; MTR Wan Cha (exit C)

This *crème de la crème* of Cantonese restaurants, opened by a local showbiz celebrity, serves home-style delicacies and offers a special seasonal menu with a dozen additional dishes. A must-try is the freshly baked Chinese roast-pork puffs. Prices are high but loyalists say it's worth the extra bucks.

HYANG CHON KOREAN RESTAURANT
Map p65 — Korean $$

☎ 2574 5142; 2nd fl, Workingfield Commercial Bldg, 408-412 Jaffe Rd, Wan Chai; ⏰ 6pm-4am; MTR Causeway Bay (exit C)

This somewhat expensive Korean restaurant attracts Korean expats and their friends with its authentic ginseng chicken and *bibimbab*, rice served in a sizzling pot topped with thinly sliced beef and cooked and preserved vegetables, which is then bound by a raw egg and flavoured with chilli-laced soy bean paste. Service is friendly and helpful.

LIU YUAN RESTAURANT
Map p65 — Shanghainese $$

☎ 2510 0483; 1st fl, CRE Bldg, 303 Hennessy Rd, Wan Chai; MTR Wan Chai (exit A2)

This stylish restaurant serves superb Shanghainese dishes, including things like crab claws cooked with duck egg; the tiny prawns steamed with tea leaves are superb. Highly recommended.

R66 Map p65 — Buffet $$

☎ 2862 6166; 62nd fl, Hopewell Centre, 183 Queen's Rd E, Wan Chai; MTR Wan Chai (exit B2)

R66 – it's on the 62nd, not the 66th floor, as you'd expect – obeys the unwritten code of revolving restaurants by playing cheesy music and serving average buffets. It's best to roll up for an afternoon tea (3pm to 5pm; $66) and go for a twirl in the daylight. To access the lipstick tube–like Hopewell Centre's outfacing bubble lifts, swap at the 17th (lifts are in the alcove opposite lift 6) and 56th floors.

THAI BASIL Map p63 — Thai $$

☎ 2537 4682; Shop 005, Lower ground fl, Pacific Place, 88 Queensway, Admiralty; ⏰ 11.30am-11pm; MTR Admiralty (exit F)

This basement-mall restaurant turns out some surprisingly authentic (and quite lovely) Thai dishes. This may not be a destination but it's not a bad stop along the way. The sticky banana pudding ($60) is the ultimate blast for the sweet tooth.

VICEROY RESTAURANT & BAR
Map p65 — Indian, Middle Eastern $$

☎ 2827 7777; Room 2B, 2nd fl, Sun Hung Kai Centre, 30 Harbour Rd, Wan Chai; MTR Wan Chai (exit A5)

The Viceroy has been an institution in Hong Kong for some two decades: an upmarket Indian restaurant with sitar music and a fun place to watch comedy (p216) at least once a month.

369 SHANGHAI RESTAURANT
Map p65   Shanghainese $
☎ 2527 2343; Ground fl, 30-32 O'Brien Rd, Wan Chai; ☺ 11am-4am; MTR Wan Chai (exit A1)
Low-key Shanghainese eatery that's nothing like five star but does the dumpling job well. It's family run and there are some comfy booths in the front window. It's open late, too, so you can come here after a draining dance. Try the signature hot-and-sour soup ($40 to $60) – almost a meal in itself – or the eggplant fried with garlic ($55).

AMERICAN RESTAURANT
Map p65   Northern Chinese $
☎ 2527 7277; Ground fl, Golden Star Bldg, 20 Lockhart Rd, Wan Chai; ☺ 11am-11.30pm; MTR Wan Chai (exit C)
The friendly American (which chose its name to attract Yank sailors cruising the Wanch for sustenance while on R&R during the Vietnam War) has been serving decent Northern Chinese cuisine for well over half a century. Famous for Peking duck ($275) and beggar's chicken ($310; order in advance).

CARRIANA CHIU CHOW RESTAURANT
Map p65   Chiu Chow $
☎ 2511 1282; 1st fl, AXA Centre, 151 Gloucester Rd, Wan Chai; ☺ 11am-11.30pm; MTR Wan Chai (exit A1)
For Chiu Chow food, the Carriana still rates right up there after all these years. Try the cold dishes (sliced goose with vinegar, crab claws), pork with tofu or Chiu Chow chicken. Enter from Tonnochy Rd.

CINTA-J Map p65   Filipino, Indonesian $
☎ 2529 6622; Shop G4, Ground fl, Malaysia Bldg, 69 Jaffe Rd, Wan Chai; ☺ 11am-3.30am Mon-Fri, 11am-5am Sat & Sun; MTR Wan Chai
This friendly restaurant and lounge has a Southeast Asian menu longer than the Book of Job, which covers all bases from *murtabak* to *gado-gado,* but with a strong emphasis on Pinoy dishes. It turns into a cocktail lounge in the late evening and stays open until 3.30am (5am on the weekend).

CHUEN CHEUNG KUI Map p74   Hakka $
☎ 2577 3833; 7-8/F, Causeway Bay Plaza 1, 489 Hennessy Rd, Causeway Bay; ☺ 11am-midnight; MTR Causeway Bay (exit B)

Enlist a Cantonese dining companion or dive in bravely: there's not much English spoken here and the food is challenging. The pulled chicken, a Hakka classic, is the dish to insist upon. ('Gizzard soup' and 'stomach titbit' may be less appealing.)

LUNG MOON RESTAURANT
Map p65   Cantonese $
☎ 2572 9888; 130-136 Johnston Rd, Wan Chai; ☺ 6am-midnight; MTR Wan Chai
The dining experience at this very basic (and friendly) Cantonese restaurant has not changed a great deal since the 1950s, and the prices, while not quite at 1950s levels, are still reasonable. Dim sum is available daily from opening till 5pm.

SABAH Map p65   Malaysian $
☎ 2143 6626; Shop 4 & 5, Ground fl, 98-108 Jaffe Rd, Wan Chai; ☺ 7.30am-midnight; MTR Wan Chai (exit A1)
Sabah in the heart of Wan Chai serves Malaysian food tempered for the Hong Kong palate. It's a favourite of office workers; try to avoid 1pm to 2pm. A choice of five set lunches ($48) is available from 11am to 3pm.

THAI SHING Map p74   Thai $
☎ 2577 3833; ☎ 2834 2500; 36 Tang Lung St, Causeway Bay; ☺ 10am-midnight; MTR Causeway Bay (exit B)
If you want the best Thai food on Hong Kong Island and you couldn't care less about eating off a Formica table top and being assaulted by cheesy Thai pop, this place is where you should be. The folks here won't give you top-notch service either, but once that delicious *tom kha gai, padthai* and *kaeng* hit the table nothing else matters.

TIM'S KITCHEN Map p65   Hong Kong Fast Food $
☎ 2527 2982; Shop C, Ground fl, 118 Jaffe Rd, Wan Chai; ☺ 7.30am-10.30pm Mon-Fri, 7.30am-7pm Sat, closed Sun; MTR Wan Chai (exit A1)
When as many Hong Kong Chinese queue up outside a restaurant at lunch time as they do at Tim's every day, you can be sure that the food is both inexpensive and of good quality. It's a mix of Cantonese staples (fried rice, noodles) with some Hong Kong–style additions (such as fried pasta).

CAUSEWAY BAY

Causeway Bay is a strange amalgam of restaurants and cuisines but, apart from a selection of rather slick and overpriced European places on Fashion Walk (otherwise known as Houston St) northeast of the Causeway MTR station, this is the place for Chinese and other Asian – particularly Southeast Asian – food. Causeway Bay also has a lot of Japanese restaurants because of all the Japanese department stores headquartered here.

FORUM Map p74 Cantonese $$$$
☎ 2891 2555; 485 Lockhart Rd; MTR Causeway Bay (exit C)

The Forum's abalone dishes have fans spread across the world and have won countless awards. What restaurant owner Yeung Koon-Yat does with these marvellous molluscs has earned him membership to Le Club des Chefs des Chefs and the moniker 'King of Abalone'. The pan-fried redfish and crunchy-skin chicken are also recommended.

HEICHINROU Map p74 Cantonese $$$
☎ 2506 2333; Shop 1003, 10th fl, Food Forum, Times Square, 1 Matheson St; 11.30am-midnight Mon-Fri, 11am-midnight Sat, 10am-midnight Sun; MTR Causeway Bay (exit A)

This stylish Cantonese restaurant is arguably the most elegant eatery in what makes up the four-level Food Forum (floors 10 to 13) in the Times Square shopping mall. The dim sum ($16 to $45) is excellent.

SUSHI HIRO Map p74 Japanese $$$
☎ 2882 8752; 10/F, Henry House, 42 Yun Ping Rd, Causeway Bay; MTR Causeway Bay (exit F)

A good example of Causeway Bay's Japanese-ness, this restaurant is one of the many authentic sushi bars hidden in the upper floors of commercial buildings, much like the way it is in Tokyo. Like other sushi bars of this grade, Sushi Hiro offers a seasonal choice of fish that changes on a weekly basis, and the chef will happily pick the best for you. Set lunch starts from $120 per head (nine pieces) and set dinner from $320 (12 pieces). For $450 you get sashimi as well.

INDONESIAN RESTAURANT 1968
Map p74 Indonesian $$
☎ 2577 9981; 28 Leighton Rd; noon-11pm; MTR Causeway Bay (exit A)

This erstwhile dive has recently got a much needed face-lift and has added the year of its founding to its name – just so you won't forget. The food? It still serves pretty authentic *rendang, gado-gado* and the like, with improved presentations but in considerably smaller portions. There's a Tsim Sha Tsui branch (Map p94; ☎ 2619 1926; 2-4A Observatory Rd) and a Sha Tin branch (☎ 2699 8777; Shop 701, Shatin New Town Plaza Phase 1).

PAK LOH CHIU CHOW RESTAURANT
Map p74 Chiu Chow $$
☎ 2576 8886; 23-25 Hysan Ave; 11am-11pm; MTR Causeway Bay (exit F)

This is one of the best Chiu Chow restaurants on Hong Kong Island, turning out the most perfect shrimp and crab balls and delectable *sek-làu-gài* (steamed egg-white pouches filled with minced chicken).

QUEEN'S CAFE Map p74 Russian $$
☎ 2576 2658; Shop D, Ground fl, Eton Tower, 8 Hysan Ave; noon-11.30pm; MTR Causeway Bay (exit F)

This eatery has been around since 1952 (though obviously not at the bottom of the same modern high-rise), which accounts for its subdued yet assured atmosphere. The borsch and meat set meals – White Russian dishes that filtered through China after WWI – are pretty good. Try the *zakuska* ($70 to $90), a mixture of Russian appetisers.

SORABOL KOREAN RESTAURANT
Map p74 Korean $$
☎ 2881 6823; 17th fl, Lee Theatre Plaza, 99 Percival St; 11.30am-midnight; MTR Causeway Bay (exit A)

This is the Korean's Korean restaurant, with helpful and informative staff. The barbecues are great and the *kimchi* dishes – notably the summer variety of the piquant and fermented cabbage – are particularly well prepared.

TAI PING KOON
Map p74 International, Chinese $$
☎ 2576 9161; 6 Pak Sha Rd; 11am-midnight; MTR Causeway Bay (exit F)

This place has been around since 1860 and offers an incredible mix of Western and Chinese flavours – what Hong Kong people called 'soy sauce restaurants' in pre-fusion days. Try the borscht ($40) and the smoked pomfret ($158) or roast pigeon ($98).

TOMOKAZU Map p74 — Japanese $$
☎ 2833 6339; Shop B, Lockhart House, 441 Lockhart Rd; sushi platter from $150; ☷ 11.30am-3pm & 6pm-4.30am; MTR Causeway Bay (exit C)
One of the longest-running Japanese haunts in town, this restaurant, for its location and well-prepared Japanese food, is a bargain. It's also the place to go for a fix of noodles or sushi in the wee hours.

TOWNGAS AVENUE Map p74 — International $$
☎ 2367 2710; Ground fl, 59-65 Paterson St; MTR Causeway Bay (exit E)
This is an odd concept in a Hong Kong restaurant, where the cook is usually to be heard and *not* seen. This restaurant, operated by a Hong Kong gas utility, allows you to watch chefs at work through a glass screen. You get to keep the recipe of the dish(es) you order and you may even spot the cooker or fridge of your heart's desire: it's also a kitchenware showroom.

W'S ENTRECÔTE Map p74 — French, Steakhouse $$
☎ 2506 0133; 6th fl, Express by Holiday Inn, 33 Sharp St East; MTR Causeway Bay (exit A)
This place serves steaks of every shape and size, but with a Gallic twist. Included in the price is a salad and as many *frites* (chips) as you can squeeze onto your plate. Starters are in the 'foie gras and snails' category. A three-course set lunch is $108 to $138, while a three-course set dinner is $278 to $318.

XINJISHI Map p74 — Shanghainese $$
☎ 2890 1122; Shop 201-203, 2nd fl, Lee Gardens Two, 28 Yun Ping Rd; MTR Causeway Bay (exit F)
This restaurant exemplifies how the world has turned upside down in Hong Kong in recent years. It's a branch of a successful mainland-based chain, with five restaurants in Shanghai, one in Taipei and another in Osaka. It offers traditional Shanghainese (the cooks are imported) in a modern, very stylish setting. Try one of the clay-pot dishes, such as braised pork meatballs with vegetables ($70).

KUNG TAK LAM Map p74 — Vegetarian $
☎ 2881 9966; Ground fl, Lok Sing Centre, 31 Yee Wo St; ☷ 11am-11pm; MTR Causeway Bay (exit E)

This long-established place, which serves Shanghai-style meatless dishes, has more of a modern feeling than most vegetarian eateries and is usually packed out. All the vegetables are 100% organic and dishes are free of MSG.

MAN FAI Map p74 — Noodles $
☎ 2890 1278; G/F, 22-24 Jardine's Bazaar, Causeway Bay, ☷ 8am-2am; MTR Causeway Bay (exit F)
Any time of day you can see people squeezed together here at the few communal tables, slurping up noodles. It's not a heaven for hygienists, but it is for noodles lovers. The signature squid balls, desired for their al dente texture, can be had alone or with a variety of noodles ($20), and with other ingredients such as beef balls, fish balls, crispy fish skin and seaweed (assorted $23). There is a Sheung Wan branch (Map p70; ☎ 2543 8468; 274 Des Voeux Rd Central; ☷ 10am-10pm).

MI-NEI SUSHI map p74 — Sushi $
☎ 3188 2440; 12 Pak Sha Rd, Causeway Bay; sushi $9-60; ☷ 11.30am-midnight; MTR Causeway Bay (exit F)
Conveyor-belt sushi *(kaiten-zushi)* has been in Hong Kong for decades, but mostly it's been done badly. Since it opened a few years ago, this place has changed everything. People want the sushi rice to be the right consistency and the morsels lovingly presented, even if they are picked from a rotating belt. A plate of salmon sushi is presented like an art installation, decorated with a 'crown' made from sliced *daikon*.

YIN PING VIETNAMESE RESTAURANT
Map p74 — Vietnamese $
☎ 2832 9038; Ground fl, 24 Cannon St; ☷ 11am-midnight; MTR Causeway Bay (exit D1)
This little place is the 'anchor' Vietnamese restaurant on a street with more than a few of those eateries. Set lunches with soup are a snip at $37.

HAPPY VALLEY
In general, the restaurants and cafés in Happy Valley cater to local residents, though two places – a little beyond the racecourse – are worth making the trip out for.

AMIGO Map p74 — French, International $$$$
☎ 2577 2202; Amigo Mansion, 79A Wong Nai Chung Rd; ☷ tram

Call us old-fashioned but this old relic with a Spanish name and Gallic twists is a place full of memories. The waiters still wear black tie and white gloves, there's a strolling guitarist and women are handed roses as they leave. Swoon city…

KISSHO Map p74 — Japanese $$$$
☎ 2836 6992; 1A Wong Nai Chung Rd; 🚋 tram
Residents of this prestigious neighbourhood swear by the seasonal selection of fish here. Be ready for anything: the chefs might drag out from the kitchen a giant octopus the size of an aerobic Swiss ball and just start slicing it up in front of you. The mini crabs in the tank are not pets, they are deep-fried for snacks.

ISLAND EAST
North Point is traditionally home to a sizeable Fujian population and there are a few good places for dishes from its native province. Quarry Bay has the largest collection of restaurants in the entire district, especially in and around Tong Chong St, a short distance southeast of the Quarry Bay MTR station. But these places offer nothing very special and their customers are mostly workers from nearby offices. The waterfront of Sai Wan Ho has a line-up of decent restaurants, and for the ambience alone they are worth visiting.

BEIRA RIO WINE BAR & GRILL
Map pp54–5 — Surf & Turf $$
☎ 2568 3993; Shop GB08-10, G/F, 45 Tai Hong St, Lei King Wan, Sai Wan Ho; set lunch from $42; 🕙 11am-midnight; MTR Sai Wan Ho (exit A)
Along the foodie waterfront of this Island East neighbourhood, this restaurant looks the classiest and the food is reliable. Kick back with a glass of chilled white wine and a seafood mountain ($268, good for two) and there should be no complaints.

KIN'S KITCHEN Map p74 — Chinese $$
☎ 2571 0913; 9 Tsing Fung St, Tin Hau; MTR Tin Hau (exit A2)
Opened by artist and gourmand Lau Kin-wai, who was behind the opening of private kitchen Sichuan Cuisine Da Ping Huo (see boxed text, p184), this unassuming restaurant is so painstaking in choosing its ingredients that the waiter can tell you why the chef needs to source a chicken from a particular region. The signature smoked

chicken (half/whole $180/360) needs to be booked a day in advance, and you will know why when it melts in your mouth.

FOOD REPUBLIC Map pp54–5 — Food Court $
☎ 2907 0521; Shop 308, Cityplaza, 18 Tai Koo Shing Rd, Tai Koo Shing; 🕙 10.30am-10.15pm; MTR Tai Koo (exit D2)
Food courts in malls have a bad rep but this one proves an exception. The choice of food covers everything from pasta and noodles to Thai and Vietnamese. There are also mini hotpots and teppanyaki. The longest queue is at the stall by Yummy Vietnamese Restaurant, which is famous for its beef *pho* ($25).

MIN NAN RESTAURANT
Map pp54–5 — Chinese $
☎ 2807 2168; 25 Kam Ping St; 🕙 7.30am-9.30pm; MTR North Point (exit B1)
This authentic Fujian restaurant is famous for its specialised noodles, porridge and snacks, which, starting from $10 per serving, are an absolute bargain.

ISLAND SOUTH
The restaurants in this district are as varied and eclectic as the villages and settlements themselves. While the choice is obviously limited in smaller places such as Shek O and Repulse Bay, you'll still manage to eat decent Thai at the former, and enjoy one of the most delightful venues on any coast in the latter. Main St in Stanley offers diners and snackers an embarrassment of choices, and in Aberdeen Harbour you'll find what is – for better or worse – Hong Kong's best-known restaurant.

Shek O
SHEK O CHINESE & THAI SEAFOOD
Map pp54–5 — Thai, Cantonese $
☎ 2809 4426; 303 Shek O Village; 🕙 11.30am-10pm; 🚌 9 from MTR Shau Kei Wan (exit A3)
This hybrid of a place is hardly authentic in either category, but the portions are generous, the staff are convivial and the cold Tsingtao beers just keep on flowing.

Stanley
Far-flung Stanley is reachable by bus 6, 6A, 6X or 260 from Exchange Square, Central.

BAYSIDE BRASSERIE Map p85   Fusion $$

☎ 2899 0818; Ground fl, 25 Stanley Market Rd; ⏰ 11.30am-11pm

This waterfront eatery offers a splendid view and an enormous menu, including everything from oysters (from $88 for three pieces) and pasta and pizzas ($68 to $158) to international and Indian main courses.

BOATHOUSE Map p85   International $$

☎ 2813 4467; 86-88 Stanley Main St; set dinner $446 for 2; ⏰ 11am-midnight Sun-Thu, 11am-1am Fri & Sat

All aboard for nautical overload. Salads, bruschetta and Med-inspired mains make up the bulk of the Boathouse's fleet. Steer for sea views; a table on the roof garden is something to covet.

LUCY'S Map p85   International $$

☎ 2813 9055; 64 Stanley Main St

This cool oasis within the hustle and bustle of Stanley Market doesn't overwhelm with choice but with quality food. The menu changes frequently as fresh produce and inspiration arrive, but the offerings tend to honest fusion rather than fancy flimflammery. There's a good selection of wines by the glass. A set dinner of two/three courses for $240/280 is available from Sunday to Thursday only.

SHU ZHAI Map p85   Chinese $$

☎ 2813 0123; 80 Stanley Main St, Stanley; dim sum $25-35; ⏰ noon-10pm

Modelled to resemble a school in ancient China, this breezy new restaurant off Stanley's waterfront serves an assortment of Chinese dishes that are as nice to look at as to eat. Braised Mandarin fish with vermicelli in salty sauce ($148) is a must-try. There is a door connecting the restaurant to a branch of Dymocks book shops (see p159).

CHILLI N SPICE Map p85   Asian $

☎ 2899 0147; Shop 101, 1st fl, Murray House, Stanley Plaza; ⏰ noon-11.30pm Mon-Fri, 11am-11.30pm Sat & Sun

A branch of the ever-growing chain – nine branches at last count – has found its way into Hong Kong's oldest (reconstructed) colonial building. Expect no surprises, but the venue and views are worth a ringside table.

TOBY INN Map p85   Cantonese $

☎ 2813 2880; U1-U2, 126 Stanley Main St; ⏰ 5.30am-10.30pm

This modest eatery is the neighbourhood restaurant of Stanley, with elderly people dropping in for early morning dim sum at the crack of dawn and family diners coming in for cheap and cheery food throughout the day.

Deep Water Bay & Repulse Bay

These little beach resorts are reachable by bus 6, 6A, 6X or 260 from Exchange Square, Central.

VERANDAH RESTAURANT

Map pp54–5   International $$$

☎ 2812 2722; 1st fl, The Repulse Bay, 109 Repulse Bay Rd; ⏰ noon-2.30pm, 3-5.30pm (tea) & 6.30-10.30pm Tue-Sat, 11am-3pm, 3.30-5.30pm (tea) & 6.30-10.30pm Sun

In the new-colonial bit of the wavy Repulse Bay condos, the Verandah is hushed and formal, with heavy white tablecloths and demurely clinking cutlery. The Sunday brunch is famous (book ahead); the afternoon tea is the south side's best. Set dinner starts at $580.

COCOCABANA Map pp54–5   Mediterranean $$

☎ 2812 2226; 2/F, Beach Bldg, Island Rd, Deep Water Bay; ⏰ noon-midnight

Clichéd as it may sound, it's all location, location, location. The service is rather lax, but with the sounds of the waves and the sea breezes, the dishes such as bouillabaisse and Spanish duck confit with olives go down well.

Aberdeen

The lively harbour of Aberdeen is reachable by bus 70 from Exchange Square, Central.

TOP DECK Map p82   International $$$

☎ 2552 3331; Top fl Jumbo Kingdom, Shum Wan Pier Dr, Wong Chuk Hang; ⏰ 6-11.30pm Tue-Thu, 6pm-1am Sat, 9am-11.30pm Sun & public holidays

Alfresco dining in a Chinese courtyard setting and with a view of the sea – you just can't beat that. Top Deck's seafood brunch, with free-flowing champagne on Sunday ($328; 11.30am to 4.30pm), is a dream.

JUMBO KINGDOM FLOATING
RESTAURANT Map p82   Cantonese $$
☎ 2553 9111; Shum Wan Pier Dr, Wong Chuk Hang; ⏱ 11am-11.30pm Mon-Sat, 7.30am-11.30pm Sun

The larger of two floating restaurants moored in Aberdeen Harbour and specialising in seafood, the Jumbo is touristy in the extreme and the food is so-so. The interior looks like Beijing's Imperial Palace crossbred with a Las Vegas casino; think of it as a spectacle – a show – and you'll have fun. There's free transport for diners from the pier on Aberdeen Promenade (p82). Dim sum is served from 7.30am to 4.30pm on Sunday. The other floating restaurant, the Tai Pak, is usually reserved for groups and spillovers.

SHAN LOON TSE KEE FISH BALL
Map p82   Noodles $
☎ 2552 3809; 80-82 Old Main St; ⏱ 10am-6pm

This place started from a nearby cave (shan loon) decades ago and it has since grown into a busy restaurant with two jointed shops. The signature fish balls are al dente and they are great eaten with ho fan (flat rice noodles). The jyu zaat (dumplings made with fish meat, minced pork, carrot and celery) is usually sold out by noon.

WANG JIA SHA Map p82   Shanghainese $
☎ 2873 3030; Shop E, 1/F, Site 5 Aberdeen Centre, 6-12 Nam Ning St; ⏱ 11am-11pm

Another mainland import to cash in on the affluent Hong Kong market, this household name from Shanghai offers delectable siú lùng bàau (steamed pork dumplings; $32 for four), daam daam mìn (noodles in savoury sauce; $28) and more.

KOWLOON

Kowloon doesn't have quite the same range of restaurants as Hong Kong Island does, but you will still find an amazing assortment of ethnic eateries in Tsim Sha Tsui. For Chinese soul food, head for Yau Ma Tei or Mong Kok. Kowloon City is renowned for its Thai eateries.

TSIM SHA TSUI

Tsim Sha Tsui can claim the lion's share of ethnic restaurants in Kowloon. If you're looking

for something fast, cheap and Chinese, Hau Fook St (Map p94) has food stalls (dishes from about $25). It's a few blocks east of Nathan Rd in Tsim Sha Tsui and isn't included on many tourist maps. Walking north from the intersection of Carnarvon and Cameron Rds, it's the first lane on your right. Most of the places don't have English menus, but you can always point to what your fellow diners are tucking into.

FELIX Map p92   Fusion $$$
☎ 2315 3188; 28th fl, Peninsula Hong Kong, Salisbury Rd; ⏱ 6pm-midnight; MTR Tsim Sha Tsui (exit E)

Felix has a fantastic setting, both inside and out. You're sure to pay as much attention to the views and the Philippe Starck–designed interior as to the fusion food (think lobster nachos, hoisin grilled ribs). Towering ceilings and copper-clad columns surround the Art Deco tables. Even the view from the men's is dizzying. A special lift will whisk you up directly. There's a set dinner for $728 (six courses) and early dinner set for $428 (three courses with a glass of wine; served 6pm to 8pm).

HUTONG Map p92   Chinese $$$
☎ 3428 8342; 28/F, 1 Peking Rd; MTR Tsim Sha Tsui (exit C1)

With the panoramic view of Hong Kong you'd feel like you're midair while eating here, and dishes such as wok-fried prawns with salty egg yolk and crab roe ($188), and crispy de-boned lamb ribs in hutong style ($248) would make you feel that way anyway. If you're adventurous, try the drunken raw crab ($188).

SPRING MOON Map p92   Cantonese $$$
☎ 2315 3160; 1st fl, Peninsula Hong Kong, Salisbury Rd; MTR Tsim Sha Tsui (exit E)

The Peninsula's flagship Chinese restaurant, Spring Moon is Japanese minimalist with bits of Art Deco thrown in. The Cantonese food is excellently prepared, and the surrounds and ambience are stunning.

ARIRANG Map p92   Korean $$
☎ 2956 3288; Shop 2306-7, 2nd fl, Gateway Arcade, Harbour City, 25-27 Canton Rd; set dinner for 2 $328; MTR Tsim Sha Tsui (exit A1)

This is a large, brightly lit restaurant that may not be the place for a romantic tête à tête but is great for a group. It's mostly given over to barbecue. If in doubt, order a set lunch ($98).

EASTERN PALACE CHIU CHOW RESTAURANT Map p92   Chiu Chow $$

☎ 2730 6011; Shop 308, 3rd fl, Marco Polo Hong Kong Hotel, 3 Canton Rd; ⏰ 11am-11pm; MTR Tsim Sha Tsui (exit C1)

Chiu Chow dim sum is served at this large hotel restaurant from 11am to 4pm daily. Particularly good are the crab and shrimp balls, as well as the sliced goose in vinegar.

GOLDEN BULL Map p92   Vietnamese $$

☎ 2730 4866; Shop 101, 1st fl, Ocean Centre, Harbour City, 3-9 Canton Rd; MTR Tsim Sha Tsui (exit C1)

The crowds who descend on this place at lunch and dinner are not coming for the atmosphere (noisy) or service (abrupt), but the excellent-quality, low-cost Vietnamese food.

WU KONG SHANGHAI RESTAURANT
Map p92   Shanghainese $$

☎ 2366 7244; Basement, Alpha House, 27-33 Nathan Rd; ⏰ 11.30am-midnight; MTR Tsim Sha Tsui (exit E)

The specialities at this Shanghainese restaurant – cold pigeon in wine sauce and crispy fried eels – are worth a trip across town. Dim sum ($20 to $48) is served all day.

CHUNGKING MANSIONS Map p92   Indian $

36-44 Nathan Rd; MTR Tsim Sha Tsui (exit D1)

The greatest concentration of cheap Indian and Pakistani restaurants in Kowloon is in this rabbit warren of hostels and guesthouses. Despite the grotty appearance of the building, many of these 'messes' are quite plush, though somewhat claustrophobic. The food varies in quality, but if you follow the recommendations below you should be in for a cheap and very filling meal. A good lunch will cost from about $50; for $80 to $100 you'll get a blowout. Only a couple of these places are licensed, but you are usually allowed to BYO.

Delhi Club (☎ 2368 1682; Flat C3, 3rd fl, C Block) does good-value Indian and Nepalese food, especially the curry and chicken tandoori ($20). Pretty flash by Chungking Mansions standards. Everest Club (☎ 2316 2718; Flat D6, 3rd fl, D Block) boasts a cornucopia of 'Everest' cuisines but, frankly, the food is less colourful compared to the other offerings in the building. The Spartan Islamabad Club (☎ 2721 5362; Flat C3, 4th fl, C Block) serves Indian and Pakistani halal food.

Swagat Restaurant (☎ 2722 5350; Flat C3-4, 1st fl, C Block) is one of the most popular messes in Chungking Mansions, probably less to do with the quality of food than its liquor licence, one of the few held by a mess in this building. Taj Mahal Club (☎ 2722 5454; Flat B4, 3rd fl, B Block) is popular with those who like truly hot curries, such as the chicken Madras ($40). This place can do you *raan mussalam* ($275), a leg of lamb cooked in the tandoor and feeding six to eight people, if given advance warning.

KYOZASA RESTAURANT
Map p92   Japanese $

☎ 2376 1888; 20 Ashley Rd; MTR Tsim Sha Tsui (exit E)

For an *izakaya* experience, this colourful and cosy Japanese restaurant is as close as you'd get in Hong Kong. It has a menu that extends from sushi to steaks via hotpots. There are reasonably priced set lunches. And unlike Gomitori (Map p94; ☎ 2367 8519; Shop LG5, Lower ground fl, Energy Plaza, 92 Granville Rd; dishes $50-250; ⏰ 7pm-1am Mon-Sat) it does not discriminate – they treat you the same whether you're Japanese or not.

WEINSTUBE Map p92   Austrian, German $

☎ 2376 1800; 1st fl, Honeytex Bldg, 22 Ashley Rd; ⏰ noon-1am Mon-Sat; MTR Tsim Sha Tsui (exit E)

Pfannengebratener fleischkäse (pan-fried meatloaf), *Schweinshaxe* (Bavarian-style pork knuckle) and other hearty mains await you at this Austro-German wine bar, which has been going strong for over two decades. Happy hour is from 3pm to 8pm Monday to Friday and from noon to 8pm on Saturday.

YUMMY VIETNAMESE RESTAURANT
Map p92   Vietnamese $

☎ 3520 4343; 9/F, Canton Plaza, 82-84 Canton Rd; ⏰ 11am-11.30pm; MTR Tsim Sha Tsui (exit A1)

This place looks like a fast-food canteen but it's actually a truly authentic Vietnamese restaurant that serves even the most exotic of dishes, such as duck foetus egg ($18). But no need to go that far if all you want is a bowl of truly satisfying *pho* (from $25) or roasted pigeon in lemongrass ($60).

TSIM SHA TSUI EAST

After a bit of a slump in the '90s, Tsim Sha Tsui East has regained much of its life with the extension of KCR East Rail line, which is connected with the MTR and has an exit right outside of Kowloon Shangri-La.

NOBU Map p94   Japanese $$$$
2/F InterContinental Hong Kong, 18 Salisbury Rd; MTR Tsim Sha Tsui (exit F)

This is the restaurant where the Hollywood set drops by whenever they are in town, like they would in London, New York and Los Angeles. The *tiradito* (scallop, white fish, live octopus or razor clam; from $195) with spicy lime dressing that highlights the seafood is world famous, and other Nobu dishes like black cod *saikyo yaki* (black cod in sweet miso; $268) are also served here.

FOOK LAM MOON Map p94   Cantonese $$$
☎ 2366 0286; Shop 8, 1st fl, 53-59 Kimberley Rd; ⏰ 11am-11pm; MTR Tsim Sha Tsui (exit B1)

One of Hong Kong's top Cantonese restaurants, the Fook Lam Moon takes care of you from the minute you walk out of the lifts, with cheongsam-clad hostesses waiting to escort you to your table. The enormous menu contains a lot of unusual and expensive dishes (shark's fin, frog, abalone), which would shoot your bill up to at least $1000 per head. You might sample the pan-fried lobster balls (from $440), which are a house speciality.

NADAMAN Map p94   Japanese $$$
☎ 2733 8751; Basement 2, Kowloon Shangri-La, 64 Mody Rd; MTR Tsim Sha Tsui (exit G)

The authentic Japanese food at this restaurant has won it a well-deserved reputation, but the décor falls somewhat short. Though it is expensive, it's worth it, and the set meals at lunch time ($120 to $480) are very good value.

SABATINI Map p94   Italian $$$
☎ 2733 2000; 3rd fl, Royal Garden Hotel, 69 Mody Rd East; MTR Tsim Sha Tsui (exit G)

Classy Sabatini is a direct copy of its namesake in Rome, with murals on the walls and ceilings and polished terracotta tiles on the floor. Even classic Italian pasta dishes ($218 to $300) such as fettuccine

carbonara come across as light in the best sense, leaving room to sample the exquisite desserts. Set lunches of two/four courses are $148/250. The wine list is excellent but pricey.

SPRING DEER Map p94   Northern Chinese $$
☎ 2366 4012; 1st fl, Lyton Bldg, 42 Mody Rd; MTR Tsim Sha Tsui (exit D2)

This is probably Hong Kong's most famous (though not best) Peking restaurant, and it serves some of the crispiest Peking duck ($280 for the whole bird) in town. This place is extremely popular, so book several days in advance.

A TOUCH OF SPICE
Map p94   Southeast Asian $$
☎ 2312 1118; 1st fl, Knutsford 10 Bldg, 10 Knutsford Tce; MTR Tsim Sha Tsui (exit B1)

This is one of several trendy restaurant-bars stacked up Japanese style at 10 Knutsford Terrace. This one does Thai curries, Indonesian and Vietnamese noodles and stir-fried dishes. Most meals are good value, unless you go for the seafood.

RED STONE BAR & GRILL
Map p94   Surf & Turf $$
☎ 2722 7050; Shop G7-G8, Tsim Sha Tsui Centre, 66 Mody Rd; ⏰ 11.45am-midnight; MTR Tsim Sha Tsui (exit G)

One of the newer restaurants that has contributed to the renaissance of Tsim Sha Tsui East, this waterfront venue serves up some truly great steaks and fresh oysters ($160 for half-dozen). For lunch, try the pizzas (small from $98, large $120).

CHANG WON KOREAN RESTAURANT
Map p94   Korean $
☎ 2368 4606; 1G Kimberley St; ⏰ noon-5am; MTR Tsim Sha Tsui (exit B1)

If you're looking for truly authentic Korean food, head for this place, just one of several restaurants along a stretch that makes up Tsim Sha Tsui's 'Little Korea'. Try the excellent *bibimbab* ($100).

GOOD SATAY Map p94   Malaysian $
☎ 2739 9808; Shop 144-148, 1st fl, Houston Centre, 63 Mody Rd; ⏰ noon-10pm; MTR Tsim Sha Tsui (exit G)

This place on the 1st floor of a shopping and office complex doesn't look promising

EATING KOWLOON

VEGGIES BEWARE

There are probably more than 101 ways to accidentally eat meat in Hong Kong. Sensitivity towards vegetarians is generally low. If you are a strict vegetarian, you may as well forget about dim sum. A plate of green would be cooked in meat stock and served with oyster sauce. Vegetable dumplings might have been seasoned with lard, and minced pork creeps in when you least expect it. You can tell the staff 'I'm a vegetarian' (*ngàw hai sik jàai ge*) but it almost never helps. In fact, Cantonese food in general is a minefield to vegetarians. Superior broth, made with chicken and Chinese ham, is a prevalent ingredient, even in dishes where no actual meat is visible. In budget Chinese restaurants, chicken powder is used liberally, often in the place of salt. The safe bet for veggies wanting to go Chinese is either a specialised vegetarian eatery or upscale Chinese establishments, especially those in hotels. The chefs would substitute the flavour of meat stock with logan fruits and mushroom broth.

but it serves some of the best (and most authentic) laksa and sate in town, as well as Hainan chicken rice ($39) that has people travelling in from other parts of town. It's packed at lunch.

WOODLANDS Map p94   Indian, Vegetarian $
☎ 2369 3718; Shops 5 & 6, Ground fl, Mirror Tower, 61 Mody Rd; MTR Tsim Sha Tsui (exit G)
If you can't handle the less-than-salubrious surrounds of Chungking Mansions (p192), this place offers an inexpensive Indian alternative.

YAU MA TEI & MONG KOK

Temple St, the area around the night market, is a traditional place for cheap eats and snacks. Market cuisine, served from a push-cart, includes fish balls or squid on skewers, and there's a large choice on offer from the nearby stalls. Anything upmarket in this part of Kowloon will usually be inside a hotel of some sort.

MING COURT Map p98   Cantonese $$
☎ 3552 3388; 6th fl, Langham Place Hotel, 555 Shanghai St, Mong Kok; MTR Mong Kok (exit C3/E1)
This hotel restaurant serves excellent modern Cantonese fare in a lovely dining room surrounded by replicas of ancient pottery unearthed in the area. Dim sum is served at lunch time daily.

BALI RESTAURANT Map p97   Indonesian $
☎ 2780 2902; 10 Nanking St; set lunch from $69; noon-11pm; MTR Jordan (exit B1)
The food is pretty good and the service friendly, but the best thing about the Bali is its superb tackiness: a permanent 'happy birthday' sign, vinyl booths separated by fake brick walls, and a 'resort'-style bar playing tunes from *South Pacific*. Try the

nasi goreng, the vegetable curry or the pork satay.

TAI PAK Map p97   Taiwanese $
☎ 2332 4673; Shop 2N, 2 Tung Choi St, Mong Kok; 11.30am-11.30pm; MTR Mong Kok (exit E2)
Diners who come here are being squashed waiting for a table on the narrow pedestrian walkway, and they are being squashed when having to share the small tables with strangers. But they are not gluttons for punishment; they are simply food lovers who enjoy a good *daam daam mìn* ($24) and drunken chicken ($48).

MIU GUTE CHEONG VEGETARIAN RESTAURANT Map p97   Vegetarian $
☎ 2771 6218; 31 Ning Po St, Yau Ma Tei; 11am-11pm; MTR Jordan (exit A)
Cheap, cheerful and family-oriented vegetarian restaurant. The tofu is fresh and firm, the vegetables are the pick of the market and the tea flows freely. Takeaway dim sum is $10 to $15 (three to five pieces).

NEW KOWLOON

There isn't really much that inner Kowloon has to offer that you wouldn't find south of Mong Kok. But the confluence of Thai restaurants in Kowloon City and a few famous local joints may be worth a visit.

MEGA BOX Map pp88–9   Shopping Mall $-$$
38 Wang Chiu Rd, Kowloon Bay; MTR Kowloon Bay (exit A)
One of the newest shopping arcades promising all forms of entertainment under one roof, the dining options here span a large spectrum of Asian cuisines, including Japanese, Vietnamese and regional Chinese. Western restaurants are few at the moment but the choice is bound to grow.

KOWLOON CITY THAI RESTAURANTS

Map pp88–9   Thai $

🚌 5C from Tsim Sha Tsui Star or 101 from Statue Square, Central

Kai Tak airport may have shut down in 1998, but the neighbourhood of Kowloon City to the northeast of Tsim Sha Tsui is still worth a journey. This is Hong Kong's Thai quarter, and the area's restaurants are the place for a tom yum and green-curry fix. Among the simplest and most authentic (attracting Thai domestics by the bucketful) eateries are those below. Kowloon City, packed with herbalists, jewellers, tea merchants and bird shops, is worth a postprandial look round.

One of the most authentic Thai restaurants in the area, Friendship Thai Food (☎ 2382 8671; 38 Kai Tak Rd; dishes $32-138; 🕙 10.30am-3pm & 6-12.30pm) is always full of Thai domestics. Golden Orchid Thai (☎ 2716 1269, 2383 3076; 12 Lung Kong Rd; dishes $35-65; 🕙 noon-1am) is slightly more expensive than the Friendship but the food is excellent.

Hot Basil Thai Cuisine (☎ 2718 1088; Ground fl, 31-33 Kai Tak Rd; mains $45-110) serves decent Thai in very upmarket (for this neighbourhood) surrounds, while the Thai Farm Restaurant (☎ 2382 0992; Ground fl, 21-23 Nam Kok Rd), with its panelled walls and banquettes, looks like a neighbourhood café in Bangkok. Wong Chun Chun Thai Restaurant (☎ 2716 6269; 23 Tak Ku Ling Rd; 🕙 11am-2am), arguably the most commercially successful, is an enormous place spread over three floors and keeps later hours than most restaurants in the area.

CHONG FAT CHIU CHOW
RESTAURANT Map pp88–9   Chiu Chow $

☎ 2383 3114, 2383 1296; 60-62 South Wall Rd, Kowloon City; 🕙 11am-midnight; 🚌 5C from Tsim Sha Tsui Star or 101 from Statue Square, Central

While this place isn't easy to get to and communications are limited, it has some of the best and freshest Chiu Chow seafood in the territory. Don't miss the crab dishes, sek-làu-gài (chicken wrapped in little egg-white sacs) and the various goose offerings.

ISLAM FOOD Map pp88–9   Halal Chinese $

☎ 2382 2822; Ground fl, 1 Lung Kong Rd, Kowloon City; 🕙 11am-11pm; 🚌 5C from Tsim Sha Tsui Star or 101 from Statue Square, Central

If you fancy trying the cuisine of the Wui (Chinese Muslims), come here. Order the

mutton with scallions on a hotplate, or minced beef with pickled cabbage stuffed into sesame rolls.

WING LAI YUEN Off Map pp88–9   Sichuanese $

☎ 2726 3818; 15-17 Fung Tak Rd, Wong Tai Sin; 🕙 11am-11.30pm; MTR Wong Tai Sin (exit E)

A household name in Hong Kong for daam daam min, this unpretentious local eatery actually offers more than that. Try the fiery beef cooked in chilli broth ($48), or for something tamer, go for the wonton chicken in clay pot (from $78). English won't work here: bring a phrase book.

NEW TERRITORIES

With very few exceptions, the New Territories is not an area offering a surfeit of culinary surprises. The following recommendations are basically to help you find sustenance along the way.

TSUEN WAN

As in most of the New Towns of the New Territories, the happiest hunting grounds for a snack or lunch in Tsuen Wan are in the shopping mall that – inevitably – tops the MTR station. But there are also often surprises further afield.

PANDA CAFÉ Map p105   International $$

☎ 2409 3218; 3rd fl, Panda Hotel, 3 Tsuen Wah St; 🕙 6.30am-midnight; MTR Tsuen Wan (exit B)

You might be in the neighbourhood exploring its indigenous culture and charm, but if the foreignness gets a little much the Panda Cafe is a decent choice for some reasonable International cuisine that includes pasta and steaks. Or dive into the buffet (lunch from $128, dinner from $248) for everything from sushi to curries.

TUEN MUN

You'll find plenty of Chinese restaurants and noodle shops in Tuen Mun town centre, but it's best to travel out a way for something unusual and delicious.

CAFE LAGOON Map pp50–1   Café $$

☎ 2452 8448; LG/F, Hong Kong Gold Coast Hotel, 1 Castle Peak Rd, Castle Peak Bay, Tuen Mun; 🕙 6.30am-midnight; 🚌 53 from Tsuen Wan Ferry Pier

Even if you are not staying at the resort, you may still want to come here and chill by the pool with the international menu that includes sushi, pasta and steak. Or have it all with the buffet, especially at the more lavish evening edition, from $298.

ASIAN KITCHEN Map pp50–1   Singaporean $
☎ 3446 1122; 49 Tin Liu New Village, Ma Wan; 🚢 from Ferry Pier No 2 or Tsuen Wan Ferry Pier
A number of foodies on the quest for the best Hainan chicken rice in town have found themselves ending up here in this far-flung place. The *bak kut teh* (herbal pork-rib soup) has also won quite a few fans.

MIU FAT MONASTERY
Map pp50–1   Vegetarian $
☎ 2461 8567; 18 Castle Peak Rd; lunch $75; ⏰ noon-3pm; Light Rail line 751
This restaurant, on the 1st floor of Miu Fat Monastery in Lam Tei, due north of Tuen Mun town centre, serves vegetarian meals at lunch time only. The range of dishes varies daily and depends on group size, starting with three dishes for two (which is the minimum number).

NANG KEE GOOSE RESTAURANT
Map pp50–1   Cantonese $
☎ 2491 0392; 13 Sham Hong Rd, Sun Tsuen, Sham Tseng; roast goose from $250; ⏰ 10.30am-10.30pm; 🚌 234A or 234B from Tsuen Wan town centre
Sham Tseng has long been famous for roost goose, and this place is the most-visited restaurant in the area. Savour the crispy skin and succulent meat of the bird with some cold beer and there can be no complaint. The San Miguel brewery is just across the street.

YUEN LONG
Besides the mall offerings at Yuen Long Plaza, this historical town has a couple of interesting dining places that are actually worth trekking up north for. See the Tai Wing Wah boxed text (p198).

PAK HEUNG KWUN YUM TEMPLE
Map pp50–1   Chinese $
☎ 2477 5168/9077 5393; 8 Sheung Tsuen, Pak Heung; ⏰ 11.30am-2pm (prior booking a must);

$768 for 10-12 people; 🚌 51 from Nina Tower, Tsuen Wan
The folks here claim that their *poon choy* is the most authentic and the recipe dates back to the end of the Southern Song dynasty (AD 1127–1279), when the defeated emperor fled from the Mongolians to what is the New Territories today. Apparently, the proof is in the duck, stewed the same way it was 800 years ago. Vegetarian food is available upon request. Booking is by the table, each seating 10 to 12.

TAI PO & SURROUNDS
Tai Po town centre features pretty decent street food, such as Shanghainese meat buns (*sheng jian bao*), and the many Chinese eateries serve up old-style dishes that more Westernised parts of Hong Kong no longer serve, such as *kam ung dan yin choi* (amaranth cooked with salted and cured eggs). Tai Mei Tuk, the springboard for the Plover Cove area some 6km to the northeast, boasts a number of interesting eateries along Ting Kok Rd, many of them Thai.

LITTLE EGRET RESTAURANT
Map pp50–1   International $$
☎ 2657 6628; Tai Po Kau Interactive Nature Centre, 2 Hung Lam Dr, Tai Po Kau; ⏰ 10.30am-6.30pm Mon-Sat, 11am-10.30pm Sun; 🚌 70 from Wui Cheung Rd bus terminus, Jordan
In the same complex as the nature centre and the Museum of Ethnology (p122) is this attractive little restaurant serving a mix of dishes, from seafood to pasta ($78 to $98).

CHUNG SHING THAI RESTAURANT
Map pp50–1   Thai $
☎ 2664 5218; 69 Lung Mei Village, Ting Kok Rd, Tai Mei Tuk; 🚌 75K from Tai Po Market KCR
This is the flagship restaurant of the restaurant strip in Tai Mei Tuk, the one that launched the entire fleet. It remains very popular for its authentic Thai curries, soups and fish dishes but caters for less adventurous locals with a few Chinese offerings.

SHA TIN
The multilevel, three-phase shopping mall New Town Plaza (Map p124), connected to the Sha Tin KCR station, has more restaurants and snack bars than you can shake a chopstick at, including a branch of the Saint's Alp Teahouse

(☎ 2693 0638; Shop A189, 1st fl, New Town Plaza Phase III; ☻ 11am-11pm), steakhouse **A-1 Restaurant** (☎ 2699 0428; Shop 140-151, 1st fl, New Town Plaza Phase I; mains $70-190; ☻ 11am-11pm) and its affiliated **A-1 Bakery Shop** (☎ 2697 6377), and **Kaga Japanese Restaurant** (☎ 2603 0545; Shop A191-A193A, 1st fl, New Town Plaza Phase III; rice & noodle dishes $52-85).

STAR SEAFOOD RESTAURANT
Map p124   Cantonese $$
☎ 2635 3788; 55 Tai Chung Kiu Rd; dim sum $11-18, dinner per person from $200; ☻ 6am-12.30am; 🚌 680 from MTR Admiralty (east bus terminus) or 85k from Sha Tin KCR

A cement building that's shaped like a giant boat, this is your quintessential tourist restaurant. The food might not be the best you've had, but the experience would certainly be one of a kind.

SUN KEUNG KEE ROASTED GOOSE & SEAFOOD RESTAURANT Map p124 Chinese $
☎ 2606 1197; 47-50 Holford Garden, Tai Wai; whole roast goose $220, regular serving $55; Tai Wai KCR

In most cases you come here for the roast goose and congee when you happen by, maybe en route to another New Territories destination. But this restaurant does have a loyal following of people making a trip here just for the bird.

SAI KUNG

Sai Kung town is chock-a-block with eateries. Here you'll find curry, pizzas, and bangers and mash just as easily as Chinese seafood, but you'd make a special trip here only for that last category. It's reachable by bus 92 from Diamond Hill MTR bus terminus (exit C2).

DIA Map p127   Indian $$
☎ 2791 4466; Shop 2, Block A, Ground fl, 42-56 Fuk Man Rd; ☻ 11am-11pm

This stylish place, all blue satin and rattan, serves North Indian cuisine. Kick off with the mixed starters platter ($120) before diving into the curries with some sensational *naan* ($15).

JASPA'S Map p127   International, Fusion $$
☎ 2792 6388; 13 Sha Tsui Path; ☻ 8am-10.30pm Mon-Sat, 9am-midnight Sun

Jaspa's is an upbeat and casual place serving international and fusion food. Weekday set lunch is $88, as is all-day breakfast on the weekend.

PEPPERONI'S PIZZA Map p127   Italian $$
☎ 2791 0394; Lot 1592, Po Tung Rd; pizzas from $75; ☻ 11am-11pm

This place serves up some decent pizza, although you are advised to stick with the classics and stay away from the hybrid recipes such as the Cajun. The atmosphere is relaxing and fun.

SAUCE Map p127   International $$
☎ 2791 2348; 9 Sha Tsui Path; ☻ 11am-11pm Mon-Fri, 10am-11pm Sat & Sun

This very stylish restaurant on a narrow pedestrian path in the centre of Sai Kung town has outside seating. There is a range of pasta dishes and the sticky toffee pudding is divine.

CHUEN KEE SEAFOOD RESTAURANT
Map p127   Chinese, Seafood $
☎ 2791 1195; 53 Hoi Pong St; ☻ 11am-11pm

Chuen Kee, the granddaddy of the Sai Kung seafood restaurants, has three several nearby branches to house customers when capacity is maxing out. A standard stir-fried clams costs $48.

HONEYMOON DESSERT
Map p127   Chinese Desserts $
☎ 2792 4991; 9, 10A, B&C Po Tung Rd; per person $30; ☻ 1pm-2.45am

This place, serving Chinese desserts such as sweet thick walnut soup and durian pudding, has become so famous that some people drive in from town for it. Some former loyalists say standards have slipped in recent times, but others remain faithful. The business has since grown to include new locations, such as Sheung Wan (Map p70; ☎ 2851 2606; Shop 4-8, G/F, Western Market, 323 Des Voeux Rd Central; ☻ noon-midnight; MTR Sheung Wan, exit C).

TAP MUN CHAU

You won't starve to death on remote Tap Mun, but you also won't have much of a choice in the way of venues. There's only one restaurant on this far-flung island, which technically belongs to the Tai Po District but is connected to Sai Kung by ferry. The food, including some local seafood, is good and the people helpful and friendly.

NEW HON KEE Map pp50–1   Chinese, Seafood $

☎ 2328 2428; 4 Tap Mun Hoi Pong St; ☻ 11am-2pm Mon-Fri, 11am-6pm Sat & Sun; ⚓ Tap Mun ferry from Ma Liu Shui (University KCR)

This seafood restaurant, popular with islanders and visitors alike, is a short walk northeast of the ferry pier on the way to the Tin Hau temple. The grilled prawns and squid are very good.

OUTLYING ISLANDS

Restaurants and other eateries vary widely from island to island. Some, like those on Lantau (and to a large extent Cheung Chau), are just convenient refuelling stations as you head for (or return from) your destination. Others, such as the seafood restaurants in Lamma's Sok Kwu Wan (opposite) or on Po Toi (p201), are destinations in their own right.

LAMMA

Lamma offers the greatest choice of restaurants and cuisines of any of the Outlying Islands. Most people head directly to Sok Kwu Wan for a fix of Cantonese-style seafood, but Yung Shue Wan has a vast and eclectic range, and there are a couple of other venues elsewhere on the island, including a famous pigeon restaurant, that are worth the trip in itself.

Yung Shue Wan

Yung Shue Wan has a large choice of places to eat. Along its main (and only) street, not only will you find Chinese restaurants, but also Western, vegetarian, Thai and even Indian ones. To get here, take a ferry from Central Pier in front of Exchange Square or from Aberdeen near the wholesale fish market.

MAN FUNG SEAFOOD RESTAURANT
Map p132   Chinese, Seafood $$

☎ 2982 0719; 5 Main St; ☻ 11am-10pm

You can't judge a book by its cover, but you can certainly judge a seafood restaurant by its tanks. The live seafood is displayed outside, all seemingly having a good life in what looks like pristine water, until you end it by sending it to the kitchen. Don't be surprised to see your fellow diners diving into basketball-size spider crabs.

PIZZA MILANO Map p132   Italian $$

☎ 2982 4848; Flat A, Ground fl, 2 Back St; small/medium/large pizzas $50/62/98; ☻ 6-11pm Mon-Fri, noon-11pm Sat & Sun

If you're looking for pizza, pasta, calzone or crostini, Lamma's only Italian restaurant is the right choice.

TAI WING WAH

In the old days every district in Hong Kong would have at least one of those gaudy and massive neighbourhood Chinese restaurants, recognisable by the characteristically cheesy décor of red velvet, glaring carpet, and the gold-plated dragon and phoenix sculptures with blinking eyes. That would be where nearby residents go for dim sum, family gatherings and wedding banquets (hence the carved mythical creatures, signifying the union of a man and a woman). Tai Wing Wah (Map pp50–1; 2/F, Koon Wong Mansion, 2-6 On Ning Rd; all dishes $48; ☻ 6am-midnight; 🚌 968 from Tin Hau bus terminus) was once the neighbourhood Chinese restaurant of Yuen Long, a New Territories township not far from the border with the mainland. But like its counterparts in other districts, changing times and changing tastes forced it into closure in the early '90s. Its head chef and managing partner Hugo Leung Man-to migrated to Canada, but made a comeback five years later. He decided that after years of being fed industrialised foods, Hong Kong diners were missing the good ol' days of no-frills dishes and seasonal produce. He reopened Tai Wing Wah and reintroduced many Cantonese and walled village dishes, which most other restaurants had stopped serving because of their labour intensiveness and low profitability.

Hugo sources local ingredients from small farms and food producers whenever possible, and compensates with his cookery skills if industrialised produce has to be used. Hugo thinks shrimps in Hong Kong, mostly farmed in China, taste bland, and he boosts them with Bexter's lobster bisque – an idea he came up with during his time in North America. His ideas work. People have been zooming into this far corner of town to line up for tables, and to savour everything from five-taste chicken (seasoned with soy sauce, star anise, Sichuan pepper, nutmeg and dried mandarin peel) and stir-fried translucent bean noodles with dried shrimps and vegetable, through to the signature steamed rice served with lard and Malay sponge cake. Leung has hosted TV food shows and writes newspaper columns on the subject. He is probably one of the few remaining chefs in Hong Kong who know how to make a dish out of pig's oviducts.

BOOKWORM CAFÉ Map p132 Café, Vegetarian $
☎ 2982 4838; 79 Main St; ☺ 10am-9pm Mon-Fri, 9am-10pm Sat, 9am-9pm Sun

This place is not just a great vegetarian café-restaurant with fruit juices and organic wine ($35 per glass), but a second-hand bookshop and an internet café ($0.50 per minute) as well.

DELI LAMMA CAFÉ Map p132 Café $
☎ 2982 1583; 36 Main St; set lunch $70; ☺ 9am-1am

This relaxed café-restaurant serves everything, and that means everything. The menu features everything from continental fare leaning towards the Mediterranean, with a fair few pasta dishes and pizzas. It has an excellent bar and views of the harbour.

Hung Shing Yeh

This popular beach southeast of Yung Shue Wan, about 500m from the pier, has a convenient waterfront hotel where you can lunch on the terrace. It also boasts one of the most famous nonseafood restaurants on the Outlying Islands.

Sok Kwu Wan

An evening meal at Sok Kwu Wan is an enjoyable way to end a trip to Lamma. The restaurants line the waterfront on either side of the ferry pier and will be chock-a-block on weekend nights with Chinese and expats who have arrived by ferry, on boats laid on by the restaurants themselves, on company junks or on the ostentatious yachts known locally as 'gin palaces'. Most of the dozen or so restaurants offer the same relatively high-quality seafood at similar prices, but a few places stand out from the pack. There's a ferry service from Central Pier in front of Exchange Square.

RAINBOW SEAFOOD RESTAURANT
Map p132 Chinese, Seafood $$
☎ 2982 8100; Shops 1A-1B, Ground fl, 23-24 First St; ☺ 11am-11pm

The Rainbow, with a waterfront location, specialises in seafood, especially steamed grouper, lobster and abalone. A plus is that when you book a table, you have the option of being transported by small ferry from Queen's Pier in Central (up to seven sailings on weekdays from 2.40pm to 9pm, and up to a dozen on weekends

from 11.30am to 9pm) or from Aberdeen (three optional sailings at 6.15pm, 7.15pm and 8pm).

TAI YUEN RESTAURANT
Map p132 Chinese, Seafood $
☎ 2982 8386, 2982 8391; 15 First St; ☺ 10am-11pm

This small, intimate place offers less frenetic, friendlier service than most of the other places in Sok Kwu Wan.

Mo Tat Wan

Surprisingly, in this relatively remote corner of Lamma there's an upmarket Western restaurant, The Bay (Map p132; ☎ 2982 8186; 7 Beach Front; mains $98-138; ☺ 11am-10pm; ⛴ from Aberdeen near the wholesale fish market).

CHEUNG CHAU

In Cheung Chau village, south of the cargo pier and at the start of Tai Hing Tai Rd, there are a number of food stalls with fish tanks where you can choose your favourite finned or shelled creatures at more or less market prices and then pay the stall holders to cook them the way you like.

Pak She Praya Rd, running northwest off Praya St, is loaded with seafood restaurants that face the typhoon shelter and its flotilla of junks and sampans.

There's a ferry service from Central Pier in front of Exchange Square.

EAST LAKE Map p143 Cantonese $
☎ 2981 3869; 85 Tung Wan Rd; ☺ 10am-10pm

This Cantonese restaurant, away from the waterfront and close to Tung Wan Beach, is popular with locals and expats, especially in the evening when tables are set up outside.

HOMETOWN TEAHOUSE Map p143 Café $
☎ 2981 5038; 12 Tung Wan Rd; ☺ noon-11pm midnight

This wonderfully relaxed place run by an amiable Japanese couple serves lunch and dinner, but the afternoon tea – sushi ($10 to $15 each), pancakes, tea – is what you should come for. It's convenient to Tung Wan Beach.

NEW BACCARAT Map p143 Chinese, Seafood $
☎ 2981 0606; 9A Pak She Praya Rd; set meals from $138; ☺ 11am-10.30pm

EATING OUTLYING ISLANDS

LAMMA & LANTAU

Spending a day over the weekend on one of the outlying islands is a popular pastime in Hong Kong, and the two that are most famous for dining are Lamma Island (p198) and Lantau Island (below). The former is famous for its waterfront seafood restaurants, found both in the most populated and cosmopolitan village of Yung Shue Wan, in the north, and more rustic Sok Kwu Wan on the east side of the island, where a handful of fish farms remain. The locally produced shrimp paste, which can be bought for about $20 a bottle from many of the shops on the village's main artery Sok Kwu Wan First St, is famous. The trail between the two villages, divided by a small hill, is popular among leisure hikers. The journey will take you through Hung Shing Ye Beach, where popular stopover Concerto Inn (Map p132; ☎ 2982-1668; 28 Hung Shing Ye Beach, Yung Shue Wan; ☽ 8am-10pm) is located. There is also the famous Kin Hing Tofu Dessert (Map p132; Yung Shue Wan Back St; ☽ 10am-6pm Sat, Sun & public holidays) and well-known pigeon restaurant Han Lok Yuen (Map p132; ☎ 2982 0608; 16-17 Hung Shing Yeh Wan; pigeon $55 each; ☽ 11.30am-8.30pm Tue-Sat, 11.30am-7pm Sun & public holidays).

Lantau Island, the largest land mass of the Hong Kong Special Administrative Region, is home to many villages, luxury residential area Discovery Bay and the new satellite town of Tung Chung. Mui Wo, the main village whose ferry pier was once the only connecting point between Lantau and the city area, offers cafés and passable seafood restaurants. The newly renovated Discovery Bay Plaza features a range of dining options, most of which are branches of restaurant chains from the city, except Hemingway's (opposite). In Tung Chung, the main shopping mall Citygate offers everything from Thai and Vietnamese to Shanghainese and Kentucky Fried Chicken, but it's nothing to write home about. The adjacent Novotel Citygate Hong Kong hotel (Map p136; ☎ 3602 8888; 20 Tai Tong Rd; MTR Tung Chung, exit C), though, has a pretty decent Mediterranean restaurant called Olea, which serves tapas and pizzas fresh from the grill. Tai O, on the far west of the island, has lost some of its fishing village charm in recent years because of thoughtless development. But it remains a relaxing place for a day trip and some seafood.

This place has been around for so long you have to believe that it's doing something right. Seafood-wise it serves everything from a steamed fish served with soy sauce, ginger and scallion to mantis shrimp cooked with peppered salt.

LANTAU

The lion's share of Lantau's restaurants is, naturally enough, in Mui Wo (Silvermine Bay), but you certainly won't starve in places further afield, such as the settlements along South Lantau Rd, on the Ngong Ping Plateau and in Tai O. Discovery Bay has its own line-up of eateries around Discovery Bay Plaza (Map p136).

Mui Wo

You'll find a slew of restaurants, noodle shops and bars to the southwest of the ferry pier. There are also some restaurants on the way to Silvermine Bay Beach and on the beach itself. For some pub recommendations, see p213. There's a ferry service from Central Pier in front of Exchange Square.

SILVERMINE BEACH HOTEL
Map p139   International $$
☎ 2984 8295; Tung Wan Tau Rd
The coffee shop and Chinese restaurant at this relatively flashy hotel is no great

shakes, but it can be recommended for its all-you-can-eat buffet ($138) from Sunday to Friday and its barbecue buffet ($198) on Saturday.

BAHÇE Map p139   Turkish $
☎ 2984 0222; Shop 19, Ground fl, Mui Wo Centre, 3 Ngan Wan Rd; kebabs from $80; ☽ 11.30am-11pm Mon-Fri, 10am-11pm Sat & Sun
'The Garden' might be a somewhat ambitious name for this small eatery but it has all our Turkish favourites, including *sigara böreği* (filo parcels filled with cheese) and *yaprak dolmasi* (stuffed vine leaves), as well as kebabs and felafel.

LA PIZZERIA Map p139   Italian $
☎ 2984 8933; Ground fl, Grand View Mansion, 11C Mui Wo Ferry Pier Rd
Most people come here for the pizza ($45 to $95), but there are lots of pasta choices and main courses such as fajitas and barbecued spareribs.

Discovery Bay

The restaurants in the circular plaza opposite the ferry pier at Discovery Bay (Map p136) offer a wide variety of cuisines. There's a ferry service from Central Pier in front of Exchange Square.

HEMINGWAY'S
Map p136   Caribbean, Barbecue $$

☎ 2987 8855; Shop G09, Block A, Discovery Bay Plaza; ⏰ 10am-2am; ⚓ Discovery Bay

It may not feel exactly like Key West or Havana here, but when the weather is clear, this beachfront restaurant makes for a great escape. Try the barbecue salmon jerky ($120) and the great cocktails ($58).

South Lantau Rd

Two of the villages along South Lantau Rd, Lantau's main east–west thoroughfare, have decent restaurants from which to choose.

GALLERY Map p136   Barbecue $$

☎ 2980 2582; 26 Tong Fuk Village; ⏰ 6pm-midnight Mon-Fri, noon-midnight Sat & Sun; 🚌 1, 2 or 3

This Middle Eastern(ish) restaurant, on a terrace with an arbour overlooking South Lantau Rd, has some good international dishes and, on the weekend, a decent barbecue, with Australian seafood, kebabs and other grills, such as the signature black Angus. Oven-baked pizzas are another must-try.

OOH LA LA! Map p136   French, Mediterranean $$

☎ 2546 3543; Pui O Beach; ⏰ 10.30am-11.30pm Mon-Sat, 10.30am-10pm Sun; 🚌 1 or 2 from Mui Wo

This simple place at the Treasure Island on Lantau hotel (Map p136) has a meat and seafood barbecue in the summer and fondue ($280 to $320 for two) in the winter. The terrace directly on the beach is a bonus, as is the Ooh La La! signature Pui-O-Punch.

STOEP RESTAURANT
Map p136   Mediterranean, South African $$

☎ 2980 2699; 32 Lower Cheung Sha Village; ⏰ 11am-10pm Tue-Sun; 🚌 1 or 2 from Mui Wo

This Mediterranean-style restaurant with a huge terrace right on Lower Cheung Sha Beach has acceptable meat and fish dishes and a South African *braai* (barbecue; $80 to $150). Be sure to book on the weekend.

Ngong Ping

An artificial Chinese village has been built alongside the ill-fated Ngong Ping Skyrail, featuring a range of casual dining options that include noodle joints, fusion restaurants, Starbucks as well as a branch of Honeymoon Des-

sert (Map p136; see also p197). For some no-frills vegetarian treats, the Po Lin Monastery is only a short walk away.

PO LIN VEGETARIAN RESTAURANT
Map p136   Vegetarian $

☎ 2985 5248; Ngong Ping; set meals regular/deluxe $60/100; ⏰ 11.30am-4.30pm; 🚌 23 from Mui Wo

The famous monastery (p135) in west-central Lantau has a good reputation for its inexpensive but substantial vegetarian food. The simple restaurant is in the covered arcade to the left of the main monastery building. Buy your ticket there or at the ticket office below the Tian Tan Buddha statue. Sittings are every half-hour.

Tai O

Tai O, a village on the western coast, is famous for its excellent seafood restaurants, many of which display their names in Chinese only. Take bus 4 from Mui Wo.

PENG CHAU

The couple of waterfront pubs and restaurants on Peng Chau used to survive on business from residents of the Discovery Bay across the narrow channel. But the renovation of Discovery Bay Plaza that has seen many new dining options springing up spells the end for them. No one is going to starve here though, with the many local Chinese places serving up noodles and rice. Take a ferry from Central Pier in front of Exchange Square.

GREENY GRASSLAND Map p147   Café $

☎ 2983 8182; 12 Po Peng St; ⏰ noon-9pm

The food here is nothing to write home about, but the ultrafriendly service is. Take a seat outside, enjoy some pasta (with soup and coffee for $28) or the signature pork loin bun ($10) and soak in the village charm.

PO TOI

MING KEE SEAFOOD RESTAURANT
Map pp50–1   Seafood $$

☎ 2849 7038; ⏰ 11am-11pm; ⚓ Po Toi ferry from Ma Liu Shui (University KCR)

This is one of a handful of restaurants in the main village of Po Toi Island, south of Hong Kong Island, and is by far the most popular with day-trippers. Make sure you book ahead on the weekend.

BLUELIST[1] (blu list) *v.*
to recommend a travel experience.
What's your recommendation? www.lonelyplanet.com/bluelist

ENTERTAINMENT

top picks

- **Aqua Spirit** (p211) Plate glass harbour panoramas, swanky surroundings.
- **Cloudnine** (p216) Listen to the local kids sing along to saccharine Cantopop. An authentic, if perhaps painful, Hong Kong experience.
- **Drop** (p214) Chilled owners, rib-rattling sound system, up-for-it crowd, bangin' choons.
- **Gecko Lounge** (p207) Lost French civilisation found in Central back alley. Great wines, chilled beats, warm atmosphere.
- **Yumla** (p214) Scruffy, unpretentious, inexpensive and late-opening club-cum-bar with cool, eclectic music.
- **Yun Fu** (p207) Kick off the night with eclectic tunes, fruity cocktails and a retro Chinese look at Yun Fu's tiny, circular bar.

Hong Kong's reputation as a cultural desert that's full of drinking holes is not entirely deserved. Certainly the clubbing and bar scene is more frantic and full of choice than it has ever been. Beyond the happy hours and the neon, though, there's a small but growing world of cultural entertainment representing drama, Cantonese opera, dance or live music.

Most weeks, half a dozen local arts companies perform anything from Cantonese opera to an English-language version of a Chekhov play. Locally cultivated drama and dance are among the most enjoyable in Asia, and the schedule of foreign performances is often stellar; recent imports have included the incomparable soprano Barbara Hendricks, composer Philip Glass and his ensemble, the Senegalese *mbalax* superstar Youssou N'Dour and Australian pop-singing sensation Kylie Minogue. There are also some very impressive new venues, especially in New Kowloon and the New Territories.

Nightlife Strips & Districts

Hong Kong Island has the lion's share of the territory's most popular pubs, bars and clubs, plus the cultural venues of Central and Wan Chai, so classical music concerts, theatre, opera and the like are within easy striking distance.

Much of Central's fun nightlife revolves around the now legendary Lan Kwai Fong, and increasingly the streets immediately above it. In the not-so-distant past it was an area of squalid tenements, rubbish and rats, but it has since been scrubbed, face-lifted and closed to traffic and these days is often full to bursting. Lan Kwai Fong's clientele tends to be young, hip, cashed up and increasingly Chinese as well as expatriate.

Soho is more geared more for dining than drinking, but a handful of bars and clubs make it worth the trek – on foot or via the Central Escalator – up the hill. Sheung Wan boasts a couple of attractive venues, including a popular gay bar (p208).

Wan Chai has been sleaze territory ever since it was the first port of call for American sailors and GIs on R&R from the battlefields of Vietnam. Much of the western part of the district has cleaned up its act, but hostess bars still line Lockhart Rd. There's lots of zippy club action and a sprinkling of late-night cover-band venues throughout the district.

Compared with Wan Chai and the Lan Kwai Fong area of Central, Causeway Bay is relatively tame after dark. Still, there are a few pubs and bars that do a thriving business. The neighbourhoods to the east are not especially attractive for their entertainment venues, though you will find a clutch of pubs and bars in Quarry Bay (especially on and around Tong Chong St).

For the most part, the entertainment scene in Kowloon plays second fiddle to the hot spots of Hong Kong Island, although there's a nascent local karaoke bar scene around the Minden Rd area and a more touristy, but no less buzzy, food-and-drink thing going on around along Knutsford Terrace in the north of Tsim Sha Tsui. Otherwise the district is littered with bars and pubs – it's just a bit tackier, less imaginative and more run-down.

What's On

To find out what's on in Hong Kong, pick up a copy of HK Magazine (www.asia-city.com), a very comprehensive entertainment-listings magazine that also has lively articles on current trends in the city, reviews of restaurants and bars, and a classified ad pull-out section called *black + white*. It's free, appears on Friday and can be picked up at restaurants, bars, shops and hotels throughout the territory.

Also worth checking out is bc magazine (www.bcmagazine.net), a biweekly guide to Hong Kong's entertainment and partying scene. One of the most useful features in this highly visual and glossy publication is its complete listing of bars and clubs. It is also free and can usually be found alongside copies of *HK Magazine*.

The Hong Kong Arts Centre (www.hkac.org.hk) publishes *Artslink,* a monthly with listings of performances, exhibitions and art-house film screenings. Another invaluable source of information is the monthly Artmap (www.artmap .com.hk), a map with listings, available free at venues throughout the territory.

Tickets & Reservations

Expect to pay around $50 for a seat up the back for the Hong Kong Philharmonic and from about $400 for a performance by the likes of Norah Jones or an international musical such as *Saturday Night Fever*. Bookings for most cultural events can be made by telephone or the internet with Urbtix (☎ 2111 5999; www .urbtix.gov.hk; ⏰ 10am-8pm). Tickets can either be reserved with a passport number and picked up within three days, or paid for in advance by credit card. There are Urbtix windows at the Hong Kong City Hall (Map p56; ⏰ 10am-9.30pm) in Central, Queen Elizabeth Stadium (Map p65) in Wan Chai and the Hong Kong Cultural Centre (Map p92) in Tsim Sha Tsui. Tickets can also be purchased from the Tom Lee Music Company Centre (Map p92; ☎ 2723 9932; 1-9 Cameron Lane, Tsim Sha Tsui; ⏰ ticketing 10am-7.30pm). The Fringe Theatre and the Academy for Performing Arts use HK Ticketing (☎ 3128 8288; www.hkticketing.com).

You can also book tickets for many films and concerts and a great variety of cultural events over the phone or internet through Cityline (☎ 2317 6666; www.cityline.com.hk).

DRINKING

Drinking venues in Hong Kong run the gamut from British-style pubs to tiny little karaoke bars aimed at a young Cantonese clientele, to stylish wine and cocktail lounges where affluent professionals don their glad rags. Much of Hong Kong's nightlife takes place in top-end hotels where inventive cocktails, skilled bar staff and some of the best views in town attract visitors and locals.

Depending on where you go, beer costs at least $40 a pint (though it's cheaper at happy hour). Overall, Lan Kwai Fong in Central is the best – and most expensive – area for bars, though it's the stomping ground of expat and Chinese suits. The pubs in Wan Chai are cheaper and more relaxed, and those in Tsim Sha Tsui tend to attract more locals than visitors.

Opening Hours

Bars generally open at noon or 6pm and close anywhere between 2am and 6am. Wan Chai bars stay open the latest.

HAPPY HOUR

During certain hours of the day, most pubs, bars and even certain clubs give discounts on drinks (usually one-third to one-half off) or offer two for every one drink purchased. Happy hour is usually in the late afternoon or early evening – 4pm to 8pm, say – but the times vary widely from place to place. Depending on the season, the day of the week and the location, some pubs' happy hours run from noon until as late as 10pm, and some start again after midnight.

HONG KONG ISLAND
Central

BAR GEORGE Map p68   Bar
☎ 2521 2202; 38-44 D'Aguilar St; ⏰ 3pm-4am, happy hour 3-9pm; MTR Central (exit D2)
This large and raucous place is probably Lan Kwai Fong's biggest meat market; if you can't make it here, you won't make it anywhere. There's a lounge section and a dance floor at the back, with a second bar at the dance floor.

BIT POINT Map p68   Bar
☎ 2523 7436; Ground fl, 31 D'Aguilar St; ⏰ noon-3am Mon-Fri, noon-4am Sat, 4pm-2am Sun, happy hour 4-9pm; MTR Central (exit D2)
Owned by the same lot as Biergarten (p211), Bit Point is essentially a German-style bar where beer drinking is taken very seriously. Most beers here are draught pilsners that you can get in a glass boot if you've got a thirst big enough to kick. Bit Point also serves some pretty solid Teutonic fare (starters from $30, mains from $60), with set lunches still a snip at $59/75 for half/full portions.

CAPTAIN'S BAR Map p56   Bar
☎ 2522 0111; Ground fl, Mandarin Oriental, 5 Connaught Rd Central; ⏰ 11am-2am Mon-Sat, 11am-1am Sun; MTR Central (exit F)
This is a clubby, suited place that serves ice-cold draught beer in chilled silver mugs,

as well as some of the best martinis in town. This is a good place to talk business, at least until the cover band strikes up at 9pm.

DRAGON-I Map p68 — Bar, Club

☎ 3110 1222; www.dragon-i.com.hk; Upper ground fl, the Centrium, 60 Wyndham St; ☾ noon-midnight Mon-Sat, happy hour 3-9pm Mon-Sat (terrace); ☐ 26

A fabulous venue on the edge of Soho serving as club, indoor bar and restaurant with a huge terrace over Wyndham St filled with caged songbirds. There's an ultra-exclusive door policy by night, so it helps to be a rock star or a supermodel.

FINDS Map p68 — Bar

☎ 2522 9318; www.finds.com.hk; 2nd fl, LKF Tower, 33 Wyndham St, Central; ☾ noon-late Mon-Sat; MTR Central (exit D2)

Scandinavian food and drink is the theme at this elegant bar-'Scandinavian tapas' joint commanding prime spot above the Lan Kwai Fong hordes. There's a fine range of Scandinavian spirits, including some fantastic Finnish Akavit–style firewater. There's a small balcony if it's a fine night.

GLOBE Map p68 — Bar

☎ 2543 1941; 39 Hollywood Rd; ☾ 7.30am-1am Mon-Fri, 10am-1am Sat & Sun, happy hour 9am-8pm & midnight-1am Mon-Sat, all day Sun; ☐ 26

This tiny, unpretentious place gets packed out after work with expats thirsting for one (or more) of the 60 lagers, beers and real ales from around the world that are available here.

LA DOLCE VITA Map p68 — Bar

☎ 2186 1888; Cosmos Bldg, 9-11 Lan Kwai Fong Lane; ☾ 11am-2am Mon-Thu, 11.30am-3am Fri, 2pm-3am Sat, 2pm-1am Sun, happy hour 5.30-8pm; MTR Central (exit D2)

This is a popular place for postwork brews, with room to prop on the heart-shaped bar or stand on the terrace and watch the preening mob crawl by.

LE JARDIN Map p68 — Bar

☎ 2526 2717; 1st fl, Winner Bldg, 10 Wing Wah Lane; ☾ noon-3am Mon-Thu, 4.30pm-3am Fri & Sat, happy hour noon-8pm Mon-Thu, 4.30-8pm Sat; MTR Central (exit D2)

Don't imagine a breezy oasis – 'The Garden' is no more than an enclosed veranda – but this is still an attractive bar with loads of atmosphere. The mostly expat crowd enjoys itself without getting too boisterous.

MO BAR Map p56 — Bar

☎ 2132 0077; The Landmark, 15 Queen's Rd, Central; ☾ 11am-2am Mon-Sat; MTR Central (exit D1)

If you can't face the crush of Central's usual drinking haunts and perhaps want to catch up with a chat, the swish MO Bar, attached to the Mandarin's new swanky outpost, offers peace, repose, soft lighting and a high-end drinks list of wines and cocktails.

RED BAR Map p56 — Bar

☎ 8129 8882; L4, Two IFC, 8 Finance St, Central; ☾ noon-midnight Mon-Thu, noon-3am Fri & Sat, noon-10pm Sun; MTR Hong Kong (exit F)

A fantastic combination of alfresco drinking and harbour views is hard to beat on Hong Kong Island. DJs playing funk and jazz turn up the volume as the weekend approaches.

SODA Map p68 — Bar

☎ 2522 8118; Upper basement, 79 Wyndham St, Central (enter from Pottinger St); ☾ 4pm-midnight Sun-Thu, 4pm-3am Fri & Sat, happy hour 6-9pm; ☐ 13, 26, 40M

This well-placed watering hole, decorated in warm yellows and oranges, and with its front open to steep Pottinger St, is also a DJ scene, notably on Wednesday and the weekend, with hip-hop and R & B.

SOLAS Map p68 — Bar

☎ 9154 4049; www.solas.com.hk; 60 Wyndham St, Central; ☾ noon-2am Mon-Sat; MTR Central (exit D2)

If the nasty man wouldn't let you into Dragon-I upstairs, never mind. Who wants to spend all night swapping small talk with characters out of *Zoolander* anyway? This relaxed, friendly place, where a DJ spins relaxed lounge sounds and the cocktails pack a punch, isn't a bad consolation prize.

TIVO Map p68 — Bar

☎ 2116 8055; www.aqua.com.hk; 43-55 Wyndham St, Central; ☾ noon-2am Mon-Sat; MTR Central (exit D2)

One of the best of a lively little string of bars that have sprung up, almost overnight it seems, along increasingly lively Wyndham St. Tivo is a cut above the peanuts and beer standard of the 'Fong, just

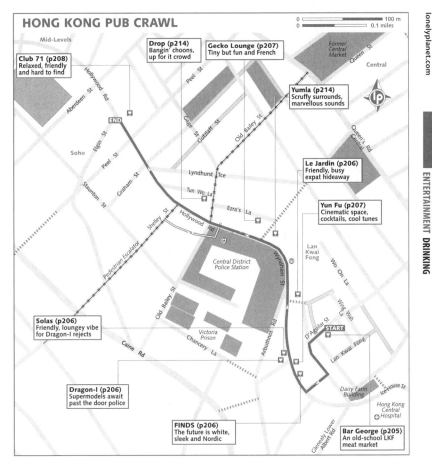

HONG KONG PUB CRAWL

0 — 100 m
0 — 0.1 miles

Mid-Levels

Club 71 (p208)
Relaxed, friendly and hard to find

Drop (p214)
Bangin' choons, up for it crowd

Gecko Lounge (p207)
Tiny but fun and French

Former Central Market

Queen St

Central

Hollywood Rd

Aberdeen St

Peel St

Gutzlaff St

Cage St

Old Bailey St

Yumla (p214)
Scruffy surrounds, marvellous sounds

Queen's Rd Central

Elgin St

Soho

Peel St

Staunton St

Graham St

Shelley St

Pedestrian Escalator

END

Lyndhurst Tce

Tun Wo La

Ezra's La

Hollywood Rd

Le Jardin (p206)
Friendly, busy expat hideaway

Yun Fu (p207)
Cinematic space, cocktails, cool tunes

Central District Police Station

Wyndham St

Lan Kwai Fong

Wo On La

Wing Wah

Solas (p206)
Friendly, loungey vibe for Dragon-I rejects

Old Bailey St

Victoria Prison

Chancery La

Arbuthnot Rd

D'Aguilar St

START

Lan Kwai Fong

Caine Rd

Dragon-I (p206)
Supermodels await past the door police

Dairy Farm Building

Ice House St

Hong Kong Central Hospital

FINDS (p206)
The future is white, sleek and Nordic

Glenealy Lower Albert Rd

Bar George (p205)
An old-school LKF meat market

around the corner. Wine and snacks Italian style (such as thin-crust pizza) is the thing (that'll be where the name comes from then). You can just have a drink without eating, though.

YUN FU Map p68 — Bar, Restaurant
☎ 2116 8855; www.aqua.com.hk; Basement 43-55 Wyndham St, Central; ☺ noon-2am Mon-Sat; MTR Central (exit D2)
Look for the Chinese characters before you reach Tivo and descend to this tiny but delightful circular bar. The fantastic Imperial China theming is actually part of the pioneering restaurant of the same name (p178), but even if you're not dining, it's well worth stopping for one of the fresh fruit cocktails and to soak up the sounds coming from the DJ's tiny cubby hole.

GECKO LOUNGE Map p68 — Lounge, Wine Bar
☎ 2537 4680; Lower ground fl, 15-19 Hollywood Rd; ☺ 4pm-2am Mon-Thu, 4pm-4am Fri & Sat, happy hour 6-9pm; MTR Central (exit D1)
Entered from narrow Ezra's Lane off Cochrane or Pottinger Sts, Gecko is an intimate lounge and wine bar run by a friendly French sommelier and wine importer with a penchant for absinthe. The well-hidden DJ mixes good sounds with kooky Parisian tunes, and there's usually live music on Tuesday and Wednesday. Great wine list, obviously.

WHISKEY PRIEST Map p68 — Pub
☎ 2869 0099; Ground & 1st fl, 12 Lan Kwai Fong; ☺ 4pm-1am Tue-Thu, 4pm-3am Fri & Sat, noon-1am Sun, happy hour 4-10pm Mon-Sat, noon-1pm Sun; MTR Central (exit D2)

The first (and so far only) Irish – thus the 'e' in 'whiskey' – pub to hit Lan Kwai Fong has Guinness, Kilkenny and Harp on tap, and 60 types of whiskey.

Soho & Sheung Wan

BAR 1911 Map p68   Bar
☎ 2810 6681; 27 Staunton St, Soho; �---- 5pm-midnight Mon-Sat, happy hour 5-9pm Mon-Sat; ☐ 26
This is a refined bar with fine details (stained glass, burlwood bar, ceiling fan) and a 1920s Chinese vibe. It's usually a tad less crowded than other nearby competitors, which makes it a great haven from the hubbub of the 'Fong.

BARCO Map p56   Bar
☎ 2857 4478; 42 Staunton St, Soho; �---- 4pm-1am Sun-Thu, 4pm-late Fri & Sat, happy hour 4-8pm; MTR Central
One of our favourite Soho bars, Barco has great staff, is small enough to never feel empty, and attracts a cool mix of locals and expats.

CLUB 71 Map p68   Bar
☎ 2858 7071; Basement, 67 Hollywood Rd, Central; �---- 3pm-2am Mon-Sat, 6pm-1am Sun, happy hour 3-9pm; ☐ 26
When Club 64, the counter-culture nerve centre of Lan Kwai Fong whose name recalled 4 June 1989, the date of the Tiananmen Square massacre in Beijing, was forced to close, some of the owners relocated to this quiet alley north of Hollywood Rd. Named after the huge protest march held on 1 July 2003, Club 71 is again one of the best drinking spots for nonposers, with a pleasant little terrace. It's accessed via a small footpath running west off Peel St.

LOTUS Map p68   Bar
☎ 2543 6290; 37-43 Pottinger St, Soho; �---- 7pm-late Tue; ☐ 26
This cool little style bar takes the art of mixing cocktails to entertaining extremes. With a nod to molecular gastronomy, it plays with taste and texture by foaming, heating and freezing various ingredients. Silly but fun.

PEAK CAFE BAR Map p68   Bar
☎ 2140 6877; 9-13 Shelley St, Soho; �---- 11am-2am Mon-Sat, 11am-midnight Sun, happy hour 5-8pm; ☐ 13, 26, 40M

The fixtures and fittings of the much-missed Peak Cafe, from 1947, have moved down the hill to this comfy bar with super cocktails and excellent nosh. The only thing missing is the view.

V-13 Map p68   Bar
☎ 9803 6650; 13 Old Bailey St, Soho; �---- 6pm-midnight Mon-Thu, 6pm-late Fri, 6pm-late Sat, happy hour 6-9pm Mon-Sat; ☐ 26
The 'v' word here could only refer to Russian mouthwash, and there are some 80 vodkas on offer – from chocolate to chilli flavoured. The bar staff know their mixes very well.

BLISS Map p68   Gay Club
☎ 3110 1222, 2147 2122; Basement & ground fl, 1 Elgin St, Soho; �---- 5.30pm-late Mon-Sat, 2-11pm Sun, happy hour 6-9pm; ☐ 26
What was a popular post-work suit hang-out called Liquid then a sophisticated lounge-dance bar called NU has metamorphosed into Hong Kong's newest low-key gay club, with two bars and ultra-sophisticated lounge. You can't miss the joint; it's next to eye-popping Rock Candy.

RICE BAR Map p70   Gay Bar
☎ 2851 4800; www.rice-bar.com; 33 Jervois St, Sheung Wan; �---- 7pm-1am Sun-Thu, 7pm-2am Fri, 8pm-3am Sat, happy hour 7-9pm Sun-Fri, 8-9pm Sat; MTR Sheung Wan (exit A2)
Rice is a popular gay bar with a lounge area that sees a bit of dancing as it gets later. It can get very crowded on the weekend.

FEATHER BOA Map p68   Lounge
☎ 2857 2586; 38 Staunton St, Soho; �---- 5pm-late Tue; ☐ 26
Feather Boa is a plush lounge hidden behind gold drapes. Part camp lounge, part bordello – part those curtains and order a mango daiquiri ($75). It was once an antiques shop – thus the odd furnishings.

STAUNTON'S WINE BAR & CAFE
Map p68   Wine Bar
☎ 2973 6611; 10-12 Staunton St, Soho; �---- 10am-2am Mon-Fri, 8am-2am Sat & Sun, happy hour 5-9pm; ☐ 26
Staunton's, on the corner with Shelley St, is swish, cool and on the ball with decent wine, a Central Escalator–cruising scene and a lovely terrace. If you're hungry,

there's light fare downstairs and a fabulously remodelled international restaurant above.

Wan Chai

Most of the best bars and pubs line the western ends of Jaffe and Lockhart Rds. As in Lan Kwai Fong, on weekend nights this area is crawling with partygoers.

BAR 109 Map p65   Bar
☎ 2861 3336; 109 Lockhart Rd; ☼ noon-3am, happy hour 3-9pm; MTR Wan Chai

Tired of rubbing, er, shoulders with working girls in the Wanch? Well, even if not, the 109 will give you 110 reasons to flock here. It's a serious chill-out zone cobbled from a 1920s-vintage bakery and divided into three sections, including a bar, a covered 'outside' area and a 1st-floor balcony.

BRIDGE Map p65   Bar
☎ 2865 5586; Shop A-B, 1st fl, Beverly House, 93-107 Lockhart Rd, Wan Chai; ☼ 24hr, happy hour noon-10pm; MTR Wan Chai (exit c)

This large and airy bar, with great windows overlooking the frenzy of Lockhart Rd, is open 24 hours, serving cocktails to the denizens and the doomed of Wan Chai. Less frenetic than most of its neighbours.

CHAMPAGNE BAR Map p65   Bar
☎ 2588 1234 ext 7321; Ground fl, Grand Hyatt Hotel, 1 Harbour Rd, MTR Wan Chai; ☼ 5pm-2am; MTR Wan Chai (exit A1)

Take your fizz in the sumptuous surrounds of the Grand Hyatt's Champagne Room, kitted out in Art Deco furnishings to evoke the Paris of the 1920s. Live blues or jazz happens most evenings and the circular main bar is always busy.

CHINATOWN Map p65   Bar
☎ 2861 3588; 78-82 Jaffe Rd, Wan Chai; ☼ noon-2.30am, happy hour noon-6pm; MTR Wan Chai (exit C)

The kitschy Chinese Brothel theming may sound a tad over the top, but fear not, this is nothing like one of the nearby go-go bars. The soft lighting and large red lanterns actually combine to make this one of the more relaxed Wan Chai watering holes. It's busy but seldom frantic, and the service from cheongsam-wearing waitresses is swift and friendly.

DELANEY'S Map p65   Bar, Pub
☎ 2804 2880; Ground & 1st fl, One Capital Place, 18 Luard Rd, Wan Chai; ☼ noon-2.30am Sun-Thu, noon-3am Fri & Sat, happy hour noon-9pm; MTR Wan Chai (exit C)

At this immensely popular Irish watering hole you can choose between the black-and-white-tiled pub on the ground floor and a sports bar and restaurant on the 1st floor. The food is good and plentiful; the kitchen allegedly goes through 400kg of potatoes a week. There's also a branch on Peking Rd in Tsim Sha Tsui (p211).

MAYA Map p65   Bar
☎ 2866 6200; 68-70 Lockhart Rd, Wan Chai; ☼ 11am-2am Sun-Thu, 11am-3am Fri & Sat, happy hour noon-9pm; MTR Wan Chai (exit C)

This lovely new bar, whose name apparently means 'illusion' in Sanskrit, is a design-minded oasis in Wan Chai. We love the bold black-and-white patterns on the wall, the bright red bar and the (almost) never-ending happy/relaxing/two-for-one hour(s).

MES AMIS Map p65   Bar
☎ 2527 6680; 81-85 Lockhart Rd, Wan Chai; ☼ noon-2am Sun-Thu, noon-6am Fri & Sat, happy hour 4-9pm; MTR Wan Chai (exit C)

This easy-going bar is in the lap of girly club land. It has a good range of wines and a Mediterranean-style snacks list. There's a DJ from 11pm on Friday and Saturday. There's also a Tsim Sha Tsui branch (Map p94); ☎ 2730 3038; 15 Ashley Rd; ☼ noon-2am Sun-Thu, noon-3am Fri & Sat, happy hour 4-9pm).

OLD CHINA HAND Map p65   Bar
☎ 2865 4378; 104 Lockhart Rd, Wan Chai; ☼ 8am-5am, happy hour noon-10pm; MTR Wan Chai (exit C)

This place is hardly recognisable as the gloomy old dive where the desperate-to-drink (no one we know) used to find themselves unhappy but never alone at 3am. Now it's got a generous happy hour, internet access and cheap set lunches.

SKITZ Map p65   Bar
☎ 2866 3277; www.skitzbar.com; 5th fl, Phoenix Bldg, 21-25 Luard Rd, Wan Chai; MTR Wan Chai (exit C)

Hong Kong's most convenient sports bar screens big sporting events on its massive plasmas. There are also pool tables and dart boards, and (depending on the night) a DJ on the decks.

KANGAROO DOWNUNDER
Map p65   Lounge Bar

☎ 2139 31111; Lower ground fl, The Broadway, 54-62 Lockhart Rd, Wan Chai; ⏱ 11am-2am, happy hour 4-9pm; MTR Wan Chai (exit C)

This well-scrubbed successor to the infamous Kangaroo Pub in Tsim Sha Tsui is more of a lounge bar-cum-restaurant than the erstwhile pub, but it's popular with young Australians and other expats nonetheless.

DEVIL'S ADVOCATE Map p65   Pub

☎ 2865 7271; 48-50 Lockhart Rd, Wan Chai; ⏱ noon-late Mon-Sat, 1pm-late Sun, happy hour noon-10pm; MTR Wan Chai (exit C)

This pleasant pub in the thick of things is as relaxed as they come. The bar spills onto the pavement and the staff is charming. 'Devilling Hour' (5pm to 7pm) is even cheaper than happy hour, and there are cheap drinks on Wednesday night.

WHITE STAG Map p65   Pub

☎ 2866 4244; Ground fl, The Broadway, 54-62 Lockhart Rd, Wan Chai; ⏱ noon-late, happy hour noon-10pm; MTR Wan Chai (exit C)

This is a somewhat subdued (suity, not snooty) pub with open frontage, and such filling dishes as sausage and beans ($65), cottage pie ($75), fish and chips ($85), and chilli ($75).

Causeway Bay

BRECHT'S CIRCLE Map p74   Bar

☎ 2576 4785; www.brechts.net; Ground fl, Rita House, 123 Leighton Rd; ⏱ 4pm-2am Mon-Thu, 4pm-4am Fri & Sat, happy hour 4-8pm Mon-Sat; MTR Causeway Bay (exit f)

A small and fairly unusual clublike bar with an arty edge, Brecht's is given more to intimate, cerebral conversation than serious raging. Thankfully the décor has been upgraded to this century.

DICKENS BAR Map p74   Bar

☎ 2837 6782; Basement, Excelsior Hong Kong, 281 Gloucester Rd; ⏱ 11am-1am Sun-Thu, 11am-2am Fri & Sat, happy hour 5-8pm; MTR Causeway Bay (exit D1)

This evergreen place has been popular with expats and Hong Kong Chinese for dec-

ades. In truth the atmosphere is nothing special and the real draw is the big-screen sports coverage.

EAST END BREWERY & INN SIDE OUT
Map p74   Pub

☎ 2895 2900; Ground fl, Sunning Plaza, 10 Hysan Ave; ⏱ 11.30am-1am Sun-Thu, 11.30am-1.30am Fri & Sat, happy hour 2.30-8.30pm; MTR Causeway Bay (exit F)

These two related pubs flank a central covered terrace where you can while away the hours on a warm evening, sipping beers and throwing peanut shells on the ground. East End has imported microbrews, and also has a Quarry Bay branch (below).

Island East & Island South

CAFÉ EINSTEIN Map pp54–5   Bar, Lounge

☎ 2960 0994; 33 Tong Chong St, Quarry Bay; 11am-1am Mon-Sat, happy hour 4-9pm Mon-Sat; Quarry Bay (exit B)

This attractive and upbeat bar-bistro, which feels more Lan Kwai Fong than Tong Chong St, has a great bar and lounge with piped jazz and R&B, and serves decent food all day from a short but inspired menu.

EAST END BREWERY Map pp54–5   Bar

☎ 2811 1907; 23-27 Tong Chong St, Quarry Bay; ⏱ 11.30am-2am, happy hour 4-8pm; Quarry Bay (exit)

This place out in Quarry Bay is a beer lover's must-visit. You can choose from more than 30 beers and lagers from around the world, including a couple of local microbrews. There's wi-fi access, too. The Causeway Bay branch (above) serves up much the same beer and fodder if you can't make it this far out.

SMUGGLERS INN Map p85   Pub

☎ 2813 8852; Ground fl, 90A Stanley Main St, Stanley; ⏱ 10am-2am, happy hour 6-9pm; 🚌 6, 6A, 6X or 260

This scruffy but good-natured place is arguably the most popular pub on the Stanley waterfront, offering perhaps the closest thing to a traditional English pub in Hong Kong. Smugglers Inn gets a good mix of people and serves a decent pint of Guinness. Pub food is also available, including steak sandwiches ($55), burritos ($75) and, to accompany your beer, finger food ($40).

KOWLOON
Tsim Sha Tsui

AQUA SPIRIT Map p92   Bar
☎ 3427 2288; 30th fl, 1 Peking Rd; ☺ 6pm-1am
Sun-Thu, 4.30pm-3am Fri & Sat; MTR Tsim Sha Tsui
(exit E)
This magnificent restaurant-bar on top of
one of Kowloon's new skyscrapers is everyone's favourite place for a brew with a view,
which is spectacular enough to take your
mind off the equally stratospheric bar bill.

BAR Map p92   Bar
☎ 2315 3163; 1st fl, Peninsula Hong Kong, Salisbury Rd; ☺ 4pm-midnight; Star Ferry, MTR Tsim
Sha Tsui (exit E)
For mellow 1940s and '50s jazz, don your
smoking jacket and sip Cognac at the
Peninsula's stylish main watering hole.
Your fellow tipplers will be serious business
blokes, coutured couples and new-money
names trying to sound old(er). The music
starts around 9.30pm.

FELIX Map p92   Bar
☎ 2315 3188; 28th fl, Peninsula Hong Kong,
Salisbury Rd; ☺ 6pm-2am; MTR Tsim Sha Tsui
(exit E)
Enjoy the fabulous view at this Philippe
Starck–designed bar connected to Felix restaurant (p191), one of the swankiest eateries
in Hong Kong's poshest hotel. Guys, the
view from the urinals in the gents' is just
one reason to fill your bladders.

TONY'S BAR Map p92   Gay Bar
☎ 2723 2726; www.tonys-bar.com; Ground fl, 7-9
Bristol Ave; ☺ 5.30pm-4am, happy hour 5.30-
10pm; Tsim Sha Tsui (exit D2)
This low-key, anonymous and rather scruffy
gay-friendly bar just behind Mirador Mansion (see boxed text, p261) is a relaxed place
to come for a drink, with none of that 'last
chance for romance' tension found in some
other gay venues.

SKY LOUNGE Map p92   Lounge
☎ 2369 1111; 18th fl, Sheraton Hong Kong Hotel
& Towers, 20 Nathan Rd; ☺ 4pm-1am Mon-Thu,
4pm-2am Fri, 2pm-2am Sat, 2pm-1am Sun; MTR
Tsim Sha Tsui (exit E)
Before you can pooh-pooh the departure-
lounge feel of this big, long lounge, you've
already started marvelling at the view.

Don't take flight: sit down in a scoop chair,
sip something shaken or stirred and scoff
international snacks.

DELANEY'S Map p92   Pub
☎ 2301 3980; Basement, Mary Bldg, 71-77 Peking
Rd; ☺ 9am-3am, happy hour 5-9pm; MTR Tsim
Sha Tsui (exit E)
This pub seems more authentically Irish
than its Wan Chai counterpart (p209), with
lots of dark wood, green felt and a long bar
that you can really settle into.

NEW WALLY MATT LOUNGE
Map p92   Pub
☎ 2721 2568; www.wallymatt.com; 5A Humphreys
Ave; ☺ 5pm-4am, happy hour 5-10pm; MTR Tsim
Sha Tsui (exit A2)
The name comes from the old Waltzing
Matilda pub, which was one of the daggi-
est gay watering holes in creation. But New
Wally Matt is an upbeat and busy place and
actually more a pub than a lounge.

Tsim Sha Tsui East & Hung Hom

BALALAIKA Map p94   Bar
☎ 2312 6222; 2nd fl, 10 Knutsford Tce, Tsim Sha
Tsui; ☺ 5pm-midnight Sun-Thu, 5pm-1am Fri &
Sat; MTR Tsim Sha Tsui
Russian theming – from the dacha-style
walls to the music, the food and, of course,
the vodka – set a fun tone here. Don a fur
hat and coat and step into the tiny ice bar
if you really want to take the experience to
the extreme.

BIERGARTEN Map p94   Bar
☎ 2721 2302; 5 Hanoi Rd; ☺ 10am-3am Mon-Fri,
noon-2am, happy hour 4-9pm; MTR Tsim Sha Tsui
(exit G)
This clean, modern place rubbing shoulders
with the expanding Minden Rd car and
club hotspot has a jukebox full of hits (and
misses) and Bitburger on tap. It's popular
with visiting Germans and others who
hanker after such hearty and filling nosh as
pork knuckle and sauerkraut.

CHILLAX Map p94   Bar
☎ 2722 4338; 8 Minden Ave; ☺ 6pm-3am Mon-
Sat; MTR Tsim Sha Tsui (exit G)
This tiny space lit by candles and mainly
patronised by young locals, is good for
simply sitting, slumping and taking refuge
from a day spent dodging through Tsim

Sha Tsui. Things get livelier later when the DJ gets going.

COURTNEY'S Map p94   Bar
☎ 2739 7777; 5th fl, The Minden, 7 Minden Ave; ☀ 5pm-2am; MTR Tsim Sha Tsui (exit G)
This hotel snack room-bar, decorated with original and attractive artwork by local painter Pauline Courtney, has a fabulous outdoor terrace, allowing you to watch the goings-on in lively Minden Ave below. Don't expect crowds, though; this is a great place for a quiet drink and some elbow room.

LA TASCA Map p94   Bar, Live Music
☎ 2723 1072; 8 Hanoi Rd; ☀ 11am-4am Mon-Fri, 5pm-4am Sat & Sun; happy hour 4-8pm; MTR Tsim Sha Tsui (exit D2)
La Tasca is more a cantina and bar than a restaurant nowadays and has live music starting from 10pm on Saturdays. But it still does a set lunch ($38 to $42) and food at night, including tasty tapas ($40 to $60) and more substantial main courses ($85 to $95).

NEW TERRITORIES
Sai Kung Town
XTREME BAR & RESTAURANT
Map p127   Bar
☎ 2791 7222; 72 Po Tung Rd; ☀ 4pm-late Mon-Fri, 11am-3am Sat & Sun, happy hour 4-9pm Mon-Fri, 11am-9pm Sat, 11am-7pm Sun; 🚌 92, 299
This uberstyled brasserie-like place has raised the bar by a few hundred metres for upmarket drinking venues in Sai Kung town. Food (starters from $48, mains from $78) is available until just before closing.

POETS Map p127   Pub
☎ 2791 7993; 55 Yi Chun St; ☀ 5pm-1am Mon-Fri, 3-4pm-2am Sat & Sun, happy hour noon-9pm Mon-Fri; 🚌 92, 299
This friendly workaday pub with literary aspirations is a pleasant place for a pint and serves typical pub meals, such as pies, chips and beans for $58.

THE DUKE Map p127   Pub
☎ 2791 6255; Ground fl, 42-56 Fuk Man Rd; ☀ 12pm-2am, happy hour 12-9pm Mon-Fri, 12-7pm Sat & Sun; 🚌 92, 299
This popular pub, just up from the waterfront, has darts, free pool and sports on the TV. Cocktails range from $35 to $60 and

there's snack food, such as curried fish balls ($25) and marinated chicken kidney ($30).

OUTLYING ISLANDS
Lamma
Yung Shue Wan has several cosy waterfront boozers worth checking out, which serve a very much local crowd in the evenings (mostly expats). In theory you may have to sign a members' book, as some operate on club licences.

DIESEL'S BAR Map p132   Bar
☎ 2982 4116; 51 Main St, Yung Shue Wan; ☀ 6pm-late Mon-Fri, noon-late Sat & Sun, happy hour 6-9pm Mon-Fri; 🚢 Lamma (Yung Shue Wan)
This place next to the Lamma Bistro attracts punters with big-screen TV during sports matches.

FOUNTAINHEAD DRINKING BAR
Map p132   Bar
☎ 2982 2118; 17 Main St, Yung Shue Wan; ☀ 5pm-2am Mon-Fri, 3pm-4am Sat & Sun, happy hour all day Mon-Fri; 🚢 Lamma (Yung Shue Wan)
The cheerfully no-frills Fountainhead has a good mix of Chinese and expats in regular attendance, decent music and beer at affordable prices.

ISLAND SOCIETY BAR Map p132   Bar
☎ 2982 1376; 6 Main St, Yung Shue Wan; ☀ 6pm-late Mon-Fri, noon-late Sat & Sun, happy hour 4-8pm; 🚢 Lamma (Yung Shue Wan)
The Island remains the bar of choice for long-term expats living on Lamma, so if you want the lowdown on what's up, head here.

Cheung Chau
MOROCCO'S BAR & RESTAURANT
Map p143   Bar
☎ 2986 9767; 71 Praya St; ☀ 12pm-3am, happy hour 4-9pm Mon-Fri; 🚢 Cheung Chau
The exodus of expats from Cheung Chau over the past years has left the island all but bereft of quality drinking venues, but there will always be Morocco's on the waterfront. It also does decent Indian food (curries $45 to $50, tandoori dishes $50 to $80).

PATIO CAFÉ Map p143   Pub
☎ 2981 8316, 2981 2772; Cheung Chau Windsurfing Water Sports Centre, 1 Hak Pai Rd; ☀ noon-7pm daily Apr-Nov, noon-7pm Sat & Sun Dec-Mar; 🚢 Cheung Chau

This open-air, café-cum-pub attached to the windsurfing centre at Tung Wan Beach, known locally as Lai Kam's in honour of its owner, is a Cheung Chau institution. Come here for a sundowner.

Lantau

CHINA BEACH CLUB Map p139　　Bar
☎ 2983 8931; 18 Tung Wan Tau Rd; ⏱ noon-10pm Thu & Fri, 11.30am-10pm Sat & Sun, happy hour all day Thu-Sun; 🚶 Lantau
This pleasant bar-restaurant has a 185-sq-metre rooftop and an open-air balcony overlooking Silvermine Bay Beach. The staff is friendly and helpful, and the food is good. There are salads and sides ($35 to $65), a large barbecue section ($110 to $150), other mains including moussaka and Thai curry ($79 to $95) and puddings ($45 to $55) too. Reservations are recommended, particularly on Sundays. The two for one cocktail 'hour' can go on well into the night.

JK'S CLUB Map p136　　Bar
☎ 2984 0220; Ground fl, 20 Lo Wai Tsuen, Pui O; ⏱ 6pm-late Tue-Sat, 4pm-late Sun; 🚌 1, 2, 3M, 4 or A35
This place is conveniently located just off the main road in Pui O. The beach is right across the street.

CHINA BEAR Map p139　　Pub
☎ 2984 9720; Ground fl, Mui Wo Centre, Ngan Wan Rd; ⏱ 10am-2am, happy hour 5-9pm Mon-Fri, 5-8pm Sat & Sun; 🚶 Lantau
The China Bear is the most popular expat pub-restaurant in Mui Wo, with a wonderful open bar facing the water. It's right by the ferry terminal, making it the perfect spot for your first and last beer in Mui Wo, and for those in between perhaps. The menu includes offerings such as salads and pizzas for around $60.

Peng Chau

FOREST BAR & RESTAURANT
Map p147　　Bar
☎ 2983 8837; 38C Wing Hing St; ⏱ 11am-late Tue-Sun; 🚶 Peng Chau
This cosy bar has five beers on tap and a large outside terrace seating area. The kitchen whips up authentic pan-Asian (mostly Thai) food (snacks from $35, mains from $62) six days a week.

NIGHTLIFE

Energetic Hong Kong has long enjoyed a big night out, and in these boom times the clubs are doing a roaring trade. There's a good spread of clubs in Hong Kong, including in Wan Chai and Causeway Bay, although Central and Soho dominate for the sheer number of venues.

The defining feature of Hong Kong's dance music scene has evolved from the impromptu, large-scale and often semi-legal dance parties held in warehouses and other remote locations a few years ago to a focus on a night spent flitting between a number of intimate little venues.

Most of the club nights take place on Friday and Saturday, but there are some good midweek venues as well. Cover charges range from $100 to as high as $350 when a big-name foreign DJ is mixing or an internationally recognised band is on stage. On some nights, you may get in free (or for a cheaper cover) if you are among the first 50 or so through the door, dressed in '70s gear (or whatever) on theme nights, or a woman.

Karaoke clubs are also becoming ever more popular with the city's young citizens, with a sprinkling of clubs in Central and a clutch of smart places springing up on and around Minden Ave in Tsim Sha Tsui.

As in any world-class city, the club scene in Hong Kong changes with the speed of summer lightning, so it would be in your interest to flip through *HK Magazine* or *bc magazine*. On the web, check out www.hkclubbing.com or www.hkentert ainment.com.

Cantopop is the name for the local pop music (p34). If you give it a chance, you'll discover some worthwhile tunes (or ones that you won't be able to get out of your head for your entire stay here).

There are usually a few decent rock bands (both local and imported) playing around town, and numerous bars that play house bands that play dance music. Hotel bars and clubs have Filipino bands that can play 'Hotel California' and 'Love Is a Many-Splendoured Thing' in their sleep (and yours).

Judging from the closure of a couple of key venues in recent years, jazz seems to be losing a lot of its traditional following in Hong Kong; there's only a couple of venues in Central and Tsim Sha Tsui. World music is generally a staged event, with big international acts booked at the Hong Kong Arts Centre or Hong Kong City Hall.

HONG KONG ISLAND
Lan Kwai Fong & Soho

CLUB 97 Map p68   Bar, Club

☎ 2186 1897; Ground fl, Cosmos Bldg, 9-11 Lan Kwai Fong, Central; 🕙 6pm-2am Mon-Thu, 6pm-4am Fri, 8pm-4am Sat & Sun, happy hour 3-8pm; MTR Central (exit D2)

This schmoozy lounge bar has a popular happy hour (it's a gay event on Friday night) and there's reggae on Sunday. It has a 'members only' policy to turn away the underdressed; make an effort and you're in.

JOYCE IS NOT HERE Map p68   Bar, Live Music

☎ 2851 2999; 38-44 Peel St, Soho; 🕙 11am-late Tue-Fri, 10am-late Sat & Sun, happy hour 3.53-8.04pm; 🚌 13, 26, 40M

'James or Ma?' we asked, trying to be clever. Alas, neither but this super-chilled café-bar in reds, whites and blacks has something for everyone – from poetry readings and live music on Thursday to booze and Sunday brunch. Love the place.

RED ROCK Map p68   Bar, Club

☎ 2868 3884; Lower ground fl, 57-59 Wyndham St, Central; 🕙 noon-3pm & 5pm-2am Mon-Thu, 11am-2pm & 5pm-5am Fri & Sat, happy hour 5-8pm Mon-Fri; MTR Central (exit)

This attractive place, backing onto the walkway above Lan Kwai Fong, is a very successful chameleon: a decent Italian restaurant at lunch and dinner (set lunch $87, mains $70 to $90) and a popular dance venue by night (cover $100). A dozen cocktails and as many shooters go for half-price at happy hour.

DROP Map p68   Club

☎ 2543 8856; www.drophk.com; Basement, On Lok Mansion, 39-43 Hollywood Rd, Central; 🕙 7pm-2am Mon & Tue, 7pm-3am Wed, 7pm-4am Thu, 7pm-5am Fri, 9pm-5am Sat, happy hour 7-10pm Mon-Fri; 🚌 26

Deluxe lounge action, excellent tunes and potent cocktails keep Drop strong on the scene. It's like walking into *Wallpaper* magazine, but the vibe here is unpretentiously inclusive and the crowd reaches a happy mutual fever pitch on big nights. The members-only policy after 10pm Thursday to Saturday is (flexibly) enforced to keep the dance floor capacity at a manageable 'packed like sardines' level. Enter from Cochrane St.

HOMEBASE Map p68   Club

☎ 2545 0023; 2nd fl, 23 Hollywood Rd, Central; 🕙 10pm-3am Mon-Fri, 10pm-9am Sat, happy hour 10pm-midnight Mon-Thu & Sat, 8pm-midnight Fri; 🚌 26

A meet 'n' greet for the styled and beautiful early on, this place turns into a bump 'n' grind after hours (cover $100). It's one of the more popular after-hours venues and one of the few places that is still partying well after dawn in a city that does, in fact, sleep. Great house and breakbeat music, small dance floor. Friday's generous happy hour is for gays and lesbians.

INSOMNIA Map p68   Club

☎ 2525 0957; Lower Ground fl, Ho Lee Commercial Bldg, 38-44 D'Aguilar St, Central; 🕙 9am-6am Mon-Sat, 2pm-5am Sun; happy hour 5-9pm; MTR Central (exit D2)

This is the place to come to when you can't sleep, as it fills up only when other nearby bars are starting to wind down. It's a people-watching place with a wide, open frontage, and there's a live Filipino band doing covers in the back. If the munchies strike in the witching hour, there's food, too.

YUMLA Map p68   Club

☎ 2147 2382; Lower basement, 79 Wyndham St; 🕙 8am-1pm Mon-Thu, 8am-3am Fri & Sat, 8am-9pm Sun, happy hour 4-8pm; 🚌 26

Tucked behind Soda, Yumla is worth seeking out not for its scruffy looks but rather for the relaxed vibe and DJs that spin an eclectic but cutting-edge mix of excellent dance, hip-hop and guitar stuff.

PROPAGANDA Map p68   Gay Club

☎ 2868 1316; Lower ground fl, 1 Hollywood Rd, Central; 🕙 9pm-4am Tue-Thu, 9pm-6am Fri & Sat, happy hour 9pm-1.30am Tue-Thu; MTR Central (exit D2)

Propaganda is still the premier gay dance club and meat market; everyone gay ends up here at some point on a weekend night. It's free from Tuesday to Thursday, but cover charges ($120 to $160) apply on Friday and Saturday (which gets you into Works, below, on Friday). Enter from Ezra's Lane, which runs between Pottinger and Cochrane Sts.

WORKS Map p68   Gay Club

☎ 2868 6102; 1st fl, 30-32 Wyndham St, Central; 🕙 7pm-2am, happy hour 7-10.30pm Mon-Fri; MTR Central (exit D2)

Propaganda's (opposite) sister club, Works is where most gay boyz out on the town start the evening, and sees some heavy FFFR (file-for-future-reference) cruising till it's time to move on to the P. There's a cover charge ($60 to $100) on the weekend.

BOHEMIAN LOUNGE Map p68   Live Music
☎ 2526 6099; 3-5 Old Bailey St, Soho ⏰ 4.30pm-12.30am Mon-Wed, 4pm-2am or 3am Thu-Sun, happy hour 5-9pm; 🚌 26
This long, narrow watering hole is a great place for a libation anytime, but try to make it on Thursday after 9pm or Friday or Saturday after 10pm when live jazz kicks in.

CAVERN Map p68   Live Music
☎ 2121 8969; Shop 1, Lower ground fl, Lan Kwai Fong Tower, 33 Wyndham St, Central; ⏰ 6pm-late Mon-Sat; MTR Central (exit D2)
Hong Kong's first (and only) supper club, the Cavern is effectively a showcase for two tribute bands: Sixties Mania Showband, done up in mop-top haircuts and bell-bottoms, and the Rolling Bones, a great Filipino band. Music starts at 9pm Monday to Saturday. There's food and the cover charge is $100. Enter from D'Aguilar St.

FRINGE GALLERY Map p68   Live Music
☎ 2521 7251; www.hkfringe.com.hk; Ground fl, Fringe Club, 2 Lower Albert Rd, Central; ⏰ noon-midnight Mon-Thu, noon-3am Fri & Sat, happy hour 3-9pm Mon-Thu, 3-8pm Fri & Sat; MTR Central (exit D1)
The Fringe, a friendly and eclectic venue on the border of the Lan Kwai Fong quadrant, has original music in its gallery-bar from 10.30pm on Friday and Saturday, with jazz, rock and world music getting the most airplay. There's a pleasant rooftop bar open in the warmer months.

Admiralty & Wan Chai

1/5 Map p63   Club
☎ 2520 2515; 1st fl, Starcrest Bldg, 9 Star St, Wan Chai; ⏰ 5pm-3am Mon-Thu, 5pm-4am Fri & Sat, 6pm-2am Sun, happy hour 6-9pm Mon-Fri; MTR Admiralty (exit)
Pronounced 'one-fifth', this sophisticated lounge bar and club has a broad bar backed by a two-storey drinks selection from which bar staff concoct some of Hong Kong's best cocktails. It gets packed on the

weekend with a dressy professional crowd but it's still a good place to chill.

JOE BANANAS Map p65   Club
☎ 2529 1811; Ground fl, Shiu Lam Bldg, 23 Luard Rd, Wan Chai; ⏰ noon-5am Mon-Thu, noon-6am Fri & Sat, 4pm-5am Sun, happy hour 11am-10pm; MTR Wan Chai (exit C)
JB's, in Wan Chai forever it seems, has dropped its long-standing wet T-shirt/boxers aesthetic and gone for more of a bamboo-bar feel. Unaccompanied females should expect a good sampler of bad pick-up lines; go with friends and have some un-PC fun. There are free drinks for women from 6pm to 3am on Wednesday and 'Crazy Hour' (6pm to 8pm daily) is even more generous than happy hour.

NEPTUNE DISCO II Map p65   Club
☎ 2865 2238; Basement, 98-108 Jaffe Rd, Wan Chai; ⏰ 4pm-6am Mon-Fri, 2pm-6am Sat & Sun, happy hour 4-9pm Mon-Fri, 2-9pm Sat; MTR Wan Chai (exit)
Neptune II is a fun club with a mostly Filipino crowd and a rockin' Pinoy covers band. If everything's closing and you can't bear to stop dancing, this is the place to come. It really rocks at the Sunday afternoon tea dance (men/women $100/50, including one drink), starting at 2pm.

NEW MAKATI PUB & DISCO Map p65   Club
☎ 2866 3928; 1st fl, 94-100 Lockhart Rd; ⏰ 4pm-5am, happy hour 4-9pm; MTR Wan Chai (exit C)
It has to be said: you can't go lower than this sleazy pick-up joint, named after a Manila neighbourhood. Imagine dimly lit booths, Filipino *amahs* and middle-aged white male booze hounds, who all just wanna have fun. It is a friendly place to dance the morning away, though.

TRIBECA Map p65   Club
☎ 2836 3690; 4th fl, Renaissance Harbour View Hotel, 1 Harbour Rd, Wan Chai; men $120; ⏰ 6pm-4am Mon-Fri, 10pm-late Sat, happy hour 6pm-midnight Mon-Wed & Fri, 6-9pm Thu; 🚌 18 MTR Wan Chai (exit A1)
No, not NYC but glitzy Hong Kong… It's an uberdecked-out club with chatting lounges, a long bar and popular theme nights (eg salsa on Sunday). It's popular with a suave Cantonese crowd, so dress to impress. There's free entry and drinks for women on Thursday night.

CARNEGIE'S Map p65 — Live Music
☎ 2866 6289; Ground fl, 53-55 Lockhart Rd, Wan Chai; ☾ 11am-late Mon-Sat, 5pm-late Sun, happy hour 11am-9pm Mon-Sat; MTR Wan Chai (exit C)
The rock memorabilia festooning the walls makes it all seem a bit Hard Rock Café-ish but it's worth a look all the same. From 9pm on Friday and Saturday, the place fills up with revellers, many of whom will end up dancing on the bar. All good clean fun.

DUSK TILL DAWN Map p65 — Live Music
☎ 2528 4689; Ground fl, 76-84 Jaffe Rd, Wan Chai; ☾ noon-5am Mon-Fri, 3pm-7am Sat & Sun, happy hour 5-9pm; MTR Wan Chai (exit C)
Live music from 10.30pm, with an emphasis on beats and vibes that will get your booty shaking. The dance floor can be packed but the atmosphere is more friendly than sleazy. The food sticks to easy fillers, such as meat pies and burgers.

WANCH Map p65 — Live Music
☎ 2861 1621; 54 Jaffe Rd, Wan Chai; ☾ noon-2am Sun-Thu, noon-4am Fri & Sat, happy hour noon-10pm Mon-Thu, noon-8pm Fri-Sun; MTR Wan Chai (exit C)
This place, which derives its name from what everyone calls the district, has live music (mostly rock and folk with the occasional solo guitarist thrown in) seven nights a week from 9pm. Jam night is Monday from 8pm. If you're not here for the music, it can be a dubious scene – the Wanch is basically a pick-up joint.

Causeway Bay

WASABISABI Map p74 — Club
☎ 2506 0009; 13th fl, Times Square, 1 Matheson St; ☾ 6pm-midnight Sun-Thu, 6pm-3am Fri & Sat, happy hour 6-8pm; MTR Causeway Bay (exit A)
This Japanese restaurant in the Times Square shopping mall, with out-of-this-world décor (cable vines, rondo lounges, faux birch forest), transforms each night into the camp Lipstick Lounge.

CAUSEWAY LOUNGE Map p74 — Live Music
☎ 2890 6665; Basement, Causeway Cnr, 18 Percival St, Causeway Bay; ☾ 5pm-2am Mon-Thu, 5.30pm-2.30am Fri-Sun, happy hour 5-9pm; MTR Causeway Bay (exit B)
This slick lounge has live folk music from 6pm to 9pm on weekdays and a resident quartet plays pop favourites from 9pm to 1am Monday to Saturday.

KOWLOON
Tsim Sha Tsui East & Hung Hom

BAHAMA MAMA'S Map p94 — Club
☎ 9803 6650, 2368 2121; 4-5 Knutsford Tce, Tsim Sha Tsui; ☾ 5pm-3am Sun-Thu, 5pm-4am Fri & Sat, happy hour 5-9pm; MTR Tsim Sha Tsui (exit)
Bahama Mama's goes for a 'Caribbean island' feel, complete with palm trees and surfboards. It's a friendly spot and stands apart from most of the other late-night watering holes in this part of town. It's also the place to come for a foosball (table soccer) showdown. On Friday and Saturday nights there's a DJ spinning and a young crowd out on the bonsai-sized dance floor.

CLOUDNINE Map p94 — Club
☎ 2723 6383; 7 Minden Ave; ☾ 6pm-3am Mon-Sat; MTR Tsim Sha Tsui (exit G)
If you want to find out what the local kids do of an evening (or at least those with some cash to burn), step through the egg-shaped doorway of this stylish little bar-cum-karaoke joint, take a seat and listen to the Cantopop classics get murdered.

HARI'S Map p92 — Live Music
☎ 2369 3111 ext 1345; Mezzanine, Holiday Inn Golden Mile, 50 Nathan Rd, Tsim Sha Tsui; ☾ 5pm-2am, happy hour 5-9pm Mon-Sat, 5pm-2am Sun; MTR Tsim Sha Tsui (exit G2)
Is it tacky or classy (or neither)? You decide after you've had a couple of speciality martinis (there are over a dozen to challenge you). There's live music from 6.15pm weekdays, 8.45pm Saturday and 7.30pm Sunday.

THE ARTS

In Hong Kong there are classical music concerts performed every week by one of the local orchestras or a foreign ensemble.

Hong Kong is stuffed with cinemas and boasts well over 150 screens. Most show local films (with English subtitles) or Hollywood blockbusters dubbed into Cantonese, but a few – Cine-Art House in Wan Chai, the Broadway Cinematheque in Yau Ma Tei and the UA Pacific Place in Admiralty – screen more interesting current releases and art-house films.

Cinemas usually screen five sessions (very roughly at 12.30pm, 2.30pm, 5.30pm, 7.30pm and 9.30pm) weekdays, with extra screenings at 4pm and 11.30pm on Saturday, Sunday and public holidays. You must select a seat when you buy a ticket, which costs between $50 and $80, depending on the location and whether you can claim a concession. Tickets are usually cheaper (eg $40 to $50) at matinees, the last screening of the day on weekends and on holidays (usually 11.30pm), or on certain days of the week, eg Tuesday at the UA Pacific Place (Map p63).

Almost all Hong Kong films screening in Hong Kong have both Chinese and English subtitles. You can confirm that the film has English subtitles by checking its Censorship Licence in the cinema.

Both the *HK Magazine* and the *South China Morning Post* have listings for film screenings.

Local theatre groups (p35) mostly perform at the Shouson Theatre of the Hong Kong Arts Centre, the Academy for Performing Arts, the Hong Kong Cultural Centre and Hong Kong City Hall (opposite). Performances are usually in Cantonese, though there are often summaries in English available. Smaller troupes occasionally present plays in English at one of the two theatres at the Fringe Club.

HONG KONG ISLAND

On Hong Kong Island some of the most important classical music venues are the Hong Kong Academy for the Performing Arts (Map p65; ☎ 2584 8500, bookings 3128 8288; www.hkapa.edu; 1 Gloucester Rd, Wan Chai; MTR Wan Chai, exit A1), Hong Kong City Hall (Map p56; ☎ 2921 2840, bookings 2734 9009; www.cityhall.gov.hk; 5 Edinburgh Place, Central; MTR Central, exit J3) and the Hong Kong Arts Centre (Map p63; ☎ 2582 0200, bookings 2734 9009; www.hkac.org.hk; 2 Harbour Rd, Wan Chai; MTR Wan Chai, exit A1).

Central

PALACE IFC CINEMA Map p56   Cinema
☎ 2388 6268; Podium L1, IFC Mall, 8 Finance St; MTR Hong Kong (exit f)
This new eight-screen cinema complex in the IFC Mall is arguably the most advanced and comfortable in the territory.

Admiralty & Wan Chai

Certain cultural organisations based in this area show foreign films from time to time, including the Alliance Française (Map p65; ☎ 2527 7825; 1st & 2nd fl, 123 Hennessy Rd, Wan Chai) and the Goethe-Institut (Map p63; ☎ 2802 0088; 13th & 14th fl, Hong Kong Arts Centre, 2 Harbour Rd, Wan Chai).

For both art-house and mainstream films, Wan Chai has two of the best and most comfortable cinemas in the territory.

AGNÈS B CINEMA Map p63   Cinema
☎ 2582 0200; Upper basement, Hong Kong Arts Centre, 2 Harbour Rd, Wan Chai; 🚌 18
This recently renamed cinema – it was the Lim Por Yen Theatre for years – is the place for classics, revivals, alternative screenings and travelling film festivals.

CINE-ART HOUSE Map p65   Cinema
☎ 2827 4820; Ground fl, Sun Hung Kai Centre, 30 Harbour Rd, Wan Chai; MTR Wan Chai (exit A5)
This alternative cinema specialises in English-language films.

MAJOR VENUES

Hong Kong has at last arrived on the big-name concert circuit, and a growing number of internationally celebrated bands and solo acts – including the likes of REM, U2, Robbie Williams, Avril Lavigne, Norah Jones, Diana Krall, Sting and k.d. lang – perform in Hong Kong regularly.

Big concerts are usually held at either the 12,500-seat Hong Kong Coliseum (Map p94; ☎ 2355 7233, 2355 7234; 9 Cheong Wan Rd, Hung Hom; 🚆 Hung Hom), located behind the KCR station, and Queen Elizabeth Stadium (Map p65; ☎ 2591 1346; www.lcsd.gov.hk/qes; 18 Oi Kwan Rd, Wan Chai; MTR Wan Chai). The sound is abysmal in the former, and you'd get better acoustics in an empty aircraft hanger than at the latter.

Two other venues are the HITEC Rotunda (Map pp88–9; ☎ 2620 2222, 2620 2838; www.hitec.com.hk; 1 Trademart Dr, Kowloon Bay; MTR Kowloon Bay) and the New Wing of the Hong Kong Convention & Exhibition Centre (HKCEC; Map p65; ☎ 2582 8888, bookings 2582 1111; www.hkcec.com; 1 Expo Dr, Wan Chai; bus 18, MTR Wan Chai). These are not huge venues, so the ticket prices are usually quite high.

Smaller acts are sometimes booked into the Ko Shan Theatre (Map pp88–9; ☎ 2740 9222; www.lcsd.gov.hk/kst; 77 Ko Shan Rd, Hung Hom; 🚆 Hung Hom). The sound at this venue isn't great either, but the back portion of the seating area is open air, and most of the seats offer a good view of the stage.

PUNCHLINE COMEDY CLUB

Map p65   Comedy

☎ 2827 7777; 2nd fl, Sun Hung Kai Centre, 30 Harbour Rd, Wan Chai; 🚌 18, alight at Wan Chai Sports Ground

The only venue with regularly scheduled comedy acts in Hong Kong at present is the Viceroy Restaurant & Bar's Punchline Comedy Club, with local and imported acts every third Thursday, Friday and Saturday from 9pm to 11pm. Entry costs $300.

Causeway Bay & Island East

Causeway Bay is packed with cinemas but, with few exceptions, most of them show Hollywood blockbusters and Hong Kong and mainland films. Further east is Hong Kong's most important film-watching venue, the Hong Kong Film Archive.

HONG KONG FILM ARCHIVE

Map pp54–5   Cinema

☎ 2739 2139, bookings 2734 9009; wwww.film archive.gov.hk; 50 Lei King Rd, MTR Sai Wan Ho

This is the place to find out what lies (or perhaps lurks) behind Hong Kong's film industry. The archive houses more than 4300 films, runs a rich calendar of screenings (local and foreign movies), and exhibits natty posters and other fine film paraphernalia.

WINDSOR CINEMA Map p74   Cinema

☎ 2577 0783; 1st fl, Windsor House, 311 Gloucester Rd, Causeway Bay; Causeway Bay (exit E)

This comfortable cineplex with four screens is just west of Victoria Park.

SUNBEAM THEATRE Map pp54–5   Theatre

☎ 2856 0161, 2563 2959; Kiu Fai Mansion, 423 King's Rd, North Point; tickets $40-320; MTR North Point (exit B)

CHINESE OPERA UNMASKED

The best time to see and hear Chinese opera – not the easiest form of entertainment to catch in Hong Kong these days – is during the Hong Kong Arts Festival (p15) in February/March, and outdoor performances are staged in Victoria Park during the Mid-Autumn Festival. At other times, you might take your chances at catching a performance at the Temple Street Night Market (p96), but the most reliable venue for opera performances year-round is the Sunbeam Theatre (above) in North Point.

Cantonese and other Chinese opera (p35) are performed here throughout the year. Performances generally run for about a week, and are usually held five days a week in the evening at 7.30pm, with occasional matinees at 1pm or 1.30pm. The theatre is directly above the North Point MTR station (exit A4), on the north side of King's Rd, near the intersection with Shu Kuk St.

Lan Kwai Fong & Soho

FRINGE STUDIO & THEATRE

Map p68   Theatre

☎ 2521 7251, bookings 3128 8288; www.hkfringe .com.hk; Ground & 1st fl, Fringe Club, 2 Lower Albert Rd; ⏰ 8pm during performances (days vary), box office noon-10pm Mon-Sat; MTR Central (exit D2)

These intimate theatres, each seating up to 100 people, host eclectic local and international performances (average ticket price is $80) in English and in Cantonese.

KOWLOON
Tsim Sha Tsui

GRAND OCEAN CINEMA Map p92   Cinema

☎ 2377 2100; www.goldenharvest.com; Marco Polo Hong Kong Hotel Shopping Arcade, Zone D, Harbour City, 3 Canton Rd, Tsim Sha Tsui; 🚢 Star Ferry

The Grand Ocean screens the usual blockbusters.

HONG KONG CULTURAL CENTRE

Map p94   Classical Music

☎ 2734 2009; www.hkculturalcentre.gov.hk; 10 Salisbury Rd, Tsim Sha Tsui; MTR Tsim Sha Tsui

Many classical music performances are held at the Hong Kong Cultural Centre (just east of the Star Ferry terminal), also home to the Hong Kong Philharmonic and the Hong Kong Chinese Orchestra. It is well worth stopping by there to pick up a monthly schedule.

Yau Ma Tei & New Kowloon

AMC FESTIVAL WALK Map pp88–9   Cinema

☎ 2265 8545; www.amccinemas.com.hk; Upper ground fl & Levels 1 & 2, Festival Walk, 80-88 Tat Chee Ave, Kowloon Tong; MTR Kowloon Tong (exit C2)

This complex with 11 screens at Hong Kong's poshest mall is the largest cinema in the territory. The films are a mix of Chinese and Western. Check ahead as the latter are sometimes dubbed, rather than subtitled in Cantonese.

BROADWAY CINEMATHEQUE
Map p97   Cinema
☎ 2388 3188; Ground fl, Prosperous Garden, 3 Public Square St, Yau Ma Tei; MTR Yau Ma Tei
This is an unlikely place for an alternative cinema, but it's worth coming up for new art-house releases and rerun screenings. The Kubrick Bookshop Café next door serves good coffee and decent pre-flick food.

NEW TERRITORIES
The New Territories also has several important cultural centres:

Kwai Tsing Theatre (Map pp50–1; ☎ 2408 0128; www.lcsd.gov .hk/ktt; 12 Hing Ning Rd, Kwai Chung; MTR Kwai Fong)

Sha Tin Town Hall (Map p124; ☎ 2694 2550; www.lcsd.gov .hk/stth; 1 Yuen Wo Rd, Sha Tin; KCR Sha Tin, East Rail)

Tuen Mun Town Hall (Map pp50–1; ☎ 2450 4202; www.lcsd .gov.hk/tmth; 3 Tuen Hi Rd, Tuen Mun; KCR Tuen Mun)

Tsuen Wan Town Hall (Map p105; ☎ 2414 0144; www.lcsd .gov.hk/twth; 72 Tai Ho Rd, Tsuen Wan; MTR Tsuen Wan)

Yuen Long Theatre (Map pp50–1; ☎ 2476 1029, bookings 2477 1462; www.lcsd.gov.hk/ylt; 9 Tai Yuk Rd, Yuen Long; KCR Yuen Long).

BLUELIST[1] (blu̱ list) *v.*
to recommend a travel experience.
What's your recommendation? www.lonelyplanet.com/bluelist

SPORTS & ACTIVITIES

top picks

- Horse Racing in Happy Valley (p230)
- Rugby Sevens (p231)
- Walking Hong Kong's trails (p224)
- Evening harbour sailing (p230)
- Waterside morning t'ai chi (p227)
- Golf on Kau Sai Chau Island (p224)
- Stretching and breathing deep at Yoga Plus (p222)

SPORTS & ACTIVITIES

Yes it can be an urban jungle, but Hong Kong is surprisingly well served by public sports facilities and other activities. Getting the heart rate going can be as simple as slipping into some swimming togs, grabbing the handlebars of a rental bike or unrolling a yoga mat.

Hong Kong's green open spaces often surprise first-time visitors with their size and relative isolation. Beyond the concrete canyons there's enough wilderness and coast to keep even the keenest hikers, bird-watchers and sailors going for a life time.

If watching rather than doing is your thing, there's a busy spectator sports calendar, too, and often plenty of atmosphere to be found (especially where there's the possibility of a having a flutter on the result).

HEALTH & FITNESS

Hong Kong is bursting at the seams with gyms, yoga studios, spas and New Age clinics offering everything from aromatherapy and foot care to homeopathy. And if your hotel doesn't have a swimming pool, there are three-dozen public ones to choose from.

GYMS & FITNESS CLUBS

Getting fit is big business in Hong Kong, with the largest slices of the pie shared out among a few big names. The South China Athletic Association (Map p74; ☎ 2890 7736; 88 Caroline Hill Rd, So Kon Po; 🚇 Happy Valley) has a massive (1000 sq metre) gym, with modern exercise machinery and an aerobics room, as well as a sauna, a steam room and massage (monthly membership $250, or $50 per visit). The following two are notable in that they offer short-term memberships.

CALIFORNIA FITNESS Map p68
☎ 2522 5229; www.californiafitness.com; 1 Wellington St, Central; daily $150; 🕑 6am-midnight Mon-Sat, 8am-10pm Sun; MTR Central exit D2
Asia's largest health club has six outlets in Hong Kong, including a Wan Chai branch (Map p65; ☎ 2877 7070; 88 Gloucester Rd; MTR Wan Chai, exit A1), which keeps the same hours.

PURE FITNESS Map p68
☎ 2970 3366; www.pure-fit.com; 1st-3rd fl, Kinwick Centre, 32 Hollywood Rd, Soho; daily $200; 🕑 6am-midnight Mon-Sat, 8am-10pm Sun; Central Escalator
This favourite of the Soho set (entered from Shelley St) has a Central branch (Map p56; ☎ 8129 8000; 3rd fl, Two IFC Mall, 8 Finance St, Central; MTR Hong Kong Station), which is open the same hours.

SWIMMING POOLS

Hong Kong has 36 swimming pools that are open to the public. There are excellent pools in Tsim Sha Tsui's Kowloon Park (p91) and in Victoria Park (p75) in Causeway Bay. Many pools are closed between November and March, but heated indoor and outdoor pools, such as the Morrison Hill Public Swimming Pool (Map p65; ☎ 2575 3028; 7 Oi Kwan Rd, Wan Chai; adult/child $19/9) and the one in the basement of the South China Athletic Association (Map p74; ☎ 2890 7736; 88 Caroline Hill Rd, So Kon Po; adult/child $22/10; 🚇 Happy Valley), are open all year.

THERAPY CLINICS

Feel like giving your tootsies a pamper? Or how about your nostrils an olfactory feast? You can at one of Hong Kong's therapy clinics.

DK Aromatherapy (Map p68; ☎ 2771 2847; www.aroma.com.hk; Ground fl, 16A Staunton St, Central, Central Escalator; 🕑 11am-10pm) Full body aromatherapy treatment $500 to $550.

Happy Foot Reflexology Centre (Map p68; ☎ 2544 1010; 11th & 13th fl, Jade Centre, 98-102 Wellington St, Central; 🕑 10am-midnight; MTR Central, exit D2) Foot/body massage starts at $198/250 for 50 minutes.

Healing Plants (Map p68; ☎ 2815 5005; info@ehealingplants.com; 13th fl, Capital Plaza, 2-10 Lyndhurst Tce, Central; 🕑 10am-8pm Mon-Sat; Central Escalator) Acupuncture, reflexology, Swedish massage and homeopathic doctors at hand.

YOGA

Yoga in all its forms is as popular in Hong Kong as it is everywhere else in the world.

Yoga Central (Map p68; ☎ 2982 4308; www.yogacentral.com.hk; 4th fl, 13 Wyndham St, Central; 🕑 variable hours; Central MTR, exit D2) Well-established studio offering Hatha with an Iyengar spin, and Pilates. Beginner and intermediate classes Monday to Saturday cost from $140/200 for one/two hours.

Yoga Fitness (Map p68; ☎ 2851 8353; www.yoga-fitness.com; 5th fl, Sea Bird House, 22-28 Wyndham St, Central; ☼ variable hours; Central MTR, exit D2) Hatha for $140 per class or from $499 for five classes in a month.

Yoga Plus (Map p68; ☎ 2521 4555; www.yogaplus.com.hk; 6th fl, LKF Tower, 55 D'Aguilar St, Central; ☼ 7am-11pm Mon-Sun; Central MTR, exit D2) Plush studio with spa treatments, Pilates and 11 styles of yoga, including Hatha and Iyengar.

ACTIVITIES

Hong Kong offers countless ways to have fun and keep fit. From tennis and squash courts to cycling and hiking trails, you'll hardly be stumped for something active to do during your visit here.

Information & Venues

One excellent, all-round option is the South China Athletic Association (SCAA; opposite), east of the Happy Valley Racecourse and south of Causeway Bay. The SCAA has facilities for badminton, billiards, bowling, tennis, squash, table tennis, gymnastics, fencing, yoga, judo, karate and golf (among other activities), and short-term membership for visitors is $50 per month. Another good place to know is the nearby Hong Kong Amateur Athletic Association (☎ 2504 8215; www.hka aa.com).

Hong Kong Outdoors (www.hkoutdoors.com) is an excellent website for all sorts of active pursuits.

BEACHES

The most accessible beaches are on the southern side of Hong Kong Island (see in particular Shek O, p86), but the best ones are on the Outlying Islands and in the New Territories. For a list of beaches deemed safe enough for swimming and their water-quality gradings, check the website of the Environmental Protection Department (www.info.g ov.hk/epd).

Hong Kong's 41 gazetted beaches are staffed by lifeguards from 9am to 6pm daily from at least April to October (from 8am to 7pm on Saturday and Sunday from June to August). A few beaches, including Deep Water Bay and Clear Water Bay, have year-round lifeguard services. Shark nets are installed and inspected at 32 beaches. From the first day of the official swimming season

top picks

ONLY IN HONG KONG

- Morning t'ai chi in the park (p227)
- Betting on the horses at uniquely urban Happy Valley (p230)
- Cheers and beers at the Rugby Sevens (p231)
- Watching (or joining in) the Dragon Boat Racing festival (p17)
- Hiking from city into jungle on the Hong Kong Trail (p224)

until the last, expect the beaches to be chock-a-block on weekends and holidays. When the swimming season is officially declared over, the beaches become deserted – no matter how hot the weather.

At most of the beaches you will find toilets, showers, changing rooms, refreshment stalls and sometimes cafés and restaurants.

For information on Hong Kong's swimming pools, see opposite.

BIRD-WATCHING

Birders in Hong Kong will have their work cut out for them: some 450 species have been spotted in the territory. The best area is Mai Po Marsh (p108), but others include Tai Po Kau Nature Reserve (p122) and Po Toi (p149). The Hong Kong Bird-Watching Society (☎ 2377 4387; www.hkbws.org.hk) is a font of information and can arrange organised visits to local birding venues. Ask for its free brochure *Bird Watching in Hong Kong.*

BOWLING

Some of the best facilities are on the 1st floor of the Sports Complex at the SCAA (opposite). About 60 lanes are open from 10am to 12.30am Monday to Thursday, from 10am to 1.30am Friday, 9.30am to 1.30am Saturday and from 9am to 12.30am on Sunday and holidays. Games cost $18 to $30, depending on the time of day and day of the week.

CLIMBING

The Hong Kong Climbing (www.hongkongclimbing.com) website is the best resource for climbers in Hong Kong. According to these guys, Tung Lung Chau (p149) has the highest concentration of quality sport climbs in Hong Kong.

CYCLING

There are bicycle paths in the New Territories, mostly around Tolo Harbour. The paths run from Sha Tin to Tai Po and continue up to Tai Mei Tuk. You can rent bicycles in these three places, but the paths get very crowded on the weekends. Bicycle rentals are also available at Shek O on Hong Kong Island and on Lamma, Cheung Chau and Lantau.

Although the Hong Kong Cycling Association (www .cycling.org.hk) mainly organises races, you can try it for information.

Mountain biking is no longer banned in Hong Kong's country parks and there is a fine, ever-growing network of trails available in 10 of them, including Sai Kung and Lantau South Country Parks. You must apply for a permit in writing, in person or by fax through the Country & Marine Parks Authority (Map pp88–9; ☎ /fax 2317 0482; 5th fl, 303 Cheung Sha Wan Rd; MTR Sham Shui Po, exit C). For information check out the website of the Hong Kong Mountain Bike Association (www.hkmba .org); for equipment (and first-hand advice) talk to the helpful staff at the Flying Ball Bicycle Co (☎ 2381 3661; Ground fl, 478 Castle Peak Rd, Cheung Sha Wan; ☻ 11am-8pm Mon-Sat; MTR Sham Shui Po, exit D).

FISHING

While there are almost no restrictions on deep-sea fishing, it's a different story at Hong Kong's 17 freshwater reservoirs, where the season runs from September to March and there are limits on the quantity and size of fish (generally various types of carp and tilapia) allowed. A licence from the Water Supplies Department (Map p65; ☎ 2824 5000; 1st fl, Immigration Tower, 7 Gloucester Rd, Wan Chai; Wan Chai MTR exit A1) costs $24 and is valid for three years.

For something a little less, well, wild, head for the Tai Mei Tuk Fish Farm (Map pp50–1; ☎ 2662 6351; Tai Mei Tuk; weekday/weekend per hr $25/30, rods rental $10; ☻ 9am-10pm; ☒ 75K), a large artificial pond by the harbour stocked with freshwater fish.

GOLF

Most golf courses in Hong Kong are private but do open to the public at certain times – usually weekdays only. Greens fees for visitors vary, but range from over $450 for two rounds at the nine-hole Deep Water Bay Golf Club (Map pp54–5; ☎ 2812 7070; 19 Island Rd, Deep Water Bay; ☒ 6, 6A) on Hong Kong Island to $1400 at its parent club, the Hong Kong Golf Club (Map pp50–1; ☎ 2670 1211;

www.hkgolfcub.org; Fan Kam Rd, Fanling, New Territories; Fanling KCR), which has three 18-hole courses. Nonmembers can play weekdays only at both clubs.

One of the most dramatic links to play in Hong Kong – for the scenery if not the par – is the 36-hole Jockey Club Kau Sai Chau Public Golf Course (Map pp50–1; ☎ 2791 3388; www.kscgolf.com) on the island of Kau Sai Chau, which is linked by regular ferry with Sai Kung town, northeast of Kowloon (see boxed text, p126). Greens fees for 18 holes of play by adult nonresidents range from $660 on weekdays to $980 on the weekend. You must be accompanied by a Hong Kong ID card holder on weekends; for weekdays be sure to bring your passport and handicap card. It costs from $160 per round to rent clubs and $35 to rent golf shoes; caddies are $175 for 18 holes.

Other courses in Hong Kong include those below.

Clearwater Bay Golf & Country Club (Map pp50–1; ☎ 2335 3888; www.cwbgolf.org; 139 Tau Au Mun Rd, Clearwater Bay; greens fees $1600-1800; ☒ 91) 27-hole course at the tip of the Clearwater Bay peninsula in the New Territories.

Discovery Bay Golf Club (Map p136; ☎ 2987 7273, automated booking 2987 2112; Discovery Bay, Lantau; greens fees $1400; ☒ Discovery Bay) Perched high on a hill, this 27-hole course has impressive views of the Outlying Islands. Nonmembers Monday, Tuesday and Friday only.

Shek O Golf & Country Club (Map pp54–5; ☎ 2809 4458; Shek O Rd, Shek O; greens fees $300-500; ☒ 3, 309) 18-hole course located on the southeastern edge of Hong Kong Island. Nonmembers must be accompanied by a member.

If you're content with just teeing off (again and again), the Jockey Club Kau Sai Chau Public Golf Course has a driving range (☎ 2791 3344; per 30 min $35, club rental $15; ☻ 7am-8pm Mon, Wed & Thu, 11am-8pm Tue, 7am-10pm Fri-Sun). In addition it offers a variety of packages where you can practise putting, chipping and bunker shots.

For more information, contact the Hong Kong Golf Association (☎ 2504 8659; www.hkg a.com).

HIKING

Hong Kong is an excellent place for hiking, and there are numerous trails on Hong Kong Island, in the New Territories (see in particular the Sai Kung Peninsula, p126) and on the Outlying Islands. The four main ones are the MacLehose Trail (p226), at 100km the longest in the territory; the 78km-long Wilson Trail (p227), which runs on both sides of Victoria Harbour; the 70km-long Lantau Trail (p226); and the Hong Kong Trail (right), which is 50km long.

When hiking or trekking in Hong Kong some basic equipment is required. Most important is a full water bottle. Other useful items include trail snacks, a weatherproof jacket, a sun hat, toilet paper, maps and a compass. Boots are not necessary; the best footwear is a good pair of running shoes.

Hikers should remember that the high humidity during spring and summer can be enervating. October to March is the best season for arduous treks. At high elevations, such as parts of the Lantau and MacLehose Trails, it can get very cold so it's essential to bring warm clothing.

Mosquitoes are a nuisance in spring and summer, so a good mosquito repellent is necessary. Snakes are rarely encountered.

Maps

Good hiking maps will save you a lot of time, energy and trouble. The Map Publication Centres (p295) stock the excellent Countryside Series of topographical maps, as well as the unfolded hiking maps ($34) produced by the Country & Marine Parks Authority for each of Hong Kong's four main trails: the 1:15,000 *Hong Kong Trail,* the 1:35,000 *Wilson Trail,* the 1:25,000 *MacLehose Trail* and the 1:20,000 *Lantau Trail.* The four trail maps are also available from the Government Publications Office (p158) in Central.

Accommodation

The Country & Marine Parks Authority (☎ 2420 0529; http://parks.afcd.gov.hk) of the Agriculture, Fisheries & Conservation Department maintains 38 no-frills camp sites in the New Territories and Outlying Islands for use by hikers. They are all free and are clearly labelled on the Countryside Series and four trail maps. Camping is prohibited on the 41 gazetted public beaches patrolled by lifeguards, but is generally OK on more remote beaches.

You can camp at the hostels managed by the Hong Kong Youth Hostels Association (HKYHA; ☎ 2788 1638; www.yha.org.hk), with the exception of the Jockey Club Mount Davis hostel on Hong Kong Island and Bradbury Lodge at Tai Mei Tuk in the New Territories. The fee, which allows you to use the hostel's toilet and washroom facilities, is $25 for HKYHA or Hostelling International (HI) members, or $35 for nonmembers.

Organised Hikes

The YWCA (☎ 3476 1300; www.ywca.org.hk) arranges group hikes around such areas as Silvermine to Pui O, Shek O to Chai Wan and other popular routes. The Hong Kong Trampers (☎ 8209 0517; www.hktrampers.com) are worth checking and arrange informal walks on Sundays. Serious hikers might consider joining in the annual Trailwalker event (www.oxfamtrailwalker.org.hk), a gruelling 48-hour race across the MacLehose Trail in the New Territories in November, organised since 1986 by Oxfam Hong Kong (☎ 2520 2525).

If you would like to do some hiking in the countryside – either individually or in a group – but you would prefer to be shown the way, Walk Hong Kong (☎ 9187 8641; www.walkhongkong.com) takes guided nature walks on Hong Kong Island (eg The Peak to Aberdeen), the New Territories (eg Plover Cove and Sai Kung Country Parks) and Lantau Island. There are half-/full-day walks, costing from $300 to $600, including lunch.

Natural Excursion Ideals (☎ 9300 5197; www.kayak-and-hike.com) offers both hiking and kayaking trips. Hikes take in such places as Plover Cove Country Park and the peak of Ma On Shan. On the water it has half-/full-day tours ($700/880) including the 'Power Boat, Kayak & Coral Explorer'. This will take you, by unique 'fast-pursuit craft', to the otherwise inaccessible Bluff Island and the fishing village of Sha Kiu Tau from where you can swim, snorkel and then kayak. All gear, including a mask and snorkel, is provided and the full-day tours include lunch.

Hong Kong Trail

Starting from the Peak Tram upper terminus (Map pp54–5) on the Peak, the 50km-long Hong Kong Trail follows Lugard Rd to the west and drops down the hill to Pok Fu Lam Reservoir near Aberdeen, before turning east and zigzagging across the ridges. The trail traverses four country parks: 2.7-sq-km Pok Fu Lam Country Park south of Victoria Peak; 4.2-sq-km Aberdeen Country Park east of the Peak; 13-sq-km Tai Tam Country Park on the eastern side of the island; and 7-sq-km Shek O Country Park in the southeast. Tai Tam is the most beautiful of the four, with its dense emerald woods and trickling streams. The Hong Kong Trail skirts the northern side of

Tai Tam Reservoir, the largest body of water on the island.

It's possible to hike the entire trail – a total of eight stages from the Peak to Big Wave Bay – in one day, but it's quite a slog and requires about 15 full hours. Most hikers pick a manageable section to suit, such as stage No 1 from the Peak to Pok Fu Lam Reservoir Rd (7km, two hours). Note that there are no designated camp sites along the Hong Kong Trail.

Apart from gaining stage No 1 of the trail on the Peak, you can reach stage No 6 (Tai Tam) on bus 6 from the Central bus terminal below Exchange Square or bus 14 from Sai Wan Ho, and stage No 7 (Tai Tam Bay and Shek O) on buses 9 and 309 (Sunday only) from Shau Kei Wan MTR station.

Lantau Trail

The 70km-long Lantau Trail (Map p136) follows the mountain tops from Mui Wo and then doubles back at Tai O along the coast to where it started. It takes just over 24 hours to walk in full, but the trail is divided into a dozen manageable stages ranging from 2.5km (45 minutes) to 10.5km (three hours).

A realistic approach is to tackle the trail's first four stages (17.5km, seven hours), which take in the highest and most scenic parts of the trail and can be accessed from Mui Wo or, conversely, from the Po Lin Monastery and SG Davis Hostel at Ngong Ping. Note that the walk can be treacherous in certain steep sections. Stage No 1 (2.5km, 45 minutes) of the Lantau Trail from Mui Wo follows boring South Lantau Rd, but there's an alternative, more scenic path from Mui Wo to Nam Shan, where stage No 2 begins, via Luk Tei Tong.

The western part of the trail, which follows the southwestern coast of Lantau from Tai O to Fan Lau and then up to Shek Pik (stage Nos 7 to 9), is also very scenic.

MacLehose Trail

The 100km MacLehose Trail (Map pp50–1), the territory's longest hiking path, spans the New Territories from Tuen Mun in the west to Pak Tam Chung on the Sai Kung Peninsula in the east. The trail follows the ridge, goes over Tai Mo Shan, at 957m Hong Kong's highest peak, and passes close to Ma On Shan (702m), the territory's fourth-tallest mountain. The trail is divided into 10 stages, ranging in length from about 4.6km (1½ hours) to 15.6km (five hours).

You can access the MacLehose Trail by public transport at many points (see the list at the end of this section), but arguably the most convenient is reached by catching bus 51 on Tai Ho Rd North, just north of the Tsuen Wan MTR station, and getting off where Route Twisk meets Tai Mo Shan Rd. This is the beginning (or the end) of stage No 9 of the trail. From there you have the choice of heading east towards Tai Mo Shan and Lead Mine Pass (9.7km, four hours) or west to the Tai Lam Chung Reservoir, through Tai Lam Country Park (54 sq km), and eventually all the way to Tuen Mun (22km, 7½ hours), which is the western end of the trail. From Tuen Mun town centre, you can catch bus 260X or 63X to Yau Ma Tei and Tsim Sha Tsui.

Another, perhaps more enjoyable, way to reach the trail is to take green minibus 82 from Shiu Wo St, due south of the Tsuen Wan MTR station. This will drop you off at Pineapple Dam, adjacent to the Shing Mun Reservoir in 14-sq-km Shing Mun Country Park; the new Shing Mun Country Park Visitor Centre (Map pp50–1; ☎ 2489 1362; ⏰ 9.30am-4.30pm Wed-Mon) is on the western edge of the reservoir. You can follow the Pineapple Dam Nature Trail past several picnic and barbecue areas and around the reservoir itself. The signposted Shing Mun Arboretum has 70 varieties of fruit and other trees, plus medicinal plants.

Running south from the Shing Mun Reservoir is stage No 6 of the MacLehose Trail, which will take you by Smugglers' Ridge and past some pretty dramatic scenery. The trail leads west and then south alongside Kowloon Reservoir to Tai Po Rd (4.6km, 1½ hours). From here stage No 5 of the trail heads east past a hill called Eagle's Nest, through woodland and up Beacon Hill, named after a lookout station positioned here under Qing-dynasty Emperor Kang Xi, which fired up a beacon when enemy ships sailed into view.

From there stage No 5 of the trail runs along a ridge to Lion Rock, from where there is a path leading north to Amah Rock (p124). The MacLehose Trail circumvents Lion Rock but you can clamber up the path leading to it. Be warned, though – it's a tough climb.

Coming down from Lion Rock, the MacLehose Trail leads you to Sha Tin Pass. From here you can either head south a short distance along the road and pick up green minibus 37M at Tsz Wan Shan estate heading for Wong Tai Sin MTR in Kowloon, or walk north along a path to Sha Tin (about 2km) and jump on the KCR. If you carry on along stage No 4 of the MacLehose Trail, it will take you into the heart of Ma On Shan Country Park via Tate's Cairn (577m) and Buffalo Hill.

Other places to access the MacLehose Trail (from east to west):

Pak Tam Chung (stage No 1) Bus 94 from Sai Kung town.

Pak Tam Au (stage Nos 2 & 3) As above.

Kei Ling Rd (stage Nos 3 & 4) Bus 299 from Sha Tin or Sai Kung town.

Ma On Shan (stage No 4) Bus 99 from Sai Kung town to Nai Chung (descend at Sai Sha Rd).

Tai Po Rd (stage No 6) Green minibus 81 from Tsuen Wan or bus 81C from the Hung Hom KCR station.

Tuen Mun (stage No 10) Buses 53 and 60M from Tsuen Wan or bus 63X from Nathan Rd in Tsim Sha Tsui or Yau Ma Tei.

Wilson Trail

Wilson Trail (Map pp50–1), which is 78km in length – 82.5km long if you include the MTR harbour crossing – is unusual in that its southern section (two stages, 11.4km, 4½ hours) is on Hong Kong Island, while its northern part (eight stages, 66.6km, 26½ hours) crosses the eastern harbour to Lei Yue Mun in New Kowloon and then carries on into the New Territories.

The trail begins at Stanley Gap Rd, about 1km to the north of Stanley; bus 6, 6A, 6X and 260 from Central pass the beginning of the trail about 2km short of Repulse Bay. The first steeply rising section of the trail is all concrete steps. You soon reach the summit of Stanley Mound (386m), topped by a pavilion. The summit is also known as the Twins (or Ma Kong Shan in Cantonese). On a clear day you'll have an excellent view of Stanley, Repulse Bay and as far as Lamma. The trail continues north over Violet Hill (Tsz Lo Lan Shan), where it meets the Hong Kong Trail, and passes by Mt Butler, drops down into the urban chaos and terminates at the Quarry Bay MTR station. Those who wish to carry on should then take the MTR across to Yau Tong on the Tseung Kwan O line and pick up the trail outside the station.

From here the trail zigzags south to Lei Yue Mun before turning sharply north again into the hills. The trail then takes a westward turn, heading over the summit of Tate's Cairn, and passes Lion Rock and Beacon Hill. The path makes another sharp turn northward, continues through Shing Mun Country Park, returns to civilisation near Tai Po, then disappears into the hills again at Pat Sin Leng Country Park before ending at Nam Chung Reservoir on the Starling Inlet, not far from Shau Tau Kok and Hong Kong's border with Shenzhen and the mainland.

Parts of the Wilson Trail overlap with the Hong Kong Trail on Hong Kong Island and with the MacLehose Trail in the New Territories, particularly in the area east of Tai Mo Shan.

HORSE RIDING

The Hong Kong Jockey Club's Tuen Mun Public Riding School (Map pp50–1; ☎ 2461 3338; Lot No 45, Lung Mun Rd, Tuen Mun; ☼ 9am-6pm Tue-Sun; Tuen Mun KCR) in the New Territories offers private lessons for about $360 per hour, as does the club's Pok Fu Lam Public Riding School (Map pp54–5; ☎ 2550 1359; 75 Pok Fu Lam Reservoir Rd) in southeastern Hong Kong Island.

KAYAKING & CANOEING

The Cheung Chau Windsurfing Water Sports Centre (Map p143; ☎ 2981 8316; www.ccwindc.com.hk) located at Tung Wan Beach rents out single/double kayaks for $60/100 per hour. These are also available at the St Stephen's Beach Water Sports Centre (off Map p85; ☎ 2813 5407; Wong Ma Kok Path; ☼ closed Tue; ☒ 6, 6A, 6X) located in Stanley.

Canoeing facilities are available through the Tai Mei Tuk Water Sports Centre (Map pp50–1; ☎ 2665 3591; ☼ closed Wed; ☒ 75K) at Tai Mei Tuk in the New Territories. You can also enquire at the Wong Shek Water Sports Centre (Map pp50–1; ☎ 2328 2311; Wong Shek pier, Sai Kung; ☼ closed Tue; ☒ 92, 299) in the New Territories.

Natural Excursion Ideals (☎ 9300 5197; www.kayak-and-hike.com) has organised kayaking trips out of its base in Sai Kung in the New Territories from $700. Dragonfly (☎ 2916 8230; www.dragonfly.com.hk) has similar excursions on offer.

MARTIAL ARTS

The HKTB (☎ 2508 1234), through its Cultural Kaleidoscope program, offers free one-hour t'ai chi lessons at 8am on Monday, Wednesday, Thursday and Friday on the waterfront promenade outside the Hong Kong Cultural Centre (Map p92) in Tsim Sha Tsui. A further class runs at 9am on Saturday on The Peak Tower rooftop. On Sunday from 2.30pm to 4.30pm a display of traditional Chinese martial arts takes place at Kung Fu Corner near Sculpture Walk in Kowloon Park (Map p92).

WALKING & NATURE GUIDES TO LEAD THE WAY

Exploring Hong Kong's Countryside: A Visitor's Companion by Edward Stokes is a well-written and illustrated 185-page guidebook distributed free by the HKTB. It provides excellent background information and the maps are good.

Peter Spurrier's new *Hiker's Guide to Hong Kong* will guide you along the four main trails and introduce you to 10 shorter ones.

Hong Kong Hikes: The Twenty Best Walks in the Territory by Christian Wright and Tinja Tsang is unique in that it consists of 20 laminated loose-leaf cards for hikes on Hong Kong Island, the Outlying Islands and the New Territories that can be unclipped and slotted into the transparent plastic folder provided.

Magic Walks, which comes in four volumes and is good for 50 relatively easy hikes throughout the territory, is written by Kaarlo Schepel, almost a legend among Hong Kong walkers.

Hong Kong Pathfinder: 23 Day-Walks in Hong Kong by Martin Williams is based on the author's 'Day Away' column in the *South China Morning Post*.

A lovely pictorial dealing with the countryside is *The MacLehose Trail* by Tim Nutt, Chris Bale and Tao Ho.

The Birds of Hong Kong and South China by Clive Viney, Karen Phillips and Lam Chiu Ying is the definitive guide for spotting and identifying the territory's feathered creatures and an excellent guide to take along while hiking in the New Territories.

A specialist title but a welcome addition to Hong Kong's walking guides bookshelf is *Ruins of War: A Guide to Hong Kong's Battlefields and Wartime Sites* by Ko Tim Keung and Jason Wordie, which includes a lot of walking in the countryside.

Fightin' Fit (Map p68; ☎ 2526 6648; www.fightinfit.com
.hk; The One Martial Gym, 23rd fl, Asia Standard Tower, 59 Queens Rd, Central; MTR Central, exit D)

Hong Kong Chinese Martial Arts Association (☎ 2504 8164)

Hong Kong Tai Chi Association (☎ 2395 4884; www
.hktaichi.com)

Hong Kong Wushu Union (☎ 2504 8226; www.hkwushuu
.com.hk) Has classes for children.

Wan Kei Ho International Martial Arts Association
(☎ 2544 1368, 9885 8336; www.kungfuwan.com)

Wing Chun Yip Man Martial Arts Athletic Association
(Map p92; ☎ 2723 2306; Flat A, 4th fl, Alpha House, 27-33 Nathan Rd, Tsim Sha Tsui; MTR Tsim Sha Tsui, exit E) Charges $500 a month for three lessons a week (two or

three hours each) and has a six-month intensive course (six hours a day, six days a week) for around $5000 depending on the student.

RUNNING

It's hot, humid, hilly, crowded, congested and the air quality can be shocking. Apart from that Hong Kong is a great place to run.

The best places to run on Hong Kong Island include Harlech and Lugard Rds on the Peak, Bowen Rd above Wan Chai, the track in Victoria Park and the Happy Valley racecourse (as long as there aren't any horse races on it!). In Kowloon a popular place to run is the Tsim Sha Tsui East Promenade. Lamma makes an ideal place for trail runners with plenty of paths and dirt trails, great views and best of all, no cars.

KUNG FU & YOU

Chinese *gùng-fù* (kung fu) is the basis for many Asian martial arts. There are hundreds of styles of martial arts that have evolved since about AD 500, including *mó-seut,* which is full of expansive strides and strokes and great to watch in competition; *wìng-chèun,* the late actor and martial-arts master Bruce Lee's original style, indigenous to Hong Kong, which combines blocks, punches and low kicks; and the ever-popular *taai-gik* (t'ai chi), the slow-motion 'shadow boxing' that has been popular for centuries.

As you can see every morning in the parks throughout Hong Kong, t'ai chi is the most visible and commonly practised form of kung fu today. Not only is it a terrific form of exercise, improving your muscle tone, developing breathing muscles and promoting good health in general, it also forms a solid foundation for any other martial-arts practice. Its various forms are characterised by deep, powerful stances, soft and flowing hand techniques and relaxed breathing.

In China martial arts were traditionally passed down through patriarchal family lines and seldom taught to outsiders, as these skills were considered far too valuable to spread indiscriminately. During the Cultural Revolution, when all teachings outside Maoist philosophy were suppressed, the practise of innocuous-looking t'ai chi was allowed, helping kung fu to live on when so much traditional culture had disappeared.

For easy runs followed by brewskis and good company, contact the Hong Kong Hash House Harriers (www.hkhash.com), the main local branch of a lively organisation with members worldwide, or the Ladies' Hash House Harriers (www.hkladies hash.com). The inappropriately named Ladies Road Runners Club (www.hklrrc.org) allows men to join in the fun. Another group that organises runs is Athletic Veterans of Hong Kong (www.avo hk.org).

Every Sunday from May to November at 8am (7.15am July to September), the Adventist Hospital (Map pp54–5; ☎ 2835 0555; Wong Nai Chung Gap Rd, Happy Valley; ⓦ Happy Valley) organises a running clinic. To sign up as a new member will cost you $350. Groups focus on full or half marathon training as well as 10km walks and runs.

SCUBA DIVING

Hong Kong has some surprisingly worthwhile diving spots, particularly in the far northeast, and there is certainly no shortage of courses. One of the best sources of information for courses and excursions is Sai Kung–based Splash Hong Kong (☎ 2792 4495, 9047 9603; www.splashhk .com). Other outfits giving lessons and organising dives include the following:

Bunn's Divers (Map p65; see p164) Organises dives in Sai Kung on Sunday for about $500 (less for members).

Ocean Sky Divers (Map p92; p169) This dive shop runs PADI courses and organises local dives from $270.

SKATING

There are several major ice-skating rinks in Hong Kong, with Cityplaza Ice Palace in Quarry Bay and Festival Walk Glacier in Kowloon Tong by far the best. They both have two separate sessions on weekdays and up to three on the weekend.

Cityplaza Ice Palace (Map pp54–5; ☎ 2844 8688; www .icepalace.com.hk; 1st fl, Cityplaza 2, 18 Tai Koo Shing Rd, Quarry Bay; admission Mon-Fri $45, Sat & Sun before/after 2.30pm $60/70; ⓦ 9.30am-10pm Mon-Fri, 7.30am-10pm Sat, 12.30-7.30pm Sun; MTR Quarry Bay, exit B)

Festival Walk Glacier (Map pp88–9; ☎ 2544 3588; www .glacier.com.hk; Upper Ground fl, Festival Walk Shopping Centre, 80-88 Tat Chee Ave, Kowloon Tong; admission Mon-Fri $40-50, Sat & Sun $60-70; ⓦ 10.30am-10pm Mon, Wed-Fri, 10.30am-8pm Tue, 8.30am-10pm Sat, 1-5.30pm Sun; MTR Kowloon Tong, exit C2)

SQUASH

There are almost 80 squash centres scattered around the territory. The Hong Kong Squash Centre

(Map p63; ☎ 2521 5072; 23 Cotton Tree Dr; per 30 min $27; ⓦ 7am-11pm) has some of the most modern facilities, with 18 courts bordering Hong Kong Park in Central. There are three squash courts at Queen Elizabeth Stadium (Map p65; ☎ 2591 1346; 18 Oi Kwan Rd, Wan Chai; ⓡ Morrison Hill Rd) and Kowloon Park Sports Centre (Map p92; ☎ 2724 3344; 22 Austin Rd, Tsim Sha Tsui; MTR Jordan exit C3).

TENNIS

The Hong Kong Tennis Centre (Map pp54–5; ☎ 2574 9122; Wong Nai Chung Gap Rd; per hr day/evening $42/57; ⓦ 7am-11pm), with 17 courts, is on the spectacular pass in the hills between Happy Valley and Deep Water Bay on Hong Kong Island. It's usually only easy to get a court during working hours. Other courts available:

Bowen Road Sports Ground (Map p63; ☎ 2528 2983; Bowen Dr, Mid-Levels; ⓦ 6am-7pm; MTR Admiralty) Four courts.

King's Park Tennis Courts (Map pp88–9; ☎ 2385 8985; 6 Wylie Path, Yau Ma Tei; ⓦ 7am-11pm; MTR Yau Ma Tei, exit D) Six courts.

Victoria Park (Map p74; ☎ 2890 5824; Hing Fat St, Causeway Bay; ⓦ 6am or 7am-11pm; MTR Causeway Bay, exit E) Fourteen courts.

WINDSURFING & WAKEBOARDING

Windsurfing is extremely popular in Hong Kong; the territory's only Olympic gold medal (Atlanta, 1996) to date was won in this sport. The best time for windsurfing is October to December, when a steady northeast monsoon wind blows. Boards and other equipment are available for rent at St Stephen's Beach Water Sports Centre (off Map p85; ☎ 2813 5407) in Stanley on Hong Kong Island, at the Windsurfing Centre (off Map p127; ☎ 2792 5605) in Sha Ha just north of Sai Kung in the New Territories, at the Cheung Chau Windsurfing Water Sports Centre (Map p143; ☎ 2981 8316; www.ccwindc.com.hk) on Cheung Chau and at Long Coast Seasports (Map p136; ☎ 2980 3222) on Lantau.

The Windsurfing Association of Hong Kong (☎ 2504 8255; www.windsurfing.org.hk) has some courses for juniors.

Wakeboarding has grown tremendously in popularity in recent years. Deep Water Bay is a popular area for the sport, but for other venues contact the Hong Kong Wakeboarding Association, which shares a website with the Hong Kong Water Ski Association (☎ 2504 8168; www .waters ki.org.hk).

YACHTING & SAILING

Even if you're not a member, you can check with any of the following yachting clubs to see if races are being held and whether an afternoon's sail is possible.

Aberdeen Boat Club (Map p82; ☎ 2552 8182; www .abcclub-hk.com; 20 Shum Wan Rd, Aberdeen; 🚌 70, 73 & 793)

Aberdeen Marina Club (Map p82; ☎ 2555 8321; www .aberdeenmarinaclub.com; 8 Shum Wan Rd, Aberdeen; 🚌 70, 73 & 793)

Hebe Haven Yacht Club (Map pp50–1; ☎ 2719 9682; www.hhyc.org.hk; 10½ Milestone, Hiram's Hwy, Pak Sha Wan; 🚌 92 or 299)

Royal Hong Kong Yacht Club (Map p74; ☎ 2832 2817; www.rhkyc.org.hk; Hung Hing Rd, Kellett Island, Causeway Bay)

A major sailing event in Hong Kong is the Hong Kong–Manila yacht race, which takes place every two years. Phone the Royal Hong Kong Yacht Club or contact the Hong Kong Sailing Federation (☎ 2504 8159; www.sailing.org.hk) for details.

If there is a group of you, you should consider hiring a junk for the day or evening. Eight hours of vessel hire (four hours for night trips), plus a captain and deck hand, are usually included in the price. Jubilee International Tour Centre (Map p56; ☎ 2530 0530; www.jubilee.com .hk; Room 2305-6, Far East Consortium Bldg, 121 Des Voeux Rd Central; 🕑 8.30am-5.30pm Mon-Fri, 8.30am-1pm Sat; MTR Sheung Wan, exit E3) hires out vessels for 10 to 25 people from $2000 on weekdays and $3000 on the weekend.

In addition, the restaurant chain Jaspa's (p197) has two junks – one carrying 26 people and the other 40 – for rent. An evening or daytime junk party, including all drinks and a full menu prepared and served on board, costs $550/200/100 for adults/children aged five to 13/children aged one to five. Note that there must be a minimum of 14 passengers. The boat can pick up or drop off guests at either Sai Kung or Causeway Bay. Ring Jaspa's Party Junk (☎ 2869 0733; www.jaspasjunk.com) or consult the website for details.

SPECTATOR SPORTS

Sporting events are well covered in the sports section of Hong Kong's English-language newspapers. Many of the annual events don't fall on the same day or even in the same month every year, so contact the Hong Kong Tourism Board (HKTB; ☎ 2508 1234; www.discoverhongkong .com) for further information.

CRICKET

Hong Kong has two cricket clubs: the very exclusive Hong Kong Cricket Club (Map pp54–5; ☎ 2574 6266; www.hkcc.org; 137 Wong Nai Chung Gap Rd; 🚌 63), above Deep Water Bay on Hong Kong Island, and the Kowloon Cricket Club (Map p94; ☎ 2367 4141; www.kcc.org.hk; 10 Cox's Rd, Tsim Sha Tsui; MTR Jordan, exit E), where the Hong Kong International Cricket Sixes is held in late October or early November. This two-day event sees teams from Australia, New Zealand, Hong Kong, England, the West Indies, India, Pakistan, Sri Lanka and South Africa battle it out in a speedier version of the game. For information contact the Hong Kong Cricket Association (☎ 2504 8102; www.hkca.cricket.org).

FOOTBALL (SOCCER)

Hong Kong has a fairly lively amateur soccer league. Games are played at the Happy Valley Sports Ground (Map p65; ☎ 2895 1523; Sports Rd, Happy Valley; 🚇 Happy Valley), a group of pitches inside the Happy Valley Racecourse, and at Mong Kok Stadium (Map p98; ☎ 2380 0188; 37 Flower Market Rd, Mong Kok; MTR Prince Edward, exit B1). For match schedules and venues, check the sports sections of the English-language newspapers or contact the Hong Kong Football Association (☎ 2712 9122; www.hkfa .com). The big football event of the year is the Lunar New Year Cup, which is held on the first and fourth days of the Chinese New Year (late January/early February).

HORSE RACING

Horse racing is Hong Kong's biggest spectator sport, probably because until recently it was the only form of legalised gambling in the territory apart from the Mark Six Lottery, and no one likes to wager like the Hong Kong Chinese. There are about 80 meetings a year at two racecourses: one in Happy Valley (p79) on Hong Kong Island, with a capacity for 35,000 punters, and the newer and larger one at Sha Tin (p125) in the New Territories accommodating around 80,000.

The racing season is from September to June, with most race meetings at Happy Valley taking place on Wednesday at 7pm or 7.30pm and at Sha Tin on Saturday or Sunday afternoon. Check the website of the Hong Kong

Jockey Club (HKJC; ☎ 2966 8111, information hotline 1817; www.hkjc.com) for details, or pick up a list of race meetings from any HKTB information centre.

You have three choices if you want to attend a meeting. You can join the crowds and pay $10 to sit in the public area or, if you've been in Hong Kong for less than 21 days and are over 18 years of age, you can buy a tourist badge ($100 to $150, depending on the meeting), which allows you to jump the queue, sit in the members' enclosure and walk around next to the finish area. These can be purchased at the gate on the day, or up to 10 days in advance at any branch of the HKJC. Make sure to bring along your passport as proof. The last choice is to join one of the racing tours (p79) sponsored by the HKTB.

The HKJC maintains off-track betting centres around the territory, including a Central branch (Map p56; Unit A1, Ground fl, CMA Bldg, 64 Connaught Rd Central; MTR Central, exit J3), a Wan Chai branch (Map p65; Ground fl, Kin Lee Bldg, 130 Jaffe Rd; MTR Wanchai, exit A1) and a Tsim Sha Tsui branch (Map p92; Ground fl, Eader Centre, 39-41 Hankow Rd; MTR Tsim Sha Tsui, exit E).

Red-letter days at the races include the Chinese New Year races in late January or early February, the Hong Kong Derby in March, the Queen Elizabeth II Cup in April and the Hong Kong International Races in December.

RUGBY

The Rugby World Cup Sevens (www.hksevens.com.hk) sees teams from all over the world come together in Hong Kong in late March for three days of lightning-fast 15-minute matches at the 40,000-seat Hong Kong Stadium (Map p74; ☎ 2895 7925; www.lcsd.gov.hk/stadium; 🚇 Happy Valley) in So Kon Po, a division of Causeway Bay. Even nonrugby fans scramble to get tickets (adult/child $880/300), because the Sevens is a giant, international, three-day party. For inquiries and tickets, contact the Hong Kong Rugby Football Union (☎ 2504 8311; www.hkrugby.com).

EXCURSIONS

Within very easy reach of Hong Kong and Macau are two of China's five original 'Special Economic Zones': Shenzhen and Zhuhai. While the former is a temple to riches with an almost lawless feel to it, Zhuhai is much more laid-back. Both offer bargain shopping, cut-rate services and a glimpse at the direction in which 21st-century China is heading.

SHENZHEN

Immediately across Hong Kong's border to the north is Shenzhen (population 10,970,000), China's wealthiest city and a 'Special Economic Zone' (SEZ). Most foreigners come here for business or to bargain hunt at the innumerable factory outlets and shops, but there is more to keep you entertained—you just have to look. You can buy a five-day, Shenzhen-only visa at the border, Americans excluded (p286).

Before the 1980s, Shenzhen's tallest building was a mere four storeys. But in 1980 this sleepy fishing village won the equivalent of the National Lottery and became a SEZ. Developers added a stock market, luxury condominiums and office towers rivalling those of Hong Kong. Consumer society now thrives here.

Today, Shenzhen – the name includes Shenzhen City (Shēzhèn Shì in Mandarin), opposite the border crossing at Lo Wu (Luóhú), the Shenzhen SEZ and Shenzhen County (Shēzhèn Xiàn), which extends several kilometres north of the SEZ – is essentially a migrant city. Indeed, two-thirds of Shenzhen's population are transients hailing from all corners of China. This constant influx of outsiders brings a highly diverse workforce, a variety of cuisines, and prostitution. The rise of the new, relatively rich middle class has nurtured some cultural scenes, though they are yet to flourish. For Hong Kong residents, Shenzhen is an extended shopping mall and a good place for a cheap massage (legitimate and otherwise) and dim sum.

For Shenzhenians, the series of theme parks stretching some 15km west of Shenzhen City are the major attractions. Window of the World (Shìjiè Zhīchuáng; ☎ 0755-2690 2840, 0755-2660 8000; www .szwwco.com; adult/child under 12 Y120/60; ☼ 9am-10.30pm; Exit I or J, Shìjiè Zhīchuáng metro, bus 90 or 245 from Shenzhen Bay Port) hosts a collection of replicas of world-famous world monuments, always filled to the brim with snap-happy Chinese tourists eager to see the highlights of the rest of the world. Reverse roles at the adjacent

Splendid China (Jǐnxiù Zhōnghuá; ☎ 0755-2660 0626; www .cn5000.com.cn; adult/child under 12 incl entry to China Folk Culture Village Y120/60; ☼ 9am-6pm; Exit B, Huáqiáo Chéng metro, bus 245 from Shenzhen Bay Port), home to miniature replicas of China's own famous sights. Included in admission is China Folk Culture Village (Zhōngguó Mínzú Wénhuà Cūn; ☎ 0755-2660 0626; www .cn5000.com.cn; adult/child under 12 incl entry to Splendid China Y120/60; ☼ 9am-10pm; Exit B, Huáqiáochéng metro), a zoo-like museum of two-dozen ethnic minority villages, with Chinese minorities on display. For tired feet, a mini-monorail run by the Shenzhen Happy Line Tour Co links the three parks, along with several other sights.

Some 12km east of Shenzhen City, a 40,000-tonne decommissioned Soviet aircraft carrier and military theme park called Minsk World (Míngsīkè Hángmǔ Shìjiè; 明思克航母世界; ☎ 0755-2535 5333; Dapeng Bay, Yantian District; adult/child under 12 Y110/55; ☼ 9.30am-6.30pm; bus 103 or 205), complete with choppers, MiG fighter planes and a troupe of Russian dancers in military costumes (and hot pants) performing bizarre erotic dances.

In this authentically inauthentic city such as Shenzhen, it is refreshing to visit Dapeng Fortress (Dàpéng Shùochéng; 大鹏所城; ☎ 0755-8431 5618; Pengcheng Village, Dapeng Town, Longgang District; adult/student & senior Y20/10; ☼ 10am-6pm), further to the east. Reminiscent of the old days as a fishing village, this preserved walled town was built 600 years ago and is best known as a key battle site in the Opium Wars in the 19th century. It is still a lively village with dwellings occupied by both the locals and migrants alike. To get there, board bus 360 at Yinhu bus terminal; it also stops near China Regency Hotel at Sǔngāngdōng Lu. The journey takes about 90 minutes. Alight at the terminal at Huilian Superstore (Huìlián Báihuò; 惠联百货) at Wangmu (Wángmǔ; 王母) and change to minibus 966. A faster and easier way to get there is to take the Sha Tou Kok Express ($60, 90 minutes, hourly departure between 6.45am and 6.30pm) at Suffolk Rd (MTR Kowloon Tong, Exit C). Once the bus arrives at Wangmu change to minibus 966.

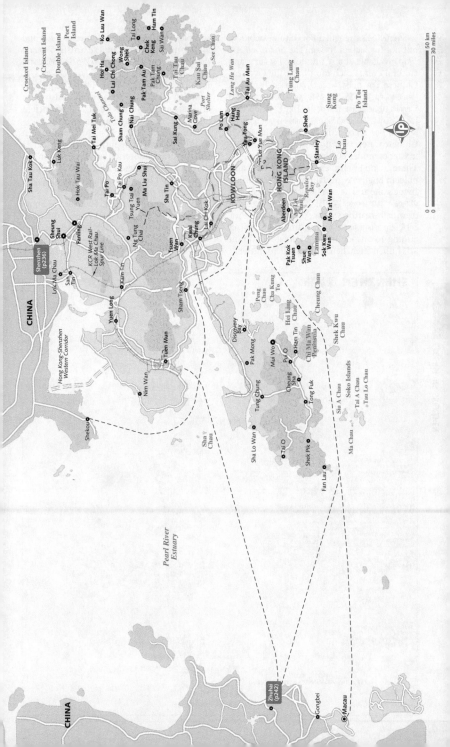

Shenzhen's strength is not cultural ambition, but not for lack of trying. The *Shenzhen Art Map*, available at any museum, lists arts and cultural events each month. At the Overseas Chinese Town, He Xiangning Art Gallery (Héxiāngníng Měishùguǎn; ☎ 0755-2660 4540; www.hxnart.com; 9013 Shennan Lu; admission Y20, free on Fri; 🕙 10am-5.30pm Tue-Sun; Exit C, Huáqiáochéng metro, bus 245 from Shenzhen Bay Port) has a collection of hybrid Japanese/Chinese water paintings by the legendary late master of modern Chinese art, He Xiangning. There are no English explanations but a pamphlet in English is available in the ticket office. In the same area, OCT-LOFT Art Terminal (Huáqiáochéng Dāngdài Yìshùzhongxīn; ☎ 0755-2691 5100; www.o-cat.net; Enping Lu, Overseas Chinese Town; 🕙 10am-5.30pm Tue-Sun; Exit A, Qiáochéng dōng metro) is an ambitious project aiming to attract artists to create a vibrant arts hub in Shenzhen. This excellent museum complex exhibits works of international and local contemporary Chinese artists. Shenzhen Museum (Shēnzhèn Bówùguǎn; ☎ 0755-8210 1036; Tongzin Lu, Futian; 🕙 9am-5pm; Exit A, Kēxué Guǎn metro, bus 3, 12, 101, 102 or 104), in Litchi Park (Lìzhī Gōngyuán), contains 20,000 jade, porcelain and bronze artefacts and has halls dedicated to ancient Shenzhen, zoology and underwater life.

Of course, for Hong Kong people Shenzhen is mostly about shopping. It doesn't matter whether it is counterfeit or pirate, so long as the price is right. And sometimes, with a little patience and luck, you can find quality at a rock bottom price. See p238.

In addition to shopping, Shenzhen offers all sorts of body perfecting services, from massage to manicure. Try Mang Bing Massage Centre (Máng Bǐng; ☎ 0755-8232 1703; Shop 2028, Luohu Commercial City, 🕙 8am-11pm), where you can expect to

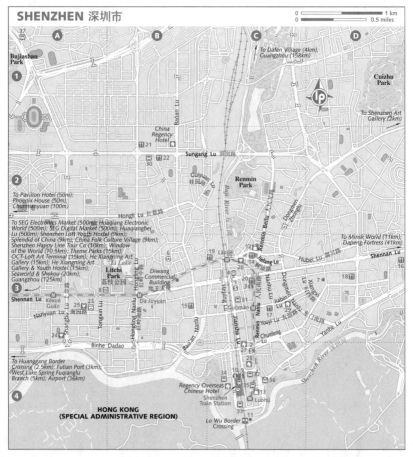

pay between Y45 to Y120 for an hour's massage, and Jian Fu Mei Health & Beauty Centre (Jiàn Fù Měi ☎ 0755-8233 8178; Shop 4028, 4th fl, Luohu Commercial City; ☻ 8.30am-11pm) in Luohu Commercial City, where you'll pay Y88 to Y100 for a massage and from Y90 for a facial. The place is a bit decrepit but the massages are great value. The new branch at the south-wing basement has a slightly cheaper rate. On the other hand, if you are looking for class, head to the regal Queen's Spa and Dining (Huángshì Jiàqí; ☎ 0755-8225 3888; B1-5th fl, Golden Metropolis Bldg, Chunfeng Lu; ☻ 24hr; Exit B, Gúomào metro) near Gúomào metro. Here a sauna costs Y98 and a massage Y168 to Y218; a minimum Y30 tip is mandatory.

Finding a venue for anything from a quiet drink to a raucous knees-up after a hard day of bargaining is easy, especially on 'Bar St' below Citic City Plaza (Zhōngxīn Chéngshì Guǎngchǎng). One that stands out is Coko bar (☎ 0755-2598 9998; Block F, Citic City Plaza, 1093 Shennan Zhonglu; ☻ 10am-2am; Exit D, Kēxuéguǎn metro). For blues or punk rock, the absolutely pop music–free Base Bar (Gēnjùdì Jiǔbā; ☎ 0755-8363 3533; 1019 Shangbu Nanlu; ☻ 7pm-2am; Exit D, Kēxuéguǎn metro) is where rebellious local bands jam every night. The music usually starts at 10pm. It's about a 10-minute walk south from the metro and Citic City Plaza. Clubbers should check out one of the locals' favourites, True Color (Běnsè; ☎ 0755-8230 1833; 4th fl, Golden World, 2001 Jiefang Lu; ☻ 9am-1am; Exit A, Lǎojiē metro), where DJs turn the beat around night after night. You can also find a cluster of pubs and restaurants with different cuisines further afield at SeaWorld (Hǎishàng Shìjiè; 海上世

界; Shekou, Nanshan) in Shekou (Shékǒu). Most pubs here are open until 2am.

INFORMATION

Bank of China (Zhōngguó Yínháng; 2022 Jianshe Lu; ☻ 8.30am-5pm Mon-Fri, 9am-4pm Sat, Sun & holidays); Renmin Nanlu branch (Zhōngguó Yínháng Fēnháng;1st fl, Fángdìchǎn Dáxià, Renmin Nanlu) This branch is just behind New Century Hotel. You can use either Chinese Renminbi (or yuan, abbreviated 'Y') or Hong Kong dollars in Shenzhen, but the rise of the Renminbi makes Hong Kong dollars less desired.

China Travel Service Shenzhen (CTS; Zhōngguó Lûxíngshè Shēnzhèn; ☎ 0755-8225 8447; 3009 Renmin Nanlu; ☻ 9am-6pm)

HSBC (Ground fl, Shangri-la Hotel, 1002 Jianshe Lu; ☻ 9am-5pm Mon-Fri)

Internet Access You can access the internet at most of the hotels listed in this chapter, for an average Y15 per hour.

Post Office (Yóujú; ☎ 0755-2516 8326; 3040 Jianshe Lu; ☻ 8am-8pm); Railway Station branch (☎ 0755-8232 0482, Shenzhen Train Station; ☻ 8am-9pm)

Public Security Bureau (PSB; gōng'ānjú; ☎ 0755-8446 3999; 4018 Jiefang Lu; ☻ 9am-noon & 2-6pm Mon-Fri)

Shenzhen Happy Line Tour Co (☎ 0755-2690 6000; adult/child under 12 Y40/20; ☻ 10am-7pm; Huáqiáo Chéng metro)

Shenzhen Tourist Consultation Centre (Shēnzhènshì Yóukè Wènxúnchù; ☎ 0755-8236 5043; Ground Fl, East Exit of Shenzhen Train Station; ☻ 9am-6pm) Free and reasonably detailed maps are available on request.

Visa Offices at Lo Wu (☎ 0755-8233 9585; ⏱ 9am-10pm); Huanggang (☎ 0755-8339 5171; ⏱ 9am-1pm & 2.30-5pm border 24hr); Shekou (☎ 0755-2669 1848, ⏱ 8.45am-12.30pm & 2.30-5.30pm) You can buy a five-day visa (restricted to Shenzhen SEZ, excluding the Longgang and Bao'an districts) at any of these offices on the spot ($150 for most nationalities, $450 for British citizens; US citizens must apply for a full Chinese visa, in advance).

Websites Visit Shenzhen (www.visitshenzhen.com) is a great website. For entertainment options, check out the expat-run Shenzhen Party (www.shenzhenparty.com).

SHOPPING

Shopping is the sole reason many people visit Shenzhen. An invaluable book to guide you is *Shop in Shenzhen: An Insider's Guide* ($95/US$12) by Ellen McNally, available in bookshops throughout Hong Kong and on-line from Amazon. You are guaranteed not to leave Shenzhen empty-handed, though the quality can vary. Be ready to haggle.

Dafen Village (Dàfēncūn; 大芬村; ☎ 0755-8473 2633; www.cndafen.com; Dafen, Buji, Longgang District) It is easy to associate China with all kinds of counterfeits, including artwork, but this village is definitely eye-opening: 600 art-packed stores, 8000 skilled artists and 5000 freshly painted Mona Lisas every week. Others include Van Goghs and Rembrandts – any famous masterpiece you can imagine. Prices range from Y200 to Y700.

Dongmen Market (Dōngmén Shìchǎng; Lǎojiē metro) This chaotic market is popular for tailored suits and skirts, electronic goods and cheap ready-to-wear clothes, with competitive prices. Most shops open from 10am to 10pm. Be extremely careful of pickpockets.

Huaqiang Bei Commercial St (Huáqiángbēi Shāngyèjiē; Exit A, Huáqiánglù metro) For those on the hunt for electronics, Huaqiang Bei is a mecca complete with the latest tech gadgets.

Huaqiang Electronic World (Huáqiáng Diànzǐshìjiè; ☎ 0755-8329 4262; 1007-1015 Huaqiangbeilu; Exit A, Huáqiánglù metro) On Huaqiang Bei Commercial St; another electronics giant to compete with the SEGs, due to open by the time you read this.

Luohu Commercial City (Luóhú Shāngyè Chéng; ☎ 0755-8233 8178; Renmin Nanlu; ⏱ 6.30am-midnight) The Hong Kong day-trippers' favourite. Over 700 shops sell gobs of goods. The 5th floor houses a cluster of fabric and tailor shops. Stephenie (Shop 5060A) and Wan Dan (Shop 48) have a reputation for their workmanship and quality clothing. Most shops are open 10.30am to 10pm.

SEG Electronics Market (Sàigé Diànzǐshìchǎng; ☎ 0755-8335 8192; ⏱ 9am-6pm) This behemoth has eight floors crammed with tiny booths selling computer components at rock bottom prices. On Huaqiang Bei Commercial St.

SEG Digital Market (Sàibóhóngdà Shùmáguǎngchǎng; ⏱ 10am-9.30pm) A good place to come for hi-tech audiovisual equipment. Also on Huaqiang Bei Commercial St.

IS THE SEZ STILL SPECIAL?

Glitzy nightclubs and cascades of neon advertising indicate the phenomenal growth that Shenzhen had experienced in the last two decades, transforming a mere village into a metropolis. The locals are quick to highlight that Shenzhen was at the forefront of capitalism in Communist China in the '80s. As the rest of mainstream China had looked on enviously at their southern neighbours enjoying the spoils of success that capitalism brings, an electrified fence bordering the northern part of the Special Economic Zone (SEZ) was all that prevented mass illegal immigrants migrating south to Shenzhen.

Deng Xiaoping, glorified as 'the father of the SEZ', bestowed numerous favourable measures to this cosseted kid, including China's first stock market. The maxim of China in the '90s – 'To get rich is glorious' – was the sole motivation to justify the existence of Shenzhen.

After three decades of pioneering capitalism, SEZ represents the prototype of nurturing a fledging city in its infancy to a shining beacon of capitalism. Today, similar favours are granted to cities like Shanghai and Chongqing, sending waves of apprehension among the people of Shenzhen that they will no longer be able to retain their favoured status.

As the barriers between Shenzhen and the rest of China crumble and the population of migrants outstrips the locals, societal problems arise. The minimum wage in Shenzhen is Y4.66 per hour, aggravating the imbalance of wealth and poverty between the haves and have nots. Human trafficking and violent robberies are widespread, and the local police are severely understaffed, overworked and insufficiently trained.

The only way for this anomalous society to retain its special status, according to a *gongan* (police officer) and a TV producer we met, is integration with Hong Kong. 'We are ready to erase the border. Hong Kong police are welcome to combat crimes for us.' As we walked along an unruly street in Shenzhen, we sensed that Shenzhen is struggling to retain its special status. It looks both to its north, at the mainland, and to the south to Hong Kong, and strives to remain the bridge between North and South.

TRANSPORT – SHENZHEN

For more detailed information about getting from Hong Kong to Shenzhen, see p284.

Distance from Hung Hom station 35km

Direction from Hung Hom station North

Travel time from Hung Hom station Forty minutes by KCR East Rail train

Distance from Macau's Inner Harbour to Shekou About 115km

Direction from Macau's Inner Harbour to Shekou Northeast

Travel time from Macau's Inner Harbour to Shekou Ninety minutes by ferry

Boat There are 13 jet-cat departures ($110 to $145, one hour) daily between Shekou port (☎ 0755-2669 1213) and Hong Kong between 7.45am and 9.30pm. Seven go to the Macau ferry pier in Central, with the rest heading for the China ferry terminal in Kowloon. The same number of boats leave Hong Kong for Shekou between 7.45am and 9pm. Thirteen ferries go to Hong Kong airport (Y200 to Y240 one way, Y390 roundtrip, 30 minutes) between 7.45am and 8.15pm. The same number of boats leave Hong Kong airport for Shekou between 9am and 9.20pm. Four ferries a day also link Shekou with Macau; for details, see p349. You can also reach Zhuhai (Y80, one hour) from Shekou every half-hour from 7.30am to 9.30pm.

Bus Buses to Huanggang run 24 hourly from various departure points in Hong Kong, including Wanchai Ferry Pier ($45 to $50, 45 minutes) and Arran St, Prince Edward ($35 to $45, 35 minutes). There are also buses going to Shenzhen International Airport from these points between 6.40am and 10.20pm. For details, see p284. With the opening of the Hong Kong–Shenzhen Western Corridor on 1 July 2007, buses started going to Shenzhen Bay (深圳湾) at Shekou from a couple of departure points in Hong Kong. Operators such as Eternal East (☎ 3760 0888; www.eebus .com) has express buses running from Grand Promenade, Sau Kei Wan (one way/roundtrip $45/$80, 65 minutes) and West Kowloon Centre, Sham Shui Po (one way/roundtrip $35/60, 45 minutes) to Shenzhen Bay and Overseas Chinese Town. New Lantao Bus and City Bus also operate bus B2 from Yuen Long KCR station ($11), B3 from Tuen Mun Ferry Pier Bus Terminus ($11) and B3X from Tuen Mun Town Centre ($11) to Shenzhen Bay Port Public Transport Interchange. In Shenzhen intercity buses depart from Luohu bus station (Luóhú qìchēzhàn) beneath Luohu Commercial City, and there are frequent departures to Cháozhōu (Y182, 5½ hours), Guangzhou (Y70, 1½ hours), Hǔmén (Y45, one hour), Shàntóu (Y150, four hours), Xiàmén (Y240 to Y303, eight hours) and Zhōngshān (Y78, 2½ hours). The bus station behind Regency Overseas Chinese Hotel has two daily departures to Guìlín (Y230 to Y305, 13 hours) at 7.30pm and 8.30pm and four departures to Nánníng (Y250 to Y370, 12 hours) between 6pm and 9pm. Shenzhen has a cheap and efficient network of buses and minibuses costing Y1.5 to Y4.

Metro At present Shenzhen has two metro lines (Y2 to Y5). Line No 1, the more useful for visitors, stretches from the Luohu border crossing to the Windows of the World theme park. Another line has a Huanggang metro in service at Futian Port where passengers can interchange from Lok Ma Chau station in Hong Kong.

Taxi In Shenzhen taxis (☎ 0755-8322 8000) cost Y12.5 (Y18.50 from 11pm to 6am) for the first 3km, with each additional 250m another Y0.60.

Train The Kowloon–Canton Railway East Rail (1st/2nd class Y69.50/36.50, 40 minutes) is the most convenient transport to Shenzhen from Hong Kong (p285). Lok Ma Chau spur line on the KCR West Rail and Huanggang metro in Shenzhen has recently opened, which is a faster way to go to western Shenzhen. From Shenzhen there are frequent high-speed trains (Y70 to Y75, 60 to 70 minutes) and bullet trains (Y80 to Y100, 52 minutes) to Guangzhou running between 6.22am and 10.46pm. Other departures include Beijing (Y257 to Y720, 24 hours), Chángshā (Y147 to Y379, 11 hours) and Guìlín (Y137 to Y379, 13 hours).

Wong Kong Oil Painting and Art Plaza (Huángjiāng Yóuhuà Yìshùguǎngchǎng; 黄江油画艺术广场; ☎ 0755-2134 2627, Dafen, Buji, Longgang; ☺ 10am-10pm) Near the entrance to Dafen Village, Wong Kong Oil Painting and Art Plaza is the founding shop of this mass production painting kingdom. Bus 106 from Luohu takes you to the village in an hour's ride. A taxi ride costs around Y40 to Y60.

EATING

As Shenzhen is comprised mainly of migrants, it is not difficult to find a wide variety of Chinese cuisines. However, a number of eating outlets worth trying still preserve their Cantonese origins.

Chūnmǎnyuán (☎ 0755-8336 6688/8336 9333; 1st-3rd fl, Pavilion Century Tower, 4002 Huaqiang Beilu; meals per person Y50-150; 🕑 7.30am-11pm; Exit A, Huáqiánglù metro) If the queue at the Phoenix House is long, this is a good alternative with excellent dim sum.

Dǐng Tài Fēng (☎ 0755-8223 8586/8230 7588; 2nd fl, Zhonghai Commercial Centre, 1 Xinyuenlu; meals per person Y8-78; 🕑 10am-10pm) Try the steamed bun stuffed with crab meat and pork. It has a nonsmoking area.

Grand Prince (Wángzǐ Guóyàn; ☎ 0755-8269 0666; Shop 45, 5th fl, The MixC, Bao'an Nanlu; lunch Y38-50, dinner Y80-150; 🕑 9am-3pm & 5-10pm; Exit C3, Dàjùyuán metro) This classy restaurant serves up a wide variety of surprisingly affordable dishes from all over China. The spacious dining hall is particularly impressive. The first branch, The Prince (Wángzǐ Fàndiàn; ☎ 0755-8248 5288; 4th fl, Zhongming Times Square, 12 Sungang Lu; 🕑 9.30am-3pm & 5-10.30pm), is equally good, although the location is a bit remote.

Ju's Fusion Restaurant (Jūbào Sīfángcài; ☎ 0755-2513 0998; 2nd fl, 999 Royal Suites and Towers, 1001 Shennan Donglu; meals per person from Y80-450; 🕑 9am-10pm) This upmarket restaurant is famous for its expensive abalone and shark fin dishes. It also has an elegant and comfy ambience.

Laurel (Dānguìxuān; ☎ 0755-8232 1888; 2nd fl, Century Plaza Hotel, 1 Chunfeng Lu; meals per person Y50-180; 🕑 7am-11pm) The Luohu branch (☎ 0755-8232 3668; Shop 5010, 5th fl, Luohu Commercial City; 🕑 7am-11pm) is a handy choice if you are shopping at Luohu Commercial City, but the main branch at the Century Plaza Hotel serves the better dim sum.

Made in Kitchen (Chúfáng Zhìzào; ☎ 0755-8261 1639; 7th fl, Kingglory Plaza, 2028 Renmin Lu; appetiser Y8-88, main Y48-208; 🕑 9.30am-11.30pm; Exit A, Gúomào metro) This attractive, stylish restaurant specialises in Southeast Asian fusion cuisine. The menu is a feast for the eyes and palate, with over 400 diverse choices, such as pad thai noodles, sashimi, steak and lamb.

Muslim Hotel Restaurant (Músìlín Bīngguǎn Dà Cānguǎn; ☎ 0755-8225 9664; 2nd fl, Muslim Hotel, 2013 Wenjing Nanlu; dishes Y22-58; 🕑 10am-11pm; Minibus 430) If you fancy trying huí (Chinese Muslim) food (eg various beef and mutton dishes), head for this halal restaurant.

Noodle King (Miàndiàn Wáng; ☎ 0755-8205 8099; 4 Jiefang Lu; dishes Y6-22; 🕑 8am-midnight) This budget noodle chain has a line of chefs from whom you request dumplings and noodles. There's also a Noodle King Renmin Nanlu branch (☎ 0755-8222 2348; 3021 Renmin Nanlu; dishes Y6-20; 🕑 8.30am-10.30pm).

Phoenix House (Fènghuánglóu; ☎ 0755-8207 6688/8207 6338; East Wing, Pavilion Hotel, 4002 Huaqiang Beilu; lunch Y60-80, dinner Y100-350; 🕑 7.30am-11pm; Exit A, Huáqiánglù metro) Phoenix House is one of the top Cantonese restaurants in town. Expect rowdy waits for a seat of a half-hour or more after 11.30am.

West Lake Spring (Xīhú Chūntiān; ☎ 0755-8211 6988; 2nd-3rd fl, Parkway Tower, 3019 Xungang Donglu; dishes Y18-180; 🕑 11am-2.30pm & 5-10pm; bus 18, get off at Xīhú Bīngguǎn) Shenzhen's middle class give a big thumbs-up to this Hángzhōu restaurant. It has no English menu but pictures of the dishes are printed. The signature dishes Lóngjǐng Xiàrén (stir-fried river shrimp with Longjing tea leaves; Y78) and Sòngsǎo Yúgēng (yellow croaker fish soup; small/large Y38/48) deserve savouring. There's also a Fuqianglu branch (☎ 0755-8385 0222; 6th fl, Zhonggang City, 3004 Fuqiang Lu; 🕑 11am-2.30pm & 5-10pm).

SLEEPING

Hotels in Shenzhen discount deeply during the week, slicing as much as 60% off the regular rack rate, though you should ask for a discount no matter when you go.

Century Plaza Hotel (Xīndū Jiǔdiàn; ☎ 0755-8232 0888; www.szcphotel.com; 1 Chunfeng Lu; s & d Y1320-1430, ste from Y2420) This is a better deal than the Shangri-La as it sometimes cuts its published rates in half and has more facilities.

Pavilion Hotel (Shēngtīngwǎn Jiǔdiàn; ☎ 0755-8207 8888; www.pavilionhotel.com; 4002 Huaqiang Beilu; s & d Y1900-2000 ste from Y2450; Exit A, Huáqiánglù metro) Stay here if you shop till you drop at Huaqiangbei. There isn't much to look at from the outside, but the rooms are comfortable. Discounts of 20% to 60% apply.

Shangri-La (Xiānggélǐlā Dàjiǔdiàn; ☎ 0755-8233 0888; www.shangri-la.com/shenzhen; 1002 Jianshe Lu; s & d Y1598-1950, ste Y2500) Despite all the competition, this luxurious hotel still keeps its prices up there in the stars, but is also still one of the best places to stay in Luohu district.

Shenzhen Loft Youth Hostel (Shēnzhèn Qiáochénglùyóu Guójì qīngniánlǚshè; ☎ 0755-2694 9443; www.yhachina .com; 3 Enping Lu, Huaqiaocheng; dorm Y60, d without bathroom Y138, s & d Y158; Exit A, Qiáochéngdōng metro) This friendly hostel is located in a tranquil residential area behind the OCT-LOFT Art Terminal (p236). The rooms are simple but spotless. The entrance is behind the Konka building.

Sunshine Hotel (Yángguāng Jiǔdiàn; ☎ 0755-8223 3888; www.sunshinehotel.com; 1 Jiabin Lu; s & d Y1600-1800; ste

WHICH WAY TO GO?

At present there are seven border crossings between Hong Kong and Shenzhen. From east to west they are Sha Tou Kok (⊙ 7am-8pm), Man Kam To (⊙ 7am-10pm), Lo Wu (⊙ 6am-12am), Lok Ma Chau/Huanggang Port (⊙ 24hr), Lok Ma Chau/Futian Port (⊙ 6.30am-10.30pm), Shekou (⊙ 7.45am-9.30pm) and Hong Kong–Shenzhen Western Corridor/Shenzhen Bay Port (⊙ 6.30am-12am). Shekou at western Shenzhen is easily accessible by ferries from Hong Kong and by buses from the new Hong Kong–Shenzhen Western Corridor. While Lok Ma Chau/Huanggang Port (not to be confused with the recently opened Huanggang metro at Futian Port) is open 24 hours, the most convenient border crossings are still Lo Wu and the new Lok Ma Chau/Futian Port, opened on 15 August 2007. You can hop on the Lo Wu–bound or Lok Ma Chau–bound KCR train in Hong Kong to the border, which is connected with the metro in Shenzhen. However, buying a visa on the spot at Futian Port remains impossible at the time of writing. If you want to travel to the rest of Guangdong province or other parts of China, Lo Wu remains the best option as Shenzhen train station and the intercity bus stations are just a stone's throw away once you cross the border. Sha Tou Kok and Man Kam To are more for truck traffic and rarely used by travellers, unless you're heading to eastern Shenzhen (such as Dapeng Fortress, see p234), where the express buses departing from Kowloon will take you through Sha Tou Kok.

Y2600-3200; Exit B, Gúomào metro) Rooms on the 8th floor or above have better views. The service is flawless.

ZHUHAI

Zhuhai is as laidback as its neighbouring former Portuguese enclave, Macau. A SEZ, this 'pearl of the sea' never reached the level of success (or excess) of the nearby Shenzhen SEZ. So much the better for residents and travellers, for this city of 1.4 million people is clean and green and has the fewest maniacal drivers in China.

A small agricultural town into the 1980s, the Zhuhai of today has not only the usual SEZ skyline of glimmering five-star hotels and big factories, but even its own ultramodern airport. Nonetheless, it manages to preserve its heritage surprisingly well.

Zhuhai is divided into three main districts: Gǒngběi, Jídà and Xiāngzhōu. Gǒngběi (拱 北), adjacent to the border with Macau, is the main tourist district, with restaurants and shops; Gongbei Port (Gǒngběi Kǒu'àn) is the large modern complex that visitors pass through en route from the SAR. To the northeast is Jídà (吉大), with its large waterfront hotels and resorts, and Jiuzhou Harbour (Jiǔzhōu Gǎng; 九州港), where Hong Kong, Shenzhen and Guǎngdōng passenger ferries arrive and depart. The northernmost district is Xiāngzhōu (香洲), with many government buildings and a busy fishing port.

Zhuhai is close enough to Macau for a day trip. Downtown, you can stroll along the waterfront Haibin Park (Hǎibìn Gōngyuán; Haibin Nanlu; ⊙ 8am-10pm) at Jídà, with hills on both sides, palm trees and an amusement park, or

through Paradise Park, noted for its 'boulder forest' covering Paradise Hill (Shíjìng Shān). In Paradise Park (Shí Jingshān Gōngyuán; Haibin Beilu; admission Y2; ⊙ 8am-9pm) the Paradise Hill Cable Car (Shíjìng Shān Suǒdào; 石景山索道; ☎ 0756-211 3058; adult one way/return Y25/50, child Y20/30; ⊙ 9am-5pm) takes you to the top. Next to the cable car there are go-karts for rent (five/10 minutes Y25/40). In the bay between the two parks is the Zhuhai Fisher Girl (Zhūhǎi Yúnǚ; Xianglu Bay; bus 99), an 8.7m-high statue of a dame holding a pearl, the symbol of the city.

The Zhuhai City Museum (Zhūhǎishì Bówùguǎn; ☎ 0756-332 4116; 191 Jianshan Lu; admission Y10; ⊙ 9am-5pm; bus 2, 30 or 26), housed on two floors of a building in Jídà, is designed to look like a Ming dynasty compound and contains a small but interesting collection of old copperware and Tibetan artefacts.

North of the museum at the eastern edge of Xiangshan Park (Xiāngshān Gōngyuán; 香山公园; Fenghuang Bei Lu), the austere Revolutionary Martyrs' Memorial (Lièshì Língyuán; 烈士陵园; ☎ 8am-6pm; bus 3, 13 or 99) is dedicated to local victims of the Japanese during WWII.

Zhuhai has a number of lesser-known sites that nonetheless played vital parts in Guangdong history. Several of these are described in the *Cultural Tour* pamphlet, issued by Zhuhai Tourism Bureau and available at most hotels. Among these, the most accessible is Yang's Ancestral Hall (Yángshì; Dàzōngcí; Beishan Village, admission free; ⊙ 8.30-11am & 12.30-5pm) at Beishan Village (Běishāncūn; 北山村), Nánpíng (南屏), a shrine built in 1868 and the largest Lingnan architecture representative of its kind in Zhuhai. This lively village still has a number of private dwellings that preserve some spectacular brick embossments. To get there, take bus 34

241

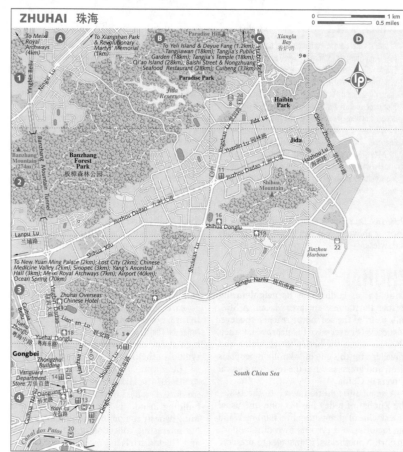

ZHUHAI 珠海

near the landmark Vanguard Department Store on Yingbin Dadao. Alight at Beìshān (the second stop after crossing Qianshan Bridge). Cross the road (be careful!) to Sinopec petrol station. Take the path beside it to Beishan village. Go straight down and turn left till you see a basketball court.

To the northwest of downtown is Meixi Royal Archways (Meíxī Paìfāng; 梅溪牌坊; ☎ 0756-865 9577; Meixi Village, Qíanshān; admission Y50; ☽ 8.30am-6pm; bus 99 or Line 1, Sightseeing Bus) at Qíanshān (前山), originally a residence of the legendary Chen Fang (Chan Afong), a philanthropist who married a sister of the Hawaiian king in the 19th century. The archways were bestowed by Emperor Guangxu but one was destroyed during the Cultural Revolution. The mansions beside them have wax works, archway models and photos on display.

To the north of Xiangzhou, two sites are worth discovering in the labyrinth-like Tángjīawān (唐家湾). Tangjia's Public Garden (Tángjīa Gònglèyuán; ☎ 0756-338 8896; Eling, Tángjīawān; adult/student Y10/5; ☽ 8.30am-5.30pm) was a private estate of the first premier of the Republic of China, Tang Shaoyi, in 1900. Now it is a wonderful tranquil garden preserving various old growth and rare species from South China. To get there, take bus 10 and alight at Tangjia Market (Tángjīashìcháng). On your way you can detour to the 300-year-old Tangjia's Temple (Tángjīa Sānmìao; cnr Datong Lu & Xindizhi Jie, Tángjīawān; admission free; ☽ 8.30am-6pm; bus 10), dedicated to Lady Golden Flower (a local deity of marriage and pregnancy), the God of War and Literature, and the Buddha. A highlight is the grim-looking Buddha statue brought from India when the temple was founded. It's a bit

ZHUHAI

difficult to locate the temples amid numerous nameless alleys. Just ask the friendly villagers where Sānmiào is.

More off the beaten track is Baishi St (Báishíjiē; 白石街; Qi'ao North, Qi'ao Island; admission Y5; 🕑 9am-6pm), literally 'white stone' street, on Qi'ao Island (Qíàodǎo; 淇澳岛), where local villagers drove the British off the island on the eve of the First Opium War and used the proceeds of a British indemnity to pave a path with white stones. Today the village preserves a 700-year-old shrine and an old fortress. To get there, board bus 10 on Yingbin Dadao at Gongbei and alight at Tángjiāshìcháng. The journey takes 45 minutes. Then change to minibus 85 to Qi'ao Island and get off at the terminus. This takes another 15 minutes.

The small village of Cuiheng (Cuìhēng; 翠亨), 33km north of Zhuhai, is the site of the Dr Sun Yat Sen Residence Memorial Museum (Sūn Zhōngshān Gùjū Jiniànguǎn; 孙中山故居纪念馆; ☎ 0760-550 1691; Cuiheng Dadao, Cuiheng; adult/child Y20/10; 🕑 9am-5pm), where the revolutionary hero and founder of the Republic of China was born in 1866. A solemn place of pilgrimage for Chinese of all political persuasions, the museum re-creates the house where Sun grew up and the village compound includes a remarkable collection of period furniture. To reach the museum, take bus 10 along Yingbin Dadao in Zhuhai. Alight at the terminus, walk 10 minutes past the gate to the next bus stop and board bus 12.

A couple of kilometres northwest of Gongbei is a 'been there, done that' icon of Zhuhai, New Yuan Ming Palace (Yuánmíng Xīnyuán; ☎ 0756-861 0388; www.ymy.com.cn; cnr Jiuzhou Dadao & Lanpu Lu; adult/child Y120/80; 🕑 9am-9pm; bus 1, 13, 60 or 99). This massive theme park is a reproduction of the original im-

perial Yuan Ming Palace in Beijing destroyed by British and French forces during the Second Opium War. There are lavish 30-minute performances staged throughout the day. The entry fee includes admission to Lost City (Mènghuàn Shuǐchéng; ☎ 0756-861 0388; 🕑 10.30am-6pm Mon-Fri, 9.30am-6.30pm Sat & Sun May, Jun, Sep & Oct, 9am-9pm Jul & Aug), a huge adventure and water park.

Next door is Chinese Medicine Valley (Zhōngyàugǔ; ☎ 0756-866 1113; cnr Lanpu Lu & Baishi Lu; adult/child Y99/49), a resort where you can soak away your fatigue in pools filled with Chinese herbs or just settle for a traditional massage. Remember to bring your own swimsuit.

For a true hot-spring experience, the newly opened Ocean Spring (Haǐchuánwān; 海泉湾; ☎ 0756-726 7788; Pingsha, Zhuhai; admission Y168-212; 🕑 8.30am-1.30am) resort in Dǒumén (斗门) has a huge ocean-side open-air pool and rooms with their own hot-spring tubs. The resort also houses a Fisherman's Wharf for dining and drinks, and an amusement park, Mysterious Island (Shénmìdǎo; 神秘岛; admission Y110; 🕑 9am-9pm).

Night owls will find Zhuhai's nightlife passable, with a boom of pubs at Shuiwan St (Shǔiwānlù). Cohiba (☎ 0758-889 2444; 203-209 Shuiwan Lu; 🕑 10am-4am; Bus 13, 99) stands out. Nearby, Lianhua St (Liánhuālù) has a cluster of open bar booths straddling the road where the drinks are cheap but the streetwalkers rampant.

INFORMATION

Bank of China (Zhōngguó Yínháng; cnr Yingbin Dadao & Yuehai Donglu; 🕑 9am-5pm Mon-Fri, 10am-4pm Sat & Sun); Lianhua Lu branch (Zhōngguó Yínháng Fēnháng; 41 Lianhua Lu; 🕑 8.30am-5pm Mon-Fri, 10am-4pm Sat &

Sun) ATMs here and elsewhere are linked to most common international money systems.

China Travel Service Guangzhou Gongbei (CTS; Zhōngguó Lǚxíngshè Guǎngzhōu Gōngběi; ☎ 0756-889 9072, 0756-889 9073; 33 Yingbin Dadao; ⊗ 8am-8pm) Located next to Zhuhai Overseas Chinese Hotel, this helpful office sells discounted tickets to a number of tourist sights.

Post office (Yóujú; 57 Jingshan Lu; ⊗ 8am-8pm); Yuehai Donglu branch (Yóujú; 1043 Yuehai Donglu; ⊗ 8am-8pm) International calling cards are sold here.

Public Security Bureau (PSB; Gōng'ānjú; ☎ 0756-887 2872; 1038 Yingbin Dadao)

Visas The visa offices on the 2nd floor of Gongbei Port (⊗ 8.30am-12.15pm, 12.45-6.15pm & 6.45-10pm) and at Jiuzhou Port (⊗ 8.30am-7pm) issue visas valid for three days only (MOP$150 for most nationalities, MOP$450 for British) and your travel is restricted to Zhuhai. US citizens have to buy a visa in advance in Macau or Hong Kong (p348). The border at Gongbei Port opens from 7.30am to midnight.

Zhuhai Tourist Information & Service Centre (Zhūhǎishì Lǚyóu Zīxùn Fúwùzhōngxīn; 珠海旅游资询服务中心; Departure Hall, Jiuzhou Port; ⊗ 7.30am-8.30pm) It has a handful of English pamphlets available as well as luggage-storage facilities (per piece Y10).

TRANSPORT – ZHUHAI

Distance from Macau ferry pier 2km

Direction from Macau ferry pier North

Travel time from Macau ferry pier Twenty minutes by bus

Distance from Hong Kong's Macau ferry pier in Central About 65km

Direction from Hong Kong's Macau ferry pier in Central West 72km

Travel time from Hong Kong's Macau ferry pier in Central Seventy minutes by high-speed ferry

Boat Jetcats between Zhuhai and Hong Kong (Y177, 70 minutes) depart seven times a day between 8am and 5.30pm from Jiuzhou Harbour (☎ 0756-333 3359, in Hong Kong 852-2858 3876) for the China ferry terminal in Kowloon, and nine times a day from 9am to 9.30pm for the Macau ferry pier in Central. Hong Kong Northwest Express (☎ 852-2441 3133) has high-speed ferries departing from Tuen Mun for Jiuzhou Harbour at 7.45am and 10.15pm ($160, 40 minutes) and the same ferries return at 9am and 8.45pm (Y140). Another high-speed ferry operates between Jiuzhou Harbour and Shenzhen's port of Shékǒu (Y80, one hour). There are departures every half-hour from 8am to 9.30pm. They leave from Shekou at the same frequency between 7.30am and 9.30pm. Local buses 3 (stopovers at Tángjiāwān and Jiuzhou City), 12 (departs from Fènghuángběi), 25 (departs from Nánpíng) and 26 (stopovers at Xiangzhou bus terminal) all go to the harbour.

Bus In Macau buses 3, 5, 9 and 10 all go to the Border Gate (Portas de Cerco). Bus 3 leaves from the ferry terminal, and the rest leave from A-Ma Temple. All of them have stopovers along Avenida do Infante Dom Henrique. You can also enter via the less-busy Cotai Frontier Post (☎ 853-898 9727; ⊗ 9am-8pm). Macau bus 15, 21 or 26 will drop you off at the crossing; a shuttle bus will then take you over the Lotus Bridge. Bus 15 leaves from Westin Resort Macau, Coloane or Estrada Governador Albano de Oliveira, Taipa; bus 21 from Macau International Airport; and bus 26 from Hác Sá Beach or Avenida do Conselheiro Borja, Macau. In Zhuhai, air-conditioned buses for Guangzhou (Y55 to Y75, 2½ hours) leave from Gongbei long-distance bus station (☎ 0756-888 5218, 0756-888 8554) on Youyi Lu every 20 minutes between 6am and 10pm. It also has one daily departure to Guìlín (Y250 to Y299, 13 hours, 6.30pm). Frequent buses to other points in China depart from either this station or the Kee Kwan bus station (☎ 0756-818 6705) and the new CTS bus station. Both are located below the shopping centre at Gongbei Port. Destinations include Dōngguǎn (Y65 to Y75, 2½ hours), Guangzhou (Y75 to Y90, 2½ hours), Fóshān (Y65 to Y80, three hours), Hǔmén (Y55 to Y70, two hours), Kāipíng (Y65 to Y77, 3½ hours), Ocean Spring (Hǎichuánwān; round-trip/one way Y40/22, one hour), Shàntóu (Y180 to Y195, seven hours), Shenzhen (Y85 to Y92, 2½ hours), Zhàoqìng (Y60 to Y80, 4½ hours), Zhōngshān (Y20 to Y23, one hour) and Héngqín (Y15, 45 minutes). Zhuhai's local buses are clean, efficient and, at Y1.5 to Y2.5, very cheap. The bus stop at Vanguard has a number of routes to most parts of the city. The Zhuhai Sightseeing Bus (☎ 0756-334 5605, 0756-337 8381) has two lines. Line 1 (Y2, every 20 minutes, 6.45am to 9pm) goes to the west and Line 2 (Y3, every 30 minutes, 7am to 7pm) to the east. Both take you to most of the sights and depart from along Yingbin Dadao and the Zhuhai City Museum in Jida.

Taxi A taxi from the Macau ferry pier to the border will cost about MOP$24. In Zhuhai taxis (☎ 863 2033) have meters; flag fall is Y10 for the first 3km and Y0.60 for each additional 250m. A taxi ride from the border with Macau to Jiuzhou Harbour costs around Y20.

EATING

Déyuè Fǎng (得月舫; ☎ 0756-217 3298; Minting Garden, Yeli Island; meals per person from Y100; ☺ 10am-3pm & 5-10.30pm Mon-Fri, 9am-3pm & 5-10.30pm Sat & Sun) This floating restaurant moored off Yeli Island in Xiangzhou Harbour specialises in seafood. A golf cart picks you up and delivers you to your table.

Jīn Yuè Xuān (☎ 0756-813 3133; 1st-3rd fl, Block B, 265 Rihua Commercial Square, Qinglu Nanlu, Gongbei; meals per person Y30-100; ☺ 9am-10pm; bus 4) This pleasant restaurant serves the best dim sum and classic Cantonese cuisine in Zhuhai. Expect a long queue after 11.30am.

Lao Beijing Restaurant (Laóběijīng Fēngwei; ☎ 0756-335 0222; 1312 Jiuzhou Dadao; meals Y30-80; ☺ 9am-2pm & 5-10pm) This small friendly restaurant serving authentic Beijing cuisine is easy to miss but worth finding.

May Flower Restaurant (Wǔyuèhuā Jiǔjiā; ☎ 0756-818 1111; 31 Shuiwan Lu; meals per person Y60-100; ☺ 7.30am-11pm) This place specialises in Cantonese seafood and clay-pot dishes.

Nongzhuang Seafood Restaurant (Laózihaò Nóngzhuāng Cāntīng; 老字号农庄餐厅; East gate of the Mangroves, Qi'ao Bei, Qi'ao Island; meals per person Y30-80; ☺ 10am-10pm) This countryside restaurant serves freshly made dishes with ingredients produced from its own farm. Try the juicy *níhuìjī* (chicken baked in clay dough) or *jiāngcōngjǔhaó* (oysters baked with ginger and onion). Located 1km north of minibus 85 terminus, look for the big advertising panels beside the water and turn right until you see the bamboo-stilt bungalow. No English menu.

Tea Palace (Chá Huángdiàn; ☎ 0756-888 3388; Ground fl, Yindo Hotel, cnr Yingbin Dadao & Yuehai Lu; meals per person from Y75; ☺ 8am-5pm) This delightful space serves traditional Chinese brews and snacks. The perfect place to chill out.

Zhen Kungfu (Zhēn gōngfū; 17 Lianhua Lu; dishes Y6-20; ☺ 8am-11pm) This budget-chain outlet serves up congee and steamed rice. There's also a Yingbin Dadao branch (1077 Yingbin Dadao; ☺ 8am-11pm).

SLEEPING

With new competition popping up left and right, most midrange to top-end hotels offer heavy discounting that can blur distinctions from budget accommodation. Some hotels add a 10% to 15% levy to the bill.

Grand Bay View Hotel (Zhūhǎi Hǎiwān Dàjǐudiàn; ☎ 0756-887 7998; fax 0756-887 8998; Shuiwan Lu; s & d Y930-Y1640, ste from Y1990) This recently renovated hotel offers some elegantly designed rooms with great views of the bay and the hill. Take bus 9 from Vanguard to get here.

Home Inn (Yújiā Jiǔdiàn; ☎ 0756-337 5111; fax 0756-337 5000; 58 Shihua Donglu, Jida; s & d Y148-Y199) This recently opened motel-like chain offers basic but neat rooms. Take bus 22 from Jiuzhou Port or bus 4 from Vanguard.

Jinye Hotel (Jīnyè Jiǔdiàn; ☎ 0756-888 2668; fax 0756-888-2788; cnr Yingbin Dadao & Qiaoguang Lu; s & d Y430-Y528, ste from Y573) This hotel's convenient proximity to the Vanguard bus stop makes up for its general lack of character.

Yindo Hotel (Yíndū Jiǔdiàn; ☎ 0756-888 3388; yindobc@pub.zhuhai.gd.cn; cnr Yingbin Dadao & Yuehai Lu; s & d Y860-1240, ste from Y1360) This is one of the best places to stay within striking distance of the border. Outlets include a decent Western restaurant called Huntress Grill (☺ 11am-2.30pm & 5.30-10.30pm) on the 2nd floor and the Tea Palace (left).

Zhuhai Holiday Resort (Zhūhǎi Dùjià cūn; ☎ 0756-333 3838; www.zhuhai-holitel.com; 9 Shihua Donglu; s & d Y572-997, ste from Y1166) The five-star complex of Zhuhai Holiday Resort has spacious grounds and some eight restaurants; it hugs the coast northeast of Gongbei near Jiuzhou Harbour. The Youth Hostel (Zhūhǎi Gúojìxuéshēng Lúguǎn) is also here, with two eight-bed dorms (Y60).

SLEEPING

top picks

- **The Four Seasons** (p250)
  Vast rooms, an extensive spa-pool complex and breath-
  taking harbour views.
- **The Fleming** (p254)
  Boutique intimacy and individuality in the heart of Wan
  Chai.
- **Hotel LKF** (p251)
  Sleep tight in lively Lan Kwai Fong.
- **Mandarin Oriental** (p251)
  The last word in style and 'face' on Hong Kong Island.
- **The Minden** (p262)
  Style and great value just off Nathan Rd.
- **Peninsula Hong Kong** (p257)
  The one and only *grande dame* of Kowloon.
- **Hong Kong Hostel** (p256)
  The best value for money on Hong Kong Island.
- **Salisbury** (p258)
  YMCA reliability with views as rich as the Peninsula's,
  next door.

SLEEPING

Money makes all the difference in Hong Kong, nowhere more so than when you're looking for a bed for the night. If you have money to spend you'll be spoiled with inspiring options, so wide is the choice of luxurious places. The midrange of the price spectrum tends to be crowded with adequate if uninspiring business hotels, while further down the price scale, the pickings get thinner still and the defining feature is hostels and guesthouses with broom cupboard–sized rooms.

But don't despair. Things have been improving of late. A few inexpensive guesthouses have raised their standards and décor lately (even if they can't do anything about their modest square footage) and a handful of new Central midrange places now offer much higher standards and far better value than of old.

Whatever your budget, accommodation costs are generally higher in Hong Kong than most other Asian cities, but cheaper than those in Europe and the USA. It is worth bearing in mind that in recent years many guesthouses and hotels have dropped their prices, and that midrange and even some top-end hotels are offering big discounts (especially to walk-ins during the shoulder and low seasons) on their posted rates, which are the ones listed in this chapter.

Although an influx of mainland visitors is buoying occupancy rates, Hong Kong hotels do still have quieter times of year. Its two high seasons have traditionally been from March to April and October to November, though things can be tight around Chinese New Year (late January or February) as well. Outside these periods, rates can drop (sometimes substantially) and little extras can come your way: room upgrades, late checkouts, free breakfast and complimentary cocktails. If the hotel seems a bit quiet when you arrive, it can be worth asking for an upgrade.

Almost every hotel in town (and even some guesthouses) offers broadband and/or wi-fi access (often free at guesthouses and usually starting at $40 per hour in the hotels).

The accommodation options in this guide are listed by price and by area.

ACCOMMODATION STYLES

Hotels

Hong Kong's luxury hotels are locked in an arms race for the dollars of affluent travellers. Their weapons are superstar restaurants; a choice of airport transit by Rolls Royce Phantom or helicopter; lavish spa complexes and harbourside infinity pools. Then, of course, there's the silky smooth service and attention to your most footling whims. A multipage pillow menu? Certainly sir. A caviar and lotus flower deluxe facial? But, of course, madam.

It doesn't come cheap though. Top-of-the-range food and beverage outlets and prices start from about $3000 per room. A few such hotels – the Four Seasons, Peninsula, Mandarin Oriental and Island Shangri-La, for example – offer comfort, amenities and service that compete with or surpass that of the world's finest five-star hotels.

Top-end hotels, starting at a minimum of $1600, are in spiffy locations; they also have smart, comfortable rooms with excellent aircon, in-house movies and a good variety of room-service options. Amenities include business facilities, bars and restaurants, and fluent English-speaking staff.

Midrange hotels tend to be generic business and/or tourist establishments with little to distinguish one from another. Rooms are spacious enough (if you don't plan on playing Twister in the evening), and usually have a bath, limited cable TV and room service. Most have some sort of business centre with internet access as well. Sometimes there is not a great deal to distinguish midrange from top-end hotels, except perhaps a certain ambience and sense of style and, of course, price.

Prices in the midrange category start anywhere from about $700 (minimum) for a double room, though the average price is closer to around $1000. At the very least, rooms will have a separate bathroom with shower, bath and toilet, plus air-con, telephone and TV.

The majority of Hong Kong's budget hotels – a dying breed (as opposed to guesthouses and hostels) – are in Kowloon, with many on or near Nathan Rd. Though most budget hotel rooms are very small, the places listed here are clean and cheerily shabby rather than grim and grimy. Most have telephones, TVs, air-con and private bathrooms; if not, we've said so. Anything under $700 should be considered budget.

Hotels in Hong Kong add 10% service and 3% government tax to your bill, something guesthouses and hostels usually do not do. The rates quoted in this book do not include these charges.

Guesthouses

Dominating the lower end of the accommodation market are guesthouses, usually a block of tiny rooms squeezed into a converted apartment or two. Often several guesthouses operate out of the same building. Your options are greater if there are two of you; find a double room in a clean guesthouse for $150 to $200 and your accommodation costs will fall sharply.

Some guesthouses are relatively swish, with doubles for up to $400. Depending on the season and location, try to negotiate a better deal as a lot of places will be eager to fill empty rooms. Most guesthouses now offer some sort of internet access.

Hostels

The Hong Kong Youth Hostels Association (HKYHA; Map pp88–9; ☎ 2788 1638; www.yha.org.hk; Room 225-227, Block 19, Upper Shek Kip Mei Estate, Shek Kip Mei St; Shek Kip Mei MTR) maintains seven hostels affiliated with Hostelling International (HI). It sells HKYHA and HI cards (p290). If you intend on buying a membership card at one of the hostels, be sure to take along a visa-sized photo and some identification.

All HKYHA hostels have separate toilets and showers for men and women, and cooking facilities, including free gas, refrigerators and utensils. They provide blankets, pillows and sheet bags, though you may prefer to take your own. Most hostels have lockers available.

Prices for a bed in a dormitory range from $30 to $65 a night, depending on the hostel and whether you are a junior (under 18 years of age) or senior member.

Only three of the hostels are open daily. Jockey Club Mount Davis Hostel (p252) allows check-in from 2pm till 11pm daily, while Bradbury Lodge (p264) and Hongkong Bank Foundation SG Davis Hostel (p267) are open to guests from 4pm to 11pm Sunday to Friday and 2pm to 11pm on Saturday. The four other hostels usually open on Saturday night and the eve of public holidays only. All hostels are shut between 11pm and 7am and checkout is between 10am and noon on weekdays and between 11am and 1pm on

Sunday. Travellers are not normally permitted to stay more than three days, but this can be extended if the hostel has room.

If making a booking more than three days in advance, ring or email the HKYHA head office. International computerised bookings are also possible. To reserve a bed less than three days before your anticipated stay, call the particular hostel directly. The phone numbers of the individual hostels are listed in the relevant sections of this chapter.

Rental Accommodation

A one-bedroom apartment in the Mid-Levels will cost anywhere from $8500 a month. That same apartment will go for somewhat less in Tsim Sha Tsui or Wan Chai. The districts on eastern Hong Kong Island, western Hong Kong Island (eg Kennedy Town) and northeastern or northwestern Kowloon are more affordable – you may even find a one-bedroom apartment (roughly 60 sq metres) for as little as $3000 a month. The most expensive place is the Peak, where rents can easily top $100,000 a month. A guide to prices and availability can be found on the website www.gohom e.com.hk.

Apartments are generally rented out with little or no furniture, but used furnishings can easily be bought from departing foreigners. Check the noticeboards at pubs and supermarkets, particularly around expatriate housing areas. Also check the classified advertisements of the weekend English-language papers and *HK Magazine* or the website www.asiaxpat.com. Estate agents usually take a fee equivalent to two weeks' rent. Other upfront expenses include a deposit, usually equal to two months' rent, and, of course, the first month's rent in advance.

Long-term accommodation on the Outlying Islands and in the Sai Kung area of the New Territories offers far better value than the equivalent on Hong Kong Island or in Kowloon. You can still rent a three-bedroom apartment with a roof terrace on Lamma for less than $7000 a month or a shared flat or room for as little as $2000 a month. Things to weigh in the balance, however, include transportation costs and the time spent commuting. A one-way ferry trip to Lamma, for example, costs a minimum of $11 from Monday to Saturday ($14 on Sunday) and takes 25 to 35 minutes. Allow 40 minutes to an hour (and $20) for the journey via the MTR and green minibus to Sai Kung from Central.

Though nowhere near as cheap, Discovery Bay on Lantau's southeast coast is another affordable option.

Those staying in Hong Kong for between one and three months may be interested in serviced apartments: relatively high-priced flats that are rented out for the short term have become more and more common, particularly in and around Central. Some of these are listed in this chapter. Many hotels (eg Garden View International Hotel in Central, the Empire Hotel Hong Kong, Harbour View International House and Wharney Guangdong Hotel in Wan Chai, and the Caritas Lodge and YMCA International House in Yau Ma Tei) offer extraordinarily good-value, long-term packages at certain times throughout the year, depending on the season.

RESERVATIONS

Making an advance reservation for accommodation is not essential outside peak periods, but it can save you a lot of time, hassle and, depending on the season, money. If you fly into Hong Kong without having booked anything, the Hong Kong Hotels Association (HKHA; Map p92; ☎ 2375 3838; www.hkha.org; 508-511 Silvercord Tower Two, 30 Canton Rd, Tsim Sha Tsui; ⚓ Star Ferry, Tsim Sha Tsui MTR), which deals with almost 90 of the region's hotels, has reservation centres located inside Halls A and B (level 5) of Hong Kong International Airport. It can book you into a midrange or top-end hotel room for as much as 50% cheaper than if you were to walk in yourself.

Booking through a travel agent can also garner substantial discounts, sometimes as much as 40% off the walk-in price. If you're in Hong Kong and want to book either a midrange or luxury hotel, call or email Phoenix Services Agency (Map p94; ☎ 2722 7378; info@phoenixtrvl .com; Room 1404, 14th fl, Austin Tower, 22-26 Austin Ave, Tsim Sha Tsui; ⏱ 9am-6pm Mon-Fri, 9am-1pm Sat) or Traveller Services (Map p94; ☎ 2375 2222; www.taketraveller.com; 1813 Miramar Tower, 132 Nathan Rd, Tsim Sha Tsui; ⏱ 9am-6pm Mon-Fri, 9am-1pm Sat).

Price Guide

$	Up to $400
$$	$400 to $1400
$$$	$1400 to $2500
$$$$	More than $2500

SLEEPING ON A BUDGET

Budget accommodation in Hong Kong amounts to guesthouses, many of which offer dormitory accommodation for those on very tight budgets, and official hostels, most of which are located in very remote areas of the New Territories. The Country & Marine Parks Authority (☎ 1823; www.afcd.gov.hk) maintains about 38 basic camp sites in the New Territories and Outlying Islands that are intended for walkers and hikers (see p225 for details).

HONG KONG ISLAND

The lion's share of Hong Kong Island's luxury hotels is in Central and Admiralty, catering predominantly to the business market. A handful of good midrange options do exist though, so don't dismiss the idea of staying in Central if your budget can stretch beyond guesthouse levels.

CENTRAL, SOHO & THE MID-LEVELS

FOUR SEASONS Map p56   Luxury Hotel $$$$
☎ 3196-8888; www.fourseasons.com; 8 Finance St, Central; r from $4200, ste from $7500; Hong Kong MTR (exit F)
The latest luxury arrival, the Four Seasons arguably edges into top place on Hong Kong Island for its amazing views, its location close to the Star Ferry and Hong Kong Station, for its palatial rooms, and its glorious pool and spa complex. The downstairs lobby lounge looking onto the harbour is a wonderful place to enjoy afternoon tea, although the likes of the Mandarin, the Peninsula and the Intercontinental have better bars and food offerings, which are a tad sterile here.

RITZ-CARLTON HONG KONG
Map p56   Luxury Hotel $$$$
☎ 2877 6666; www.ritzcarlton.com; 3 Connaught Rd Central; s & d $3900-4600, ste from $7800; MTR Central (exit J3); ⚓
The attentive service, cosy rooms and the decorous atmosphere distinguish the Ritz-Carlton as one of the leading hotels on the Island. The décor is understatedly lavish, although perhaps a little muted and masculine. Views from harbour-side rooms are – surprise, surprise – breathtaking, but the best view in the hotel may have to be the

one from the outdoor pool. Lie back and soak up the skyline.

MANDARIN ORIENTAL
Map p56   Luxury Hotel $$$$
☎ 2522 0111; www.mandarinoriental.com; 5 Connaught Rd Central; s & d $3400-4300, ste from $5500, Landmark rooms d from $4300, ste $8800; MTR Central (exit J3); ⬙

The venerable Mandarin set the standard on the island and continues to be a contender for top spot despite the competition from the likes of the Four Seasons. The styling, service, food and atmosphere are stellar throughout and a recent revamp has managed to retain its sense of gracious old-world charm. If you're on business and want to give or get good face, splash out and stay here. It's also home to one of Hong Kong's great bars, Captain's Bar (p205), and restaurants, Pierre (p177). Its sleek new rooms in the Landmark Building (Map p56) just across the way, offer more modern luxury and are designed down to their door knobs.

HOTEL LKF
Map p68   Hotel $$$
☎ 3518 9688; www.hotel-lkf.com.hk; 33 Wyndham St, Central; r from $1900; MTR Central (exit D2)

A great upper-to-midrange addition to your options in Central, Hotel LKF is in the thick of the Lan Kwai Fong action (but far enough above it not to be disturbed by it), and has spacious rooms in muted earth tones containing all the trimmings: fluffy dressing gowns, espresso machines, free water, and free bed-time milk and cookies. The staff is eager to please, and there's a plush spa and yoga studio (p222) in the building.

LAN KWAI FONG HOTEL
Map p70   Hotel $$$
☎ 3650 0000; www.lankwaifonghotel.com.hk; 3 Kau U Fong, Central; r from $1600, ste from $2800; MTR Sheung Wan (exit E2)

Not to be confused with Hotel LKF, which is a notch up in terms of quality, service and location (not to mention the fact that this place is nowhere near Lan Kwai Fong), this hotel nonetheless offers good value if you can secure a better online deal than the rates published. The Chinese décor is done with a modern flair that avoids chintz and the rooms are reasonably spacious. The rooms are well equipped with flat-screen TV, cable, broadband and most other conveniences you'd expect.

CENTRAL PARK HOTEL Map p70   Hotel $$$
☎ 2850 8899; www.centralparkhotel.com.hk; 263 Hollywood Rd, Central; s & d $1450-1950, ste from $3200; MTR Sheung Wan (exit A2)

A smart, small hotel, with brightly decorated rooms is handy for Hollywood Rd's antique hunting grounds. Sister to the nearby Lan Kwai Fong Hotel, it's worth considering given that there can be some great deals (starting at around $650).

BISHOP LEI INTERNATIONAL HOUSE
Map p77   Hotel $$
☎ 2868 0828; www.bishopleihtl.com.hk; 4 Robinson Rd, the Mid-Levels; s/d from $1250/1480, ste from $2480; ⬙ 23 or 40; ⬙ ⬙

It's out of the way on the Mid-Levels, the rooms are neither large nor luxurious, but consider BLIH all the same for its good service, swimming pool and gym, and the proximity to the Zoological & Botanical Gardens. Rates can fall by more than half during the low season.

EDEN Map p56   Hotel $$
☎ 2851 0303; 148 Wellington St, Central; s & d $800-1100; MTR Central (exit D2)

It may call itself a 'boutique hotel in Central', but with rates posted as '3 hours extended (sic) session' and the like, we know what this place is up to... Still, it is probably the most luxurious knock-up shop you've ever stayed in. Rooms are comfortable but small, with down-filled bedding and spa baths in some.

HANLUN HABITATS
Map p68   Serviced Apartments $$
☎ 2868 0168; www.hanlunhabitats.com; 21st fl, Winway Bldg, 50 Wellington St, Central; MTR Central (exit D2)

This agency has three properties with serviced and furnished flats within striking distance of each other in the Mid-Levels and easily accessible via the Central Escalator to Central and Soho. Daisy Court (Map p77;

☎ 2533 7203; 31 Shelley St, the Mid-Levels; MTR Central, exit D1) has one-bedroom flats measuring about 45 sq metres from $22,000 a month, depending on the floor and the view. Peach Blossom (Map p77; ☎ 2234 8202; 15 Mosque St, the Mid-Levels; MTR Central, exit D1) has one- and two-bedroom flats of about 50 or 60 sq metres for between $30,000 and $33,000. Lily Court (Map p77; ☎ 2822 9508; 28 Robinson Rd, the Mid-Levels; 🚌 26) has two-bedroom flats of about 65 sq metres for between $33,000 and $40,000 a month.

ICE HOUSE Map p68   Serviced Apartments $$
☎ 2836 7333; www.icehouse.com.hk; 38 Ice House St, Central; 250/350/450-sq-m studios per night $1000/1200/$1500; MTR Central (exit G)
Next to the Fringe Club and up the hill from Lan Kwai Fong, Ice House offers open-plan 'suites' spread over 13 floors that are bright, colourfully decorated, and have a small kitchenette and a work area with broadband access. It's become a favourite of visiting journalists, who water at the Foreign Correspondents' Club next door. The down side is that some of the rooms on the top floors are very noisy, and service can be cavalier. Monthly rates start at $17,000.

YWCA BUILDING
Map p70   Serviced Apartments $$
☎ 2915 2345; www.ywca.org.hk; 38C Bonham Rd, the Mid-Levels; s/d $460/900, ste from $1900, monthly packages from $6900; 🚌 23, 40 or 40M
This large block of serviced apartments, arguably the only budget 'hotel' on the island, is not in the most convenient of locations, but it's accessible via bus from Admiralty and Central, open to men and women, and reasonably cheap. There are TVs, phones and broadband in the rooms, a laundry and a decent coffee shop on the 1st floor. All rooms require a minimum stay of seven nights.

BAUHINIA FURNISHED SUITES
Map p70   Serviced Apartments $$
☎ 2156 3000; www.apartments.com.hk; 119-120 Connaught Rd Central; per month 1-bedroom $13,000-18,000, 2-bedroom $18,000-36,000; MTR Sheung Wan (exit A1)
This very central outfit has more than 110 furnished and serviced flats on offer. Prices usually depend on whether you want an open or enclosed kitchen, and include daily cleaning, broadband access, all cooking

utensils and crockery, and laundry facilities. Enter from Man Wah Lane.

JOCKEY CLUB MOUNT DAVIS HOSTEL
Map pp54–5   Hostel $
☎ 2817 5715; www.yha.org.hk; Mt Davis Path, Kennedy Town; dm under/over 18 $60/90, 2-/3-/4-/6-bed r $240/280/420/560; 🚌 5A, minibus 54
Hong Kong Island's only official hostel is a very clean and quiet property occupying a prime spot atop Mt Davis, in the northwest part of the island. It has great views of Victoria Harbour and there are cooking and laundry facilities, a TV and recreation room, and secure lockers. The only problem is that it's so far away from everything; call ahead to make sure there's a bed before you make the trek out. The hostel is open daily throughout the year; check-in time is from 3pm to 11pm. You can checkout at noon any day of the week. Camping is prohibited.

Get there aboard the hostel shuttle bus ($10) from the Shun Tak Centre (Map p70; 200 Connaught Rd Central, Sheung Wan). It departs five times a day: 9.30am, 4.30pm, 7pm, 9pm and 10.30pm. (Buses leave the hostel for the Shun Tak Centre at 7.30am, 9am, 10.30am, 1pm and 6.30pm daily.) Alternatively, you can catch bus 5A from Admiralty or minibus 54 from the Outlying Islands ferry terminal and alight at Felix Villas, at the junction of Victoria and Mt Davis Rds. From there, walk back 100m. Look for the hostel association sign and follow Mt Davis Path (not Mt David Rd). The walk is about 2km. A taxi from Central costs about $30.

ADMIRALTY & WAN CHAI
Admiralty is home to two of the best high-end hotels in Hong Kong and that's your lot. Wan Chai is generally all about midrange accommodation, with a sprinkling of cheaper guesthouses and a couple of high-end options at the Convention Centre.

CONRAD HONG KONG
Map p63   Luxury Hotel $$$$
☎ 2521 3838; www.conradhotels.com; Pacific Place, 88 Queensway, Admiralty; r $3800-4700, ste from $7000; MTR Admiralty (exit F) via Pacific Place; 🖳
This elegantly unstuffy hotel above Pacific Place gets enthusiastic reviews for its attention to business travellers' needs despite its vast size, and for its restaurants, including Nicholini's (p183).

STANDBY HOTELS

At busy times (when the big conferences and exhibitions are in full swing, for example) the best hotels can get booked out. The following are some standby, midrange alternatives that should have rooms and will do if you do get stuck without a bed for the night.

Hong Kong Island

Regal Hongkong Hotel   Map p74   Hotel $$$

☎ 2890 6633; www.regalhongkong.com; 88 Yee Wo St; s & d $2400-5000, ste from $7000; MTR Causeway Bay (exit F); 🚇

A Sino-baroque palace dripping with gilt and rooftop Roman-style *piscina* (pool). Over the top in the nicest possible way. Deals available.

Luk Kwok Hotel   Map p65   Hotel $$$

☎ 2866 2166; www.lukkwokhotel.com; 72 Gloucester Rd, Wan Chai; s $1700-2200, d $1900-2400, ste from $4000; 🚌 18

Few frills but an attentive staff, and you're close to the convention centre and the bustle (and hustle) of Wan Chai. Low-season deals from $1015.

Wesley Hong Kong   Map p63   Hotel $$

☎ 2866 6688; 22 Hennessy Rd, Wan Chai; s & d $1000-2400, monthly packages $9500-29,000; MTR Wan Chai (exit B1)
Central and inexpensive but with very few facilities, virtually nonexistent service and bare, stuffy rooms.

Newton Hotel Hong Kong   Map p74   Hotel $$

☎ 2807 2333; www.newtonhk.com; 218 Electric Rd; s & d $900-2000, ste from $2600; MTR Fortress Hill (exit A)
A great little hotel. Just a shame it's in less-than-sexy North Point. Fortress Hill MTR station is just opposite. Causeway Bay is a pleasant walk away through Victoria Park.

Express by Holiday Inn   Map p74   Hotel $$

☎ 2295 6509; www.ichotelsgroup.com; 33 Sharp St East; s & d $780-1500; MTR Causeway Bay (exit A)
Delivers what it promises: consistent and affordable accommodation, and it's right next to the Times Square shopping mall.

Kowloon

Harbour Plaza Metropolis   Map p94   Hotel $$$

☎ 3160 6888; www.harbour-plaza.com/hpme; 7 Metropolis Dr, Hung Hom; s $1600-2700, d $1700-2800, ste from $3200; 🚌 5C or 8

Directly behind the Hong Kong Coliseum and just southeast of the Hung Hom train station, it's handy if you expect to be travelling into China at the crack of dawn.

Royal Pacific Hotel & Towers   Map p92   Hotel $$

☎ 2736 1188; www.royalpacific.com.hk; China Hong Kong City, 33 Canton Rd; s $1300-2700, d $1400-2900, ste from $2700; MTR Tsim Sha Tsui (exit E)
An easy stroll to Kowloon Park and the China and Macau ferry terminal. Reception is on the 3rd floor. Service can be both slow and harried at times.

Dorsett Seaview Hotel   Map p97   Hotel $$

☎ 2782 0882; www.dorsettseaview.com.hk; 268 Shanghai St, Yau Ma Tei; s $880-1280, d $1280-1580, ste from $2400; MTR Yau Ma Tei (exit B2)
Packed with Chinese tour groups. Temple St and Nathan Rd retail area are all within easy reach.

Newton Hotel Kowloon   Map p98   Hotel $$

☎ 2787 2338; www.newtonkln.com; 66 Boundary St, Mong Kok; s & d $650-1300, ste from $2200; MTR Prince Edward
In a noisy neighbourhood close to Prince Edward MTR and the Mong Kok market, clothes stalls and noodle shops. Reasonable value but no surprises.

New Kings Hotel   Map p97   Hotel $$

☎ 2780 1281; newkings@netvigator.com; 473 Nathan Rd, Yau Ma Tei; s $550-600, d $650-750; MTR Yau Ma Tei (exit C)
The newly upgraded New Kings Hotel may look somewhat off the track, but it's hard by the Yau Ma Tei MTR station (you enter the hotel from Wing Sing Lane).

ISLAND SHANGRI-LA HONG KONG
Map p63   Luxury Hotel $$$$

☎ 2877 3838; www.shangri-la.com; Pacific Place, Supreme Court Rd, Admiralty; s $3200-4000, d $3500-4300, ste from $6000; MTR Admiralty (exit F) via Pacific Place mall; 🖭

The monolithic exterior does not prepare you for the sophistication awaiting inside. The guestrooms are among the loveliest in Hong Kong and the public spaces almost match up to them. Take a quick ride up the bubble lift linking the 39th and 56th floors; you'll catch a glance of the hotel's signature 60m-high painting, a mountainous Chinese landscape said to be the largest in the world. Facilities include an outdoor spa, a 24-hour business centre and a good selection of food outlets.

RENAISSANCE HARBOUR VIEW HOTEL
Map p65   Luxury Hotel $$$$

☎ 2802 8888; www.renaissancehotels.com; 1 Harbour Rd, Wan Chai; r from $3200-3900, ste from $5000; 🚌 18, MTR Wan Chai

This spectacular hotel with a cavernous marble lobby adjoins the almost-in-the-water Hong Kong Convention & Exhibition Centre, ensuring steady suit-and-tie custom and marvellous harbour views from 65% of the guestrooms. Leisure travellers will appreciate turbaned doormen, informed concierges, and a huge outdoor pool and activities complex with a golf driving range and tennis courts. Rates drop significantly in off-peak periods.

GRAND HYATT HOTEL
Map p65   Luxury Hotel $$$$

☎ 2588 1234; www.hongkong.grand.hyatt.com; 1 Harbour Rd, Wan Chai; s $2600-4000, d $2650-4250, ste from $4400; 🚌 18, MTR Wan Chai; 🖭

Vast and unrestrained luxury in the public and private areas is the defining characteristic here. Subtle it is not. The rooms are huge, sporting desks bristling with technology, marble-clad bathrooms and some great views. Its Champagne Bar (p209) is one of the classiest places to tipple in town. The stunning Plateau, a 7500-sq-metre spa complex with every treatment imaginable (available to both hotel guests and visitors), is an oasis on the 11th floor with its own zenlike residential rooms – think light wood fittings, futon-style beds and balconies.

SOUTH PACIFIC HOTEL HONG KONG
Map p65   Hotel $$$

☎ 2572 3838; www.southpacifichotel.com.hk; 23 Morrison Hill Rd, Wan Chai; r $1500-2300, ste from $2300; MTR Wan Chai or Causeway Bay

An odd location in southern Wan Chai and an odd exterior may not recommend this place but the rooms, well equipped and with warm splashes of colour and a distinctly uncorporate feel, together with the competitive deals, just might. Ignore the rack rates outside busy times; you could secure a room for as little as $600.

EMPIRE HOTEL HONG KONG
Map p65   Hotel $$$

☎ 2866 9111; www.empirehotel.com.hk; 33 Hennessy Rd, Wan Chai; s $1480-2200, d $1580-2400, ste from $3000; MTR Wan Chai (exit A2); 🖭

With its sunny staff, pleasant rooms, outdoor swimming pool and fitness centre on the 21st-floor terrace, the 360-room Empire is a good option and an easy hop from the Hong Kong Convention & Exhibition Centre. Enter from Fenwick St.

THE FLEMING Map p65   Boutique Hotel $$

☎ 3607 2288; www.thefleming.com; 41 Fleming Rd, Wan Chai; r $1400-2300; MTR Wan Chai (exit A2)

Forgive this new 'urban lifestyle concept' marketing drivel. It is just the kind of stylish, small-ish hotel Wan Chai needs. Located on a quiet road set back from all the Wan Chai night-time madness, the rooms strike a good balance with smart minimalism and a cosy homeliness. Executive rooms come complete with a home office, kitchenette and yoga mats, and there's also a secure, women-only floor and Cubix, an intimate little bar-restaurant. Free use of the nearby California gym. Rates as low as $1000 in low season.

HARBOUR VIEW INTERNATIONAL HOUSE Map p65   Hotel $$

☎ 2802 0111; www.harbour.ymca.org.hk; 4 Harbour Rd, Wan Chai; r $1400-1950, biweekly/monthly packages from $6500; 🚌 18, MTR Wan Chai; 🖭

Right next door to the Hong Kong Arts Centre and a mere stroll to the Hong Kong Convention & Exhibition Centre and Wan Chai ferry terminal, this 320-room, YMCA-run hotel is excellent value. It offers simply furnished but adequate rooms, most of which look out over Victoria Harbour, and exceptionally friendly and helpful staff.

Room rack rates drop by as much as 45% in the slower months.

GARDEN VIEW INTERNATIONAL HOUSE Map p63   Hotel $$

☎ 2877 3737; www.ywca.org.hk; 1 MacDonnell Rd, Central; s & d from $1350, ste from $2500, weekly packages from $5600; 🚌 green minibus 1A; 🚇
Straddling the border of Central and the Mid-Levels, the YWCA-run Garden View (133 rooms) overlooks the Zoological & Botanical Gardens. Accommodation here is plain but comfortable enough (there's good air-con) and there's an outdoor swimming pool on the roof. Daily rates drop substantially in the low season, typically from $800 to $950 for a single or double.

WHARNEY GUANGDONG HOTEL HONG KONG Map p65   Hotel $$

☎ 2861 1000; www.gdhhotels.com; 57-73 Lockhart Rd, Wan Chai; s & d $1000-1800, ste from $3800; MTR Wan Chai (exit C)
Yes OK, the atmosphere is a tad corporate but the combination of rooftop swimming pool, appealingly updated rooms, low midrange rates and a location in the heart of Wan Chai make this well worth considering. Competitive weekly and monthly packages.

CHARTERHOUSE HOTEL Map p65   Hotel $$

☎ 2833 5566; www.charterhouse.com; 209-219 Wan Chai Rd, Wan Chai; s $800-1600, d $1600-1800, ste from $2000; MTR Wan Chai 🚋 Morrison Hill Rd Tram
You'll find pretty good deals here on the leafy side of Wan Chai. You're almost getting top-end accommodation for midrange rates (as little as $800 if it's quiet). And if you feel up to it, you can always sing for your supper at the fun Nightingale karaoke bar on the 2nd floor. The 'signature' floor is a rather bleak attempt at a modern 'boutique' look and feel. The standard rooms, with quality fittings and restful décor complete with plenty of dark wood detailing, will do just fine.

YING KING APARTMENT
Map p65   Guesthouse $

☎ 2753 2049; 9th fl, Mei Wah Mansion, 172-176 Johnston Rd; s & d $300; MTR Wan Chai (exit A3)
Marooned somewhat across from the business end of Wan Chai, this little place trims its prices accordingly. The rooms are squeaky clean, with air-con and bath.

CAUSEWAY BAY

As well as some good-value midrange options, Causeway Bay is also relatively well served by inexpensive guesthouses, especially on or around Paterson St. During the low season, guesthouses often struggle to fill beds and rooms; most will offer discounts to anyone staying longer than a few nights.

LANSON PLACE Map p74   Hotel $$$

☎ 3477 6888; www.lansonplace.com; 133 Leighton Rd; rm $2300-3600, ste from $4500; MTR Causeway Bay (exit F)
The best new address in Hong Kong, this plush new hotel is an oasis of calm and class amid the Causeway Bay din. The spacious rooms blend classic style with modern fittings on which money has been plentifully spent, including in the lavish bathrooms. There's plenty of public lounging space and a concierge service. All in all this is a graceful, homey alternative to the jazzy JIA around the corner.

PARK LANE HONG KONG
Map p74   Hotel $$$

☎ 2293 8888; www.parklane.com.hk; 310 Gloucester Rd; s & d $2000-3600, ste from $5000; MTR Causeway Bay (exit E)
With restful views of Victoria Park to the east and the shoppers' paradise of Causeway Bay to the west, the Park Lane is the perfect hotel for those who want to be both in and out of the action. The rooms are spacious, the fittings of good quality, and the décor in soothing greens and earth tones. There's also a large gym. Depending on the season, you should be able to get at least a third off the rack rate.

JIA Map p74   Boutique Hotel $$$

☎ 3196 9000; www.jiahongkong.com; 1-5 Irving St; s & d $1600, ste from $2800; MTR Causeway Bay (exit F)
The style mags have gushed about this chi-chi little place in part conceived by French design guru Philippe Starck and you can see why. Every aspect right down to the staff's Shanghai Tang uniforms, postmodern/baroque furnishings, and the latest in music and internet technology is designed to fit with its sleek, whimsical aesthetic. 'Home' (its name in Mandarin) is above all else a friendly place and the service here and upstairs in Opia, the Asian-fusion food

bar-restaurant, is great. Downsides? Well the rooms are what Monsieur Starck would call *serré* (cramped) and the location is traffic choked.

ROSEDALE ON THE PARK
Map p74   Hotel $$
☎ 2127 8606; www.rosedale.com.hk; 8 Shelter St; s $1180-1480, d $1280-1580, ste from $2200/2400, weekly/monthly packages from $4888/18,800; MTR Causeway Bay (exit E)
Attractively appointed rooms and a position overlooking Victoria Park make this place worth considering. Free broadband is included in the rates. Generous weekly and monthly packages are available.

METROPARK HOTEL   Map p74   Hotel $$
☎ 2600 1000; www.metroparkhotel.com; 148 Tung Lo Wan Rd; s & d $900-1700, ste from $3600; MTR Causeway Bay (exit E)
This flashy tower, overlooking Victoria Park and managed by a department of China Travel Service, makes the most of its easterly location, with 70% of its 243 rooms boasting sweeping city-harbour views through floor-to-ceiling windows. Bright, appealing open-plan rooms offer generous work space and broadband internet. Expect some substantial discounts – often 50% – during the low season. The small pool and gym makes a great harbour grandstand.

SHAMA   Map p74   Serviced Apartments $$
🕒 2202 5555; www.shama.com; 7th fl, 8 Russell St, Causeway Bay; studios per month from $23,500, 1-/2-bedroom apt per month from $31,500/68,000; MTR Causeway Bay (exit A)
Among the most attractive serviced apartments in Hong Kong, in a block opposite Times Square shopping mall. Ranging from fairly spacious studio flats to two-bedroom apartments, they're all tastefully furnished and exceedingly comfortable. Features and extras include broadband internet connection, VCD and DVD equipment, laundry facilities on each floor and membership to a half-dozen California Fitness Centres scattered around the territory. There are also branches in Central, Soho and Wan Chai; contact the Shama main office (Map p68; ☎ 2522 3082; www.shama.com; 8th fl, Shama Pl, 30 Hollywood Rd, Central) for details.

NOBLE HOSTEL   Map p74   Guesthouse $
☎ 2576 6148; www.noblehostel.com.hk; Flat A3, 17th fl, Great George Bldg, 27 Paterson St; s/d $280/340; MTR Causeway Bay (exit E)

This is certainly one of the best-value guesthouses on Hong Kong Island. Each one of the 45 rooms is squeaky clean and is equipped with a private phone, fridge and air-con. Some cheaper rooms have shared bathrooms.

ALISAN GUEST HOUSE
Map p74   Guesthouse $
☎ 2838 0762; http://home.hkstar.com/~alisangh; Flat A, 5th fl, Hoito Ct, 275 Gloucester Rd; s $280-320, d $320-350, tr $390-450; MTR Causeway Bay (exit D1)
This excellent and spotlessly clean, family-run place has 21 rooms with air-con, private showers and toilets, and free internet access. The multilingual owners are willing to please and can organise China visas (see p303 for costs). Enter from 23 Cannon St.

CAUSEWAY BAY GUEST HOUSE
Map p74   Guesthouse $
☎ 2895 2013; www.cbgh.net; Flat B, 1st fl, Lai Yee Bldg, 44A-D Leighton Rd; s/d/tr $250/350/450; MTR Causeway Bay (exit A)
On the south side of Causeway Bay and wedged between a pub and a church (enter from Leighton Lane), this comfortable, seven-room guesthouse can get booked up quickly so phone ahead. All rooms are quite clean and have private bathrooms.

HONG KONG HOSTEL
Map p74   Hostel, Guesthouse $
☎ 2895 1015, 9353 0514; www.wangfathostel.com.hk; Flat A2, 3rd fl, Paterson Bldg, 47 Paterson St; dm $120, s/d/tr from $240/280/420; MTR Causeway Bay (exit E)
This excellent series of ever-expanding hostels and guesthouses, incorporating the long-established Wang Fat Hostel on the same floor and the Asia Hostel on the 6th floor, is just about the best deal on Hong Kong Island. It's quiet and clean and most of the rooms have private phone, TV and fridge. There are also cooking and laundry facilities, a computer room with three terminals offering free internet access, safe-deposit boxes and phonecards for sale. Dorm rooms have between four and five beds. Cheaper rooms with shared bathrooms are available.

CHUNG KIU INN   Map p74   Guesthouse $
☎ 2895 3304; www.chungkiuinn.com.hk; Flat P, 15th fl, Hong Kong Mansion, 1 Yee Wo St; s $220-

280, d $280-350, tr $400-450; MTR Causeway Bay (exit E)

This hostel, with three-dozen rooms spread over the 9th and 15th floors of the same building, is tidy but the rooms are small and basic. Cheaper rooms with shared bathrooms are available. You may have trouble communicating as the owner speaks no English.

ISLAND EAST
North Point

CITY GARDEN HOTEL HONG KONG
Map pp54–5 — Hotel $$

☎ 2887 2888; www.citygarden.com.hk; 9 City Garden Rd; s & d $850-2500, ste from $3000; MTR Fortress Hill (exit A)

It may be in gritty Fortress Hill but readers have nice things to say about this exceptionally well-turned-out hotel, not only for its service and generous discounting policy (biweekly/monthly packages from $8200/13,800). There are several appealing food and drink outlets, including Satay Inn serving Malaysian and Singapore flavours, and the Garden Café serving an afternoon tea buffet. The closest MTR stop is Fortress Hill (exit A) on the Island line. Enter the hotel from the corner of Electric Rd and Power St.

KOWLOON

Splendour rubs shoulders with squalor in Kowloon. Hong Kong's poshest hotel, the Peninsula, is here in Tsim Sha Tsui, within spitting distance of the infamous Chungking Mansions, a crumbling block stacked with dirt-cheap hostels and guesthouses. Of course, a huge range of other hotels and guesthouses can be found in Kowloon catering to all budgets between these two extremes.

When you mention the words 'hotel' and 'Hong Kong', many people think of the Peninsula, which opened in 1928 and is the *grande dame* of the territory's luxury hotels. Across from the Peninsula is the Inter-Continental, which has a much more modern feel to it and fabulous views. These are Kowloon's two 'face' hotels.

Tsim Sha Tsui East, an area of reclaimed land to the northeast of Tsim Sha Tsui, is weighted down with mostly anonymous top-end hotels. It's not very convenient for the MTR, but the terminus of the KCR East Rail (East Tsim Sha Tsui station) is nearby and most of the hotels run shuttle buses to Tsim

Sha Tsui proper and/or to Central. You'll find many more top-end hotels lining Nathan Rd as it travels north from the harbour.

TSIM SHA TSUI
PENINSULA HONG KONG
Map p92 — Luxury Hotel $$$$

☎ 2920 2888; www.peninsula.com; Salisbury Rd; s & d $3700-4900, ste from $6000; MTR Tsim Sha Tsui (exit E); 🖾

Lording it over the southern tip of Kowloon, Hong Kong's finest hotel evokes colonial elegance. Your main dilemma will be how to get there: landing on the rooftop helipad or arriving in one of the hotel's 14-strong fleet of Rolls Royce Phantoms. Some 300 classic European-style rooms boast wi-fi internet access, CD and DVD players, as well as the requisite (and sumptuous) marble bathrooms. Many rooms in the Pen's 20-storey annexe offer spectacular harbour views; in the original building, you'll have to make do with the glorious interior décor. There's a top-notch spa and swimming pool The outlets, such as the fusion legend Felix (p211) and the Cantonese Spring Moon (p192), are the best eating spots of their class in the territory.

MARCO POLO HONGKONG HOTEL
Map p92 — Luxury Hotel $$$$

☎ 2113 0088; www.marcopolohotels.com; Harbour City, 3-9 Canton Rd; s & d $2450-4520, ste from $4900; 🚢 Star Ferry, MTR Tsim Sha Tsui (exit E)

This is the daddy of the Marco Polo Hotel group's Canton Rd trio, all of which are in the Harbour City complex. It is closest to the Star Ferry and the most highly priced; it has an outdoor pool and a well-regarded Japanese restaurant Nishimura. The rooms are large and well appointed. The 433-room Marco Polo Gateway (Map p92; ☎ 2113 0088; 13 Canton Rd; s $2050-2350, d $2150-2450, ste from $3650) and the smaller Marco Polo Prince (Map p92; ☎ 2113 0088; 23 Canton Rd; s $2050-2350, d $2150-2450, ste from $3650), at the northern end of Harbour City, are both a step down in terms of luxury and room size but both have good business facilities and some of the rooms in the Prince have harbour views.

LANGHAM HOTEL HONG KONG
Map p92 — Luxury Hotel $$$

☎ 2375 1133; www.langhamhotels.com/langham /hongkong; 8 Peking Rd; s & d $2200-3600, ste from $6000; MTR Tsim Sha Tsui (exit E); 🖾

The elder sister of the Langham Place Hotel (p263), the Langham serves up five-star luxury in the heart of Tsim Sha Tsui. The rooms are classic and simple, there's a 24-hour gym and open-air pool, and there are several cafés and restaurants here and just round the corner on Ashley and Peking Rds.

SHERATON HONG KONG HOTEL & TOWERS Map p92   Hotel $$$

☎ 2369 1111; www.sheraton.com/hongkong; 20 Nathan Rd; s $2200-4200, d $2400-4400, ste hotel/towers from $4200/5600; MTR Tsim Sha Tsui (exit F); 🏊

This large, very American hostelry (the ground floor is the 1st floor, escalators travel on the right), at the start of Nathan Rd, is as central as you'll find in Tsim Sha Tsui and offers a high level of comfort and great facilities. The tower rooms command superior harbour views (and higher prices). The Sky Lounge (p211), on the 18th floor, is worth a visit for the stunning harbour views and there's a rooftop pool and gym. Reception is on the 2nd floor. During the low season you can score a room for less than $1500.

HOLIDAY INN GOLDEN MILE
Map p92   Hotel $$$

☎ 2369 3111; www.ichotelsgroup.com; 50 Nathan Rd; s $2100-3050, d/tw $2500-3150, ste from $5800; MTR Tsim Sha Tsui (exit G)

The guestrooms are pricey for what they are inside a rather dreary multistory car-park exterior, but they're Holiday Inn–reliable. Among the excellent outlets is the schmoozy Hari's (p216).

KOWLOON HOTEL HONG KONG
Map p92   Hotel $$$

☎ 2929 2888; www.thekowloonhotel.com; 19-21 Nathan Rd; s $1800-2700, d $1900-2650, ste from $3900; MTR Tsim Sha Tsui (exit E)

The Kowloon Hotel has a dated feel about it, with its over-the-top lobby, the so-out-dated-it's-almost-cool-again 1990s techno aesthetic and views of the back of the Peninsula. Nevertheless, the hotel is popular for its unflappable service, central location and decent if rather small rooms. Rates drop dramatically off season.

HOTEL MIRAMAR HONG KONG
Map p92   Hotel $$

☎ 2368 1111; www.miramarhk.com; 118-130 Nathan Rd; s & d $1100-2000, ste from $3800; MTR Tsim Sha Tsui

This landmark (and very central hotel) is good value for its category and location. It has some fine food outlets and the Miramar Shopping Centre is just across Kimberley Rd. Avoid the rather tired looking non-executive rooms, which lack style and broadband access.

BP INTERNATIONAL HOTEL
Map p92   Hotel $$

☎ 2376 1111; www.bpih.com.hk; 8 Austin Rd; r $1150-2400, ste from $3500; MTR Jordan

This enormous hotel, owned by the Scout Association of Hong Kong and named after Robert Baden-Powell, founder of the World Scout Movement, overlooks Kowloon Park from its northwest corner and is relatively convenient to most places of interest in Tsim Sha Tsui. The public areas are quite flash, the rooms have finally been upgraded to a reasonable standard and some of the more expensive ones have good harbour views. There are family rooms with bunk beds available, making this a good option if you're travelling with kids. A self-service laundry room and free broadband access are on site. Haggle before you book; depending on the season and day of the week, prices are often reduced by 50%.

SALISBURY Map p92   Hostel $, Hotel $$

☎ 2268 7000; www.ymcahk.org.hk; 41 Salisbury Rd; dm/s $230/800, d $750-1100, ste from $1500; 🚢 Star Ferry; 🏊

If you can manage to book a room at the fabulously located, YMCA-run Salisbury, you'll be rewarded with professional service and excellent exercise facilities, including a six-lane swimming pool and fitness centre on the 1st floor and a climbing wall on the 2nd floor. The rooms and suites are comfortable but simple, so keep your eyes on the harbour; that view would cost you at least five times as much at the Peninsula next door. The four-bed dormitory rooms on the 9th floor are a bonus, but there are restrictions: check-in is at 2pm; no one can stay more than seven consecutive nights; and walk-in guests aren't accepted if they've been in Hong Kong for more than 10 days.

WONDERFUL INN Map p92   Guesthouse $

☎ 2302 4812; www.wonderfulinn.com; 5th fl, Mirador Mansion, 66-70 Nathan Rd; s & d from $350-580; MTR Tsim Sha Tsui

For once some money has been spent on design and fittings, making the rooms here much more appealing than the usual guesthouse boxes. The rooms are still small, but this is a good compromise for budgets that don't quite stretch to a hotel.

SEALAND HOUSE Map p92 Guesthouse $
☎ 2368 9522; www.sealandhouse.com.hk; Flat D, 8th fl, Majestic House, 80 Nathan Rd; s $250-300, d $300-450; MTR Tsim Sha Tsui (exit B2)
This eight-room place, towering above Nathan Rd, is small but clean and very bright. It's a great independent choice over the guesthouses in Mirador Mansion or Chungking Mansions and wi-fi internet is include in rates. Enter from Cameron Rd.

FIRST-CLASS GUEST HOUSE
Map p92 Guesthouse $
☎ 2724 0595; fax 2724 0843; Flat D1, 16th fl, Mirador Mansion, 58-62 Nathan Rd; s/d $160/200; MTR Tsim Sha Tsui (exit D2)
While its name may be a little ambitious, the First-Class Guest House is clean and fresh and the staff friendly. All 20 rooms have private bathrooms.

MEI LAM GUEST HOUSE
Map p92 Guesthouse $
☎ 2721 5278, 9095 1379; fax 2723 6168; Flat D1, 5th fl, Mirador Mansion, 62 Nathan Rd; s/d from $160/200; MTR Tsim Sha Tsui (exit D2)
A few notches above the usual standard, this excellent guesthouse has modern, comfortable rooms packed with extras including internet access.

CHUNGKING HOUSE Map p92 Guesthouse $
☎ 2366 5362; chungkinghouse@yahoo.com.hk; 4th & 5th fl, A Block, Chungking Mansions, 36-44 Nathan Rd; s $150-250, d $300-400; MTR Tsim Sha Tsui (exit F)
This place covering two floors – with two receptions and a total of 80 rooms – is pretty swish by the standards of Chungking Mansions, with phones and TVs included.

TOM'S GUEST HOUSE
Map p92 Guesthouse $
☎ 2722 6035, 9194 5923; fax 2366 6706; Flat B7, 16th fl, B Block, Chungking Mansions, 36-44 Nathan Rd; s $150-160, d $150-250; MTR Tsim Sha Tsui (exit F)
A friendly and popular place. Can also be entered from C Block (Flat C1, 16th fl). There's another large branch located in

A Block (☎ 2722 4956; Flat A5, 8th fl), so you should always be able to find a room here.

YAN YAN GUEST HOUSE
Map p92 Guesthouse $
☎ 2366 8930, 9489 3891; fax 2721 0840; Flat E1, 8th fl, E Block, Chungking Mansions, 36-44 Nathan Rd; s $130, d $180-250; MTR Tsim Sha Tsui (exit F)
This is one of the last of the Chinese-owned guesthouses in the overwhelmingly sub-continental E Block of Chungking Mansions. The swish New Yan Yan Guesthouse (☎ 2723 5671; Flat E5, 12th fl), in the same block, is managed by the same people.

PEKING GUEST HOUSE
Map p92 Guesthouse $
☎ 2723 8320, 9464 3684; fax 2366 6706; Flat A1-A2, 12th fl, A Block, Chungking Mansions, 36-44 Nathan Rd; s $130-150, d $160-200, tr $280; MTR Tsim Sha Tsui (exit F)
Peking has friendly management, the place is cluttered but clean and all rooms have a private bathroom.

NEW SHANGHAI GUEST HOUSE
Map p92 Guesthouse $
☎ 2311 2515; Flat D2, 16th fl, D Block, Chungking Mansions, 36-44 Nathan Rd; s/d from $120/260; MTR Tsim Sha Tsui (exit F)
This is an old-style guesthouse run by pleasant Mrs Cheung. It's clean and there's a laundry service.

GARDEN GUEST HOUSE
Map p92 Guesthouse $
☎ 2368 0981, 9057 5265; Flat C5, 16th fl, C Block, Chungking Mansions, 36-44 Nathan Rd; s $120, d $180; MTR Tsim Sha Tsui (exit F)
This is a clean, quiet place much favoured by backpackers. There's another branch (☎ 2366 0169; Flat C5, 7th fl) in the same block.

HUNG KIU GUEST HOUSE
Map p92 Guesthouse $
☎ 2312 1505, 9370 2325; fax 2311 4258; Flat C3, 8th fl, Mirador Mansion, 58-62 Nathan Rd; s $120, d $180-200; MTR Tsim Sha Tsui (exit D2)
Merely adequate facilities but very clean, with an affable and helpful young Chinese manager. Free wi-fi internet.

MAN HING LUNG HOTEL
Map p92 Guesthouse $
☎ 2722 0678, 2311 8807; http://home.hkstar.com /~mhlhotel; Flat F2, 14th fl, Mirador Mansion, 58-62

Nathan Rd; s $120-150, d $150-200, tr $210-240; MTR Tsim Sha Tsui (exit D2)
This decent place, which likes to call itself a hotel, has clean if rather spartan rooms, broadband and laundry facilities. If you need a roommate to share costs, the very friendly manager, Mr Chan, will put you in with another traveller for $80. He can also arrange China visas (for costs, see p303).

PARK GUEST HOUSE Map p92   Guesthouse $
☎ 2368 1689; fax 2367 7889; Flat A1, 15th fl, A Block, Chungking Mansions, 36-44 Nathan Rd; s with shared bathroom $108, s/d with private bathroom $100/150; MTR Tsim Sha Tsui (exit F)
All 45 rooms in this basic but welcoming guesthouse have air-con. It comes recommended by readers. Room 1509 has a sliver of a sea view.

WELCOME GUEST HOUSE
Map p92   Guesthouse $
☎ 2721 7793, 9838 8375; Flat A5, 7th fl, A Block, Chungking Mansions, 36-44 Nathan Rd; s with shared shower $100, s with private shower $100-150, d with private shower $190-200; MTR Tsim Sha Tsui (exit F)
This place is a cut above the rest in Chungking Mansions and its name says it all. The owner, John Wah, is exceptionally friendly, speaks excellent English, and operates a small souvenir shop and gem showroom on site. What's more, it has a laundry service.

KYOTO GUEST HOUSE
Map p92   Guesthouse $
☎ 2721 3574, 9077 8297; Flat A8, 15th fl, A Block, Chungking Mansions, 36-44 Nathan Rd; s with shared shower $90, s & tw with private shower from $140; MTR Tsim Sha Tsui (exit F)
This guesthouse, run by Mrs Kam, is very basic but comfortable.

GARDEN HOSTEL
Map p92   Hostel, Guesthouse $
☎ 2311 1183; fax 2721 2085; Flat F4, 3rd fl, Mirador Mansion, 58-62 Nathan Rd; dm $60, s & d with shower $200, d with shared shower $180; MTR Tsim Sha Tsui (exit D2)
It's on the scruffy side and the air-con seems to be rationed but this remains a good place for meeting other travellers. There are laundry facilities, the lockers are like Fort Knox and the staff speaks good English.

COSMIC GUEST HOUSE
Map p92   Hostel, Guesthouse $
☎ 2369 6669; www.cosmicguesthouse.com; Flats A1-A2, F1-F4, 12th fl, Mirador Mansion, 58-62 Nathan Rd; dm $60, s & d $166-200, large d $220-240; MTR Tsim Sha Tsui (exit D2)
This is a very clean and quiet guesthouse with big and bright rooms and a very helpful owner. The security is top grade and there's internet access in every room.

TRAVELLERS HOSTEL
Map p92   Hostel, Guesthouse $
☎ 2368 7710; mrspau@yahoo.com.hk; Flat A1-A4, 16th fl, A Block, Chungking Mansions, 36-44 Nathan Rd; dm $60-65, s/d with shared shower $80/100, d with private shower $120; MTR Tsim Sha Tsui (exit F)
A good place to meet fellow travellers in Chungking Mansions, it's popular despite being scruffy and grubby. Cooking facilities, cable TV, student discounts and internet access are all available.

TSIM SHA TSUI EAST & HUNG HOM

HOTEL INTER-CONTINENTAL HONG KONG Map p94   Luxury Hotel $$$$
☎ 2721 1211; www.hongkong-ic.intercontinental .com; 18 Salisbury Rd; s & d $2900-4390, ste from $5500; MTR Tsim Sha Tsui (exit F); 🖭
Occupying arguably the finest waterfront position in the territory, the Inter-Continental tilts at modernity while bowing to colonial traditions, such as a fleet of navy-blue Rolls Royces, doormen liveried in white and incessant brass polishing. The emphasis on service ensures a lot of return custom from rock stars and business VIPs. The restaurants – including the superb Nobu (p191) – are top class, and the Lobby Lounge bar has comfy armchairs and the best view in Hong Kong. Even if you don't stay here, drop by for a drink and the jaw-dropping evening Harbour vista.

ROYAL GARDEN HOTEL
Map p94   Luxury Hotel $$$$
☎ 2721 5215; www.rghk.com.hk; 69 Mody Rd, Tsim Sha Tsui East; s $2900-3900, d $3100-4100, ste from $4800; 🚌 5C or 8; 🖭
The 422-room Royal Garden, often overlooked, is one of the best-equipped hotels in Tsim Sha Tsui East and one of the ter-

SLEEPING KOWLOON

SLEEPING CHEAP IN CHUNGKING

Say 'budget accommodation' and 'Hong Kong' in the one breath and everyone thinks of Chungking Mansions (Map p92; 36-44 Nathan Rd, Tsim Sha Tsui; MTR Tsim Sha Tsui exit F), a place like no other. Still the cheapest place to stay in Hong Kong, it is the place to meet fellow travellers and soak up a unique souk-like atmosphere. This huge, ramshackle high-rise dump of a place in the heart of Tsim Sha Tsui caters for virtually all needs – from finding a bed and a cheap curry lunch to buying a backpack and getting your hair cut.

The sense of sleaze and the peculiar odours are not for everyone, nor are the lifts – they're like steel coffins on cables. Perhaps the best introduction to Chungking is Wong Kar Wai's cult film *Chungking Express* (1994), which captures all the squalor in a haunting series of stories.

The entrance to Chungking Mansions is via Chungking Arcade, a parade of shops that faces Nathan Rd. You will find lifts labelled A to E with hostels in each block listed. There are just two cramped and overworked lifts for each 17-storey block, and long queues form at 'rush hour'. Otherwise there're always the less-than-salubrious stairs. Be grateful for the stray cats as they keep the rats in check.

Despite the dilapidated appearance, most of the little guesthouses are OK – generally clean and often quite comfortable, though rooms are usually the size of cupboards. Standards do, however, vary significantly.

Bargaining for a bed or room is always possible, though you won't get very far in the high season. You can often negotiate a cheaper price if you stay more than, say, a week, but never try that on the first night – stay one night and find out how you like it before handing over more rent. Once you pay, there are usually no refunds.

The rooms will typically come with air-con and TV and, sometimes, phone. Many guesthouses can get you a Chinese visa quickly, most have internet access and some have a laundry service. Also, be prepared for varying levels of English fluency among guesthouse owners and concierges. Mobile-phone numbers have been included here as many of the guesthouse owners and managers engage in all sorts of other businesses and often lock their establishments during the day.

Chungking Mansions is not the only budget block in Tsim Sha Tsui. Mirador Mansion (Map p92; 58-62 Nathan Rd, Tsim Sha Tsui; MTR Tsim Sha Tsui), above an arcade of that name between Mody and Carnarvon Rds, is a scaled-down version of Chungking Mansions, but considerably cleaner and roomier. Much of the backpacker clientele has moved here in recent years, with the result that there can be heavy queues for the lifts during peak hours. Golden Crown Court (Map p92; 66-70 Nathan Rd, Tsim Sha Tsui; MTR Tsim Sha Tsui), opposite the southeast corner of Kowloon Park, has undergone a transformation in recent years and now offers a host of clean, smart guesthouses.

ritory's most attractive options. From the chic blonde-wood-and-chrome lobby and atrium to the rooftop sports complex (25m pool, putting green and tennis court with million-dollar views), the Royal Garden ticks all the boxes. The rooms are highly specced with plasma screens and large, comfortable beds. You should be able to secure large discounts off the quoted rates. Sabatini (p193), on the 3rd floor, is one of the best Italian restaurants in Hong Kong.

GRAND STANFORD INTER-CONTINENTAL
Map p94   Luxury Hotel $$$$

☎ 2721 5161; www.hongkong.intercontinental.com; 70 Mody Rd, Tsim Sha Tsui East; s & d $2700-3800, ste from $4800; 🚇 5C or 8

This large five-star palace is one of the nicest top-range hotels in Tsim Sha Tsui East and offers excellent discounts, depending on the season and the day of the week. Unfortunately part of its harbour view is marred by the unsightly Hung Hom Bypass.

KOWLOON SHANGRI-LA
Map p94   Luxury Hotel $$$$

☎ 2721 2111; www.shangri-la.com; 64 Mody Rd, Tsim Sha Tsui East; s & d $2650-4200, ste from $4300; 🚇 5C or 8

Almost (but not entirely) as swish as its sister hotel in Admiralty, the Island Shangri-La Hong Kong (p254), the views and its eight bars and restaurants, including the Japanese Nadaman (p193), are excellent. We love the enormous murals of imperial Chinese scenes in the lobby.

EMPIRE KOWLOON
Map p94   Hotel $$$

☎ 2685 3000; www.empirehotel.com.hk; 62 Kimberley Rd; s & d $1600-2400, ste from $3000; MTR Tsim Sha Tsui (exit B1); 🚇

This sister hotel of the Empire (p254) on Hong Kong Island offers modern, comfortable rooms and an excellent indoor atrium swimming pool and spa. It's an easy stroll from here to just about anywhere in Tsimsy. Check the website for promotions.

LUXE MANOR Map p94   Boutique Hotel $$$

☎ 3763 8888; www.theluxemanor.com; 39 Kimberley Rd; s & d $1600-2200, ste from $2600; MTR Tsim Sha Tsui (exit B1)

Tsim Sha Tsui's latest stab at a style-led boutique hotel is a tad self-conscious perhaps but works pretty well. The rather Dali-esque public areas hint at what's to come in the boldly done rooms, which are modern and loaded with technology, including wi-fi internet and in-room entertainment systems. Go elsewhere for food and drink, though. Discounts are frequently available off the published rates.

KIMBERLEY HOTEL Map p94   Hotel $$$

☎ 2723 3888; www.kimberleyhotel.com.hk; 28 Kimberley Rd; s & d $1500-2350, ste from $2800; MTR Tsim Sha Tsui (exit B1)

The Kimberley isn't a glamorous property, but it's one of the better midrange hotels in Tsim Sha Tsui. You'll find assured staff and large, chintz-free rooms with good facilities, including broadband. The hotel also has golf nets and a health spa. The lobby, a leafy and cool oasis up from the bustle, is on the 2nd floor. Summer rates are half the quoted ones.

PARK HOTEL Map p94   Hotel $$

☎ 2731 2100; www.parkhotel.com.hk; 61-65 Chatham Rd South; s $1100-1900, d $1200-2000, ste from $2600; MTR Tsim Sha Tsui (exit B2)

A vibrant renovation has given the spacious rooms here a welcoming feel, a sense backed up by the warm service on offer. Family suites are available from $4000, the history and science museums are just over the road, and the hustle of Granville Rd is a block away. Enter from Cameron Rd.

STANFORD HILLVIEW HOTEL
Map p94   Hotel $$

☎ 2722 7822; www.stanfordhillview.com; 13-17 Observatory Rd; s & d $1000-1680, ste from $2480; MTR Tsim Sha Tsui (exit B1)

Set back from Nathan Rd in a quiet, leafy little corner of Tsim Sha Tsui, the location is great just down the road from the food, fun and frolicking of Knutsford Tce. The rooms are forgettable but clean and well maintained. Enter from Knutsford Tce.

THE MINDEN Map p94   Hotel $$

☎ 2739 7777; www.theminden.com; 7 Minden Ave; s & d $900-1500, ste from $2500; MTR Tsim Sha Tsui (exit G)

This almost boutique 64-room hotel, tucked away on relatively quiet Minden Ave, is one of our favourites. It's central, being well located for both Tsim Sha Tsui and Tsim Sha Tsui East stations, and very reasonable value. The lobby is stuffed with Chinese antiques and paintings, while the rooms are serene and comfortable with all the amenities you'd expect, including broadband internet access included in the rates. The bar-cum-breakfast room Courtney's (p212) is a great place to go for a quiet alfresco drink.

PINNACLE APARTMENT
Map p94   Serviced Apartments $$

☎ 2734 8288; www.pinnacleapartment.com; 8 Minden Ave; per month 1-bedroom apt $16,500-26,000, 2-bedroom apt $24,000-38,000; MTR Tsim Sha Tsui (exit G)

This elegant block of serviced apartments, on lively Minden Ave in the heart of the Tsim Sha Tsui nightlife area, has four different size apartments available ranging in size from 47 to 90 sq metres. Some have harbour views. The staff here is delightful.

STAR GUEST HOUSE Map p94   Guesthouse $

☎ 2723 8951; www.starguesthouse.com; Flat B, 6th fl, 21 Cameron Rd; s/d with shared bathroom $250, s/d with private bathroom from $300/400, tr with private bathroom $500; MTR Tsim Sha Tsui

This excellent guesthouse and its sister property just up the road, the Lee Garden Guest House (Map p94; ☎ 2367 2284; charliechan@iname.com; 8th fl, D Block, 36 Cameron Rd), with a total of 45 rooms, are owned and run by the charismatic Charlie Chan, who can arrange most things for you, including China visas ($300) delivered in a day. Long-term stayers get good discounts. The pricier rooms have satellite TV, phone and broadband connection.

YAU MA TEI

Things start getting much cheaper up in this part of Kowloon. There are several cheap, basic hotels and a good range of guesthouses, many of them occupying New Lucky House (Map p97; 300-306 Nathan Rd, Yau Ma Tei), with its main entrance on Jordan Rd. Accommodation located here includes the Hakka's and Ocean guesthouses.

EATON HOTEL Map p97   Hotel $$$

☎ 2782 1818; www.eaton-hotel.com; 380 Nathan Rd, Yau Ma Tei; s & d $1950-4200, ste from $4000; MTR Jordan (exit B1)

Leave the chaos of Nathan Rd behind as you step into the Eaton's grand lobby. The rooms are large and comfortable, while downstairs the glass-fronted Planter's Bar (☎ 2710 1866; ⏰ 4pm-1am Mon-Thu, 5pm-2am Fri-Sat, happy hour 5-9pm) on the 4th floor sits next to an improbably pleasant and leafy courtyard given the proximity of all that traffic. Booking on the internet can halve the quoted rates. Enter the hotel from Pak Hoi St.

NATHAN HOTEL Map p97   Hotel $$

☎ 2388 5141; www.nathanhotel.com; 378 Nathan Rd, Yau Ma Tei; s & d $1080-1580, ste from $1880; MTR Jordan (exit B1)

The just-renovated Nathan Hotel is surprisingly quiet and pleasant; even the cheapest of its 166 rooms are spacious, clean and serene. It's in a good location, right near the Jordan MTR station and Temple St; we like the moustachioed and turbaned doorman. All in all good value for what you get. Enter from Pak Hoi St.

YMCA INTERNATIONAL HOUSE
Map p97   Hostel $, Guesthouse $$

☎ 2771 9111; www.intlhouse.ymca.org.hk; 23 Waterloo Rd, Yau Ma Tei; dm $230, s & d $880-1380, ste from $2080; weekly/monthly packages from $3400/9000; MTR Yau Ma Tei (exit A2)

Though a bit out of the way, the YMCA, with all the mod cons, is a steal for what it offers, so book well in advance. It is open to men and women. All rooms have a full range of facilities, including broadband.

CARITAS BIANCHI LODGE
Map p97   Guesthouse $$

☎ 2388 1111; cblresv@bianchi-lodge.com; 4 Cliff Rd, Yau Ma Tei; s/d/tr $650/740/920; MTR Yau Ma Tei (exit D)

This 90-room hotel-cum-guesthouse is run by a Catholic social-welfare organisation. Though it's just off Nathan Rd (and a goalie's throw from Yau Ma Tei MTR station), the rear rooms are very quiet and some have views onto King's Park. All rooms have private bathroom and breakfast is included. Promotional rates throughout the year bring rates even further down.

BOOTH LODGE Map p97   Guesthouse $$

☎ 2771 9266; http://boothlodge.salvation.org.hk; 11 Wing Sing Lane, Yau Ma Tei; s & d $620-1500; MTR Yau Ma Tei (exit D)

Run by the Salvation Army, this 53-room place is spartan and clean but comfortable, too. Promotional rates for standard singles and doubles are a rock-bottom $420 to $540. Rates include breakfast. Reception is on the 7th floor.

RENT-A-ROOM HONG KONG
Map p97   Guesthouse $

☎ 2366 3011, 9023 8022; www.rentaroomhk.com; Flat A, 2nd fl, Knight Garden, 7-8 Tak Hing St, Tsim Sha Tsui; dm $160, s/d/tr/q with shared bathroom from $310/370/490/620, with private bathroom from $360/460/720/920; MTR Jordan (exit E)

This fabulous place has 50 positively immaculate rooms in a block around the corner close to Jordan MTR station. Each room has TV, telephone (free local calls), high-speed internet access and a fridge.

HAKKA'S GUEST HOUSE
Map p97   Guesthouse $

☎ 2771 3656; fax 2770 1470; Flat L, 3rd fl, New Lucky House, 300 Nathan Rd, Yau Ma Tei; s $200-250, d $250-300, tr $300-350; MTR Jordan (exit B1)

This is the nicest guesthouse of those found in New Lucky House and each of the nine ultraclean guestrooms has a telephone, TV, air-con and shower. The affable and helpful owner, Kevin Koo, is a keen hiker and he will often invite guests out along with him for country walks on Sunday.

OCEAN GUEST HOUSE
Map p97   Guesthouse $

☎ 2385 0125; fax 2771 4083; Flat G, 11th fl, New Lucky House, 300 Nathan Rd, Yau Ma Tei; s/d $200/250; MTR Jordan (exit B)

All eight rooms in this rather comfy place have TV, telephone, air-con and private shower.

MONG KOK

LANGHAM PLACE HOTEL
Map p98   Hotel $$$$

☎ 3552 3388; www.langhamhotels.com/langham place/hongkong; 555 Shanghai St, Mong Kok; s & d $2600-3200, ste from $3900; MTR Mong Kok (exit C3); ♿

Peering out from one of the guestrooms of this colossal tower hotel, you'd never suspect for a moment that you were in Mong Kok. It's a triumph for the district. The special guestroom features include multifunction IP phones, DVD players, marble bathrooms with 'rain shower' plus bath, and room safes that can fit (and recharge) a laptop. Ming Court (p194) serves excellent dim sum, while the backyard offers alfresco snacking. Reception is on the 4th floor and the hotel is linked to the Langham Place Mall (p169). The 20m rooftop pool, gym and spa all command great views over Kowloon.

ROYAL PLAZA HOTEL Map p98 Hotel $$$

☎ 2928 8822; www.royalplaza.com.hk; 193 Prince Edward Rd West, Mong Kok; s $1800-3200, d $2000-3400, ste from $4800; KCR Mong Kok East Rail;

The plushness is a bit overdone, but the 671-room Royal Plaza is comfortable and central; the bird and flower markets are on the other side of Prince Edward Rd. The rooms come well equipped, even with heated no-steam bathroom mirrors, and some with kitchenettes. The large outdoor pool with underwater music is a lounge lizard's nirvana and some rooms have wireless internet access. The Mong Kok KCR station is accessible through the adjoining Grand Century Place shopping centre, making this a handy spot if you've business in the New Territories or China.

ANNE BLACK GUEST HOUSE

Map pp88–9 Guesthouse $$

☎ 2713 9211; www.ywca.org.hk; 5 Man Fuk Rd, Yau Ma Tei; s & d with shared bath $600, with private bathroom $900-1100, monthly packages from $6000; MTR Yau Ma Tei (exit D)

This YWCA-run guesthouse, which accommodates both women and men, is located near Pui Ching and Waterloo Rds in Mong Kok, behind and uphill from a petrol station. There are laundry facilities and a decent restaurant here. Conveniently almost half of the rooms are singles.

CARITAS LODGE Map pp88–9 Guesthouse $

☎ 2339 3777; www.caritas-chs.org.hk; 134 Boundary St, Mong Kok; s/d/tw $350/400/560, s weekly/monthly packages from $1960/5940, d from $2310/7140; KCR Mong Kok East Rail

With just 40 rooms, this place is a lot smaller and just as nice as its sister guesthouse, Caritas Bianchi Lodge, but it's a bit further afield. Still, you couldn't get much closer to the bird market, and the New Territories is (officially) just across the road. Breakfast is included in the price of the room.

NEW TERRITORIES

The New Territories does not offer travellers a tremendous choice of accommodation, but there are five official and independent hostels, most in the more remote parts of the region. Remember, too, that walkers and hikers can pitch a tent at any one of 28 New Territories camp sites managed by the Country & Marine Parks Authority (☎ 1823; www.afcd .gov.hk).

TAI MO SHAN

SZE LOK YUEN HOSTEL

Map pp50–1 Hostel $

☎ 2488 8188; www.yha.org.hk; Tai Mo Shan, New Territories; camping members/nonmembers $25/35, dm under/over 18 yr $35/50; 51

This 92-bed hostel, a few kilometres north of Tsuen Wan, is usually only open on Saturday and on the eve of public holidays but you may get lucky midweek (telephone the HKYHA in advance on ☎ 2788 1638). It's in the shadow of Hong Kong's highest peak and at this elevation it can get pretty chilly at night, so come prepared. There are cooking facilities, but you should buy food supplies while in Tsuen Wan as none are available at the hostel. Check-in is usually from 3pm to 11pm. To get here take bus 51 from the Tsuen Wan MTR station (exit A) and alight at Tai Mo Shan Rd. Follow Tai Mo Shan Rd for about 4km, pass the car park and turn onto a small concrete path on the right-hand side. This leads directly to the hostel.

TAI MEI TUK

BRADBURY LODGE Map pp50–1 Hostel $

☎ 2662 5123; www.yha.org.hk; 66 Tai Mei Tuk Rd; dm under/over 18 yr $35/55, d/q $240/280; 75K

Bradbury Lodge (not to be confused with Bradbury Hall in Sai Kung) is the HKYHA's flagship hostel in the New Territories. It has 72 beds and is open seven days a week year-round. Check-in is from 4pm to 11pm (from 3pm on Saturday). Bradbury Lodge is next to the northern tip of the Plover Cove Reservoir dam wall, a few hundred metres south of Tai Mei Tuk. Camping is not permitted. To get here take bus 75K (or 275R on Sundays or public holidays) from Tai Po Maket KCR East station to the Tei Mei Tuk bus terminus. The hostel can be found along the road leading to the reservoir.

SHA TIN

REGAL RIVERSIDE HOTEL
Map p124   Hotel $$$

☎ 2649 7878; www.regalriverside.com; 34-36 Tai Chung Kiu Rd; s & d $1500-2000, ste from $3800; KCR Sha Tin Wai East Rail; 🦽

This enormous hotel overlooks the Shing Mun River, northeast of Sha Tin town centre. It's not very appealing from the outside but inside the rooms are well decorated and surprisingly spacious for Hong Kong. Those overlooking the river have excellent views. The hotel also has five restaurants, two bars, and a pleasant outdoor swimming pool on a terrace. It's worth calling to check prices as promotions can cut quoted rates in half.

ASCENSION HOUSE Map p124   Hotel $

☎ 2691 4196; www.achouse.com; 33 Tao Fong Shan Rd; dm $125; KCR Sha Tin East Rail

This cosy 11-bed place, affiliated with the Lutheran Church, is one of the best deals in Hong Kong as the price of a bed includes free laundry service and three meals. It's set on a peaceful hill side above the town. To get here, take the KCR East Rail to Sha Tin station, leave via exit B and walk down the ramp, passing a series of old village houses on the left. To the left of these houses is a set of steps signposted 'To Fung Shan'. Go up these, follow the path and when you come to a roundabout, go along the uphill road – signposted 'To Pak Lok Path' – to your right. After about 150m you'll come to a small staircase and a sign pointing the way to Ascension House on the right. When you reach the fork in the path and the Tao Fong Shan Christian Centre, bear to the right and you'll soon come to more steps leading up to Ascension House. The walk should take between 15 and 20 minutes. A taxi from the station in Sha Tin will cost around $20.

SAI KUNG PENINSULA

BRADBURY HALL Map pp50–1   Hostel $

☎ 2328 2458; www.yha.org.hk; Chek Keng, Sai Kung; camping members/nonmembers $25/35; dm members under/over 18 yr $35/50; 🚌 94

This 90-bed HKYHA hostel is right on the harbour facing Chek Keng pier. It's always open on the weekend and on the eve of public holidays but is often open on weekdays, too; telephone the HKYHA on ☎ 2788

1638 in advance to check. To reach Chek Keng by bus from Sai Kung town, catch bus 94 headed for Wong Shek and alight at Pak Tam Au (it's the fourth bus stop after the entrance to Sai Kung Country Park near the top of a hill). Take the footpath at the side of the road heading east and walk for about half an hour to Chek Keng. Bradbury Hall is another 10 minutes to the northeast.

PAK SHA O HOSTEL Map pp50–1   Hostel $

☎ 2328 2327; www.yha.org.hk; Hoi Ha Rd, Sai Kung; camping members/nonmembers $25/35, dm members under/over 18 yr $35/50; 🚌 94

This large HKYHA hostel with 112 beds is southwest of Hoi Ha Bay and the marine park. Like Bradbury Hall, it is not necessarily open every weekday. Call the HKYHA on ☎ 2788 1638 for details. To reach the hostel, from Sai Kung town take green minibus 7 to Hoi Ha alighting at the hostel shortly before the turn-off to Pak Sha O village. A taxi from Sai Kung will cost around $105.

OUTLYING ISLANDS

There are not many hotels per se on the Outlying Islands, though you'll find one each on Lamma and Cheung Chau and several on Lantau. There are guesthouses on these three islands as well.

During the warmer months and on the weekends throughout most of the year, estate agencies set up booking kiosks for rental apartments and holiday villas near the ferry piers on Cheung Chau and at Mui Wo (Silvermine Bay) on Lantau.

The HKYHA has two hostels on Lantau, and the Country & Marine Parks Authority (☎ 1823; www.afcd.gov.hk) maintains 10 basic camp sites for hikers along the Lantau Trail and a single one on Tung Lung Chau.

LAMMA

CONCERTO INN Map p132   Hotel $$

☎ 2982 1668; www.concertoinn.com.hk; 28 Hung Shing Yeh Beach, Hung Shing Yeh; s & d Sun-Fri $480-630, tr & q $730, s & d Sat & public holidays $780-930, tr & q $1060; ⚓ Lamma (Yung Shue Wan)

This cheerful beach-front hotel, southeast of Yung Shue Wan, is quite some distance from the action, so you should stay here only if you really want to get away from it all. There's also a decent beach-side café-restaurant.

MAN LAI WAH HOTEL Map p132 Guesthouse $
☎ 2982 0220; Manlaiwahhotel@yahoo.com; 2 Po Wah Garden, Yung Shue Wan; r Mon-Fri $300-350, Sat & Sun $500; 🛳 Lamma (Yung Shue Wan)
This eight-room hotel (or, rather, guesthouse) greets you as you get off the ferry and begin to walk up Main St. All rooms have air-con and private shower and some have little balconies.

JACKSON PROPERTY AGENCY
Map p132   Holiday Homes $
☎ 2982 0606, 9055 3288; fax 2982 0636; 15 Main St, Yung Shue Wan; 🛳 Lamma (Yung Shue Wan)
This property agency has studios and apartments for rent on Lamma. All of them have TV, private bathroom, microwave and fridge; some also offer sea views. Rooms start at $300 per night for two people from Sunday to Friday and go up to between $450 and $550 on Saturday.

BALI HOLIDAY RESORT
Map p132   Holiday Homes $
☎ 2982 4580; fax 2982 1044; 8 Main St, Yung Shue Wan; s/d Sun-Fri $280/380, Sat $560/760; 🛳 Lamma (Yung Shue Wan)
An agency rather than a resort as such, Bali Holiday Resort has about 30 studios and apartments sprinkled around the island. All have TV, fridge and air-con and some have sea views.

CHEUNG CHAU
Cheung Chau is not particularly well set up for overnighters. Depending on the day of the week and the season, up to half a dozen booths just opposite the ferry pier and another couple north along Praya St rent out studios and apartments. There is also the Warwick Hotel on Tung Wan Beach.

WARWICK HOTEL Map p143   Hotel $$
☎ 2981 0081; www.warwickhotel.com.hk; Cheung Chau Sports Rd, Tung Wan Beach; s & d with mountain/sea view Mon-Fri $740/840, Sat & Sun $1090/1190, ste from $1340/1890, weekly/monthly packages from $4300/16,800; 🛳 Cheung Chau
This six-storey, 71-room carbuncle on the butt of Tung Wan Beach is the only game in town, but it does offer wonderful views across the sea to Lamma and Hong Kong

Islands. Ignore the rack rates; heavy discounts are available here, so call to check.

CHEUNG CHAU B&B Map p143 Guesthouse $
☎ 2986 9990; www.bbcheungchau.com.hk; 12-14 Tung Wan Rd; s & d Sun-Thu $390/590, Fri $490/690, Sat $690/890; 🛳 Cheung Chau
This B&B offers an alternative to the island's only hotel and the rooms offered by kiosks. The 16 rooms are very well decorated with private bathrooms, although some are rather compact so you might want to look first. There's a lovely little terrace on the roof from where you can catch both the sunset and the sunrise.

CHEUNG CHAU ACCOMMODATION KIOSKS Map p143   Holiday Homes $
Cheung Chau Ferry Pier; 🛳 Cheung Chau
Agents with booking kiosks on the Cheung Chau *praya* (waterfront promenade) include Bela Vista Miami Resort (☎ 2981 7299; www.miamicheungchau.com.hk), Holiday Resort (☎ 2981 0093) and Sea View Holiday Flats (☎ 2986 9368), but unless you have a smattering of Cantonese or a Chinese friend in tow, you may have difficulty getting what you want at a fair price (though there are photo albums illustrating what's on offer both outside and in). Expect to pay $200 to $250 a night for a studio accommodating two people from Sunday to Friday, and $300 to $500 on Saturday.

LANTAU
As on Lamma and Cheung Chau during the summer, and on weekends the rest of the year, you can rent holiday rooms and apartments from kiosks set up at the Mui Wo ferry pier.

The HKYHA has two hostels on Lantau, one a stone's throw from the Tian Tan Buddha in Ngong Ping and the other in a remote area of the Chi Ma Wan Peninsula. The hostels are open to HKYHA/HI cardholders only, but membership is available if you pay the nonmember's rate for six nights here or at other HKYHA hostels.

You can also find another three decent accommodation options along Silvermine Bay Beach.

REGAL AIRPORT HOTEL Map p136 Hotel $$$
☎ 2286 8888; www.regalairport.com; 9 Cheong Tat Rd, Hong Kong International Airport; s & d $2400-4500, ste from $8000; MTR Airport Express; 🛳

A simple undercover shuffle from the airport terminal is this stylish hotel with more than 1100 sleek and easily accessible rooms, many with futuristic runway views. There's a splashy indoor/outdoor pool complex, half a dozen restaurants and fun games rooms (one for adults, one for kids). Soundproofing ensures the only noise is that of your own making. Discounts to the above rates can often be found on the hotel's website. Rooms also available for day use (four hours and more between 8am and 9pm) cost from $600.

SILVERMINE BEACH HOTEL
Map p139   Hotel $$
☎ 2984 8295; www.resort.com.hk; Tung Wan Tau Rd, Silvermine Bay Beach; s & d $980-1480, monthly packages from $7288; 🚇 Lantau
This 128-room hotel has rooms that look out to the hills, sideways to the bay and directly onto the bay. A good-value barbecue buffet is held in the coffee shop and Chinese restaurant on Saturday evenings, and there's an attractive pool. Eschew the rooms in the South Wing for those in the superior New Wing. Rates are negotiable, depending on the day of the week and the season.

MUI WO INN Map p139   Hotel $$
☎ 2984 7225; fax 2984 1916; Tung Wan Tau Rd, Silvermine Bay Beach; s & d Sun-Fri $450, Sat $750; 🚇 Lantau
This is the last hotel on the beach and can be identified by the ring of faux-classical statues at the front. At the time of writing the hotel had been reduced in size to nine rooms (some in the main building and a few out the back) and these were being renovated. Those completed were tastefully decorated and inviting. It's a friendly place to stay and rates include breakfast.

LONG COAST SEASPORTS
Map p136   Guesthouse $
☎ 2980 3222; www.longcoast.hk; 29 Lower Cheung Sha Village; r winter/summer Sun-Thu $400/500, Fri & Sat $480/600, 20% weekly discounts; 🚌 1, 2, 3M, 4 or A35
This water-sports centre (see p138), opened in 2004, offers accommodation in four double rooms with private bathrooms. The rooms are simple but clean, air-conditioned, have wi-fi internet access and two have sea views. This is a great deal for

water-sports fans as the rooms are 'free' when you purchase an activity voucher at the quoted rates. The voucher can then be used for sports and beach equipment. Breakfast is also included.

MUI WO ACCOMMODATION KIOSKS
Map p139   Holiday Homes $
Mui Wo Ferry Pier; 🚇 Lantau
There are several kiosks run by different outfits (☎ 2984 8982, 2984 2282) on the ferry pier that let out rooms and apartments on Lantau and have photos of them on display. Expect to pay $150 on weekdays and $250 on the weekend for a double room or studio. Not all the places are in Mui Wo (ie within walking distance of the ferry pier); many are along Cheung Sha Beach and in Pui O village.

JOCKEY CLUB MONG TUNG WAN
HOSTEL Map p136   Hostel $
☎ 2984 1389; www.yha.org.hk; Mong Tung Wan; camping members/nonmembers $25/35, dm members under/over 18 yr $35/50, nonmembers +$30; 🚌 1, 2, 3M, 4 or A35
This tranquil property, along the waterfront on the southeastern side of the Chi Ma Wan Peninsula, is jointly operated by the HKYHA and the Hong Kong Jockey Club. In the past it's been open on the weekend and on the eve of public holidays only, so telephone the HKYHA on ☎ 2788 1638 in advance for advice. From Mui Wo, take bus 1 or 4 (or bus A35 from Hong Kong International Airport) and jump out at Pui O. Follow the footpath across the fields from the bus stop and continue along Chi Ma Wan Rd until it leaves the sea edge. At a sharp bend in the road at Ham Tin, turn right onto the footpath by the sea and follow it to the hostel – about a 45-minute walk. Alternatively, you can take a ferry to Cheung Chau and hire a sampan (this should cost about $150, it will be more in the evening) to the jetty at Mong Tung Wan.

HONGKONG BANK FOUNDATION SG
DAVIS HOSTEL Map p136   Hostel $
☎ 2985 5610; www.yha.org.hk; Ngong Ping; camping members/nonmembers $25/35, dm members under/over 18 yr $35/50, nonmembers +$30; 🚌 2, 21 or 23
This 46-bed hostel (open daily) is a 10-minute walk from the bus stop near the Tian Tan Buddha statue in Ngong Ping and

is the ideal place to stay if you want to watch the sun rise at nearby Lantau Peak. Check-in is from 4pm to 11pm (from 3pm on Saturday). From the Ngong Ping bus terminus, take the paved path to your left as you face the Tian Tan Buddha, pass the public toilets on your right and the Lantau Tea Garden on your left and follow the signs to the maze-like steps going up to the hostel. If you visit in winter, be sure to bring warm clothing for the evenings and early mornings.

TRANSPORT

Amazingly well connected, Hong Kong's sea, air, road and rail links make getting there and away easy and largely stress free. Its excellent, modern infrastructure makes it a breeze to get around within the Special Administrative Region (SAR). Flights, tours and rail tickets can be booked online at www.lonelyplanet.com/travel_services.

AIR

Hong Kong's importance as an international hub for China and much of East and Southeast Asia ensures excellent international air connections, and competition keeps the fares relatively low (to most places except China).

A proliferation of budget airlines in recent years has only increased competition and downward pressure on many shorter haul fares in particular. Specific information on air travel to and from Macau and China can be found on p348 and p284, respectively.

Tickets are normally issued the day after booking, but you can usually pick up really cheap tickets (actually group fares) at the airport from the 'tour leader' just before the flight. Check these tickets carefully as there may be errors (eg the return portion of the ticket being valid for only 60 days from when you paid for a ticket valid for six months).

You can generally get a good idea of what fares are available at the moment by looking in the classified section of the *South China Morning Post*. Otherwise try any of the following websites:

Bargain Holidays (www.bargainholidays.com)

ebookers (www.ebookers.com)

Last Minute (www.lastminute.com)

Skyscanner (www.skyscanner.net)

Travelocity (www.travelocity.com)

You'll find travel agencies everywhere in Hong Kong but the following are among the most reliable and offer the best deals on air tickets:

Aero International (Map p56; ☎ 2545 6669, 2543 3800; www.ticketscentre.com; Room 603, 6th fl, Cheung's Bldg, 1-3 Wing Lok St, Sheung Wan; ☾ 9.15am-5.30pm Mon-Fri, 9.15am-1pm Sat) Convenient to Central; enter from Wing Wo St.

Concorde Travel (Map p68; ☎ 2526 3391; www.concorde-travel.com; 1st fl, Galuxe Bldg, 8-10 On Lan St, Central; ☾ 9.30am-5.30pm Mon-Fri, 9am-1pm Sat) This is a long-established and highly dependable agency owned and operated by expats.

Natoria Travel (Map p68; ☎ 2810 1681; fax 2810 8190; Room 2207, Melbourne Plaza, 33 Queen's Rd Central; ☾ 9am-7pm Mon-Fri, 9am-4pm Sat) Readers have long used and recommended this place.

Phoenix Services Agency (Map p94; ☎ 2722 7378; www.statravel.hk; Room 1404, 14th fl, Austin Tower, 22-26 Austin Ave, Tsim Sha Tsui; ☾ 9am-6pm Mon-Fri, 9am-1pm Sat) Phoenix is one of the best places in Hong Kong to buy air tickets, get China visas and seek travel advice. It is also the agent for student and discount group STA Travel in Hong Kong.

Traveller Services (Map p92; ☎ 2375 2222; www.taketraveller.com; 1813 Miramar Tower, 132 Nathan Rd, Tsim Sha Tsui; ☾ 9am-6pm Mon-Fri, 9am-1pm Sat) Very reliable for good-value air tickets.

Airlines

More than 70 international airlines operate between Hong Kong International Airport and some 130 destinations around the world. You can check flight schedules and real-time flight information for both Macau and Hong Kong airports at www.hktime table.com.

Regional short-haul operators flying to Hong Kong include Singapore-based Jetstar (www.jetstar.com), which flies to Jakarta and Singapore.

Among the major airlines serving Hong Kong are the following:

Air New Zealand (NZ; Map p56; ☎ 2862 8988; www.airnewzealand.com.hk; Ste 1701, 17th fl, Jardine House, 1 Connaught Pl, Central)

British Airways (BA; Map p56; ☎ 2822 9000; 24th fl, Jardine House, 1 Connaught Pl, Central)

China Eastern/China Southern Airlines (MU/CZ; Map p56; ☎ 2861 0322; 4th fl, CNAC Group Bldg, 10 Queen's Rd Central)

Dragonair (KA; Map p56; ☎ 3193 3888; Room 4611, Cosco Tower, 183 Queen's Rd Central)

Hong Kong Express (UO; Map p70; ☎ 3152 3777; www .hongkongexpress.com; Room 1417, 14/F China Merchants Tower, Shun Tak Centre, 200 Connaught Rd, Central)

Northwest Airlines (NW; Map p56; ☎ 2810 4288; Room 1908, 19th fl, Cosco Tower, 183 Queen's Rd Central)

Qantas Airways (QF; Map p56; ☎ 2822 9000; 24th fl, Jardine House, 1 Connaught Pl, Central)

Singapore Airlines (SQ; Map p63; ☎ 2520 2233; 17th fl, United Centre, 95 Queensway, Admiralty)

Virgin Atlantic Airways (VS; Map p56; ☎ 2532 6060; 8th fl, Alexandra House, 16-20 Chater Rd, Central)

Airport

Hong Kong International Airport (Map p136; ☎ 2181 0000; www.hkairport.com), which was the world's largest civil engineering project when it opened in mid-1998, is on Chek Lap Kok, a largely man-made island off the northern coast of Lantau. It is connected to the mainland by several spans. Among them is the 2.2km-long Tsing Ma Bridge, which is one of the world's largest suspension bridges and is capable of supporting both road and rail transport, including the 34km-long Airport Express high-speed train from Hong Kong Island to Chek Lap Kok via Kowloon.

The futuristic passenger terminal, designed by British architect Sir Norman Foster, consists of eight levels, with check-in on level seven, departures on level six and arrivals on level five. Outlets (including bank branches, moneychangers and five ATMs) total 150, and there are more than 30 cafés, restaurants and bars, and more than 280 check-in counters.

The Hong Kong Tourism Board (HKTB; ☎ 2508 1234; www.discoverhongkong.com) maintains information centres on level five. On the same level you'll also find branches of China Travel Service (CTS; ☎ 2261 2472, 2261 2062; www.chinatravel1 .com; 🕙 8.45am-10pm), which can issue China visas, and counters run by the Hong Kong Hotels Association (HKHA; ☎ 2383 8380, 2769 8822; www .hkha.org; 🕙 6am-midnight); for details see p250. Be advised that the HKHA deals with midrange and top-end hotels only and does not handle hostels, guesthouses or other budget accommodation.

If you are booked on a scheduled (but *not* a charter) flight and are taking the Airport Express to the airport, most airlines allow you to check in your bags and receive your boarding pass a day ahead of your flight at the in-town check-in counters at the Hong Kong Island or Kowloon Airport Express stations between 5.30am and 12.30am. You are required, however, to check yourself in at least 90 minutes before your flight. Some airlines, including Cathay Pacific Airways, China Airlines and Thai Airways, allow check-in a

---

CLIMATE CHANGE & TRAVEL

Climate change is a serious threat to the ecosystems that humans rely upon, and air travel is the fastest-growing contributor to the problem. Lonely Planet regards travel, overall, as a global benefit, but believes we all have a responsibility to limit our personal impact on global warming.

Flying & Climate Change

Pretty much every form of motor transport generates CO_2 (the main cause of human-induced climate change) but planes are far and away the worst offenders, not just because of the sheer distances they allow us to travel, but because they release greenhouse gases high into the atmosphere. The statistics are frightening: two people taking a return flight between Europe and the US will contribute as much to climate change as an average household's gas and electricity consumption over a whole year.

Carbon Offset Schemes

Climatecare.org and other websites use 'carbon calculators' that allow travellers to offset the greenhouse gases they are responsible for with contributions to energy-saving projects and other climate-friendly initiatives in the developing world – including projects in India, Honduras, Kazakhstan and Uganda.

Lonely Planet, together with Rough Guides and other concerned partners in the travel industry, supports the carbon offset scheme run by climatecare.org. Lonely Planet offsets all of its staff and author travel.

For more information check out our website: www.lonelyplanet.com.

full day before your flight. See the airport's website for details.

DEPARTURE TAX
Hong Kong's airport departure tax – $120 for everyone over the age of 12 – is always included in the price of the ticket. Those travelling to Macau by helicopter (see p348) must pay the same amount.

To/From the Airport
The Airport Express line of the Mass Transit Railway (MTR) is the fastest – and most expensive – way to get to and from Hong Kong International Airport. A gaggle of much cheaper buses connects the airport with Lantau, the New Territories, Kowloon and Hong Kong Island.

AIRPORT EXPRESS
Airport Express (AEL; ☎ 2881 8888; www.mtr.com.hk) has trains departing from Hong Kong station in Central every 10 to 12 minutes from 5.50am to 12.48am, calling at Kowloon and Tsing Yi stations before arriving at Airport station. The last train leaves the airport for all three stations at 12.48am. Running at speeds of up to 135km/h, trains make the journey from Central/Kowloon/Tsing Yi in only 23/20/12 minutes.

From Central/Kowloon/Tsing Yi one-way adult fares are $100/90/60, with children three to 11 years paying half-fare. Adult return fares, valid for a month, are $180/160/110. A same-day return is equivalent to a one-way fare.

Airport Express has two shuttle buses on Hong Kong Island (H1 and H2) and five in Kowloon (K1 to K5), with free transfers for passengers between Hong Kong and Kowloon stations and major hotels. The buses run every 12 to 24 minutes between 6.20am and 11.10pm. Schedules and routes are available at Airport Express and MTR stations and on the Airport Express website.

BOAT
High-speed ferries run by New World First Ferry Services (☎ 2131 8181; www.nwff.com.hk) link Tung Chung New Development ferry pier opposite the airport (and accessible from the terminal on bus S56) with Tuen Mun in the New Territories. Ferries depart from Tuen Mun every 20 to 30 minutes between 5.40am and 11pm; the first ferry from Tung Chung pier leaves at 6am and the last at 11.20pm and the journey takes 18 minutes (one way adult/child and senior $15/10).

LONG HAUL, LOW PRICE
Hong Kong's first long-haul budget airline Oasis (www.oasishongkong.com) launched in late 2006 flying to London Gatwick and Vancouver, with plans to expand its network by the time you read this (it hopes) to Berlin, Oakland near San Francisco and Chicago.

Tickets are sold through the company website and travel agents. One-way economy fares for the Hong Kong–London route start at UK£75 or $1000 (excluding taxes and charges) for at least 10% of the seats available and include hot meals and in-flight entertainment. Business-class fares start at UK£470 or $6600 (excluding taxes and charges). Return economy-class fares for Vancouver start at $3980 (excluding taxes and charges) for at least 10% of the seats available. Return business-class fares start at $18,000 (excluding taxes and charges).

A fast ferry service called the Skypier (☎ 2307 0880) links Hong Kong airport with five Pearl River Delta destinations: Shekou near Shenzhen, Shenzhen Fuyong, Humen in Dongguan, Zhongshan and Macau.

One of the companies operating from the Skypier is Turbojet Sea Express (☎ 2859 3333; www .turbojetseaexpress.com.hk), sailing four times daily to Macau ($180) and at least seven times daily to Shenzhen ($200).

The service enables travellers to board ferries directly without clearing Hong Kong customs and immigration. Book a ticket prior to boarding from the ticketing desks located in the transfer area on Arrivals Level 5 close to the immigration counters. An air-side bus then takes you to the ferry terminal. A planned expansion of the service by late 2008 should mean more Pearl River Delta destinations and a dedicated MTR station on the airport express line.

BUS
Most major areas of Hong Kong Island, Kowloon, the New Territories and Lantau are connected to the airport by buses, of which there is a huge choice. The buses are run by quite a few different companies.

The most useful for travellers are the Citybus 'airbuses' A11 ($40) and A12 ($45), which go to or near the major hotel and guesthouse areas on Hong Kong Island, and the A21 ($33), which serves similar areas in Kowloon. These buses have plenty of room for luggage, and announcements are usually made in English, Cantonese and Mandarin notifying passengers of hotels at each stop. But they are also the most expensive; there are cheaper options, such as taking 'external' bus E11 ($21) to Hong Kong Island or 'shuttle' bus S1 ($3.50) to Tung Chung and then the MTR to Kowloon or Central. There are also quite a few night (designated 'N') buses costing from $20 to $31.

Bus drivers in Hong Kong do not give change, but it is available at the ground transportation centre at the airport, as are Octopus cards (p283). Normal returns are double the one-way fare. Unless otherwise stated, children aged between three and 11 and seniors over 65 pay half-fare.

Some of the New Territories buses terminate at MTR stations, from where you can reach destinations in Kowloon and on Hong Kong Island at a lower cost than the more direct buses. You can also reach Shenzhen and other points in southern China directly from the airport (p284).

The following lists give the bus numbers, service providers, routes, one-way fares and frequencies for the airport buses most useful for visitors. For full route details see www.cityb us.com.hk.

Buses to Hong Kong Island:

A11 (Citybus) Sheung Wan, Central, Admiralty, Wan Chai, Causeway Bay, North Point Ferry pier; $40; every 15 to 30 minutes from 6.10am to midnight.

A12 (Citybus) Tsing Ma, Kowloon Station, Wan Chai, North Point, Quarry Bay, Sai Wan Ho, Shau Kei Wan, Chai Wan, Siu Sai Wan; $45; every 20 to 30 minutes from 6am to 12.10am.

E11 (Citybus) Tung Chung, Tsing Ma, Kowloon Station, Sheung Wan, Central, Admiralty, Wan Chai, Causeway Bay, Tin Hau MTR; $21; every 15 to 20 minutes from 5.20am to midnight.

N11 (Citybus) Same routing as E11; $31; every 30 minutes from 12.50am to 4.50am.

Buses to Kowloon:

A21 (Citybus) Sham Shui Po, Mong Kok, Yau Ma Tei, Jordan, Tsim Sha Tsui MTR, Tsim Sha Tsui East, Hung Hom KCR; $33; every 10 to 15 minutes from 6am to midnight.

N21 (Citybus) Tung Chung, Mei Foo Sun Chuen, Lai Chi Kok MTR, Mong Kok, Tsim Sha Tsui Star Ferry pier; $23; every 20 minutes from 12.20am to 5am.

Buses to Lantau:

A35 (New Lantao) Tong Fuk village, Mui Wo; $14 ($23 on Sunday and public holidays); every 40 to 60 minutes from 6.30am to 12.25am.

DB02R (Discovery Bay Transportation Services) Discovery Bay; $28; every 30 minutes, 24 hours.

N35 (New Lantao) Same routing as A35; $20 ($30 on Sunday and public holidays); departures at 1.30am and 4am.

S1 (Citybus) Tung Chung MTR; $3.50; every six to 10 minutes from 5.30am to midnight.

S56 (Citybus) Tung Chung New Development pier (ferries to/from Tuen Mun); $3.50; every 30 minutes from 9am to 10.40pm.

Buses to the New Territories:

A31 (KMB) Tsing Yi, Kwai Chung, Tsuen Wan MTR; $17; every 15 to 20 minutes from 6am to midnight.

N31 (KMB) Same routing as A31; $20; every 20 to 30 minutes from 12.20am to 5.05am.

TAXI

In addition to the fares listed, passengers taking a taxi to or from the airport at Chek Lap Kok are required to pay the $30 toll for using the Lantau Link road and bridge network in both directions.

Destination	Fare ($)
Aberdeen (Hong Kong Island)	380
Causeway Bay (Hong Kong Island)	340
Central (Hong Kong Island)	340
Kwun Tong MTR (Kowloon)	320
Mui Wo (Lantau)	130
Sai Kung (New Territories)	355-370
Sha Tin (New Territories)	300
Tsim Sha Tsui Star Ferry (Kowloon)	270
Tsuen Wan (New Territories)	200-235
Tung Chung (Lantau)	30-40

There are limousine service counters in the arrivals hall and at the ground transportation centre, including Parklane Limousine Service (☎ 2261 0303; www.hongkonglimo.com) and Intercontinental Hire Cars (☎ 3193 9333; www.trans-island.com.hk). In a car seating up to four people, expect to pay from $450 to destinations in urban Kowloon and from $550 to Hong Kong Island.

BICYCLE

Cycling in urbanised Kowloon or Hong Kong Island would be suicide, but in the quiet areas of the islands (including southern Hong Kong Island) or the New Territories, a bike can be a lovely way to get around. It's not really a form of transport, though – the hilly terrain will slow you down (unless you're mountain biking) – but more recreational. Be advised that bicycle-rental shops and kiosks tend to run

FERRY ANGRY

The Star Ferry is an institution dear to the hearts of its passengers. Mess with it and you risk getting Hong Kong's ordinarily phlegmatic folk worked up into a fury.

Take 1966, for example, when Communist China was in the grip of the Cultural Revolution. Agitators used the ferry company's fare increase of 5c as a pretext for fomenting violent demonstrations. The disturbances continued for almost a year.

More recently the demolition of the rather functional, but nonetheless iconic, 1950s Central Ferry pier in 2006 to make way for new development and land reclamation provoked more fury. In the days running up to the pier's demolition, thousands of emotional Hong Kong residents arrived to post banners and plead for the conservation of a rare piece of Hong Kong's historical architecture. Their efforts were in vain.

Mention of the Star Ferry service between Pedder's Wharf (now reclaimed land) and Tsim Sha Tsui first appeared in an 1888 newspaper article. At that time, boats sailed 'every 40 minutes to one hour during all hours of the day' except on Monday and Friday, when they were billeted for coal delivery. Service has continued ever since, with the only major suspension occurring during WWII. The Star Ferry was something of a war hero: during the Japanese invasion, boats were used to evacuate refugees and Allied troops from the Kowloon peninsula before the service was suspended for more than four years.

Until the Cross-Harbour Tunnel opened in 1978 and the first line of the MTR two years later, the Star Ferry was the only way to cross the harbour. At rush hour long queues of commuters would back up as far as the General Post Office on the Hong Kong Island side and Star House in Kowloon.

out of bikes early on weekends if the weather is good (see p224).

BOAT

Despite Hong Kong's comprehensive road and rail public-transport system, the territory still relies very much on ferries to get across the harbour and to reach the Outlying Islands.

Hong Kong's cross-harbour ferries are faster and cheaper than buses and the MTR. They're also great fun and afford stunning views. Since the opening of the Lantau Link, ferries are not the only way to reach Lantau, but for the other Outlying Islands, they remain the only game in town.

Smoking is prohibited on all ferries inside or out; the fine is a hefty $5000. With the exception of Star Ferry services from Central to Hung Hom and Wan Chai to Hung Hom, the cross-harbour ferries ban the transport of bicycles. You can, however, take bicycles on the ordinary ferries to the Outlying Islands.

Star Ferry

You can't say you've 'done' Hong Kong until you've taken a ride on a Star Ferry (☎ 2367 7065; www.starferry.com.hk), that wonderful fleet of a dozen electric-diesel vessels with names like *Morning Star, Celestial Star* and *Twinkling Star*. Try to take your first trip on a clear night from Kowloon to Central. It's not half as dramatic in the opposite direction.

The Star Ferry operates on four routes, but the most popular one is the run between Tsim Sha Tsui and Central (pier 7). The coin-operated turnstiles do not give change, but you can get it from the ticket window (unnecessary, of course, if you're carrying an Octopus card).

For details on the special four-day tourist pass valid on trams and the Star Ferry, see p283.

Star Ferry routes:

Central (Star Ferry pier 7)–Tsim Sha Tsui Adult lower/upper deck $1.70/2.20, child $1.20/1.30, seniors free; seven minutes; every six to 12 minutes from 6.30am to 11.30pm.

Central (Star Ferry pier 8)–Hung Hom Adult/child $5.30/2.70, seniors free; 15 minutes; every 15 to 20 minutes from 7am to 7.20pm Monday to Friday, every 20 minutes from 7am to 7pm Saturday and Sunday.

Wan Chai–Hung Hom Adult/child $5.30/2.70, seniors free; 10 minutes; every 15 to 20 minutes from 7am to 8pm Monday to Friday, every 20 to 22 minutes from 7.08am to 7.10pm Saturday and Sunday.

Wan Chai–Tsim Sha Tsui Adult/child $2.20/1.30, seniors free; eight minutes; every eight to 20 minutes from 7.30am to 11pm Monday to Saturday, every 12 to 20 minutes from 7.40am to 11pm Sunday.

Other Cross-Harbour Ferries

Two other ferry companies operate cross-harbour ferries: New World First Ferry (☎ 2131 8181; www.nwff.com.hk) has ferries from North Point to Hung Hom and Kowloon City; and the Fortune

Ferry Co (☎ 2994 8155) has a service linking North Point and Kwun Tong.

North Point–Hung Hom Adult $4.50, child and senior $2.30; seven minutes; every 20 minutes from 7.20am to 7.20pm.

North Point–Kowloon City Adult $4.50, child and senior $2.30; 11 minutes; every 20 minutes from 7.10am to 7.30pm.

North Point–Kwun Tong Adult $5, child and senior $2.50; 12 minutes; every 30 minutes from 7am to 7.30pm.

New Territories Ferries
SAI KUNG PENINSULA & TAP MUN CHAU

Boats operated by the Tsui Wah Ferry Service (☎ 2527 2513, 2272 2022; www.traway.com.hk) link the east-central New Territories near Chinese University with the Sai Kung Peninsula and Tap Mun Chau. From the pier at Ma Liu Shui, ferries cruise through Tolo Harbour to Tap Mun Chau and back, calling at various villages on the Sai Kung Peninsula both outbound and inbound.

Ferries leave Ma Liu Shui at 8.30am and 3pm daily, arriving at Tap Mun Chau at 10am and 4.20pm respectively, from where they continue on to Ko Lau Wan, Chek Keng and Wong Shek (weekdays/weekend $16/25). They leave for Ma Liu Shui at 11.10am and 5.30pm. On Saturday, Sunday and public holidays an extra ferry leaves Ma Liu Shui at 12.30pm, arriving and departing from Tap Mun Chau at 1.45pm.

An easier – and faster – way to reach Tap Mun Chau, with many more departures, is by kaido (p277) from Wong Shek pier, which is the last stop on bus 94 from Sai Kung town. The kaidos, operated by Tsui Wah Ferry Service, run about once every two hours (there's a total of six sailings, with two callings at Chek Keng) from 8.30am to 6.30pm Monday to Friday ($8), and hourly (there are 12 sailings, with two stops at Chek Keng) between 8.30am and 6.35pm on the weekend and on public holidays ($12). Be aware that the last sailing back from Tap Mun Chau is at 6pm from Monday to Friday and 6.05pm at the weekend.

If you've missed the boat or can't be bothered waiting for the next, the private sampans at Wong Shek pier, which seat up to three people in addition to the driver, charge from $70 per trip to or from the island.

TUNG PING CHAU

You can reach Tung Ping Chau from Ma Liu Shui, near the Chinese University, on ferries operated by Tsui Wah Ferry Service (☎ 2527 2513; www .traway.com.hk), but only on the weekend and on public holidays. Ferries depart from Ma Liu Shui at 9am and 3.30pm on Saturday, returning at 5.15pm. The single ferry on Sunday and public holidays leaves Ma Liu Shui at 9am, returning from Tung Ping Chau at 5.15pm. Only return tickets ($80) are available, and the trip takes 1¾ hours. The Sunday morning ferry could well be booked out, so call ahead to check availability.

Outlying Islands Ferries

The main Outlying Islands are all linked to Hong Kong by regular ferry services. Fares are cheap and the ferries are comfortable and usually air-conditioned. They have toilets, and some have a basic bar that serves snacks and cold drinks. The ferries can get very crowded on Saturday afternoon and all day Sunday, especially in the warmer months. They depart early and return in the evening.

There are two types of ferries: the large 'ordinary ferries', which, with the exception of those to Lamma, offer ordinary and deluxe classes; and the smaller 'fast ferries' – hovercraft that have one class only and cut travel time by between 10 and 20 minutes, but cost between 50% and 100% more. 'Weekday' fares apply from Monday to Saturday; prices are higher on Sunday and public holidays. Unless stated otherwise, children aged three to 11 years, seniors over 65 years and people with disabilities pay half-fare on both types of ferries and in both classes. Return is double the single fare.

The main operator serving the Outlying Islands is New World First Ferry (NWFF; ☎ 2131 8181; www.nwff.com.hk), which has a customer service centre (Map p56; pier 6, Outlying Islands ferry pier; ☒ 10am-2pm & 3-7pm Mon & Wed-Fri, 10am-1.30pm Tue, 10.30am-3.30pm Sat & Sun). NWFF boats sail to/from Cheung Chau, Peng Chau and Lantau, and connect all three via an interisland service. The Hong Kong & Kowloon Ferry Co (HKKF; ☎ 2815 6063; www.hkkf.com.hk) serves destinations on Lamma only and also has a customer service centre (Map p56; pier 4, Outlying Islands ferry pier; ☒ 9am-6pm).

Ferry timetables are subject to slight seasonal changes. They are prominently displayed at all ferry piers, or you can read them on the ferry companies' websites.

Tickets are available from booths at the ferry piers, but avoid queuing at busy times by using an Octopus card or putting the exact change into the turnstile as you enter.

If your time is limited, you can go on an organised tour (p298) or even hire your own junk (p230).

The NWFF's Island Hopping Pass allows unlimited rides for a day on ordinary ferries to Lantau, Cheung Chau and Peng Chau. The pass costs $30 Monday to Saturday and $40 on Sunday. For $10 per trip you can upgrade to deluxe class or the fast ferry.

LAMMA

For travelling to/from Central, both Yung Shue Wan and Sok Kwu Wan are served by HKKF ferries from pier 4 (Map p56) at the Outlying Islands ferry pier in Central. Ordinary and fast ferries depart Central for Yung Shue Wan approximately every half-hour to an hour (with additional sailings around 8am and 6pm) from 6.30am to 12.30am. The last boat to Central from Yung Shue Wan leaves at 11.30pm. The trip on the ordinary ferry takes 35 minutes, and the adult one-way fare is $11 ($14 on Sunday and public holidays). The fast ferries, which take just 20 minutes, cost $16 ($20 on Sunday and public holidays).

From Central, fast ferries (only) reach Sok Kwu Wan in 25 minutes and cost $14 ($18 on Sunday and public holidays). Ferries leave every 1½ hours or so, with the first departing Central at 7.20am and the last at 11.30pm. The last ferry to Central from Sok Kwu Wan is at 10.40pm.

To/from Aberdeen, fast ferries (only) link the pier at Aberdeen Promenade with Yung Shue Wan ($12) via Pak Kok Tsuen ($6) some 10 times a day, with the first ferry leaving Aberdeen at 6.30am and the last at 8.15pm Monday to Saturday. There are up to 15 ferries on Sunday and public holidays, with the first leaving Aberdeen at 7.30am and the last at 7.30pm. The last ferry for Aberdeen leaves Yung Shue Wan at 8.45pm and Pak Kok Tsuen at 9pm Monday to Saturday. On Sunday and public holidays, the last sailing times are 8pm from Yung Shue Wan and 8.10pm from Pak Kok Tsuen.

There is also a smaller ferry – more like a *kaido,* really – run by Chuen Kee Ferry (☎ 2982 8225, 2375 7883; www.ferry.com.hk) between Aberdeen and Sok Kwu Wan; all but two stop at Mo Tat Wan along the way. The journey between Aberdeen and Mo Tat Wan takes 23 minutes, and it's another seven minutes from there to Sok Kwu Wan. The adult fare is $8 ($12 in the evening and on Sunday and public holidays); between Mo Tat Wan and Sok Kwu Wan it costs $3 ($4).

There are up to 13 departures from Aberdeen to Sok Kwu Wan from Monday to Saturday between 6.40am and 10.50pm, leaving roughly every 1½ hours. In the other direction there are the same number of daily departures from Monday to Saturday between 6am and 10.10pm. On Sunday and public holiday, the service increases to 19 trips in each direction. Boats depart approximately every 45 minutes; the earliest and latest boats from Aberdeen are 6.40am and 10.50pm. From Sok Kwu Wan, the earliest and latest trips are 6am and 10.10pm.

A sampan (p277) from Aberdeen to Sok Kwu Wan/Yung Shue Wan will cost from $100/120 during the day and double that or more in the wee hours, when drunken revellers who have missed the last ferry back from Central are trying to get home. If you should be in the same boat – as it were – don't panic; there's usually at least one other person willing to split the cost.

CHEUNG CHAU

For travelling to/from Central, ordinary and fast ferries for Cheung Chau depart from pier 5 (Map p56) at the Outlying Islands ferry pier in Central approximately every half-hour between 6.30am and 12.30am. There are then fast ferries at 1.30am and 4.15am until normal daytime services begin again.

The trip on the ordinary ferry takes 48 minutes, and the adult one-way fare in ordinary class is $11.30 ($16.70 on Sunday and public holidays). The fares for deluxe class, which allows you to sit on the open-air deck at the stern, are $17.80 and $26, respectively. The fast ferries, which run as frequently as the ordinary ones and take just 32 minutes, cost $22.20 ($32 on Sunday and public holidays).

An ordinary interisland ferry ($9.20 all sectors) links Cheung Chau with Mui Wo (usually via Chi Ma Wan on Lantau) and Peng Chau seven days a week. The first ferry leaves Cheung Chau at 6am, and the last ferry is at 10.50pm; boats depart approximately every 1½ hours. From Cheung Chau, it takes 20 minutes to reach Chi Ma Wan, 30 to 45 minutes to Mui Wo and 50 to 75 minutes to Peng Chau.

LANTAU

The main entry port for vessels serving Lantau proper is Mui Wo, which is known as Silvermine Bay in English. You can, however, also reach Lantau destinations from other ports: Discovery Bay from Central; the Chi Ma Wan Peninsula from Cheung Chau; the Trappist Monastery from Peng Chau; and Tai O and Tung Chung from Tuen Mun in the New Territories.

For travelling between Mui Wo and Central, both ordinary and fast ferries depart for Mui Wo from pier 6 (Map p56) at the Outlying Islands ferry pier in Central approximately every half-hour between 6.10am (7am on Sunday and public holidays) and 12.30am. There is also a 3am fast ferry to Mui Wo via Peng Chau. The last ferry from Mui Wo to Central is at 11.30pm, though there is a fast ferry at 3.40am, which calls at Peng Chau along the way.

The journey on the ordinary ferry takes 48 minutes, and the adult one-way fare is $11.30/16.70 in ordinary/deluxe class ($16.70/26 on Sunday and public holidays). The fast ferries, which take 31 minutes, cost $22.20 ($32 on Sunday and public holidays).

The ordinary interisland ferry ($9.20) links Mui Wo with Cheung Chau (via Chi Ma Wan mostly) and Peng Chau 20 times a day. The first ferry leaves Mui Wo for Cheung Chau at 6am and for Peng Chau at 6.35am; the last ferry to Cheung Chau is at 10.20pm and to Peng Chau at 11.20pm. From Mui Wo it takes 20 to 25 minutes to reach Peng Chau, 15 to 20 minutes to Chi Ma Wan and 40 to 50 minutes to Cheung Chau.

For details on how to reach the Trappist Monastery on Lantau's northeast coast, see right.

To/from Discovery Bay, high-speed ferries run by the Discovery Bay Transportation Service (☎ 2987 7351; www.hkri.com) leave from pier 3 (Map p56) at the Outlying Islands ferry pier in Central every 10 to 30 minutes between 6.30am and 1am; after that time there are additional sailings at 1.30am (on weekends only), 2am, 2.30am (on weekends only), 3.30am and 5am until the daytime schedule resumes. Similar services run from Discovery Bay to Central. Tickets are $27 and the trip takes 25 to 30 minutes.

Ferries run by Peng Chau Rental Kaito (☎ 9033 8102) depart from Mui Wo for Discovery Bay between 7.45am and 6.45pm Monday to Friday and up to nine times on the weekend. From Discovery Bay to Mui Wo, sailings are between 7.15am and 6.15pm Monday to Friday, and there are up to nine sailings on Saturday and Sunday. Tickets cost $10 and the trip takes between 15 and 20 minutes.

You can also reach Discovery Bay from Peng Chau (opposite).

For travelling to/from Chi Ma Wan, the ordinary interisland ferry ($9.20) linking Cheung Chau and Mui Wo calls at the Chi Ma Wan ferry pier on the northeastern corner of the peninsula six times a day heading for Cheung Chau (with the first at 6.15am and the last at 8.30pm), and five times a day going to Mui Wo (the first at 6.55am and the last at 7.05pm), from where it carries on to Peng Chau.

To/from Tai O, there are NWFF ferries linking the Tai O berthing pier on Wing On St and Tuen Mun in the New Territories (via Sha Lo Wan and the Tung Chung New Development pier on Lantau's north coast) daily at 9.45am, 12.15pm, 4.15pm and 7.15pm, with an additional sailing at 2.15pm on Sunday. The trip takes between 50 minutes and an hour and costs $15 ($25 on Sunday). On Sunday and public holidays there are three direct sailings ($25, 30 minutes) to Tuen Mun at 10.45am, 1.45pm and 5.45pm, departing from Tai O's Shek Tsai Po pier, which is about 1.2km west of the centre.

For travelling to/from Tung Chung, another service run by NWFF links Tung Chung New Development pier with Tuen Mun in the New Territories. Ferries depart from Tuen Mun every 20 minutes from 5.40am to 11pm, with the return boats leaving Tung Chung between 20 and 30 minutes later (6am to 11.20pm). The trip takes 17 minutes and costs $15 ($10 for concession).

PENG CHAU

Ordinary and fast ferries leave for Peng Chau approximately once every 45 minutes between 7am and 12.30am from pier 6 (Map p56) at the Outlying Islands ferry pier in Central. There's also a 3am fast ferry to Peng Chau that carries on to Mui Wo on Lantau. The last ferry from Peng Chau to Central is at 11.30pm (11.35pm on Sunday), though there is a fast ferry at 3.25am.

The journey on the ordinary ferry takes 38 minutes, and the adult one-way fare is $11.30/17.80 in ordinary/deluxe class ($16.70/26 on Sunday and public holidays). The fast ferries, which take 25 minutes, cost $22.20 ($32 on Sunday and public holidays).

An ordinary interisland ferry ($9.20) links Peng Chau with Mui Wo and (frequently) Chi Ma Wan on Lantau, as well as Cheung Chau, up to 11 times a day. The first ferry leaves Peng Chau at 5.40am for all three destinations; the last ferry to Mui Wo is at 11.40pm. Boats take 20 minutes to reach Mui Wo, 40 minutes to Chi Ma Wan and 70 minutes to Cheung Chau.

Peng Chau is the main springboard for the Trappist Monastery, with up to 10 sailings a day. Peng Chau Rental Kaito (☎ 9033 8102) sails sampans to Tai Shui Hang pier from the auxiliary pier southeast of the main Peng Chau ferry pier daily between 7.45am and 5pm. They return from the monastery between 8.10am and 5.10pm.

Peng Chau Rental Kaito (☎ 9033 8102) links Peng Chau with Discovery Bay every 30 minutes to an hour, with up to 20 sailings a day between 6.30am and 10pm, from the pier southeast of the main Peng Chau ferry. The last boat from Discovery Bay sails at 10.15pm.

MA WAN

For travelling to/from Central, ferries run by Park Island Transport (☎ 2946 8888; www.pitcl.com .hk), which essentially service the high-end residential community on Ma Wan, depart from pier 2 (Map p56) at the Outlying Islands ferry pier in Central every 15 to 30 minutes from 7am to 1.30am and then run hourly until the normal schedule resumes. The one-way fare is $16 and the trip takes 22 minutes.

To/from Tsuen Wan, boats run by Park Island Transport leave the ferry pier in Tsuen Wan, which is due south of the KCR West Rail's Tsuen Wan West station in the New Territories, for Ma Wan every 15 to 30 minutes between 5.57am and 1.02am (5.40am to 12.45am from Ma Wan to Tsuen Wan). The one-way fare is $5 and the trip takes just 10 minutes.

TUNG LUNG CHAU

On the weekend only, ferries run by Lam Kee Kaido (☎ 2560 9929) heading for Joss House Bay on the Clearwater Bay Peninsula from Sai Wan Ho, east of Quarry Bay on Hong Kong Island, stop at Tung Lung Chau en route. On Saturday boats sail from Sai Wan Ho at 9am, 10.30am, 3.30pm and 4.45pm, departing from Tung Lung Chau a half-hour later. On Sunday and public holidays there are boats from Sai Wan Ho at 8.30am, 9.45am, 11am, 2.15pm, 3.30pm and 4.45pm; they return from Tung Lung Chau at 9am, 10.20am, 1.45pm, 3pm, 4pm and 5.30pm. The trip takes a half-hour, and the one-way fare is $28/14 for adults/children under 12.

To catch the ferry, take the MTR's Island line to Sai Wan Ho and then use exit A. Follow Tai On St north until you reach the quayside. The ride to Joss House Bay from Tung Lung Chau is significantly shorter than the one from Sai Wan Ho. If you're in a hurry coming back, get off there and catch bus 91 to the Choi Hung MTR station.

PO TOI ISLAND

A ferry run by Po Toi Kaido Services (☎ 2554 4059) leaves Aberdeen for Po Toi on Tuesday, Thursday and Saturday at 9am, returning from the island at 10.30am. On Sunday a single boat leaves Aberdeen at 8am, but there are also departures at 10am and 1.30am from St Stephen's Beach & Water Sports Centre (off Map p85; ☎ 2813 5407; Wong Ma Kok Path) in Stanley. Boats return from Po Toi at 3pm, 4.30pm and 6pm. A same-day return fare is $40 and the journey takes about 35 minutes.

Other Boats

Sea and harbour transport is not limited to scheduled ferries in Hong Kong. You may encounter several other types of boats as you travel further afield.

Kaidos (small- to medium-sized 'ferries') are able to make short runs on the open sea. Only a few *kaido* routes operate on regular schedules (eg the ones from Peng Chau to the Trappist Monastery and Discovery Bay, and from Aberdeen to Sok Kwu Wan on Lamma); most simply adjust supply to demand. *Kaidos* run most frequently on weekends and public holidays.

Sampans are motorised launches that can only accommodate a few (usually four) people. Sampans are generally too small to be considered seaworthy, but they can safely zip you around typhoon shelters like the ones at Aberdeen and Cheung Chau.

Bigger than a sampan but smaller than a *kaido, walla wallas* (water taxis that operate in Victoria Harbour) are a dying breed. Most of the customers are sailors stationed on ships anchored in the harbour. On Hong Kong Island look for them at Queen's pier on the east side of the Star Ferry pier. On the Kowloon side, they can sometimes be found southeast of the Star Ferry pier in Tsim Sha Tsui.

BUS

Hong Kong's extensive bus system offers a bewildering number of routes that will take you just about anywhere in the territory. Since Kowloon and the northern side of Hong Kong Island are so well served by the MTR, most visitors use the buses primarily to explore the southern side of Hong Kong Island and the New Territories.

Although buses pick up and discharge passengers at stops along the way, on Hong Kong Island the most important bus stations are the bus terminus below Exchange Square in Central (Map p56; at the time of writing there were plans to move the terminus to Sheung Wan in 2009) and the one at Admiralty (Map p63). From these stations you can catch buses to Aberdeen, Repulse Bay, Stanley and other destinations on the southern side of Hong Kong Island. In Kowloon the bus terminal at the Star Ferry pier in Tsim Sha Tsui (Map p92) is the most important, with buses to Hung Hom station and points in eastern and western Kowloon. Almost all New Towns in the New Territories are important transport hubs, though Sha Tin is particularly so, with buses travelling as far afield as Sai Kung, Tung Chung and Tuen Mun.

Bus fares range from $1.70 to $48, depending on the destination and how many sections you travel. Fares for night buses cost from $14 to $31. Payment is made into a fare box upon entry so, unless you're carrying an ever-so-convenient Octopus card, have plenty of coins handy, as the driver does not give change.

Hong Kong's buses are usually double-deckers. Many buses have easy-to-read LCD displays of road names and stops in Chinese and sometimes in English, and TV screens to entertain (or annoy) you as you roll along. Buses serving the airport and Hung Hom train station have luggage racks.

Hong Kong's buses are run by a half-dozen private operators, carrying more than four million passengers a day. Though it's much of a muchness as to who's driving you from A to B, you may want to check the routings on their websites.

Citybus (☎ 2873 0818; www.citybus.com.hk)

Discovery Bay Transportation Services (☎ 2987 7351; www.hkri.com)

Kowloon Motor Bus Co (☎ 2745 4466; www.kmb.com.hk)

Long Win Bus Co (☎ 2261 2791; www.kmb.com.hk)

New Lantao Bus Company (☎ 2984 9848; www.kmb.com .hk)

New World First Bus Services (☎ 2136 8888; www.nwfb .com.hk)

Routes & Schedules

There are no good bus maps and, because buses are run by so many different private operators, there is no longer a comprehensive directory for the whole territory. Your best option is Universal Publications' *Hong Kong Public Transport Atlas* ($50).

The HKTB has useful leaflets on the major bus routes, and the major bus companies detail all their routes on their websites.

Night Buses

Most buses run from about 5.30am or 6am until midnight or 12.30am, but there are a handful of useful night bus services in addition to the ones linking the airport with various parts of the territory. Citybus' N121, which operates every 15 minutes between 12.45am and 5am, runs from the Macau ferry bus terminus through Central and Wan Chai on Hong Kong Island and through the Cross-Harbour Tunnel to Chatham Rd North in Tsim Sha Tsui East before continuing on to eastern Kowloon and Ngau Tau Kok ($12.80).

Bus N122, also run by Citybus with the same fare and schedule, runs from North Point ferry bus terminus on Hong Kong Island, through the Cross-Harbour Tunnel to Nathan Rd and on to Mei Foo Sun Chuen in the northwestern part of Kowloon. You can catch these two buses near the tunnel entrances on either side of the harbour.

Other useful night buses that cross the harbour include the N118, which runs from Siu Sai Wan in the northeastern part of Hong Kong Island to Sham Shui Po in northwest Kowloon via North Point and Causeway Bay ($12.80); and the N170, which runs from Wah Fu, a large estate near Aberdeen in the southwest of Hong Kong Island, through Wan Chai and Causeway Bay before crossing over to Kowloon and travelling as far as Sha Tin in the New Territories ($23).

Useful night buses on Lantau include the N1 ($16; $25 on Sunday and public holidays) linking Mui Wo and Tai O at 3.45am and the N35 ($20; $30 on Sunday and public holidays) between Mui Wo (1.30am and 4.30am) and the airport (1.30am and 5am).

CAR & MOTORCYCLE

It would be sheer madness for a newcomer to consider driving in Hong Kong. Traffic is heavy, the roads can get hopelessly clogged and the ever-changing network of highways and bridges with its new numbering system is complicated in the extreme. And if driving the car doesn't destroy your holiday sense of spontaneity, parking the damn thing will. If you are determined to see Hong Kong under your own steam, do yourself a favour and rent a car with a driver.

Driving Licence & Permits

Hong Kong allows most foreigners over the age of 18 to drive for up to 12 months with their valid local licenses. It's still a good idea to carry an International Driving Permit (IDP) as well, though. This can be obtained from your local automobile association for a reasonable fee.

Anyone driving in the territory for more than a year will need to get a Hong Kong licence, which will be valid for 10 years ($900). Apply to the Licensing Division of the Transport Department (Map p63; ☎ 2804 2600; www.info.gov.hk/td; 3rd fl, United Centre, 95 Queensway, Admiralty; ⏰ 9am-5pm Mon-Fri).

Hire

Car-hire firms accept IDPs or driving licences from your home country. Drivers must usually be at least 25 years of age. Daily rates for small cars start at just under $700, but there are weekend and weekly deals available. For example, Avis (Map p94; ☎ 2890 6988; www.avis .com.hk; Ground fl, Shop 46, Peninsula Centre, 67 Mody Sq, Tsim Sha Tsui East; ⏰ 9am-6pm Mon-Fri, 9am-4pm Sat & Sun) will rent you a Toyota Corolla or Honda Civic for the weekend (from 2pm on Friday to 10.30am Monday) for $1360; the same car for a day/week costs $680/3000. Rates include unlimited kilometres.

If you're looking for a car with a driver, contact Ace Hire Car Service (Map pp54–5; ☎ 2572 7663; www.acehirecar.com.hk; 16 Min Fat St, Happy Valley), which charges between $160 and $250 per hour (minimum three to five hours, depending on the location). Avis' chauffeur-driven cars are much more expensive: $300 to $1000 with a minimum of three hours.

Road Rules

Vehicles drive on the left-hand side of the road in Hong Kong, as in the UK, Australia and Macau, but *not* in mainland China. Seat belts must be worn by the driver and all passengers, in both the front and back seats. Police are strict and give out traffic tickets at the drop of a hat.

MINIBUS

Minibuses are vans with no more than 16 seats. They come in two varieties: red and green. The red minibuses are cream coloured with a red roof or stripe, and pick up and discharge passengers wherever they are

hailed or asked to stop (but not in restricted zones or at busy bus stops). Maxicabs, commonly known as 'green minibuses', are also cream coloured but with a green roof or stripe, and operate on fixed routes. As with red minibuses there are set stops for green minibuses, but where circumstance allows and no traffic restrictions apply, you may also flag one down.

There are 4350 minibuses running in the territory. About 40% are red minibuses and 60% green.

Red Minibus

Red minibuses can be handy for short distances, such as the trip from Central to Wan Chai or Causeway Bay, and you can be assured of a seat – by law, passengers are not allowed to stand. The destination is displayed on the front in large Chinese characters, usually with a smaller English translation below.

Minibus fares range from $2 to $22. The price to the final destination is displayed on a card propped up in the windscreen, but this is often only written in Chinese numbers. Fares are equal to or higher than those on the bus, but drivers often increase their fares on rainy days, at night and during holiday periods. You usually hand the driver the fare when you get off, and change is given. You can use your Octopus card on certain routes.

If you're in Central, the best place to catch minibuses to Wan Chai and other points east is the Central bus terminus below Exchange Square (Map p56). If heading west towards Kennedy Town, walk to Stanley St, near Lan Kwai Fong.

There are a few minibuses that cross the harbour late at night, running between Wan Chai and Mong Kok. In Wan Chai minibuses can be found on Hennessy and Fleming Rds. In Kowloon you may have to trudge up Nathan Rd as far as Mong Kok before you'll find one. Minibuses to the New Territories can be found at the Jordan and Choi Hung MTR stations in Kowloon.

Green Minibus

Green minibuses operate on some 352 routes, more than half of which are in the New Territories, and serve designated stops. Fares range from $2.50 to $24, according to distance. You must put the exact fare in the cash box as you descend (no change is given) or, on some routes, use your Octopus card.

MASS TRANSIT RAILWAY

The Mass Transit Railway (MTR; ☎ 2881 8888; www.mtr .com.hk), Hong Kong's underground rail system and universally known as the 'MTR', is a phenomenon of modern urban public transport. Sleek, pristine and *always* on time, it is also rather soulless.

Though it costs more than other forms of public transport in Hong Kong, the MTR is the quickest way to get to most destinations in the urban areas. Trains run every two to 10 minutes from around 6am to sometime between 12.30am and 1am.

The MTR travels on more than 85km of track and is made up of seven lines, including the Airport Express and the new Disneyland Resort line. It serves 53 stations and carries 2.3 million passengers a day.

The Island line (blue) extends along the northern coast of Hong Kong Island from Sheung Wan in the west to Chai Wan in the east. The Tsuen Wan line (red) runs from Central station and travels alongside the Island line as far as Admiralty, where it crosses the harbour and runs through central Kowloon, terminating at Tsuen Wan in the New Territories.

The Kwun Tong line (green), which begins at Yau Ma Tei, shares that and two subsequent stations with the Tsuen Wan line; at Prince Edward it branches off and heads for eastern Kowloon, crossing the KCR East Rail line at Kowloon Tong before joining the Tseung Kwan O line at Yau Tong and terminating at Tiu Keng Leng in the southeastern New Territories.

The Tseung Kwan O line (purple) starts at North Point and hits Quarry Bay before crossing the eastern harbour and terminating at Po Lam in the southeastern New Territories. The Tung Chung line (orange) shares the same rail lines as the Airport Express, but stops at two additional stations in Kowloon (Kowloon and Olympic) along the way. It terminates at Tung Chung, a New Town on Lantau that offers cheaper transport options to and from the airport.

The MTR connects with the KCR East Rail at Tsim Sha Tsui and Kowloon Tong stations. It meets the KCR West Rail at Nam Cheong and Mei Foo.

For short hauls, the MTR is not great value. If you want to cross the harbour from Tsim Sha Tsui to Central, for example, at $9/4.5 per adult/child (or $7.90/4 with an Octopus card) the MTR is more than four times the price of the Star Ferry, with none of the views, and the journey is only marginally faster. If your destination is further away – North Point, say, or Kwun Tong – the MTR is considerably faster than a bus or minibus and about the same price. If possible, it's best to avoid the rush hours: 7.30am to 9.30am and 5pm to 7pm weekdays and Saturday morning, when 85% of the 1050 MTR carriages are in use.

Travelling by the MTR is so easy: everything, from the ticket-vending machines to the turnstiles, is automated. The system uses the stored-value Octopus card (p283), really the only way to go, and single-journey tickets with a magnetic coding strip on the back. When you pass through the turnstile, the card is encoded with the station identification and time. At the other end, the exit turnstile sucks in the ticket, reads where you came from, the time you bought the ticket and how much you paid. If everything is in order, it will let you through. If you have underpaid (by mistake or otherwise), you can make up the difference at an MTR service counter; there are no fines since no one gets out without paying. Once you've passed through the turnstile to begin a journey you have 90 minutes to complete it before the ticket becomes invalid.

Ticket prices range from $4 to $26 ($3.80 and $23.10 with an Octopus card); children and seniors pay between $3 and $13 ($2.40 and $11.60 with a card), depending on the destination. Ticket machines accept $10 and $20 notes and $10, $5, $2, $1 and 50c coins, and they dispense change. The machines have a touch screen with highlighted destinations. You can also buy tickets from MTR service counters and get change from the Hang Seng bank branches located in most stations.

Smoking, eating and drinking are not permitted in MTR stations or on the trains, and violators are subject to a fine of $5000. You are not allowed to carry large objects or bicycles aboard trains either, though backpacks and suitcases are fine.

There are no toilets in any of the MTR stations. Like the 90-minute limit on a ticket's validity, the reasoning behind this is to get bodies into stations, bums on seats (or hands on straps) and bodies out onto the street again as quickly as possible. The system works, and very few people complain.

MTR exit signs use an alphanumerical system and there can be as many as a dozen to choose from. We give the correct exit for sights and destinations wherever possible, but you may find yourself studying the exit table from time to time and scratching your head. There are always maps of the local area at each exit.

Should you leave something behind on the MTR, you can contact the lost property office (☎ 2861 0020; ⏱ 8am-8pm) at Admiralty MTR station.

TAXI

Hong Kong taxis are a bargain compared with those in other world-class cities. With more than 18,000 cruising the streets of the territory, they're easy to flag down.

When a taxi is available, there should be a red 'For Hire' sign illuminated on the meter that's visible through the windscreen. At night the 'Taxi' sign on the roof will be lit up as well. Taxis will not stop at bus stops or in restricted zones where a yellow line is painted next to the kerb.

The law requires that everyone in a vehicle wears a seat belt. Both driver and passenger(s) will be fined if stopped by the police, and most drivers will gently remind you to buckle up before proceeding.

'Urban taxis' – those in Kowloon and on Hong Kong Island – are red with silver roofs. New Territories taxis are green with white tops, and Lantau taxis are blue.

Hong Kong Island and Kowloon taxis tend to avoid each others' turf as the drivers' street geography on the other side of the harbour can be pretty shaky. Hong Kong Island and Kowloon taxis maintain separate ranks at places such as Hung Hom train station and the Star Ferry pier, and will sometimes refuse to take you to the 'other side'. In any case, if you're travelling from Hong Kong Island to Kowloon (or vice versa), choose the correct taxi as you'll save on the tunnel toll. New Territories taxis are not permitted to pick up passengers in Kowloon or on Hong Kong Island at all.

The rate for taxis on Hong Kong Island and Kowloon is $15 for the first 2km and $1.40 for every additional 200m; waiting costs $1.40 per minute. In the New Territories it's $12.50 for the first 2km and $1.20 for each additional 200m; waiting costs $1.20 per minute. On Lantau the equivalent charges are $12 and $1.20, and $1.20 per minute for waiting. There is a luggage fee of $5 per bag but, depending on the size, not all drivers insist on this payment. It costs an extra $5 to book a taxi by telephone. Try to carry smaller bills and coins; most drivers are hesitant to make change for anything over $100. You can tip up to 10%,

but most Hong Kong people just leave the little brown coins and a dollar or two.

Passengers must pay the toll if a taxi goes through the many Hong Kong harbour or mountain tunnels or uses the Lantau Link to Tung Chung or the airport. Though the Cross-Harbour Tunnel costs only $10, you'll have to pay $20 if, say, you take a Hong Kong taxi from Hong Kong Island to Kowloon. If you manage to find a Kowloon taxi returning 'home', you'll pay only $10. (It works the other way round as well, of course.) If you cross the harbour via the Western Harbour Tunnel, you must pay the $25 toll plus $25 for the return unless you can find a taxi heading for its base. Similarly, if you use the Eastern Harbour Crossing, you may have to pay the $20 toll twice.

There's no way of avoiding the whopping great toll of $30 in both directions when a taxi uses the Lantau Link.

There is no double charge for the other roads and tunnels: Aberdeen ($5); Lion Rock ($8); Shing Mun ($5); Tate's Cairn ($10); Tai Lam ($22); and Tseung Kwan O ($3).

You may have some trouble hailing a taxi during rush hour, when it rains or during the driver shift-change period (around 4pm daily). Taxis are also in higher demand after midnight. There are no extra late-night charges and no extra passenger charges, though some taxis are insured to carry four passengers and some five. You can tell by glancing at the licence plate.

Some taxi drivers speak English well; others don't have a word of the language. It's never a bad idea to have your destination written down in Chinese.

Though most Hong Kong taxi drivers are scrupulously honest, if you feel you've been ripped off, take down the taxi or driver's licence number (usually displayed on the sun visor in front) and call the taxi complaints hotline (☎ 2889 9999), the police report hotline (☎ 2527 7177) or the Transport Department hotline (☎ 2804 2600) to lodge a complaint. Be sure to have all the relevant details: when, where and how much. If you leave something behind in a taxi, ring the Road Co-op Lost & Found hotline (☎ 187 2920); most drivers turn in lost property.

TRAIN

The MTR underground system notwithstanding, Hong Kong has two 'real' train systems that are crucial for travellers getting around in the New Territories and/or heading for China.

Kowloon-Canton Railway

Also known as the 'KCR', the Kowloon-Canton Railway (☎ 2929 3399; www.kcrc.com) is made up of two lines. The KCR East Rail, which commenced in 1910, is a single-line, 43km-long commuter railway running from the new East Tsim Sha Tsui station in southern Kowloon to Lo Wo on the border with mainland China and a new spur to Lok Ma Chau, also on the border. The terminus of the new spur connects to the new Shenzhen Metro system at Huanggang station via a pedestrian bridge across the Shenzhen River.

The tracks are the same as those used by the express trains to cities in Guangdong province as well as to Shanghai and Beijing, but the trains are different and look more like MTR carriages. Ma On Shan Rail, which branches off from the KCR East Rail at Tai Wai and serves nine stations, opened in December 2004 but is of limited use to travellers.

The KCR West Rail, a separate 30.5km-long line, links Nam Cheong station in Sham Shui Po with Tuen Mun via Yuen Long, stopping at nine stations. Eventually it will be linked to the KCR East Rail at East Tsim Sha Shui, with stops at Kowloon West and Canton Rd. At time of writing an extension of the line south from Nam Cheong to East Tsim Sha Tsui via a new station at West Kowloon was scheduled to open in 2009.

The KCR is a quick way to get to the New Territories, and the ride offers some nice vistas, particularly between the Chinese University and Tai Po Market stations on the KCR East Rail. You can transfer from the MTR to the KCR East Rail at Tsim Sha Tsui and Kowloon Tong stations. On the KCR West Rail, there is interchange with the Tung Chung MTR line at Nam Cheong, with the Tsuen Wan line at Mei Foo and with the Light Rail (see right) at Yuen Long, Tin Shui Wai, Siu Hong and Tuen Mun.

KCR trains run every five to eight minutes, except during rush hour, when they depart every three to eight minutes. The first KCR East Rail train leaves East Tsim Sha Tsui at 5.28am and the last departs from Lo Wu at 12.30am. The KCR West Rail runs from 6am to sometime between 12.15am and 12.40am. The trip from Nam Cheong to Tuen Mun on the KCR West Rail takes 30 minutes.

KCR fares are cheap, starting at $3.50, with a half-hour ride to Sheung Shui from East Tsim Sha Tsui costing just $12.50 (1st class is $25) and the 40-minute trip to Lo Wu $36.50

(1st class $73). Children and seniors pay reduced fares of between $1.80 and $17.40. Paying with an Octopus card brings down fares considerably.

The KCR runs some 129 feeder buses on 18 routes via its KCRC Bus Service (☎ 2602 7799; www .kcrc.com), but these are generally of interest only to residents of housing estates within striking distance of the KCR East and West Rails and the Light Rail.

Light Rail

The KCR's Light Rail (☎ 2929 3399; www.kcrc.com) system began operations in 1988 and has been extended several times since. It is rather like a modern, air-conditioned version of the trams in Hong Kong, but it's much faster, reaching speeds of up to 70km/h. It runs along 36km of track parallel to the road and stops at 68 designated stations, carrying some 320,000 passengers a day.

Until recently, only those travellers visiting the temples of the western New Territories made much use of the Light Rail as it essentially was just a link between the New Towns of Tuen Mun and Yuen Long. But with the opening of the KCR West Rail, it is an important feeder service for the KCR and, by extension, the MTR.

There are 11 Light Rail lines connecting various small suburbs with Tuen Mun to the south and Yuen Long to the northeast, both of which are on the KCR West Rail. The system operates from about 5.30am to between 12.15am and 12.45am. Trams run every four to 20 minutes, depending on the line and time of day. Fares are $4 to $5.80, depending on the number of zones (from 1 to 5) travelled; children aged three to 11 and seniors over 65 pay from $2 to $2.90. If you don't have an Octopus card, you can buy single-journey tickets from vending machines on the platforms.

The system of fare collection is unique in Hong Kong: there are no gates or turnstiles and customers are trusted to validate their ticket or Octopus card when they board and exit. That trust is enforced by frequent spot checks, however, and the fine is 50 times the maximum adult fare – $290 at present.

TRAM

Hong Kong's venerable old trams, operated by Hongkong Tramways Ltd (☎ 2548 7102; www.hktramways .com), are tall and narrow double-decker streetcars, the only all double-deck wooden-sided tram fleet in the world. They roll (and rock) along the northern coast of Hong Kong Island on 16km of track, carrying some 240,000 passengers daily.

The electric tramline first began operating in 1904 on what was then the shoreline of Hong Kong Island. This helps explain why roads curve and dogleg in ways that don't seem quite right. Try to get a seat at the front window on the upper deck for a first-class view while rattling through the crowded streets: tall passengers will find it uncomfortable standing up as the ceiling is low, but there is more space at the rear of the tram on both decks.

Trams operate from 6am to between 12.30am and 1am daily and run every two to 10 minutes, but they often arrive bunched together. Be prepared to elbow your way through the crowd to alight, particularly on the lower deck.

Hong Kong's trams are not fast but they're cheap and fun; in fact, apart from the Star Ferry (p273), no form of transport is nearer and dearer to the hearts of most Hong Kong people. For a flat fare of $2 ($1 for children aged three to 11 and seniors over 65) dropped into a box beside the driver as you descend, you can go as far as you like, whether it's one block or to the end of the line. You can also use your Octopus card.

Tram routes often overlap. Some start at Kennedy Town and run to Shau Kei Wan, while others run only part of the way; one turns south and heads for Happy Valley. The longest run, covering the entire length of the system from Shau Kei Wan to Kennedy Town (with a change at Western Market), takes about 1½ hours. The six routes from west to east are: Kennedy Town–Western Market; Kennedy Town–Happy Valley; Kennedy Town–Causeway Bay; Sai Ying Pun (Whitty St)–North Point; Sheung Wan (Western Market)–Shau Kei Wan; and Happy Valley–Shau Kei Wan.

Peak Tram

The Peak Tram is not really a tram but a cable-hauled funicular railway that has been scaling the 396m ascent to the highest point on Hong Kong Island since 1888. It is thus the oldest form of public transport in the territory.

While a few residents on the Peak and in the Mid-Levels actually use it as a form of transport – there are four intermediate stops before you reach the top – the Peak Tram is intended to transport visitors and locals to the

attractions, shops and restaurants in the Peak Tower and Peak Galleria (p78).

The Peak Tram (☎ 2522 0922, 2849 7654; www .thepeak.com.hk; one way/return adult $22/33, child 3-11yr $8/15, senior over 65 yr $8/15) runs every 10 to 15 minutes from 7am to midnight, making between one and four stops (Kennedy Rd, MacDonnell Rd, May Rd and Barker Rd) along the way in about seven minutes. It's such a steep ride that the floor is angled to help standing passengers stay upright. Running for more than a century, the tram has never had an accident – a comforting thought if you start to have doubts about the strength of that vital cable. It carries 8500 passengers a day.

The Peak Tram lower terminus (Map p56) is behind the St John's Building. The upper tram terminus is in the Peak Tower (off Map p56; 128 Peak Rd). Avoid going on Sunday and public holidays when there are usually long queues. Octopus cards can be used.

Between 10am and 11.45pm, open-deck (or air-conditioned) bus 15C takes passengers between the Star Ferry pier and Pedder St in Central and the lower tram terminus.

TRAVEL & TOURIST PASSES

The Octopus card (☎ 2266 2222; www.octopuscards.com), originally designed for the MTR and seven other forms of transport (thus the eight-armed 'octopus' connection), is valid on most forms of public transport in Hong Kong and will even allow you to make purchases at retail outlets across the territory (such as 7-Eleven convenience stores and Wellcome supermarkets). All you do is touch fare-deducting processors installed at stations and ferry piers, on minibuses, in shops etc with the Octopus card and the fare is deducted, indicating how much credit you have left.

The Octopus card comes in three basic denominations: $150 for adults, $100 for students aged 12 to 25, and $70 for children aged three to 11 and seniors ('elders' here) over 65. All cards include a refundable deposit of $50. If you want to add more money to your card, just go to one of the add-value machines or the ticket offices located at every MTR station. The maximum amount you can add is $1000, and the card has a maximum negative value of $30, which is recovered the next time you reload (thus the $50 deposit). Octopus fares are between 5% and 10% cheaper than ordinary fares on the MTR, KCR, Light Rail systems and certain green minibuses.

You can purchase Octopus cards at ticket offices or customer service centres in MTR, KCR and LRT stations, New World First Bus customer service centres as well as Outlying Islands ferry piers on both sides.

The much-advertised Airport Express Tourist Octopus card is not really worth the microchip embedded into it. The card costs $220 (including $50 deposit) and allows one trip on the Airport Express, three days' un-limited travel on the MTR and $20 usable value on other forms of transport. For $300 you get two trips on the Airport Express and the same benefits. At the end of your trip you can claim your deposit back (plus any part of the $20 'usable value' still on the card). For shorter stays there's the Tourist MTR 1-Day Pass ($50), valid on the MTR for 24 hours.

TRANSPORT TO/FROM CHINA

Air

Competition of sorts is driving prices down slightly but expect to pay a premium to fly between Hong Kong and China as the govern-ment regulates the prices. Depending on the season, seats can be difficult to find due to the enormous volume of business travellers and Chinese tourists, so book well in advance. Some sample adult return fares valid for a year from Hong Kong are Beijing $2520, Chengdu $1970, Kunming $1890 and Shanghai $2200. One-way fares are a bit more than half the return price.

You should be able to do better than that, however, on both scheduled and charter flights, especially in summer. If you plan to fly to a destination in China from Hong Kong, you can save at least 30% on the above fares by heading for Shenzhen by bus or ferry and boarding the aircraft at Huangtian airport there.

Land

The only way in and out of Hong Kong by land is to cross the 30km border with main-land China. The options for surface travel to and from China have increased dramatically since the handover, with buses and trains de-parting throughout the day to destinations as close as Shenzhen and as far as Beijing. Travellers should be aware that, although the Hong Kong Special Administrative Region (SAR) is an integral part of China, visas are still required to cross the border to the main-land (see p286).

The border crossing at Lo Wu opens at 6.30am and closes at midnight. The crossing at Lok Ma Chau is open round the clock. The terminus of the new KCR spur line connects to the new Shenzhen Metro system at Huang-gang station via a pedestrian bridge across the Shenzhen River.

BUS

You can reach virtually any major destina-tion in neighbouring Guangdong province by bus from Hong Kong. With KCR East Rail services so fast and cheap, however, few buses call on Shenzhen proper, though most of the big hotels run minivans to and from that des-tination for around $100 one way. One-way fares from Hong Kong to other mainland destinations include Changsha $280, Dong-guan $70 to $100, Foshan $100, Guangzhou $80 to $100, Huizhou $100, Kaiping $130, Shantou $180 to $200, Shenzhen's Huangtian airport $150, Xiamen $370 and Zhongshan $100 to $150.

Buses are run by a multitude of transport companies and depart from locations around the territory; the list that follows is only a sam-pling. Schedules vary enormously according to carrier and place, but buses leave through-out the day and departures are frequent.

CTS Express Coach (☎ 2764 9803, 2365 0118; http://cts bus.hkcts.com) Buses depart from locations throughout Hong Kong, including the CTS Wan Chai branch (Map p65; ☎ 2832 3888; Southorn Centre, 130-138 Hennessy Rd) on Hong Kong Island and from just south of the CTS Mong Kok branch (Map p98; ☎ 2789 5888; 62-72 Sai Yee St) in Kowloon.

Eternal East Cross Border Coach (Map p92; ☎ 3412 6677, 3760 0888; 13th fl, Kai Seng Commercial Centre, 4-6 Hankow Rd, Tsim Sha Tsui; ☷ 7am-8pm) Buses leave from just outside the Hang Seng Bank next door.

Motor Transport Company of Guangdong and Hong Kong (GDHK; ☎ 2317 7900) Buses bound for destina-tions throughout Guangdong leave from the Cross-Border Coach Terminus (Map p92; ☎ 2317 7900; Ground fl, Hong Kong Scout Centre, 8 Austin Rd, Tsim Sha Tsui; ☷ 6.30am-7pm), which is entered from Scout Path.

Trans-Island Chinalink (Map p98; ☎ 2336 1111; www .trans-island.com.hk) Buses depart from Prince Edward MTR next to the Metropark Hotel. Cars and vans leave from Portland St opposite the Hotel Concourse Hong Kong.

In addition, at Chek Lap Kok buses run by CTS Express Coach (☎ 2261 2472), Eternal East Cross Bor-der Coach (☎ 2261 0176) and Trans-Island (☎ 2261

0296; www.trans-island.com.hk) link Hong Kong International Airport with many points in southern China, including Dongguan ($100), Foshan ($150 to $220), Guangzhou ($100 to $200) and Shenzhen ($100 to $180).

TRAIN

You can now book cross-border train tickets online via the website of KCR (www.it3.kcrc .com). You have to sign up, but it's a useful service. Reaching Shenzhen is a breeze. Just board the KCR East Rail at East Tsim Sha Tsui station (1st/2nd class $73/36.50) or at any other KCR East Rail station along the way (such as Hung Hom, Kowloon Tong or Sha Tin) and ride it to Lo Wu; China is a couple of hundred metres away. The first train to Lo Wu leaves East Tsim Sha Tsui station at 5.28am, the last at 11.05pm, and the trip takes about 40 minutes. For more details on KCR services, see p282.

The most comfortable way to reach Guangzhou by land is via the Kowloon–Guangzhou express train (usually via Dongguan), which covers the 182km route in approximately 1¾ hours. High-speed intercity trains leave Hung Hom station for Guangzhou East train station 12 times a day between 7.28am and 7.20pm, returning from that station the same number of times from 8.18am to 9.32pm. One-way tickets cost $230/190 in 1st/2nd class for adults and $115/95 for children aged five to nine. Adults/children are allowed one piece of luggage, weighing up to 20/10kg. Additional bags cost $3.90 per 5kg.

There are also direct rail links between Hung Hom and both Shanghai and Beijing. Trains to Beijing West train station (hard/soft sleeper from $574/934, 24 hours) depart on alternate days at 3pm and travel via Guangzhou East, Changsha and Wuhan, arriving at 3.18pm the following day. Trains to Shanghai (hard/soft sleeper from $508/825, 23 hours) also depart on alternate days at 3pm and pass through Guangzhou East and Hangzhou East stations, arriving at 1.38pm the following day.

There is one daily departure to Zhaoqing (adult/child $235/117.50) via Dongguan, Guangzhou East and Foshan at 12.30pm, arriving in Zhaoqing at 4.27pm. The train departs Zhaoqing at 4.56pm, reaching Hung Hom at 8.53pm.

Immigration formalities at Hung Hom are completed before boarding; you won't get on the train without a visa for China. Passengers are required to arrive at the station 45 minutes before departure. To reach Hung Hom station from Tsim Sha Tsui by public transport, take the KCR East Rail for one stop, bus 5C from the Star Ferry pier, or the green minibus 6 or 8 from Hankow Rd.

One-way and return tickets can be booked 60 days in advance through CTS (p286), including at CTS Hung Hom station branch (☎ 2334 9333; 6.30am-8pm) and at KCR East Rail stations in Hung Hom, Mong Kok, Kowloon Tong and Sha Tin. Tickets booked with a credit card via the Tele-Ticketing Hotline (☎ 2947 7888) must be collected at least one hour before departure.

A cheaper but much less convenient option is to take the KCR East Rail train to Lo Wu (or to the Shenzhen Metro via Lok Ma Chau), cross through immigration into Shenzhen and catch a local train from there to Guangzhou. There are frequent local trains (Y70, two hours) and high-speed trains (Y80, 55 minutes) throughout the day.

Sea

Regularly scheduled ferries link the China ferry terminal (Map p92; Canton Rd, Tsim Sha Tsui) in Kowloon and/or the Macau ferry pier (Map p70; 200 Connaught Rd, Sheung Wan) on Hong Kong Island with a string of towns and cities on the Pearl River Delta – but not central Guangzhou or Shenzhen. For sea transport to/from Macau, see p348.

TurboJet (☎ 2921 6688, 2859 3333; www.turbojet.com .hk) runs high-speed ferries ($200, one hour) leaving the China ferry terminal for Fuyong ferry terminal (Shenzhen airport) five to seven times a day between 7.30am and 6pm. There are five return sailings from Fuyong ($185) starting at 9am, with the last at 4.30pm. One boat a day leaves the Macau ferry pier in Central at 8am. Return sailings are at 5.50pm and 7.30pm.

CMSE Passenger Transport (☎ 2858 0909) runs some 13 Jetcats (day/night sailing $110/145, one hour) that link Hong Kong with Shekou, a port about 20km west of Shenzhen town and easily accessible by bus or taxi to the town centre, from 7.45am to 9pm daily. Seven of these (between 7.45am and 7pm) leave from the China ferry terminal in Kowloon, while the rest (9am to 9pm) go from the Macau ferry pier on Hong Kong Island. Return sailings from Shekou are from 7.45am to 9.30pm.

Zhuhai can also be reached from Hong Kong on seven ferries a day ($177, 70 minutes) from the China ferry terminal in Tsim Sha Tsui (from 7.30am to 5.30pm) and on the same number from the Macau ferry pier in

Sheung Wan (8.40am to 9.30pm) on ferries operated by the Chu Kong Passenger Transportation Company (☎ 2858 3876; www.cksp.com.hk). The 14 return sailings from Zhuhai ($158) run between 8am and 9.30pm.

Chu Kong also has ferries from the China ferry terminal in Tsim Sha Tsui to a number of other ports in southern Guangdong province, including Humen (Taiping; $177, 90 minutes, three a day at 9am, 1.45pm and 5.30pm), Kaiping ($212, four hours, daily at 8.30am), Shunde ($185, 110 minutes, six sailings between 7.30am and 6pm) and Zhongshan ($196, 90 minutes, eight or nine sailings from 8am to 8pm).

Ferries run by Expert Fortune (☎ 2375 0688, 2517 3494) link the China ferry terminal with Nansha ($138, five sailings daily) between 8am and 3.30pm, with return sailings ($100) between 9.30am and 5pm or 5.30pm. One daily ferry departs from the Macau ferry pier at 8.20am.

DEPARTURE TAX
The $26 departure tax levied when leaving Hong Kong by sea is usually included in the ticket price.

Visas
Everyone except Hong Kong Chinese residents must have a visa to enter mainland China. Holders of Canadian, Australian, New Zealand and most EU passports – but *not* American ones (at the time of writing) – can get a visa on the spot for $150 at the Lo Wu border crossing, the last stop on the Kowloon–Canton Railway's East Rail. This particular visa limits you to a maximum stay of seven days within the confines of the Shenzhen Special Economic Zone (SEZ) *only*. The queues for these visas can be interminable, so it is highly recommended that you shell out the extra money and get a proper China visa before setting off even if you're headed just for Shenzhen.

If you would like to arrange your visa yourself, you can go to the Visa Office of the People's Republic of China (Map p65; ☎ 3413 2424; 7th fl, Lower Block, China Resources Centre, 26 Harbour Rd, Wan Chai; ☺ 9am-noon & 2-5pm Mon-Fri). Visas processed in one/two/three days for 'reciprocal countries' cost $480/360/210. Visas for double/multiple entry valid six months cost $350/850, or if you require express/urgent service the double-entry visa costs $500/620 and the multiple entry $1150/1400. You must supply two photos, which can be taken at photo booths in the MTR or at the visa office for $35. Any photo-processing shop can also oblige.

Visas can be arranged by China Travel Service (CTS; ☎ 2851 17000, 2789 5401; www.ctshk.com), the mainland-affiliated agency; a good many hostels and guesthouses; and most Hong Kong travel agents, including those listed on p269.

CHINA TRAVEL SERVICES OFFICES
There are almost three-dozen China Travel Services (CTS) offices in Hong Kong, including the five listed below.

Offices in Hong Kong Island:

Causeway Bay (Map p74; ☎ 2808 1131; Room 606, 6th fl, Hang Kung Centre, 2-20 Paterson St; ☺ 9am-8.30pm Mon-Fri, 10am-7pm Sat)

Central (Map p56; ☎ 2522 0450; Ground fl, China Travel Bldg, 77 Queen's Rd Central; ☺ 9am-7.30pm Mon-Sat, 9.30am-5pm Sun)

Wan Chai (Map p65; ☎ 2832 3888; Ground fl, Southorn Centre, 130-138 Hennessy Rd; ☺ 9am-7pm Mon-Sat, 9.30am-6pm Sun)

Offices in Kowloon:

Mong Kok (Map p98; ☎ 2789 5888, 2789 5970; 1st & 2nd fl, Tak Po Bldg, 62-72 Sai Yee St; ☺ 9am-7pm Mon-Fri, 9am-5pm Sat, 9.30am-12.30pm & 2-5pm Sun)

Offices in New Territories:

Sha Tin (Map p124; ☎ 2692 7773; Shop 233, 2nd fl, New Town Plaza; ☺ 9am-9pm)

DIRECTORY

ADDRESSES

Addresses in Hong Kong are fairly straightforward. In general the apartment (or office) number and floor precede the name of the building, street address and district. There are no postal codes. In Hong Kong (and in this book), the 1st floor is the floor above the ground floor. Virtually every business and residential building here has a guard or concierge and a table displaying the names of the occupants.

About the only problem you may have in finding your way around Hong Kong is determining the appropriate exit for your destination from the Mass Transit Railway (MTR; p280).

BUSINESS

Hong Kong is not all about business, but it remains an important aspect of its ethos and character. Some useful business contacts:

American Chamber of Commerce (Map p56; ☎ 2530 6900; www.amcham.org.hk; Room 1904, 19th fl, Bank of America Tower, 12 Harcourt Rd, Central) The most active overseas chamber of commerce in Hong Kong.

Chinese General Chamber of Commerce (Map p56; ☎ 2525 6385; www.cgcc.org.hk; 4th fl, Chinese General Chamber of Commerce Bldg, 24-25 Connaught Rd, Central) Authorised to issue Certificates of Hong Kong origin for trade.

Chinese Manufacturers' Association of Hong Kong (Map p56; ☎ 2545 6166; www.cma.org.hk; 3rd fl, CMA Bldg, 64-66 Connaught Rd, Central) Operates testing laboratories for product certification and can also issue Certificates of Hong Kong origin.

Hong Kong General Chamber of Commerce (Map p63; ☎ 2529 9229; www.chamber.org.hk; 22nd fl, United Centre, 95 Queensway, Admiralty) Services for foreign executives and firms, such as translation, serviced offices, secretarial help and printing.

Hong Kong Labour Department (Map p56; ☎ 2717 1771; www.labour.gov.hk; 16th fl, Harbour Bldg, 38 Pier Rd, Central) Contact this department for labour-relations problems and queries.

Hong Kong Trade & Industry Department (Map p98; ☎ 2392 2922; www.tid.gov.hk; Room 908, 700 Nathan Rd, Trade & Industry Department Tower, Mong Kok)

This department is a key source for trade information, statistics, government regulations and product certification (enter from Fife St).

Hong Kong Trade Development Council (HKTDC; Map p65; ☎ 1830 668; www.tdctrade.com; 38th fl, Office Tower, Convention Plaza, 1 Harbour Rd, Wan Chai) Cosponsors and participates in trade fairs, and publishes a wealth of material on Hong Kong markets.

TDC Business InfoCentre (Map p65; ☎ 2248 4000; http://infocentre.tdctrade.com; New Wing, Hong Kong Convention & Exhibition Centre, 1 Expo Dr, Wan Chai; ☎ 10am-7pm Mon-Fri, 10am-5pm Sat) Run by the HKTDC, the centre is well stocked with relevant books, periodicals and reference materials.

BUSINESS HOURS

Office hours in Hong Kong are from 9am to either 5.30pm or 6pm on weekdays and often (but increasingly less so) from 9am to noon or 1pm on Saturday. The weekday lunch hour is usually from 1pm to 2pm. Banks are open from 9am to 4.30pm or 5.30pm weekdays and 9am to 12.30pm on Saturday.

Shops that cater to tourists keep longer hours, but almost nothing opens before 9am. As a rule of thumb, assume a place will be open from 10am to 7pm daily. For specifics, see p152.

Museums are generally open from 10am to between 5pm and 9pm and are closed one day a week (usually Monday, Tuesday or Thursday).

Restaurants are open from noon to 3pm; dinner is usually from 6pm to 11pm.

CHILDREN

Hong Kong is a great travel destination for kids (see the boxed text, p138), though the crowds, traffic and pollution might be off-putting to some parents. Food and sanitation is of a high standard, and the territory is jam-packed with things to entertain the young 'uns. As a starting point, get a copy of the *Hong Kong Family Fun Guide* from the *Hong Kong Tourism Board* (HKTB) or download it from the HKTB website www .discoverhongkong.com/eng/travelneeds/family/index.jhtml.

Lonely Planet's *Travel with Children* includes all sorts of useful advice for those travelling with their little ones.

Most public transport and museums offer half-price fares and admission fees to children under the age of 12, but combination family tickets are rare. Hotels can recommend babysitters if you've got daytime appointments or want a night out sans child. Otherwise call Rent-A-Mum (☎ 2523 4868; rentamum@netvigator .com; per hr $110-140 plus transport charges depending on the location).

CLIMATE

Both Hong Kong and Macau have a subtropical climate characterised by hot, humid summers and cool, relatively dry winters.

October, November and most of December are the best months to visit. Temperatures are moderate, the skies are clear and the sun shines. January and February are cloudy and cold but dry. It's warmer from March to May, but the humidity is high, and the fog and drizzle can make getting around difficult. The sweltering heat and humidity from June to August can make sightseeing a sweaty proposition, and it is also the rainy season. September is a grand month if you like drama; the threat of a typhoon seems to loom every other day.

The very informative Hong Kong Observatory (Map p94; ☎ 2926 8200; www.hko.gov.hk; 134A Nathan Rd, Tsim Sha Tsui) issues weather reports on ☎ 1878 200 and on its website. The hotline for cyclone warnings is ☎ 2835 1473.

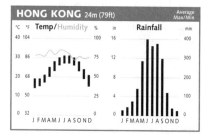

TYPHOON!

Typhoons – massive tropical cyclones often tens of kilometres high and hundreds of kilometres wide – sometimes hit Hong Kong. When they hit, the place all but shuts down. Flights are grounded, ferries are cancelled, shops and offices close (although happily a handful of enterprising bars have been known to stay open).

Cyclones can last for as long as a few weeks, but not all will mature into typhoons. Feeding off moisture, tropical cyclones can only survive over warm oceans – once typhoons hit land, they quickly die out. The 'eye' of the cyclone is generally tens of kilometres wide and is basically a column of descending air, which is much calmer than the surrounding vortex.

Only about half the cyclones in the South China Sea ever reach typhoon ferocity. The gradation of tropical cyclones ascends as follows: tropical depression (with winds up to 62km/h); tropical storm (up to 87km/h); severe tropical storm (up to 117km/h); and typhoon (118km/h or more).

About a dozen typhoons develop in the South China Sea each year, although Hong Kong is a small target, so the chances of a direct hit – within 100km – are reasonably slim.

There is a numbering system to warn of typhoons broadcast on all media. No 1 (its visual symbol being the letter 't') means that a tropical cyclone is within 800km of Hong Kong. No 3 (an upside-down 't') – there is no No 2 – warns that winds of up to 62km are blowing, or expected to blow, generally in Hong Kong near sea level, and there is a risk of Hong Kong being hit and that people should take precautions such as securing flower pots on balconies and terraces. The system then jumps to No 8 (a triangle), which means that there are sustained winds of between 63km/h and 117km/h. People are instructed to stay indoors and to fix adhesive tape to exposed windows to reduce the damage caused by broken glass, while businesses shut down and ferries stop running. No 9 (a double triangle) warns that gale- or storm-force winds are increasing, and No 10 (a cross) is the most severe, with winds reaching upwards of 118km/h and gusts exceeding 220km/h.

Only 13 typhoons have reached No 10 since the end of WWII. The most famous ones in recent years were Typhoon Wanda (1962), the most ferocious of all, delivering hourly mean wind speeds of 133km/h and peak gusts of 259km/h; Typhoon Ellen (1983), which killed 22 people and injured over 300; and Typhoon York (1999), which had the No 10 signal up the longest of any other typhoon – 11 hours.

Rain, which can fall so heavily in Hong Kong that it sounds like a drum roll as it hits the pavement, can cause deadly landslips. Hong Kong also has a 'heavy rain warning system' that is colour-coded – in ascending degrees of severity – amber, red and black.

CONSULATES

Hong Kong is definitely one of the world's most consulate-clogged cities. You'll find a complete list of consulates in the *Yellow Pages*.

Australia (Map p65; ☎ 2827 8881; 23rd fl, Harbour Centre, 25 Harbour Rd, Wan Chai)

Canada (Map p56; ☎ 2810 4321; 11th-14th fl, Tower I, Exchange Sq, 8 Connaught Pl, Central)

France (Map p63; ☎ 3196 6100; 26th fl, Tower II, Admiralty Centre, 18 Harcourt Rd, Admiralty)

Germany (Map p63; ☎ 2105 8788; 21st fl, United Centre, 95 Queensway, Admiralty)

Ireland (Map p65; ☎ 2527 4897; 6th fl, Chung Nam Bldg, 1 Lockhart Rd, Wan Chai) Honorary consulate.

Japan (Map p56; ☎ 2522 1184; 46th-47th fl, Tower I, Exchange Sq, 8 Connaught Pl, Central)

Netherlands (Map p56; ☎ 2522 5127; Room 5702, 57th fl, Cheung Kong Centre, 2 Queen's Rd Central, Central)

New Zealand (Map p65; ☎ 2877 4488; Room 6508, 65th fl, Central Plaza, 18 Harbour Rd, Wan Chai)

South Africa (Map p65; ☎ 2577 3279; Room 2706-2710, 27th fl, Great Eagle Centre, 23 Harbour Rd, Wan Chai)

UK (Map p63; ☎ 2901 3000; 1 Supreme Court Rd, Admiralty)

USA (Map p56; ☎ 2523 9011; 26 Garden Rd, Central)

COURSES

The Community Advice Bureau (Map p56; ☎ 2815 5444; www.cab.org.hk; Room 16C, Right Emperor Commercial Bldg, 122-126 Wellington St, Central; ⏰ 9.30am-4.30pm Mon-Fri) is a fabulous source of information on courses of all kinds in Hong Kong. The YMCA (☎ 2771 9111; www.ymca.org.hk) and the YWCA (☎ 3476 1300; www.ywca.org.hk) both offer a range of cultural classes and three-month courses, from basic Cantonese and mahjong to yoga and t'ai chi.

For visual arts, check with the Hong Kong Museum of Art (☎ 2721 0116), the Hong Kong Visual Arts Centre (☎ 2521 3008) or the Hong Kong Arts Centre (☎ 2582 0200). The Fringe Club (☎ 2521 7251; www.hkfringe.com.hk; 2 Lower Albert Rd, Central) offers any number of courses and workshops.

The Cultural Kaleidoscope Meet the People program organised by the HKTB (☎ 2508 1234; www.discoverhongkong.com) will whet your appetite to learn more about everything from Chinese tea and opera to t'ai chi and jade. It is unique in that it allows you to visit galleries, antique shops, jewellers to grade pearls and jade, tea-houses, even a feng shui master's studio and a t'ai chi class. It's an excellent way to learn first-hand about Hong Kong Chinese culture. For details on times and locations see the HKTB website.

Language

The New Asia-Yale-in-China Chinese Language Centre at the Chinese University of Hong Kong (Map pp50–1; ☎ 2609 6727; www.cuhk.edu.hk/clc; Fong Shu Chuen Bldg, Ma Liu Shui, New Territories) offers regular courses in Cantonese and Mandarin. There are four terms a year – four- and 11-week summer sessions and two regular 15-week terms in spring and autumn. The cost of the four-week summer term is $8000, the 11-week session $18,960, while the 15-week semesters are $23,700. In addition there are shorter two-week introductory courses such as Elementary Cantonese for $5400.

Another good place for learning Cantonese, Mandarin and other Asian languages is the School of Professional and Continuing Education at Hong Kong University (Map pp54–5; ☎ 2559 9771; http://hkuspace.hku.hk; Room 304, 3rd fl, TT Tsui Bldg, Pok Fu Lam Rd, Pok Fu Lam).

A number of private-language schools cater to individuals or companies. These schools offer more flexibility and even dispatch teachers to companies to teach the whole staff. For one-on-one instruction, expect to pay $200 plus per hour. Language schools to consider:

Essential Chinese Language Centre (Map p56; ☎ 2544 6979; http://eclc.com.hk; 8th fl, Man On Commercial Bldg, 12-13 Jubilee St, Central)

Hong Kong Institute of Languages (Map p68; ☎ 2877 6160; www.hklanguages.com; 6th fl, Wellington Plaza, 56-58 Wellington St, Central)

CULTURAL CENTRES

Opening hours for cultural centres vary according to the department (library, media centre, gallery etc) and what's exhibiting.

Alliance Française (Map p65; ☎ 2527 7825; www.alliancefrancaise.com.hk; 1st & 2nd fl, 123 Hennessy Rd, Wan Chai) This place has a library and offers a wide range of cultural activities.

British Council (Map p63; ☎ 2913 5100; www.britishcouncil.org.hk; 3 Supreme Court Rd, Admiralty) Provides English-language classes, sponsors cultural programmes, has internet access and a useful Customer Services Centre (⏰ 9am-8.30pm Mon-Fri, 9am-6pm Sat).

Goethe-Institut (Map p65; ☎ 2802 0088; www.goethe .de/hongkong; 13th & 14th fl, Hong Kong Arts Centre, 2 Harbour Rd, Wan Chai) German classes, films, exhibitions and lectures.

CUSTOMS REGULATIONS

Even though Hong Kong is a duty-free port, there are items on which duty is still charged. Import taxes on cigarettes and, in particular, alcohol are high (100% on spirits, 40% on wine, 20% on beer).

The duty-free allowance for visitors arriving into Hong Kong (including those coming from Macau and mainland China) is 60 cigarettes (or 15 cigars or 75g of tobacco) and 1L of alcohol (wine or spirits). Apart from these limits there are few other import taxes, so you can bring in reasonable quantities of almost anything.

Firecrackers and fireworks are banned in Hong Kong but not in Macau and mainland China, and people crossing the border are sometimes thoroughly searched for these. Customs officers are on high alert for drug smugglers. If you're arriving from Thailand or Vietnam, be prepared for a rigorous examination of your luggage.

DISCOUNT CARDS

Hong Kong Museums Pass

This pass allows multiple entries to six of Hong Kong's museums: Hong Kong Museum of Coastal Defence on Hong Kong Island; the Hong Kong Science Museum, Hong Kong Museum of History, Hong Kong Museum of Art and Hong Kong Space Museum (excluding Space Theatre) in Kowloon; and the Hong Kong Heritage Museum in the New Territories. Passes valid for seven consecutive days cost $30; passes valid for a half-year cost $50/25 for adults/seniors over 60 and students; and a full-year pass is $100/50. Passes are available from HKTB outlets and participating museums. Please note that these half-dozen museums are all free on Wednesdays.

Hostel Card

A Hostelling International (HI) card or the equivalent is of relatively limited use in Hong Kong as there are only seven HI-affiliated hostels here and most are in remote locations in the New Territories. If you arrive without a card and want to stay in one of these hostels, you can buy one from the Hong Kong Youth Hostels Association (HKYHA; Map pp88–9; ☎ 2788 1638; www.yha .org.hk; Room 225-227, Block 19, Shek Kip Mei Estate, Nam Cheong St, Kowloon) for $110/50 over/under 18 years.

You are allowed to stay at any of Hong Kong's HKYHA hostels without a membership card, but you will have to buy a 'Welcome Stamp' ($30) for each night of your stay. Once you've stayed six nights, you are issued your own card.

Seniors Card

Many attractions in Hong Kong offer discounts for people aged over 60 or 65. Most of Hong Kong's museums are either free or half-price for those over 60 and most forms of public transport offer a 50% discount to anyone over 65. A passport or ID with a photo should be sufficient proof of age.

Student, Youth & Teacher Cards

The International Student Identity Card (ISIC), a plastic ID-style card with your photograph, provides discounts on some forms of transport and cheaper admission to museums and other sights. If you're aged under 26 but not a student, you can apply for an International Youth Travel Card (IYTC) issued by the Federation of International Youth Travel Organisations (FIYTO), which gives much the same discounts and benefits. Teachers can apply for the International Teacher Identity Card (ITIC).

Hong Kong Student Travel, based at Sincerity Travel (Map p92; ☎ 2730 3269; Room 833-834, 8th fl, East Block, Star House, 3 Salisbury Rd, Tsim Sha Tsui; ☒ 10am-7pm Mon-Sat), can issue you any of these cards instantly for $100. Make sure you bring your student ID or other credentials along with you.

ELECTRICITY

The standard is 220V, 50Hz AC. Hong Kong's plug and socket system can be a bit confusing at first. The vast majority of electric outlets are designed to accommodate the British three square pins, but some take three large round prongs and others three small pins. Unsurprisingly, inexpensive plug adaptors are widely available in Hong Kong, even in supermarkets.

EMERGENCY

Hong Kong is generally a very safe place but, as everywhere, things can go awry. Although it is safe to walk around just about anywhere in the territory after dark, it's best to stick to well-lit areas. Tourist districts such as Tsim Sha Tsui are heavily patrolled by the police. In the event of a real emergency, ring ☎ 999.

Hong Kong does have its share of local pickpockets and thieves. Carry as little cash and as few valuables as possible, and if you put a bag down, keep an eye on it. This also applies to restaurants and pubs, particularly in touristed areas such as the Star Ferry piers and the Peak Tram. If your bag doesn't accompany you to the toilet, don't expect to find it when you return.

If you are robbed, you can obtain a loss report for insurance purposes at the police station in the area in which the crime occurred. For locations and contact details of police stations in Hong Kong, visit www.info.gov.hk/police and click on 'Contact Use' and then 'Report Rooms'.

If you run into legal trouble, call the Legal Aid Department (☎ 2537 7677; www.lad.gov.hk; ☺ 8.45am-1pm & 2-5.15pm Mon-Fri, 9am-noon Sat, 24hr hotline), which provides residents and visitors with representation, subject to a means and merits test. Other important numbers include the following:

Auxiliary Medical Service (AMS) hotline (☎ 2762 2033)

Bushfire Control Centre hotline (☎ 2720 0777)

Police (☎ general enquiries 2860 2000, report hotline 2527 7177)

St John Ambulance Brigade (Hong Kong Island ☎ 2576 6555, Kowloon ☎ 2713 5555, New Territories ☎ 2639 2555, territory-wide ☎ 2530 8032)

Tropical Cyclone Warning (☎ 2835 1473)

GAY & LESBIAN TRAVELLERS

Those travelling to Hong Kong will find a small but vibrant and growing gay and lesbian scene in the Special Administrative Region (SAR). It may not compete with the likes of London or Sydney but Hong Kong has come a long way all the same.

It was, after all, only in 1991 that the Crimes (Amendment) Ordinance removed criminal penalties for homosexual acts between consenting adults over the age of 18. Since that time gay groups have been lobbying for legislation to address the issue of discrimination on the grounds of sexual orientation. Despite these changes, however, Hong Kong Chinese society remains fairly conservative, and it can

still be risky for gays and lesbians to come out to family members or their employers.

Useful organisations:

Chi Heng Foundation (☎ 2517 0564; www.chihengfoundation.com; GPO Box 3923, Central, Hong Kong) Umbrella unit for gay and lesbian associations and groups in Hong Kong.

Horizons (☎ 2815 9268, 9776 6479; www.horizons.org.hk; GPO Box 6837, Central, Hong Kong; ☺ hotline 7.30-10.30pm Thu) Phone service that can provide information and advice to local and visiting gays, lesbians and bisexuals.

Queer Sisters (☎ 2314 4348; www.qs.org.hk; ☺ hotline 8-10pm Tue) Information and assistance organisation for lesbians. You can call and leave a voicemail message outside of hotline hours and staff will get back to you.

HEALTH

The Severe Acute Respiratory Syndrome (SARS) outbreak of 2003 notwithstanding, health conditions in the region are good. Travellers have a low risk of contracting infectious diseases, apart from travellers' diarrhoea, which is common throughout Asia. The health system (p295) is generally excellent.

Diseases
DENGUE FEVER

This is caught from mosquito bites. Until recently it was unheard of in Hong Kong, yet some 30 cases were reported in 2004 (the outbreak claimed no lives).

This viral disease is transmitted by mosquitoes but unlike the malaria mosquito, the *Aedes aegypti* mosquito, which transmits the dengue virus, is most active during the day, and is found mainly in urban areas, in and around human dwellings. Signs and symptoms of dengue fever include a sudden onset of high fever, headache, joint and muscle pains (hence its old name, 'breakbone fever'), and nausea and vomiting. A rash of small red spots sometimes appears three to four days after the onset of fever.

You should seek medical attention as soon as possible if you think you may be infected. A blood test can exclude malaria and indicate the possibility of dengue fever. There is no specific treatment for dengue. Aspirin should be avoided, as it increases the risk of haemorrhaging. The best prevention is to avoid mosquito bites at all times by covering up, using insect repellents containing the compound DEET and mosquito nets.

GIARDIA

This is a parasite that often jumps on board when you have diarrhoea. It then causes a more prolonged illness with intermittent diarrhoea or loose stools, bloating, fatigue and some nausea. There may be a metallic taste in the mouth. Avoiding potentially contaminated foods and always washing your hands can help to prevent giardia.

HEPATITIS A

This virus is common in Hong Kong and Macau and is transmitted through contaminated water and shellfish. It is most commonly caught at local island seafood restaurants. Immunisation and avoiding local seafood restaurants should prevent it.

HEPATITIS B

Whilst this is common in the area, it can only be transmitted by unprotected sex, sharing needles, treading on a discarded needle, or receiving contaminated blood in very remote areas of China.

INFLUENZA

Hong Kong has a bad flu season over the winter months from December to March. Symptoms include a cold (runny nose etc) with a high fever and aches and pains. You should wash your hands frequently, avoid anybody you know who has the flu and think about getting a flu shot before you travel.

TRAVELLERS' DIARRHOEA

To prevent diarrhoea, avoid tap water unless it has been boiled, filtered or chemically disinfected (eg with iodine tablets); only eat fresh fruits and vegetables if they're cooked or peeled; be wary of dairy products that might contain unpasteurised milk; and be highly selective when eating food from street vendors.

If you develop diarrhoea, be sure to drink plenty of fluids, preferably an oral rehydration solution containing lots of salt and sugar. A few loose stools don't mean you require treatment but, if you start experiencing more than four or five stools a day, you should start taking an antibiotic (usually a quinolone drug) and an antidiarrheal agent (such as loperamide). If diarrhoea is bloody, or persists for more than 72 hours, or is accompanied by fever, shaking chills or severe abdominal pain, you should seek medical attention.

Environmental Hazards

INSECTS

Mosquitoes are prevalent in Hong Kong. You should always use insect repellent and if bitten use hydrocortisone cream to reduce swelling. Lamma Island is home to large red centipedes, which have a poisonous bite that causes swelling and discomfort in most cases, but can be more dangerous (and supposedly in very rare cases deadly) for young children.

MAMMALS

Wild boars and aggressive dogs are a minor hazard in some of the more remote parts of the New Territories. Wild boars are shy and retiring most of the time but dangerous when they feel threatened, so give them a wide berth and avoid disturbing thick areas of undergrowth.

SNAKES

There are many snakes in Hong Kong and some are deadly, but you are unlikely to encounter any. Still, always take care when bushwalking, particularly on Lamma and Lantau Islands. Go straight to a public hospital if bitten; private doctors do not stock antivenin.

WATER

Avoid drinking the local water as its quality varies enormously and depends on the pipes in the building you're in. Bottled water is a safer option or you can boil tap water for three minutes.

Online Resources

The World Health Organization (WHO) publishes a superb book called *International Travel and Health*, which is revised annually and is available free online at www.who .int/ith.

Recommended Immunisations

There are no required vaccinations for entry into Hong Kong or Macau unless you have travelled from a country infected with yellow fever. In this case, you will have to show your yellow-fever vaccination certificate. Hong Kong is a highly developed city and as such immunisations are not really necessary unless you will be travelling on to the mainland or elsewhere in the region.

Since most vaccines don't produce immunity until at least two weeks after they're given, visit a physician four to eight weeks before departure. Ask your doctor for an International Certificate of Vaccination (or 'yellow booklet'), which will list all of the vaccinations you've received.

If your health insurance doesn't cover you for medical expenses abroad, consider supplemental insurance (see www.lonelyplanet .com/travel_links for more information).

HOLIDAYS

Western and Chinese culture combine to create an interesting mix – and number – of public holidays in Hong Kong and Macau. Determining the exact date of some of them is tricky as there are traditionally two calendars in use: the Gregorian solar (or Western) calendar and the Chinese lunar calendar.

The following are public holidays in both Hong Kong and Macau (unless noted otherwise). For Macau-specific holidays, see p351.

New Year's Day 1 January

Chinese New Year 7 February 2008, 26 January 2009, 14 February 2010

Easter 21-24 March 2008, 10-13 April 2009, 2-5 April 2010

Ching Ming 5 April

Labour Day 1 May

Buddha's Birthday 12 May 2008, 2 May 2009, 21 May 2010

Dragon Boat (Tuen Ng) Festival 8 June 2008, 28 June 2009, 16 June 2010

Hong Kong SAR Establishment Day 1 July (not Macau)

Mid-Autumn Festival 14 September 2008, 3 October 2009, 22 September 2010

China National Day 1 October

Cheung Yeung 7 October 2008, 26 October 2009

Christmas Day 25 December

Boxing Day 26 December

IDENTITY CARD

Hong Kong residents are required to carry a government-issued Hong Kong Identity Card with them at all times and this rule is strictly enforced. As a visitor, you are required to carry your passport; it is the only acceptable form of identification as far as the police are concerned.

Anyone over the age of 11 who stays in Hong Kong for longer than 180 days must apply for a Hong Kong ID. Enquire at the ID-issuing office of the Hong Kong Immigration Department (Map p65; ☎ 2824 6111; www.immd.gov

.hk; 8th fl, Immigration Tower, 7 Gloucester Rd, Wan Chai; ☺ 8.45am-4.30pm Mon-Fri, 9-11.30am Sat). Be sure to take your passport and other documents with you.

INTERNET ACCESS

The internet is very popular in computer-literate Hong Kong, and the territory was the first place in the world to be totally accessible by broadband. Virtually every business has a website and just about anyone you're likely to do business with can be contacted by email.

Internet service providers (ISPs) most often used in Hong Kong include PCCW's Netvigator (☎ 183 3833; www.netvigator.com), HKNet (☎ 2110 2288; www.hknet.com), CPCNet (☎ 2331 8930; www.cpc net-hk.com) and Yahoo (☎ 2895 5769; www.yah oo.hk).

Most hotels and hostels have internet access. You'll also be able to log on for free at major MTR stations (eg Central and Causeway Bay) and many public libraries, including the Causeway Bay branch of the Central Library (p76). All it takes to log on to one of up to a half-dozen terminals at the Pacific Coffee Company (www.pacificcoffee.com) is the purchase of a coffee ($21 to $36) or a piece of cake ($12 to $26).

Among some of the best (ie fast machines, good locations, number of terminals) private internet cafés:

Cyber Clan (Map p65; ☎ 2723 2821; Luen Tai Bldg, 93-99 Wan Chai Rd, Wan Chai; membership $5, per hr members $12, nonmembers $13; ☺ 24hr) Round-the-clock place located where Johnston and Wan Chai Rds meet.

Cyber Pro Internet (Map p74; ☎ 2836 3502; Basement, 491-499 Lockhart Rd, Causeway Bay; per hr 11am-midnight/midnight-7am Sun-Thu $16/10, Fri & Sat $18/13; ☺ 11am-7am) This huge place is packed with young 'uns playing games.

IT. Fans (Map p56; ☎ 2542 1868; Ground & mezzanine fl, Man On Commercial Bldg, 12-13 Jubilee St, Central; membership $10, per hr members/nonmembers Mon-Thu $16/20, Fri-Sun $18/22; ☺ 10am-5am) This massive and very central place has 100 monitors and serves real food.

Pacific Coffee Company (Map p92; ☎ 2735 0112; Shop G31-G32A, Miramar Shopping Centre, 132 Nathan Rd, Tsim Sha Tsui; ☺ 7am-midnight Mon-Thu, 7am-1am Fri & Sat, 8am-midnight Sun) Internet is free for customers. In addition, there are dozens of other branches throughout Hong Kong.

Shadowman Cyber Cafe (Map p92; ☎ 2366 5262; Ground fl, 21A Ashley Rd, Tsim Sha Tsui; ☺ 8am-midnight Mon-Sat, 10am-midnight Sun) This is a small but convivial place to check emails, surf the web and have lunch (sandwiches $28 to $100, set meal $45). The first 20 minutes are free with your purchase, then it's $10 every 15 minutes.

LAUNDRY

Laundries are easy to find everywhere in Hong Kong – hey, this *is* China – though they're *never* self-service. Most hotels, guesthouses and even some hostels have a laundry service. Prices at local laundries are normally $28 to $35 for the first 3kg, and then $8 to $12 for each additional kilogram.

Dry cleaners are easy to spot and some laundries offer that service as well. Both prices and quality vary enormously, but expect to pay from $25 for a dress shirt, from $35 for a skirt and from $60 for a suit.

The following are recommended laundries and dry-cleaners:

Martinizing (Map p56; ☎ 2525 3089; Ground fl, 7 Glenealy, Central; ☷ 8.30am-7pm Mon-Sat)

New Furama Dry-Cleaning (Map p56; ☎ 2537 2217; Shop 1C, Ground fl, Bank of America Tower, 12 Harcourt Rd, Central; ☷ 8am-7pm Mon-Sat)

Wei Wei Dry Cleaner & Laundry (Map p68; ☎ 2522 9818; 26 Old Bailey St, Soho; ☷ 7.30am-7.45pm Mon-Sat)

LEFT LUGGAGE

There are left-luggage lockers in major KCR train stations, including the Hung Hom station, the West Tower of the Shun Tak Centre in Sheung Wan, from where the Macau ferry departs, and the China ferry terminal in Tsim Sha Tsui. Luggage costs between $20 and $30 for up to two hours (depending on the locker size) and between $25 and $35 for every 12 hours after that. The Hong Kong Airport Express station has a left-luggage office open from 6am to 1am. There's also a counter on level 5 (arrivals hall) of Hong Kong International Airport (☎ 2261 0110; ☷ 5.30am-1.30am). Storage here costs $35 for up to three hours, $50 for up to 24 hours and $120 for up to 48 hours. It's $80 for each 24-hour period after that.

Generally the machines don't use keys but spit out a numbered ticket when you have deposited your money and closed the door. You have to punch in this number when you retrieve your bag, so keep it somewhere safe or write the number down. Some lockers have a maximum storage time of three days, so read the instructions carefully.

If you're going to visit Macau or the mainland and you'll be returning to Hong Kong, most hotels and even some guesthouses and hostels have left-luggage rooms and will let you leave your gear behind, even if you've already checked out and won't be staying on your return. There is usually a charge for this service, so be sure to enquire first.

LEGAL MATTERS

Hong Kong has a serious drug problem, much of it supplied by the Triads. There are estimated to be more than 40,000 drug addicts in Hong Kong, 75% of whom are hooked on heroin, which they generally smoke – the process is called 'chasing the dragon' – rather than inject. Some female addicts finance their habit by working in the sex industry; others resort to pickpocketing, burglary and robbery.

Professional smugglers often target Westerners to carry goods into countries like Vietnam and India, where those goods are prohibited or the import taxes are high. The theory is that customs agents are less likely to stop and search foreigners. These small-time smuggling expeditions, or 'milk runs', either earn the Westerner a fee or a free air ticket to another destination. But smuggling is very, very risky.

Most foreigners who get into legal trouble in Hong Kong are involved in drugs. *All* forms of narcotics are illegal in Hong Kong. It makes no difference whether it's heroin, opium, 'ice', ecstasy or marijuana – the law makes no distinction. If police or customs officials find dope or even smoking equipment in your possession, you can expect to be arrested immediately. If you do run into legal trouble, contact the Legal Aid Department (☎ 2537 7677; ☷ 24hr hotline).

LIBRARIES

Hong Kong has an extensive public library system – some 66 in total – and you will find a list on the internet at www.hkpl.gov.hk. The most useful for travellers is the City Hall Public Library (Map p56; ☎ 2921 2555; ☷ 10am-7pm Mon-Thu, 10am-9pm Fri, 10am-5pm Sat & Sun & some public holidays), spread over eight floors of the High Block of City Hall, opposite Queen's Pier in Central. With a passport and a deposit of $130 per item, foreign visitors can get a temporary library card (3rd floor), which allows them to borrow up to six books and other materials from the library for 14 days at any one time.

In Causeway Bay the even larger Central Library (Map p74; ☎ 3150 1234; 66 Causeway Rd; ☷ 10am-9pm Thu-Tue, 1-9pm Wed, 10am-7pm some public holidays) has lending sections, children's and young adult libraries, some two-dozen terminals with internet available to the public and a wonderful reading room on the 5th floor with around 4000 international periodicals.

MAPS

Decent tourist maps are easy to come by in Hong Kong, and they're usually free. The HKTB hands out copies of the bimonthly *The Hong Kong Map* at its information centres. It covers the northern coast of Hong Kong Island from Sheung Wan to Causeway Bay and part of the Kowloon peninsula, and has inset maps of Aberdeen, Hung Hom, Kowloon City, Kowloon Tong, Sha Tin, Stanley and Tsuen Wan.

Another free map you'll find everywhere is the *AOA Street Map*, but it's full of advertising and difficult to use.

Lonely Planet's *Hong Kong City Map* has five separate maps with varying scales, a street index and an inset map of Hong Kong's rail network.

Universal Publications (UP; www.up.com.hk) produces many maps of Hong Kong, including the 1:80,000 *Hong Kong Touring Map* ($22) and the 1:9000 *City Map of Hong Kong & Kowloon* ($25). It publishes detailed street maps of Hong Kong Island and Kowloon ($22 each), with scales below 1:8000.

The *Hong Kong Official Guide Map* ($45), produced by the Survey and Mapping Office of the Lands Department (www.info.gov.hk/landsd/mapping), has both street and district maps and is available from most bookshops.

If you're looking for greater detail, topographical accuracy and good colour reproduction, it's worth investing in the *Hong Kong Guidebook* ($60), a street atlas to the entire territory published by UP and updated annually. Compiled in English and Chinese, it also includes useful information on public transport and a host of other listings. A larger format version of this, the *Hong Kong Directory* ($70) is available as well as the pocket-size *Palm Atlas of Hong Kong* ($42). The *Public Transport Atlas* ($50) shows detailed information on all land public transport routes in Hong Kong, displaying all of the stops on maps.

Along with everything from flying charts to plans of the New Towns in the New Territories, the Survey and Mapping Office produces a series of eight *Countryside Series* maps that are useful for hiking in the hills and country parks. They are available from two Map Publication Centres: the North Point branch (Map pp54–5; ☎ 2231 3187; 23rd fl, North Point Government Offices, 333 Java Rd; ◷ 9am-5.30pm Mon-Fri) and the Yau Ma Tei branch (Map p97; ☎ 2780 0981; 382 Nathan Rd; ◷ 9am-5.30pm Mon-Fri).

Each of the six *Countryside Series* maps is 1:25,000, with larger-scale inset maps. One of them covers Hong Kong Island and surrounds: *Hong Kong Island & Neighbouring Islands* ($50). Three maps are devoted to the New Territories: *North-West New Territories* ($62); *North-East & Central New Territories* ($50); and *Sai Kung & Clearwater Bay* ($50). For the islands, there's *Outlying Islands* ($45), with large-scale maps of Cheung Chau, Lamma, Peng Chau, Ma Wan, Tung Lung Chau and Po Toi, and *Lantau Island & Neighbouring Islands* ($62), essentially a 1:25,000-scale map of Hong Kong's largest island, with several larger-scale inset maps.

Most bookshops stock UP's 1:32,000-scale *Lantau Island, Cheung Chau & Lamma Island* ($25), which is laminated and contains useful transport information, and its 1:54,000 *Tseung Kwan O, Sai Kung, Clearwater Bay* ($25).

If you're heading for any of Hong Kong's four major trails, you should get a copy of the trail map produced by the Country & Marine Parks Authority, which is available at the Map Publication Centres.

MEDICAL SERVICES

The standard of medical care in Hong Kong is generally excellent but expensive. Always take out travel insurance before you travel. Healthcare is divided into public and private, and there is no interaction between the two. In the case of an emergency, all ambulances (☎ 999) will take you to a government-run public hospital where, as a visitor, you will be required to pay $570 for using emergency services. Treatment is guaranteed in any case; people who cannot pay immediately will be billed later. While the emergency care is excellent, you may wish to transfer to a private hospital once you are stable.

There are many English-speaking general practitioners, specialists and dentists in Hong Kong, who can be found through your consulate (p289), private hospital or the *Yellow Pages*. If money is tight, take yourself to the nearest public hospital emergency room and be prepared to wait. The general enquiry number for hospitals is ☎ 2300 6555.

Public and private hospitals with 24-hour accident and emergency departments:

HONG KONG ISLAND

Hong Kong Central Hospital (Map p68; ☎ 2522 3141; 1B Lower Albert Rd, Central) Private.

Matilda International Hospital (Map pp54–5; ☎ 2849 0111, 24hr help line 2849 0123; 41 Mt Kellett Rd, The Peak) Private.

Queen Mary Hospital (Map pp54–5; ☎ 2855 3838; 102 Pok Fu Lam Rd, Pok Fu Lam) Public.

KOWLOON

Hong Kong Baptist Hospital (Off Map pp88–9; ☎ 2339 8888; 222 Waterloo Rd, Kowloon Tong) Private.

Princess Margaret Hospital (Map pp50–1; ☎ 2990 1111, 24hr help line 2990 2000; 2-10 Princess Margaret Hospital Rd, Lai Chi Kok) Public.

Queen Elizabeth Hospital (Map p97; ☎ 2958 8428; 30 Gascoigne Rd, Yau Ma Tei) Public.

NEW TERRITORIES

Prince of Wales Hospital (Map p124; ☎ 2632 2415; 30-32 Ngan Shing St, Sha Tin) Public.

There are many pharmacies in Hong Kong and Macau. They bear a red-and-white cross outside and there should be a registered pharmacist available inside. Though many medications can be bought over the counter without a prescription in Hong Kong, you should always check it is a known brand and that the expiry date is valid. Birth-control pills, pads, tampons and condoms are available over the counter in these dispensaries, as well as in stores such as Watsons and Mannings.

MONEY

Consult the inside front cover for a table of exchange rates and refer to the boxed text on p18 for information on costs.

ATMs

Hong Kong Automated Teller Machines (ATMs) can be found almost everywhere and are usually linked up to international money systems such as Cirrus, Maestro, Plus and Visa Electron. Some HSBC so-called Electronic Money machines offer cash withdrawal facilities for Visa and MasterCard holders; American Express (Amex) cardholders have access to Jetco ATMs and can withdraw local currency and travellers cheques at the Express Cash ATMs in town.

Changing Money

One of the main reasons why Hong Kong has become a major financial centre is because it has no currency controls; locals and foreigners can bring/send in or take out as much money as they like.

Banks in Hong Kong generally offer the best rates, though two of the biggest ones – Standard Chartered and the Hang Seng Bank – levy a $50 commission for each transaction on nonaccount holders. Avoid HSBC where this charge is $100. If you're changing the equivalent of several hundred US dollars or more, the exchange rate improves, which usually makes up for the fee.

There are licensed moneychangers, such as Chequepoint, abundant in touristed areas, including Tsim Sha Tsui and the Shun Tak Centre, from where ferries depart for Macau. While they are convenient (usually open on Sunday and holidays and late into the evenings) and take no commission per se, the less-than-attractive exchange rates offered are equivalent to a 5% commission. These rates are clearly posted, though if you're changing several hundred US dollars or more you might be able to bargain for a better rate. Before the actual exchange is made, the moneychanger is required by law to give you a form to sign that clearly shows the amount due to you, the exchange rate and any service charges. And try to avoid the exchange counters at the airport: they offer some of the worst rates in Hong Kong. The rates offered at hotels are only marginally better.

One moneychanger that we've been using since the ink was still wet on the Treaty of Nanking is Wing Hoi Money Exchange (Map p92; ☎ 2723 5948; Ground fl, shop No 9B, Mirador Mansion Arcade, 58 Nathan Rd, Tsim Sha Tsui; ✆ 8.30am-8.30pm Mon-Sat, 8.30am-7pm Sun). It will change just about any currency as well as travellers cheques.

No foreign currency black market exists in Hong Kong. If anyone on the street does approach you to change money, assume it's a scam.

Credit Cards

The most widely accepted credit cards in Hong Kong are Visa, MasterCard, Amex, Diners Club and JCB – and pretty much in that order. When signing credit card receipts, make sure you always write 'HK' in front of the dollar sign if there isn't one already printed there.

If you plan to use a credit card, make sure you have a high enough credit limit to cover major expenses such as car hire or airline tickets. Alternatively, leave your card in credit when you start your travels. And don't just carry one card, go for two: an Amex or Diners Club card with a MasterCard or Visa card. Better still, combine cards and travellers cheques so you have something to fall back on if an ATM swallows your card or the bank won't accept it.

Some shops in Hong Kong may try to add a surcharge to offset the commission charged by credit companies, which can range from 2.5% to 7%. In theory, this is prohibited by the credit companies, but to get around this many shops will offer a 5% discount if you pay cash. It's your call.

If a card is lost or stolen, you must inform both the police (☎ 2527 7177) and the issuing company as soon as possible; otherwise, you may have to pay for the purchases that the unspeakable scoundrel has racked up on your card. Some 24-hour numbers for cancelling cards:

American Express (☎ 2811 6888)

Diners Club (☎ 2860 1888)

JCB (☎ 001 800 0009 0009 toll free)

MasterCard (☎ 800 966 677)

Visa (☎ 800 900 782)

The Visa number may be able to help you (or at least point you in the right direction) should you lose your Visa card but, in general, you must deal with the issuing bank in the case of an emergency. Round-the-clock emergency bank numbers:

Chase Manhattan Bank (☎ 2881 0888)

Citibank (☎ 2860 0333)

HSBC (☎ 2748 4848)

Standard Chartered Bank (☎ 2886 4111)

Currency

The local currency is the Hong Kong dollar (HK$), which is divided into 100 cents. Bills are issued in denominations of $10, $20, $50, $100, $500 and $1000. There are little copper coins worth 10¢, 20¢ and 50¢, silver-coloured $1, $2 and $5 coins, and a nickel and bronze $10 coin.

Hong Kong notes are issued by three banks: HSBC (formerly the Hongkong & Shanghai Bank), the Standard Chartered Bank and the Bank of China (all but the $10 bill).

For exchange rates see the inside front cover, or check out the FXConverter website (www .oanda.com/convert/classic).

Personal Cheques

Personal cheques are still widely used (and accepted) in Hong Kong; a group of diners will often write separate cheques to pay for their share of a meal. If you plan to stay for a while in Hong Kong – or even travel around Asia and return here – you might want to open a bank account here. There is no need to be a Hong Kong resident, and current and savings accounts can be opened in Hong Kong dollars or most other major currencies.

Travellers Cheques

Travellers cheques offer protection from theft but are becoming less common due to the preponderance of ATMs. Most banks will cash travellers cheques, and they all charge a fee, often irrespective of whether you are an account holder or not. HSBC, Standard Chartered and Hang Seng banks all charge commissions, whether this be a flat amount or a percentage of the total exchanged.

If any cheques go missing, contact the issuing office or the nearest branch of the issuing agency immediately. American Express (☎ 3002 1275) can usually arrange replacement cheques within 24 hours.

NEWSPAPERS & MAGAZINES

There are two principal English-language newspapers available in Hong Kong. The daily broadsheet *South China Morning Post* (www .scmp.com), which has always toed the government line – before and after the handover – has the larger circulation and is read by more Hong Kong Chinese than expatriates. Its classified advertisement sales have placed it among the world's most profitable newspapers in the past. The tabloid *Hong Kong Standard* (www .thestandard.com.hk), published from Monday to Saturday (weekend edition), is generally more rigorous in its local reporting. It dubs itself 'Greater China's Business Newspaper', though it's hard to see how it can claim that sobriquet. The Beijing mouthpiece *China Daily* (www .chinadaily.com.cn) also prints out a Hong Kong English-language edition of its paper.

The *Asian Wall Street Journal* as well as regional editions of *USA Today*, the *International Herald Tribune* and the *Financial Times* are printed and are available in Hong Kong.

Hong Kong also has its share of English-language periodicals, including a slew of home-grown (and Asian-focused) business magazines. *Time, Newsweek* and the *Economist* are all available in the current editions.

ORGANISED TOURS

Despite its size a profusion of organised tours operates in Hong Kong. There are tours available to just about anywhere in the territory and they can make good options if you only have a short time in Hong Kong or don't want to deal with public transport. Some tours are standard excursions covering major sights on Hong Kong Island such as the Peak and Hollywood Rd, while other tours take you on harbour cruises, out to the islands or through the New Territories. For tours to Macau, see p313.

Air

If you hanker to see Hong Kong from on high – and hang the expense – Heliservices (☎ 2802 0200; www.heliservices.com.hk) has chartered Aerospatiale Squirrels for up to five passengers available for $6000/9000 for each 15-/30-minute period. They depart from rooftop helipads atop the Peninsula Hong Kong (p257) annexe.

Boat

Several operators offer Harbour Tours. If you're on a budget, the Hong Kong Tourism Board (HKTB; p301) offers a one-hour free ride on the *Duk Ling,* a traditional Chinese junk complete with red triangular sails, departing Kowloon Public pier at 2pm and 4pm Thursday and 10am and noon on Saturday. It also picks up from Central pier 9 at 3pm and 5pm on Thursday, and at 11am and 1pm Saturday.

The easiest way to see the full extent of Victoria Harbour from sea level is to join a circular Star Ferry Harbour Tour (☎ 2118 6201, 2118 6202; www.starferry.com.hk/harbour tour), of which there are a number of different options. A single daytime round trip, departing from the Star Ferry pier in Tsim Sha Tsui hourly between 2.05pm and 5.05pm daily, costs $45/40 for adults/concessions (children aged three to 12 and seniors over 65). A full-/half-day hopping pass, available from 11.05am to 7.05pm/5.05pm respectively, costs $165/70 for adults and $148/63 for concessions. At night, a two-hour round trip (at 7.05pm and 9.05pm) is $115/104 for adults/concessions. A single night ride taken between 6.05pm and

11.05pm costs $95/85. There are also departures from the piers at Central, Wan Chai and Hung Hom; see the website for details.

Many agents, including Gray Line (☎ 2368 7111; www.grayline.com.hk), Splendid Tours & Travel (☎ 2316 2151; www.splendidtours.com) and Hong Kong Dragon Cruise (☎ 2131 8181; www.nwft.com.hk), run by New World First Travel, offer tours of Victoria and Aberdeen Harbours, but the company with the longest experience in these is Watertours (Map p92; ☎ 2926 3868; www.watertours.com.hk; Shop 5C, Ground fl, Star House, 3 Salisbury Rd, Tsim Sha Tsui; ☀ 9am-9pm). Some eight different tours of the harbour and the Outlying Islands, as well as dinner and cocktail cruises, are available. Prices range from $220 ($130 for children aged two to 12) for the Morning Harbour & Noon Day Gun Firing Cruise, to $390 ($360 for children) for the Harbour Lights & Lei Yue Mun Seafood Village Dinner Cruise.

For the Outlying Islands, HKKF Travel (☎ 2533 5339, 2533 5315; info@hkkf.com.hk) has a five-hour Outlying Islands Escapade ($360) that takes in Cheung Chau and Lamma Island. Departure is from pier 4 at the Outlying Islands ferry terminal in Central.

Bus

For first-time visitors to Hong Kong trying to get their bearings, Splendid Tours & Travel (☎ 2316 2151; www.splendidtours.com) runs some interesting 'orientation' tours of Hong Kong Island, Kowloon and the New Territories. The tours last four to five hours and cost $320/220 per adult/child aged three to 12 years. Another tour company to try is the old stalwart Gray Line (☎ 2368 7111; www.grayline.com.hk), which has a five-hour tour ($320/215) taking in Man Mo Temple, Victoria Peak, Aberdeen and Repulse Bay.

Some of the most popular surface tours of the New Territories are offered (or sub-contracted) by the Hong Kong Tourism Board (p301). The ever-popular Land Between Tour takes in the Yuen Yuen Institute temple complex in Tsuen Wan and Tai Mo Shan lookout, as well as several other sights. The full-day tour (adult/child under 16 or senior over 60 $420/370) takes 6½ hours and includes lunch; the half-day tour ($320/270) is five hours, without lunch. The five-hour Heritage Tour ($320/270), which does not include lunch, takes in such New Territories sights as Man Mo Temple in Tai Po, the Tang Chung Ling Ancestral Hall in Leung Yeuk Tau village and the walled settlement of Lo Wai. Contact the HKTB tours reservation hotline (☎ 2368 7112; ☼ 7am-9pm) for information and bookings.

Walking

For tailor-made, personal walking tours of both urban and rural Hong Kong, contact Walk Hong Kong (☎ 9187 8641, 9359 9071; www.walkhongkong.com), which is run by a couple of long-term expatriates.

An unusual way of touring Hong Kong with a 'guide' is on offer from an outfit called Walk the Talk (☎ 2380 7756; www.mobileadventures.net). It's effectively an audioguide that uses your mobile phone. For $150 (or $88 if you don't need a Hong Kong SIM card), you get guided tours of Central, Tsim Sha Tsui and Macau. Each is made up of 15 to 20 segments that last two to three minutes each and contain history and stories, as well as suggestions on where to eat, shop and visit the loo. You can buy Walk the Talk tour packages, which include a pocket-size map, access code and/or SIM card, from any HKTB information centre.

PASSPORT

A passport is essential for visiting Hong Kong, and if yours is within six months of expiration get a new one. If you'll be staying for some time in Hong Kong, it's wise to register with your consulate. This makes the replacement process much simpler if you lose your passport or it is stolen.

Hong Kong residents are required to carry an officially issued identification card at all times (p293). Visitors should carry their passports with them at all times, as the immigration authorities do frequent spot checks to catch illegal workers and those who overstay their visas, and this is the only form of identification acceptable to the Hong Kong police.

PHOTOGRAPHY

Almost everything you could possibly need in the way of photographic accessories is available in Hong Kong. Stanley St on Hong Kong Island is the place to look for reputable camera shops.

Photo developing is relatively inexpensive; to develop a roll of 36 exposures and have them printed costs from $50 for size 3R and from $60 for size 4R. Processing and mounting slide film is $50. Most photo shops will take four passport-size photos of you for $35

or $40. Some of the best photo-processing in town is available at Color Six (Map p68; ☎ 2526 0123; www.colorsix.com; Ground fl, 28A Stanley St, Central; ☼ 8.30am-7pm Mon-Fri, 8.30am-4pm Sat). Not only can colour slides be professionally processed in just three hours, but many special types of film, unavailable elsewhere in Hong Kong, are on sale here. Most photography shops are well geared up for printing from digital formats and for copying onto CDs.

POST

Hong Kong Post (☎ 2921 2222; www.hongkongpost.com) is generally excellent; local letters are often delivered the same day they are sent and there is Saturday delivery. The staff at most post offices speak English, and the lavender-coloured mail boxes with lime-green posts are clearly marked in English.

Receiving Mail

If a letter is addressed c/o Poste Restante, GPO Hong Kong, it will go to the GPO on Hong Kong Island. Pick it up at counter No 29 from 8am to 6pm Monday to Saturday only. If you want your letters to go to Kowloon, have them addressed as follows: c/o Poste Restante, Tsim Sha Tsui Post Office, 10 Middle Rd, Tsim Sha Tsui, Kowloon. Mail is normally held for two months.

Sending Mail

On Hong Kong Island, the General Post Office (Map p56; 2 Connaught Place, Central; ☼ 8am-6pm Mon-Sat, 9am-2pm Sun) is just west of the Star Ferry pier. In Kowloon, the Tsim Sha Tsui Post Office (Map p92; Ground fl, Hermes House, 10 Middle Rd, Tsim Sha Tsui; ☼ 9am-6pm Mon-Sat, 9am-2pm Sun) is just east of the southern end of Nathan Rd. Post office branches elsewhere keep shorter hours and usually don't open on Sunday.

You should allow five days for delivery of letters, postcards and aerogrammes to the UK, Continental Europe and Australia, and five to six days to the USA.

COURIER SERVICES

Private companies offering courier delivery service include the following. All four companies have pick-up points around the territory. Many MTR stations have DHL outlets, including the DHL Central branch (☎ 2877 2848) next to exit F, and the Admiralty MTR branch (☎ 2529 5778) next to exit E.

DHL International (☎ 2400 3388)

Federal Express (☎ 2730 3333)

TNT Express Worldwide (☎ 2331 2663)

UPS (☎ 2735 3535)

POSTAL RATES
Local mail is $1.40 for up to 30g. Airmail letters and postcards for the first 20/30g are $2.40/4.50 to Asia (excluding Japan) and $3/5.30 elsewhere, and $1.20 and $1.30 respectively for each additional 10g. Aerogrammes are a uniform $2.30.

SPEEDPOST
Letters and small parcels sent via Hong Kong Post's Speedpost (☎ 2921 2288; www.hongkongpost.com /speedpost) should reach any of 210 destinations worldwide within four days and are automatically registered. Speedpost rates vary enormously according to destination; every post office has a schedule of fees and a timetable.

RADIO
Hong Kong's most popular English-language radio stations are RTHK Radio 3 (current affairs and talkback; 567AM, 1584AM, 97.9FM and 106.8FM); RTHK Radio 4 (classical music; 97.6-98.9FM); RTHK Radio 6 (BBC World Service relays; 675AM); AM 864 (hit parade; 864AM); and Metro Plus (news; 1044AM). The *South China Morning Post* publishes a daily schedule of radio programmes.

RELOCATING
Several companies offer relocation services in Hong Kong. One of the larger ones is Santa Fe Transport (☎ 2574 6204; www.santaferelo.com), which operates in cities around Asia and also offers online quotations. For a fuller list of relocation agents, see yp.com.hk.

See also the sections in this book on working in Hong Kong (p303) and long-term rental accommodation options (p249).

TAXES & REFUNDS
There is no sales tax in Hong Kong. The only 'visible' tax visitors are likely to encounter is the 3% government tax on hotel rates.

TELEPHONE
International Calls & Rates
Hong Kong's country code is ☎ 852. To call someone outside Hong Kong, dial ☎ 001,

then the country code, the local area code (you usually drop the initial zero if there is one) and the number. Country codes:

Australia (☎ 61)

Canada (☎ 1)

China (mainland) (☎ 86)

France (☎ 33)

Germany (☎ 49)

Japan (☎ 81)

Macau (☎ 853)

Netherlands (☎ 31)

New Zealand (☎ 64)

South Africa (☎ 27)

UK (☎ 44)

USA (☎ 1)

Remember that phone rates in Hong Kong are cheaper from 9pm to 8am on weekdays and throughout the weekend. If the phone you're using has the facility, dial ☎ 0060 first and then the number; rates will be cheaper at any time.

International Direct Dial (IDD) calls to almost anywhere in the world can be made from most public telephones in Hong Kong, but you'll need a phonecard. There's a wide range available, both in terms of the denominations and the service providers, including PCCW's Hello card. You can buy phonecards at any PCCW branch, 7-Eleven or Circle K convenience stores, Mannings pharmacies or Wellcome supermarkets.

PCCW (☎ 2888 2888, 1000 hotline; www.pccw.com), the erstwhile Hong Kong Telecom and now known as Pacific Century Cyber Works, has retail outlets called i.Shops (☎ 2888 0008; www .pccwshop.com) throughout the territory, where you can buy phonecards, mobile phones and accessories. The most convenient shops for travellers are the Central branch (Map p56; Ground fl, 113 Des Voeux Rd Central; ☿ 10am-8pm Mon-Sat, noon-7pm Sun) and the Tsim Sha Tsui branch (Map p92; Shop G3, Ground fl, Hotel Miramar, 118-130 Nathan Rd; ☿ 10am-10pm). There's also a Causeway Bay branch (Map p74; G3, Ground fl, McDonalds Bldg, 46-54 Yee Wo St; ☿ 10am-10pm Mon-Sat, 11am-9pm Sun).

Local Calls & Rates
All calls made from private phones in Hong Kong are local calls and therefore free. From public pay phones calls cost $1 for five min-

utes. The pay phones accept $1, $2, $5 and $10 coins. Hotels charge between $3 and $5 for local calls.

All land-line numbers in the territory have eight digits (except ☎ 800 toll-free numbers and specific hotlines), and there are no area codes.

Mobile Phones

Hong Kong has one of the world's highest per-capita usage of mobile telephones, and they work everywhere, including in tunnels and on the MTR. Any GSM-compatible phone can be used here.

PCCW i.Shops have mobile phones and accessories along with rechargeable SIM chips for sale at $180 and $280. Local calls work out to cost between 30¢ and 50¢ a minute (calls to the mainland are about $1 to $2 a minute) and top-up cards are $88 and $180. Handsets can be hired for as little as $35 a day from Hong Kong CSL (☎ 2888 1010; www.hkcsl.com), which maintains 1010 outlets in Hong Kong, including a 1010 CSL Central branch (Map p68; ☎ 2918 1010; Ground fl, Century Square, 1-13 D'Aguilar St; ☺ 8.30am-11pm) and a 1010 CSL Tsim Sha Tsui branch (Map p92; ☎ 2910 1010; Ground fl, Canton House, 82-84 Canton Rd; ☺ 8.30am-10pm). CSL's prepaid SIM cards come in a variety of price options, depending if and where you need roaming services; top-up cards are also available at 7-Eleven and Circle K convenience stores.

Useful Numbers

The following are some important telephone numbers and codes; for emergency numbers, see p290. Both the telephone directory and the *Yellow Pages* can be consulted online (www.yp.com.hk).

Coastal Waters & Tidal Information (☎ 187 8200)

International Dialling Code (☎ 001)

International Directory Enquiries (☎ 10015)

International Fax Dialling Code (☎ 002)

Local Directory Enquiries (☎ 1081)

Reverse-Charge/Collect Calls (☎ 10010)

Time & Temperature (☎ 18501)

Weather (☎ 187 8200)

TELEVISION

Hong Kong's four free terrestrial TV stations are run by two companies: Television Broad-

casts (TVB) and Asia Television (ATV). Each runs a Cantonese-language channel (TVB Jade and ATV Home) and an English one (TVB Pearl and ATV World). Programmes are listed daily in the *South China Morning Post* and in a weekly Sunday supplement.

There are also numerous pay cable channels and a variety of satellite channels.

TIME

Hong Kong does not have daylight-saving time. Hong Kong time is eight hours ahead of GMT and London; 13 hours ahead of New York; 16 hours ahead of San Francisco; the same time as Singapore, Manila and Perth; and two hours behind Sydney.

TIPPING

Hong Kong isn't particularly conscious of tipping and there is no obligation to tip, say, taxi drivers; just round the fare up or you can throw in a dollar or two more. It's almost mandatory to tip hotel staff $10 to $20, and if you make use of the porters at the airport, $2 to $5 a suitcase is normally expected. The porters putting your bags on a push cart at Hong Kong or Kowloon Airport Express station do not expect a gratuity, though; it's all part of the service.

Most hotels and many restaurants add a 10% service charge to the bill. Check for hidden extras before you tip; some midrange hotels charge $3 to $5 for each local call when they are actually free throughout the territory, and some restaurants consistently get the bill wrong. If using the services of a hotel porter, it's customary to tip them at least $10.

TOILETS

Hong Kong has never had as many public toilets as other world-class cities but that is changing rapidly, with new ones being built and old ones refurbished and reopened. They are always free to use. Almost all public toilets have access for people with disabilities, and baby-changing shelves in both men's and women's rooms. Equip yourself with tissues, though; public toilets in Hong Kong are often out of toilet paper.

TOURIST INFORMATION

The enterprising and energetic Hong Kong Tourism Board (HKTB; ☎ 2508 1234; www.discoverhongkong.com) is one of the most helpful and useful in the world. Staff are welcoming and have reams of information. Most of its literature is free, though it also sells a few useful publications and books, as well as postcards, T-shirts and souvenirs.

Before you depart, check the HKTB website, which should be able to answer any question you could possibly have. While on the ground and in Hong Kong phone the HKTB Visitor Hotline (☎ 2508 1234; ⏰ 8am-6pm) if you have a query, a problem or you're lost. Staff are always able (and, what's more, keen) to help.

HKTB Visitor Information & Service Centres can be found on Hong Kong Island, in Kowloon, at Hong Kong International Airport on Lantau, and in Lo Wu on the border with the mainland. Outside these centres and at several other places in the territory you'll be able to find iCyberlink screens from which you can conveniently access the HKTB website and database 24 hours a day.

Hong Kong International Airport HKTB Centres (Map p136; Chek Lap Kok; ⏰ 7am-11pm) There are centres in Halls A and B on the arrival level and the E2 transfer area.

Hong Kong Island HKTB Centre (Map p74; Causeway Bay MTR station, near exit F; ⏰ 8am-8pm)

Kowloon HKTB Centre (Map p92; Star Ferry Concourse, Tsim Sha Tsui; ⏰ 8am-8pm)

Lo Wu HKTB Centre (Map pp50–1; 2nd fl, Arrival Hall, Ko Wu Terminal Bldg; ⏰ 8am-6pm)

Other excellent sources for information:

Community Advice Bureau (Map p56; ☎ 2815 5444; www.cab.org.hk; Room 16C, Right Emperor Commercial Bldg, 122-126 Wellington St, Central; ⏰ 9.30am-4.30pm Mon-Fri) Will answer questions for anyone about anything but primarily directed at new Hong Kong residents trying to get their feet on the ground.

Hong Kong Information Services Department (☎ 1823 hotline; www.info.gov.hk) Can answer specific questions or direct you to the appropriate government department.

TRAVELLERS WITH DISABILITIES

People with disabilities have to cope with substantial obstacles in Hong Kong, including the stairs at many MTR and KCR stations, as well as pedestrian overpasses, narrow and crowded footpaths, and steep hills. On the other hand, some buses are accessible by wheelchair, taxis are never hard to find, most buildings have lifts (many with Braille panels) and MTR sta-

tions have Braille maps with recorded information. Wheelchairs can negotiate the lower decks of most ferries.

For further information about facilities and services for travellers with disabilities in Hong Kong, contact either of the following:

Hong Kong Paralympic Committee & Sports Association for the Physically Disabled (☎ 2602 8232; www .hkparalympic.org)

Joint Council for People with Disabilities (Map p65; ☎ 2864 2931; www.hkcss.org.hk; Room 1204, 12th fl, Duke of Windsor Bldg, 15 Hennessy Rd, Wan Chai)

UNIVERSITIES

Hong Kong has a total of eight universities. Hong Kong University (Map pp54–5; ☎ 2859 2111; www .hku.hk), established in 1911, is the oldest and most difficult to get into. Its campus is in Pok Fu Lam on the western side of Hong Kong Island. The Chinese University of Hong Kong (Map pp50–1; ☎ 2609 6000; www.cuhk.edu.hk), established in 1963, is most applicants' second choice. It is situated on a beautiful campus at Ma Liu Shui, which is north of Sha Tin in the New Territories.

The Hong Kong University of Science & Technology (Map pp50–1; ☎ 2358 6000; www.ust.hk) admitted its first students in 1991, and is situated at Tai Po Tsai in Clearwater Bay in the New Territories.

The other five universities are based in Kowloon and include the Hong Kong Polytechnic University (Map p94; ☎ 2766 5111; www.polyu.edu.hk) in Hung Hom, which was set up in 1972.

USEFUL ORGANISATIONS

Hong Kong Consumer Council (Map p56; ☎ 2929 2222; www.consumer.org.hk; Ground fl, Harbour Bldg, 38 Pier Rd, Central) Can help with complaints about dishonest shopkeepers and other rip-offs. See its website for locations of other offices around Hong Kong.

Royal Asiatic Society (☎ 2813 7500; www.royalasiatic society.org.hk; GPO Box 3864, Central) Organises lectures, field trips of cultural and historical interest, and puts out publications.

Royal Geographical Society (☎ 2583 9700; www.rgshk .org.hk; GPO Box 6681, Central) Organises lectures by high-profile local and foreign travellers, as well as hikes and field trips.

World Wide Fund for Nature Hong Kong (WWFHK; ☎ 2526 1011; www.wwf.org.hk; 1 Tramway Path, Central)

VISAS

The vast majority of travellers, including citizens of Australia, Canada, the EU, Israel, Japan, New Zealand and the USA, are allowed to enter the Hong Kong SAR without a visa and stay for 90 days. Holders of British passports can stay up to 180 days without a visa, but British Dependent Territories and British Overseas citizens not holding a visa are only allowed to remain 90 days. Holders of many African (including South African), South American and Middle Eastern passports do not require visas for a visit of 30 days or less.

If you do require a visa, you must apply beforehand at the nearest Chinese consulate or embassy; for addresses and contact information consult the website www.immd.gov.hk/e html/embassy.htm.

If you plan on visiting mainland China, you must have a visa, although American citizens must apply for their visas prior to crossing the border; for further details, see p286.

Visitors may have to prove they have adequate funds for their stay (a credit card should do the trick) and that they hold an onward or return ticket. Ordinary visas cost $160 (or the equivalent in local currency), while transit visas are $84.

Visitors are not permitted to take up employment, establish any sort of business or enrol as students while visiting on a tourist visa. If you want to work or study, you must apply for an employment or student visa beforehand. It is very hard to change your visa status after you have arrived in Hong Kong. Anyone wishing to stay longer than the visa-free period must apply for a visa before travelling to Hong Kong. For details on applying for a work permit, see p304.

Visa Extensions

In general, visa extensions ($160) are not readily granted unless there are special or extenuating circumstances, such as cancelled flights, illness, registration in a legitimate course of study, legal employment, or marriage to a local.

For more information contact the Hong Kong Immigration Department (Map p65; ☎ 2824 6111; www .immd.gov.hk; 5th fl, Immigration Tower, 7 Gloucester Rd, Wan Chai; 🕓 8.45am-4.30pm Mon-Fri, 9-11.30am Sat).

VOLUNTEERING

Being small and developed, the scope for volunteering schemes is rather limited. Volunteerabroad.com contains a handful of listings for Hong Kong aimed at incoming volunteers. Ho-Sum ('Good Heart'; www.ho-sum.org) tends to list scores of schemes, most of them more short-term volunteering projects aimed at local residents.

WEIGHTS & MEASURES

Although the international metric system (see the inside front cover) is in official use in Hong Kong, traditional Chinese weights and measures are still common. At local markets, meat, fish and produce are sold by the *léung,* equivalent to 37.8g, and the *gàn* (catty), which is equivalent to about 600g. There are 16 *léung* to the *gàn*. Gold and silver are sold by the tael, which is exactly the same as a *léung*.

WOMEN TRAVELLERS

Respect for women is deeply ingrained in the Chinese culture. Despite the Confucian principle of the superiority of men, women in Chinese society often call all the shots and can wield a tremendous amount of influence at home, in business and in politics.

Hong Kong is a safe city for women, although common-sense caution should be observed, especially at night. Few women – visitors or residents – complain of bad treatment, intimidation or aggression. Having said that, some Chinese men regard Western women as 'easy' and have made passes at foreigners – even quite publicly. If you are sexually assaulted, call the Hong Kong Rape Hotline (☎ 2375 5322).

Other useful organisations:

Hong Kong Federation of Women (Map p65; ☎ 2833 6131; hkfw.org; Ground fl, 435 Lockhart Rd, Wan Chai)

International Women's League (Map p97; ☎ 2782 2207; 2nd fl, Boss Commercial Bldg, 28 Ferry St, Jordan)

WORK

Travellers on tourist visas are barred from accepting employment in Hong Kong. It is possible to obtain work 'under the table', but there are stiff penalties for employers who are caught hiring foreigners illegally. Still, to earn extra money many foreigners end up teaching English or doing some other kind of work – translating, modelling, acting in Chinese films, waiting on tables or bartending. Few – if any – restaurants or bars will take the risk and hire you if you don't have a Hong Kong ID card these days.

For professional jobs, registering with Hong Kong personnel agencies or head-hunters is important; check out Jobs DB (www.jobsdb.com /hk). Drake International (Map p56; ☎ 2848 9288; www .drakeintl.com; 19th fl, Chekiang First Bank Centre, 1 Duddell St, Central) is an international employment agency that often advertises work in Hong Kong. You can always check the classified advertisements in the local English-language newspapers. The Thursday and Saturday editions of the *South China Morning Post* or the Friday edition of the *Hong Kong Standard* are particularly helpful. *HK Magazine* also has a jobs section.

Recruit (www.recruit.com.hk) and *Jiu Jik* (Job Finder; www.jiujik.com) are free job-seeker tabloids available on Wednesdays and Fridays at the majority of MTR stations. There are also the *Job Market Weekly* (www.jobmarket.com.hk) and *Career Times* (www.careertimes.com.hk), for sale at most newsagents.

Work Permits

To work legally here you need to have a work permit. The Hong Kong authorities require proof that you have been offered employment, usually in the form of a contract. The prospective employer is obligated to show that the work you plan to do cannot be performed by a local person. If you're planning on working or studying in Hong Kong, it could be helpful to have copies of transcripts, diplomas, letters of reference and other professional qualifications in hand.

In general, visitors must leave Hong Kong in order to obtain a work permit, returning only when it is ready; unfortunately Macau and the mainland do not qualify as interim destinations. Exceptions are made, however, especially if the company urgently needs to fill a position. Work visas are generally granted for between one and three years. Extensions should be applied for at least a month before the visa expires.

From overseas, applications for work visas can be made at any Chinese embassy or consulate (p289). In Hong Kong, contact the Immigration Department (Map p65; ☎ 2824 6111; www .immd.gov.hk; 24th fl, Immigration Tower, 7 Gloucester Rd, Wan Chai; ☺ 8.45am-4.30pm Mon-Fri, 9-11.30am Sat) for information on how to apply.

MACAU

top picks

- Ruins of the Church of St Paul (p315)
- Monte Fort (p319)
- Avenida da República (p324)
- Temples (p322)
- A-Ma Temple (p324)
- Taipa House Museum (p329)
- Coloane Village (p331)
- Casinos (p340)

The zodiac sign of Macau is Gemini. It is a city of duality. The fortresses, the churches and food of former colonial Portuguese masters speak to a uniquely Mediterranean style on the China coast, intermixed with numerous alleys, temples and shrines along the way. On the other hand, you'll find yourself in a self-styled Las Vegas of the East. Amazingly, all of these different parts of Macau are within a stone's throw of each other.

Lying 65km to the west of Hong Kong, Macau was the first European enclave in Asia, 450 years ago. When China resumed sovereignty over what is now called the Special Administrative Region (SAR) of Macau in 1999, it was by far the oldest colony. During the past few years, the charismatic-but-sleepy traits of that little Macau have undergone an intensive transformation, fuelled by the gambling industry's boost to the economy. Super-sized by massive reclamation projects for Vegas-style megacasinos and hotels, Macau has been turned into an enormous construction site. The fast pace of growth and economic prosperity have resulted in a labour shortage, skyrocketing rents and air pollution, along with a nostalgia among the people of Macau for the past – and life before 'Hongkongisation' – when people earned less money but enjoyed a better quality of life.

Though Macau remains the one and only place where casinos are legal in China, there is much more to do than just gambling. Largo do Senado on Macau Peninsula plus the islands of Coloane and Taipa form a colourful palette of pastels and ordered greenery. The Portuguese influence is everywhere: cobbled backstreets, baroque churches, ancient stone fortresses, Art Deco apartment buildings, and restful parks and gardens. The cemeteries of Macau are the final resting places of many European and American missionaries, painters, soldiers and sailors who died at 'Macao Roads'. It's a unique fusion of East and West that has been recognised by Unesco, which in 2005 named 30 buildings and squares collectively as the Historic Centre of Macau World Heritage Site.

If you travel to Hong Kong, it is well worth a short trip to Macau. Travel between the two territories has never been easier, with high-speed ferries now running virtually every 15 minutes (as well as frequent helicopter services). With time and patience you will be rewarded with something new at each step and on every visit, but even spending just a night or two will let you discover this hybrid city's unique lifestyles, temperaments and food that make it so much fun.

BACKGROUND
HISTORY
Early Settlement

Archaeological finds from digs around Hác Sá and Ká Hó Bays on Coloane Island suggest that Macau has been inhabited since Neolithic times (from 4000 BC). Before the arrival of the Portuguese, Macau had a relatively small number of inhabitants, mainly Cantonese-speaking farmers and fisherfolk from Fujian.

The Arrival of the Portuguese

In 1510 and 1511 the Portuguese routed Arab fleets at Goa on the west coast of India and Malacca on the Malay Peninsula. At Malacca they encountered several junks with Chi-

nese captains and crews. Realising that the so-called Chins, about whom Portuguese mariners and explorers had heard reports a century earlier, were not a mythical people but natives of 'Cathay' (the land that Marco Polo had visited and written about 2½ centuries earlier), a small party sailed northwards to try to open up trade with China.

The first Portuguese contingent, led by Jorge Álvares, set foot on Chinese soil in 1513 at a place they called Tamaõ, today known as Shangchuan Island, about 80km southwest of the mouth of the Pearl River. However, it wasn't until 1553 that an official basis for trading was set up between the two countries, and the Portuguese were allowed to settle on Shangchuan. The exposed anchorage there forced the Portuguese traders to abandon the island that same year, and they moved to Lampacau, an island closer to the Pearl River estuary.

To the northeast of Lampacau was a small peninsula where the Portuguese had frequently dropped anchor. Known variously as Amagau, Aomen and Macau (see the boxed text, below), the peninsula had two natural harbours – an inner one on the Qianshan waterway facing the mainland, and an outer one in a bay on the Pearl River – and two sheltered islands to the south. In 1557 officials at Guangzhou let the Portuguese build temporary shelters on the peninsula in exchange for customs dues and rent. The Portuguese also agreed to rid the area of the pirates that were endemic at the time.

A Trading Powerhouse

Macau grew rapidly as a trading centre, largely due to the fact that Chinese merchants were forbidden to leave the country by imperial decree. Acting as agents for the Chinese merchants, Portuguese traders took Chinese goods to Goa and exchanged them for cotton and textiles. The cloth was then taken to Malacca, where it was traded for spices and sandalwood. The Portuguese would then carry on to Nagasaki in Japan, where the cargo from Malacca was exchanged for Japanese silver, swords, lacquerware and fans that would be traded in Macau for more Chinese goods.

During the late 16th century the Portuguese in Macau were at the forefront of all international commerce between China and Japan. Macau's growing status was evidenced when the Holy See established the bishopric of Macau in 1576, which included both China and Japan under its jurisdiction. By 1586 Macau was important enough for the Portuguese Crown to confer upon it the status of a city: Cidade de Nome de Deus (City of the Name of God).

The Golden Years

By the beginning of the 17th century, Macau supported several thousand permanent resi-

dents, including about 900 Portuguese. The rest were Christian converts from Malacca and Japan and a large number of slaves from colonial outposts in Africa, India and the Malay Peninsula. Many Chinese had moved into Macau from across the border, and they worked there as traders, craftspeople, hawkers, labourers and coolies; by the close of the century, their numbers had reached about 40,000.

Besides trading, Macau had also become a centre of Christianity in Asia. Priests and missionaries accompanied Portuguese ships, although the interests of traders and missionaries were frequently in conflict.

Among the earliest missionaries was Francis Xavier (later canonised) of the Jesuit order, who spent two years (1549 to 1551) in Japan attempting to convert the local population before turning his attention to China. He was stalled by the Portuguese, who feared the consequences of his meddling in Chinese affairs, but made it as far as Tamaõ, where he developed a fever and died in December 1552 at age 46.

The Portuguese who stayed in Macau, along with their Macanese descendants, created a home away from home. Their luxurious villas overlooking the Praia Grande, now the enclosed Baia da Praia, and splendid baroque churches were paid for with the wealth generated by their monopoly on trade with China and Japan. These buildings included the Jesuit Church of Madre de Deus (later the Church of St Paul, p315), hailed as the greatest monument to Christianity in the Far East when dedicated in 1602.

Portuguese Decline

Portugal's decline as an imperial power came as quickly as its rise. In 1580 Spanish armies occupied Portugal and for more than 60 years

WHAT'S IN A NAME?

The name Macau is derived from the name of the goddess A-Ma, better known in Hong Kong as Tin Hau. At the southwestern tip of Macau Peninsula stands the A-Ma Temple, which dates back to the early 16th century. Many people believe that when the Portuguese first arrived and asked the name of the place, 'A-Ma Gau' (Bay of A-Ma) was what they were told.

According to legend, A-Ma, a poor girl looking for passage to Guangzhou, was turned away by wealthy junk owners. Instead a poor fisherman took her on board; shortly afterwards a storm blew up, wrecking all the junks but leaving the fishing boat unscathed. When it returned to the Inner Harbour, A-Ma walked to the top of nearby Barra Hill and, in a glowing aura of light, ascended to heaven. The fisherman built a temple on the spot where they had landed (which was, in fact, on the water's edge until land reclamation early in the last century set it further inland).

In modern Cantonese, Macau is Ou Mun (Aomen in Mandarin), meaning Gateway of the Bay.

three Spanish kings ruled over the country and its empire. In the early years of the 17th century, the Dutch, embroiled in the Thirty Years' War with Spain, moved to seize the rich Portuguese enclaves of Macau, Nagasaki and Malacca. In June 1622 some 13 Dutch warships carrying 1300 men attacked Macau but retreated when a shell fired by a Jesuit priest from one of the cannons on Monte Fort hit a stock of gunpowder and blew the Hollanders out of the water.

The Japanese soon became suspicious of Portuguese and Spanish intentions and closed its doors to foreign trade in 1639. Two years later, Dutch harassment of Portuguese commerce and trading interests ended with the capture of Malacca. The Portuguese would no longer be able to provide the Chinese with the Japanese silver needed for their silk and porcelain or with spices from the Malay Peninsula.

A Change of Status

A flood of refugees unleashed on Macau when the Ming dynasty was overthrown in 1644. In 1684 the most corrupt of the new Manchu rulers, the so-called *hoppo* (*hói poi* in Cantonese) – the customs superintendent who held the monopoly on trade with foreigners – set up an office in the Inner Harbour.

At the same time religious infighting weakened the status of Macau as a Christian centre. In what became known as the Rites Controversy, the Jesuits maintained that central aspects of Chinese belief – such as ancestor worship and Confucianism – were not incompatible with the Christian faith. The Dominicans and Franciscans, equally well represented in Macau, disagreed. It took an edict by Pope Clement XI in 1715 condemning the rites as idolatrous to settle the matter and this stopped further missionary expansion into China.

In the mid-18th century Chinese authorities created the *cohong,* a mercantile monopoly based in Guangzhou that dealt with foreign trade. Numerous restrictions were placed on Western traders, including limitations on the amount of time they could reside in Guangzhou. Macau in effect became an outpost for all European traders in China, a position it held until the British took possession of Hong Kong in 1841.

Until the mid-19th century the history of Macau was a long series of incidents involving the Portuguese, Chinese and British as the Portuguese attempted to maintain a hold on the territory. But as time progressed and the troublesome British wrestled concession after concession out of China, the Portuguese grew bolder.

The Treaty of Nanking (1842) ceded the island of Hong Kong in perpetuity to the British; the Treaty of Tientsin (1860) gave them Kowloon on the same terms. The Portuguese felt that they, too, should take advantage of China's weakness and push for sovereignty over the territory they had occupied for three centuries. Negotiation began in 1862, although it was not until 1887 that a treaty was signed in which China effectively recognised Portuguese sovereignty over Macau forever.

With the advent of the steamship, there were fewer transshipments from Chinese ports through Macau and more direct transactions between the mainland and Hong Kong. Macau's future economy was greatly assisted by the legalisation of gambling in the 1850s, but by the close of the 19th century the ascent of the British colony and the decline of the Portuguese territory had become irreversible.

Macau in the 20th Century

By the turn of the 20th century Macau was little more than an impoverished backwater, its glory days all but forgotten. It did, however, continue to serve as a haven for Chinese refugees fleeing war, famine and political oppression. Among them was Sun Yat Sen, founder of the republic of China, who lived in Macau before the 1911 Revolution. Even the birth of the Portuguese republic in 1910 had little effect on the sleepy outpost.

In the mid-1920s large numbers of Chinese immigrants doubled the number of Macau residents to 160,000. A steady stream of refugees from the Sino-Japanese War meant that by 1939 the population had reached 245,000. During WWII many people from Hong Kong and China, as well as Asian-based Europeans, took refuge in Macau, as the Japanese respected Portugal's neutrality; by 1943 the population stood at 500,000. There was another influx of Chinese refugees in 1949 when the Communists took power in China, and from 1978 until about 1981 Macau was a haven for Vietnamese boat people. Macau was made an overseas province of Portugal in 1951.

Macau's last great upset occurred in 1966 and 1967, when China's Cultural Revolution spilled over into the territory. Macau was stormed by Red Guards, and violent riots resulted in some of them being shot and killed by Portuguese troops. The government proposed that Portugal abandon Macau forever, but China refused to hear of it, fearing the loss of foreign trade through the colony.

In 1974 a revolution restored democracy in Portugal and the new left-wing government began to divest Portugal of the last remnants of its empire, including Mozambique and Angola in Africa and East Timor in the Indonesian archipelago. Power brokers in Lisbon tried to return Macau to China as well, but the word from Beijing was that China wished Macau to remain as it was – at least for the time being.

The End of Portuguese Rule

Once the Joint Declaration over Hong Kong had been signed by Britain and China in 1984, the latter turned its attentions to the future of Macau. Talks began in 1986 and an agreement was signed the following April.

Under the so-called Sino-Portuguese Pact, Macau would become a Special Administrative Region of China. The date set was 20 December 1999, ending 442 years of Portuguese rule. Like Hong Kong, the Macau SAR would enjoy a 'high degree of autonomy' for 50 years in all matters except defence and foreign affairs, under the slogan 'one country, two systems'.

The basic law for Macau differed from its Hong Kong equivalent in that holders of foreign passports were not excluded from holding high-level posts in the post-handover administration (apart from the position of chief executive). There was also no stipulation that China would station troops of the People's Liberation Army (PLA) in Macau after the return of the territory to China, though it did just that.

Macau had directly elected some of the members of its Legislative Assembly since the assembly's founding in 1976 but, unlike Hong Kong, it did not rush through proposals to widen the franchise or speed up democratisation at the last minute. The existing legislature continued to serve throughout the handover, unlike that in the British territory.

But not everything went so smoothly. Macau residents were pleased when Portugal gave everyone born in Macau the right to a Portuguese passport, allowing them to live anywhere in the EU – something the UK had refused Hong Kong Chinese people. However, not everyone in Macau benefited from Portugal's move. Until 1975 any Chinese refugee reaching Macau could obtain residency. As a result, as much as 70% of the population had not actually been born in Macau and therefore didn't qualify for Portuguese citizenship.

The years 1996 to 1998 were a grim showdown for Macau and its all-important tourism industry – an escalating number of gangland killings took place. Some 40 people were killed as senior Triad leaders jostled for control of the lucrative gambling rackets, and one international hotel was raked with AK-47 gunfire. On 8 May 1998 alone, 14 cars and motorcycles and a couple of shops were engulfed in flames when Triad members, protesting the arrest of their boss, Wan Kwok 'Broken Tooth' Koi, let off a string of firebombs. The violence scared tourists off in a big way; arrivals fell by some 36% in August 1997.

As the handover approached, China put pressure on Portugal to clean up its act. The government issued a new anti-Triad law calling for a lengthy prison term for anyone found to be a senior leader. Koi was arrested and sentenced to 15 years, and many other Triad members fled overseas.

The Handover & Macau after 1999

The handover ceremony on 20 December 1999 was as stage-managed as the one held 2½ years earlier in Hong Kong. The following day 500 PLA soldiers drove down from Zhuhai. There are now an estimated 10,000 troops stationed here, though they have no responsibility for internal security.

In the past decade or so, Macau has launched a series of enormous public works and land-reclamation projects. The US$11.8-billion airport built in 1995 and Cotai, a reclaimed area almost the size of Taipa with a six-lane highway, are among the most ambitious ones.

The deregulation of gambling laws in 2001 has further boosted the expansion of Macau's land reclamation and economy, though problems have followed this surge. On the one hand Macau has suffered a severe shortage of labour because of the galloping growth of the gambling industry, forcing casinos to raise wages dramatically to attract card dealers; on the other hand the boom doesn't really benefit the local workers, as cheap illegal labourers are often hired for construction. A protest on May day in 2007 that resulted in a brutal police suppression reflected the undercurrents of dissatisfaction in the city. Macau's image has been further tarnished by government officials selling public land cheaply to financial giants for commercial development and receiving bribes in return. The notorious Ao Man Long case, in which the former transportation minister was accused of taking 800 million patacas in bribes – 57 times his legal income from his seven-year term of office – from a number of public-works projects, is believed to be just the tip of the iceberg.

Other grand projects continue forward, including the megaresort City of Dreams in Cotai. But the most ambitious project by far is the proposed 36km-long, US$3.7-billion, six-lane cross-delta bridge linking Macau and Zhuhai with Hong Kong via Tai O on Lantau Island. The Y-shaped bridge would reduce the present four-hour journey by car between Zhuhai and Hong Kong to 20 minutes.

ARTS
Painting

Macau can lay claim to having spawned or influenced a number of artists. Their work is on display in the Gallery of Historical Pictures of the Macau Museum of Art (p323).

The most important Western artist to have lived in Macau was George Chinnery (see the boxed text, below). Other influential European painters who spent time in Macau include the Scottish physician Thomas Watson (1815–60), who was a student of Chinnery and lived in

Macau from 1845 to 1856; Frenchman Auguste Borget (1808–77), who spent some 10 months in 1838 and 1939 painting Macau's waterfront and churches; and watercolourist Marciano António Baptista (1856–1930), who was born in Macau.

Guan Qiaochang (1825–60), another of Chinnery's pupils, was a Chinese artist who painted in the Western style and worked under the name Lamqua. His oil portraits of mandarins and other Chinese worthies are particularly fine.

Two of the best galleries for viewing contemporary Macau and other art are Tap Seac Gallery (p326) and Ox Warehouse (p326).

Architecture

Portuguese architectural styles reflect a variety of forms, from Romanesque and Gothic through to baroque and neoclassical, and these are best seen in Macau's churches. Two excellent examples are the Chapel of St Joseph Seminary (p322), completed in 1758, and the Church of St Dominic (p321), a 17th-century replacement of a chapel built in the 1590s.

Civic buildings worth close inspection are the Leal Senado (p319), erected in 1784 but rebuilt after it was damaged by a typhoon a century later; and the Government House (p322), dating from 1849.

Macau has seen a surge of skyscrapers go up, changing its skyline drastically. Macau Tower (p324) is a 338m-tall copy of the Sky Tower in Auckland, New Zealand. The landmark Grand Lisboa Casino (p341), an ugly, 52-storey lotus-shaped golden structure, will be the tallest building in Macau upon its completion in late 2007.

GEORGE CHINNERY: CHRONICLER OF MACAU

Though George Chinnery may enjoy little more than footnote status in the history of world art, as a chronicler of his own world (colonial Macau) and his times (the early 19th century) he is without peer. In the absence of photography, taipans ('big bosses' of large companies) and mandarins turned to trade art (commissioned portraiture), and Chinnery was the master of the genre. Today he is known less for his formal portraits and paintings of factory buildings and clipper ships than for his landscapes and sometimes fragmentary sketches of everyday life.

Chinnery was born in London in 1774 and studied at the Royal Academy of Arts before turning his hand to portrait painting in Dublin. He sailed for India in 1802 and spent the next 23 years in Madras and Calcutta, where he earned substantial sums (up to UK£500 a month) as a popular portrait painter to British colonial society and spent most of it on his opium addiction. He fled to Macau in 1825 to escape spiralling debts, Calcutta's 'cranky formality' and his wife (whom he described as 'the ugliest woman I ever saw in my life'), and took up residence at 8 Rua de Inácio Baptista (Map p320), just south of the Church of St Lawrence. He lived at this address until his death from stroke in 1852.

Although Chinnery is sometimes 'claimed' by Hong Kong (the Mandarin Oriental hotel even has a bar named after him), he visited the colony only once, during the hot summer of 1846. Although he was unwell and did not like it very much, he managed to execute some vivid sketches of the place.

MACAU CALENDAR

You're likely to find a festival or some special event taking place in Macau no matter when you visit. Chinese New Year (see the boxed text, p16) is chaotic in Macau, and hotel rooms are a prized commodity during this period. Still, it's a colourful time to visit, as the city literally explodes with bangers and fireworks – they're legal here – and the streets are filled with a carnival atmosphere. The Macau Formula 3 Grand Prix (p345) is also a peak time for visitors. The website of the Macau Government Tourist Office (MGTO; www.macautourism.gov.mo) has a list of events in Macau. For dates of Macau's public holidays, see p351. For information on festivals and events celebrated both here and in Hong Kong, see p15.

February/March

Procession of the Passion of Our Lord A 400-year-old tradition on the first Saturday of Lent in which a colourful procession bears a statue of Jesus Christ from Macau's Church of St Augustine to Macau Cathedral, where it spends the night and is carried back the following day. This will fall on 9 February in 2008, 28 February in 2009 and 20 February in 2010.

April/May

A-Ma Festival This festival honours Tin Hau (known here as A-Ma), the patroness of fisherfolk and one of the territory's most popular goddesses. The best place to see the festival is at the A-Ma Temple in the Inner Harbour. This festival will fall on 28 April in 2008, 18 April in 2009 and 6 May in 2010.

Birthday of the Lord Buddha/Feast of the Drunken Dragon Buddha's statue is taken from monasteries and temples and ceremoniously bathed in scented water on this day. It also marks the Feast of the Drunken Dragon, which features dancing dragons in the streets of the Inner Harbour and a lot of legless merrymakers. 12 May in 2008, 2 May in 2009 and 21 May in 2010.

Procession of our Lady of Fatima The procession goes from Macau Cathedral to the Chapel of Our Lady of Penha to commemorate a series of apparitions by the Virgin Mary to three peasant children at Fatima in Portugal in 1917. This falls on 13 May each year.

Macau Arts Festival (www.icm.gov.mo) Macau's red-letter arts event kicks off the cultural year with music, drama and dance from both Asia and the West.

Macau Open Golf Tournament (www.sport.gov.mo) Part of the Asian PGA Tour, this event is held at the Macau Golf & Country Club on Coloane and attracts the region's best golfers.

June

Dragon Boat Festival This festival is also known as Tuen Ng (Double Fifth) as it falls on the fifth day of the fifth moon. It commemorates the death of Qu Yuan, a poet-statesman of the 3rd century BC, who hurled himself into the Mi Lo River in Hunan province to protest against a corrupt government; dragon-boat races take place and traditional rice dumplings are eaten in memory of the event. The festival will fall on 8 June in 2008, 28 May in 2009 and 16 June 2010.

Macau Lotus Flower Festival The symbol of Macau is the focus of this festival, which sees lotuses blossoming in parks and gardens throughout Macau.

July

FIVB Women's Volleyball Grand Prix (www.sport.gov.mo) This is one of the most important women's volleyball tournaments in the region.

September/October

Macau International Fireworks Display Contest This event, the largest of its kind in the world, adds a splash of colour to the Macau night sky in autumn.

October/November

Macau International Music Festival (www.icm.gov.mo) This two-week festival is a heady mix of opera, musicals, visiting orchestras and other musical events.

Macau Formula 3 Grand Prix (www.macau.grandprix.gov.mo) Approximately 30 national championship drivers compete to take the chequered flag in Macau's premier sporting event. The Grand Prix is held in the third week of November.

December

Macau International Marathon (www.sport.gov.mo) Like its Hong Kong counterpart, this running event, which takes place on the first Sunday in December, also includes a half-marathon.

MACAU **BACKGROUND**

ONE-DAY ITINERARY

If you only have a day in Macau, start by following the walking tour (p314) to get a feel for the lay of the land and Macau's living history. Spend an hour or so in the Macau Museum (p319) to answer all the questions you'll now have, and walk to the ruins of the Church of St Paul (p315). In the afternoon, hop on a bus for Taipa (p327) and stroll through the village to Avenida da Praia and the three-part Taipa House Museum (p329). In the evening you should also walk along peninsula Macau's more dramatic Avenida da Praia Grande, stopping for a while at the Lisboa Casino (p341) to see what all the fuss is about. Have a sundowner drink or two along the Lan Kwai Fong (p342) strip in NAPE and dinner at the atmospheric Clube Militar de Macau (p336) before catching the ferry back to Hong Kong.

The feverish construction in Macau has also given rise to a public outcry for heritage conservation, especially since the Unesco-protected Guia Lighthouse (p325) will be overshadowed by skyscrapers in the NAPE area if they are built as planned.

Literature

Macau's home-grown writers are not insignificant; you'll sample their work at the Macau Museum (p319).

First and foremost in literature was Portugal's national poet, Luís de Camões (1524–80), who was banished from Portugal to Goa and then apparently to Macau in the 16th century. He is said to have written part of his epic poem *Os Lusiadas* (The Lusiads), which recounts the 15th-century voyage of Vasco da Gama to India, during the two years he lived in the enclave, but there is no firm evidence that he was ever in Macau.

The teacher, judge, opium addict and Symbolist poet Camilio de Almeida Pessanha (1867–1926; author of such works as *Clepsidra*) lived in Macau for the last 30 years of his life; he is buried in the Cemetery of St Michael the Archangel (p325). Local-born writers include Henrique de Senna Fernandes (1923–), author of the *Nam Wan* collection of short stories and the novel *The Bewitching Braid*, and the much-beloved Macanese writer José dos Santos Ferreira (1919–93), known as Adé, who wrote in *patuá*, a dialect forging Portuguese and Cantonese. A statue in honour of Adé, who wrote plays, operettas and poems, stands in the Jardim des Artes along Avenida da Amizade, opposite the Landmark Macau building, and you can hear a recording of him reading his poetry in the Macau Museum.

CULTURE

Traditional culture among the Chinese of Macau is almost indistinguishable from that of Hong Kong. However, the Portuguese minority has a vastly different culture that has evolved under a number of different influences through the centuries. Colonial Portuguese architecture survives throughout Macau, and Portuguese food is to be found in abundance.

Macanese culture is different again. Unlike the Portuguese and Chinese communities elsewhere in the world, the Macanese community, a tiny community of the descendents of intermarriages between Portuguese and Asians, is very distinct and exists solely in Macau. They have a unique cuisine, set of festivals and traditions, and even their own dialect called *patuá*. The *do* (traditional woman's outfit) has long disappeared, though you may catch a glimpse of it at certain festivals.

Portuguese and Chinese – Cantonese being the more widely spoken dialect – are both official languages of Macau. For key phrases and words in Cantonese and Portuguese, see p353.

For the vast majority of Macau Chinese people, Taoism and Buddhism are the dominant religions (see the boxed text, p43). Four and a half centuries of Portuguese Christian rule left its mark, however, and the Roman Catholic Church is very strong in Macau, with an estimated 30,000 (about 6% of the population) adherents. Macau consists of a single diocese, directly responsible to Rome.

ECONOMY

Tourism and gambling still drive Macau's economy, and the latter remains Macau's major cash cow; today gambling concessions contribute some 70% of government revenue through betting tax.

Tourism usually generates almost half of Macau's GDP, and about a third of the labour force works in some aspect of it. In 2006 Macau welcomed some 21 million tourists and visitors, an increase of 31% over the previous year and almost 42 times its population.

Visitors from the mainland accounted for 52% of total arrivals, with most of the balance coming from Hong Kong, Taiwan, Japan and the USA. As a result of this phenomenal boost, Macau's economy expanded a record 23% in 2006.

Macau has some light industries, such as textile, garment, toy and fireworks production, but factories have slowed down and many companies have moved across the border. Unemployment in Macau is currently around 3.8%.

GOVERNMENT & POLITICS

The executive branch of the Macau SAR government is led by the chief executive, who is chosen by an electoral college made up of 200 local representatives. Edmund Ho, a popular Macau-born banker, was selected for his second (and, by law, final) five-year term in 2004.

The Legislative Assembly, which sits in its own purpose-built assembly hall on reclaimed land in the Nam Van Lakes area, now permanently consists of 29 members, 12 of whom are directly elected in geographical constituencies, 10 chosen by interest groups and seven appointed by the chief executive.

Like Hong Kong, Macau has primary courts, intermediate courts and a Court of Final Appeal.

NEIGHBOURHOODS & SIGHTS

For such a tiny city, Macau is packed with many important cultural and historical sights, including eight squares and 22 historic buildings that have collectively been named the Historic Centre of Macau World Heritage

Site by Unesco. The best way to see the sights and to feel the uniqueness of Macau is to wander through the squares and narrow alleys. Remember to pick up the excellent series of pamphlets by the Macau Government Tourist Office (MGTO) before you set off.

Macau is divided into three main sections: the Macau Peninsula, which is attached to mainland China to the north; the middle island of Taipa, directly south of the peninsula and linked to it by the 2.5km-long Ponte Governador Nobre de Carvalho (Macau–Taipa Bridge), the 4.5km-long Ponte da Amizade (Friendship Bridge) and the new 2.2km-long covered, typhoon-proof Sai Van Bridge; and Coloane Island, south of Taipa and connected to it by recent massive land-reclamation efforts.

ORGANISED TOURS

Tours booked on the ground in Macau are generally much better value than those booked in Hong Kong, though the latter include transportation to and from Macau and sometimes a side trip across the border to Zhuhai. Tours from Hong Kong are usually one-day whirlwind tours, departing for Macau in the morning and returning to Hong Kong on the same evening. Gray Line (☎ in Hong Kong 2368 7111; www.grayline.com.hk) offers such a tour for HK$690/$720 on weekdays/weekends (child under 10 HK$620/$650).

Quality Tours organised by the MGTO and tendered to agents such as Gray Line (Map pp316–17; ☎ 2833 6611; Rua do Campo; 🕑 9.30am-6.30pm Mon-Sat) take around 6½ hours (adult/child under 10 including museum and Macau Tower tickets MOP$200/$150).

The Tour Machine, run by Avis Rent A Car (Map pp316–17; ☎ 2833 6789; www.avis.com.mo; Room 1022, Ground fl, Macau ferry terminal; 🕑 8am-7pm), is a replica 1920s-style English bus that seats nine people and runs on fixed routes in about two hours past some of Macau's most important sights (adult/child under 12 MOP$150/$80). You're allowed to disembark, stretch your legs and take photos along the way. There are two departures a day (11am and 3pm) from the Macau ferry terminal.

MACAU PENINSULA

You'll find the lion's share of Macau's museums, churches, gardens, old cemeteries and important colonial buildings on the peninsula and, in July 2005, Unesco recognised this wealth by adding the Historic Centre of Macau, comprising 25 distinct sites, to its World Heritage list. If you're after more active pursuits, such as cycling, hiking and swimming, head for the islands (p343).

MACAU PENINSULA WALKING TOUR

1 Largo do Senado Begin your tour of the peninsula in the beautiful 'Square of the Senate' in the heart of Macau, which is accessible from the ferry terminal on bus 3. On the south side of the square facing Avenida de Almeida Ribeiro is the main post office, built in 1931, and nearby is the restored Museum of the Holy House of Mercy (p319). From here, walk to the northeastern end of the square.

2 Church of St Dominic Overlooking Largo de São Domingos is this church (p321), with its distinctive green shutters and doors.

3 Macau Cathedral On the southern side of the square, you'll spot a narrow road called Travessa de São Domingos. Follow this up to Largo da Sé and Macau Cathedral (p319).

4 Lou Kau Mansion Housed on Travessa da Sé is Lou Kau Mansion (p321), built in 1889. The street leads down into Rua de São Domingos. Take a right at the bottom of the hill and follow Rua de São Domingos and its extension, Rua de Pedro Nolasco da Silva, to the corner with Calçada do Monte. Just visible across the garden to the east is the Consulate General of Portugal, housed in an exquisite colonial mansion.

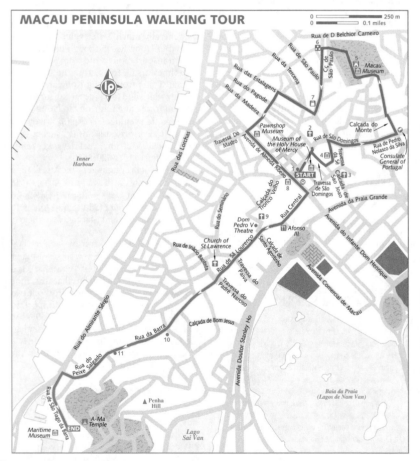

MACAU PENINSULA WALKING TOUR

5 Monte Fort Begin climbing up Calçada do Monte, and once you reach Travessa do Artilheiros, turn left. A cobbled path leads up to the Monte Fort (p319) and the Macau Museum (p319).

6 Ruins of the Church of St Paul Take the escalator down from the museum and walk west to the façade of the Church of St Paul (right); there's a platform offering stunning views over the town on the north side leading to the former choir loft.

7 Antique & Chinese Shops Walk down the impressive stone steps in front of the façade and continue south along Rua de São Paolo, which is lined with antique shops (p332). Turn right onto Rua das Estalagens, which is full of traditional Chinese shops and, once you reach Rua de Camilo Pessanha, turn left. At the western end of this street, turn left again into Avenida de Almeida Ribeiro and immediately on your left you'll pass the Pawnshop Museum (p322).

8 Leal Senado Continue along Avenida de Almeida Ribeiro. After passing the Leal Senado (p319), turn right onto Rua Central, which changes names several times as it heads southwest for the Inner Harbour. If you're feeling peckish, you may want to stop for a bowl of *caldo verde* at Afonso III (p336).

9 Church of St Augustine Towering above this end of Rua Central is the Church of St Augustine (p322) and opposite that the Dom Pedro V Theatre (p321).

10 Largo do Lilau Follow Rua Central's extensions, Rua de São Lourenço and Rua da Barra, passing the Church of St Lawrence (p321) and Largo do Lilau; according to local folklore, should you drink from the fountain in this romantic square, it's a given that you'll return to Macau one day.

11 Moorish Barracks Further on are these enormous barracks, completed in 1874 and now housing the offices of the maritime po-

lice. Rua do Peixe Salgado (Street of Salted Fish) debouches into Rua do Almirante Sérgio, where you should turn left. A short distance south is the ever-active A-Ma Temple (p324) and opposite, across Rua de São Tiago da Barra, is the Maritime Museum (p324). From here, you can follow Avenida da República to Avenida da Praia Grande and Avenida de Almeida Ribeiro or hop on bus 5 or 7.

Central Macau Peninsula

Avenida de Almeida Ribeiro – called San Ma Lo (New St) in Cantonese, together with its southern extension, Avenida do Infante Dom Henrique – is the peninsula's main thoroughfare. It effectively divides the narrow southern peninsula from central and northern Macau. In the centre of this long thoroughfare is the charming square, Largo do Senado. Bus 3 will bring you to the city centre, or take a free casino shuttle to Grand Lisboa from the ferry terminal. The sights are within walking distance from the casino.

RUINS OF THE CHURCH OF ST PAUL
Map p320
Ruinas de Igreja de São Paulo; Travessa de São Paulo; admission free
The most famous sight in Macau, the façade and stairway are all that remain of this early-17th-century Jesuit church, called Tai Sam Ba in Cantonese. With its wonderful statues, portals and engravings that effectively make up a 'sermon in stone' and a *Biblia pauperum* (Bible of the poor), some consider the ruins to be the greatest monument to Christianity in Asia to help the illiterate understand the Passion of Christ and the lives of the saints.

The church was designed by an Italian Jesuit and completed by early Japanese Christian exiles and Chinese craftsmen in 1602. It was abandoned after the expulsion of the Jesuits in 1762 and a military battalion was stationed here. In 1835 a fire erupted in the kitchen of the barracks, destroying everything, except what you see today.

At the top is a dove, representing the Holy Spirit, surrounded by stone carvings of the sun, moon and stars. Beneath the Holy Spirit is a statue of the infant Jesus surrounded by stone carvings of the implements of the Crucifixion (the whip, crown of thorns, nails, ladder and spear). In the centre of the 3rd tier stands the Virgin Mary being assumed bodily into heaven along with angels and two

WALK FACTS
Start Largo do Senado
End Maritime Museum
Distance 4km
Duration Three to four hours
Fuel Stops Many along the way

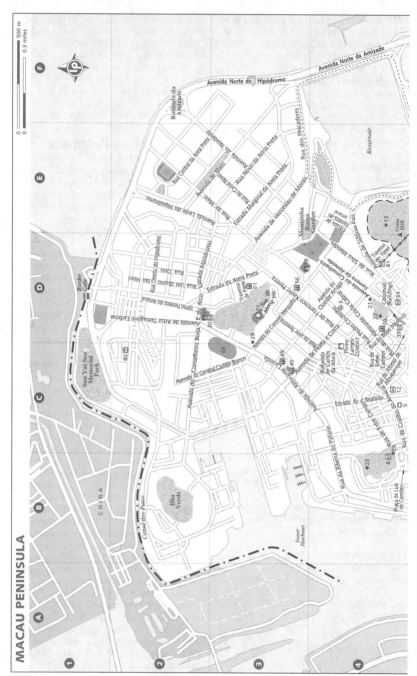

MACAU PENINSULA

0 500 m
0 0.3 miles

CHINA

Canal dos Patos

Sun Yat Sen Memorial Park

Border Gate

Ilha Verde

Inner Harbour

Avenida do Conselheiro Borja

Avenida do General Castelo Branco

Istmo Ferreira do Amaral

Rua Direita do Hipódromo

Rua Dois

Rua Um (Bairro Iao Hon)

Avenida de Artur Tamagnini Barbosa

Estrada Mipódromo

Estrada da Areia Preta

Avenida do Norte do Hipódromo

Avenida Leste do Hipódromo

Rua Central da Areia Preta

Rua Nova da Areia Preta

Avenida de Vercelau de Morais

Avenida de Maio

Rua de Maio

Avenida do Chan Norte

Estrada Marginal da Areia Preta

Rotunda da Amizade

Avenida Norte do Hipódromo

Avenida Norte da Amizade

Rua dos Pescadores

Reservoir

Montanha Russa Garden

Avenida de Silva Mendes

Estrada de Cacilhas

Travessa do Túnel

Guia Hill

Avenida do Conselheiro Ferreira de Almeida

Colonial Buildings

Avenida do Ouvidor Arriaga

Avenida Sidónio Pais

Rua do Campo

Rua de Francisco Xavier Pereira

Rua de Pedro Coutinho

Avenida de Almirante Costa Cabral

Rua de Tomás da Rosa

Três Lamps District

Rotunda de Carlos da Maia

Rua de Entre

Rua do Bispo Medeiros

Rua de Afonso de Albuquerque

Rua de Cosme

Estrada do s Repouso

Rua da Ribeira do Patane

Rua de Luís de Camões

Praça de Luís de Camões

Rua da Entre Campo

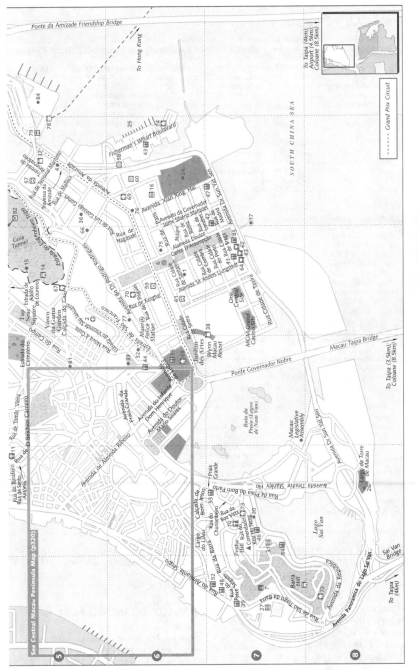

See Central Macau Peninsula Map (p320)

Grand Prix Circuit

MACAU PENINSULA

flowers: the peony, representing China, and the chrysanthemum, a symbol of Japan. To the right of the Virgin is a carving of the tree of life and the apocalyptic woman (Mary) slaying a seven-headed hydra; the Chinese characters next to her read 'the holy mother tramples the heads of the dragon'. To the left of the central statue of Mary, a 'star' guides a ship (the Church) through a storm (sin); a carving of the devil is to the left.

The 4th tier has statues of four Jesuit doctors of the Church (from left to right):

Blessed Francisco de Borja; St Ignatius Loyola, the founder of the order; St Francis Xavier, the apostle of the Far East; and Blessed Luís Gonzaga.

MUSEUM OF SACRED ART & CRYPT
Map p320

Museu de Arte Sacra e Cripta; Travessa de São Paolo; admission free; [icon] **9am-6pm**
This small museum behind the ruins of the Church of St Paul contains polychrome carved wooden statues, silver chalices,

monstrances and oil paintings, including a copy of a 17th-century painting depicting the martyrdom of 26 Japanese Christians by crucifixion at Nagasaki in 1597. The adjoining crypt contains the remains of the martyrs, as well as those of Vietnamese and other Japanese Christians killed in the 17th century. Also here is the recently unearthed tomb of Alessandro Valignano, the Jesuit who founded the College of the Mother of God and is credited with establishing Christianity in Japan.

LEAL SENADO Map p320
163 Avenida de Almeida Ribeiro
Facing Largo do Senado to the west is Macau's most important historical building, the 18th-century 'Loyal Senate', which now houses the Instituto para os Assuntos Cívicos e Municipais (IACM; Civic and Municipal Affairs Bureau) and the mayor's office. It is so-named because the body sitting here refused to recognise Spain's sovereignty during the 60 years that it occupied Portugal.

In 1654, a dozen years after Portuguese sovereignty was re-established, King João IV ordered a heraldic inscription to be placed inside the senate's entrance hall, and this can still be seen today. To the right of the entrance hall is the IACM Gallery (☎ 988 4180; admission free; ◷ 9am-9pm Tue-Sun), which features changing exhibits. On the 1st floor is the Senate Library (☎ 2857 2233; admission free; ◷ 1-7pm Mon-Sat), which has a collection of some 18,500 books, and wonderful carved wooden furnishings and panelled walls.

MONTE FORT Map p320
Fortaleza do Monte; ◷ 7am-7pm
On a hill and accessible by an escalator just east of the ruins of the Church of St Paul, Monte Fort was built by the Jesuits between 1617 and 1626 as part of the College of the Mother of God. Barracks and storehouses were designed to allow the fort to survive a two-year siege, but the cannons were fired only once: during the aborted attempt by the Dutch to invade Macau in 1622 (p307).

MACAU MUSEUM Map p320
Museu de Macau; ☎ 2835 7911; Praceta do Museu de Macau, Fortaleza do Monte; adult/child under 11, student & senior over 60 MOP$15/8, 15th of month admission free; ◷ 10am-6pm Tue-Sun

This wonderful museum housed in the fort tells the story of the hybrid territory of Macau through a host of multimedia exhibits.

On the 1st level, the Genesis of Macau exhibit takes you through the early history of the territory, with parallel developments in the East and the West compared and contrasted. The section devoted to the territory's religions is excellent.

On the 2nd level (Popular Arts & Traditions of Macau), you'll see and hear everything from a re-created firecracker factory, and a *chá gordo* (fat tea) of 20 dishes enjoyed on a Sunday, to the recorded cries of street vendors selling items such as brooms, tea and scrap metal. You can also hear a recording of the poet José dos Santos Ferreira (1919–93), known as Adé, reading from his work in local dialect.

The top-floor Contemporary Macau exhibit focuses on the latest architecture, literature and urban-development plans.

MACAU CATHEDRAL Map p320
A Sé Catedral; Largo da Sé; ◷ 8am-6pm
East of Largo do Senado is the cathedral, a not particularly attractive structure consecrated in 1850 to replace an earlier one badly damaged in a typhoon. The cathedral, which was completely rebuilt in 1937, has some notable stained-glass windows and is very active during major Christian festivals and holy days in Macau.

MUSEUM OF THE HOLY HOUSE OF MERCY Map p320
Núcleo Museológico da Santa Casa da Misericórdia; ☎ 2857 3938; 2 Travessa da Misericórdia; adult/ student & senior over 65 MOP$5/free; ◷ 10am-5.30pm Mon-Sat
Established in 1569, it is the oldest social institution in Macau, serving as a home to orphans and prostitutes in the 18th century. Today it is a two-room museum containing items related to the house, including religious artefacts; Chinese, Japanese and European porcelain; the skull of its founder and Macau's first bishop, Dom Belchior Carneiro; and a portrait of Martha Merop, an orphan who became a tycoon and a patron of the House, painted shortly before her death. Its restaurant (☎ 2833 5220; ◷ 10am-6pm Mon-Sat) at the basement serves very affordable and decent meals during lunch time.

MACAU **NEIGHBOURHOODS & SIGHTS**

CENTRAL MACAU PENINSULA

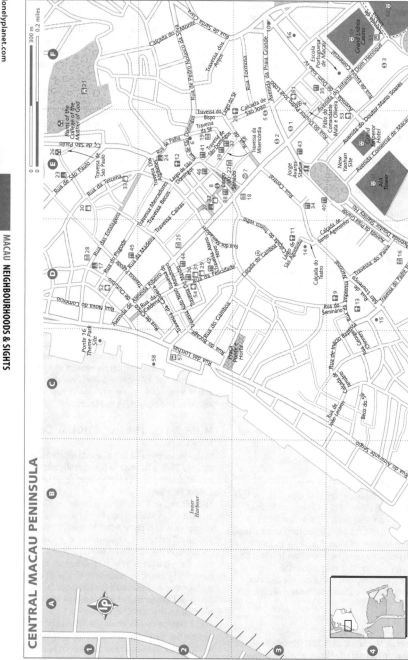

CHURCH OF ST DOMINIC Map p320
Igreja de São Domingos; Largo de São Domingos; ⏰ 10am-6pm
Northeast of Largo do Senado, this 17th-century baroque church is a replacement of a chapel built by the Dominicans in the 1590s. Today it contains the Treasury of Sacred Art (Tresouro de Arte Sacra; ☎ 2836 7706; admission free; ⏰ 10am-6pm), an Aladdin's cave of ecclesiastical art and liturgical objects exhibited on three floors.

LOU KAU MANSION Map p320
Casa de Lou Kau; ☎ 399 6699; 7 Travessa da Sé; admission free; ⏰ 9am-7pm Tue-Mon & public holidays, 10am-7pm Sat & Sun
Near the Macau Cathedral is this well-preserved traditional Cantonese-style mansion built in 1889. It belonged to tycoon Lou Wa Sio, father of Lou Lim Ioc, who made his fortunes in Macau during the 19th century. The mansion has kept its elaborated brick relief

and lattice carvings on windows, as well as some hybrid East-West architecture. Interestingly there is no kitchen in the mansion, as the owner's concubines were supposed to bring him pleasure rather than cook.

DOM PEDRO V THEATRE Map p320
Teatro Dom Pedro V; ☎ 2893 9646; Calçada do Teatro
Opposite the Church of St Augustine, this colonnaded, neoclassical theatre built in 1858 is the oldest European theatre in China and is sometimes used for cultural performances.

CHURCH OF ST LAWRENCE Map p320
Igreja de São Lourenço; Rua de São Lourenço; ⏰ 10am-4pm
Enter Macau's most fashionable church from Rua da Imprensa Nacional. The original was built of wood in the 1560s but was

---

CENTRAL MACAU PENINSULA

INFORMATION (pp350-2)
Banco Comercial de Macau 澳門國際銀行 1 E3
Banco Nacional Ultramarino 大西洋銀行 2 E3
Bank of China 中國銀行大廈 3 F4
CTM Branch 澳門電訊 4 F3
HSBC 匯豐銀行 5 E3
Livararia 6 E2
Main Post Office 郵政總局 7 E3
MGTO Branch 旅遊諮詢處 ....(see 26)
MGTO Branch 旅遊諮詢處 8 E2

SIGHTS (pp315-22)
Chapel of St Joseph Seminary 聖約翰修院及聖堂 9 D4
Chinese Reading Room 八角亭圖書館 10 F3
Church of St Augustine 聖奧斯定教堂 11 D3
Church of St Dominic 玫瑰堂 12 E3
Church of St Lawrence 聖老楞佐教堂 13 D4
Cultural Club 文化會館 ....(see 25)
Dom Pedro V Theatre 崗頂劇院 14 D3
George Chinnery House 錢納利故居 15 D4
Government House 特區政府總部 16 D4
Hong Kung Temple 康公廟 17 D1
IACM Gallery 民政總署展覽廳 ....(see 18)
Leal Senado 民政總署 18 E3
Lou Kau Mansion 盧家大屋 19 E2
Macau Cathedral 大堂 (主教座堂) 20 E3
Macau Museum 澳門博物館 ....(see 21)

Monte Fort 大炮台 21 F1
Museum of Sacred Art & Crypt 天主教藝術博物館與墓室 ....(see 26)
Museum of the Holy House of Mercy 仁慈堂博物館 22 E2
Na Tcha Temple 哪吒廟 23 E1
Nu Wa Temple 女媧廟 24 E2
Pawnshop Museum 典當業展示館 25 D2
Ruins of the Church of St Paul 大三巴 26 E1
Sam Kai Vui Kun Temple 三街會館 27 E2
Senate Library 民政總署圖書館 ....(see 18)
Sound of the Century Museum (Tai Peng Electronics) 留聲歲月音響博物館 (太平電器) 28 D1
Treasury of Sacred Art 聖物寶庫 ....(see 12)

SHOPPING (pp332-3)
Choi Heong Yuen 咀香園 29 D2
Flea Market 30 E1
Koi Kei 鉅記 31 D2
Main Post Office 郵政總局 ....(see 7)
St Dominic Market 營地街市 32 E2
Traditional Shops 33 E1

EATING (pp333-8)
Afonso III 亞豐素三世餐廳 34 E3
Caravela 35 F3
Don Alfonso 1890 ....(see 49)
Fat Siu Lau 佛笑樓 36 D2
La Bonne Heure 良辰法國餐廳 37 E2
Long Kei 龍記 38 E2

Ou Mun Café 39 E2
Pavilions Supermercado 百利來超級市場 40 E3
Platão 九如坊 41 E2
Sai Nam 西南飯店 42 D2
Solmar 沙利文餐廳 43 E3
The Eight 8 餐廳 ....(see 49)
Tou Tou Koi 陶陶居 44 D2
U Tac Hong 頤德行 45 D1
Wong Chi Kei 黃枝記 46 E2

ENTERTAINMENT (pp340-2)
Crazy Paris Show 瘋狂巴黎艷舞團 ....(see 49)
D2 ....47 E4
Emperor Palace Casino 英皇宮殿娛樂場 48 E4
Grand Lisboa Casino 新葡京 49 F4
Lisboa Casino 葡京娛樂場 50 F4
Sky 21 ....(see 47)

SLEEPING (pp345-7)
Augusters Lodge 51 F3
East Asia Hotel 東亞酒店 52 D1
Hotel Sintra 新麗華酒店 53 E4
San Va Hospedaria 新華旅店 54 D2

TRANSPORT (pp348-50)
Buses to Islands 55 F4
China National Aviation Corporation 中國航空 56 F3
Kee Kwan Motor Road Co 歧關客運站 57 C2
Pier 14 十四號碼頭 58 C2

reconstructed in stone in the early 19th century and has a magnificent painted ceiling. One of the church towers once served as an ecclesiastical prison.

CHAPEL OF ST JOSEPH SEMINARY
Map p320

Capela do Seminário São José; Rua do Seminário; ⏰ 10am-5pm

To the southwest of the Dom Pedro V Theatre is the Chapel of St Joseph, consecrated in 1758 as part of a Jesuit seminary. Its 19m-high domed ceiling has exceptionally fine acoustics, and the church is used as a concert venue.

CHURCH OF ST AUGUSTINE Map p320

Igreja de Santo Agostinho; Largo de São Agostinho; ⏰ 10am-6pm

Southwest of Largo do Senado via Rua Central is the Church of St Augustine. Though its foundations date from 1586, the present church was built in 1814. The high altar has a statue of Christ bearing the cross, which is carried through the streets during the Procession of the Passion of Our Lord on the first Saturday of Lent (p311). At the time of writing, the church was closed for maintenance.

SAM KAI VUI KUN TEMPLE Map p320

Sam Kai Vui Kun; Rua Sui do Mercado de São Domingos; ⏰ 8am-6pm

Literally 'a community hall for three streets', this temple was a meeting place for merchants then an adjudication court before the Chinese Chamber of Commerce came into existence in 1912. Also known as Kwan Tai Temple, dedicated to Kwan Yu, the god of war and justice (see p67), it gets particularly busy in May, June and July when locals celebrate three festivals in the god's honour.

TEMPLES

Macau has several interesting Chinese temples dedicated to some important but lesser worshipped deities. Na Tcha Temple (Map p320; Nat Tcha Miu; Rua de São Paolo; free admission; ⏰ 8am-5pm), sitting quietly beside the Ruins of the Church of St Paul, was built in 1888 and dedicated to the child god of war to halt the plague occurring at that time. The Nu Wa Temple (Map p320; Nui Wo Miu; cnr Rua das Estalagens & Travessa Dos Algibebes; free admission; ⏰ 9am-5pm), also built in 1888, was consecrated to the Chinese equivalent of Gaia.

The 200-year-old Hong Kung Temple (Map p320; Hong Kung Miu; cnr Rua das Estalagens & Rua de Cinco de Outubro; ⏰ 8am-6pm) is for worshipping Li Lie, a general during the Han dynasty. The boat-shaped sculpture in the middle of the main hall is for offering wine to the deities during religious festivities.

GOVERNMENT HOUSE Map p320

Sede do Governo; cnr Avenida da Praia Grande & Travessa do Padré Narciso

South of the Church of St Lawrence is monumental Government House, a pillared, rose-coloured building erected for a Portuguese noble in 1849. It's now the headquarters of the Macau SAR government. It is open to the public for a day, usually scheduled in September or October.

CHINESE READING ROOM Map p320

Rua de Santa Clara; ⏰ 9am-noon & 7-10pm Tue-Sat, 9am-10pm Sun

This attractive octagonal structure, with its double stone staircase and little round tower, is a wonderful mix of Chinese and Portuguese styles that could only be found in Macau.

PAWNSHOP MUSEUM Map p320

Casa de Penhores Tradicional; ☎ 2892 1811; 396 Avenida de Almeida Ribeiro; admission MOP$5; ⏰ 10.30am-7pm, closed 1st Mon of month

Housed in the former Tak Seng On (Virtue and Success) pawnshop built in 1917, the museum incorporates the fortresslike eight-storey granite tower with slotted windows where goods were stored on racks or in safes. Sharing the same building is the Cultural Club (Map p320; Clube Cultural; ☎ 2892 1811; www.culturalclub.net; 390 Avenida de Almeida Ribeiro; admission free; ⏰ 10.30am-8pm), which claims to look at various aspects of everyday life in Macau but is little more than a souvenir shop.

SOUND OF THE CENTURY MUSEUM
Map p320

☎ 2892 1389; www.tai-peng.com/antique; support@tai-peng.com; 3rd fl, 13-15 Rua Das Estalagens; admission MOP$30; ⏰ 11am-5pm

Whether you are a phonograph enthusiast or not, this private museum is eye-opening. The personal collections of the owner of Tai Peng Electronics include 200 items, from antique phonographs to tournaphones and echophones dating back to as early as 1882. Prior appointment is required.

Southern Macau Peninsula

Southern Macau Peninsula encompasses three areas: that around the extensively renovated Macau Forum, a conference and exhibition space, and Tourist Activities Centre housing two worthwhile museums; the rectangle of reclaimed land called NAPE to the south; and the southwest corner of the peninsula. While buses 8, 12 and 17, leaving from Ilha Verde, the ferry terminal and Luís de Camães Garden respectively, will take you to NAPE, the free casino shuttles provided by Sands, Babylon, Wynn Macau and Star World are an alternative.

MACAU CULTURAL CENTRE Map pp316–17

Centro Cultural de Macau; ☎ 2870 0699, 2855 5555; www.ccm.gov.mo; Avenida Xian Xing Hai; ⏰ 9am-7pm Tue-Sun

This US$100-million centre is the territory's prime venue for theatre, opera and other cultural performances.

MACAU MUSEUM OF ART Map pp316–17

Museu de Arte de Macau; ☎ 791 9814; www.artmuseum.gov.mo; Avenida Xian Xing Hai; adult/child under 12 & student/senior over 65 MOP$5/3/free, Sun admission free; ⏰ 10am-7pm Tue-Sun

This vast five-storey complex within the Macau Cultural Centre houses some excellent exhibits and permanent collections of Chinese traditional art and paintings by Western artists who lived in Macau, such as George Chinnery (p310). There's a library with art-related titles on the ground floor.

KUN IAM STATUE Map pp316–17

Estátua de Kun Iam; Avenida Doutor Sun Yat Sen

This 20m-high bronze figure, emerging Virgin Mary–like from a 7m-high lotus in the outer harbour, is probably the only statue of the goddess of mercy in the world not facing the sea. It is quite relaxing once you've entered Kun Iam's 'blossom' – the Kun Iam Ecumenical Centre (Centro Ecuménico Kun Iam; ☎ 2875 1516; admission free; ⏰ 10am-6pm Sat-Thu). Information is available on Buddhism, Taoism and Confucianism.

GRAND PRIX MUSEUM Map pp316–17

Museu do Grande Prémio; ☎ 798 4108; Basement, CAT, 431 Rua de Luís Gonzaga Gomes; adult/child under 11 & senior over 60/child under 19 MOP$10/free/5, adult with Macau Wine Museum MOP$20; ⏰ 10am-6pm Wed-Mon

Cars from the Macau Formula 3 Grand Prix, including the bright-red Triumph TR2 driven by Eduardo de Carvalho that won the first Grand Prix in 1954, are on display, while simulators let you test your racing skills.

MACAU SECURITY FORCES MUSEUM Map pp316–17

Museu das Forças de Segurança de Macau; ☎ 2855 9999; Calçada dos Quartéis; admission free; ⏰ 9am-5.45pm Mon-Fri, 9am-5pm Sat & Sun

Housed in the 17th-century St Francis Barracks (Quartéis de São Francisco; Map pp316–17), this museum has two rooms of exhibits relating to the police and their work. The building is set in the lovely St Francis Garden (Jardim de São Francisco; Map pp316–17).

MACAU WINE MUSEUM Map pp316–17

Museu do Vinho de Macau; ☎ 798 4188; Basement, CAT, 431 Rua de Luís Gonzaga Gomes; adult/child under 11 & senior over 60/child under 19 MOP$15/free/5, adult with Grand Prix Museum MOP$20; ⏰ 10am-6pm Wed-Mon

This museum is a rather inert display of wine racks, barrels, presses and tools used by wine makers, as well as a rundown of Portugal's various wine regions. Some of the recent wines of the more than 1300 on display are available for tasting, which is included in the entry fee.

MACAU FISHERMAN'S WHARF Map pp316–17

Doca dos Pescadores; www.fishermanswharf.com.mo

Bordering the east of NAPE (pronounced 'NA-pay'), a rectangular area of reclaimed land, is Macau Fisherman's Wharf, a rather tacky 'theme park' built partially on reclaimed land. It combines attractions, hotels, shops, and restaurants, and is divided into three sections. Tang Dynasty focuses on Chinese history and culture; East Meets West is a 30m-high working volcano, an Africa Fort funfair for kids, and the Greek Square leisure and performance park; and Legend Wharf features landmarks from around the world.

HANDOVER OF MACAU GIFTS MUSEUM Map pp316–17

Museu das Ofertas sobre a Transferência de Soberania de Macau; ☎ 791 9800; Avenida Xian Xing Hai; admission free; ⏰ 10am-7pm Tue-Sun

This new museum, next to the Macau Cultural Centre, is a crowd-pleaser among visitors from the mainland. It displays art pieces and handicrafts presented by China's various provinces and regions to Macau to mark the return of Chinese sovereignty in 1999. Some exhibits are kitsch in the extreme.

SOUTHWEST CORNER

The southwestern tip of the Macau Peninsula has a number of important historical sights, as it should – it was the first area of territory to be settled.

A-MA TEMPLE Map pp316–17
Templo de A-Ma; Rua de São Tiago da Barra; 7am-6pm; 1, 1A, 5

North of Barra Hill, this temple – called Ma Kok Miu in Cantonese – is dedicated to the goddess A-Ma, who is better known as Tin Hau (see the boxed text, p307). The original temple on this site was probably already standing when the Portuguese arrived, although the present one may only date back to the 17th century. At the main entrance is a large boulder with a coloured relief of a *lorcha*, a traditional sailing vessel of the South China Sea. The faithful make a pilgrimage here during the A-Ma Festival sometime between late April and early May.

AVENIDA DA REPÚBLICA Map pp316–17
Avenida da Praia Grande and Rua da Praia do Bom Parto form an arc that leads into Avenida da República, the oldest section of Macau. Along here are several grand colonial villas not open to the public. The former Bela Vista Hotel, one of the most-storied hotels in Asia, is now the residence of the Portuguese consul general. Nearby is the ornate Santa Sancha Palace (Palacete de Santa Sancha; Estrada de Santa Sancha), once the residence of Macau's Portuguese governors and now used to accommodate state guests.

PENHA HILL Map pp316–17
Colina da Penha

Towering above the colonial villas along Avenida da República is Penha Hill, from where you'll get an excellent view of the central area of Macau and across the Pearl River into China. The Bishop's Palace (built in 1837) is here, as is the lovely Chapel of Our Lady of Penha (Capela de Nostra Señora da Penha; 9am-5.30pm), once a place of pilgrimage for sailors.

MACAU TOWER Map pp316–17
Torre de Macau; 2893 3339; www.macautower.com.mo; Largo da Torre de Macau; 10am-9pm Mon-Fri, 9am-9pm Sat & Sun; 9A, 32, AP1

Macau Tower, at 338m, is the 10th-tallest freestanding structure in the world; it stands on the narrow isthmus of land southeast of Avenida da República. The squat building at its base is the Macau Convention & Entertainment Centre.

The tower houses observation decks (adult/child 3-12 & senior over 65 MOP$70/35) on the 58th and 61st floors; restaurants and bars such as the revolving 360° Café (11.30am-3pm, 3.30-4.15pm & 6-11pm) on the 60th floor; and the 180° Lounge (minimum charge MOP$100; noon-1am), a floor below it.

If none of this takes your fancy, you might be interested in the activities of the New Zealand–based extreme-sports company AJ Hackett (988 8656), which organises all kinds of adventure climbs up and around the tower.

The truly intrepid will go for the Mast Climb (MOP$700 to MOP$1000), in which you go up and down the mast's 100m of vertical ladders to the top in two hours. The Skywalk (weekdays/weekends MOP$100/$120) is a twirl around the covered walkway – you're attached to a lanyard – under the pod of the tower (on the 57th floor) and 216m above ground. The Skywalk X (MOP$160/$190) is a railless walk around the *outer* rim, some 233m high, on the 61st floor. The faint-hearted may try something closer to terra firma: the Flying Fox (MOP$30) is a 70m 'flight' on a zip line from one of the tower legs into a large net; the Ironwalk (MOP$60) is an 8m-high walk via rope ladder around the legs of the tower, with a Flying Fox finish; and Long Ironwalk (MOP$80) is a vertical version of the Ironwalk, some 23m up. Bungy (MOP$888) is the world's highest free fall, from a 233m-high platform, and the Sky Jump (MOP$588 to MOP$1088) is a slower version of Bungy.

MARITIME MUSEUM Map pp316–17
Museu Marítimo; 2859 5481; 1 Largo do Pagode da Barra; adult/senior over 65/child 10-17 Mon & Wed-Sat MOP$10/free/5, Sun MOP$5/free/3; 10am-5.30pm Wed-Mon

Opposite the A-Ma Temple, the Maritime Museum has interesting boats and artefacts from Macau's seafaring past, a mock-up of a Hakka fishing village and displays of the long, narrow boats that are raced during the Dragon Boat Festival (p311) in June.

Northern Macau Peninsula

The northern part of the peninsula, encompassing everything northwards from the Luís de Camões Garden in the west and Guia Fort in the east to the border with the mainland, has a few important historic sites and divine gardens. With fewer tourists than other parts of the peninsula, it's an agreeable area for just wandering about.

GUIA FORT Map pp316–17
Colina da Guia
The fortress, built in 1638 atop the highest point on the peninsula, was originally designed to defend the border with China, but it soon came into its own as a lookout post. Storm warnings were sounded from the bell in the quaint Chapel of Our Lady of Guia (Capela de Nostra Señora da Guia; 🕙 10am-5pm Tue-Sun), built in 1622. The walls of the little church have interesting frescoes only discovered recently, and there's a colourful choir loft above the main entrance. On the floor below is a tombstone with the inscription (in Latin): 'Here lies at this gate the remains of a Christian, by accident, for his body does not deserve such an honourable sepulchre'. It's believed the deceased was buried here in 1687. The 15m-tall Guia Lighthouse (Farol da Guia; 1865) is the oldest lighthouse on the China coast. It's open on 18 May annually. On clear days you can see Lantau Island from the fort, but the new skyscrapers in NAPE now block some of the view.

The 52m-long Guia Hill Air Raid Shelter (Abrigos Antiaéreos da Colina a Guia; 🕙 10am-5pm Tue-Sun), an old military installation, was constructed in 1931 and was off-limits until 1962. Photos of the history of the shelter and an electricity generator used during WWII are on display.

The easiest way to reach the top of Guia Hill is to hop on the little Guia Cable Car (Teleférico da Guia; one way/return MOP$2/3) that runs from 8am to 6pm Tuesday to Sunday from just outside the entrance of the attractive Flora Garden (Rua do Túnel; 🕙 6am-7pm), off Avenida de Sidónio Pais.

CASA GARDEN Map pp316–17
13 Praça de Luís de Camões; 🚌 8A, 12, 26
This colonial villa, east of the Luís de Camões Garden, was the headquarters of the British East India Company when it was based in Macau in the early 19th century. Today the villa houses the Oriental Foundation (Fundação Oriente; ☎ 2855 4699; www.foriente.pt), an organisation founded in 1996 to promote Portuguese culture worldwide, and an exhibition gallery (☎ 398 1126; admission free; 🕙 10am-5.30pm Mon-Fri, 10am-7pm daily during special exhibitions), which houses both exhibits of Chinese antiques, porcelain and contemporary art.

OLD PROTESTANT CEMETERY
Map pp316–17
15 Praça de Luís de Camões; 🕙 8.30am-5.30pm
To the east of the Casa Garden is the final resting place of many early non-Portuguese residents of Macau. As Church law forbade the burial of non-Catholics on hallowed ground, there was nowhere to inter Protestants who died here, and they were often buried clandestinely in the nearby hills. The governor finally allowed the British East India Company to establish the cemetery in 1821. A number of old graves were then transferred to the cemetery, which explains the earlier dates on some of the tombstones.

Among the better-known people interred in this well-kept cemetery are the artist George Chinnery (see the boxed text, p310) and Robert Morrison (1782–1834), the first Protestant missionary to China and author of the first Chinese-English dictionary.

CHURCH OF ST ANTHONY   Map pp316–17
Igreja de Santo António; cnr Rua de Santo António & Rua do Tarrafeiro; 🕙 7.30am-5.30pm
Located just outside the Casa Garden and next to the roundabout, this church, built from 1558 to 1608, is considered to be the oldest in Macau and was the Jesuit's earliest headquarters. The local Portuguese used to hold wedding ceremonies here, hence its name in Cantonese: Fa Vong Tong (Church of Flowers). It burnt down three times and the present architecture is a restoration from 1930.

CEMETERY OF ST MICHAEL THE ARCHANGEL Map pp316–17
Cemitério de São Miguel Arcanjo; 2A Estrada do Cemitério; 🕙 8am-6pm

This cemetery, northeast of Monte Fort, contains tombs and sepulchres that can only be described as baroque ecclesiastical works of art. Near the main entrance is the Chapel of St Michael (Capela de São Miguel; ☾ 10am-6pm), a doll-sized, pea-green church with a tiny choir loft and pretty porticoes.

LOU LIM IOC GARDEN Map pp316–17
Jardim de Lou Lim Ioc; 10 Estrada de Adolfo de Loureiro; ☾ 6am-9pm; 🚍 12
The cool and shady Lou Lim Ioc Garden is the only Chinese-style garden you can find in Macau. Local people use the park to practise t'ai chi or play traditional Chinese musical instruments.

The renovated Victorian-style Lou Lim Ioc Garden Pavilion (Pavilhão do Jardim de Lou Lim Ioc; ☎ 988 4128; admission free; ☾ 9am-9pm Tue-Sun) is used for temporary exhibits and for recitals during the Macau International Music Festival (p311) in late October/November.

Adjacent to the garden is the recently opened Macao Tea Culture House (Caultura do Chá em Macau; ☾ 9am-7pm Tue-Sun), displaying the Guangdong tea culture with exhibits of various teapots.

LIN FUNG TEMPLE Map pp316–17
Lin Fung Miu; Avenida do Almirante Lacerda; ☾ 10am-6.30pm; 🚍 12
Built in 1592 as a Taoist temple but now dedicated to Kun Iam, it's where mandarins from Guangdong province would stay when they visited Macau. The most celebrated of these visitors was Lin Zexu (p21), the commissioner charged with stamping out the opium trade, who stayed here in September 1839. The Lin Zexu Memorial Hall (Museu de Lin Zexu; ☎ 2855 0166; tourist adult/local adult/child under 8 & senior over 65 MOP$10/5/3; ☾ 9am-5pm Tue-Sun), with its old photographs, a model of a Chinese war junk and opium-smoking paraphernalia, recalls his visit.

KUN IAM TEMPLE Map pp316–17
Kun Iam Tong; Avenida do Coronel Mesquita; ☾ 10am-6pm; 🚍 1A, 12
Dating from 1627, this is the most active Buddhist temple in Macau. It also honours the goddess of mercy with a collection of pictures and scrolls. Some of the reliefs were damaged during the Cultural Revolution.

The first treaty of trade and friendship between the USA and China (1844) was signed at a stone table in the terraced gardens at the back; a tablet marks the spot.

SUN YAT SEN MEMORIAL HOME
Map pp316–17
Casa Memorativa de Doutor Sun Yat Sen; ☎ 2857 4064; 1 Rua de Silva Mendes; admission free; ☾ 10am-5pm Wed-Mon
Around the corner from the Lou Lim Ioc Garden, this museum is dedicated to the founder of the Chinese Republic, Dr Sun Yat Sen (1866–1925). Dr Sun practised medicine at the Kiang Wu Hospital on Rua Coelho do Amaral for a few years before turning to revolution to overthrow the Qing dynasty. The house, built in the mock Moorish style popular at the time, contains a collection of flags, photos and documents relating to the life and times of the 'Father of the Nation'. It replaces the original house, which blew up while being used as an explosives store. Sun's first wife, Lu Muzhen, died in the upstairs back bedroom in 1952.

TAP SEAC GALLERY Map pp316–17
Galeria Tam Seac; www.macauart.net/TS; 95 Avenida Conselheiro Ferreira de Almeida; ☾ 10am-6pm Tue-Sun; 🚍 9, 12
Also housed in a Moorish-style mansion dating back to the 1920s, this gallery is arguably the best place to view contemporary art in Macau, and exhibitions change regularly. Check its website for details. The gallery keeps the original patio in the middle of the house, which creates a light-filled, relaxed setting.

OX WAREHOUSE Map pp316–17
Armazem de Boi; ☎ 2853 0026; www.oxware house.blogspot.com; cnr Avenida do Coronel Mesquita & Avenida do Almirante Lacerda; ☾ noon-7pm Wed-Mon; 🚍 1A, 12
Near the Canidrome is the Ox Warehouse, home to a group of avant-garde artists working in a variety of media. It's also known as Old Ladies' House Art Space, where a number of installations and performances are hosted in the two exhibition halls. The lovely courtyard makes it a cheerful rest area amid the densely populated northern Macau.

LUÍS DE CAMÕES GARDEN Map pp316–17
Jardim de Luís de Camões; Praça de Luís de Camões; ☾ 6am-10pm; 🚍 8A

This lovely garden is popular with local Chinese, who use it to 'walk' their caged songbirds or play Chinese chequers. In the centre of the park is the Camões Grotto (Gruta de Camões), which contains a 19th-century bust of the one-eyed national poet of Portugal, Luís de Camões (see p312).

FIRE SERVICES MUSEUM Map pp316–17
Museu de Bombeiros; ☎ 2857 2222; 2-6 Estrada de Coelho do Amaral; admission free; ✆ 10am-6pm daily; ☐ 8
Housed in the former headquarters of the Macau fire brigade, the museum holds a small but interesting collection of old fire trucks from the 1940s and '50s, a manual pump from 1877, lots of helmets and boots.

TAIPA & COLOANE ISLANDS
Connected to the Macau mainland by three bridges and joined together by Cotai (an ever-growing area of reclaimed land), Coloane and, to a lesser extent, Taipa, are oases of calm and greenery, with striking, pastel-coloured colonial villas, quiet lanes, decent beaches, and fine Portuguese and Macanese restaurants. By contrast, the Cotai Strip is development central, with several new megacasinos sprouting up.

TAIPA WALKING TOUR
1 Taipa House Museum Bus 28A from the ferry terminal will take you to Taipa. Begin your tour by visiting the beautiful Macanese villa built in 1921, which is now converted to the Taipa House Museum (p329).

WALK FACTS
Start Taipa House Museum
End Largo de Camões
Distance 1km
Duration One to 1½ hours
Fuel Stop Many along Rua do Regedor

2 Church of Our Lady of Carmel Walk up the steps to the 1885 Church of Our Lady of Carmel from the western end of Avenida da Praia. The colonial library, opposite, is a recent reproduction, replacing the original that had been pulled down illegally. Surrounding it are the pretty Carmel Gardens and just north is Calçada do Carmo, a positively delightful stepped lane lined with ancient banyans.

3 Temples Following Avenida de Carlos da Maia will take you past an old police school and into Rua da Correia Silva, which leads to a small early-19th-century Tin Hau temple on Largo Governador Tamagnini Barbosa. Northeast, just off Rua do Regedor, is Pak Tai Temple, dedicated to the guardian of peace and order.

4 Markets The Taipa market is housed in a building at the end of the street. There's a weekly crafts market (✆ noon-9pm Sun) in Largo de Camões.

Taipa Island
When the Portuguese first sighted Taipa (Tam Chai in Cantonese, Tanzai in Mandarin), it was actually two islands. Over the centuries the pair

MACAU NEIGHBOURHOODS & SIGHTS

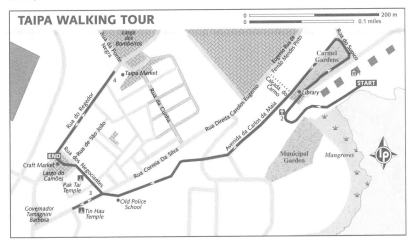

TAIPA WALKING TOUR

lonelyplanet.com

TAIPA

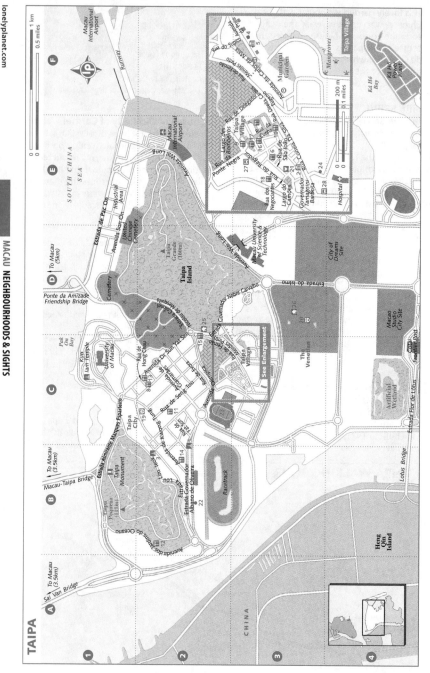

was joined together by silt pouring down from the Pearl River. Reclamation has succeeded in doing the same thing to Taipa and Coloane.

Traditionally an island of duck farms and boat yards, with enough small fireworks factories to satisfy the insatiable demand for bangers and crackers, Taipa is rapidly becoming urbanised and now boasts major casino-hotels, a university, a racecourse and stadium, high-rise apartments and an airport. But a parade of baroque churches and buildings, Taoist and Buddhist temples, overgrown esplanades and lethargic settlements means it's still possible to experience the traditional charms of the island. Buses 11 and 28A leave from A-Ma Temple and the ferry terminal respectively and have stops at almost all the sights in Taipa.

TAIPA HOUSE MUSEUM Map p328
Casa Museum da Taipa; ☎ 2882 7103; Avenida da Praia; adult/child under 12 & senior over 65/student MOP$5/free/2, Sun admission free; 🕙 10am-6pm Tue-Sun
The five lime-green villas facing the water were built in 1921 by wealthy Macanese as summer residences and three of them collectively form this unusual museum. The two houses east of where Avenida da Praia meets Rua do Supico are used for receptions and special exhibitions; the three to the west house permanent collections.

The House of the Regions of Portugal (Casa das Regiões de Portugal) contains costumes and examines traditional ways of life in Portugal. The House of the Islands (Casa das Ilhas) looks at the history of Taipa and Coloane, with interesting displays devoted to the islands' traditional industries: fishing and the manufacture of oyster sauce, shrimp paste and fireworks.

The last is the Macanese House (Casa Macaense), a residence done up in traditional local style that looks like the *dom e doña* (husband and wife) residing here just left. The mix of furnishings – heavy blackwood furniture and Chinese cloisonné with statues and pictures of saints and the Sacred Heart – offers a snapshot of life in Macau in the early 20th century.

TAIPA VILLAGE Map p328
This village in the south of the island is a window to the island's past. It is a tidy sprawl of traditional Chinese shops and some excellent restaurants, punctuated here and there by grand colonial villas, churches and ancient temples. Down along what was once the seafront and is now an artificial lake, Avenida da Praia is a tree-lined esplanade with wrought-iron benches and old-world charm. It's the perfect place for a leisurely stroll.

POU TAI TEMPLE Map p328
Pou Tai Un; 5 Estrada Lou Lim Ieok; 🕙 9am-6pm
This Buddhist temple is the largest temple complex on the islands. The main hall, dedicated to the Three Precious Buddhas, contains an enormous bronze statue of Lord Gautama, and there are brightly coloured prayer pavilions and orchid greenhouses scattered around the complex. The temple also has a popular vegetarian restaurant (p339).

MUSEUM OF TAIPA & COLOANE HISTORY Map p328
Museu da História da Taipa e Coloane; ☎ 2882 7103; Rua Correia da Silva; adult/student & senior MOP$5/2, Tue admission free; 🕙 10am-6pm Tue-Sun

TAIPA

SIGHTS (pp327-31)	
Four-Faced Buddha Shrine	
四面佛 1 C2	
Museum of Taipa & Coloane History	
路氹歷史館 2 E3	
Pou Tai Temple 菩提禪院.....3 B2	
Reception House	
龍環葡韻住宅式博物館 4 F3	
Taipa House Museum 5 F3	

EATING 🍴 (pp338-9)	
A Petisqueira 葡國美食天地....6 E3	
Amagao 阿馬交美食 7 E3	
Chun Yu Fang 春雨坊............8 C2	
Cozinha Pinocchio	
木偶葡國餐廳 9 E3	

Galo 公雞餐廳 10 E3
Gourmet Fine Foods............11 C2
Hyper Gourmet...................12 B2
Kapok Cantonese Restaurant
六棉酒家......................13 C2
O Capítulo 花窗餐廳 14 B2
O Manel 阿曼諾葡國餐....15 D2
O Santos
山度士葡式餐廳 16 E3
Pou Tai Temple Restaurant ....(see 3)
Seng Cheong 誠昌飯店........17 E3
Serrdura 沙厘娜..................18 E3

ENTERTAINMENT 🎭 (pp340-1)
Crown Macau 澳門皇冠 19 C2
Venetian Macau 20 D3

DRINKING 🍸 (p342)
Old Taipa Tavern 21 E3

SPORTS & ACTIVITIES (pp343-5)
Macau Jockey Club 澳門賽馬會....22 B2
Macau Stadium
澳門氹仔運動場 23 C2
Mercearia Bicileta Aluguer....24 E3

SLEEPING 🛏 (p347)
Crown Macau 澳門皇冠 ....(see 19)
Hotel Taipa 澳門格蘭酒店 25 D2
Venetian Macao Resort Hotel
澳門威尼斯人渡假村酒店........26 D3

TRANSPORT (pp348-50)
Bus Stop 27 E3
Main Bus Stop....................28 E3

COLOANE

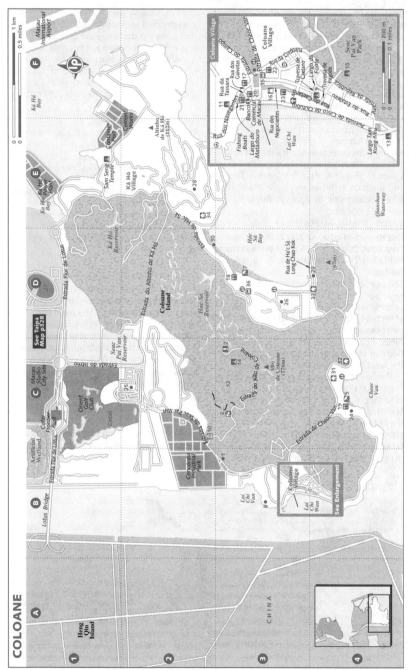

The museum is built on the remnants of the former Island Municipal Council and tries to be a mini-Macau Museum with a focus on Taipa and Coloane, although the collections are not nearly as good as those on Monte Fort. There is a display of excavated relics and other artefacts on the 1st floor that represent the earlier cultural history of Taipa and Coloane, while the 2nd floor contains religious objects, handicrafts and architectural models.

FOUR-FACED BUDDHA SHRINE
Map p328

O Buda de Quatro Faces; cnr Estrada Governador Albano de Oliveira & Rua de Fat San
Northeast of the Macau Jockey Club race-track's main entrance is the Buddhist shrine guarded by four stone elephants and fes-tooned with gold leaf and Thai-style floral bouquets. It's a popular place to pray and make offerings before race meetings.

Coloane Island
A haven for pirates until the start of the 20th century, Coloane (Lo Wan in Cantonese) fought off the last assault by buccaneers on the South China Sea in 1910, and the island still celebrates the victory every 13 July. Nowadays it's the only part of Macau that doesn't seem to be changing at a head-spinning rate. To visit Coloane Island board bus 21A at A-Ma Tem-ple or bus 25 at Portas do Cerco. Both head to Hác Sá Beach and have stops at Avenida do Infante Dom Henrique and Coloane Village.

COLOANE VILLAGE Map p330
The only true settlement on the island, Coloane Village is still largely a fishing village in character, although tourism has given the local economy a big boost. The village is a fascinating relic of the Macau that once was, and strolling along the narrow lanes flanked by temples and colourful shops is a joy.

The bus drops you off in the village's at-tractive main square; Coloane market is on the eastern side. To the west is the waterfront; China is just across the channel. From here a sign points the way north to the Sam Seng Temple (2 Rua dos Navegantes), which is so small it's more like a family altar. Just past the temple is the village pier and beyond that, to the northeast, about a dozen junk-building sheds – a fire in 1999 destroyed many of the sheds.

CHAPEL OF ST FRANCIS XAVIER
Map p330

Capela de São Francisco Xavier; Avenida de Cinco de Outubro; 🕑 10am-8pm
This delightful little church on the water-front was built in 1928 to honour St Francis Xavier, a missionary in Japan. Today Japa-nese Catholics still come to Coloane to pay their respects. For many years a fragment of the saint's arm bone was kept in the chapel, but it has now been moved to St Joseph Seminary on the Macau Peninsula. Have a look in the room to the right of the chapel, where an interesting painting of a Kum Iam–like Virgin Mary is on display.

COLOANE

In front of the chapel are a monument and fountain surrounded by four cannon-balls that commemorate the successful – and final – routing of pirates in 1910.

TEMPLES Map p330

Southeast of the Chapel of St Francis Xavier, between Travessa de Caetano and Travessa de Pagode, is a small Kun Iam Temple – just an altar inside a little walled compound. If you walk just a little further to the southeast, you'll find the considerably larger Tin Hau Temple up in Largo Tin Hau Miu.

At the southern end of Avenida de Cinco de Outubro in Largo Tam Kong Miu, the Tam Kong Temple is dedicated to the Taoist god of seafarers, who may be a deification of the Song-dynasty boy emperor Duan Zong (see p20). To the right of the main altar is a long whale bone, which has been carved into a model of a boat, complete with a dragon's head and a crew of men in pointed hats. Stroke the dragon's head and tail for good luck.

HÁC SÁ BEACH Map p330

Hác Sá (Black Sand) is the most popular beach in Macau. The sand is indeed a grey to blackish colour and makes the water look somewhat dirty (especially at the tide line), but it's perfectly clean. Lifeguards keep the same schedule here as on Cheoc Van Beach.

A-MA STATUE Map p330

Estátua da Deusa A-Ma; Estrada do Alto de Coloane

This colossal 20m statue of the goddess who gave Macau its name (see the boxed text, p307), atop Alto de Coloane (176m), is hewn from a form of white jade quarried near Beijing and was erected in 1998. Below it is enormous Tian Hou Temple (8am-7.30pm), which, together with the statue, form the core of A-Ma Cultural Village, a religious complex containing a museum, retreat and medical centres, a vegetarian restaurant and handicraft shops. It's rather commercial and you'll probably see more traders than prayers, selling different kinds of products supposedly meant to bring luck and wealth, including turtles and birds. Still, it's a good spot to get a birds-eye view of Hác Sá beach on a clear day.

A free bus runs from the A-Ma ornamental entrance gate on Estrada de Seac Pai Van every half-hour from 8am to 6pm.

Otherwise you can reach both by following the Coloane Trail (Trilho de Coloane; p343) from Seac Pai Van Park.

CHEOC VAN BEACH Map p330

Estrada de Cheoc Van

About 1.5km down Estrada de Cheoc Van, which runs east and then southeast from Coloane Village, is the beach at Cheoc Van (Bamboo Bay). There are public changing rooms and toilets and, in season, lifeguards (10am-6pm Mon-Sat, 9am-6pm Sun May-Oct) on duty.

SEAC PAI VAN PARK Map p330

☎ 2887 0277; Estrada de Seac Pai Van; admission free; 9am-6pm Tue-Sun

At the end of Cotai, this 20-hectare park, built in the wooded hills on the western side of the island, has somewhat unkempt gardens sprouting species of plants and trees from around the world, a children's zoo, a lake with swans and other waterfowl, and a decaying walk-through aviary (9am-5pm Tue-Sun), which contains a number of rare birds. The Museum of Nature & Agriculture (Museu Natural e Agrário; ☎ 2882 7277; admission free; 10am-6pm Tue-Sun) has traditional farming equipment, dioramas of Coloane's ecosystem, and displays cataloguing a wide range of the island's fauna and flora.

SHOPPING

The main shopping areas in Macau Peninsula are along Avenida do Infante Dom Henrique and Avenida de Almeida Ribeiro. Other shopping zones can be found along Rua da Palha, Rua do Campo and Rua Pedro Nolasco da Silva.

The largest shopping complex in Macau is the newly opened Venetian Macau (Map p328). Same as the Wynn Macau (Map pp316–17; Rua Cidade de Sintra, NAPE), it has a number of luxury retailers selling high-end fashion. The more family-friendly Japanese-owned department store New Yaohan (Map pp316–17; Avenida da Amizade), opposite the ferry terminal, is expected to relocate behind the Grand Emperor Hotel (Map p320) in 2008.

ANTIQUES & CURIOS

While exploring Macau's back lanes and streets you'll stumble across bustling markets and traditional Chinese shops. Rua da

Madeira is a charming market street, with many shops selling carved Buddha heads and other religious items.

Rua dos Mercadores, which leads up to Rua da Tercena, will lead you past tailors, tiny jewellery stores, incense and mahjong shops, and other traditional businesses (Map p320). At the far end of Rua da Tercena, where the road splits, is a flea market (Map p320), where you can pick up baskets and other rattan ware, jade pieces and old coins.

Great streets for antiques, ceramics and curios (eg traditional Chinese kites) are Rua de São Paulo, Rua das Estalagens and Rua de São António, and the lanes off them; most shops are open from 10.30am or 11am to 6pm or 7pm, with a one-hour lunch some time between 12.30pm and 2pm.

Coloane Village has a few shops selling bric-a-brac, traditional goods and antiques. Asian Artefacts (Map p330; ☎ 2888 1022; 9 Rua dos Negociantes; ◷ 10am-7pm) is one of the best.

CLOTHING

For cheap clothing, go to the St Dominic Market (Map p320), in an alley just north of Largo do Senado, or the Three Lamps District, especially around Rotunda de Carlos da Maia (Map pp316–17), near the Almirante Lacerda City Market in northern Macau Peninsula.

SPECIALTY FOODS

On Rua da Felicidade, 'street of happiness' and once Macau's red-light district, a cluster of shops sell Chinese pastries original to Macau. Koi Kei (Map p320; 74 Rua de Felicidade), just next to Fat Siu Lau, specialises in phoenix rolls (shredded pork wrapped with seaweed) and peanut candies. Choi Heong Yuen (Map p320; ☎ 2835 5966; 70-72 Rua de Felicidade), going strong for over 70 years, is Macau's most popular place for *hang-yàn-béng* (almond-flavoured biscuits). Both shops have numerous outlets but Felicidade has the most elaborate choices. Other Macau specialties you might want to try include nougats, preserved apricots and *yuk-gàwn*, dried sweet strips of pork and other meats. The shops usually open from 10am to 10pm.

STAMPS

Macau produces some wonderful postage stamps, real collector's items that include images of everything from key colonial landmarks to roulette tables and high-speed

ferries. Mint sets and first-day covers are available from counters 17 and 18 at the main post office (Map p320) facing Largo do Senado.

EATING

Eating – be it Portuguese or Macanese 'soul food', Chinese dim sum or the special treats available from street stalls and night markets – is one of the most rewarding aspects of a visit to Macau. One thing to remember, though: people eat dinner relatively early here, and in some restaurants the dining room is all but empty by 9pm.

The most popular alcoholic tipple in Macau is *vinho verde,* a crisp, dry, slightly effervescent 'green' wine from Portugal that goes down a treat with salty Portuguese food and spicy Macanese dishes. You may also try one of the fine wines from Dão, Douro or Alenquer.

Portuguese & Macanese Cuisine

Portuguese cuisine is meat-based and not always particularly refined. It makes great use of olive oil, garlic and *bacalhau* (dried salted cod), which can be prepared in many different ways. The cuisine sometimes combines meat and seafood in one dish, such as *porco à Alentejana,* a tasty casserole of pork and clams. Some favourite dishes are *caldo verde* (a soup of green kale – a type of cabbage – thickened with potatoes), *pasteis de bacalhau* (codfish croquettes), *sardinhas grelhadas* (grilled sardines), and *feijoada* (a casserole of beans, pork, spicy sausages, potatoes and cabbage).

Macanese food borrows a lot of its ingredients and tastes from Chinese and other Asian cuisines, as well as from those of former Portuguese colonies in Africa and India. It is redolent of coconut, tamarind, chilli, jaggery (palm sugar) and shrimp paste.

The most famous Macanese speciality is *galinha áfricana* (African chicken), in which the bird is prepared in coconut, garlic and chillies.

MACAU EATING

PRICE GUIDE

This price guide is for the approximate cost of a two-course meal, with drinks.

$$$	over MOP$400 a meal
$$	MOP$150-400
$	under MOP$150

As well as cod, there are plenty of other fish and seafood: shrimps, prawns, crabs, squid and white fish. Sole, a tongue-shaped flat fish, is a Macanese delicacy. The contribution from the former Portuguese enclave of Goa, on the west coast of India, is spicy prawns.

Other Macanese favourites include *casquinha* (stuffed crab), *porco balichão tamarino* (pork cooked with tamarind and shrimp paste), *minchi* (minced beef or pork cooked with potatoes, onions and spices), and baked rice dishes made with cod, prawns or crab. Macanese desserts include *pudim,* which is basically crème caramel, *pastéis de nata,* a scrumptious egg-custard tartlet eaten warm, and *serradura,* a calorie-rich 'sawdust' pudding made with crushed biscuits, cream and condensed milk. If you want to try the latter while touring around, visit the mistakenly spelled Serrdura (p338).

Dining in Macau (www.dininginmacau.com) is a quarterly advertorial freebie, but a good source of information about restaurants nonetheless. You may also like to have a read of the Macau Food Guide (www.cityguide.gov.mo/food/food_e.htm), available for free at the tourist office.

Other Cuisines

Macau is not just about Macanese and Portuguese food. Some people swear that the dim sum here is far better than anything you'll find in Hong Kong. Burmese cuisine can also be found in the Three Lamps District, a contribution of the sizeable Burmese community living there.

MACAU PENINSULA

Macau is known for its distinct culinary pleasures, no matter whether for Chinese, Portuguese or Macanese cuisines. Most of the restaurants in Macau open from noon to around 3pm, and re-open again at 6pm till 10pm. Good news for foodies – the 5% government tax levied on food and beverage in restaurants was recently lifted.

Macau Peninsula's *dàai-pàai-dawng* (open-air street stalls) serve up excellent stir-fried dishes; try any of those along Rua do Almirante Sérgio.

Macau has about 10 *mercados* (markets) selling fresh fruit, vegetables, meat and fish from 6am to 8pm daily. The largest is the Almirante Lacerda City Market (Mercado Municipal Almirante Lacerda; Map pp316–17; 130 Avenida do Almirante Lacerda), in northern Macau, commonly known as the

Red Market. The old historic St Lawrence City Market (Mercado Municipal de São Lourenço; Rua de João Lecaros) in the south was demolished in 2006, but a new market complex at the same location is expected to be complete in 2009.

Pavilions Supermercado (Map p320; ☎ 2833 3636; 421 Avenida da Praia Grande; ☯ 10am-9pm Mon-Sat, 11am-8pm Sun), a supermarket in the centre of the Macau Peninsula, has a wide selection of imported food and drinks, including a Portuguese section in the basement. Hyper Gourmet (Map p328; ☎ 2881 3452; Ground fl, Magnolia Court, Ocean Gardens, Avenida dos Jardins do Oceano, Taipa; ☯ 10am-10pm), another supermarket on Taipa, and Gourmet Fine Foods (Map p328; ☎ 2884 1436; Ground fl, Block 25, Nava Taipa Garden, 393 Rua de Seng Tou, Taipa; ☯ 10am-9pm), a deli-style store, feature Portuguese, French and Italian foods.

ROBUCHON A GALERA
Map pp316–17   French $$$
☎ 2837 7666; 3rd fl, New/West Wing, Lisboa Hotel, 2-4 Avenida de Lisboa; starters MOP$190-290, mains MOP$330-570; ☯ noon-2.30pm & 6.30-10.30pm
Joël Robuchon, Michelin-starred French chef and serious *bon vivant,* opened this restaurant featuring *haute cuisine* and world-class wines. For possibly the best fine-dining experience in Macau, try the sublime 12-course tasting menu for MOP$1400. Even if you don't hit the jackpot at the casinos, the three-course set lunch for MOP$288 is very affordable.

DON ALFONSO 1890 Map p320   Italian $$$
☎ 2828 3838; Avenida de Lisboa, Grand Lisboa; starters MOP$180-230, mains MOP$120-540; ☯ noon-2pm & 6.30pm-2am
This new restaurant opened by another colourful Michelin-starred chef, Alfonso Iaccarino, is an alternative for fine dining in Macau, with a dégustation menu for MOP$1200.

MANG PAN KOI
Map pp316–17   Cantonese, Seafood $$$
☎ 2856 9256, 687 7296; 26F Rua do Bispo Medeiros; mains MOP$300-400, abalone & shark's fin plate MOP$90-450; ☯ noon-12am
This pocket-sized, homely restaurant is a hidden gem near Lou Lim Iok Garden and gets a thumbs up among the Chinese in Macau. The food specialties here include

SAMPLING THE MENU

These are a few of the dishes you're likely to encounter on your travels through Macau.

Entradas	Appetisers
chouriço assado	grilled Portuguese sausage
croquetes de carne	minced beef croquettes
pastéis de bacalhau	dried Portuguese cod cakes

Sopas	Soups
caldo verde	Portuguese kale soup with *chouriço*, thickened with potato
sopa de marisco	seafood soup

Marisco	Shellfish
açorda de marisco	seafood and mashed bread casserole
ameijoas 'Bulhão Pato'	clams with garlic, coriander and olive oil
arroz de marisco	mixed seafood rice
camarão frito com alho e piri-piri	deep-fried prawns with garlic and chilli
caril de carangueijo	crab curry
casquinha	stuffed crab

Peixe	Fish
bacalhau á 'Brás'	sautéed bacalhau with potatoes and egg
bacalhau á 'Zé do Pipo'	baked, dried cod with mashed potato
lulas recheadas	stuffed squid
sardinhas na brasa	grilled sardines

Carne	Meat
bife de vitela grelhado na brasa com batata frita	grilled veal steak and chips
caldeirada de borrego	lamb, potato and white-wine stew
carne de porco á Alentejana	sautéed pork and clams
coelho á caçadora	rabbit stew
feijoada	pork knuckle, *chouriço*, red bean and cabbage stew
galinha á Africana	grilled chicken cooked with coconut, garlic and chillies
minchi	minced beef or pork cooked with potato
porco balichão tamarino	pork cooked with tamarind and shrimp paste

Sobremesas	Desserts
fatias de tomar	cake-like dessert made with egg yolks and syrup
pudim de ovos	caramel egg pudding
serradura	cream and condensed milk pudding topped with crumbled biscuits

abalone and shark fin and are all carefully prepared with fresh ingredients by the wonderful, hospitable chef Mr Dai, cooking with heart and soul. If possible, bring a Chinese friend for communication.

SAI NAM Map p320   Chinese, Seafood $$$
☎ 2857 4072; 36 Rua da Felicidade; abalone & shark's fin plate from MOP$350; ⏱ 5.30-10.15pm
Handily located in the specialty foods shopping area and housed in a character-

istic former two-storey shop house, this is another decent place to sample abalone, though it's a bit overpriced.

FURUSATO Map pp316–17   Japanese $$$
☎ 2837 7666; 2nd fl, East Wing, Lisboa Hotel; lunch MOP$240-280, dinner MOP$400-700; ⏱ noon-3pm & 6-11pm
Unlike in Hong Kong, good Japanese restaurants are never easy to find in Macau. Furusato is an exception. It is one of the

335

best and most impressive Japanese restaurants in town, and is a good choice for classy and delicate fine Japanese dining.

TOU TOU KOI Map p320 Cantonese $$$
☎ 2857 2629; 6-8 Travessa do Mastro; mains MOP$58-150, seafood MOP$150-488; ☯ 8am-3pm & 5pm-12am
Located down the alley just opposite the Pawnshop Museum, this nominally Chinese restaurant serves some very traditional Cantonese dishes you can no longer find in other Chinese restaurants. Among the wide range of sumptuous dishes is its signature deep-fried stuffed crab with shrimp.

WING LEI Map pp316–17 Chinese $$$
☎ 986 3688; Ground fl, Wynn Macau; dim sum MOP$20-30, mains MOP$80-450; ☯ 11.30am-3pm & 6-11pm
This is one of the top Chinese restaurants on the casino strip. Its ambience may not be as good as the Eight in Grand Lisboa but its dim sum definitely is.

THE EIGHT Map p320 Cantonese $$$
☎ 2888 3838; 2nd fl, Grand Lisboa, Avenida e Lisboa; mains MOP$150-200; ☯ 11.30am-2.30pm & 6.30-10.30pm
Elegantly designed in black, the main dining hall will impress you at first sight with its water-lily pool; at first taste, so will its dim sum.

CAMÕES Map pp316–17 Portuguese $$
☎ 2873 8818; 1st fl, 3 Lisboa Bldg, Fisherman's Wharf; starters MOP$48-180, mains MOP$98-178; ☯ noon-3pm & 6-11.30pm
Camões is the best place to dine on the Fisherman's Wharf. The menu features a wide range of bacalhau dishes to suit everybody's fancy, along with some excellent and good-value house wine (per glass/half litre MOP$20/50). Ask for a table on the balcony.

CLUBE MILITAR DE MACAU
Map pp316–17 Portuguese $$
☎ 2871 4000; 975 Avenida da Praia Grande; starters MOP$38-98, mains MOP$120-150, lunch buffet MOP$90; ☯ noon-3pm & 7-11pm
The Portuguese dishes may not be the best in town, but the Military Club is one of Macau's most distinguished colonial buildings and its restaurant is as atmospheric

as you'll find in Macau. Be sure to dress smartly.

SOLMAR Map p320 Portuguese, Macanese $$
☎ 2888 1881; 512 Rua da Praia Grande; starters MOP$45-88, mains MOP$95-190; ☯ 11am-11pm
While Macau is changing at a crazy pace, this 40-year-old restaurant in the city centre has a nostalgic atmosphere filling every corner. It is particularly well known for its galinha à Africana (Africa Chicken).

BON APETITE Map pp316–17 Macanese $$
☎ 2875 7725; 73 Rua de Madrid, Wan Yu Villas, NAPE; starters MOP$35-50, mains MOP$88-150; ☯ noon-3pm & 6-11pm Wed-Mon
Grab a seat near the window for a view of the Kum Iam Statue and some home-style Macanese fare. The regularly changing menu features such palette-tempting delights as carne de porco à alentejana (fried pork meat with clams) and pasteis e bacalhau (codfish cakes).

AFONSO III Map p320 Portuguese $$
☎ 2858 6272; 11A Rua Central; starters MOP$55-85, mains MOP$75-155; ☯ noon-3pm & 6.30-10.30pm Mon-Sat
This simple authentic Portuguese restaurant, a short stroll southwest of the Leal Senado, has won a well-deserved reputation among the Portuguese community in Macau. Tables are often in short supply, so phone ahead.

LA BONNE HEURE Map p320 French $$
☎ 2833 1209; 12A-B Travessa de São Domingos; starters MOP$68-148, mains MOP$98-228, 1-/2-/3-course set lunch MOP$60/75/85; ☯ noon-3pm & 5.30-10pm Sun-Wed, 5.30-11.30pm Thu-Sat
This affordable French restaurant is in a charming old building just up from the Largo do Senado. The set lunches are a par-

top picks

MACAU RESTAURANTS

- A Lorcha (opposite)
- Robuchon A Galera (p334)
- Amagao (p339)
- Tou Tou Koi (left)
- Espaço Lisboa (p340)

ticularly good value. The bar area extends its opening hours until 1.30am on Fridays. There is a tiny gallery (tall people mind your head!) upstairs exhibiting artwork from local young artists.

PRAIA GRANDE Map pp316–17   Portuguese $$

☎ 2897 3022; 10A Praça Lobo d'Avila; starters MOP$35-65, mains MOP$80-200; ☻ noon-11pm Mon-Fri, 11.45am-11pm Sat & Sun; ☒ 6, 9, 32
Get a table by the window upstairs for a view of the boulevard. This stylish place serves adequate Portuguese dishes on the historic Praia Grande.

PLATÃO Map p320   Portuguese $$

☎ 2833 1818; www.plataomacau.com; 3 Travessa de Sao Domingos; starters MOP$28-40, mains MOP$94-206; ☻ noon-11pm Tue-Sun
This restaurant is renowned for its chef, who once worked for the governors of Macau. Dishes worth trying include the baked duck rice and the rack of lamb with mustard. The giant *serradura* (MOP$52) is a must.

OS GATOS
Map pp316–17   Portuguese, Mediterranean $$
☎ 2837 8111; Avenida da República, Pousada de São Tiago; mains MOP$88-380; ☻ 7am-11.30pm
You might go inside this restaurant just for a cup of coffee and no one could blame you, as its romantic ambience is unbeatable. Not to be missed is its afternoon tea set (MOP$110), served from 3pm to 6pm.

A LORCHA Map pp316–17   Portuguese $$

☎ 2831 3193; 289A Rua do Almirante Sérgio; starters MOP$38-56, mains MOP$78-146; ☻ 12.30-3pm & 6.30-11pm Wed-Mon
'The Sailboat', right by the A-Ma Temple, is a benchmark of Portuguese food on the peninsula. Try the pork-ear salad and deep-fried *bacalhau* cakes. If you can only try one Portuguese restaurant in Macau, make it this one.

ANTICA TRATTORIA DA ISA
Map pp316–17   Italian $$
☎ 2875 5102; 1st fl, Vista Magnífica Bldg, 40-46 Avenida Sir Anders Ljungstedt; starters MOP$38-70, mains MOP$78-120; ☻ noon-10.45pm
This Italian restaurant in NAPE has an extensive menu of well-prepared dishes, lovely décor and warm, helpful service.

Pizzas (MOP$78 to MOP$95) and pasta (MOP$70 to MOP$95) are popular.

LITORAL Map pp316–17   Macanese, Portuguese $$

☎ 2896 7878; 261A Rua do Almirante Sérgio; starters MOP$30-50, mains MOP$60-120; ☻ noon-3pm & 6-10.30pm
This authentic Macanese restaurant attracts both locals and tourists alike. Apart from the delightful Macanese fare, including baked duck rice, it's renowned for its home-made crab soup and shrimp soup served in a bread bowl.

O PORTO INTERIOR
Map pp316–17   Macanese, Portuguese $$
☎ 2896 7770; 259B Rua do Almirante Sérgio; mains MOP$55-130; ☻ noon-11.30pm
If you can't get a table at A Lorcha, this lovely restaurant is a good alternative for both Portuguese and Macanese fare. The juicy African chicken deserves savouring.

RESTAURANTE TENIS CIVIL LEON
Map pp316–17   Macanese, Portuguese $$
☎ 2830 1189; 1st fl, 14 Avenida da República; starters MOP$40-75, mains MOP$88-150; ☻ 11am-3pm & 6-11pm
This restaurant may not serve the best Portuguese food but it definitely has a lovely ambience with a wonderful view overlooking Sai Van lake. Though housed in a tennis club, the restaurant welcomes both members and nonmembers.

HENRI'S GALLEY Map pp316–17   Macanese $$

☎ 2855 6251; 4G-H Avenida da República; starters MOP$38-72, mains MOP$60-135; ☻ 11am-11pm
Located on the waterfront at the southern end of the Macau Peninsula, this 30-year-old institution serves up specialities of African chicken and Macau sole with a unique recipe expertly prepared by the cheerful Macanese chef Henri Wong.

FAT SIU LAU Map p320   Macanese $$

☎ 2857 3580; cnr Rua da Felicidade & Travessa Do Mastro; mains MOP$42-156; ☻ noon-11pm
At least three generations in Macau would have heard about this charming century-old restaurant. Try its signature dish *pombo assado* (roasted pigeon). The chic Fat Siu Lau 2 (Map pp316–17; ☎ 2872 2922; Ef Vista Magnifica Ct, Avenida Dr Sun Yat Sen; ☻ noon-3pm & 6.30pm-12am), its first and only branch after a century, has some fusion initiatives in its menu.

PORTAS DO SOL Map pp316–17   Cantonese $$
☎ 2888 3888; 2nd fl, East Wing, Lisboa Hotel; dim sum MOP$14-30, mains MOP$68-188; ⏰ 9.30am-3pm & 6.30-11.30pm
Portas do So changes its dim sum menu regularly to keep you surprised every time you visit and it has a very spacious dining hall. Make sure you have a reservation if you go on the weekend as it gets pretty full during lunch time when families get together for dim sum.

LONG KEI Map p320   Cantonese $$
☎ 2858 9508; 7B Largo do Senado; dishes MOP$48-138; ⏰ 11.30am-3pm & 6-11.30pm
This landmark place is a straightforward Cantonese restaurant with more than 300 dishes on offer. The food may not be the best, but its location makes it a handy choice.

LA COMEDIE CHEZ VOUS
Map pp316–17   French $
☎ 2875 2021; Shop G, Ground fl, Edf Zhu Kuan, Avenida Xian Xing Hai; mains MOP$42-250; ⏰ noon-2.30pm & 7-10.30pm Mon-Thu, noon-2.30pm & 7-11pm Fri & Sat
A favourite with business executives for its excellent-value set lunch (MOP$65) and, presumably, its comfy chairs. It's also a handy place to hang out after watching a performance at the cultural centre.

CARAVELA Map p320   Café $
☎ 712 080; Ground fl, Kam Loi Bldg, 7 Pátio do Comandante Mata e Oliveira; cakes MOP$10-25, set lunch MOP$60; ⏰ 8am-10.30pm
This excellent *pastelaria* (pastry shop), just north of Avenida de Dom João IV, is the hang-out of choice for Portuguese residents on the peninsula. Grab a *befe a Caravela* (Caravela beef) if craving something more substantial.

O PORTO Map pp316–17   Macanese, Portuguese $
☎ 2859 4643; 17 Travessa de Paria; mains MOP$55-100; ⏰ 12.30pm-2.30pm & 7-10.30pm
This unmarked place is actually a soccer club, evident from its soccer banners on display. It's out of the way, but good value for a unique Portuguese experience with robustly flavoured cuisine.

SERRDURA Map pp316–17   Macanese Dessert $
☎ 2833 2880; Ground fl, Tin Fok Bldg, 15 Avenida do Coronel Mesquita; ⏰ noon-11pm

This shop sells bite-sized (MOP$11) and large (MOP$88) versions of *serradura*, a rich local dessert made with crushed biscuits, cream and condensed milk. It also has a branch in Taipa (Map p328; ☎ 2833 2880; Rua do Regedor; ⏰ noon-10pm), next to Cozinha Pinocchio.

OU MUN CAFÉ Map p320   Café $
☎ 2837 2207; 12 Travessa de São Domingos; sandwiches MOP$12-25, dishes MOP$50; ⏰ 8am-8pm Tue-Sun
This is a rather flashy little café with the rather imaginative name of 'Macau'. While the former is often clustered with Cantonese, this is a Macanese hang-out spot, serving a range of decent sandwiches, cakes and coffees.

LONG WA Map pp316–17   Cantonese, Tea House $
☎ 2857 4456; 3 Avenida do Almirante Lacerda; dishes MOP$12-25; ⏰ 7am-2pm
Next to the red market, this yellowish two-storey tea house's ambience and age-old tiled floors tell you it's a rare survivor of the traditional Cantonese tea houses in Macau. There is no English menu, but you can just point to the dim sum carts. No smoking, no pets, no alcohol.

WONG CHI KEI Map p320   Cantonese $
☎ 2833 1313; 17 Largo do Senado; rice & noodle dishes MOP$18-36; ⏰ 8am-midnight
Visit this centrally located Chinese eatery for a fix of cheap late-night noodles. It is particularly renowned for its noodle soup with wontons.

U TAC HONG Map p320   Cantonese Dessert $
☎ 2892 0598; 19D Rua da Madeira; snacks & drinks MOP$4-10; ⏰ 7am-7pm
Also known as Lee Hong Kee, U Tac Hong is a tiny local place that has been selling soya-bean products for 50 years, and is reputable for its silky *tofufa*, sweet bean-curd with evaporated milk (MOP$4), and soya-bean milk.

TAIPA & COLOANE ISLANDS
The number of restaurants in Taipa has grown by leaps and bounds in just a few short years. While much of the choice is restricted to Portuguese and Macanese cuisine, you'll also find some excellent Cantonese eateries here, too.

Coloane is not the treasure-trove of restaurants and other eateries that Taipa is, but there are a few decent options offering a variety of cuisines at various price levels.

Taipa Island

A PETISQUEIRA Map p328   Portuguese $$
☎ 2882 5354; 15A-B Rua de São João; starters MOP$25-85, mains MOP$85-180; ⊗ noon-3pm & 7-10.30pm
'The Snackery', an excellent restaurant set in a little alley that is easy to overlook, is considered to have the best Portuguese food in Taipa. It serves its own *queijo fresca da casa* (homemade cheese; MOP$22). Try the baked seafood with rice.

AMAGAO Map p328   Macanese $$
☎ 2882 7627; Rua Ho Lin Vong; starters MOP$24-60, mains MOP$60-120; ⊗ 6-10pm Thu-Tue
Located in a side alley off Rua da Cunha, Amagao is a 10-seat family-style Macanese restaurant, probably the best in Macau. It continues to wow crowds with its fabulously flavourful Portuguese chicken (MOP$88), and the hospitality of its store owner/chef.

O MANEL Map p328   Portuguese $$
☎ 2882 7571; 90 Rua de Fernão Mendes Pinto; starters MOP$25-30, mains MOP$60-135; ⊗ noon-3.30pm & 6-11pm Wed-Mon
Another family-run restaurant, though a bit isolated from Taipa Village, it still attracts both locals and expats alike with its splendid Portuguese dishes such as grilled *bacalhau*.

O SANTOS Map p328   Portuguese $$
☎ 2882 7508; 20 Rua da Cunha; mains MOP$62-120; ⊗ noon-3pm & 6.30-10.30pm
Head here for the *sapateira recheada*, a type of crab flown in fresh from Portugal, and *maçã assada*, a special baked apple. Expect a crowd.

O CAPÍTULO Map p328   Portuguese $$
☎ 2882 1519; Ground fl, Nam San Bldg, Avenida de Kwong Tung; starters MOP$30-140, mains MOP$70-165; ⊗ noon-10pm
O Capítulo's home-made Portuguese dishes are as fresh as its recent renovation. Try the superb suckling pig and *fatias de Tomar*, a rich dessert made with egg yolks and syrup.

KAPOK CANTONESE RESTAURANT
Map p328   Cantonese $
☎ 2883 3333; 60 Rua de Hong Chau, Hoi Yee Garden; mains MOP$60-150; ⊗ 11am-5pm & 5.30-11pm Mon-Sat, 9am-3pm & 5.30-11pm Sun
Next to the peaceful tea house Chun Yu Fang is this bustling restaurant, which is arguably the best place for dim sum in Taipa, and is always full during the weekends.

COZINHA PINOCCHIO Map p328   Macanese $$
☎ 2882 7128; 195 Rua do Regedor; starters MOP$40-62, mains MOP$52-135; ⊗ 11.45am-11pm
The well-known Cozinha Pinocchio, after its relocation to Rua do Regedor, is less atmospheric than before. But on the weekends it's still packed with local and tourists alike enjoying the stir-fried curried crab and grilled fresh sardines.

GALO Map p328   Macanese, Portuguese $$
☎ 2882 7423; 45 Rua da Cunha; starters MOP$20-48, mains MOP$48-120; ⊗ 11am-3pm & 6-10.30pm
You can easily recognise this place by the picture of a red-combed *galo* (rooster) above the door. The food is adequate and the service flawless.

CHUN YU FANG Map p328   Chinese, Tea House $
☎ 2883 9093; 42 Rua de Hong Chau; snacks MOP$28-38, tea for 2 MOP$40-88; ⊗ 12.30-9.30pm Wed-Mon
Located behind Crown Macau, this graceful tea house is a paradise amid the rapid changes in Taipa. Its serenity offers you a delectable tea experience.

SENG CHEONG Map p328   Cantonese $
☎ 2882 5323; 28 30 Rua da Cunha; mains MOP$80; ⊗ noon-midnight
This simple Chinese restaurant is celebrated for its fried fish balls, steamed eel and *congee* (rice porridge with savoury titbits).

POU TAI TEMPLE RESTAURANT
Map p328   Chinese, Vegetarian $
☎ 893 0321; 5 Estrada Lou Lim Ieok; dishes MOP$36-55; ⊗ 11am-8pm Mon-Sat, 9am-9pm Sun & the 1st & 15th day of the lunar calendar month
If you get tired of the meat-laden Portuguese cuisine, this strictly vegetarian restaurant, set in a Buddhist temple in northern Taipa, is a great find for the health conscious. It's housed in the basement of the building next to the main hall.

LISBOA Map p330   Portuguese $$

6; 8 Rua dos Gaivotas; starters
, mains MOP$98-288; ☺ noon-3pm &
6.30-10pm Tue-Fri, noon-10.30pm Sat & Sun
The 'Lisbon Space' restaurant, located in
a charming village house over two floors,
serves some of the most thoughtfully
prepared Portuguese dishes in Macau. Get
a table on the balcony. Daily specials cost
MOP$88 to MOP$168, and the wine list is
superb.

KWUN HOI HEEN Map p330   Cantonese $$
☎ 899 1320; 3rd fl, Westin Resort Macau, 1918
Estrada de Hác Sá; rice & noodle dishes MOP$28-78,
mains MOP$35-210; ☺ lunch 11am-3pm Mon-Fri,
9.30am-4pm Sat & Sun, dinner 6.30-11pm daily
Though it boasts alfresco dining and
sumptuous views, it's the superb Cantonese cuisine that makes Kwun Hoi Heen
stand out among the hotel restaurants
on Coloane Island. Dim sum is MOP$18
to MOP$22. The Saturday buffet lunch
(MOP$180) and dinner (from MOP$198)
are excellent value.

LA GONDOLA Map p330   Italian $$
☎ 2888 0156; Cheoc Van Beach; mains MOP$55-
180; ☺ 11am-11pm
Next to the swimming pool at Cheoc Van
Beach, La Gondola is a good spot to soak
up some beach-side views from the terrace
while enjoying your meal. It offers some
excellent pizzas cooked in a wood-fired
oven.

FERNANDO Map p330   Portuguese $$
☎ 2888 2264; 9 Hác Sá Beach; starters MOP$22-
26, mains MOP$66-148, rice dishes MOP$60-66;
☺ noon-9.30pm
Fernando has a devoted clientele and is
famed for its seafood. It's the perfect place
for a protracted, boozy lunch by the sea.
The bar stays open till midnight.

RESTAURANTE PARQUE HÁC SÁ
Map p330   Portuguese $
☎ 2888 2297; Hác Sá Sports & Recreation Park,
Estrada Nova de Hác Sá; snacks & sandwiches
MOP$16-30, mains MOP$30-90; ☺ noon-11pm
This is a pleasant place for meals by the
beach at Hác Sá, with barbecue dishes
figuring prominently on the menu. Dine
inside or out on the terrace.

NGA TIM CAFÉ Map p330   Cantonese, Portuguese $
☎ 2888 2086; 1 Rua Caetano; mains MOP$100;
☺ 11am-1am
This café itself is no work of art, but it has
a unique and laidback setting just in front
of the Chapel of St Francis Xavier. Enjoy the
scene, and the hybrid Sino-Portuguese food.

LORD STOW'S CAFÉ Map p330   Café $
☎ 2888 2174; 9 Largo do Matadouro; sandwiches
& quiches MOP$22-35, desserts MOP$10-26;
☺ 10.30am-7pm
Though the celebrated English baker
Andrew Stow passed away recently, his
café and Lord Stow's Bakery (☎ 2888 2534; 1
Rua da Tassara; ☺ 7am-10pm Thu-Tue, 7am-7pm
Wed) keeps his memory well alive by serving his renowned *pastéis de nata*, a warm
egg-custard tart (MOP$6) and cheesecake
(MOP$14) in unusual flavours, including
black sesame and green tea. The Lord Stow's
Garden Café (☎ 2888 1851; 105 Rua da Cordoaria;
☺ 10.30am-7pm) near the Coloane bus stop
has a very relaxed atmosphere on its patio.

ENTERTAINMENT

The Macau Cultural Centre (p323) is the territory's
premier venue for classical music concerts,
dance performances and studio film screenings. To book tickets ring ☎ 2855 5555 or,
in Hong Kong ☎ 2380 5083, or check the
website www.macauticket.net. The mammoth
Venetian Macau (p347) hosts a 15,000-seat indoor
arena that will likely be a great place for live-
music performances.

Macau Travel Talk, a free bimonthly available at MGTO outlets and larger hotels, has
useful entertainment listings at the back.

CASINOS

As of late 2007, Macau had 27 casinos. Most
of them are located at big hotels on the 'casino
strip' along Avenida da Amizade, and provide
frequent free shuttle service (☺ 9.30am-midnight) to
and from both the ferry terminal and Portas
do Cerco. All casinos are open 24 hours.

The legal gambling age in Macau is 18
years (21 for Macau residents). Photography
is absolutely prohibited inside the casinos.
Men cannot wear shorts, even relatively long
ones, or a singlet (undershirt) unless they
have a shirt over it. Women wearing shorts
or sleeveless tops are refused entry, the same
for anyone wearing thongs (flip-flops).

CROWN MACAU Map p328 Casino
☎ 2886 8888; www.crown-macau.com; Avenida de Kwong Tung, Taipa
This self-proclaimed six-star hotel-casino has 220 gaming tables and targets high rollers. Ostentatiousness is readily displayed.

EMPEROR PALACE CASINO
Map p320 Casino
☎ 2888 9988; 299 Avenida Comerical De Macau, Grand Emperor Hotel, Macau Peninsula
The Emperor Palace is worth a visit, if only for its entrance. The princely concourse, with incantation on the marble columns and pure gold bricks on the floor, is where you'll find deployment of the art of feng shui to make fortunes, if not to show off.

GRAND LISBOA CASINO Map p320 Casino
☎ 2838 2828; Avenida de Lisboa, Macau Peninsula
Connected to the Lisboa Casino by a footbridge is the new, plush Grand Lisboa, with its glowing golden bulb and truly kitschy lotus-shaped towering structure. The interior ventilation works much better here.

LISBOA CASINO Map p320 Casino
☎ 2837 5111; Hotel Lisboa, 2-4 Avenida de Lisboa, Macau Peninsula
This once-monopolistic old-timer used to be a bizarre icon in Macau. Those days are gone, but the tightly packed baccarat tables and pungent clouds of smoke still live on.

MANDARIN ORIENTAL CASINO
Map pp316–17 Casino
☎ 2856 4297; Mandarin Oriental, 956-1110 Avenida da Amizade, Macau Peninsula
Though the Mandarin cannot compete with the other casinos listed here, in terms of size and riches, its gentility earns it a name.

SANDS MACAU Map pp316–17 Casino
☎ 2888 3377; www.sands.com.mo; 23 Largo de Monte Carlo, Macau Peninsula
Run by the consortium from Vegas leading Macau's gambling business renaissance, it has a spacious atrium allowing natural lighting together with a fantastic array of crystal lights. Only high rollers with US$10,000 minimum bets are invited to stay in its hotel.

VENETIAN MACAU Map p328 Casino
☎ 2882 8888; www.venetianmacao.com; Cotai Strip
As the world's largest casino and three times the size of its Vegas counterpart,

you're guaranteed to get lost in this behemoth. Gambling tables are omnipresent in its labyrinth-like complex. Expect throngs of gamblers from the mainland. Its free shuttle service also goes to Cotai Frontier Post.

WYNN MACAU Map pp316–17 Casino
☎ 2888 9966; Rua Cidade de Sintra, NAPE, Macau Peninsula
Mimicking its counterpart in Vegas, Wynn Macau has the most glamorous and elegant ambience, albeit a bit low-ceilinged. This is the first casino with a nonsmoking area.

OTHER CASINOS
Other casinos you might consider for a visit (and, perhaps, a laugh) include the mediocre Star World Casino (Map pp316–17; ☎ 2838 3838; Avenida da Amizade), a favourite for the mainland Chinese punters, and Pharaoh's Palace Casino (Map pp316–17; ☎ 2878 8111; 3rd fl, Landmark Macau, Avenida da Amizade), where a failed attempt to re-create an ancient Egyptian palace makes you feel like you are gambling inside a tomb.

CLUBBING
The club scene in Macau is flourishing with more opening every day. The trendiest spots are clustered near the pubs in the NAPE area, while the tacky nightclub floorshows and hostess clubs are on the casino strip.

D2 Map p320 Club
☎ 2872 3777; 2nd fl, AIA Tower, 301 Avenida Comercial de Macau, Macau Peninsula; ⏰ 10pm-7am, happy hour 11pm-2am
To strut your stuff on the dance floor, head to the latest incarnation of DD, the former (in)famous bar and dance club. It's smaller than its predecessor but more fashionable. It's full of young women dancing by 3am. A place to revel, and to flirt.

NICOLE FASHION CLUB Map pp316–17 Club
☎ 2872 8922; Block 1, Trinidad, Fisherman's Wharf, Macau Peninsula; ⏰ 10pm-6am
This glitzy bar is where partiers dress to impress or be impressed. Resident and visiting DJs host dance parties almost every night, making it the best place on the Wharf.

SKY 21 Map p320 Club
☎ 2822 2122, 2872 3344; www.sky21macau.com; 21st fl, AIA Tower, 301 Avenida Comercial de Macau; ⏰ noon-11.30pm 21st-22nd fl, noon-3am bar area, 5pm-2am 23rd fl

Located in the same building as D2, this three-storey multiplex flashy club has a more distinguished atmosphere, and ambitiously caters to people from all walks of life. DJs from Portugal host dancing parties and Troupe from Amsterdam dances everything from hip-hop to salsa. A big plus is its superb view of Nam Van Lake and Macau Tower.

DRINKING

The southern end of the NAPE area on Macau Peninsula (what locals call Lan Kwai Fong) is where to head for pub crawls. For a quieter drink, the local Portuguese and Macanese have some wonderful, low-key places that are hidden away from the usual tourist haunts; in the unassuming buildings near the Flora Garden (Map pp316–17) and Kiang Wu Hospital (Map pp316–17), you'll need patience to unearth them, but you'll be rewarded with the discovery of some pleasingly authentic local watering holes.

Macau Beer has a couple of its own brews: the citrus-tasting Blond Ale and Amber Ale, which is quite hoppy. All sorts of 'ruby' ports are available in Macau – the Parador is particularly fine – but go for something different, such as the evocatively named Lágrima do Christo (Tears of Christ), a white port. Some Portuguese *aguardentes* (brandies) are worthwhile, such as Adega Velha and Antqua VSOP Aliança.

CASABLANCA CAFÉ Map pp316–17   Bar
☎ 2875 1281; Ground fl, Vista Magnífica Court Bldg, Avenida Doutor Sun Yat Sen, Macau Peninsula; ☽ 6pm-4am, happy hour 6-8pm
Next to the famous Moonwalker is this favourite hang-out for the Portuguese. It has a long list of cocktails, plays cold jazz in the background and is considered the best spot to chill out in NAPE.

MOONWALKER BAR Map pp316–17   Bar
☎ 2875 1326; Ground fl, Vista Magnífica Court Bldg, Avenida Doutor Sun Yat Sen, Macau Peninsula; ☽ 4pm-4am, happy hour 4-8pm
Moonwalker features fun live entertainment on most nights (usually Filipina chanteuses), and is considered the most famous (and expensive) one among its neighbours.

MP3 Map pp316–17   Bar
☎ 2875 1306; www.mp3barlounge.com; Ground fl, Vista Magnífica Court Bldg, 1333 Avenida Doutor Sun Yat Sen, Macau Peninsula; ☽ 6pm-4am, happy hour 6-9pm

With live shows, music and the unbeatable MOP$100 all-you-can-drink during happy hour, MP3 has become a popular spot along the strip. DJs spin all kinds of music; drag queens and pose dancers dazzle your eyes.

OLD TAIPA TAVERN Map p328   Bar, Live Music
☎ 2882 5221; Rua dos Negociantes, Taipa; ☽ noon-1am, happy hour 5-8pm
Known as 'OTT', its location next to the Pak Tai Temple at Taipa Village makes this bar delightful. A wonderful band plays every Saturday. You can also have a sip while watching ritual performances at the temple.

VASCO Map pp316–17   Bar
☎ 793 3830; Ground fl, Mandarin Oriental, 956-1110 Avenida da Amizade, Macau Peninsula; ☽ 2pm-2am
For a quiet place to drink, the Vasco lounge in the Mandarin Oriental Hotel is populated mostly by beautiful urbanites. In the afternoon it serves *tapas*-style afternoon tea.

WHISKY BAR Map pp316–17   Bar
☎ 2838 3838; 16th fl, Star World Hotel, Avenida da Amizade, Macau Peninsula; ☽ 11am-2am Sun-Thu, 11am-3am Fri & Sat
The tacky Star World casino-hotel somehow has a cheerful bar where you can have a pleasant glimpse of the Guia Lighthouse flashing at night. Get a window seat.

THEATRE

There's very little in the way of legitimate theatre in Macau, though, as in Las Vegas, floorshows – including the following two – are popular.

CRAZY PARIS SHOW Map p320   Theatre
☎ 2838 2828; Grand Lisboa Casino, Avenida de Lisboa, Macau Peninsula; ☽ 9pm-midnight
The Crazy Paris Show features a multitude of leggy women onstage strutting around in a couple of beads and a feather or two.

JAI ALAI SHOW PALACE
Map pp316–17   Theatre
☎ 2872 6126; 3rd fl, Jai Alai Complex, Travessa do Reservatório, Macau Peninsula; ☽ 7pm-2am
Come here to witness lots of women wannabes (it's a transvestite show) doing what the girls in the Crazy Paris Show do – only much better.

SPORTS & ACTIVITIES
ACTIVITIES
Cycling

You can rent bicycles (MOP$12 to MOP$18 per hour) in Taipa Village from Mercearia Bicileta Aluguer (Map p328; ☎ 2882 7975; 36 Largo Governador Tamagini Barbosa), next to the Don Quixote restaurant. There's no English spoken.

Biking across the Macau–Taipa Bridges is prohibited. Although biking across the Cotai road linking Taipa and Coloane is allowed, it is also suicidal – and definitely not recommended – due to the many heavy trucks plying the road.

Gambling

In 2007 Macau overtook Las Vegas as the world's casino capital. The story begins with the end of a casino monopoly held by Stanley Ho's Sociedade de Turismo Diversoes de Macau (STDM) in 2002. The gambling industry was shaken up with the subsequent arrival of consortia from Las Vegas. Revenue from gambling reached US$7.2 billion in 2006, but the passing of the baton to Macau is not without problems. The number of addicted gamblers has increased drastically in Macau and the neighbouring mainland. Very little has been done to curb gambling addiction so far. Other side-effects, such as money laundering, domestic violence and prostitution, have also shot up.

Although the games in Macau are somewhat different from those played in Las Vegas and elsewhere (see the boxed text, p344), the same basic principles apply. No matter what the game, the casino enjoys a built-in mathematical advantage. In the short term, anyone can hit a winning streak and get ahead, but the longer you play, the more certain it is that the odds will catch up with you.

Go-Karting

The Coloane Kartodrome (Map p330; ☎ 2888 2126; Estrada de Seac Pai Van; ☽ 11.30am-7pm Mon-Fri, 11am-8.30pm Sat & Sun), run by the Macau Motorsports Club, is the region's most popular venue for go-karting. There's a choice of seven circuits. It costs MOP$100/$180 for 10/20 minutes; a two-seater is MOP$150 for 10 minutes. Races are held on Sunday.

Golf

The 18-hole, par-71 course at Macau Golf & Country Club (Map p330; ☎ 2887 1188; 1918 Estrada de Hác Sá),

connected to the Westin Resort Macau on Coloane by walkway on the 9th floor, is open to foreigners through the hotel. Green fees are MOP$800/$1500 on weekdays/weekends, and you must have a handicap certificate to tee off. There's also a driving range (☎ 2887 1111; per 40 balls MOP$40), from where you drive balls into the ocean.

Hiking

There are two trails on Guia Hill (Map pp316–17), in central Macau Peninsula, which are good for a stroll or jog. The Walk of 33 Curves (1.7km) circles the hill; inside this loop is the shorter Fitness Circuit Walk, with 20 exercise stations. You can access these by Guia Cable Car.

The Little Taipa Trail (Trilho de Taipa Pequena; Map p328) is a 2km-long circuit around a hill (111m) of that name in northwestern Taipa reachable via Estrada Lou Lim Ieok. The 2.2km-long Big Taipa Trail (Trilho de Taipa Grande; Map p328) rings Taipa Grande, a 160m-high hill at the eastern end of the island. You can access the trail via a short paved road off Estrada Colonel Nicolau de Mesquita.

Coloane's longest trail, the Coloane Trail (Trilho de Coloane; Map p330), begins at Seac Pai Van Park and is just over 8km long; the main trailhead is called the Estrada do Alto de Coloane. The shorter Northeast Coloane Trail (Trilho Nordeste de Coloane), near Ká Hó, runs for about 3km. Other trails that offer good hiking include the 1.5km-long Altinho de Ká Hó Trail and the 1.5km-long Hác Sá Reservoir Circuit (Circuito da Barragem de Hác Sá), which both loop around the reservoir to the northwest of Hác Sá Beach.

SPECTATOR SPORTS

The Macau Stadium (Estádio de Macau; Map p328; ☎ 2883 8208; www.sport.gov.mo; Avenida Olímpica), next to the Macau Jockey Club on Taipa Island, seats 16,250 people and hosts international soccer matches and athletics competitions. On the first Sunday in December the Macau International Marathon starts and finishes here. The impressive Macau Dome (Map p330) on Coloane was built to host the 2005 East Asian Games and the 2007 Indoor Asian Games. Its main arena seats more than 7000 spectators.

For details of forthcoming events, contact the Macau Sports Institute (Instituto do Desporto de Macau; Map pp316–17; ☎ 2858 0762, 2888 1836; Macau Forum, Avenida do Doutor Rodrigo Rodrigues).

SOME FUN & GAMES IN MACAU

Baccarat

Also known as *chemin de fer* (railroad), this has become the card game of choice for the upper crust of Macau's gambling elite. Baccarat rooms are always the classiest part of any casino, and the minimum wager is high – MOP$1000 at some casinos. Two hands are dealt simultaneously: a player hand and a bank hand. Players can bet on either (neither is actually the house hand), and the one that scores closest to nine is the winner. The casino deducts a percentage if the bank hand wins, which is how the house makes its profit. If the player understands the game properly, the house enjoys only a slightly better than 1% advantage over the player.

Blackjack

Also known as 21, it is an easy game, although it requires some skill to play it well. The dealer takes a card and gives another to the players. Face cards count as 10, aces as one or 11. Cards are dealt one at a time – the goal is to get as close as possible to 21 (blackjack) without going over. If you go over 21 you 'bust', or lose. Players are always dealt their cards before the dealer, so if they bust they will always bust before the dealer does. This is what gives the casino the edge over the player. If the dealer and player both get 21, it's a tie and the bet is cancelled. If players get 21, they win even money plus a 50% bonus. Dealers must draw until they reach 16, and stand on 17 or higher. The player is free to decide when to stand or when to draw.

Boule

This is very similar to roulette, except that boule is played with a ball about the size of a billiard ball, and there are fewer numbers – 24 numbers plus a star. The payoff is 23 to one on numbers. On all bets (numbers, red or black, odd or even), the casino has a 4% advantage over players.

Daai-sai

Cantonese for 'big little', this game is also known as *sìk-bó* (dice treasure) or *chàai sìk* (guessing dice) and remains popular in Macau. Three dice are placed in a covered glass container, the container is then shaken and you bet on whether the toss will be from three to nine (small) or 10 to 18 (big). However, you lose on combinations where all three dice come up the same (2-2-2, 3-3-3 etc) unless you bet directly on three of a kind. For betting *daai-sai* the house advantage is 2.78%. Betting on a specific three of a kind gives the house a 30% advantage.

Fàan-tàan

This ancient Chinese game is practically unknown in the West. The dealer takes an inverted silver cup and plunges it into a pile of porcelain buttons, then moves the cup to one side. After all bets have been placed, the buttons are counted out in groups of four. You have to bet on how many will remain after the last set of four has been taken out.

Pàai-gáu

This is a form of Chinese dominoes similar to mahjong. One player is made banker and the others compare their hands against the banker's. The casino doesn't play, but deducts a 3% commission from the winnings for providing the gambling facilities.

Roulette

The dealer spins the roulette wheel in one direction and tosses a ball the other way. Roulette wheels have 36 numbers plus a zero, so your chance of hitting any given number is one in 37. The payoff is 35 to one, which is what gives the casino its advantage. Rather than betting on a single number, it's much easier to win if you bet odd versus even, or red versus black numbers, which only gives the house a 2.7% advantage. If the ball lands on zero, everyone loses to the house (unless you also bet on the zero).

Dog Racing

Macau's Canidrome (Map pp316–17; ☎ 2822 1199, racing information hotline 2833 3399, Hong Kong hotline 800 932 199; www.macauyydog.com; Avenida do General Castelo Branco; admission MOP$10; 🚌 1, 1A, 3, 25), in the northern part of the Macau Peninsula, is the only facility for greyhound racing in Asia. Greyhound races are held on Monday, Thursday, Friday, Saturday and Sunday at 7.30pm. There are 16 races per night, with six to eight dogs chasing a mechanical rabbit around the 455m oval track at speeds of up to 60km/h. If you want to sit in the members' stands, it costs MOP$80 weekdays and MOP$120 on the weekend.

Grand Prix

The biggest sporting event of the year is the Macau Formula 3 Grand Prix, held in the third week of November. The 6.2km Guia circuit (Map pp316–17) starts near the Lisboa Hotel and follows the shoreline along Avenida da Amizade, going around the reservoir and back through the city. It is a testing series of twists and turns – including the infamous Melco hairpin – that calls on drivers' reserves of skill and daring.

Certain zones in Macau are designated as viewing areas for the races. Streets and alleys along the track are blocked off, so it's unlikely that you'll be able to find a decent vantage point without paying for it. Prices for seats in the Reservoir Stand are MOP$250/350 for a single day/package (which includes practise days and qualifying events before the start of the actual races) and from MOP$450 to MOP$650 at the Lisboa and Grand Stands (MOP$900 for the package). To watch just the practise days and qualifying events costs MOP$50. For ticket enquiries and bookings call ☎ 796 2268 or consult www.macau.grandprix.gov.mo.

Horse Racing

Regular flat racing takes place at the Taipa racetrack (Hipodromo da Taipa) of the Macau Jockey Club (Jockey Clube de Macau; Map p328; ☎ 2882 1188, racing information hotline 2882 0868, Hong Kong hotline 800 967 822; www.macauhorse.com; Estrada Governador Albano de Oliveira; admission MOP$20; 🚍 11, 15, 22) through most of the year, usually on Saturday or Sunday from 2pm, and midweek (generally Tuesday or Wednesday) from 5pm. Summer recess lasts from late August to mid-September.

WATER SPORTS

The Hác Sá Sports & Recreation Park (Map p330; ☎ 2888 2296; Estrada Nova de Hác Sá, Coloane; 🕐 8am-9pm Sun-Fri, 8am-11pm Sat), by the beach, has an outdoor swimming pool (adult/child/student MOP$15/5/7; 🕐 8am-noon & 1-9pm Sun-Fri, 8am-noon & 1-11pm Sat).

The Cheoc Van swimming pool (Map p330; ☎ 2887 0277), which costs the same for entry and keeps the same hours as the Hác Sá pool, is at the southern end of the beach.

There are watersports equipment stands where you can hire windsurfing boards, jet skis and water scooters at either end of Hác Sá Beach.

SLEEPING

With a host of new hotels on the way, Macau will have some great hotel rooms with cheap rates in the coming years. Usually hotels with casinos attached charge lower rates, and substantial discounts (30% or more) are available for hotels of three stars and above if you book through a travel agency. In Hong Kong many of these agents are at the Shun Tak Centre (Map p70; 200 Connaught Rd Central, Sheung Wan), from where the ferries to Macau depart. You can book your room upon arrival at one of the many hotel desks in the ferry terminal pier in Macau, but be aware that hotel prices can double or even treble on the weekend, on public holidays or during the summer high season.

Most large hotels add a 10% service charge and 5% government tax to the bill. Prices listed here are the rack rates quoted to walk-in customers.

MACAU PENINSULA

You can find a wide range of choices from cheap hotels and guesthouses through to top-end resorts in Macau. From 2008 to 2009 consortia will add a number of big names here, such as Hotel Sofitel at Ponte 16, and a new Mandarin Oriental at MGM Grand Macau.

WYNN MACAU Map pp316–17 Hotel $$$
☎ 2888 9966; www.wynnmacau.com; Rua Cidade de Sintra, NAPE; r MOP$3000-3700, ste from MOP$7800
This five-star American-style resort has huge, impressive rooms with high ceilings, and almost everything automated. Bonuses include its outdoor swimming pool and some very serious restaurants.

POUSADA DE SÃO TIAGO
Map pp316–17 Hotel $$$
☎ 2837 8111; www.saotiago.com.mo; Avenida da República; r MOP$2600-3200, ste from MOP$4200
The landmark São Tiago is built into the ruins of the 17th-century Barra Fort and is one of the most romantic places to stay in Macau.

MANDARIN ORIENTAL Map pp316–17 Hotel $$$
☎ 2856 7888; www.mandarinoriental.com; 956-1110 Avenida da Amizade; r MOP$2000-2600, ste from MOP$5300

This classy hotel is notable for its impeccable service and its spa with impressive natural surroundings. As a long-standing favourite with tourists, it's always full during the weekends.

ROCKS HOTEL Map pp316–17 Hotel $$$
☎ 295 6528; www.rockshotel.com.mo; Macau Fisherman's Wharf; r MOP$1880-2580, ste from MOP$4080

This elegant Victorian boutique hotel is set amid a tribal-hut African restaurant and Babylon Casino, reminding you that you're in the middle of a theme park. The rooms are decent and most have a view of the waterfront. It also has very affordable shuttle services with its Nissan Cefiro (MOP$30/60/90 to Macau/Taipa/Coloane) and Benz-Mercedes (MOP$150/250/350 to Macau/Taipa/Coloane).

LISBOA HOTEL Map pp316–17 Hotel $$$
☎ 2837 7666; www.hotellisboa.com; 2-4 Avenida de Lisboa; r MOP$1650-3000, ste from MOP$3800

The Hotel Lisboa, one of Macau's most famous landmarks, is known locally for its unrestrained outlandishly gaudy looks and its raunchy atmosphere. For many punters its casino remains the only game in town, and hookers hunt for clients at the shopping arcade. At the time of writing, the hotel was under renovation; hopefully its facilities and services will be upgraded.

METRO PARK HOTEL Map pp316–17 Hotel $$
☎ 2878 1233; www.metroparkmacau.com; 199 Rua de Pequim; r MOP$1680-2300, ste from MOP$2800

Rooms are small and the service so-so, but this is a good-value casino-free option along the casino strip. A plus is a regular substantial discount (40% or more).

HOTEL SINTRA Map p320 Hotel $$
☎ 2871 0111; www.hotelsintra.com; Avenida de Dom João IV; r MOP$1160-1760, ste from MOP$2360

PRICE GUIDE
The price guide for rooms in Macau. Breakfast is usually included with hotels marked $$ and $$$.

$$$	Over MOP$1650
$$	MOP$500-1650
$	Under MOP$500

This centrally located three-star hotel often has a 50% discount and is a better place to stay than Metro Park. Rooms are spotless, but those facing Grand Emperor Hotel may find the big LED screen disturbing. It provides a shuttle service to the ferry terminal every 15 minutes.

RITZ HOTEL Map pp316–17 Hotel $$
☎ 2833 9955; www.ritzhotel.com.mo; 11-13 Rua do Comendador Kou Ho Neng; r MOP$1080-1380, ste from MOP$2080

This palace of a place, in a quiet street high above Avenida da República, is as close as you'll get to staying at the legendary Bela Vista across the road. This good-value, five-star hotel has a wonderful recreation centre, with a huge heated pool.

GUIA HOTEL Map pp316–17 Hotel $$
☎ 2851 3888; guia@macau.ctm.net; 1-5 Estrada do Engenheiro Trigo; r MOP$850-1080, tr MOP$980, ste from MOP$1480

If you want something smaller and a bit 'isolated', choose this place at the foot of Guia Hill. The recently renovated rooms are extremely clean and comfortable. The friendly and accommodating staff speak fairly adequate English.

POUSADA DE MONG HÁ
Map pp316–17 Inn $$
☎ 2851 5222; www.ift.edu.mo; Colina de Mong Há; s/d Mon-Fri MOP$500/600, Sat & Sun MOP$600/800, ste Mon-Fri MOP$1000, Sat & Sun MOP$1200

This traditional-style Portuguese inn sits atop Mong Há Hill, near the ruins of a fort built in 1849. It is run by students at the Instituto de Formação Turística (Institute for Tourism Studies), so service is more than eager. Rates include breakfast. The restaurant here is open from noon to 3pm for lunch on weekdays, from 7pm to 10.30pm on Friday for a Macanese buffet (MOP$160). Afternoon tea (3pm to 6pm) and cake-of-the-month is served at its atmospheric café.

EAST ASIA HOTEL Map p320 Hotel $
☎ 2892 2433; fax 922 431; 1A Rua da Madeira; s MOP$270-370, d MOP$400-500, ste MOP$720

The East Asia is housed in a classic green-and-white colonial-style building and, though it's been remodelled, has not lost all of its charm. The rooms are simple but spacious.

AUGUSTERS LODGE Map p320 Guesthouse $

☎ 2871 3242; www.augusters.de; Flat 3J, Block 4, Edif Kam Loi, 24 Rua Do Dr Pedro José Lobo; dm MOP$80, d MOP$150, tr MOP$200; 🚌 3, 3A, 10, 10A, 10B, AP1

If you're looking for something similar to a backpackers hub, head to this tiny, friendly guesthouse. Rooms are basic but clean, with shared bathrooms. It's located above the CTM shop.

SAN VA HOSPEDARIA Map p320 Guesthouse $

☎ 2857 3701; www.sanvahotel.com; 67 Rua de Felicidade; r MOP$70-100

This traditional-style guesthouse has survived since 1873 and definitely has character, though the cupboard-like rooms, separated by filmsy cardboard partitions, are pretty spartan and a few rooms are occupied by the homeless. Even if you don't stay here overnight, it can be a great cheap place to hang out on an afternoon if you get the very affordable room with balcony (MOP$90), buy some Chinese pastries and some drinks at the specialty food stores downstairs (p333), and relax on the balcony as you people-watch over this older part of Chinese Macau.

TAIPA & COLOANE ISLANDS

Taipa is a very happening place with the commencement of massive land-reclamation projects on the Cotai strip bringing in a bunch of top-end accommodation options. Coloane offers quite a diversity of places to stay – from two budget hostels to a 'cosy' inn to the territory's most exclusive resort.

Taipa Island

CROWN MACAU Map p328 Hotel $$$

☎ 2886 8888; www.crown-macau.com; Avenida de Kwong Tung; r MOP$3080, ste from MOP$4180

Located next to the notorious Regency Hotel (the hotel staff are terribly rude) is this recently opened 'six-star hotel', where you are supposed to feel like a king, with three servants per guest. This has yet to prove itself, but the rooms are indeed impressive and spacious, and each has its own lounge area.

VENETIAN MACAO RESORT HOTEL

Map p328 Hotel $$$

☎ 2882 8888; www.venetianmacao.com; Cotai Strip; ste MOP$1600-4500

At the time of writing only this landmark hotel was complete and ready for service in the Venetian Macau megaresort. The 32-storey tower has 3000 luxurious suites. Other amenities include a bizarre replica of the Venice canals, afloat with gondola and Chinese sampans. Four Seasons, Shangrila and Sheraton etc are all on their way.

HOTEL TAIPA Map p328 Hotel $$

☎ 2882 1666; www.hoteltaipa.com; 822 Estrada Governador Nobre Carvalho; r MOP$880-1680, ste MOP$2280-4280

If you want to avoid the casino-hotels on Taipa, this hotel's a decent place to stay, though it's lacking in character. It's an air-crew's favourite and has less tourist groups staying here.

Coloane Island

WESTIN RESORT MACAU

Map p330 Hotel $$$

☎ 2887 1111; www.westin.com/macau; 1918 Estrada de Hác Sá; r MOP$2200-2700, ste from MOP$5000

This 'island resort' complex is on the eastern side of Hác Sá Beach. Each room has a large terrace. The overall atmosphere is that of a country club, with an attached 18-hole golf course (p343), two swimming pools, an outdoor spa, and sauna and fitness centre on 60 hectares of land. The resort's Panorama Lounge (☎ 899 1020; 🕙 11am-1am) is a delightful spot for a sundowner.

POUSADA DE COLOANE Map p330 Inn $$

☎ 2888 2143; fax 2882 251; Estrada de Cheoc Van; s & d MOP$680-750, tr MOP$880-950

This inn has rooms furnished with some fantastic Portuguese-style décor overlooking Cheoc Van Beach and has a relaxed atmosphere. It serves a good Sunday lunch buffet (MOP$120) and the restaurant has a nice bar area.

POUSADA DE JUVENTUDE DE CHEOC VAN Map p330 Hostel $

☎ 2888 2024; Rua de António Francisco; dm/d Sun-Fri MOP$40/70, Sat MOP$50/100

To stay either here or at the hostel at Hác Sá, you must book through the Education & Youth Services Department (☎ 2855 5533, 397 2640; www.dsej.gov.mo) and have a Hostelling International (HI) card. During the high season (summer and holidays) competition for beds is high and it might be shut altogether in August. The hostel has a garden and a small kitchen for making hot drinks.

POUSADA DE JUVENTUDE DE HÁC SÁ
Map p330   Hostel $
☎ 2888 2701; Rua de Hác-Sá Long Chao Kok; dm/d/q Sun-Fri MOP$40/50/70, Sat MOP$50/70/100
This circular, grey-tiled building, at the southern end of Hác Sá Beach, is more modern than the Cheoc Van hostel, though it's sometimes reserved for groups only.

TRANSPORT
MACAU TO HONG KONG
Air
Travel to Macau by helicopter is a viable option and is becoming increasingly popular for residents and visitors alike.

Heli Express (☎ 2872 7288, in Hong Kong 2108 9898; www.heliexpress.com) runs a 16-minute helicopter shuttle service between Macau and Hong Kong (HK$1900, tax included) with up to 28 daily flights leaving between 9am and 10.30pm (9.30am to 11pm from Hong Kong). Flights arrive and depart in Macau from the roof of the ferry terminal (Map pp316–17; ☎ 790 7240). In Hong Kong departures are from the helipad atop the ferry pier that is linked to the Shun Tak Centre (Map p70; ☎ 2859 3359; 200 Connaught Rd Central) in Sheung Wan.

Sea
The vast majority of people make their way from Macau to Hong Kong by ferry. The journey takes just an hour and there are frequent departures throughout the day, with reduced service between midnight and 7am. Two ferry companies operate services to and from Macau, one from Hong Kong Island for the most part and the other usually from Tsim Sha Tsui.

TurboJet (☎ 790 7039, in Hong Kong information 2859 3333, bookings 2921 6688; www.turbojet.com.hk) operates three types of vessels (economy/superclass Monday to Friday HK$142/$244, Saturday to Sunday MOP$154/260, night crossing MOP$176/275), from the ferry terminal in Macau and the Shun Tak Centre in Hong Kong, which take between 55 and 65 minutes.

New World First Ferry (NWFF; ☎ 2872 7676, in Hong Kong 2131 8181; www.nwff.com.hk) operates high-speed catamarans from the Macau ferry terminal every half-hour or so between 7am and 8.30pm. In Hong Kong they leave the China ferry terminal (Map p92; Canton Rd, Tsim Sha Tsui) on the half-hour from 7am to 9pm or 10pm. The trip takes 60 to 75 minutes and tickets cost HK$140/175 on weekdays/nights (ie from 6pm to 9pm or 10pm from Hong Kong and 6.30pm to 8.30pm from Macau), and HK$155/175 on weekends and public holidays. Deluxe class is HK$245/275 on weekdays/nights and HK$260/275 on weekends and public holidays.

Macau is also linked directly to Hong Kong International Airport by the TurboJet Sea Express (☎ 2859 3333; www.turbojetseaexpress.com.hk), which leaves at 9.45am, 1pm, 3pm, 4.30pm and 8pm. It costs MOP$200/155/110 per adult/child/infant and takes 45 minutes.

The new Macau Express Link (☎ 2886 1111, in Hong Kong 2859 3401), run by Turbojet and seven airlines operating in Macau, connects Macau International Airport to Hong Kong. Passengers are able to check-in and transit straight through to Macau from Shop G02 at the ferry terminal at Shun Tak Centre. Make sure you arrive at the ferry terminal three hours before flight departure. You'll be given a temporary boarding pass after you check in. When you arrive at the ferry terminal in Macau, you do not need to go through immigration, but instead, proceed to the Express Link waiting room at Berth 2, and a transit bus (four daily from 11am to 6.30pm; from Macau airport, six departures between noon and 8pm) will take you directly to the airport. The fare is the same as the normal Turbojet service.

Tickets can be booked up to 28 days in advance at the ferry terminals, many travel agencies or online. You can also simply buy tickets on the spot, though advance booking is recommended if you travel on weekends or public holidays. There is a standby queue for passengers wanting to travel before their ticketed sailing. You need to arrive at the pier at least 15 minutes before departure, but you should allow 30 minutes because of occasional long queues at immigration.

You are limited to 10kg of carry-on luggage in economy class, but oversized or overweight bags can be checked.

MACAU TO CHINA
Nationals of Australia, Canada, EU, New Zealand and most other countries (but not US citizens) will be able to purchase their

visas at the border with Zhuhai, but it will ultimately save you time if you buy one in advance. These are available in Hong Kong (see p286) or in Macau from China Travel Service (CTS; Map pp316–17; ☎ 2870 0888; 207 Avenida do Dr Rodrigo Rorigues, Nam Kwong Bldg; ☼ 9am-6pm), usually in one day.

Air

Air Macau (NX; Map pp316–17; ☎ 396 5555; www.airmacau .com.mo; Ground fl, Nam Ngan Garden Bldg, 398 Alameda Doutor Carlos d'Assumpção; ☼ 9am-6pm) and/or several carriers of the China National Aviation Corporation (CNAC; Map p320; ☎ 2878 8034; fax 2878 8036; 5th fl, lat Teng Hou Bldg, Avenida de Dom João IV) group link Macau International Airport (Map p328; ☎ 2886 1111; www .macau-airport.gov.mo) with at least five flights a week to Beijing, Fuzhou, Guilin, Hangzhou, Kunming, Shanghai, Xiamen and Xian. The departure tax for adults is MOP$80 and for children aged two to 12 MOP$50.

Heli Express (☎ 2872 7288, in Hong Kong 2108 9898; www.heliexpress.com) has a helicopter shuttle linking Macau with Shenzhen five times a day from 9.45am to 7.45pm (11.45am to 8.30pm from Shenzhen) for HK$1900 (HK$1990 from Shenzhen). The trip takes 25 minutes.

Land

Macau is an easy gateway by land into China. Simply take bus 3, 5 or 9 to the border gate (Portas do Cerco; off Map pp316–17; ☼ 7am-midnight) and walk across. A second – and much less busy crossing – is the Cotai Frontier Post (Map p330; ☼ 9am-8pm) on the causeway linking Taipa and Coloane, which allows visitors to cross over the Lotus Flower Bridge by shuttle bus (MOP$4) to Zhuhai. Buses 15, 21 and 26 will drop you off at the crossing.

If you want to travel further afield in China, buses run by the Kee Kwan Motor Road Co (Map p320; ☎ 2893 3888; ☼ 7.15am-9pm) leave the bus station on Rua das Lorchas. Buses for Guangzhou (MOP$55, 2½ hours) depart about every 15 minutes and for Zhongshan (MOP$25, one hour) every 20 minutes between 8am and 6.30pm. There are many buses to Guangzhou (MOP$75) and Dongguan (MOP$80) from Macau International Airport.

Sea

A daily ferry run by the Yuet Tung Shipping Co (☎ 2877 4478) connects Macau with the port of Shekou in Shenzhen. The boat departs from Macau at 10am, 2pm, 6pm and 8.15pm and takes 1½ hours; they return from Shekou at 8.15am, 11.45am, 3.45pm and 6.30pm. Tickets (adult/child MOP$114/$67) can be bought up to three days in advance from the point of departure, which is pier 14 (Map p320) in the Inner Harbour. A departure tax of MOP$20 applies.

Sampans and ferries also leave from the same pier for Wanzai (MOP$12.50) on the mainland, crossing the Inner Harbour. Departures are every half-hour between 8am and 4.15pm, returning a half-hour later.

MACAU TO ASIA

Apart from AirAsia (☎ in Hong Kong 3167 2299; www .airasia.com), new budget airline Viva Macau (www.fly vivamacau.com) is expected to service destinations including Mumbai, Delhi, Jakarta, Manila and Sydney by the time you read this. The website www.gomacau.com acts as a consolidator. The departure tax for adults is MOP$130 and for children aged two to 12 MOP$80.

CAR & MOTORCYCLE

The streets of Macau Peninsula are a gridlock of cars and mopeds that will cut you off at every turn. A Moke (a brightly coloured Jeeplike convertible) can be a convenient way to explore the islands, as can a motorbike.

Hire

Happy Rent A Car (Map pp316–17; ☎ 2872 6868; fax 2872 6888), in room 1025 of the ferry terminal arrivals hall, has four-person Mokes available for hire for MOP$450 a day. Mokes seating six are available from Avis Rent A Car (Map pp316–17; ☎ 2833 6789; www.avis.com.mo; Room 1022, Ground fl, Macau ferry terminal; ☼ 8am-7pm), which also has an office at the Mandarin Oriental hotel car park; they cost MOP$500/$600 per day on weekdays/weekends.

PUBLIC TRANSPORT

Public buses and minibuses run by TCM (☎ 2885 0060) and Transmac (☎ 2877 1122) operate on 40 routes from 6.45am till shortly after midnight. Fares – MOP$2.50 on the peninsula, MOP$3.30 to Taipa Village, MOP$4 to Coloane Village, MOP$5 to Hác Sá Beach – are dropped into a box upon entry; there's no change given.

The Macau Tourist Map (p351) has a full list of both bus companies' routes. The two most useful buses on the peninsula are buses 3 and 3A, which run between the ferry terminal and the city centre, near the post office. Bus 3 continues up to the border crossing with the mainland, as does bus 5, which can be boarded along Avenida Almeida Ribeiro. Bus 12 runs from the ferry terminal, past the Lisboa Hotel and then up to the Lou Lim Ioc Garden and Kun Iam Temple.

The best services to Taipa and Coloane are buses 21, 21A, 25 and 26A. Bus 22 goes to Taipa, terminating at the Macau Jockey Club. Buses to the airport are AP1, 26, MT1 and MT2.

Macau is suffering from a severe shortage of drivers, so you may have to wait at least 20 minutes for a bus. Expect buses to be very crowded. Hopping aboard the free casino shuttles (p340) to some of the sights is a viable alternative. The shuttles depart from both the ferry terminal and Portas do Cerco every 10 minutes between 9.30am and midnight. Originally they were designed to bring Hong Kong and the mainland gamblers to spend money, but in reality nobody checks whether you go gambling or not, and now Macau citizens use them regularly instead of waiting for the never-coming buses.

TAXI

Flag fall is MOP$10 for the first 1.5km and MOP$1 for each additional 200m. There is a MOP$5 surcharge to go to Coloane; travelling between Taipa and Coloane is MOP$2 extra. Journeys starting from the airport incur an extra charge of MOP$5. A taxi from the airport to the centre of town should cost about MOP$40. Large bags cost an extra MOP$3. For yellow radio taxi call ☎ 2851 9519 or ☎ 2893 9939. Again, flagging a taxi in the downtown area can be as difficult as getting a bus. Good luck.

DIRECTORY

Much of the advice given for Hong Kong applies to Macau as well. If you find any sections missing here, refer to the ones in the Hong Kong Directory chapter (p287).

BOOKS

Macau: The Imaginary City: Culture and Society, 1577 to Present, by Jonathan Porter, provides a vivid account of Macau's history. Novels set in Macau are rare, but Austin Coates' *City of Broken Promises,* a fictionalised account of 18th-century Macanese trader Martha Merop (p319), is a classic. *Lights and Shadows of a Macao Life: the Journal of Harriett Low, Travelling Spinster,* by Harriett Low Hillard, is an American woman's account of Macau from 1829 to 1834. For short stories, you won't do better than *Visions of China: Stories from Macau,* edited by David Brookshaw, which includes works by writers with strong Macau connections, including Henrique de Senna Fernandes. If you want to learn more about Macau's distinctive hybrid cuisine, try Annabel Jackson's *Taste of Macau: Portuguese Cuisine on the China Coast.*

These books can be found at Livararia (Map p320; ☎ 2856 6442; 18-20 Rua de São Domingos; 11am-7pm Mon-Sat) or BookaChino (Map pp316–17; ☎ 2872 3362; 434 Rua Cidade de Santarém; 11am-8pm).

BUSINESS HOURS

Most government offices are open from 9am to 1pm and 2.30pm to 5.30pm or 5.45pm on weekdays. Banks normally open from 9am to 5pm weekdays and to 1pm on Saturday.

CLIMATE

Macau's climate is similar to Hong Kong's (p288), with one major difference: there is a delightfully cool sea breeze on warm summer evenings along the waterfront.

CUSTOMS

Customs formalities are virtually nonexistent here, but Hong Kong only allows you to import small amounts of duty-free tobacco and alcohol (see p290).

DISCOUNT CARDS

The Macau Museums Pass, a card allowing you entry to Grand Prix Museum, the Macau Wine Museum, the Maritime Museum, Lin Zexu Memorial Hall in Lin Fung Temple, the Macau Museum of Art and the Macau Museum, valid for five days, is available for MOP$25/12 for adults/concessions, from the MGTO or any participating museum.

EMERGENCY

In the event of any emergency, phone the central SOS number (☎ 999) for the fire services, police or an ambulance. Important numbers:

Ambulance (☎ 2837 8311)

Consumer Council (☎ 988 9315)

Fire service (☎ 2857 2222)

Police (☎ 2857 3333)

Tourist Assistance Hotline (☎ 2834 0390) From 9am to 6pm.

HOLIDAYS

In Macau half-days are allowed on the day before the start of Chinese New Year and on the day of New Year's Eve. For holidays celebrated in both Hong Kong and Macau, see p293. The following are public holidays in Macau only.

All Souls' Day 2 November

Feast of the Immaculate Conception 8 December

Macau SAR Establishment Day 20 December

Winter Solstice 22 December

INTERNET ACCESS

In NAPE, you can check your email at the Unesco Internet Café (Map pp316–17; ☎ 2872 7066; Alameda Doutor Carlos d'Assumpção; per 30/60min MOP$5/10; ☺ noon-8pm Wed-Mon), and for free at two terminals in the MGTO (Map p320; ☎ 397 1120; ☺ 9am-6pm) at Largo do Senado.

LEFT LUGGAGE

There are electronic lockers on both the arrivals and departure levels of the Macau ferry terminal. They cost MOP$20 or MOP$25, depending on the size, for the first two hours and MOP$25/30 for each additional 12-hour period. There is also a left-luggage office on the departures level that's open from 6.45am to midnight daily. It charges MOP$10 for the first six hours and another MOP$10 till midnight. Each additional day costs MOP$10.

MAPS

The MGTO distributes the excellent (and free) *Macau Tourist Map*, with major tourist sights and streets labelled in English, Portuguese and Chinese characters, small inset maps of Taipa and Coloane, and bus routes marked.

MEDICAL SERVICES

Macau's two hospitals both have 24-hour emergency services.

Conde São Januário Central Hospital (Map pp316–17; ☎ 2831 3731; Estrada do Visconde de São Januário) Southwest of the Guia Fort.

Kiang Wu Hospital (Map pp316–17; ☎ 2837 1333; Rua de Coelho do Amaral) Northeast of the ruins of the Church of St Paul.

MONEY

Macau's currency is the pataca (MOP$), which is divided up into 100 avos. Bills are issued in denominations of MOP$10, MOP$20, MOP$50, MOP$100, MOP$500 and MOP$1000. There are little copper coins worth 10, 20 and 50 avos, and silver-coloured MOP$1, MOP$2, MOP$5 and MOP$10 coins.

The pataca is pegged to the Hong Kong dollar at the rate of MOP$103.20 to HK$100. As a result, exchange rates for the pataca are virtually the same as for the Hong Kong dollar, which is accepted everywhere in Macau. When you spend Hong Kong dollars in big hotels, restaurants and department stores, usually your change will be returned in that currency. Try to use up all your patacas before leaving Macau.

Most ATMs allow you to choose between patacas and Hong Kong dollars, and credit cards are readily accepted at Macau's hotels, larger restaurants and casinos. You can also change cash and travellers cheques at the banks lining Avenida da Praia Grande and Avenida de Almeida Ribeiro, as well as at major hotels.

Banco Comercial de Macau (Map p320; ☎ 2879 1000; 572 Avenida da Praia Grande; ☺ 9am-5pm Mon-Fri, 9am-12.30pm Sat)

Banco Nacional Ultramarino (Map p320; ☎ 2835 5111; 22 Avenida de Almeida Ribeiro; ☺ 9am-5.30pm Mon-Fri)

Bank of China (Map p320; ☎ 2878 1828; Avenida do Doutor Mario Soares; ☺ 9am-5pm Mon-Fri)

HSBC (Map p320; ☎ 2855 3669; 639 Avenida da Praia Grande; ☺ 9am-5pm Mon-Fri, 9am-1pm Sat)

POST

Correios de Macau, Macau's postal system, is efficient and inexpensive.

The main post office (Map p320; ☎ 2832 3666; 126 Avenida de Almeida Ribeiro; ☺ 9am-6pm Mon-Fri, 9am-1pm Sat) faces Largo do Senado; pick up poste restante from counter 1 or 2. There are other post offices in Macau Peninsula, including a Macau ferry terminal branch (Map pp316–17; ☎ 2872 8079; ☺ 10am-7pm Mon-Sat).

Domestic letters cost MOP$1.5/2 for up to 20/50g, while those to Hong Kong are MOP$2.50/$4. For international mail, Macau divides the world into zones: zone 1 (MOP$4/$5 for up to 10/20g) is east and Southeast Asia; zone 2 (MOP$5/$6.50) is everywhere else except for the mainland (MOP$3.50/$4.50) and Portugal (MOP$4/$5.50).

EMS Speedpost (☎ 2859 6688) is available at the main post office. Other companies that can arrange express forwarding are DHL (☎ 2837 2828), Federal Express (☎ 2870 3333) and UPS (☎ 2875 1616).

TELEPHONE

Macau's telephone service provider is Companhia de Telecomunicações de Macau (CTM; ☎ inquiry hotline 1000; www.ctm.net). Note that from 2007, the initial digits of '28' were added to all six-digit telephone numbers and fax numbers, and '6' was added to mobile phone numbers. But seven-digit telephone numbers remain unchanged.

Local calls are free from private telephones, while at a public payphone they cost MOP$1 for five minutes. Most hotels will charge you at least MOP$3. All payphones permit International Direct Dialling (IDD) using a phonecard available from CTM for between MOP$50, MOP$100 and MOP$200. Rates are cheaper from 9pm to 8am during the week and all day Saturday and Sunday.

The international access code for every country, except Hong Kong, is ☎ 00. If you want to phone Hong Kong, dial ☎ 01 first, then the number you want; you do not need to dial Hong Kong's country code (☎ 852). To call Macau from abroad – including Hong Kong – the country code is ☎ 853.

Convenient CTM branches in Macau include the following:

CTM branch (Map p320; 22 Rua do Doutor Pedro José Lobo; ⌚ 10.30am-7.30pm) South of Avenida da Praia Grande.

CTM main office (Map pp316–17; 25 Rua Pedro Coutinho; ⌚ 10.30am-7.30pm) Two blocks northeast of the Lou Lim loc Garden.

Useful Numbers

The following is a list of some important telephone numbers. For numbers to call in the case of an emergency, see p350.

International directory assistance (☎ 101)

Local directory assistance (☎ 181)

Macau ferry terminal (☎ 790 7240)

New World First Ferry (☎ 2872 6301)

Tourist Hotline (☎ 2833 3000)

TurboJet (☎ 790 7039)

TOURIST INFORMATION

The Macau Government Tourist Office (MGTO; ☎ 2831 5566; www.macautourism.gov.mo) is a well-organised and helpful source of information. It has a half-dozen outlets scattered around town, including ones in the Largo do Senado (Map p320; ☎ 397 1120; ⌚ 9am-6pm), at the Guia Lighthouse (Map pp316–17; ☎ 2856 9808; ⌚ 9am-1pm & 2.15-5.30pm), at the ruins of the Church of St Paul (Map p320; ☎ 2835 8444; ⌚ 10am-6pm) and in the Macau ferry terminal (Map pp316–17; ☎ 2872 6416; ⌚ 9am-10pm), which dispense information and a large selection of free literature, including pamphlets on everything from Chinese temples and Catholic churches to fortresses, gardens and walks. The MGTO also runs a tourist assistance unit (☎ 2834 0390; ⌚ 9am-6pm) to help travellers who may have run into trouble.

MGTO also has a Hong Kong branch (Map p70; ☎ 2857 2287; 11th Fl, Yue Thai Commercial Bldg, 128 Connaught Rd Central, Sheung Wan, Hong Kong; ⌚ 9am-1pm & 2.15-5.30pm).

VISAS

Most travellers, including citizens of the EU, Australia, New Zealand, the USA, Canada and South Africa, can enter Macau with just their passports for between 30 and 90 days.

Travellers who do require them can get visas valid for 30 days on arrival in Macau. They cost MOP$100/$50/$200 for adults/children under 12/families.

You can get a single one-month extension from the Macau Immigration Department (Map pp316–17; ☎ 2872 5488; Ground fl, Travessa da Amizade; ⌚ 9am-12.30pm & 2.30-5pm Mon-Fri).

WEBSITES

Useful Macau websites:

Cityguide (www.cityguide.gov.mo) Good source of practical information, such as transport routes.

Macau Cultural Institute (www.icm.gov.mo) Macau's cultural offerings month by month.

Macau Government Information (www.macau.gov.mo) The No 1 source for nontourism information about Macau.

Macau Government Tourist Office (www.macautourism .gov.mo) The best source of information for visiting Macau.

Macau Yellow Pages (www.yp.com.mo) Telephone directory – with maps.

LANGUAGE

The Official Languages Ordinance of 1974 names Hong Kong's two official languages as English and Cantonese. Cantonese, a southern Chinese dialect (or language, depending on your definition), is spoken in Guangdong and Guangxi provinces on the mainland as well as in Hong Kong and Macau. Cantonese preserves many archaic features of spoken Chinese that date back to the Tang dynasty, which is why Tang and Sung dynasty poetry can sound better in Cantonese than in Mandarin.

While Cantonese is used in Hong Kong in everyday life by the vast majority of the population, English remains the lingua franca of commerce, banking and international trade, and is still used in the law courts. There has been a noticeable decline in the level of English-speaking proficiency in the territory, however, due to emigration and the switch by many secondary schools to Chinese vernacular education, although some schools see it as a sign of prestige to keep teaching English, and many parents believe it is better for their children to have learnt English. In general, most Hong Kong Chinese, even those taught in English, cannot hold a candle to their cousins in Singapore, who can often speak English almost as a first language.

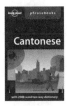

On the other hand, the ability to speak Mandarin is on the increase due to the political realities. For a Cantonese native speaker, Mandarin is far easier to learn than English. It's not uncommon these days to hear Cantonese and Mandarin being spoken in a sort of fusion-confusion.

Get Some Lingo

It's true – anyone can speak another language. Don't worry if you haven't studied languages before or that you studied a language at school for years and can't remember any of it. It doesn't even matter if you failed English grammar. After all, that's never affected your ability to speak English! The key to picking up a language in another country is just to start speaking.

Learn a few key phrases before you go. Write them on pieces of paper and stick them on the fridge, by the bed – anywhere that you'll see them often.

You'll find that locals appreciate travellers trying their language, no matter how muddled you may think you sound. If you want to learn more Cantonese than we've included here, pick up a copy of Lonely Planet's comprehensive but user-friendly *Cantonese Phrasebook*.

PRONUNCIATION
Vowels & Vowel Combinations

a	as the 'u' in 'but'
eu	as the 'er' in 'fern'
ew	as in 'blew' (short and pronounced with tightened lips)
i	as the 'ee' in 'deep'
o	as in 'go'
u	as in 'put'
ai	as in 'aisle' (short sound)
au	as the 'ou' in 'out'
ay	as in 'pay'
eui	as in French *feuille* (eu with i)
iu	as the 'yu' in 'yuletide'
oy	as in 'boy'
ui	as in French *oui*

Consonants

In Cantonese, the ng sound can appear at the start of the word. Practise by saying 'sing along' slowly and then do away with the 'si' at the beginning.

Note that words ending with the consonant sounds p, t, and k must be clipped in Cantonese. This happens in English as well – say 'pit' and 'tip' and listen to how much shorter the p sound is in 'tip'.

Many Cantonese speakers, particularly young people, replace an n sound with an l if it begins the word – náy (you), is often heard as láy. Where relevant, this change is reflected in the words and phrases in this language guide.

Tones

The use of tones in Cantonese can be quite tricky for an English speaker. The 'tone' is the pitch value of a syllable when you pronounce it. The same word, pronounced with different tones can have a very different meaning, eg gwat means 'dig up' and gwàt means 'bones'.

In our simplified pronunciation guide there are six tones: high, high rising, level, low falling, low rising and low. They can be divided into two groups: high and low pitch. High-pitch tones involve tightening your vocal muscles to get a higher note, whereas lower-pitch tones are made by relaxing the vocal chords to get a lower note. These tones are represented as accents and diacritics as shown in the list below; the low tones are all underlined in the Romanisations. Tones in Cantonese fall on vowels (a, e, i, o, u) and on n.

à	high
á	high rising
a	level
à̲	low falling
á̲	low rising
a̲	low

SOCIAL
Meeting People
Hello.
你好。 láy·hó
How are you?
你幾好啊嗎? láy gáy hó à maa
Fine, and you?
幾好, 你呢? gáy hó láy lè
Good morning.
早晨。 jó·sàn
Goodbye./Bye.
再見/拜拜。 joy·gin/bàai·baai
What's your name?
你叫乜嘢名? láy giu màt·yé méng aa
My name is …
我叫… ngáw giu …
Please …
唔該… ǹg·gòy …
Thank you.
唔該。 ǹg·gòy
多謝。 (for a gift) dàw·je
You're welcome.
唔駛客氣。 ǹg·sái haak·hay
Yes.
係。 hai
No.
唔係。 ǹg·hai
Excuse me. (to get attention)
對唔住。 deui·ǹg·jew
Excuse me. (to get past)
唔該借借。 ǹg·gòy je·je

I'm sorry.
對唔住。 deui·ǹg·jew
Do you speak (English)?
你識唔識講 láy sìk·ǹg·sìk gáwng
(英文)啊? (yìng·mán) aa
Do you understand?
你明唔明啊? láy mìng·ǹg·mìng aa
Yes, I do understand.
明白。 mìng·baak
No, I don't understand.
我唔明。 ngáw ǹg mìng

Could you please …?
唔該你…? ǹg·gòy láy …
  repeat that
  再講一次 joy gáwng yàt chi
  write it down
  寫落嚟 sé lawk lài

Going Out
What's on …?
…有乜嘢活動? … yáu màt·yé wut·dung
  locally
  呢度附近 lày·do fu·gan
  this weekend
  呢個週末 lày·gaw jàu·mut
  today
  今日 gàm·yat
  tonight
  今晚 gàm·máan

I feel like going to (a/the) …
我想去… ngáw séung heui …
Where can I find …?
邊度有…? bìn·do yáu …
  clubs
  夜總會 ye·júng·wuí
  gay venues
  同志吧 tung·ji·bàa
  places to eat
  食飯嘅地方 sik·faan ge day·fàwng
  pubs
  酒吧 jáu·bàa

Is there a local entertainment guide?
有冇本地娛樂指南?
yáu mó bún·day yèw·lawk jí·làam

Local Lingo
Beautiful!	靚啊!	jeng aa
Excellent!	冇得頂!	mó·dàk·díng
Great!	冇得頂!	mó·dàk·díng
It's OK.	OK。	ò·kày
Maybe.	可能。	háw·làng

| No way! | 無得傾！ | mó·dàk·kìng |
| No problem. | 無問題。 | mó·man·tài |

PRACTICAL

Accommodation

Where's a …?

| 邊度有…? | bìn·do yáu … |

guesthouse

| 賓館 | bàn·gún |

hotel

| 酒店 | jáu·dim |

hostel

| 招待所 | jiù·doy·sáw |

Do you have a … room?

| 有冇…房? | yáu·mó … fáwng |

double

| 雙人 | sèung·yàn |

single

| 單人 | dàan·yàn |

How much is it per (night/person)?

(晚/個人)幾多錢?

yàt (máan/gaw yàn) gáy·dàw chín

Banking

Where can I …?

我喺邊度可以…?

ngáw hái bìn·do háw·yí …

I'd like to …

我要…

ngáw yiu …

cash a cheque

| 兌一張支票 | deui yàt jèung jì·piu |

change money

| 換錢 | wun chín |

Where's the nearest …?

最近嘅…喺邊度?

jeui kán ge … hái bìn·do

automatic teller machine (ATM)

| 自動提款機 | ji·dung tài·fún·gày |

foreign exchange office

| 換外幣嘅 | wun ngoy·bai ge |
| 地方 | day·fàwng |

Days

Monday	星期一	sìng·kày·yàt
Tuesday	星期二	sìng·kày·yi
Wednesday	星期三	sìng·kày·sàam
Thursday	星期四	sìng·kày·say
Friday	星期五	sìng·kày·ńg
Saturday	星期六	sìng·kày·luk
Sunday	星期日	sìng·kày·yat

Internet

Where's the local internet café?

附近有冇網吧?

fu·gan yáu·mó máwng·bàa

I'd like to …

我想…

ngáw séung …

check my email

睇下我嘅電子信箱

tái háa ngáw ge din·jí yàu·sèung

get internet access

上網

séung·máwng

Numbers

0	零	lìng
1	一	yàt
2	二	yi
3	三	sàam
4	四	say
5	五	ńg
6	六	luk
7	七	chàt
8	八	baat
9	九	gáu
10	十	sap
11	十一	sap·yàt
12	十二	sap·yi
13	十三	sap·sàam
14	十四	sap·say
15	十五	sap·ńg
16	十六	sap·luk
17	十七	sap·chàt
18	十八	sap·baat
19	十九	sap·gáu
20	二十	yi·sap
21	二十一	yi·sap·yàt
22	二十二	yi·sap·yi
30	三十	sàam·sap
40	四十	say·sap
50	五十	ńg·sap
60	六十	luk·sap
70	七十	chàt·sap
80	八十	baat·sap
90	九十	gáu·sap
100	一百	yàt·baak
200	兩百	léung·baak
1000	一千	yàt·chìn
10,000	一萬	yàt·maan

Phones & Mobile Phones

Where's the nearest public phone?

呢度附近有冇公眾電話呀?

lày·do fu·gan yáu·mó gùng·jung din·wáa aa

I want to …
我想…
ngáw séung …
  buy a phonecard
  買張電話卡
  máai jèung dịn·wáa·kàat
  call (Singapore)
  打電話去(新加坡)
  dáa dịn·wáa heui (sàn·gaa·bàw)

I'd like a …
我想買個…
ngáw séung máai gaw …
  charger for my phone
  手機充電器
  sáu·gày chùng·dịn·hay
  mobile/cell phone for hire
  出租手機
  chèut·jò sáu·gày
  prepaid mobile/cell phone
  預付手機
  yew·fụ sáu·gày
  SIM card for your network
  你地網絡用嘅SIM卡
  láy·dạy máwng·làwk yụng ge sím·kàat

Post

Where is the post office?
郵局喺邊度?   yàu·gúk hái·bìn·dọ

I want to send a …
我想…   ngáw séung …
  parcel
  寄包裹   gay bàau·gwáw
  postcard
  寄明信片   gay mịng·seun·pín

I want to buy a/an …
我想買…   ngáw séung máai …
  aerogram
  個航空   gaw hàwng·hùng
   郵柬   yàu·gáan
  envelope
  個信封   gaw seun·fùng
  stamp
  張郵票   jèung yàu·piu

Shopping

I'd like to buy...
我想買…   ngáw séung máai...
I'm just looking.
睇下。   tái hạa
How much is it?
幾多錢?   gáy·dàw chín

Can I pay by credit card?
可唔可以用信用卡埋單呀?
háw·ṅg·háw·yí yụng seun·yụng·kàat máai·
  dàan aa

less
少啲   siú dì
more
多啲   dàw dì
bigger
更大   gang dạai
smaller
細啲   sai dì

Transport

Where's the…?
…喺邊度?   … hái bìn·dọ
  airport
  機場   gày·chèung
  bus stop
  巴士站   bàa·sí·jạam
  China Ferry terminal
  中國客運碼頭   jùng·gawk haak·wạn
                máa·tàu
  subway station
  地鐵站   dạy·tit·jạam

Is this the … to (…)?
呢班…係唔係去(…)㗎?
lày bàan … hại·ṅg·hại heui (…) gaa
Which … goes to (…)?
去(…)坐邊班…?
heui (…) cháw bìn·bàan …
  bus
  巴士   bàa·sí
  ferry
  渡輪   dọ·lèun
  train
  火車   fáw·chè
  tram
  電車   dịn·chè

What time does it leave?
幾點鐘出發?
gáy·dím jùng chèut·faa
How much is a (soft-seat) fare to …?
去…嘅(軟座飛)幾多錢?
heui … ge (yẹwn·jạw fày) gáy·dàw chín
I'd like to get off at (Panyu).
我要喺(番禺)落車。
ngáw yiu hái (pùn·yẹw) lạwk·chè
Please stop here. (eg taxi, minibus)
唔該有落
ṅg·gòy yau lawk

Let me know when we arrive at (Causeway Bay).
唔該喺(銅鑼灣)叫我落車。
ǹg·gòy hái (Tùng Làw Wàn) giu ngáw lawk chè
Where is …?
…喺邊度?
… hái·bìn·do
How far is it?
有幾遠?
yáu gáy yéwn

By …
…去。   … heui
bus
坐車   cháw·chè
foot
行路   hàang·lo
train
坐地鐵   cháw dai·tit

Can you show me (on the map)?
你可唔可以(喺地圖度)指俾我睇我喺邊度?
láy háw·ǹg·háw·yí (hái day·to do) jí báy ngáw tái ngáw hái bìn·do

EMERGENCIES
Help!
救命!   gau·meng
Could you please help?
唔該幫幫忙?   ǹg·gòy bàwng bàwng màwng
Call the police!
快啲叫警察!   faai·dì giu gíng·chaat
Call a doctor!
快啲叫醫生!   faai·dì giu yì·sàng
Call an ambulance!
快啲叫救傷車!   faai·dì giu gau·sèung·chè

HEALTH
Where's the nearest …?
最近嘅…喺邊度?
jeui kán ge … hái bìn·do
dentist
牙醫   ngàa·yì
doctor
醫生   yì·sàng
hospital
醫院   yì·yéwn
(night) pharmacist
(晝夜)藥房   (jau·ye) yeuk·fàwng

I'm sick.
我病咗。
ngáw beng·jáw

I need a doctor (who speaks English).
我要睇(識講英文嘅)醫生。
ngáw yiu tái (sìk gáwng yìng·mán ge) yì·sàng

Symptoms
I have (a/an) …
我有…   ngáw yáu …
asthma
哮喘   hàau·chéwn
diarrhoea
肚痾   tó·ngàw
fever
發燒   faat·siù
headache
頭痛   tàu·tung
sore throat
喉嚨疼   hàu·lùng·tung

FOOD & DRINK
Useful Phrases
Where would you go for (a) …?
你會去邊度…?
láy wuí heui bìn·do …
banquet
食大餐   sik daai chàan
cheap meal
食平嘢   sik pèng·yé
local specialities
地方小食   day·fàwng siú·sik
yum cha
飲茶   yám·chàa

Can you recommend a …?
有乜好…介紹?
yáu màt hó … gaai·xiu
bar
酒吧   jáu·bàa
canteen
快餐廳   faai·chàan·tèng
cooked food stall
熟食檔   suk·sik·dawng
restaurant
茶樓   chàa·làu
snack shop
零食店   lìng·sik·dim
tea house
茶館   chàa·gún

I'd like …, please.
唔該我要…
ǹg·gòy ngáw yiu …
a menu (in English)
(英文)菜單   (yìng·màn) choy·dàan

357

a table for (five)
（五位）嘅檯 (ńg wái) ge tóy
the set lunch
套餐 to·chàan
the bill
埋單 màai·dàan
a fork
叉 chàa
a knife
刀 dò
a spoon
羹 gàng

I'd like a local speciality.
我想食地方風味菜
ngáw séung sik day·fàwng fùng·may choy
What would you recommend?
有乜嘢好介紹？
yáu màt·yé hó gaai·siu
I'm (a) vegetarian.
我係食齋嘅
ngáw hai sik jàai ge

Food Glossary
FISH & SHELLFISH

baak·cheuk·hàa 白灼蝦
steamed fresh prawns
chìng jìng yèw 清蒸魚
whole steamed fish, usually grouper, served with spring
  onion, ginger and soy sauce
jìn hò béng 煎蠔餅
oyster omelette
jiù yìm yàu·yéw 椒鹽魷魚
squid dry-fried with salt and pepper in a wok
lùng hàa 龍蝦
rock lobster
siù yéw chi 燒魚翅
braised shark's fin
tìm sèwn yéw 甜酸魚
sweet-and-sour fish, usually yellow croaker
yéw dáan 魚蛋
fish balls, usually made from pike

MEAT & POULTRY

chàa siù 叉燒
roast pork
hò yàu ngàu yuk 蠔油牛肉
sliced beef with oyster sauce
hùng siù jèw sáu 紅燒豬手
red simmered pork knuckle
hùng siù pàai guàt 紅燒排骨
braised pork spareribs
jaa jí gài 炸子雞
crispy-skin chicken
jèung chàa ngáap 樟茶鴨
camphor-smoked duck

jui gài 醉雞
'drunken chicken'; poached chicken that has been
  marinated in broth and rice wine and served cold as an
  appetiser
lìng mùng gài 檸檬雞
lemon chicken
muj choi kau yuk 霉菜扣肉
twice-cooked pork with pickled cabbage
si jiù cháau pàai gwàt 豉椒炒排骨
beef spareribs in black bean sauce
siù ngáap 燒鴨
roast duck
siù ngáw 燒鵝
roast goose
siù yéw jèw 燒乳豬
roast suckling pig
tìm sèwn pàai gwàt 甜酸排骨
sweet-and-sour pork spareribs
yìm guk gài 鹽焗雞
salt-baked Hakka-style chicken

RICE & NOODLE DISHES

chàa·siù faan 叉燒飯
barbecued pork with rice
cháau·faan 炒飯
fried rice
cháau·min 炒麵
fried noodles
fán·sì 粉絲
cellophane noodles or bean threads
gài juk 雞粥
chicken congee
gòn siù yì·min 乾燒伊麵
dry-fried noodles
hàam·yéw cháau·faan 鹹魚炒飯
fried rice with salted fish
háw·fán 河粉
wide, white, flat rice noodles that are usually pan fried
hói·nàam gài 海南雞
Hainanese steamed chicken served with chicken-flavoured
  rice
sìng·jàu cháau·min 星州炒麵
Singapore noodles; rice noodles stir-fried with curry
  powder
sìn·hàa hàa wàn·tàn 鮮蝦餛飩
won tons made with prawns
wàn·tàn min 餛飩麵
won ton noodle soup
yáu·jaa·gwái 油炸鬼
'devils' tails'; dough rolled and fried in hot oil
yèung·jàu cháau·min 揚州炒麵
Cantonese-style fried rice
yèw dáan 魚蛋
fish balls
yéw pín juk 魚片粥
congee with sliced fish

SAUCES

gaai laat	芥辣
hot mustard	
hò yàu	蠔油
oyster sauce	
laat jiù jeung	辣椒醬
chilli sauce	
si yàu	豉油
soy sauce	

SOUPS

baak·choy tàwng	白菜湯
Chinese cabbage soup	
dáan·fàa·tàwng	蛋花湯
'egg flower' (or drop) soup; light stock into which a raw egg is dropped	
dùng·gwàa tàwng	冬瓜湯
winter-melon soup	
áai yuk sùk mái gàng	蟹肉粟米羹
crab and sweet corn soup	
wàn·tàn tàwng	餛飩湯
won ton soup	
yèw·chi tàwng	魚翅湯
shark's-fin soup	
yin wàw gàng	燕窩羹
bird's-nest soup	

VEGETARIAN DISHES

chìng dàn bàk gù tòng	清燉北菇湯
black mushroom soup	
chùn géwn	春卷
vegetarian spring rolls	
gài ló máy	雞滷味
mock chicken, barbecued pork or roast duck	
gàm gù sún jìm	金菇筍尖
braised bamboo shoots and black mushrooms	
law hon jàai yì mìn	羅漢齋伊麵
fried noodles with braised vegetables	
law hon jàai	羅漢齋
braised mixed vegetables	
yè choi gún	耶菜卷
cabbage rolls	

CANTONESE DISHES

baak cheuk hàa	白灼蝦
poached fresh prawns served with dipping sauces	
chìng cháau gàai láan	清炒芥蘭
stir-fried Chinese broccoli	
chìng jìng sek bàan yéw	清蒸石班魚
steamed grouper with soy sauce	
gèung chùng guk háai	薑蔥焗蟹
baked crab with ginger and spring onions	
háai yuk pàa dau miù	蟹肉扒豆苗
sautéed pea shoots with crab meat	
háai yuk sùk mái gàng	蟹肉粟米羹
crab and sweet corn soup	

hò yàu choi sàm	蠔油菜心
choisum with oyster sauce	
hò yàu ngàu yuk	蠔油牛肉
stir-fried sliced beef with oyster sauce	
jiù yìm pàai gwàt	椒鹽排骨
deep-fried spareribs served with coarse salt and pepper	
sài làan fàa daai jí	西蘭花帶子
stir-fried broccoli with scallops	
sè gàng	蛇羹
snake soup	
si jiù sìn yáu	豉椒鮮魷
stir-fried cuttlefish with black bean and chilli sauce	
siù yéw gaap	燒乳鴿
roast pigeon	

DIM SUM

chàa siù bàau	叉燒包
steamed barbecued pork buns	
chéung fán	腸粉
steamed rice-flour rolls with shrimp, beef or pork	
chìng cháau sì choi	清炒時菜
fried green vegetable of the day	
chiù·jàu fán gwáw	潮州粉果
steamed dumpling with pork, peanuts and coriander	
chùn géwn	春卷
fried spring rolls	
fán gwáw	粉果
steamed dumplings with shrimp and bamboo shoots	
fu pày géwn	腐皮卷
crispy beancurd rolls	
fung jáau	鳳爪
fried chicken feet	
hàa gáau	蝦餃
steamed shrimp dumplings	
law mai gài	糯米雞
sticky rice wrapped in lotus leaf	
pàai gwàt	排骨
small braised spareribs with black beans	
sàan jùk ngàu yuk	山竹牛肉
steamed minced beef balls	
siù máai	燒賣
steamed pork and shrimp dumplings	

CHIU CHOW DISHES

bàk gù sài làan fàa	北菇西蘭花
stewed broccoli with black mushrooms	
bìng fàa gwùn yin	冰花官燕
cold sweet bird's-nest soup served as a dessert	
chèng jiù ngàu yuk sì	青椒牛肉絲
fried shredded beef with green pepper	
chiù·jàu ló séui ngáw	潮州滷水鵝
Chiu Chow soyed goose	
chiù·jàu yéw tòng	潮州魚湯
aromatic fish soup	
chiù·jàu yì mìn	潮州伊麵
pan-fried egg noodles served with chives	

dung jìng háai 凍蒸蟹
cold steamed crab
fòng yéw gàam laam 方魚甘藍
fried kale with dried fish
jeung hèung ngáap 醬香鴨
deep-fried spiced duck
jìn jeui gài 煎醉雞
diced chicken fried in a light sauce
sek láu gài 石榴雞
steamed egg-white pouches filled with minced chicken
tìm·sèwn hùng·siù hàa/ 甜酸紅燒蝦/
háai kàu 蟹球
prawn/crab balls with sweet, sticky dipping sauce

NORTHERN DISHES
bàk gù pàa géwn 北菇扒卷
baak choi 白菜
Tianjin cabbage and black mushrooms
bàk·gìng fùng jàu 北京封州
làai mìn 拉麵
noodles fried with shredded pork and bean sprouts
bàk·gìng tìn ngáap 北京填鴨
Peking duck
chòng bàau yèung yuk 蔥爆羊肉
sliced lamb with onions on sizzling platter
chòng yáu béng 蔥油餅
pan-fried spring onion cakes
dáa bìn lò 打邊爐
Chinese hotpot or steamboat
fu gwai gài/ 富貴雞/
hàt yì gài 乞丐雞
'beggar's chicken'; partially deboned chicken stuffed with
pork, Chinese pickled cabbage, onions, mushrooms,
ginger and other seasonings, wrapped in lotus leaves,
sealed in wet clay or pastry and baked for several hours
in hot ash
gòn cháau ngàu yuk sì 乾炒牛肉絲
dried shredded beef with chilli sauce
sàam sìn tòng 三鮮湯
clear soup with chicken, prawn and abalone

SHANGHAINESE DISHES
chùng pày háai 重皮蟹
hairy crabs (an autumn dish)
chùng séw wòng yéw 松鼠黃魚
sweet-and-sour yellow croaker fish

fáw téui siù choi 火腿燒菜
Shanghai cabbage with ham
hùng siù jèw sáu 紅燒豬手
simmered pigs knuckle
jaa jí gài 炸子雞
deep-fried chicken
jeui gài 醉雞
drunken chicken
lùng jéng hàa jàn 龍井蝦仁
shrimps with 'dragon-well' tea leaves
m hèung ngàu yuk 五香牛肉
cold spiced beef
sęung·hói chò cháau 上海粗炒
fried Shanghai-style (thick) noodles with pork and cabbage
siú lùng bàau 小籠包
steamed minced pork dumplings

SICHUAN DISHES
cheui páy wòng yèw pín 脆皮黃魚片
fried fish in sweet-and-sour sauce
ching jiu ngau yok si 青椒牛肉絲
sautéed shredded beef and green pepper
daam daam mìn 擔擔麵
noodles in savoury sauce
gòn jìn say gwai dáu 乾煎四季豆
pan-fried spicy string beans
gòng baau gài ding 宮爆雞丁
sautéed diced chicken and peanuts in sweet chilli sauce
jèung chàa hàau ngáap 樟茶烤鴨
duck smoked in camphor wood
máa ngái séung sęw 螞蟻上樹
'ants climbing trees'; cellophane noodles braised with
seasoned minced pork
màa pàw dau fù 麻婆豆腐
stewed beancurd with minced pork and chilli
say·chèwn mìng hàa 四川明蝦
Sichuan chilli prawns
sèwn laat tòng 酸辣湯
hot-and-sour soup with shredded pork (and sometimes
congealed pig's blood)
wuì gwàw yuk 回鍋肉
slices of braised pork with chillies
yèw hèung ké jí 魚香茄子
sautéed eggplant in a savoury, spicy sauce

GLOSSARY

amah – literally 'mummy'; a servant, traditionally a woman, who cleans houses, sometimes cooks and looks after the children

arhats – Buddhist disciple freed from the cycle of birth and death

Bodhisattva – Buddhist striving toward enlightenment

chàu – Cantonese for 'island'

cheongsam – a fashionable, tight-fitting Chinese dress with a slit up the side (*qípáo* in Mandarin)

chìm – bamboo sticks shaken out of a cylindrical box usually at temples, and used to divine the future

chop – see *name chop*

daai-pàai-dawng – open-air eating stalls, especially popular at night, but fast disappearing in Hong Kong

dim sum – literally 'touch the heart'; a Cantonese meal of various titbits eaten as breakfast, brunch or lunch and offered from wheeled steam carts in restaurants; see also *yum cha*

dragon boat – long, narrow skiff in the shape of a dragon, used in races during the Dragon Boat Festival

feng shui – Mandarin spelling for the Cantonese *fung sui* meaning 'wind water'; the Chinese art of geomancy that manipulates or judges the environment to produce good fortune

gàwn-buì – literally 'dry glass'; 'cheers' or 'bottoms up'

godown – a warehouse, originally on or near the waterfront, but now anywhere

gùng-fú – Chinese for 'kung fu'

gwái-ló/-páw (m/f) – literally 'ghost person'; a derogatory word for 'foreigner', especially a Caucasian Westerner, but now used jocularly

Hakka – a Chinese ethnic group who speak a different Chinese language from the Cantonese; some Hakka people still lead traditional lives as farmers in the New Territories

hawng – major trading house or company, often used to refer to Hong Kong's original trading houses, such as Jardine Matheson and Swire

hell money – fake-currency money burned as an offering to the spirits of the departed

HKTB – Hong Kong Tourism Board

Hoklo – boat dwellers who originated in the coastal regions of present-day Fujian province

II – illegal immigrant

joss – luck or fortune

joss sticks – incense

junk – originally Chinese fishing boats or war vessels with square sails; diesel-powered, wooden pleasure yachts that can be seen on Victoria Harbour

kaido – small to medium-sized ferry that makes short runs on the open sea, usually used for non-scheduled services between small islands and fishing villages; sometimes spelled *kaito*

KCR – Kowloon-Canton Railway

KMB – Kowloon Motor Bus Company

kung fu – the basis of many Asian martial arts

LRT – Light Rail Transit, former name for the KCR's Light Rail system

màai-dàan – bill (in a restaurant)

mahjong – popular Chinese game played among four persons using tiles engraved with Chinese characters

makee learnee – Anglo-Chinese pidgin for 'apprentice' or 'trainee'; rarely heard in Hong Kong today

name chop – carved seal; the stamp it produces when dipped into red ink paste often serves as a signature

nullah – uniquely Hong Kong word referring to a gutter or drain and occasionally used in place names

PLA – People's Liberation Army

PRC – People's Republic of China

Punti – the first Cantonese-speaking settlers in Hong Kong

sampan – motorised launch that can only accommodate a few people and is too small to go on the open sea; mainly used for inter-harbour transport

SAR – Special Administrative Region of China; both Hong Kong and Macau are now SARs

SARS – Severe Acute Respiratory Syndrome

SEZ – Special Economic Zone of China that allows more unbridled capitalism but not political autonomy; both Shenzhen and Zhuhai have SEZ status

shroff – Anglo-Indian word meaning 'cashier'

sitting-out area – Uniquely Hong Kong word meaning open space reserved for passive or active recreation

snakehead – a smuggler of *IIs*

t'ai chi – slow-motion shadow boxing and form of exercise; also spelled *tai chi*

tai tai – any married woman but especially the leisured wife of a businessman

taijiquan – Mandarin for *t'ai chi*; usually shortened to *taiji*

taipan – 'big boss' of a large company

Tanka – Chinese ethnic group that traditionally lives on boats

Triad – Chinese secret society originally founded as patriotic associations to protect Chinese culture from the influence of usurping Manchus, but today Hong Kong's equivalent of the Mafia

wàan – bay

walla walla – motorised launch used as a water taxi and capable of short runs on the open sea

wet market – local word for an outdoor market selling fruit, vegetables, fish and meat

yum cha – literally 'drink tea'; common Cantonese term for *dim sum*

BEHIND THE SCENES

THIS BOOK

The first edition was written in 1978 by the mighty Nicko Goncharoff. The previous edition was updated by Steve Fallon; this edition was written by Andrew Stone, Reggie Ho and Chung Wah Chow. This guidebook was commissioned in Lonely Planet's Melbourne office, and produced by the following:

Commissioning Editors Rebecca Chau, George Dunford

Coordinating Editor Nigel Chin

Coordinating Cartographer Joshua Geoghegan

Coordinating Layout Designer Jim Hsu

Managing Editors Katie Lynch, Suzannah Shwer

Managing Cartographer David Connolly

Managing Layout Designer Celia Wood

Assisting Editors Daniel Corbett, Michael Day, Penelope Goodes, Charlotte Harrison, Rosie Nicholson, Kristin Odijk, Jeanette Wall

Assisting Cartographers Hunor Csutoros, Diana Duggan, Jacqueline Nguyen

Assisting Layout Designers Aomi Hongo, Jacqui Saunders

Cover Designer Marika Kozak

Project Manager Sarah Sloane

Language Content Coordinator Quentin Frayne

Thanks to Imogen Bannister, Sasha Baskett, Yvonne Byron, Chiu-yee Fred Cheung, Bruce Evans, Huw Fowles, Martin Heng, Lauren Hunt, Liang Jianxin, Evan Jones, Lisa Knights, Wayne Murphy, Maryanne Netto, Raphael Richards, Julie Sheridan

Cover photographs Noodle maker stretching dough, James Marshall (top); Duk Ling Traditional Chinese sailing Junk and Hong Kong Convention Centre, Hong Kong, Allen Brown/Dbimages (bottom).

Internal photographs by Lonely Planet Images, and by Greg Elms except p6(#2), p11(#3) Andrew Burke; p7(#7) Michael Coyne; p11(#4) Richard I'Anson; p10(#3) Holger Leue; p6(#3) Chris Mellor; p12(#4) Ian Trower/Alamy; p113 Phil Weymouth.

All images are copyright of the photographer unless otherwise indicated. Many of the images in this guide are available for licensing from Lonely Planet Images: www .lonelyplanetimages.com.

LONELY PLANET: TRAVEL WIDELY, TREAD LIGHTLY, GIVE SUSTAINABLY

The Lonely Planet Story

The story begins with a classic travel adventure: Tony and Maureen Wheeler's 1972 journey across Europe and Asia to Australia. There was no useful information about the overland trail then, so Tony and Maureen published the first Lonely Planet guidebook to meet a growing need.

From a kitchen table, Lonely Planet has grown to become the largest independent travel publisher in the world, with offices in Melbourne (Australia), Oakland (USA) and London (UK). Today Lonely Planet guidebooks cover the globe. There is an ever-growing list of books and information in a variety of media. Some things haven't changed. The main aim is still to make it possible for adventurous individuals to get out there – to explore and better understand the world.

The Lonely Planet Foundation

The Lonely Planet Foundation proudly supports nimble nonprofit institutions working for change in the world. Each year the foundation donates 5% of Lonely Planet company profits to projects selected by staff and authors. Our partners range from Kabissa, which provides small nonprofits across Africa with access to technology, to the Foundation for Developing Cambodian Orphans, which supports girls at risk of falling victim to sex traffickers.

Our nonprofit partners are linked by a grass-roots approach to the areas of health, education or sustainable tourism. Many – such as Louis Sarno who works with BaAka (Pygmy) children in the forested areas of Central African Republic – choose to focus on women and children as one of the most effective ways to support the whole community. Louis is determined to give options to children who are discriminated against by the majority Bantu population.

Sometimes foundation assistance is as simple as restoring a local ruin like the Minaret of Jam in Afghanistan; this incredible monument now draws intrepid tourists to the area and its restoration has greatly improved options for local people.

Just as travel is often about learning to see with new eyes, so many of the groups we work with aim to change the way people see themselves and the future for their children and communities.

BEHIND THE SCENES

SEND US YOUR FEEDBACK

We love to hear from travellers – your comments keep us on our toes and help make our books better. Our well-travelled team reads every word on what you loved or loathed about this book. Although we cannot reply individually to postal submissions, we always guarantee that your feedback goes straight to the appropriate authors, in time for the next edition. Each person who sends us information is thanked in the next edition – and the most useful submissions are rewarded with a free book.

To send us your updates – and find out about Lonely Planet events, newsletters and travel news – visit our award-winning website: www.lonelyplanet.com/contact.

Note: We may edit, reproduce and incorporate your comments in Lonely Planet products such as guidebooks, websites and digital products, so let us know if you don't want your comments reproduced or your name acknowledged. For a copy of our privacy policy visit www.lonelyplanet.com/privacy.

THANKS

ANDREW STONE

My fellow authors Chung Wah and Reggie helped me out in so many ways on this title with ideas, suggestions, contacts and with their excellent company. I am indebted to them. Thanks guys. Thanks also to my commissioning editor Rebecca Chau for her patience and help throughout. To Colette Koo, Calvin Yeung and everyone else who either entertained or generally led me astray, thanks for making it such fun. To Jaki and Marianne, my love and thanks for everything during write up in Sydney. Finally, thanks to Steve Fallon, whose dedication and sparkling writing on previous editions of this book left it in such great shape. I owe you all a drink (please take small sips though as there are quite a few of you).

CHUNG WAH CHOW

I owe big debts of gratitude to Calvin Kok for putting me up and giving invaluable tips in Macau. Thanks to Liz Lam and Sérgio Perez from MGTO for countless pieces of information and priceless advice; to Walter Ng and Mark Mak for keeping me company; to Trey Menefee for

LONELY PLANET AUTHORS

Why is our travel information the best in the world? It's simple: our authors are independent, dedicated travellers. They don't research using just the internet or phone, and they don't take freebies in exchange for positive coverage. They travel widely, to all the popular spots and off the beaten track. They personally visit thousands of hotels, restaurants, cafés, bars, galleries, palaces, museums and more – and they take pride in getting all the details right, and telling it how it is. Think you can do it? Find out how at **lonelyplanet.com**.

showing me the nightlife in Shenzhen. Thanks also go to Rebecca Chau and Andrew Stone for showing a novice the ropes. Contributions from Joseph Merchlinsky, Winston Wong and fellow author Reggie Ho are appreciated. A special thanks to my partner, David Rheinheimer, for his love and support.

REGGIE HO

A few hairs of mine have been lost juggling my job and researching for and writing the Eating chapter, but it's all been worth it. I had the most enjoyable times meeting with Rebecca and Andrew, and I sincerely appreciated their patience in guiding me through my first Lonely Planet gig. Also thanks to the management of the *South China Morning Post* for making an exception to the rule and allowing me to take on this exciting project. And finally to Nigel, Michael and Joshua, and all of you at Lonely Planet, your queries made my head ache sometimes, but you're all very professional and a joy to work with.

OUR READERS

Many thanks to the travellers who used the last edition and wrote to us with helpful hints, useful advice and interesting anecdotes:

Belinda Barnett, Richard Baylis, Hilda Bouma, David Boyall, Steve Brookwell, Andy Cheng, John Cheng, Yvonne Cheung, John Conlin, Cameron Cresswell, Bob Cromwell, Louise Deadman, Carlo Di Goro, Thorbjorn Eilertsen, John Emerson, Nadia Gambetta, Neil Glentworth, Ludwig Heussler, Thng Hui Hong, Benjamin Knor, Linda Kokanovich, Wing Lai, Jimmy Lam, Richard Lambourne, Reiner Lenz, Philip Lowe, Anna Malczyk, F Mclean, Tien Mcnair, Kirsti Mitchell, Jason Morrissey, Antoinette Nania, Andre Oaland, Jan Pennington, Laura Rafiqi, Rachelle Stout, Tamas Visegrady, Suraj Wagh, Paul Wylie, Amy Yates.

Notes

Notes

Notes

INDEX

INDEX

INDEX

000 map pages
000 photographs

000 map pages
000 photographs

INDEX

000 map pages
000 photographs

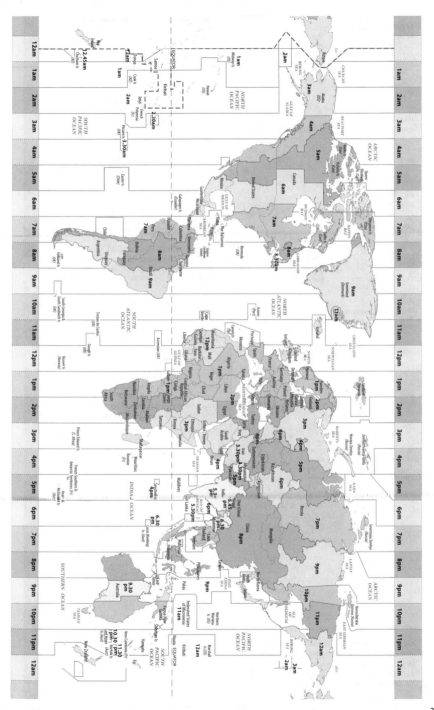

MAP LEGEND

ROUTES

	Freeway		Mall/Steps
	Primary		Tunnel
	Secondary		Pedestrian Overpass
	Tertiary		Walking Tour
	Lane		Walking Tour Detour
	Under Construction		Walking Trail
	Unsealed Road		Walking Path
	One-Way Street		Track

TRANSPORT

	Ferry		Rail (Underground)
	Metro		Tram
	Rail		Cable Car, Funicular

HYDROGRAPHY

	River, Creek		Canal
	Mangrove		Water

BOUNDARIES

	International		Regional, Suburb
	State, Provincial		Ancient Wall

AREA FEATURES

	Airport		Forest
	Area of Interest		Land
	Beach, Desert		Mall
	Building		Market
	Campus		Park
	Cemetery, Christian		Sports
	Cemetery, Other		

POPULATION

◎ CAPITAL (NATIONAL)	◉	CAPITAL (STATE)
● Large City	●	Medium City
● Small City	●	Town, Village

SYMBOLS

Sights/Activities
- Beach
- Buddhist
- Castle, Fortress
- Christian
- Islamic
- Jewish
- Monument
- Museum, Gallery
- Point of Interest
- Pool
- Ruin
- Shinto
- Zoo, Bird Sanctuary

Eating
- Eating

Drinking
- Drinking
- Café

Entertainment
- Entertainment

Shopping
- Shopping

Sleeping
- Sleeping

Transport
- Airport, Airfield
- Border Crossing
- Bus Station
- General Transport
- Parking Area
- Taxi Rank

Information
- Bank, ATM
- Embassy/Consulate
- Hospital, Medical
- Information
- Internet Facilities
- Police Station
- Post Office, GPO
- Telephone
- Toilets

Geographic
- Lighthouse
- Lookout
- Mountain, Volcano
- National Park
- Picnic Area
- Waterfall

Published by Lonely Planet Publications Pty Ltd
ABN 36 005 607 983

Australia Head Office, Locked Bag 1, Footscray, Victoria 3011, ☎ 03 8379 8000, fax 03 8379 8111, talk2us@lonelyplanet.com.au

USA 150 Linden St, Oakland, CA 94607, ☎ 510 893 8555, toll free 800 275 8555, fax 510 893 8572, info@lonelyplanet.com

UK 2nd Floor, 186 City Road, London, ECV1 2NT, ☎ 020 7106 2100, fax 020 7106 2101, go@lonelyplanet.co.uk